The Historical Jesus in
Recent Research

Sources for Biblical and Theological Study

General Editor:
David W. Baker
Ashland Theological Seminary

The Historical Jesus in Recent Research

edited by

James D. G. Dunn and Scot McKnight

Eisenbrauns
Winona Lake, Indiana
2005

www.eisenbrauns.com

Sources for Biblical and Theological Study (New
Testament series) logo (p. ii, cover) is after
Albrecht Dürer's *St. Jerome in His Study*, adapted
by Michael Brown.

Library of Congress Cataloging-in-Publication Data

The historical Jesus in recent research / edited by James D. G. Dunn and
   Scot McKnight.
      p.   cm. — (Sources for biblical and theological study)
   Includes bibliographical references and indexes.
   ISBN 1-57506-100-7 (hardback : alk. paper)
      1. Jesus Christ—Historicity.   2. Jesus Christ—History and criticism.
   I. Dunn, James D. G., 1939–   . II. McKnight, Scot.   III. Series.
   BT303.2.H485   2005
   232.9′08—dc22

                                                         2005024554

05   06   07   08   10   11   12   13   14   15   16   17   18   19   20
                 1   2   3   4   5   6   7

CONTENTS

Part 3
Teachings of Jesus:
God, Kingdom, Ethics, Parables, and Old Testament

Part 4
Jesus: Who Was He?

Part 5
Jesus: Major Events

Part 6

Jesus and Others

Part 7

Conclusion

SERIES PREFACE

Biblical and theological scholarship are well served by several recent works which detail, to a greater or lesser degree, the progress made in the study of these disciplines. Some survey the extent of the field as it developed over extended periods of time, while others concern themselves more narrowly with smaller chronological, geographical, or topical segments. There are also brief entrés into various subdisciplines of Old Testament, New Testament, and theology in the standard introductions as well as in several useful series. All of these provide helpful secondary syntheses of various aspects of biblical and theological research. All refer to, and base their discussions upon, various seminal scholarly works which have proven pivotal in the development and flourishing of the various aspects of the disciplines.

The main avenue into the various areas of inquiry, especially for the novice, has been until now through the filter of these interpreters. Even on a pedagogical level, however, it is beneficial for a student to be able to interact with foundational works firsthand. This contact will not only provide insight into the content of an area but hopefully also lead to the sharpening of critical abilities through interacting with various viewpoints. This series seeks to address this need by including not only key, ground-breaking works but also significant responses to these. This allows the reader to appreciate the process of scholarly development through interaction.

The series is also directed toward scholars. In a period of burgeoning knowledge and significant publication in many places and languages around the world, this series will endeavor to make easily accessible significant, but at times hard to find, contributions. Each volume will contain essays, articles, extracts, and the like, presenting in a manageable scope the growth and development of one of a number of different aspects of biblical and theological studies. Most volumes will contain previously published material, with synthetic essays by the editor(s) of the individual volume. Some volumes, however, are expected to contain significant, previously unpublished work. To facilitate access for students and scholars, all entries will appear in English and will be newly typeset. If students are excited by the study of the breadth

of Bible and theology, and scholars are encouraged in amicable dialogue, this
series will have fulfilled its purpose.

David W. Baker, *series editor*
Ashland Theological Seminary

Publisher's Note

Articles republished here are reprinted without alteration, except for minor
matters of style not affecting meaning. Page numbers of the original publication are marked with double brackets ([[267]], for example). Other editorial
notes or supplementations are also marked with double brackets, including
editorially-supplied translations of foreign words. The NRSV is primarily used
for translations of Greek and Hebrew citations from the Bible. Footnotes are
numbered consecutively throughout each article, even when the original
publication used another system. No attempt has been made to bring trans-
literation systems into conformity with a single style.

EDITORS' PREFACE

"The quest of the historical Jesus" has been a major preoccupation for theological scholarship for two centuries. It has absorbed countless hours of study and reflection and the books and articles devoted to it have consumed several forests. It has become a whole discipline in itself, posing major issues for philosophical and systematic theology, and often troubling the faith of everyday believers and even causing schisms in churches and colleges. Why so? Obviously, because Jesus is such a significant historical figure: not simply the individual from whom Christianity sprang, that major shaping force in world, especially Western history and culture; but also the human person in whom, Christians believe, the revelation of the one creator God came to fullest and definitive expression. Of course Christians, especially Christians though not exclusively Christians, were and should be concerned to know more about this Jesus.

The problem was that the overwhelming significance of this one man had for centuries also overwhelmed any impulse to ask questions about the historical figure. For most Christians for most of Christianity's history, there was something offensive, even blasphemous, in asking how this Jesus might have lived, even in envisaging him eating ordinary food, or laughing and joking with his friends, or in burping or being sick.

The carapace of such forbidding reverence began to be cracked in the late 1700s. The portrayal of Jesus as the Pantocrator in Orthodox art, or as the final judge, as in Michelangelo's riveting fresco in the Sistine chapel, had made Jesus a remote and frightening figure. The Catholic tradition might find sufficient solace in the thought that Mary, the mother of God, could intervene with such an awe-inspiring Son. But for Protestants such comfort had to be found in Jesus himself, not just in the thought of his atoning death and heavenly intercession, but in Hebrews' depiction of a man, tested in every respect as we are, and who, precisely because he had lived a human life, is able out of his own experience to give us the help we need (Heb 4:15–16; 5:7–10). To learn more of this Jesus, to realize afresh that Jesus provided a pattern for life, including life under stress, as well as a focus for worship, was a wholly understandable impulse behind the "quest."

All this needs to be said, because the "quest" is regularly characterized as motivated by skepticism or plain unbelief. It has been seen as a means of rebutting (or escaping) faith. And, sure enough, most of the memorable moments in the "quest" have been marked by some form of antithesis between faith and history. But the desire to see and hear Jesus as he was seen and heard by the fishermen and villagers of first-century Galilee is not in itself antithetical to faith. On the contrary, the Jesus whose call and the impact of whose ministry transformed fishermen and tax collectors into disciples and apostles is a Jesus that any who are looking for meaning in their lives, whether with faith or without faith, should want to learn about if not to encounter (historically) for themselves.

It is out of such convictions and concerns that the following essays and extracts have been put together. The huge expense of time and effort, mentioned at the beginning, has resulted in an almost endless list of books and articles, a library in itself, and highly daunting to those who have only recently begun to think about such matters or who have plunged into the midst and are in danger of being deafened by a cacophony of competing voices. Scot McKnight therefore had the very good idea of putting together an anthology of significant contributions to the quest as an introduction and way into the maze that is the "quest." And he found in me a ready collaborator.

We divided the extracts and articles under the six headings in the following pages. Over one hundred possible candidates were considered for inclusion. The criteria for inclusion were (1) representativeness, (2) importance in the history of discussion, (3) specific contribution or overview, (4) major players in the discussion, even if the piece was dated, (5) accessibility to students who need to be alerted to major works and key issues, and (6) length and availability of the material. The final choices were the items that measured up when set against all six criteria, but the decision in several cases was far from easy; and no doubt other experienced questers would have chosen differently.

There is, of course, no single definitive list of the most representative and important and useful contributions to the "quest." But for those wanting an introduction to the "quest" or to get into the heart of the "quest" or to refresh a student acquaintance with the "quest" or to have a sample of key contributions readily to hand for reference, this will be a welcome volume.

Although the editors' contribution to the volume, in terms of their own writing (the introductions to each section), is modest, the work involved in putting together such a volume is considerable. Special thanks are due to Sarah and Hauna Ondrey, two of Scot's students, who did the lion's share of the scanning of the original pieces. And the quest for permissions to reprint items still in copyright took several twists and provided another hurdle for inclusion, at which some more of our favored mounts tumbled out of consideration. In all this we have had the benefit of Jim Eisenbraun's input and advice, which at several points brought the decision-making through to successful conclusion.

It is our combined wish and prayer that readers will find this an instructive guide and helpful companion in their own attempts to engage in the "quest" for themselves.

JAMES D. G. DUNN   SCOT MCKNIGHT
University of Durham, England *North Park University*

ABBREVIATIONS

General

AV	Authorized Version (also known as King James Version)
ET	English translation
EVV	English versions
frag(s).	fragment(s)
KJV	King James Version
LXX	Septuagint
MT	Masoretic Text
MS(S)	manuscript(s)
NEB	New English Bible
NJPSV	New Jewish Publication Society Version
NRSV	New Revised Standard Bible
NT	New Testament
OT	Old Testament
REB	Revised English Bible
RSV	Revised Standard Bible

Reference Works

AB	Anchor Bible
ABD	Freedman, D. N. (editor). *The Anchor Bible Dictionary*. 6 vols. Garden City, N.Y.: Doubleday, 1992
ABRL	Anchor Bible Reference Library
Arch. f. Rel. Wiss.	*Archiv für Religionswissenschaft*
ARN	*'Abot de Rabbi Nathan*
ATR	*Anglican Theological Review*
BAGD	Bauer, W., W. F. Arndt, F. W. Gingrich, and F. W. Danker. *Greek-English lexicon of the New Testament and Other Early Christian Literature.* 2nd ed. Chicago, 1979
BBR	*Bulletin for Biblical Research*

BDAG	Bauer, W. *Greek-English lexicon of the New Testament and Other Early Christian Literature.* 3rd rev. ed. of BAGD by F. W. Danker. Chicago: University of Chicago, 2000
BETL	Bibliotheca ephemeridum theologicarum lovaniensium
Bib	*Biblica*
BJS	Brown Judaic Studies
BNTC	Black's New Testament Commentaries
BR	*Biblical Research*
BS	Biblical Seminar
BTB	*Biblical Theology Bulletin*
BWANT	Beiträge zur Wissenschaft vom Alten und Neuen Testament
BZNW	Beihefte zur Zeitschrift für die Neutestamentliche Wissenschaft
CBQ	*Catholic Biblical Quarterly*
CurBS	*Currents in Research: Biblical studies*
CSCO	Corpus scriptorum christianum orientalium
DSSSE	García Martínez, F., and Tigchelaar, E. J. C. (editors). *The Dead Sea Scrolls Study Edition.* 2 vols. Leiden: Brill, 1997–98 [revised, 2000]
ED	*Euntes Docete* (Rome)
EDNT	Balz, H., and G. Schneider (editors). *Exegetical Dictionary of the New Testament.* 3 vols. Grand Rapids: Eerdmans, 1990–99
EKK	Evangelisch-Katholischer kommentar zum Neuen Testament
ExpTim/Exp.T.	*Expository Times*
FB	*Forschung zur Bibel*
FRLANT	Forschungen zur Religion und Literatur des Alten und Neuen Testaments
GCS	Griechischen christlichen Schriftsteller
HJ	*Historisches Jahrbuch*
HTKNT	Herders theologischer Kommentar zum Neuen Testament
HT(h)R	*Harvard Theological Review*
HUCA	*Hebrew Union College Annual*
ICC	International Critical Commentary
IKZ	*Internationale kirchliche Zeitschrift*
JAAR	*Journal of the American Academy of Religion*
JR	*Journal of Religion*
JSNT	*Journal for the Study of the New Testament*

JSNTS(up)	Journal for the Study of the New Testament Supplement Series
JSPSS	Journal for the Study of the Pseudepigrapha Supplement Series
JSOTSS	Journal for the Study of the Old Testament Supplement Series
JTS	*Journal of Theological Studies*
LEP	Laertius, *The Lives and Opinions of Eminent Philosophers*
MTZ	*Münchener theologische Zeitschrift*
NCBC	New Century Bible Commentary
NICNT	New International Commentary on the New Testament
NIGTC	New International Greek Testament Commentary
NovT	*Novum Testamentum*
NTOA	Novum Testamentum et Orbis Antiquus
NTS	*New Testament Studies*
NTTS	New Testament Tools and Studies
OTP	Charlesworth, J. H. (editor). *The Old Testament Pseudepigrapha*. Garden City, N.Y.: Doubleday, 1983–85
PTMS	Pittsburgh Theological Monograph Series
QD	Quaestiones disputatae
R.B.	*Revue biblique*
RevSR	*Revue des sciences religieuses*
RGG[3]	Galling, K. (editor). *Die Religion in Geschichte und Gegenwart*. 7 vols. 3rd ed. Tübingen: Mohr, 1957–65
SBLDS	Society of Biblical Literature Dissertation Series
SBLMS	Society of Biblical Literature Monograph Series
SBS	Stuttgarter Bibelstudien
SBT	Studies in Biblical Theology
SBU	Symbolae biblicae upsalienses
SE	Aland, K., et al. *Studia Evangelica: Papers Presented to the International Congress on "The Four Gospels in 1957" Held at Christ Church, Oxford, 1957*
SJLA	Studies in Judaism in Late Antiquity
SJT	*Scottish Journal of Theology*
SNTSMS	Society for New Testament Study Monograph Series
Str-B	Strack, H. L., and P. Billerbeck, *Kommentar zum Neuen Testament aus Talmud und Midrasch*. 6 vols. Munich: Beck, 1965–69
S(t)T(h)	*Studia theologica*
SUNT	Studien zur Umwelt des Neuen Testaments

TDNT	Kittel, G., and G. Friedrich (editors). *Theological Dictionary of the New Testament*. 10 vols. Grand Rapids, Mich.: Eerdmans, 1964–76
T(h)Bl	*Theologische Blätter*
ThQ	*Theologische Quartalschrift*
Th.R.	*Theologische Rundschau*
T.S.K.	*Theologische Studien und Kritiken*
ThW(AT)	Botterweck, G. J., and H. Ringgren (editors). *Theologisches Wörterbuch zum Alten Testament*. Stuttgart: Kohlhammer, 1973
TJT	*Toronto Journal of Theology*
TLOT	Jenni, E. (editor), and M. E. Biddle (translator). *Theological Lexicon of the Old Testament*. 3 vols. Peabody, Mass., 1997
TLZ	*Theologische Literaturzeitung*
TRu	*Theologische Rundschau*
T.S.K.	*Theologische Studien und Kritiken*
TU	Texte und Untersuchungen
TW/TWNT/Th.Wb.z.N.T.	Kittel, G., and G. Friedrich (editors). *Theologisches Wörterbuch zum Neuen Testament*. Stuttgart: Kohlhammer, 1932–
T(h)Z	*Theologische Zeitschrift*
TynBul	*Tyndale Bulletin*
WBC	Word Biblical Commentary
WMANT	Wissenschaftliche Monographien zum Alten und Neuen Testament
WUNT	Wissenschaftliche Untersuchungen zum Alten und Neuen Testament
ZAW	*Zeitschrift für die Alttestamentliche Wissenschaft*
ZNW	*Zeitschrift für die Neutestamentliche Wissenschaft*
ZT(h)K	*Zeitschrift für Theologie und Kirche*

Part 1

Classic Voices

Introduction

JAMES D. G. DUNN

Albert Schweitzer described "the quest of the historical Jesus" as "the greatest achievement of German theology." The claim is somewhat "over the top," treating the "quest" as an almost exclusively German enterprise. But it does reflect a period, roughly one hundred years from the mid-nineteenth to the mid-twentieth century, when it was indeed German theology that led the way in pushing through old frontiers and in setting the agenda for biblical and theological scholarship. This is reflected in our choice of three German out of four illustrative "classic voices."

More importantly, however, Schweitzer's comment reflects the crucial importance of Jesus in Christian theology and the priority that inevitably must be given in historical study to achieving as clear as possible a picture of Jesus in his own time and context. It is this priority that has motivated the "quest" from the first. The motivation has often been mixed with less commendable features—not least, an enlightenment dismissal of the "supernatural," hostility to tradition, and suspicion of anything that smacked of faith. But the desire itself to see Jesus as he was, or at least, as he was apprehended in his own time by his own contemporaries, is not easy to fault. Even a supernaturalist, traditional faith can share the objective of trying to see and hear Jesus with the eyes and ears of the first disciples. The underlying assumption of the "quest" was that the Jesus of first-century Galilee must have been a figure of epochal importance. And if the "superstition" of the time and the subsequent faith of orthodox (and heterodox) Christianity has in any measure obscured the impact he really made, then it must be worth pushing through the clouds of piety to reexperience something of that impact afresh.

The extract from H. J. Cadbury (below, pp. 56–66) nicely illustrates the sense of disillusion that must come upon many when they first realize that great paintings and classic treatments of Jesus' life and episodes from his ministry have "modernized" Jesus. Not that we should find fault with such presentations, because their objective was usually to show how relevant Jesus was to their "modern" times. But for anyone with a sense of what life in first-century Palestine was like, these presentations must jar somewhat. Cadbury's challenge comes quite late in the "quest." His observation that the process of "modernizing" Jesus must have begun almost immediately in Christian circles was more characteristic of the twentieth-century phase of the "quest," when it was realized that even the earliest Gospel or sources for our knowledge of Jesus have already been shaped by the perspectives and needs of the generation after Jesus. But the basic desire of the "quest" has always been to see Jesus with all "modernizing" spectacles removed.

Other classic voices from the nineteenth century could have been chosen: Hermann Reimarus, whom Schweitzer credits with beginning the "quest," David Friedrich Strauss, who is remembered in his alma mater as "a scandal and offence for theology and church," and Ernest Renan, whose *Life of Jesus* went through 61 editions in France. But Schweitzer's history of the "quest" still provides an unsurpassed overview of the first phase (or two phases) of the "quest" and serves as the obvious leader of our little procession (below, pp. 6–49). The extract also has three benefits: (1) It provides a good example of the way scholars went about constructing their "Lives of Jesus" in the preceding century. Schweitzer's critique of his predecessors at times was devastating, but his own attempts at reconstruction were highly vulnerable to an equivalent critique. (2) The clue for Schweitzer is summed up in the word "eschatology." His critique commends those who gave some recognition to the importance of eschatology and criticizes those who missed that key, because they missed it. But for Schweitzer it was Jesus' expectations about the coming of the kingdom of God and of the Son of man that explained the what and the why of Jesus' ministry. That claim—eschatology as the key to unlocking the "quest"—dominated the "quest" for the next 80 years. (3) The extract also illustrates the quality of Schweitzer's prose. Even though dated now, it still has the power to captivate— and occasionally shock.

Martin Kähler had also responded to the "quest" a decade or so earlier, but in a different way, a way that posed afresh the tension between history and faith. Does faith in Christ prevent a clear perception of Jesus of Nazareth, or is it the only appropriate or possible perception for the Christian? If the later creeds and confessions tell us who Jesus truly is, then they tell us who Jesus of Nazareth truly was. The hope of writing the life of a different Jesus, more amenable to nineteenth-century sensibilities, is hopeless. The Gospels do not provide sufficient evidence to fulfill the hope. The would-be biographers of "the historical Jesus" have to fill in the gaps from their own resources—their own principles and values. The only Jesus who can be known is the Christ of faith, the Christ who is preached. The historical Jesus, the Jesus reconstructed by historians who abstract him from the faith of the church, is not worth knowing. The real Jesus is the historic Jesus—Jesus seen in the light of the influence he actually exercised.

Rather surprisingly, the conservative Kähler greatly influenced the radical Rudolf Bultmann at this point. The reason was that Bultmann, for all his work as a historian of Christianity's beginnings (he was the most influential New Testament scholar of the twentieth century), was primarily a theologian. And more than that, he was an evangelist. He believed the gospel was an existential power that brought the hearer to himself (he was pre–gender-sensitive) and brought the hearer to the reality of his situation in the here and now. He wanted that gospel to be heard afresh. He believed that Jesus and the New Testament writers (particularly Paul and John) proclaimed that gospel in their own times, in the language and with the imagery that was the language and the imagery of their time. That language and imagery now obscured the gospel and dulled its existential cutting edge. His objective was therefore not to write another "Life of Jesus." Like Kähler, he did not think the Gospels provided sufficient information for that. What critical scholarship could provide was a grasp of Jesus' *message*, a grasp sufficient for us to appreciate afresh something of its existential power, a message through which the existential challenge of the gospel could still confront the hearer.

These four extracts will give readers a good flavor of the "quest" at the height of its fascination.

Bibliography

Bultmann, R.
   1957   New Testament and Mythology (1941). Pp. 1–44 in *Kerygma and Myth*, ed. H. W. Bartsch. London: SPCK.
Reimarus, H. S.
   1970   *Fragments*, ed. C. H. Talbert; trans. R. S. Fraser. Philadelphia: Fortress. [original pub., 1778]
Renan, E.
   1864   *The Life of Jesus*. London: Trebner. [original pub., 1863]
Strauss, D. F.
   1972   *The Life of Jesus Critically Examined*, trans. G. Eliot. Philadelphia: Fortress. [original pub., 1835–36; trans., 1846]

ALBERT SCHWEITZER

The Solution of Thoroughgoing Eschatology

[[315]] How is it to be explained that Wrede, in spite of his successful recognition of the eschatological approach, in critically investigating the connections in the life of Jesus could simply leave eschatology out of account? Johannes Weiss and his followers were to blame for that. They applied the eschatology only to the preaching of Jesus, and not even to the whole of this, but only to the messianic secret, instead of using it also to throw light upon his whole public work, the connection and lack of connection between the events. Jesus was represented as thinking and speaking eschatologically in some of the most important passages of his teaching, but for the rest his life was presented as uneschatologically as modern historical theology had presented it. The teaching of Jesus and the history of his activity were set in different keys. Instead of destroying the modern-historical scheme of the life of Jesus, or at least subjecting it to a rigorous examination, and thereby performing a highly valuable service for criticism, eschatology confined itself within the limits of New Testament theology, and left it to Wrede to reveal critically one after another the difficulties which from its point of view could have been grasped historically at a single glance. It inevitably follows that Wrede is unjust to Johannes Weiss and Johannes Weiss to Wrede.[1]

Reprinted, with permission, from Albert Schweitzer, *The Quest of the Historical Jesus* (ed. J. Bowden; trans. W. Montgomery et al.; Minneapolis: Fortress, 2001) 315–54, 521–27. Original German edition: *Geschichte der Leben-Jesu-Forschung* (Tübingen: Mohr, 1906).

  1. That the eschatological school showed a certain timidity in taking seriously its recognition of the character of the preaching of Jesus and examining the tradition from the eschatological standpoint can be seen from Johannes Weiss, *Das älteste Evangelium*, Göttingen 1903, 414 pp. Ingenious and interesting as this work is in detail, one is surprised to find the author of the "Preaching of Jesus" here endeavouring to distinguish between Mark and an "Ur-Mark," in order to demonstrate Pauline influence and to bring out the "tendencies" which guided, respectively, the original evangelist and the redactor, as if in his eschatological view of the preaching of Jesus he did not have a central view which would lead him to a quite

It is quite inexplicable that the eschatological school, with its clear perception of the eschatological element in the preaching of the kingdom of
God, did not also hit upon the thought of the "dogmatic" element in the history of Jesus. Eschatology is simply "dogmatic history," which breaks in upon
the natural course of history and abrogates it. Is it not even *a priori* the only
conceivable view that the one who expected his messianic parousia in the
near future should be determined, not by the natural course of events, but by
that expectation? The chaotic confusion of the narratives ought to have suggested that the events had been thrown into this confusion by the volcanic
force of an unfathomable self-awareness, not by some kind of carelessness or
freak of the tradition. The evangelist is supposed to have been compelled by
"community theology" to represent Jesus as thinking dogmatically and actively "making history": if the poor evangelist can make him do it on paper,
why should not Jesus have been quite capable of doing it himself?

[[316]] We know very little about Jesus' early life and upbringing. When
he went back to Nazareth with the disciples, the people were amazed to see
their carpenter as teacher and prophet (Mark 6:1–16), from which we can be
fairly certain that they thought he lacked the education needed for such
work, and thus had little in the way of learning. This comment also tells us he
had never taught there before.

We cannot be certain whether he practised his trade in his home town
until he went to the Baptist, or had been elsewhere in the meantime, doing
other things.

When did he join the Baptist and for how long did he follow him? Did he
have personal contact with the preacher by the Jordan? At what moment did
he leave him?

To these questions too there is no answer. We do not even know when
the Baptist began his activity nor how long it lasted. The conjecture that Jesus
heard of him on the Passover journey and joined him then has some degree
of probability.

It is quite uncertain whether Jesus himself was already convinced that the
kingdom of God was near, or whether it was the preaching of the Baptist
which brought him to believe so. And the possibility that he already knew
himself to be the future Messiah before he went to the shores of the Jordan
should not be dismissed outright.

Jesus first steps into the light of history when he proclaims in Galilee that
the kingdom of God is near.

According to the two first evangelists it was after his baptism that he believed himself to be the coming Messiah. Whether this visionary experience

---

different psychologizing from that which he actually applies. Against Wrede he has advanced
some arguments which are worthy of attention, but he has not refuted him. In general we
need to abandon the view that some "Ur-Mark" theory could remove the problems demonstrated by the critic from Breslau. That can be achieved only by an investigation of the public
activity of Jesus which explains the "concealment theory" and everything connected with it
as "historical" and thus does away with the view that this is a later literary fiction. For Weiss's
study of Mark see also [[Schweitzer, *Quest of the Historical Jesus*,]] 517.

belongs to the assured part of the tradition will always remain open to doubt. That Mark describes the event as seen and heard only by Jesus and not by the surrounding people indicates that it might well be historical.[2] Wrede is wrong to assert that this report, as well as those of the other Gospels, intimates that the baptismal experiences should be interpreted as a public miracle; this is so only in Matthew and Luke. In the Fourth Gospel (John 1:29–34) the report describes a vision in which neither Jesus nor the people took part, but only the Baptist, so that he could be led to see the Galilean as the Son of God and preach accordingly.

Whether the experience Jesus had at his baptism was really the birth of his knowledge of himself as the Messiah, as modern psychology assumes, must remain undecided. Modern psychiatry and psychology are not generally inclined to allow solitary hallucinations to bring about such a complete transformation of a man's consciousness of himself and his whole outlook. They see them simply as incidental accompaniments of the thought-processes which are going on at the time.

There is some evidence in Jesus of specific as well as general preconceptions and reflections which suggest that he could have had some idea of his messianic destiny. In common with the Baptist he expects the kingdom to come in the very [[317]] near future and with it that supernatural state of being into which the world and the elect would then be raised. Thus he assumes that he will enter it with the rest of the elect like an angel or in some heavenly form.

Further, he thought that when the transition was made into this supernatural condition, hierarchical differences in rank would come into force among the elect whereby some would be among the greatest and some among the least great in the kingdom of heaven.[3] Thus to him it was theoretically possible that even the most supreme of all, the Messiah-Son of man, could arise from an ordinary human being. Assuming as he does that there will be a reversal of values, whereby the now would be replaced by the then, the greatest by the least and the least by the greatest, he was bound to expect that while the ruler of the messianic period passed through his earthly existence he would belong to the poor and lowly.

With the combining of the prophetic and Danielic eschatology, a great problem arose about the personality of the Messiah. How could he come

---

2. The "temptations" described in Matthew (4:1–11) are not real visions but literary productions. There are no delusions which take their course in such logical dialogues, nor have there ever been. Whether Mark's general note that Jesus lived in the wilderness with the wild beasts and the angels and was tested by Satan (Mark 1:12, 13) in any way goes back to information from the Lord must remain questionable. Given the whole nature of Jesus there is no reason to suppose that he had a whole series of visionary experiences. In general it has to be said that the experiences at his baptism and in the wilderness belong more to the uncertain prehistory.

3. For what follows see the remarks about the relationship between the messianic eschatology of Jesus and that of late Judaism and the rabbis, [[in Schweitzer, *Quest*,]] 236–59. For ranks in the kingdom of heaven see p. 256.

from the house of David yet at the same time be the supernatural Son of man? The puzzle with which Jesus vexes the Pharisees (Mark 12:35–37) about the opening words of Psalm 110 shows that this problem had occurred to him. But once acknowledged, its only solution lay in making the Christ be born in the last generation of the house of David, letting him only later, at the dawn of the messianic period, be transformed into the supernatural Son of man. This solution accords in the best manner possible with all the other information we have of Jesus' eschatology.[4]

If he believed that the messianic event was about to take place, he must also have assumed that the descendant of David who was to be the coming Son of man had already been born.

To these general theoretical assumptions there belongs another, and one which is substantiated by fact: the prophet of Nazareth himself belonged to the house of David.

There seems no reason to doubt the particulars about this which are given by the first two evangelists and Paul. The fact that the Davidic genealogies of Matt 1:1–17 and Luke 2:23–31 were drawn up later and cannot be correct does not necessarily mean that Jesus' family did not come from this royal house. A branch of the house of David had returned from exile in the person of Zerubbabel. His political role, which was encouraged to take on messianic proportions by the prophets Haggai (2) and Zechariah (3 and 4), was soon played out. But it is unthinkable that the descendants will not have remembered their lineage. Whether they could recite it in all detail is another question altogether.

Modern theology should not be permitted to consider the title son of David given to Jesus in both the earliest Gospels to be intended as messianic and therefore to be a later insertion. In fact, the surprising thing about the title is that the evangelists in no way link it with the rank which is claimed for Jesus, [[318]] but merely present it as the much-honoured family name of the prophet of Nazareth.

According to Matt 15:22, the Canaanite woman addresses him as "Lord, son of David." When the blind beggar of Jericho hears that Jesus of Nazareth is coming, he cries out to the son of David to have mercy on him (Mark 10:47–48). Those around try to quiet him, not because they object to the title son of David, but because they find his clamour disagreeable. That the beggar does not know him as the Messiah can be seen by his later addressing him simply as rabbi (Mark 10:51).

The people, too, who in Matt 12:22–23 are amazed at the healing of a demoniac by the "son of David," have no notion of his being the Messiah but only of the exorcism he has accomplished, This follows from the fact that they are told by the Pharisees immediately afterwards that the power of the Galilean comes from the prince of devils (Matt 12:24).

---

4. For the problem of the Davidic sonship of the Messiah and its great significance see [[ibid.]], 252–53 and 258–59.

At the entry into Jerusalem, according to Matt 21:9, the crowd chant Hosannas to the son of David. But it is by no means their intention to accord him a messianic ovation. When the local inhabitants ask who the man they are honouring might be, they answer, "This is the prophet Jesus from Nazareth in Galilee" (Matt 21:11).

The chief priests and the scribes object to Jesus allowing the children to offer him homage in the temple with cries of "Hosanna to the son of David" (Matt 21:15–16). But they have no notion of accusing him of claiming to be the Messiah.

That a later generation intended to show that Jesus suddenly, either naively or in some veiled way, came to be seen as the Messiah by his own generation by inserting the son of David at these points must therefore be ruled out. How could they have come so to obstruct their own purpose that in the narratives about the blind man at Jericho and the entry into Jerusalem they immediately go on to report that he was held by those who honoured him to be merely a rabbi and the prophet of Nazareth?

All attempts to make the references to Jesus as the son of David the result of later views in the community are finally invalidated by the definite evidence we are given by Paul. The apostle to the Gentiles makes the Lord of the seed of David according to the flesh (Rom 1:3). How could he have risked such a statement two or three decades after the death of Jesus if it had not been told him by those who knew of the family circumstances? And what interests would have led him to make such a dogmatic assertion when he otherwise shows such complete indifference to the facts of Jesus' earthly existence?

Brief mention must also be made of the fact that according to Hegesippus (Eusebius, 3.19, 20) at the time of Domitian (81–96) two relations of Jesus, descendants of his brother Judah, are spoken of as being of the house of David.

Modern theology would not have been so insistent on doubting the details [[319]] given about Jesus' descent if it had clearly thought through the late-Jewish ideas of the Messiah and had thus freed itself of the preconception that a prophet of Davidic descent who worked miracles could not have been active for more than a couple of weeks without the suspicion arising that he was the Messiah. Added to this, they interpreted the puzzle Jesus put to the Pharisees about Psalm 110 (Mark 12:25–37) as a clear deviation from the usual doctrine and asserted that Jesus was poking fun at the idea of the Messiah as the Son of David because he was not of this descent himself. They do not consider the other possibility, that it was precisely because he was aware of his own descent that he brought the question up.

Hitherto the view has been that it was the primitive Christian community which made the Lord into the Son of David because it held him to be the Messiah. It is time to consider seriously whether it was not rather Jesus who held himself to be the Messiah because he was descended from David.

In the kingdom of God, all the elect were to be transformed into supernatural beings and allotted widely varying ranks; the Messiah-Son of man, to be David's son as well, had to have been born of the royal house and to have lived an earthly existence; as the messianic events were imminent, it was to be expected that he had already begun this first form of existence. Given these presuppositions, it is conceivable up to a point that an outstanding religious personality of Davidic descent could see himself as the chosen one, who in the great transformation of things which was about to take place would be elevated to the rank of the Messiah-Son of man.

This realistic interpretation does not satisfy the prejudices and interests of modern theology quite so well as the other interpretation, which makes the typically Jewish pretension to messiahship arise from the consciousness of a general son-relationship to God; but it is simpler and more natural.

The question why Jesus made a secret of his expectation that he would be revealed as the Messiah cannot be answered with any accuracy. All we can determine from his behaviour is that he seriously intended to preserve this secret; we cannot make out motives for this. Generally it could well be a matter of the widely-held but nevertheless inexplicable belief that the Messiah-Son of man must spend his earthly existence unrecognized and in all humility. That Jesus did not make himself known because he did not want to be exposed to the possible ridicule of unbelievers is hardly plausible. It is more likely, even though at first sight the idea seems strange, that he thought he should not reveal himself because by doing so he would have indicated with too great a certainty and clarity that the kingdom was near, thus converting some who were not predestined for salvation, who would be saved through faith in him.

According to Mark and Matthew, Jesus' ministry lasted barely a year.[5] As they talk of only one Passover journey, it must be assumed that this festival occurred only once during the time of his activity. Had it been otherwise, it [[320]] would have been unaccountable for him not to have gone up to Jerusalem. His enemies who taxed him about rubbing ears of corn on the sabbath and the washing of hands would certainly have made much of such a major offence. As our information tells us nothing of a debate on this subject we must assume that no such thing took place. All this implies is that the burden of proof lies with those who maintain that Jesus was active over a long period of time.

But the period between his first public action and his death is only to a very small degree devoted to public activity. Jesus' preaching in Galilee lasted until he sent out the disciples, that is, at the most a matter of weeks. Thereupon, at the height of his success, he leaves the people and journeys north, to spend the period before his departure to Jerusalem alone with his disciples.

---

5. Luke is not mentioned in this account because for the most part he agrees with the first two evangelists. What he reports in addition to them does not give the impression of being particularly trustworthy, as in part it rests on impossible presuppositions—the journey from Galilee to Jerusalem goes through Samaria—and is partly biased by certain social views which are well-disposed towards the Gentiles. The literary problems of this Gospel have not yet been solved. No satisfactory answer has yet been given to the question where the Lukan special material comes from. However, it can be recognized that this is a purely literary and not a historical problem.

It is only when he reaches Jerusalem that he appears again before the people for a short time.

Thus a large part of his "public activity" is veiled from us, in inexplicable concealment. It dwindles to the weeks of preaching in Galilee and the few days he spent in Jerusalem.

Why did Jesus leave the people in Galilee?

Even in the period between his first appearance and his departure north his behavior is not immediately intelligible. There are certain indications that he already felt an odd aversion for publicity. His journeys do not all appear to be motivated by the wish to preach the kingdom and repentance in the land about him, but give the impression that they are an attempt to evade the people. That is why the reports of his journeys have an odd unease and aimlessness about them.

His behaviour after his first appearance in Capernaum is typical of this. That sabbath he had successfully exorcized a man possessed of a demon who had shouted at him in the synagogue that he was the "Holy One of God"; afterwards he had healed Peter's wife's mother, and in the evening had demonstrated his powers on many people who were either ill or possessed. In the early morning he escapes to a solitary place, is finally discovered by Simon Peter and other followers, but cannot be persuaded to return to the town where all await him. He goes to the surrounding villages and only later returns to Galilee (Mark 1:21–29).

When he tells Peter and his associates that the reason for his escape is that he wishes to preach the gospel elsewhere (Mark 1:38), he cannot in fact be voicing his real thoughts. Had that been so, there would have been no need to slip away secretly under cover of darkness. Nor is the usual interpretation, that he wanted to avoid the external fruits of success so that the people should learn to believe his word and not his works, or something of the kind, sufficient to explain his action.

Why his escape?

Later he tries to gain solitude by crossing the lake with his disciples to spend some time in Transjordan. But when he lands on the shore of the country of the Gerasenes he is met by a demon-possessed man who addresses him as the Son of [[321]] God. He exorcises him. Thereupon the inhabitants come to him and beg him to leave their land. The healed man wants to accompany him, but Jesus forbids it (Mark 4:35–5:20).

Scarcely has he landed on the western shore when he is again surrounded by the crowd (Mark 5:21–43). He sets off on a journey which later takes him to Nazareth. Then he sends the disciples out on their mission (Mark 6:1–13).

After their return he wants to be alone with them and uses a boat as their means of escape. But the people run after him along the shore of the lake (Mark 6:30–33). He is persuaded to land and spend the day with them. That evening the five thousand are fed. But afterwards, he crosses the mouth of the Jordan to prevent the people following him further along the shore. He goes to Bethsaida on the eastern shore.[6] Later he returns again to the north-western shore to the region of Gennesaret, straightway to be surrounded by people again (Mark 6:53–7:23). From there he departs to the region of Tyre and Sidon, which brings his "Galilean ministry" to an end.

Jesus' journey northwards is thus merely the accomplishment of what he had been unable to do earlier: he wants to escape the people. The Gospel accounts of his doings are unsettled and erratic because there was no question of a considered plan to his teaching and his "mission" journeys. Thus this cannot be blamed on those who report the events. They describe a series of uncorrelated episodes, not because they have extracted odd phrases from a complete report of his doings, but because that was how it was, and it could be represented in no other way.

The situation is this: that when Jesus is with the people he instructs them, but does not go out of his way to find them, evading them more and more until he finally goes to a Gentile land for a long time, in the hope that there he will remain unrecognized. His appearances are to proclaim the kingdom of God and its prerequisite repentance. But at the same time certain inhibiting motives are evident which prevent this aim from dominating entirely; they are in fact in conflict with it, bringing about a surprising end to his public activity.

His first escape took place after the great day in Capernaum. Thus the experience which Jesus underwent on that day must somehow have been the cause of his behaviour. The only new element in the day, which was additional to his message of the kingdom of God, and which could well have surprised even Jesus himself, was the healings and his confrontation with the man possessed by a demon. Hence the cause must lie in these.

The decisive thing seems to have been the knowledge of the demon-possessed man and the way he behaved. In the synagogue at Capernaum the possessed man calls Jesus "the Holy One of God"; Jesus immediately tries to silence him (Mark 1:24–25). His behaviour is similar in all his contacts with those possessed by demons. In Mark 3:11–12 they cry that he is the Son of God but he warns them most severely "that they should not make him known." The demon-possessed [[322]] man on the western shore also greets him as the "Son of the Most High God" (Mark 5:7).

Thus where Jesus is confronted in public by those possessed by demons the secret of his dignity is endangered. It is surprising that no suspicion of this rank arose in the minds of those who were present; on the other hand this is proof of how little the people were inclined to relate the coming of the

---

6. Bethsaida-Julias. See D. F. Buhl, *Geographie des alten Palästina*, Freiburg and Leipzig 1906, 300 pp., pp. 241–43. Remarkably, in this work it is assumed that Jesus is on the east shore as early as Mark 6:45. It is not said in the report how long he spent in this place and whether he remained alone or was surrounded by the people. There is a great temptation to put the healing of the blind man in Bethsaida (Mark 8:22–26) and possibly also the passage Mark 8:34–9:29 in these days. See pp. [[38–40 below and Schweitzer, *Quest of the Historical Jesus*, 524–25]].

Messiah to a figure whose appearance was normal in human terms. Only the "spirits" whose authority he threatened knew with whom they were dealing. It is scarcely possible that we shall ever be able to explain how the demon-possessed knew and why they believed as they did; but there is no evidence to lead us to doubt the reported facts. And that Jesus considered their reaction significant can be seen from Mark's note that he did all he could to silence these dangerous utterances which revealed his dignity.

The conjecture that Jesus was induced by the threat posed by the dubious behavior of the demon-possessed man to restrict his public activity wherever possible can be justified from the Gospel reports. It was because of these circumstances that the urge to teach and the duty he felt to preserve the secret of his person conflicted.

Moreover, Jesus is by no means governed by the need to preach the message of the coming of the kingdom of God and the need for repentance as urgently as possible, or to enforce it with the whole resources of his personality. It is as if from the first there were some bounds within which he had to work, even in those things which were not to do with his person. He teaches, but like one who knows that he should not do so too clearly or too convincingly.

If one extracts all that he said in disputes with others, and all those utterances and decisions which were forced on him by events, there is little remaining in the transmitted mass of discourses in which he actually instructs or proclaims his message. But his manner of procedure, too, is not that of a real "teacher." He preaches in parables which, according to Mark 4:10–12, are not intended to reveal but rather to veil, and refrains from giving details in terms intelligible to all of how and when the kingdom of God would come (Mark 4:34).

It is wrong to say that because the "concealment" theory is developed in connection with Jesus' first parable it should apply to all he ever said. The idea is never referred to again. It can scarcely be applied to the threatening parables which he uttered in Jerusalem, in which he openly implores the people to prepare themselves for the coming of the judgment and the kingdom of God. In the main, it is likely to apply only to the group of parables of Mark 4. The question which does arise is whether what must remain secret here should ever be allowed to become public, and if so, when this time comes.

But why the concealment?

One significant reason for this limitation in teaching is distinctly stated in Mark 4:10–12, viz. predestination! Jesus knows that the truth which he offers is [[323]] exclusively for those who have been definitely chosen, that the general and public announcement of his message could only thwart the plan of God, since the chosen are already winning their salvation from God. Only the phrase "Repent for the kingdom of God is at hand" and its variants belong to the public preaching. And this, therefore, is the only message which he commits to his disciples when sending them out. In the Sermon on the Mount he explains in positive terms what this repentance supplementary to the Law, the interim ethic before the coming of the kingdom, is. But whatever goes beyond that simple phrase must be publicly presented only in parables, in order that only those who are shown to possess predestination by having the initial knowledge which enables them to understand the parables may receive a more advanced knowledge, is imparted to them to a degree corresponding to their original degree of knowledge: "To him who has shall be given, and from him who does not have shall be taken away even what he has" (Mark 4:24–25).

The predestinarian view goes along with the eschatology. It is pushed to its utmost consequences in the closing incident of the parable of the marriage of the king's son (Matt 22:1–14), where the man who in response to a publicly issued invitation sits down at the table of the king, but is recognized from his appearance not to have been invited, is thrown out into perdition.

This ethical idea of salvation and the predestinarian limitation of acceptance to the elect are constantly in conflict in the mind of Jesus. In one case, however, he finds comfort in predestination. When the rich young man went away, not having had the strength to give up his possessions for the sake of following Jesus as he had been commanded to do, Jesus and his disciples were forced to draw the conclusion that like other rich men, he was lost, and could not enter into the kingdom of God. But immediately afterwards Jesus objects, "With men it is impossible, but not with God, for with God all things are possible" (Mark 10:17–27). That is, he will not give up hope that the young man, in spite of appearances, which are against him, will be found to belong to the kingdom of God, solely by virtue of the secret all-powerful will of God. Of an expected "conversion" of the young man there is no mention.

In the Beatitudes, on the other hand, the argument is reversed: the predestination is inferred from its outward manifestation. It may seem to us inconceivable, but they are predestinarian in form. Blessed are the poor in spirit! Blessed are the meek! Blessed are the peacemakers!—that does not mean that by virtue of their being poor in spirit, meek, peace-loving, they deserve the kingdom. Jesus does not intend the saying as an injunction or exhortation, but as a simple statement of fact: in their being poor in spirit, in their meekness, in their love of peace, it is made manifest that they are predestined to the kingdom. By the possession of these qualities they are marked as belonging to it. In the case of others (Matt 5:10–12), the predestination to the kingdom is made manifest by the persecutions which befall them in this world. These are the light of [[324]] the world, which already shines among men for the glory of God (Matt 5:14–15).

The kingdom cannot be "earned"; one is called to it and shows oneself to be called to it. On closer examination it appears that the idea of reward in the sayings of Jesus is not really an idea of reward, because it is set against a background of predestination. For the present it is sufficient to note that the eschatological-predestinarian view brings a mysterious element of dogma not merely into the teaching, but also into the public ministry of Jesus, with the restraint that is called for by the dangerous knowledge and crying of those possessed by demons. How notably and thoroughly the Gospels would have to have been worked over if, as Wrede and others want to assume, they originally reported the activity of a simple teacher!

What is the mystery of the kingdom of God? It must consist of something more than just its nearness, and something of extreme importance; otherwise Jesus here would be indulging in mere mystery-mongering. The saying about the light which is put on the stand, so that what was hidden may be revealed to those who have ears to hear, implies that he is making a tremendous revelation in the parables about the seed and the harvest and the growth and the unfolding (Mark 4). The mystery must in some way express why the kingdom must come now, and how people see how near it is. For both the Baptist and Jesus had proclaimed why it is very near. The mystery, therefore, must consist of something more than that.

In these parables it is not the idea of development, but the immediacy which occupies the foremost place. The description aims at raising the question how, and by what power, incomparably great and glorious results can be infallibly produced by an insignificant act without human aid. A man sowed seed. Much of it was lost, but the little that fell into good ground brought forth a harvest—thirty-, sixty-, a hundredfold—which left no trace of the loss in the sowing. How did that come about?

A man sows seed and does not trouble any further about it—cannot indeed do anything to help it. But he knows that after a definite time the glorious harvest which arises out of the seed will stand before him. By what power?

An extremely minute grain of mustard seed is planted in the earth and there necessarily arises out of it a great bush, which certainly cannot have been contained in the grain of seed. How was that?

What the parables emphasize is therefore, so to speak, the intrinsically negative, inadequate character of the initial fact which, as by a miracle, in the appointed time, through the power of God, is followed by the other. The parables do not stress the natural, but the miraculous character of such occurrences.

But what is the initial fact of the parables? It is the sowing.

It is not said that by the man who sows the seed Jesus means himself. The man [[325]] has no importance. In the parable of the mustard seed he is not even mentioned. All that is asserted is that the initial fact is already present, as certainly present as the time of the sowing is past at the moment when Jesus speaks. That being so, the kingdom of God must follow as certainly as harvest follows sowing. As a man believes in the harvest without being able to explain how from one seed first tall grass and then hundreds of grains form but expectantly awaits them in their time, because they have been sown, so with the same necessity he may believe in the kingdom of God.

And the initial fact? Jesus can mean only one thing: the movement of repentance evoked by the Baptist and now intensified by his own preaching. That compels the bringing in of the kingdom by the power of God, as man's sowing necessitates the giving of the harvest by the same infinite Power. Anyone who knows this sees with different eyes the corn growing in the fields and the harvest ripening, for he sees the one fact in the other, and awaits along with the earthly harvest the heavenly harvest, the revelation of the kingdom of God.

If we look into the thought more closely, we see that the coming of the kingdom of God is connected with the harvest not only symbolically or analogically, but also really and temporally. The harvest ripening upon earth is the last! With it comes the kingdom of God which brings in the new age. When the reapers are sent into the fields, the Lord in heaven will cause his harvest to be reaped by the holy angels.

If the parables of Mark 4 contain the mystery of the kingdom of God, and are therefore capable of being summed up in a single formula, this can be none other than the joyful invitation, "You who have eyes to see, read in the harvest which is ripening upon earth what is being prepared in heaven!" The eager eschatological hope which believed the end to be so near inevitably regarded the natural process as the last of its kind, and gave it a special significance in view of the event which it was to set off.

The logical and temporal congruence becomes complete if we assume that the movement initiated by the Baptist began in the spring, and notice that Jesus, according to Matt 9:37 and 38, before sending out the disciples to make a speedy proclamation of the nearness of the kingdom of God, uttered the remarkable saying about the rich harvest. It seems like a final expression of the thought contained in the parables about the seed and its promise, and finds its most natural explanation in the supposition that the harvest had come. The fact that in preaching to the disciples Jesus is besieged by a great host of people who do not want to leave him can be understood more easily if it is assumed that the harvest had already been brought in.

The above interpretation of the parables of the mystery of the kingdom of God is of course an *a posteriori* one. Make of it what you will. But one thing is certain: the initial fact to which Jesus points, under the figure of the sowing, [[326]] must be somehow or other connected with the eschatological preaching of repentance which had been begun by the Baptist.

That may be the more confidently asserted because Jesus in another mysterious saying describes the days of the Baptist as a time which has an effect on the coming of the kingdom of God. "From the days of John the Baptist," he says in Matt 11:12, "until now, the kingdom of heaven is subjected to violence, and the violent wrest it to themselves."

The saying has nothing to do with individuals entering the kingdom; it simply asserts that since the appearance of the Baptist a certain number of persons are engaged in forcing on and compelling the coming of the kingdom. Jesus' expectation of the kingdom is an expectation based upon a fact which exercises an active influence upon the kingdom of God. It is not he, nor the Baptist who are "working at the coming of the kingdom"; it is the host of penitents which is wringing it from God, so that it may now come at any moment.

The eschatological insight of Johannes Weiss made an end of the modern view that Jesus founded the kingdom. It did away with all "activity" towards the kingdom of God and made the part of Jesus purely a waiting one. Now the activity comes back into the preaching of the kingdom, but this time eschatologically conditioned. The secret of the kingdom of God which Jesus unveils in the parables about confident expectation in Mark 4, and declares in so many words in the eulogy on the Baptist (Matthew 11), amounts to this, that in the movement to which the Baptist gave the first impulse, and which still continued, there was an initial fact which drew after it the coming of the kingdom, in a fashion which was miraculous, unintelligible, but unfailingly certain, since the sufficient cause for it lay in the power and purpose of God.

It should be observed that in these parables, as well as in the related saying at the sending out of the Twelve, Jesus uses the formula, "He who has ears to hear, let him hear" (Mark 4:23 and Matt 11:15), thereby signifying that in this utterance there lies concealed a supernatural knowledge of the plans of God, which only those who have ears to hear—that is, the foreordained—can detect. For others these sayings are unintelligible.

If this genuinely "historical" interpretation of the mystery of the kingdom of God is correct, Jesus must have expected the coming of the kingdom at harvest time. And that is just what he did expect. That in fact is why he sends his disciples out. They are to make known in Israel, as speedily as may be, what is about to happen.

Now what was veiled in the parables may be disclosed, and what was to be kept a secret is no longer one. That explains the remark in the discourse at the sending out: "What I say to you in the darkness, speak out in the light, and what you hear in the ear, proclaim from the rooftops" (Matt 10:27). The secret which is to be made manifest is that the kingdom is coming now, at harvest time. The "is near" has become "is here."

[[327]] That in the sending out of the disciples Jesus was activated by a dogmatic idea becomes clear when we notice that according to Mark the mission of the Twelve followed immediately on the rejection at Nazareth. The unreceptiveness of the Nazarenes had made no impression upon him; he was only astonished at their unbelief (Mark 6:6). This passage is often interpreted to mean that he was astonished to find his miracle-working power fail him. There is no hint of that in the text. But he may have been astonished that in his native town there were so few believers, that is, elect, knowing as he did that the kingdom of God could appear at any moment. But that hardening makes no difference whatever to the nearness of the coming of the kingdom.

The evangelist, therefore, places the rejection at Nazareth and the mission of the Twelve side by side, simply because he found them in this temporal connection in the tradition. If he had been working by "association of ideas," he would not have arrived at this order. What is historical is the lack of connection, the impossibility of applying any natural explanation, because the course of the history was determined, not by outward events, but by decisions governed by dogmatic, eschatological considerations.

To how great an extent this was the case in regard to the mission of the Twelve is clearly seen from the "charge" which Jesus gave them. He tells them in plain words (Matt 10:23) that he does not expect to see them back in the present age. The parousia of the Son of man, which is logically and temporally identical with the dawn of the kingdom, will take place before they have completed a hasty journey through the cities of Israel to announce it. That the words mean this and nothing else, that they ought not to be in any way toned down, should be sufficiently evident. This is the form in which Jesus reveals to the disciples the secret of the kingdom of God. A few days later, he utters the saying about the violent who, since the days of John the Baptist, are forcing on the coming of the kingdom.

It is equally clear, and here the dogmatic considerations which guided the resolutions of Jesus become still more prominent, that this prediction was not fulfilled. The disciples returned to him and the appearing of the Son of man had not taken place. The actual history disavowed the dogmatic history on which the action of Jesus had been based. An event of supernatural history which had to take place, and to take place at that particular point of time, failed to come about. For Jesus, who lived wholly in the dogmatic history, that was the first "historical" occurrence, the central event which closed the former period of his activity and gave the coming period a new forward orientation.

To this extent modern theology is justified when it distinguishes two periods in the life of Jesus: an earlier one, in which he is surrounded by the people, and a later one, in which he is "deserted" by them, and travels about only with the Twelve. To explain this difference of attitude, which they thought themselves [[328]] bound to account for on natural historical grounds, modern theologians invented the theory of growing opposition and waning support. Weisse had directly opposed this theory.[7] Keim, the scholar who devised it, was aware that in setting it up he was going against the plain sense of the texts. Later writers lost this consciousness, just as in the First and Third Gospels the significance of the messianic secret in Mark gradually faded away; they imagined that they could find the basis of fact for the theory in the texts, and did not realize that they only believed in the desertion of the crowd and the "flights and withdrawals" of Jesus because they could not otherwise explain historically the alteration in his conduct, his withdrawal from public work, and his resolve to die.

The thoroughgoing eschatological school makes better work of it. It recognizes in the non-occurrence of the parousia promised in Matt 10:23 the

---

7. Weisse thought that there was no hint in the texts of the desertion of the people, since according to these, Jesus was opposed only by the Pharisees, never by the people. The abandonment of the activity in Galilee and the departure to Jerusalem must, he thought, have been due to some unrecorded fact which revealed to Jesus that the time had come to act in this way. Perhaps, he adds, it was the waning of Jesus' miracle-working power which caused the change in his attitude, since it is remarkable that he performed no further miracles during his stay in Jerusalem. The discussion about washing hands (Mark 7:1–23), which is always adduced to explain Jesus' "flight," in reality represents a defeat of the Pharisees. Really the theory of the "apostasy of the Galileans," which is varied in a more or less tasteful way in the modern Lives of Jesus, does not owe its existence to any facts that could be adduced with a semblance of justification, but only to Mark's simple report "And Jesus set out and went to the neighbourhood of Tyre" (7:24). For the assumption of a "happy" and an unhappy period in the activity of Jesus see Albert Schweitzer, *Das Leidens- und Messianitätsgeheimnis. Eine Skizze des Lebens Jesu*, 1901, 3ff., on the four presuppositions of the modern historical attempt at a solution.

"historical fact," in the estimation of Jesus, which was added to other reasons for limiting his public activity and caused the definitive "evasion."

The whole history of "Christianity" down to the present day, that is to say, the real inner history of it, is based on the "delay of the parousia," i.e., the failure of the parousia to materialize, the abandonment of eschatology, and the progress and completion of the "de-eschatologizing" of religion which has been connected with it. It should be noted that the non-fulfilment of Matt 10:23 is the first postponement of the parousia [['advent']]. We therefore have here the first significant date in the "history of Christianity"; it gives to the work of Jesus a new direction, otherwise inexplicable.

Here we recognize at the same time why the Markan hypothesis, in constructing the "Life of Jesus," found itself obliged to have recourse more and more to the help of modern psychology, and thus necessarily became more and more unhistorical. The fact which alone makes possible an understanding of the whole is lacking in this Gospel. Without Matthew 10 and 11 everything remains enigmatic. For this reason Bruno Bauer and Wrede are in their own way the only consistent representatives of the Markan hypothesis from the point of view of historical criticism, when they arrive at the result that the Markan account is inherently unintelligible. Keim, with his strong sense of historical reality, rightly felt that the plan of the life of Jesus should not be constructed exclusively on the basis of Mark.

The recognition that Mark alone gives an inadequate basis is more important than any "Ur-Mark" theories, for which it is impossible to discover a literary foundation or find an historical use. A simple observation of events takes us beyond Mark. In the discourse material of Matthew, which the modern-historical school thought they could scatter in here and there, wherever there seemed to be room for it, there lie hidden certain facts—unfulfilled facts, but all the more important for that.

Why Mark describes the events and discourses around the mission of the Twelve with such careful authentication is a literary question which the [[329]] historical study of the life of Jesus may leave open; the more so since, even as a literary question, it is insoluble.

The prediction of the parousia of the Son of man is not the only one which remained unfulfilled. There is the prediction of suffering which is connected with it. To put it more accurately, the prediction of the appearing of the Son of man in Matt 10:23 leads up to a prediction of sufferings, which, working up to a climax, forms the remainder of the discourse at the sending out of the disciples. This prediction of sufferings has as little to do with objective history as the prediction of the parousia. Consequently, none of the Lives of Jesus which follow the lines of a natural psychology, from Weisse down to Oskar Holtzmann, can make anything of it.[8] They either strike it out, or transfer it to the last "gloomy epoch" of the life of Jesus, regard it as an unintelligible anticipation, or put it down to the account of "community theol-

---

8. Bousset is most consistent in assessing the sending out and all that is attached to it as "unclear and obscure tradition."

ogy," which serves as a scrap-heap for everything for which they cannot find a place in the "historical life of Jesus."

But in the texts it is quite evident that Jesus is not speaking of suffering and tribulation after his death, but of suffering which will befall them as soon as they have gone from him. The death of Jesus is not presupposed here, but only the parousia of the Son of man, and it is implied that this will occur jut after these sufferings and bring them to a close. Had "community theology" remoulded the tradition, as is always being asserted, it would have made Jesus give his followers directions for their conduct after his death. That we never find anything of this kind is the best proof that there can be no question of such a deep, later remoulding of the life of Jesus. How easy it would have been to scatter here and there through the discourses of Jesus directions which were to be applied only after his death! But "community theology," which is made responsible for so much, did not do so, just as it is also innocent of much of what it is accused of.

The sufferings of which the prospect is held out at the sending out of the disciples are doubly, trebly, indeed four times incomprehensible. First—and this is the only point which modern historical theology has noticed—there is not a shadow of a suggestion in the outward circumstances of anything which could form a natural occasion for such predictions of, and exhortations relating to, suffering. Secondly—and this has been overlooked by modern theology because it had already declared that prediction of sufferings to be unhistorical in its own characteristic fashion, viz., by striking it out—because it was not fulfilled. Thirdly—and this has not entered into the mind of modern theology at all—because these sayings were spoken in the closest connection with the promise of the parousia and are placed in the closest connection with that event. Fourthly, because the description of what will befall the disciples is quite without any basis in experience. A time of general dissension will begin, in which brothers will rise up against brothers, and fathers against sons and children against their parents, to cause them to be put to death (Matt 10:21). And the disciples "will be hated of all men for his name's sake." Let them strive to hold out to the "end," [[330]] that is, to the coming of the Son of man, in order that they may be saved (Matt 10:22).[9]

In the same discourse Jesus predicts to the disciples that to their own surprise a supernatural wisdom will suddenly speak from their lips, so that it will not be they but the Spirit of God who will answer the great ones of the earth. Since for Jesus and early Christian theology the Spirit is a reality which is to descend upon the elect among mankind only in consequence of a definite event—the outpouring of the Spirit which, according to the prophecy of Joel, would precede the day of judgment—Jesus must have supposed that this would occur during the absence of the disciples, in the midst of the time of strife and confusion.

---

9. For dying and surviving in the pre-messianic tribulation see [[Schweitzer, *Quest*,]] 249–52.

To put it differently, the whole of the discourse at the sending out of the Twelve, taken in the clear sense of the words, is a prediction of the events of the "end time," events which are immediately at hand, in which the supernatural eschatological course of history will break through into the natural course of history. The expectation of sufferings is therefore dogmatic and unhistorical, as is, precisely in the same way, the expectation of the outpouring of the Spirit uttered at the same time. According to the messianic dogma, the parousia of the Son of man is to be preceded by a time of strife and confusion—as it were, the birth-pangs of the Messiah—and the outpouring of the Spirit. It should be noticed that according to Joel 3 and 4 the outpouring of the Spirit, along with the miraculous signs, forms the prelude to the judgment; and also, that in the same context, Joel 4:13, the judgment is described as the harvest-day of God.[10] Here we have a remarkable parallel to the saying about the harvest in Matt 9:38, which forms the introduction to the discourse at the sending out of the disciples.

There is only one point in which the predicted course of eschatological events is incomplete: the appearance of Elijah is not mentioned. Jesus could not prophesy to the disciples the parousia of the Son of man without pointing them, at the same time, to the pre-eschatological events which must first occur. He had to open to them a part of the secret of the kingdom of God, viz., the nearness of the harvest, so that they were not taken by surprise and caused to doubt by these events. Thus this discourse is historical as a whole and down to the smallest detail precisely because, according to the view of modern theology, it must be judged unhistorical. It is eschatological and dogmatic. Jesus had no need to instruct the disciples about what they were to teach. They had only to utter a cry. But he had to enlighten them about the events which were to take place. Therefore the discourse does not consist of instruction, but talks of sufferings and of parousia.

10. Joel 4:13: "Put in the sickle, for the harvest is ripe!" The last judgment is also described as the heavenly harvest in the Apocalypse of John: "Thrust in your sickle and reap; for the time is come to reap; for the harvest of the earth is ripe. And the one who sat on the cloud cast his sickle over the earth; and the earth was reaped" (Rev 14:15, 16). The most striking parallel to the discourse at the sending out of the disciples is offered by the Syriac Apocalypse of Baruch: "Behold, the days come when the time of the world shall be ripe, and the harvest of the sowing of the good and of the evil shall come, when the Almighty shall bring upon the earth and upon its inhabitants and upon their rulers confusion of spirit and terror that makes the heart stand still; and they shall hate one another and provoke one another to war; and the despised shall have power over those of repute, and the mean shall exalt themselves over those who are highly esteemed. And the many shall be at the mercy of the few . . . and all who are saved and escape the above-mentioned (dangers) shall be given into the hands of my servant, the Messiah" (chap. 70). The connection between the ideas of harvest and judgment was therefore one of the stock features of the apocalyptic writings. As the Apocalypse of Baruch dates from the period about A.D. 70, it may be assumed that this association of ideas was also current in the Jewish apocalyptic of the time of Jesus. Here is a basis for understanding the secret of the kingdom of God in the parables of sowing and reaping historically and in accordance with the ideas of the time. What Jesus did was to make known to those who understood him that the coming earthly harvest was the last, and was also the token of the coming heavenly harvest.

That being so, we may judge with what right modern theology dismisses the great Matthean discourses out of hand as mere "composite discourses." Just let anyone try to show how the evangelist, when he was racking his brains over the [[331]] task of making a "discourse at the sending out of the disciples," half piecing it together out of sayings in the tradition and "community theology" and half inventing it, lit on the curious idea of making Jesus speak entirely of inopportune and unpractical matters, and of then going on to provide the evidence that they never happened.

The announcement of the suffering as holding out the prospect of the eschatological distress is part and parcel of the preaching of the nearness of the kingdom of God. It is the practical version of the notion of the secret of the kingdom of God. It is for that reason that the notion of suffering appears at the end of the beatitudes and in the closing petition of the Lord's Prayer. For the *peirasmos* [['trial']] which is in view there is not an individual psychological temptation, but the general eschatological time of tribulation. God in his almighty grace is besought to spare those who pray so earnestly for the coming of the kingdom the bitter time of testing and proving and save them immediately from the power of the evil forces which rage in that tumult.

There followed neither the sufferings, nor the outpouring of the Spirit, nor the parousia of the Son of man. The disciples returned safe and sound and full of a proud satisfaction (Mark 6:30).

From the moment when they rejoined him, all his thoughts and efforts were devoted to getting rid of the people in order to be alone with them (Mark 6:30–33). Previously, during their absence, he had almost openly taught the multitude about John the Baptist, about what was to precede the coming of the kingdom, and about the judgment which would come upon the impenitent, even upon whole towns (Matt 11:20–24), because, in spite of the miracles which they had witnessed, they had not recognized the day of grace and used it for repentance. At the same time he had rejoiced before them over all those whom God had enlightened so that they saw what was happening and had called them to his side (Matt 11:25–30). In this hymn, in the unique knowledge and perfection of power bestowed on him by God, he goes so far that he almost discloses the mystery of his own person.[11]

And now suddenly, the moment the disciples return, his one thought is to get away from the people. However, they follow him and run along the

---

11. With what right does modern critical theology tear apart even the discourse in Matthew 11 in order to make the "cry of jubilation" into the cry with which Jesus greeted the return of his disciples, and to accommodate the curse on Chorazin and Bethsaida somewhere in an appropriately gloomy context? Is not all this apparently disconnected material held together by belief in the imminent fulfilment of the mystery of the kingdom of God? And how could Jesus have greeted the return of the disciples with a "cry of jubilation"? According to the prospects that he had held out for them in the discourse when he sent them out, their return must have been a bitter disappointment for him. It should also be noted how remarkably briefly the end of this action, which had such a great introduction, is reported. It is simply related that the disciples returned to Jesus. There is nothing about the area that they travelled through and the time that they spent. Matthew does not even mention the return.

shores of the lake. After staying with them for a day he crosses over to Beth-saida[12] and returns from there to the west bank. Finally he "slips away" to the north, because he cannot be alone in Galilee and yet he must be alone. Modern theology is right: he really does flee; not, however, from hostile scribes, but from the people, who dog his footsteps in order to await in his company the revelation of the kingdom of God and of the Son of man . . . in vain.

In his first Life of Jesus Strauss raises the question whether, in view of Matt 10:23, Jesus did not think of his parousia as a transformation which would take place during his lifetime. Ghillany bases his work on this possibility as an established historical fact. Dalman takes this assumption to be the necessary [[332]] correlative of the interpretation of the self-designation Son of man on the basis of Daniel and the apocalypses. If Jesus, he argues, designated himself in this futuristic sense as the Son of man who comes from heaven, he must have assumed that he would first be transported there. "A man who had died or been transported from the earth might perhaps be brought into the world again in this way, or one who had never been on earth might descend there in such a fashion." But as this conception of transformation and transportation seems untenable to Dalman in the case of Jesus, he treats it as a *reductio ad absurdum* of the eschatological interpretation of the title Son of man.

But why? If Jesus as a man walking in a natural body on earth predicts to his disciples the parousia of the Son of man in the immediate future, with the secret conviction that he himself was to be revealed as the Son of man, he must have made precisely this assumption that he would first be supernaturally removed and transformed. He thought of himself as anyone must who

---

12. Erich Klostermann in his commentary on Mark, Tübingen 1907, 53, joins other exegetes in being amazed that the people going along the shore get to the other shore of the Jordan by the beach of Bethsaida before Jesus and wants to conclude from this that this cannot have been a "particularly good tradition." Here he overlooks the fact that it is not said in the text that the instruction by the sea and the meal took place on the other shore. He does not even allow himself to be deterred by the information that in the evening (Mark 6:45) Jesus wants to use the boat to get "over" (*eis to peran*) to Bethsaida. He wants to assume that this was not a real crossing but merely a journey to a place close by on the same shore. But in that case why did the evangelist write *eis to peran*? And how could Jesus expect to get rid of the people this way? If we let the information speak as it stands, it says that Jesus went away from the western shore with the intention of seeking a solitary place (Mark 6:32). Whether this destination lay on the western or the eastern shore we are not told. From the boat he sees the crowd following on the shore on foot. Whether Jesus then lands at the place originally planned or on seeing the crowd decides to land again is not explicitly stated. All that is certain is that the people cannot have crossed the Jordan at this place and that the place of coming together must therefore be sought on the western shore. The continuation of the narrative also indicates this. In the evening Jesus makes the disciples go ahead, while he remains with the people a while longer and instructs them later to take him into the boat at a particular place in order to cross over to Bethsaida. If it was a short stretch on the same shore, they too could have gone back on foot. But the important thing is to cross the Jordan and thus put an obstacle in the way of those following. So the tradition is not "artificial," nor is it "not particularly good," but pertinent and clear.

believes in the immediate coming of the last things, as living in two different conditions: the present, and the future condition into which he is to be transformed at the coming of the new supernatural world. We learn later that the disciples on the way up to Jerusalem were entirely possessed by the thought of what they should be when this transformation took place. They dispute over who shall have the highest position (Mark 9:33); James and John wish Jesus to promise them in advance the thrones on his right hand and on his left (Mark 10:35–37).

However, Jesus does not rebuke them for indulging such thoughts, but only tells them that much service, humiliation and suffering in the present age is necessary to constitute a claim to such places in the future age, and that in the last resort it is not for him to allot the places on his left and on his right. They are for those for whom they are prepared; and so perhaps not for any of the disciples (Mark 10:40). At this point, therefore, the knowledge and will of Jesus are thwarted and limited by the predestinarianism which is bound up with eschatology.

It is quite wrong, however, to speak, as modern theology does, of the "service" required here as belonging to the "new ethic of the kingdom of God." For Jesus there is no morality of the kingdom of God, for in the kingdom of God all natural relationships, even, for example, the distinction of sex (Mark 12:25), are abolished. Temptation and sin no longer exist. All is "ruling," a "ruling" which has gradations—Jesus speaks of the "least in the kingdom of God"—as it has been determined in each individual case from eternity, and as each by his self-humiliation and renunciation of rule in the present age has proved his fitness for bearing rule in the future kingdom. For the loftier positions, however, it is necessary to have proved oneself in persecution and suffering. Accordingly, Jesus asks the sons of Zebedee whether, since they claim these thrones on his right hand and on his left, they feel themselves strong enough to drink of his cup and be [[333]] baptized with his baptism (Mark 10:38). To serve, to humble oneself, to incur persecution and death belong to "the interim ethic" just as much as penitence. They are indeed only a higher form of penitence.

An intense eschatological expectation is therefore impossible to conceive apart from the idea of a metamorphosis. The resurrection is only a special case of this metamorphosis, the form in which the new condition of things is realized in the case of those who are already dead. The resurrection, the metamorphosis and the parousia of the Son of man take place simultaneously and in one and the same act. It is therefore quite unimportant whether a man loses his life shortly before the parousia in order to "find his life," if that is what is ordained for him; it only means that he will experience the eschatological metamorphosis with the dead instead of with the living.

But what was to be the fate of the future Son of man during the messianic woes of the last times? It appears as if he was destined to share the persecution and the suffering. He says that those who want to be saved must take their cross and follow him (Matt 10:38), that his followers must be willing to lose their lives for his sake, and that only those who in this time of terror confess their allegiance to him will be confessed by him before his heavenly Father (Matt 10:32). Similarly, in the last of the Beatitudes, he had pronounced those blessed who were despised and persecuted for his sake (Matt 5:11, 12). As the future bearer of the supreme rule he must undergo the deepest humiliation. There is a danger that his followers may doubt him. Therefore the last words of his message to the Baptist, just at the time when he had sent out the Twelve, are "blessed is he who is not offended in me" (Matt 11:6).

If he familiarizes others with the thought that in the time of tribulation they may even lose their lives, he must have recognized that this possibility was still more strongly present in his own case. It is possible that there is a hint of what Jesus expected in the enigmatic saying about the disciples fasting "when the bridegroom is taken away from them" (Mark 2:20). In that case suffering, death and resurrection must have been closely united in his messianic consciousness from the first. This much, however, is certain, that at the time of the sending out of the disciples the thought of suffering formed part of the mystery of the kingdom of God and of the messiahship of Jesus, in the form that Jesus and all the elect were to be brought low in the *peirasmos* [['trial']] at the time of the death-struggle against the evil world-power rising up against them, if God willed, even to death. It mattered as little in his own case as in that of others whether he would experience the parousia as one transformed or as one who had died and risen again. But how could this self-awareness of Jesus remain concealed? It is true that the miracles had nothing to do with the messiahship of Jesus, since no one expected the Messiah to come as an earthly miracle-worker in the present age. On the contrary, it would have been the greatest of miracles if anyone had recognized the Messiah in an earthly miracle-worker. How far the cries of those [[334]] possessed by demons who addressed him as Messiah were intelligible to the people must remain an open question. What is clear is that his messiahship did not become known in this way even to his disciples.

And yet in all Jesus' speech and action the messianic consciousness shines out. One might, indeed, speak of the acts of his messianic consciousness. The beatitudes, indeed the whole of the Sermon on the Mount, with the authoritative "I" forever breaking through, are a manifestation of the high dignity which he ascribed to himself. Did not this "I" set the people thinking?

What did it mean when, at the close of this discourse, he mentioned people who, at the Day of Judgment, would call on him as "Lord," and appeal to the works that they had done in his name, and who yet were destined to be rejected because he would not recognize them (Matt 7:21–23)?

What did it mean when right at the beginning he pronounced those blessed who were persecuted and despised for his sake (Matt 5:11, 12)?

By what authority did this man forgive sins (Mark 2:5ff.)?

John the Baptist had not made such statements.

In the mission discourse, Jesus' "I" is still more prominent. He requires people to confess him, to love him more than father or mother, to bear their cross after him, and follow him to the death, since it is only for such that he can entreat his heavenly Father (Matt 10:32ff.). Admitting that the expression "Heavenly Father" contained no riddle for the listening disciples, since he had taught them to pray "Our Father which art in heaven,"[13] we have still to ask who he was whose yes or no would prevail with God to determine people's fate at the judgment.

The choosing of the twelve disciples is also a messianic act on the part of Jesus. They were not chosen to assist him in his work of teaching. Nor did he instruct them merely so that they should continue his work after his death. The very fact that they number twelve means that the choice is governed by a dogmatic purpose. He selects them to be those who are destined to come forward at the great moment to proclaim the event, and afterwards to be present at the messianic judgment. They are promised that they will sit upon twelve thrones and judge (Matt 19:28). Their future role is also related to the power to bind and to loose which is promised first to Peter (Matt 16:19), and then later to all twelve (Matt 18:18). Even sentences which they pronounce now will be valid at the coming judgment: the town which they have "marked" by shaking its dust off their feet will be worse off on the day of judgment than the land of Sodom and Gomorrah (Matt 10:14–15).

It is wrong to doubt the historicity of Jesus' words, "You are Peter and upon this rock I will build my church; and the gates of hell will not prevail against it. I will give you the keys of the kingdom of heaven, and whatever you bind on earth will be bound in heaven, and whatever you loose on earth will be loosed in heaven" (Matt 16:18–19). No one has yet been able to demonstrate why this [[335]] comment should have been inserted by those who wished to trace Petrine or Roman claims back to the Gospels. It has absolutely nothing to do with the empirical church and does not mean that Peter should decide what is to be allowed or not allowed in the "community" . . . for Jesus had not considered the existence of a community after his death. Nor is mythological material from Mithras worship and the Babylonian cults enough to explain it. The saying is about the very special authority which will be conferred upon the disciples in the imminent days of judgment when the Son of man comes to rule, because Peter was the first of men to address him by his title (with the man possessed of a demon it was the "spirits" who spoke!). The "church," moreover, is the pre-existent church which will appear at the end of time, and is synonymous with the kingdom.

Modern ethical ideas are not an appropriate criterion for evaluating this passage. It concerns the authority which Jesus wields and with which he endows others. It must also be remembered that their master expects that the twelve will pay for their position by grave persecution in the time of tribulation.

---

13. Jesus did not teach that all are children of God. This grace comes only to the elect. Moreover it becomes real only in the coming kingdom. As earthly men and women they are not yet children of God, any more than he is already the Messiah. But to the degree that they are destined for the kingdom and this imminently awaits them their status as children of God is already predated on the last days on earth.

The disciples, too, by reason of the status they are to be given, can save people who have no notion of what is taking place. Whoever receives him is saved, as if he had received the Son of man himself (Matt 10:40); their greeting is a real power for a house (10:13); whoever gives a man a cup of water "in the name of a disciple" will in no way lose his reward (Matt 10:42).

It is interesting that when the twelve were sent out by Jesus they had not yet been told of the great role they would play in the judgment. They learned their own destiny only after they had learned that of their master.

Jesus, too, already uses the power of judgment that he will later have. He pronounces judgment on the cities of Chorazin, Bethsaida and Capernaum (Matt 11:20–24), and proclaims that Jerusalem will be left desolate (Matt 23:37–38). Even a fig-tree is condemned by him, so that it will have no part in the messianic fruitfulness (Mark 11:12–14).[14]

As for the people, they had only the smallest knowledge of these strange and portentous words of Jesus. Before Jesus sent out his disciples, he practised the greatest reserve; moreover, most of what he said was to them only. And what he did say in public did not fully reveal the meaning which lay behind it; his words were by no means sufficient to convince his hearers that he could somehow be one with the awaited Messiah.

Therefore some thought him to be a prophet, some Elijah, and some John the Baptist risen from the dead, as appears clearly from the answer of the disciples at Caesarea Philippi (Mark 8:28).[15] The Messiah was a supernatural personality who was to be manifested at the end of days, and who was not expected upon earth before that.

At this point a difficulty presents itself. How could Jesus be Elijah for the people? Did they not hold John the Baptist to be Elijah? Not in the least! Jesus [[336]] was the first and the only person to attribute this office to him. Moreover, he declares it to the people as something mysterious, difficult to understand: "If you can receive it, this is Elijah, who is to come. Whoever has ears to hear, let him hear" (Matt 11:14, 15). In making this revelation he is communicating to them a piece of supernatural knowledge, opening up a part of the mystery of the kingdom of God. Therefore he uses the same for-

---

14. For the meaning of the saying about Jerusalem and the fig tree see [[Schweitzer, *Quest*,]] 255.

15. That Jesus could be taken for the Baptist risen from the dead shows how short the time of his activity before the death of the Baptist must have been. As the Baptist's question also shows, he became known only after the sending out of the disciples; Herod heard of him only after the death of the Baptist. Had he known anything of Jesus beforehand, it would have been impossible for him suddenly to identify him with the Baptist risen from the dead (Mark 6:16). This most elementary consideration is absent from all calculations of the length of the public ministry of Jesus. How chaotic the course of events must have been and how remarkable the thought-world of those days that Jesus could be regarded by the Galileans as the Baptist who had just died and risen again! Or is this remarkable piece of information also to be attributed to the "Pauline influence" on Mark or even to "community theology"?

mula of emphasis as when making known in parables the mystery of the kingdom of God (Mark 4).

The disciples were not with him at this time, and therefore did not learn what was the role of John the Baptist. When a little later, in descending from the Mount of Transfiguration, he predicted to the three who formed the inner circle of his followers the resurrection of the Son of man, they came to him with difficulties about the rising from the dead—how could this be possible when, according to the Pharisees and scribes, Elijah must first come? Thereupon Jesus explains to them that the preacher of repentance whom Herod had put to death had been Elijah (Mark 9:11–13).

Why did the people not take the Baptist to be Elijah? First, because he had not described himself as such. Secondly, because he did no miracle. He was only a natural man without any evidence of supernatural power, only a prophet. Thirdly, and that was the decisive point, he had himself pointed forward to the coming of Elijah. He who was to come, he whom he preached, was not the Messiah, but Elijah.

He describes Elijah, not as a supernatural personality, not as a judge, not as one who will be manifested at the unveiling of the heavenly world, but as one whose work resembles his own. The one who is to come is much more exalted than the one who proclaims him and yet is similar to him. He baptizes, but with the Holy Spirit. Since when had the Messiah baptized? No such activity is ever attributed to him in late Judaism and also in the Talmud.

It was inferred from Joel that before the last judgment the great outpouring of the Spirit would take place; before the last judgment, Malachi taught, Elijah would come. Until these events had occurred, the manifestation of the Son of man was not to be looked for. People's thoughts were fixed, therefore, not on the Messiah, but on Elijah and the outpouring of the Spirit.[16] John the Baptist in his preaching combines both ideas, and predicts the coming of the Great One who will "baptize with the Holy Spirit," i.e., who brings about the outpouring of the Spirit. His own preaching was only designed to ensure that the Great One at his coming would find a community sanctified and prepared to receive the Spirit.

When John heard in prison of one who did great wonders and signs, he desired to learn with certainty whether this was "he who should come." If this question is taken as referring to the messiahship, the whole narrative loses its meaning, and it upsets the theory of the messianic secret, since in this case at least one person had become aware, independently, of the office which belonged [[337]] to Jesus, not to mention all the ineptitudes needed to make John the Baptist here speak in doubt and confusion. Moreover, on this false interpretation of the question the point of Jesus' discourse is lost, since in that case it is not clear why he says to the people afterwards, "If you can receive it, John himself is Elijah." This revelation presupposes that Jesus and the

---

16. That had already been rightly noted by Colani. Later, however, theology lost sight of the fact because it did not know how to make any historical use of it.

people, who had also heard the question, also gave it its only natural meaning, referring it to Jesus as the bearer of the office of Elijah.

That the First Evangelist gives the episode a messianic setting by introducing it with the words "When John heard in the prison of the works of the Christ" does not alter the facts in the text. The sequel directly contradicts the introduction.

This interpretation also fully explains the evasive answer of Jesus, in which exegesis has always recognized a certain reserve without ever being able to explain why Jesus did not simply send him the message, "Yes, I am he"—to which, however, according to modern theology, he would have needed to add, "but another kind of Messiah from the one whom you expect."

The fact was that John the Baptist had put him in an impossible position. Jesus could not answer that he was Elijah if he held himself to be the Messiah; on the other hand he could not, and would not, disclose to him, still less to the messengers and the listening multitude, the secret of his messiahship. Therefore he sends this obscure message, which only contains a confirmation of the facts that John had already heard and closes with a warning, come what may, not to be offended in him. Of this the Baptist was to make what he could. It did not matter much how John understood the message. The time was much more advanced than he supposed; the hammer of the world's clock had risen to strike the last hour. All that he needed to know was that he had no cause to doubt.

In revealing to the people the true dignity of John the Baptist, Jesus unveiled to them almost the whole mystery of the kingdom of God, and nearly disclosed the secret of his messiahship. For if Elijah was already present, what stage had the coming of the kingdom reached? And if John was Elijah, who was Jesus? As two great prophets were not foreseen for the days before the end-time, there could only be one answer: the Messiah. But this seemed impossible, because the Messiah was expected as a supernatural personality. Viewed historically, the eulogy on John the Baptist is identical in content with the prediction of the parousia in the discourse on the sending out of the disciples. For the judgment and the other events belonging to the last time must follow immediately after the coming of Elijah. Now we can also understand why in the enumeration of the events of the last time in the mission discourse the coming of Elijah is not mentioned.

At the same time we recognize here how for Jesus, messianic doctrine forces its way into history and simply abolishes the historical aspect of the events. The Baptist had not held himself to be Elijah; the people had not thought of attributing [[338]] this office to him; the description of Elijah did not fit him at all, since he had done none of those things which Elijah was to do: and yet Jesus makes him Elijah simply because he expected his own revelation as Son of man, and before that it was necessary for Elijah first to have come. And even when John was dead, Jesus still told the disciples that in him Elijah had come, although the death of Elijah was not contemplated in the eschatological doctrine, and was in fact unthinkable. But Jesus somehow had to drag or force the eschatological event into the framework of the actual occurrences.[17]

Thus the concept of the "dogmatic element" in the narrative widens in an unsuspected fashion. And on closer examination even what before seemed natural becomes dogmatic. The Baptist is made into Elijah solely by the force of Jesus' messianic consciousness.

A short time afterwards, immediately upon the return of the disciples, he spoke and acted before their eyes in a way which presupposed the notion of the kingdom of God and his own messiahship. The people had been pursuing him; at a lonely spot on the shores of the lake they surrounded him, and he "taught them many things" (Mark 6:30, 34). The day was drawing to a close, but they held closely to him without troubling about food. In the evening, before sending them away, he fed them.

Weisse had already constantly pointed out that the feeding of the multitude was one of the greatest historical problems, because this narrative, like that of the transfiguration, is very firmly riveted to its historical setting and therefore imperatively demands explanation.

How is the historical element in it to be got at? Certainly not by seeking to explain the miraculous in it on natural lines, by suggesting that at the bidding of Jesus people brought out the baskets of provisions which they had been concealing. This imports into the tradition a natural fact which, so far from being hinted at in the narrative, is actually excluded by it.

Everything is historical, except the closing remark that they were all filled. Jesus distributed the provisions which he and his disciples had with them among the multitude so that each received a very little, after he had first offered thanks over them. The significance lies in the giving of thanks and in the fact that they had received consecrated food from him. Because he is the future Messiah, without their knowledge this meal becomes the messianic feast. With the morsel of bread which he gives his disciples to distribute to the people he consecrates them as partakers in the coming messianic feast, and gives them the guarantee that they who had shared his table in the time of his obscurity would also share it in the time of his glory. In the thanksgiving he gave thanks not only for the food, but also for the coming kingdom and all its blessings. It is the counterpart of the Lord's Prayer, where he so strangely inserts the petition for daily bread between the petitions for the coming of the kingdom and for deliverance from the *peirasmos*.[18]

[[339]] The feeding of the multitude was more than a love-feast, a fellowship-meal. From the point of view of Jesus it was a sacrament of salvation.

---

17. Jesus even asserted that what people had done with the Baptist was written about Elijah (Mark 9:13). It is impossible to discover what passage he can have meant. Nor can we assume that he read such a thing in an apocalypse which is lost to us. It is impossible that the returning Elijah was ever imagined as a suffering figure.

18. Many riddles would be solved if we knew what Jesus said when at this meal and the meal celebrated before his death he "gave thanks," and also what he taught the people by the sea at such length (Mark 6:34).

We never realize sufficiently that in a period when the judgment and the glory were expected as close at hand, one thought arising out of this expectation must have acquired special prominence—how, namely, in the present time a man could obtain a guarantee of coming unscathed through the judgment, of being saved and received into the kingdom, of being signed and sealed for deliverance amid the coming trial, as the chosen people in Egypt had a sign revealed to them from God by means of which they might be manifest as those who were to be spared.

The thought of signing and sealing runs through the whole of the apocalyptic literature. It is found as early as Ezekiel 9. There, God is making preparations for judgment. The day of the visitation of the city is at hand. But first the Lord calls to "the man clothed with linen who had the writer's ink-horn by his side" and says to him, "Go through the midst of the city, through the midst of Jerusalem, and set a mark on the middle of the foreheads of the men who sigh and cry over all the abominations that are done in its midst." Only after that does he give those who are charged with the judgment the command to begin, adding, "But do not come near any man on whom is the mark" (Ezek 9:4 and 6).

In *Psalms of Solomon* 15, the last eschatological writing before the movement initiated by the Baptist, it is expressly said in the description of the judgment that "the saints of God bear a sign upon them which saves them."

In Pauline theology very striking prominence is given to the thought of being sealed to salvation. The apostle is conscious of bearing about with him in his body "the marks of Jesus" (Gal 6:17), the "dying" of Jesus (2 Cor 4:10). This sign is received in baptism, since it is a baptism "into the death of Christ"; in this act the recipient is in a certain sense really buried with him, and thenceforth walks among men as one who belongs, even here below, to risen humanity (Rom 6:1ff.). Baptism is the seal, the earnest of the spirit, the pledge of what is to come (2 Cor 1:22; Eph 1:13, 14; 4:30).

This conception of baptism as "salvation" in view of what was to come dominates the whole of early theology. Its preaching might really be summed up in the words, "Keep your baptism holy and without blemish."

In the Shepherd of Hermas even the spirits of the men of the past must receive "the seal, which is the water" in order that they may "bear the name of God upon them." That is why the tower is built over the water, and the stones which are brought up out of the deep are rolled through the water (*Visions* 3 and *Similitudes* 9, 16).

In the Apocalypse of John the notion of the sealing stands prominently in the foreground. The locusts receive power to hurt only those who have not the seal of God on their foreheads (Rev 9:4, 5). The beast (Rev 13:16ff.) compels men to bear his mark; only those who will not accept it are to reign with Christ (Rev 20:4). [[340]] But the chosen hundred and forty-four thousand bear the name of God and the name of the Lamb upon their foreheads (Rev 14:1).

"Assurance of salvation" in a time of eschatological expectation demanded some kind of security for the future of which the pledge could be possessed in the present. And with this the predestinarian notion of election was in complete accord. If we find the thought of being sealed to salvation previously in the *Psalms of Solomon,* and subsequently in the same meaning in Paul, in the Apocalypse of John, and down to the Shepherd of Hermas, it may be assumed in advance that it will be found in some form or other in the strongly eschatological teaching of Jesus and John the Baptist.

Indeed, it may be said completely to dominate the eschatological preaching of John the Baptist, for this preaching does not confine itself to the declaration of the nearness of the kingdom and the demand for repentance, but at the same time performs an act to which it gives a special reference in relation to the forgiveness of sins and the outpouring of the Spirit. It is a mistake to regard baptism with water as a "symbolic act" in the modern sense, and make the Baptist decry his own wares by saying, "I baptize only with water, but the other can baptize with the Holy Spirit." He is not contrasting the two baptisms, but connecting them—whoever is baptized by him has the certainty that he will share in the outpouring of the Spirit which will precede the judgment, and at the judgment will receive forgiveness of sins, as one who is signed with the mark of repentance. The object of being baptized by him is to secure baptism with the Spirit later. The forgiveness of sins associated with baptism is proleptic; it is to be realized at the judgment. The Baptist himself did not forgive sin.[19] Had he done so, how could such offence have been taken when Jesus claimed for himself the right to forgive sins in the present (Mark 2:10)?

The washing practised by John was therefore an eschatological sacrament pointing forward to the outpouring of the Spirit and to the judgment, a provision for "salvation." Hence the wrath of the Baptist when he saw Pharisees and Sadducees crowding to his baptism: "You generation of vipers, who has warned you to flee from the wrath to come? Bring forth now fruits fit for repentance" (Matt 3:7, 8). By receiving baptism, that is, they are saved from the judgment.

As a washing for salvation it is a divine institution, a revealed means of grace. That is why Jesus' question whether the baptism of John was from heaven or from men placed the scribes in Jerusalem in so awkward a dilemma (Mark 11:30).

The authority of Jesus, however, goes further than that of the Baptist. The deliverance which is communicated at the Jordan by the holy washing is lost in Galilee by the relationship which the people enter into with the unrecognized future Messiah. Whoever confesses him and does not deny him in the persecution is justified at the judgment. For his part he gives those who throng around [[341]] him a right to the messianic meal by distributing food to them; only, they do not know what is happening to them and he cannot

---

19. That the baptism of John was essentially an act which made a claim to something in the future may also be seen from the fact that Jesus speaks of his sufferings and death as a special baptism and asks the sons of Zebedee whether they are willing, for the sake of gaining the thrones on his right hand and his left, also to undergo this baptism (Mark 10:37–39). If the baptism of John had had no real sacramental significance it would be unintelligible for Jesus to have used this metaphor.

solve the riddle for them. The supper at Lake Gennesaret was a veiled eschatological sacrament. Neither the disciples nor the multitude understood what was happening, since they did not know who he was who had thus made them his guests.[20]

This misunderstood meal has been transformed by tradition into a miracle. Allusions to the wonder of the messianic meal which perhaps occurred in the "thanksgiving" can have contributed something to this transformation, not to mention the feverish eschatological tension which then prevailed universally. Did not the disciples believe that on the same evening, when they had been commanded to take Jesus into their ship at the mouth of the Jordan, to which point he had walked along the shore, they saw him come walking towards them upon the waves of the sea? The impulse to the introduction of the miraculous into these reports came from the incomprehensible element which the men who surrounded Jesus at this time experienced and expected.[21]

The last supper at Jerusalem had the same sacramental significance as that at the lake. Towards the end of the meal Jesus, after giving thanks, makes a distribution. This has as little to do with satisfying hunger as the distribution to the Galilean believers. The meaning of the celebration rests on the fact that the Lord himself makes the distribution. In Jerusalem, however, they understood what he meant, and he declared it to them explicitly by telling them that he would drink no more of the fruit of the vine, until he drank it new in the kingdom of God. The mysterious images for the atoning significance of his death which he used at the time of the distribution do not touch the essence of the ceremony of the distribution; they are only discourses accompanying it (Mark 14:17–25).

From the beginning, baptism and the Lord's Supper existed as eschatological sacraments in the movement which later detached itself from Judaism under the name of Christianity. That explains why we find them both in Paul and in the earliest theology as sacramental acts, not as symbolic ceremonies, and in fact find them dominating the whole of dogma.[22] Because the history of dogma does not reckon with originally eschatological sacraments, it has to assume that right at the beginning of the development an originally pure, unsacramental theology descended to the depths of magical notions. Neither reasons nor evidence for this theology can be adduced. That after Jesus' death baptism and the Lord's Supper were still regarded for a while as purely "sym-

---

20. For the messianic meal in late-Jewish thought see [[Schweitzer, *Quest*,]] 255f.

21. Weisse very rightly observes that the historian's enterprise in Mark must be directed towards explaining how such "myths" could have been accepted by a reporter who was still as relatively close to events as our Mark.

22. For the difference between the primitive Christian sacraments and the "mysteries" of the oriental-Greek cult see Albert Schweitzer, *Paul and His Interpreters*, 1912, 206–30. Baptism and the eucharist were Hellenized in the second century. This process was made possible by the fact that intrinsically they were already sacraments. So their eschatological significance, which was automatically fading, was replaced by an evaluation corresponding to the Greek "mysteries." In Paul the eschatological character is still clearly marked.

bolic actions" is refuted by the testimony of Paul, who presupposes the sacramental view as the primitive Christian view.

In any case, the adoption of the baptism of John in Christian practice cannot be explained except on the assumption that it was the sacrament of the eschatological community, a revealed means of securing "salvation" which was not altered in the slightest by the messiahship of Jesus. How else could we explain the fact that baptism, without any commandment of Jesus, and without Jesus' [[342]] ever having baptized, was taken over into Christianity as a matter of course and was given a special reference to the receiving of the Spirit?

It is no use proposing to explain it as having been instituted as a symbolic repetition of the baptism of Jesus, thought of as "an anointing to the messiahship." There is not a single passage in early theology to support such a theory. And we may also point to the fact that Paul never refers to the baptism of Jesus in explaining the character of Christian baptism; he never, in fact, makes any distinct reference to it. And how could baptism, if it had been a symbolic repetition of the baptism of Jesus, ever have acquired this magic-sacramental sense of "salvation"?

The dual significance of ancient baptism, which makes it the guarantee both of the bestowal of the Spirit and of deliverance from the judgment, indicates that it is none other than the eschatological baptism of John. The only difference between the two actions is that in the Christian era baptism with water and the gift of the Spirit are connected not only logically, but also in time, seeing that since the day of Pentecost the period of the outpouring of the Spirit is present. The two portions of the eschatological sacrament which in the Baptist's preaching were distinguished in point of time—because he did not expect the outpouring of the Spirit until some future period—are now brought together, since one eschatological condition—the baptism with the Spirit—has become present. The "Christianizing" of baptism consisted in this and in nothing else; though Paul carried it a stage further when he formed the conception of baptism as a mystic partaking in the death and resurrection of Jesus.

Thus the thoroughgoing eschatological interpretation of the life of Jesus puts into the hands of those who are reconstructing the history of dogma in the earliest times an explanation of the concept of the sacrament, of which they had been able hitherto only to note the presence as an x of which the origin was undiscoverable, and for which they possessed no equation by which it could be evaluated. If Christianity as the religion of historically revealed mysteries was able to lay hold of the spirits of the East and of Hellenism, this was because already in its purely eschatological beginnings it was a sacramental religion.

The feeding of the multitude by the lake also belongs to the dogmatic element in the history. But no one had previously recognized it as what it really was, an indirect disclosure of the messianic secret, just as no one had understood the full significance of Jesus' descriptions of the Baptist as Elijah.

But how does Peter at Caesarea Philippi (Mark 8:27–32) know the secret of his Master? What he declares there is not a conviction which had gradually dawned on him and slowly grown through various stages of probability and certainty.

The real character of this incident has been interpreted with remarkable penetration by Wrede. The incident itself, he says, is to be understood in quite as [[343]] supernatural a fashion in Mark as in Matthew. But on the other hand one does not receive the impression that the writer intends to represent the confession as a merit or a discovery of Peter. "For according to the text of Mark, Jesus shows no trace of joy or surprise at this confession. His only answer consists of the command to say nothing about his person." Keim, whom Wrede quotes, had received a similar impression from the Markan account, and had supposed that Jesus had actually found the confession of Peter inopportune.

How is all this to be explained—the supernatural knowledge of Peter and the rather curt fashion in which Jesus receives his declaration?

It might be worthwhile putting the story of the transfiguration side by side with the incident at Caesarea Philippi, since there the divine sonship of Jesus is "once again" revealed to the "three," Peter, James and John, and the revelation is made supernaturally by a voice from heaven. It is characteristic that Mark's account does not seem to presuppose that those granted this confidence are experiencing something that they know already. At the beginning of the "transfiguration" Peter still addresses Jesus simply as "rabbi" (Mark 9:5). And what does it mean when Jesus, during the descent from the mountain, forbids them to speak to anyone about what they have seen until after the resurrection of the Son of man? That would exclude even the other disciples who knew only the secret of his messiahship. But why should they not be told of the divine confirmation of what Peter had declared at Caesarea Philippi and Jesus had "admitted"?

What has the transfiguration scene to do with the resurrection of the dead? And why are the thoughts of the disciples suddenly occupied, not with what they have seen, with the fact that the Son of man is to rise from the dead, but simply with the impossibility of the resurrection of the dead before the coming of Elijah? Those who see in the transfiguration a projection of Pauline theology backwards into the Gospel history do not realize the principal points and difficulties of the narrative. The problem lies in the conversation during the descent. Against the messiahship of Jesus, against his rising from the dead, they have only one objection to suggest: Elijah had not yet come.

We see here, in the first place, the importance of the revelation which Jesus had made to the people in declaring to them as a secret that the Baptist is Elijah. From the standpoint of the eschatological expectation no one could recognize Elijah in the Baptist unless he knew of the messiahship of Jesus. And no one could believe in the messiahship and "resurrection" of Jesus, that is, in his parousia, without presupposing that Elijah had in some way or other already come. This was therefore the primary difficulty of the disciples, the stumbling-block which Jesus had to remove for them by making the same revelation about the Baptist to them as to the people.

It is also once more abundantly clear that expectation was directed at that time primarily to the coming of Elijah.[23] But since the whole eschatological movement arose out of the Baptist's preaching, the natural conclusion is that in [[344]] preaching about him "who is to come" and baptize with the Holy Spirit John did not mean the Messiah, but Elijah.

But if the non-appearance of Elijah was the primary difficulty of the disciples in connection with the messiahship of Jesus and all that it implied, why does it strike the "three" and moreover all three of them together only now, and not at Caesarea Philippi?[24] How could Peter there have declared it and here still be labouring with the rest over the difficulty which stood in the way of his own declaration?

For intrinsic reasons, we should thus assume that in reality the "transfiguration" represented a manifestation of the messiahship of Jesus and that the scene at Caesarea Philippi in fact preceded it in time rather than following it.

Note the context in which it actually occurs. It falls in that inexplicable section Mark 8:34–9:30, in which the believing multitude suddenly appears in the company of Jesus who is staying in a Gentile district, only to disappear again, equally enigmatically, afterwards, when he sets out for Galilee, instead of accompanying him back to their own country.

In this section everything points to the situation after the return of the disciples from their mission. Jesus is surrounded by the people and has a need to be alone with his immediate followers. The disciples make use of the healing powers which he had bestowed upon them, and find that they are not enough in all cases (Mark 9:14–29). So the events reported take place in Galilee—whether east or west of the mouth of the Jordan it is impossible to decide.

But how could this story be torn out of its natural context and transposed to Caesarea Philippi, where both on external and internal grounds it is impossible? In the Markan account of the events which followed the sending out of the disciples we note remarkable disorder. We have two stories of feedings of the multitude with a crossing of the lake after each (Mark 6:31–56; Mark 8:1–22); two stories of Jesus going away towards the north with the same motive, that of being alone and unrecognized. The first time, after the controversy about the washing of hands, his journey is towards Tyre (Mark 7:24–30); the second time, after the demand for a sign, he goes into the district of Caesarea Philippi (Mark 8:27). The scene of the controversy about the washing of hands is some locality in the plain of Gennesaret (Mark 6:53ff.); Dalmanutha is named as the place where the sign was demanded (Mark 8:10ff.); this is probably similarly to be sought on the west bank.

23. Note too that the "Eli, Eli" of Jesus on the cross is also immediately interpreted in terms of Elijah (Mark 15:35).

24. We immediately see from this objection how utterly impossible it was for someone of their own accord "slowly to come to the knowledge of the messiahship of Jesus."

The most natural conclusion is to see the two cases of feeding the multitude and the two journeys northwards as identical. In that case, in the section Mark 6:31–9:30 we would have two sets of narratives worked into each other.

The seams in the account can be recognized in Mark 7:31, where Jesus is suddenly transferred from the north to the Decapolis, and in the saying in Mark 8:14ff., which makes explicit reference to the two feedings. Whether the [[345]] evangelist himself worked these two sets of narratives together or whether he found them already united cannot be determined, and is not of any direct historical importance. The disorder is in any case so complete that we cannot fully reconstruct each of the two narrative cycles.

The external reasons why the narratives of Mark 8:34–9:30, of which the scene is on the northern shore of the lake, are placed in this way after the incident of Caesarea Philippi are not difficult to grasp. The section contains an impressive discourse to the people on following Jesus in his sufferings, crucifixion and death (Mark 8:34–9:1). For this reason the whole series of scenes is attached to the revelation of the secret of the suffering of the Son of man; the redactor did not stop to think how the people could suddenly appear, and as suddenly disappear again. The statement "He called the people with the disciples" (Mark 8:34) could also have been an occasion for putting the section at this point, because previously Jesus had been alone with the twelve.

The whole scene therefore belongs to the days after the return of the disciples. We can no longer determine the point in time from which the six days are to be reckoned. The only certain thing is that the scene in Caesarea Philippi cannot be relevant here. Probably it was that Jesus was with the people for six days at a particular place.[25]

25. Some of the narratives contained in the passage Mark 6:31–9:30 take place in the Decapolis (the healing of the deaf and dumb man, Mark 7:32–37) and in Bethsaida (Mark 8:22–26), i.e., on the eastern shore. And indeed Jesus is surrounded by people here as well. Thus it is possible that Mark 8:23–9:29, where there is no indication of place, also presupposes the eastern shore as a locality. Accordingly we should assume that when Jesus crossed the Jordan after the return of the disciples he spent some days in Bethsaida. The people would then have consisted of the inhabitants of this place, which was a town he had already visited, as he had cursed it at the time of John's enquiry (Matt 11:21), and possibly also of the crowd, which had meanwhile crossed over from the western shore. But there are also reasons for supposing that the "transfiguration" and the scenes which frame it (Mark 8:34–9:29) took place on the western shore. In that case the mountain would not be near Bethsaida but identical with the one to which Jesus withdrew alone on the evening of the feeding (Mark 6:46) and the "house" (Mark 9:2) his usual lodgings in Capernaum. Thus the reported events took place in the days after their return from the eastern shore, during which Jesus stayed in the region of Gennesaret (Mark 6:53–56) until, after the discussion about the washing of hands, he departed north (Mark 7:1–24). This assumption is probably the more likely. Those who do not wish to accept the theory that the same events must have been reported twice must picture what happened as follows. Jesus went from the western shore to the region of Tyre (Mark 7:24), from there to the Decapolis, returned to the eastern shore (Mark 7:31–8:8), from there went over to the western shore (Mark 8:10–13), returned again to the eastern shore (Mark 8:14), stayed in Bethsaida (Mark 8:22), and from there set out for Caesarea Philippi. That he again visited the shores of the lake when he came from the north and then again tried to find solitude is not in itself impossible. Also the possibility of a second feeding,

What is contradictory about the scene in Caesarea Philippi where Peter tells the Lord who he really is and Jesus shows himself neither surprised nor particularly delighted by the knowledge of his disciple is thus not completely incomprehensible. The transfiguration had, in fact, been the revelation of the secret of the messiahship to the three who constituted the inner circle of the disciples. And Jesus had not himself revealed it to them; rather, in a state of rapture common to them all, in which they had seen the Master in transfigured light, they had seen him talking with Moses and Elijah and had heard a voice from heaven saying, "This is my believed Son, hear him."

We must continually make a fresh effort to realize that Jesus and his immediate followers were at that time in an enthusiastic state of intense eschatological expectation. We must picture them among the people, who were filled with penitence for their sins and with faith in the kingdom were expecting its coming hourly. The expectant multitude itself provided the certainty that the reckoning of time was right. This provided the psychological presuppositions for a shared visionary experience of the kind depicted in the transfiguration. It is interesting that primarily we have illusions on the part of the three disciples. Finally they see and hear and look on their Lord alone again and in his usual form and this brings the vision to an end. Jesus himself probably took part in the event only as an object. Peter played the active role.

In this ecstasy the "three" heard the voice from heaven saying who he was. Therefore the Matthaean report, in which Jesus praises Simon "because flesh and [[346]] blood have not revealed it to him, but the Father who is in heaven," is not really at variance with the briefer Markan account, since it rightly indicates the source of Peter's knowledge.

Nevertheless Jesus was astonished. For Peter here disregarded the command given during the descent from the mount of transfiguration. He had "betrayed" his Master's messianic secret to the Twelve. It could be that Jesus did not put the question to the disciples in order to reveal himself to them as Messiah, and that by the impulsive speech of Peter, upon whose silence he had counted because of his command, and to whom he had not specially addressed the question, he was forced to take a different line of action in regard to the Twelve from what he had intended. Perhaps he had never intended to reveal the secret of his messiahship to the disciples. Otherwise he would not have kept it from them at the time of their mission, when he did not expect

---

this time on the eastern shore (Mark 8:1–8), cannot be summarily dismissed, even though the nature of the narration—as if no such similar event had occurred before—makes for a strong prejudice against such an assumption and suggests positing a double account. Whether the riddle of the reporting of the events is solved one way or another is ultimately of secondary importance, for it has no bearing on the main question why Jesus is suddenly surrounded by people in Caesarea Philippi (Mark 8:34) and then just as surprisingly is alone again (Mark 9:30). It must be conceded from both external and internal evidence that the passage Mark 8:34–9:29 belongs to another place and to an earlier period. Thus the "transfiguration" precedes Jesus' appearance at Caesarea Philippi. This is the most important thing to establish. To assume the existence of a second Bethsaida lying on the western shore would complicate rather than remove the difficulties raised by Mark 7:31–9:29.

them to return before the Parousia. Even at the transfiguration the "three" do not learn it from his lips, but in a state of ecstasy. At Caesarea Philippi it is not he, but Peter, who reveals his messiahship. We may say, therefore, that Jesus did not voluntarily give up his messianic secret; it was wrung from him by the pressure of events.

Be that as it may, from Caesarea Philippi onwards the twelve know through Peter who he is . . . the secret of his suffering.

Pfleiderer and Wrede were quite right in pointing to the clear and definite predictions of the suffering, death and resurrection as the historically inexplicable element in our reports. The necessity of Jesus' death, by which modern theology endeavours to make his resolve and his predictions intelligible, is not a necessity which arises out of the historical course of events. There was no natural reason at that time for such a resolve on the part of Jesus. Had he returned to Galilee, he would immediately have had the multitudes flocking after him again.

In order to make the historical possibility of Jesus' resolve to suffer and his prediction of the sufferings in some measure intelligible, modern theology has to ignore the prediction of the resurrection which is bound up with them, for this is "dogmatic." However, that is illegitimate. We must, as Wrede insists, take the words as they are, and must not even indulge in ingenious explanations of the "three days." Therefore it is concluded that the resolve to suffer and to die is dogmatic; therefore, according to him, this is unhistorical, and only to be explained by a literary hypothesis.

But the thoroughgoing eschatological school says that it is dogmatic, and therefore historical. We understand Jesus' resolve to suffer only if we have first recognized that a mystery of suffering is also involved in the mystery of the kingdom of God, since the kingdom cannot come until the *peirasmos* [['trial']] has taken place. This certainty of suffering is quite independent of the historical circumstances, as is clearly shown by the beatitude on the persecuted in the Sermon on the Mount and the predictions in the discourse at the sending out of the Twelve. [[347]] Jesus' prediction of his own sufferings at Caesarea Philippi is precisely as unintelligible, precisely as dogmatic, and therefore precisely as historical as the prediction to the disciples at the time of their mission. The "must be" of the sufferings is the same—the coming of the kingdom and of the parousia [['advent']], which are dependent upon the *peirasmos* having first taken place.

In the first period Jesus' thoughts about his own sufferings were included in the more general thought of the suffering which formed part of the mystery of the kingdom of God. The exhortations to hold steadfastly to him in the time of trial, and not to lose faith in him, certainly tended to suggest that he thought of himself as the central point amid these conflicts and confusions, and reckoned on the possibility of his own death as much as on that of others. Upon this point nothing more definite can be said, since the mystery of Jesus' own sufferings does not detach itself from the mystery of the sufferings connected with the kingdom of God until after the messianic secret is made known at Caesarea Philippi. What is certain is that for him, suffering was always associated with the messianic secret, since he placed his parousia at the end of the pre-messianic tribulations in which he was to have his part.

The suffering, death and resurrection of which the secret was revealed at Caesarea Philippi are not therefore in themselves new or surprising.[26] The novelty lies in the form. The tribulation, so far as Jesus is concerned, is now connected with a historical event: he will go to Jerusalem, there to suffer death at the hands of the authorities.

For the future, however, he no longer speaks of the general tribulation which he is to bring upon the earth, nor of the sufferings which await his followers, nor of the sufferings in which they must gather round him and confess

---

26. The question remains how Jesus thought of the sequence of dying, rising and coming as Son of man. It would be intrinsically possible that he imagined the three events taking place consecutively in such a way that the supernatural course of events began as he was dying or even at the moment of his death agony, and that he would be revealed in his glory as Son of man. The cry of despair on the cross (Mark 15:34) would support this. The divine intervention which the Lord had expected in the moment of supreme need did not come. It is more probable that Jesus thought of his dying, rising and coming as Son of man as three separate acts despite their intrinsic connection. This is suggested above all by the saying on the way to Gethsemane: "After I am risen I will go before you into Galilee" (Mark 14:28). This cannot mean that he will appear to them in Galilee, but means that as the Risen One he will return at their head from Jerusalem to the lake, just as he led the procession to Jerusalem as one who was to die. The "go before you" is meant literally and locally and corresponds to the "and Jesus was going before them" of Mark 10:32. Far from pointing the disciples to Galilee, the saying keeps them in Jerusalem and bids them await the resurrection in this city. When the "young man" at the tomb has the women tell the disciples that they are going to Galilee because the Risen One is awaiting them there (Mark 16:7), this is a correction of the saying of the Lord which remained unfulfilled, and cannot be used for the theory of the "Galilee visions." According to the saying on the way to Gethsemane Jesus thus expects to die, then to rise and to go to Galilee. He probably also assumes that then the further events, his transformation into the Son of man, his advent in the clouds, the judgment and the descent of the glory of the kingdom of God will be played out there. It would accord with this that he has Jerusalem, which according to the usual messianology was regarded as the centre of the coming world, rejected (Matt 23:37 and 38, see also [[Schweitzer, *Quest*,]] 253f.). When he promises the judges that they will see his coming on the clouds of heaven (Mark 14:62) it seems most likely to assume as the place of this event the city in which they dwell; but it can also be that it was thought of as visible everywhere. If Jesus kept apart the three acts it is quite possible that he spoke to his disciples of his resurrection in specific words. There is no reason to regard the sayings Mark 8:31; 9:31 and 10:34 as inauthentic or worked over. Why should Jesus not also have prophesied his death and resurrection if on the basis of dogmatic notions he also envisaged other events? Even the "three days" could have figured in what he said. The only surprising thing is that this time his words are fulfilled to the degree that he really died and his disciples saw him "appear" after three days. The scene on the mountain (Mark 9:2–8) gives sufficient evidence of the ecstatic disposition of Peter and the two other disciples; of the rest of the disciples it is sufficiently attested by the glossolalia on the day of Pentecost. If the prophecies of Jesus' death and resurrection were edited after the event, how could it be explained that the special feature of dying on the cross is not mentioned and that the involvement of the "Gentiles" is not thought of? Note also that according to the saying of Jesus he will be mocked and scourged by the priests, elders and scribes and this will represent a main act in the expected drama, the humiliation before all the people. These difficulties in assuming a later origin of the sayings of Jesus are usually overlooked.

him. In the predictions of the passion to the disciples there is no word of that; at Jerusalem there is no word of that. This thought disappears once for all.

In the secret of his passion which Jesus reveals to the disciples at Caesarea Philippi the pre-messianic tribulation for others is set aside, abolished, concentrated upon himself alone, and that in the form that they are fulfilled in his own passion and death at Jerusalem. That was the new conviction that had dawned upon him. He must suffer for others . . . that the kingdom may come.

This change was due to the non-fulfilment of the promises made in the discourse at the sending out of the Twelve. He had thought then that he was letting loose the final tribulation and so compelling the coming of the kingdom. But the cataclysm had not occurred. He still expected it after the return of the disciples. He referred the crowd around him to the things to come and conjured them to endure with him, to give their lives, not to be ashamed of him in his humiliation, since otherwise the Son of man would be ashamed of them when he came in glory (Mark 8:34–9:1).[27]

On leaving Galilee he abandoned the hope that the final tribulation would begin of itself. If it delayed, that meant that there was still something to be done, [[348]] and that yet another of the violent had to lay violent hands upon the kingdom of God. The repentance movement had not been sufficient. When, in accordance with his commission, by sending forth the disciples with their message he hurled the firebrand which was to have kindled the fiery trials, the flame went out. He had not succeeded in sending the sword on earth and stirring up the conflict. And until the time of trial had come, the coming of the kingdom and his own manifestation as Son of man were impossible.

That meant, not that the kingdom was not near, but that God had resolved otherwise in regard to the time of trial. He had heard the "Lord's Prayer" in which Jesus and his followers prayed for the coming of the kingdom—and at the same time for deliverance from the *peirasmos* [['temptation, trial']]. The tribulation had not come; therefore God in his mercy and omnipotence had eliminated it from the series of eschatological events, and designated him, whose commission had been to bring it about, instead to accomplish it in his own person. As the one who was to rule over the members of the kingdom in the future age, he was appointed to serve them in the present, to give his life for them, the many (Mark 10:45 and 14:24), and to make in his own blood the atonement which they would have had to render in the tribulation.

The kingdom could not come until the debt which weighed upon the world was discharged. Until then, not only the believers living now but the chosen of all generations since the beginning of the world wait for their manifestation in glory: Abraham, Isaac and Jacob and all the countless unknown

27. Here at the same time we see specifically from the form of the proclamation of suffering that the passage Mark 8:34ff. is impossible after the disclosure at Caesarea Philippi. For the same reason the promises of suffering and tribulation in the Synoptic apocalypse Mark 13 cannot come from Jesus.

who are to come from the east and from the west to sit at tables with them at the messianic feast (Matt 8:11). The enigmatic *polloi*, the many for whom Jesus dies, are those predestined to the kingdom, since his death must at least compel the coming of the kingdom.[28]

Jesus probably read this in the sayings of the prophet Isaiah, which prophesied the suffering Servant of the Lord. The mysterious description of the one who in his humiliation was despised and misunderstood, who nevertheless bears the guilt of others and afterwards is made manifest in what he has done for them, pointed to him.

The Baptist's end, too, could well have indicated to Jesus the form his own would take. The preacher of repentance was set upon and killed by men, but this did not bring about the great persecution. His end was simply an incident in the normal course of events. From this Jesus could perceive that what had happened to Elijah was destined for him too; and it could also have revealed to him that the coming Son of man would suffer and even die, not in the great messianic time of tribulation, but in the natural course of things.

When Jesus came to realize this cannot be ascertained. Whether at the time of his transfiguration he had already seen how things would go is not clear from the words with which as he came down from the mountain he compared his fate to that of the Baptist (Mark 9:12–13). In any case, such an allusion was lost on [[349]] Peter; otherwise he would not have been so surprised at Caesarea Philippi when Jesus announced his resolve to suffer and to die.

Perhaps, when the disciples returned, Jesus still counted for some time on being revealed in glory as the Son of man and on the coming of the kingdom, and hence expected neither a general time of tribulation nor his own isolated suffering and death; rather, because the prophecies which he had

28. Weisse and Bruno Bauer had pointed out how enigmatic it was that Jesus in the sayings about his sufferings spoke of the many instead of his own or believers. Weisse found in the words the thought that Jesus died for the people as a whole; Bruno Bauer thought that the "for many" figured in the sayings of Jesus because it was produced from the standpoint of later community theology. This explanation is certainly wrong, for as soon as the sayings of Jesus come into contact with early theology the "many" disappear to give place to the believers. In the Pauline words of institution the form is "My body for you" (1 Cor 11:24)! Johannes Weiss follows in the footsteps of Weisse when he interprets the "many" as the people (*Die Predigt Jesu vom Reich Gottes*, [2]1900, 201). However, he gives quite a false twist to this interpretation by arguing that the "many" cannot include the disciples, since those "who in faith and penitence have received the message of the kingdom of God no longer need a special means of deliverance such as this. They are the elect; for them the kingdom is assured. But a ransom, a special means of salvation, is needed by the mass of the people, who in their blindness have incurred the guilt of rejecting the Messiah. For this grave sin, which is nevertheless to some extent excused as caused by ignorance, there is a unique atoning sacrifice, the death of the Messiah." This theory is based on a distinction of which there is no hint in the teaching of Jesus and it takes no account of the element of predestination which is an integral part of eschatology and which in fact dominated the thoughts of Jesus. The Lord is conscious that he dies only for the elect. His death cannot benefit the others, not even their repentance. Moreover, he does not die in order that one or another may enter the kingdom of God, but he provides atonement so that the kingdom itself may come. Until the kingdom comes, even the elect cannot possess it.

uttered as he sent out the disciples had not been fulfilled, he simply assumed that the plea of the Lord's Prayer for deliverance from the *peirasmos* had been heard.

Because it was written in Isaiah that the servant of God must suffer unrecognized and that those for whom he suffered would doubt him, his suffering could, and indeed had to, remain a mystery. In that case those who doubted him would not bring condemnation upon themselves. He no longer needed to adjure them for their own sakes to be faithful to him and to stand by him even amid reproach and humiliation; he could calmly predict to his disciples that they would all be offended in him and flee (Mark 14:26, 27); he could tell Peter, who boasted that he would die with him, that before dawn he would deny him thrice (Mark 14:29–31); all that was willed thus by scripture. They had to doubt him. But now they would not lose their blessedness, for he bore all sins and transgressions. Everything was buried in the atonement that he offered.

Therefore, also, there was no need for them to understand his secret. He spoke of it to them without any explanation. It was sufficient that they should know why he was going up to Jerusalem. They, for their part, were thinking only of the coming transformation of all things, as their conversation showed. The prospect which he had opened up to them was clear enough; the only thing that they did not understand was why he first had to die in Jerusalem. The first time that Peter ventured to speak to him about it, he had turned on him with cruel harshness, had almost cursed him (Mark 8:32, 33); later they no longer dared to ask him anything about it (Mark 9:32).

The new notion of his passion therefore has its basis in Jesus' authority to bring in the tribulation. In ethical terms, his taking the suffering upon himself was an act of mercy and compassion towards those who would otherwise have had to bear these tribulations, and perhaps would not have stood the test. In historical terms, the thought of his sufferings involves the same forced treatment both of history and eschatology as was manifested in the identification of the Baptist with Elijah. For now Jesus identifies his natural condemnation and execution with the predicted pre-messianic tribulations. This imperious forcing of eschatology into history is also its destruction; at the same time its assertion and abandonment.

Towards Passover, therefore, Jesus set out for Jerusalem, solely in order to die there.[29] "It is," says Wrede, "beyond question the opinion of Mark that Jesus went to Jerusalem because he had decided to die; that is obvious even from the details of the story."

[[350]] It is therefore a mistake to speak of Jesus as really "teaching" in Jerusalem. He has no intention of doing so. As a prophet he foretells in veiled parabolic form the offence which must come (Mark 12:1–12), exhorts people to watch for the parousia, pictures the nature of the judgment which the Son

29. The Lives of Jesus could be classified by whether they make Jesus go to Jerusalem to work or to die there. Here too Weisse's clear and certain perception is surprising. According to him Jesus' journey was a journey to death, not to the Passover.

of man will hold and, for the rest, thinks only how he can so provoke the Pharisees and the rulers that they will be compelled to get rid of him. That is why he violently cleanses the temple and attacks the Pharisees, in the presence of the people, with passionate invective.

For the revelation at Caesarea Philippi on, only the events which lead up to his death or, to put it more accurately, the events in which he himself is the sole agent, and brings about his own death, belong to the history of Jesus, in the strict sense. The other things that happen, the observations that are made, the questions that are laid before him for decision, the episodic incidents that occur in those days, have nothing to do with the real life of Jesus since they contribute nothing to the decisive issue, but merely form the anecdotal fringes of the real outward and inward event, the deliberate bringing down of death upon himself.

It is really amazing that Jesus succeeded in transforming into history this resolve which had its roots in dogma, and really dying alone. Is it not almost incomprehensible that his disciples were not involved in his fate? Not even the disciple who smote with the sword was arrested along with him (Mark 14:47); Peter, recognized in the courtyard of the high priest's house as one who had been with Jesus the Nazarene, was allowed to go free.

For a moment indeed, Jesus believes that the "three" are destined to share his fate, not from any outward necessity, but because they had professed themselves able to suffer the last extremities with him. When he asked the sons of Zebedee whether, in order to sit at his right hand and his left, they were prepared to drink his cup and be baptized with his baptism, they had declared that they were, and thereupon he had predicted that they should do so (Mark 10:38, 39). Peter had again on that last night, in spite of Jesus' warning, sworn that he would go even to death with him (Mark 14:31). So there was a possibility that these three could be taken at their word and would go through the trial with him. He takes them with him to Gethsemane and bids them remain near him and watch with him. And since they do not perceive the danger of the hour, he adjures them to watch and pray. They are to pray that they may not have to pass through the *peirasmos* since, though the spirit is willing, the flesh is weak. Amid his own sore distress he is anxious about them and their capacity to share his trial as they had declared their willingness to do.[30]

At the same time it is once more made clear that for Jesus the overall necessity of his death is grounded in dogma, not in external historical facts. Above the dogmatic eschatological necessity, however, there stands the omnipotence of God, which is bound by no limitations. As Jesus in the Lord's Prayer had taught his followers to pray for deliverance from the *peirasmos*, and as in his fears for [[351]] the three he bids them pray for the same thing, so now he himself prays for deliverance, even in this last moment when he knows that the armed band which is coming to arrest him is already on the

---

30. "That you fall not into temptation" is the content of the prayer in which they are to watch.

way. Ordinary history does not exist for him, only the will of God; and this stands above even eschatological necessity.

But how did this exact agreement between the fate of Jesus and his promise come about? Why did the authorities strike only at him and not as his whole following, not even at the disciples?

He was arrested and condemned on account of his messianic claims. But how did the high priest know that Jesus claimed to be the Messiah? And why does he put the accusation as a direct question without calling witnesses in support of it? Why was the attempt first made to produce witnesses to a saying about the temple which could be interpreted as blasphemy, in order to condemn him on this ground (Mark 14:57–59)?

Before that, as is evident from Mark's account, they had brought up a whole crowd of witnesses in the hope of securing sufficient evidence to justify his condemnation. And the attempt had not succeeded.

It was only after all these attempts had failed that the high priest brought his accusation concerning the messianic claim, and did so without citing the three necessary witnesses. Why? Because he had none. The condemnation of Jesus depended on his own admission. That was why they had endeavoured to convict him on other charges.[31]

This utterly unintelligible feature of the trial confirms what is evident also from the discourses and attitude of Jesus at Jerusalem, viz., that he had not been held by the multitude to be the Messiah, that the idea of his making such claims had not for a moment occurred to them—in fact for them it was quite beyond the bounds of possibility. Therefore he cannot have made a messianic entry.

According to Havet, Brandt, Wellhausen, Dalman, and Wrede, the ovation at the entry had no messianic character whatever. It is wholly perverse, as Wrede quite rightly remarks, to represent matters as if the messianic ovation was forced upon Jesus—as if he accepted it with inner repugnance and in silent painful passivity. For that would presuppose that the people had for a moment regarded him as Messiah and then afterwards had shown themselves as completely unsuspecting of his messiahship as if in the interval they had drunk of the waters of Lethe. The exact opposite is true: Jesus himself made the preparations for the messianic entry. Its messianic features were due to his arrangements. He made a point of riding upon the ass, not because he was weary, but because he wanted the messianic prophecy of Zech 9:9 to be secretly fulfilled.

---

31. The issue is not even whether the condemnation was thus legitimate or illegitimate; only the fact that the high priest brought no witnesses is significant. Why not? Nor can we now decide on the question whether the confession of future messianic dignity really amounts to blasphemy. Jesus' judges regarded it as such because they wanted to get rid of him. That the nocturnal session took place—even in the night of the Passover meal or the night preceding it and not a day later—was against the law, if the regulations of the Mishnah were then in force. However, we cannot conclude against the historicity as such from this; we simply have to note that when church bodies believe that their authority or the religion is in danger, they can quite easily set themselves above legal regulations.

The entry is therefore a messianic act on the part of Jesus, an action in which his consciousness of his office breaks through, as it did at the sending out of the disciples, in the explanation that the Baptist was Elijah, and in the feeding of the multitude. But those who joined in the procession rejoicing can have had no inkling of the messianic significance of what was going on before their eyes. The [[352]] entry into Jerusalem was therefore messianic for Jesus, but not messianic for the people.

But what was Jesus on that day for the people? Here Wrede's theory that he was a "teacher" again refutes itself. In the triumphal entry there is more than the ovation offered to a teacher. The jubilation refers to him "who is to come"; it is to him that the acclamations are offered and because of him that the people rejoice in the nearness of the kingdom, as the cries of jubilation in Mark show; for here, as Dalman rightly remarks, there is actually no mention of the Messiah.

Jesus therefore made his entry into Jerusalem as the Prophet, and as Elijah.

Was Mark conscious, one wonders, that it was not a messianic entry that he was reporting? We do not know. It is not inherently impossible that, as Wrede asserts, "he had no real view of the historical life of Jesus," did not know when Jesus was recognized as Messiah, and took no interest in the question from a historical point of view. Fortunately for us! For that is why he simply hands on tradition and does not write a Life of Jesus.

The Markan hypothesis went astray in conceiving this Gospel as a Life of Jesus written with either complete or partial historical consciousness, and interpreting it on these lines, simply because it introduces the designation Son of man only twice prior to Caesarea Philippi. The life of Jesus cannot be arrived at by following the arrangement of a single Gospel, but only on the basis of the tradition which is preserved more or less faithfully in the two earliest Synoptic Gospels.

In the last report, as Keim remarked long ago, questions of literary priority, indeed literary questions in general, have nothing to do with the gaining of a clear idea of the course of events, since the evangelists did not themselves have a clear idea of it in their minds; it can be arrived at only hypothetically by an experimental reconstruction based on the necessary inner connection of events.

But who in early times could possibly have had a clear conception of the life of Jesus? Its most critical moments were totally unintelligible even to the disciples who had themselves shared in the experiences, and who were the only sources for the tradition. They were simply swept through these events by the momentum of the purpose of Jesus. That is why the tradition is incoherent. The reality had been incoherent too, since it was only the secret messianic self-consciousness of Jesus which created both the events and their connection. Every Life of Jesus therefore remains a reconstruction on the basis of a more or less accurate insight into the nature of the dynamic self-consciousness of Jesus which created the history.

Whatever Mark may have thought, the people did not offer Jesus a messianic ovation at all; it was he who, in the consciousness that they were simply unable to recognize it, played with his messianic self-awareness before their eyes, just as he did at the time after the sending out of the disciples, when he similarly thought that the end was at hand. He also did the same thing when he concluded [[353]] the invective against the Pharisees with the words, "I say to you, you shall see me no more until you say, Blessed is he who comes in the name of the Lord" (Matt 23:39). This saying implies his parousia.

Jesus is similarly playing with his secret in the provocative question about David's son and David's lord. But no one outside the twelve knows this.

Suddenly he is in the hands of the high priest. How? Through Judas' betrayal.

For a hundred and fifty years the question has been historically discussed why Judas betrayed his Master. That the main question for history was what he betrayed was suspected by few and they touched on it only in a timid kind of way—indeed the problems of the trial of Jesus may be said to have been non-existent for criticism.

The betrayal by Judas cannot have consisted in informing the Sanhedrin where Jesus was to be found at a suitable place for an arrest. They could have had that information more cheaply by causing Jesus to be watched by spies. But Mark expressly says that when Judas betrayed Jesus he did not yet know of a favourable opportunity for the arrest, but was seeking such an opportunity. Mark 14:10, 11: "And Judas Iscariot, one of the Twelve, went to the chief priests, to betray him to them. And when they heard it, they were glad, and promised to give him money. And he sought how he might conveniently betray him."

In the betrayal, therefore, there were two points, one more general and one more specific: the general fact by which Judas gave Jesus into their power, and specifically the undertaking to let them know of the next opportunity when they could arrest him quietly, without publicity. But the decisive thing was the betray of the messianic secret. Jesus died because two of his disciples had broken his command of silence: Peter when he made known the secret of the messiahship to the Twelve at Caesarea Philippi; Judas Iscariot by communicating it to the high priest. But the difficulty was that Judas was the sole witness. Therefore the betrayal was useless as far as the actual trial was concerned unless Jesus admitted the charge. So they first tried to secure his condemnation on other grounds, and only when these attempts broke down did the high priest put, in the form of a question, the charge in support of which he could have brought no witnesses.

Jesus immediately admitted it, and strengthened the admission by an allusion to his parousia in the near future as Son of man.

The betrayal and the trial can be rightly understood only when it is realized that the public suspected nothing whatever of the messianic secret.[32]

---

32. If one assumes that the messianic claims of Jesus were generally recognized during those last days, one is tempted to explain the lack of witnesses for the charge of being Messiah by saying that this was something that was generally known. But in that case why would not the high priest have fulfilled the prescribed formalities? Why the attempts first to bring

The same is true of the scene in the presence of Pilate. The people on that morning knew nothing of the trial of Jesus, but came to Pilate with the sole object of asking the release of a prisoner, as was the custom at the feast (Mark 15:6–8). The idea then occurred to Pilate, who was just about to hand over, willingly enough, this troublesome fellow and prophet to the priestly faction, to [[354]] play off the people against the priests and work on the multitude to petition for the release of Jesus.

In this way he would have safeguarded himself on both sides. He would have condemned Jesus to please the priests, and after condemning him would have released him to please the people. The priests were greatly embarrassed by the presence of the multitude. They had done everything so quickly and quietly that they might well have hoped to get Jesus crucified before anyone knew what was happening or had had time to wonder at his non-appearance in the temple.

The priests therefore go among the people and induce them not to agree to the procurator's proposal.

How? By telling them why he was condemned, by revealing to them the messianic secret. That changes him at once from a prophet worthy of honour into a deluded enthusiast and blasphemer.

But it could also be that the "people" before Pilate's house were the mob of which the priests were certain, and whom they directed there early in the morning in order to put pressure on the governor and secure confirmation of the verdict as soon as possible.

At midday of the same day—it was 14 Nisan, and in the evening the Passover lamb would be eaten—Jesus cried aloud and expired. He had refused the sedative drink (Mark 15:23) in order to remain fully conscious to the last.

---

another charge? Thus the obscure and incomprehensible trial is ultimately the clearest proof that at that time the public had no inkling of Jesus' messiahship.

Rudolf Bultmann

View-Point and Method

[[3]] In strict accuracy, I should not write *"view-point"*; for a fundamental presupposition of this book is that the essence of *history* cannot be grasped by "viewing" it, as we view our natural environment in order to orient ourselves in it. Our relationship to history is wholly different from our relationship to nature. Man, if he rightly understands himself, differentiates himself from nature. When he observes nature, he perceives there something objective which is not himself. When he turns his attention to history, however, he must admit himself to be a part of history; he is considering a living complex of events in which he is essentially involved. He cannot observe this complex objectively as he can observe natural phenomena; for in every word which he says about history he is saying at the same time something about himself. Hence there cannot be impersonal observation of history in the same sense that there can be impersonal observation of nature. Therefore, if this book is to be anything more than information on interesting occurrences in the past, more than a walk through a museum of antiquities, if it is really to lead to our seeing Jesus as a part of the history in which [[4]] we have our being, or in which by critical conflict we achieve being, then this book must be in the nature of a continuous *dialogue with history*.

Further, it should be understood that the dialogue does not come as a conclusion, as a kind of evaluation of history after one has first learned the objective facts. On the contrary, the actual encounter with history takes place only in the dialogue. We do not stand outside historical forces as neutral observers; we are ourselves moved by them; and only when we are ready to listen to the *demand* which history makes on us do we understand at all what history is about. This dialogue is no clever exercise of subjectivity on the observer's part, but a real *interrogating* of history, in the course of which the his-

---

"View-Point and Method" first appeared in English in R. Bultmann, *Jesus and the Word* (trans. L. P. Smith and E. H. Lantero; New York: Scribner's, 1934) 3–15. When Bultmann speaks of "this book," it is to *Jesus and the Word* that he is referring.

torian puts this subjectivity of his in question, and is ready to listen to history as an authority. Further, such an interrogation of history does not end in complete relativism, as if history were a spectacle wholly dependent on the individual standpoint of the observer. Precisely the contrary is true: whatever is relative to the observer—namely all the presuppositions which he brings with him out of his own epoch and training and his individual position within them—must be given up, that history may actually speak. History, however, does not speak when a man stops his ears, that is, when he assumes neutrality, but speaks only when he comes seeking answers to the questions which agitate him. Only by this attitude can we discover [[5]] whether an objective element is really present in history and whether history has something to say to us.

There is an approach to history which seeks by its *method* to achieve objectivity; that is, it sees history only in a perspective determined by the particular epoch or school to which the student belongs. It succeeds indeed, at its best, in escaping the subjectivity of the individual investigator, but still remains completely bound by the subjectivity of the method and is thus highly relative. Such an approach is extremely successful in dealing with that part of history which can be grasped by objective method, for example in determining the correct chronological sequence of events, and in so far forth is always indispensable. But an approach so limited misses the true significance of history. It must always question history solely on the basis of particular presuppositions, of its own method, and thus quantitatively it collects many new facts *out* of history, but learns nothing genuinely new *about* history and man. It sees in history only as little or as much of man and of humanity as it already explicitly or implicitly knows; the correctness or incorrectness of vision is always dependent on this previous knowledge.

An example may make this clear. A historian sets himself the aim of making a historical phenomenon or personality *"psychologically comprehensible."* Now this expression implies that such a writer has at his disposal complete knowledge of the psychological possibilities [[6]] of life. He is therefore concerned with reducing every component of the event or of the personality to such possibilities. For that is what making anything "comprehensible" means: the reduction of it to what our previous knowledge includes. All individual facts are understood as specific cases of general laws, and these laws are assumed to be already known. On this assumption the criticism of the tradition is based, so that everything which cannot be understood on that basis is eliminated as unhistorical,

So far as purely psychological facts of the past are the objects of investigation, such a method is (for the psychological expert) quite correct. There remains, however, the question whether such a method reveals the essential of history, really brings us face to face with history. Whoever is of the belief that only through history can he find enlightenment on the contingencies of his own existence, will necessarily reject the psychological approach, however justified that method is in its own sphere. He must reject it if he is in earnest in his attempt to understand history. In such a belief this book is written.

Hence no attempt is here made to render Jesus as a historical phenomenon psychologically explicable, and nothing really biographical, apart from a brief introductory section, is included.

Thus I would lead the reader not to any *view* of history, but to a highly personal *encounter* with history. But because the book cannot in itself be for the [[7]] reader *his* encounter with history, but only information about *my* encounter with history, it does of course as a whole appear to him as a *view*, and I must define for him the point of observation. Whether he afterward remains a mere spectator is his affair.

If the following presentation cannot in the ordinary sense claim objectivity, in another sense it is all the more objective; for it refrains from *pronouncing value judgments*. The "objective" historians are often very lavish with such pronouncements, and they thus introduce a subjective element which seems to me unjustified. Purely formal evaluations of the meaning of an event or a person in the immediate historical sequence are of course necessary; but *a judgment of value* depends upon a point of view which the writer imports into the history and by which be measures the historical phenomena. Obviously the criticisms which many historians deliver, favorable or unfavorable, are given from a standpoint beyond history. As against this I have especially aimed to avoid everything beyond history and to find a position for myself *within* history. Therefore evaluations which depend on the distinction between the historical and the super-historical find no place here.

Indeed, if one understands by the historical process only phenomena and incidents determinable in time—"what happened"—then he has occasion to look for something beyond the historical fact which can motivate [[8]] the interest in history. But then the suspicion becomes most insistent that the essential of history has been missed; for the essential of history is in reality nothing super-historical, but is event in time. Accordingly this book lacks all the phraseology which speaks of Jesus as great man, genius, or hero; he appears neither as inspired nor as inspiring,[1] his sayings are not called profound, nor his faith mighty, nor his nature child-like. There is also no consideration of the eternal values of his message, of his discovery of the infinite depths of the human soul, or the like. Attention is entirely limited to what be *purposed*, and hence to what in his purpose as a part of history makes a present demand on us.

For the same reason, *interest in the personality of Jesus* is excluded—and not merely because, in the absence of information, I am making a virtue of necessity. I do indeed think that we can now know almost nothing concerning the life and personality of Jesus, since the early Christian sources show no interest in either, are moreover fragmentary and often legendary; and other sources about Jesus do not exist. Except for the purely critical research, what has been written in the last hundred and fifty years on the life of Jesus, his personality and the development of his inner life, is fantastic and romantic. Whoever reads Albert Schweitzer's brilliantly written *Quest of the Historical*

---

1. Literally, "neither as daemonic nor as fascinating."

Jesus[2] must vividly realize this. The same impression is made by a survey [[9]] of the differing contemporary judgments on the question of the Messianic consciousness of Jesus, the varying opinions as to whether Jesus believed himself to be the Messiah or not, and if so, in what sense, and at what point in his life. Considering that it was really no trifle to believe oneself Messiah, that, further, whoever so believed must have regulated his whole life in accordance with this belief, we must admit that if this point is obscure we can, strictly speaking, know nothing of the personality of Jesus. I am personally of the opinion that Jesus did not believe himself to be the Messiah, but I do not imagine that this opinion gives me a clearer picture of his personality. I have in this book not dealt with the question at all—not so much because nothing can be said about it with certainty as because I consider it of secondary importance.

However good the reasons for being interested in the personalities of significant historical figures, Plato or Jesus, Dante or Luther, Napoleon or Goethe, it still remains true that this interest does not touch that which such men had at heart; for *their* interest was not in their personality but in their *work*. And their work was to them not the expression of their personality, nor something through which their personality achieved its "form," but the cause to which they surrendered their lives. Moreover, their work does not mean the sum of the historical effects of their acts; for to this their view could not be directed. Rather, the "work" from *their* [[10]] standpoint is the end they really sought, and it is in connection with their purpose that they are the proper objects of historical investigation. This is certainly true if the examination of history is no neutral orientation about objectively determined past events, but is motivated by the question how we ourselves, standing in the current of history, can succeed in comprehending our own existence, can gain clear insight into the contingencies and necessities of our own life purpose.

In the case of those who like Jesus have worked through the medium of *word*, what they purposed can be reproduced only as a group of sayings, of ideas—as *teaching*. Whoever tries, according to the modern fashion, to penetrate behind the teaching to the psychology or to the personality of Jesus, inevitably, for the reasons already given, misses what Jesus purposed. For his purpose can be comprehended only as teaching.

But in studying the teaching there is again danger of misunderstanding, of supposing such teaching to be a system of general truths, a system of propositions which have validity apart from the concrete life situation of the speaker. In that case it would follow that the truth of such statements would necessarily be measured by an ideal universal system of truths, of eternally valid propositions. In so far as the thought of Jesus agreed with this ideal system, one could speak of the super-historical element in his message. But here it would again become clear that one has missed the [[11]] essential of history, has not met with anything really new in history. For this ideal system would not be learned from history; it implies rather a standard beyond history by which the particular historical phenomena are measured. The study of history

2. Translated by W. Montgomery. London, 1910.

would then at best consist in bringing this pre-existent ideal system to clearer recognition through the observation of concrete "cases." Historical research would be a work of "recollection" in the Platonic sense, a clarifying of knowledge which man already possesses. Such a view would be essentially rationalistic; history as event in time would be excluded.

Therefore, when I speak of the teaching or thought of Jesus, I base the discussion on no underlying conception of a universally valid system of thought which through this study can be made enlightening to all. Rather the ideas are understood in the light of the concrete situation of a man living in time; as his interpretation of his own existence in the midst of change, uncertainty, decision; as the expression of a possibility of comprehending this life; as the effort to gain clear insight into the contingencies and necessities of his own existence. When we encounter the words of Jesus in history, *we* do not judge *them* by a philosophical system with reference to their rational validity; *they* meet *us* with the question of how we are to interpret our own existence. That we be ourselves deeply disturbed by the problem of our own life is therefore the indispensable condition of our inquiry. Then the examination [[12]] of history will lead not to the enrichment of timeless wisdom, but to an encounter with history which itself is an event in time. This is dialogue with history.

There is little more to say in introduction. The subject of this book is, as I have said, not the life or the personality of Jesus, but only his teaching, his message. Little as we know of his life and personality, we know enough of his *message* to make for ourselves a consistent picture. Here, too, great caution is demanded by the nature of our sources. What the sources offer us is first of all the message of the early Christian community, which for the most part the church freely attributed to Jesus. This naturally gives no proof that all the words which are put into his mouth were actually spoken by him. As can be easily proved, many sayings originated in the church itself; others were modified by the church.

Critical investigation shows that the whole tradition about Jesus which appears in the three synoptic gospels is composed of a series of layers which can on the whole be clearly distinguished, although the separation at some points is difficult and doubtful. (The Gospel of John cannot be taken into account at all as a source for the teaching of Jesus, and it is not referred to in this book.) The separating of these layers in the synoptic gospels depends on the knowledge that these gospels were composed in Greek within the Hellenistic Christian community, while Jesus and the oldest Christian [[13]] group lived in Palestine and spoke Aramaic. Hence everything in the synoptics which for reasons of language or content can have originated only in Hellenistic Christianity must be excluded as a source for the teaching of Jesus. The critical analysis shows, however, that the essential content of these three gospels was taken over from the Aramaic tradition of the oldest Palestinian community. Within this Palestinian material again different layers can be distinguished, in which whatever betrays the specific interests of the church or reveals characteristics of later development must be rejected as secondary. By means of this critical analysis an oldest layer is determined, though it can be marked off with only relative exactness. Naturally we have no absolute assurance that the exact words of this oldest layer were really spoken by Jesus. There is a possibility that the contents of this oldest layer are also the result of a complicated historical process which we can no longer trace.

Of course the doubt as to whether Jesus really existed is unfounded and not worth refutation. No sane person can doubt that Jesus stands as founder behind the historical movement whose first distinct stage is represented by the oldest Palestinian community. But how far that community preserved an objectively true picture of him and his message is another question. For those whose interest is in the personality of Jesus, this situation is depressing or destructive; for our purpose [[14]] it has no particular significance. It is precisely this complex of ideas in the oldest layer of the synoptic tradition which is the object of our consideration. It meets us as a fragment of tradition coming to us from the past, and in the examination of it we seek the encounter with history. By the tradition Jesus is named as bearer of the message; according to overwhelming probability he really was. Should it prove otherwise, that does not change in any way what is said in the record. I see then no objection to naming Jesus throughout as the speaker. Whoever prefers to put the name of "Jesus" always in quotation marks and let it stand as an abbreviation for the historical phenomenon with which we are concerned, is free to do so. Further I need say only that I have in what follows seldom given the critical considerations; they can be found in their context in my book *Die Geschichte der synoptischen Tradition*[3] in connection with my own critical analysis.

After a historical introduction, this presentation of the message of Jesus is developed in three concentric circles of thought. In each circle we are concerned with the same question; but this common centre can first be clearly recognized only in the smallest circle. The smallest circle is, however, comprehensible only when one has passed through the two outer circles.

Finally I wish to say that this book does not deal with especially complicated or difficult matters, but with [[15]] extremely simple ones, so far as theoretical understanding is concerned. Of course the understanding of simple things can be difficult, but such difficulty is due not to the nature of the things but to the fact that we have forgotten how to see directly, being too much burdened with presuppositions. This is so characteristic of our contemporary situation that the following discussion may appear difficult simply because it is trying to gain for the author as well as for the reader the right method of seeing. If I am wrong in anticipating difficulty, so much the better; but the reader should realize that no end is gained by making the matter seem easier than it really is, in relation to the intellectual attitude of the present day. The essential difficulty in this book, however, lies not in the theoretical understanding nor in the acceptance of it as a "point of view," but in the actual encounter with reality which it demands. Now for a great end one must be ready to pay the price, and I would rather frighten a reader away than attract one who wants something for nothing.

3. Göttingen, Vandenhoeck and Ruprecht, 2nd ed., 1931.

HENRY J. CADBURY

The Cause and Cure of Modernization

[[28]] The tendency to modernize Jesus is not difficult to account for. It is natural and often unconscious. Writers and teachers about him have the same reasons as have the painters to attempt to interpret him in terms that will seem real, that is, modern and congenial to the modern mind. Few of them trouble themselves to acquire an intimate knowledge of the thinking categories of the ancient world, and until recent times, with the development of historical science and the study of contemporary materials, an attempt to place Jesus in his own setting would be neither thought of nor, if thought of, feasible.

Anachronism in thinking about Jesus has been largely due to an excusable ignorance. The gospels do not give us all the information we need, especially for the inner life of Jesus. The earliest gospels are singularly objective in their presentation of his life, so that when psychological biography becomes the style, not [[29]] only in novels but even in our thought of historical persons, great gaps are left to be filled by inference and conjecture if we would know the mind of Christ. These lacunae are naturally filled by modern persons with modern content. They infer what Jesus would have thought and felt from what we should think and feel. No other analogy occurs to them as needed, or as available. They do not notice that, to use the gospel metaphor, they are stitching a new patch on an old garment.

The curiosity and interest which give rise to this treatment of Jesus are not unnatural about any ancient personage. In his case there are special reasons due to his position in religion. If he is regarded as divine, while we admit that his thoughts are not like our thoughts, we have no other than human psychology to judge him by. The supreme deity is always anthropomorphized. Anthropomorphism involves not merely assigning to the deity human form. That is recognized and often resisted. It involves assigning to deity like thoughts and passions with ourselves. If anthropopathy is almost inescapable in think-

---

"The Cause and Cure of Modernization" first appeared in H. J. Cadbury, *The Peril of Modernizing Jesus* (New York: Macmillan, 1937) 28–48.

ing of the god or gods of purely divine nature, it is much more certain to take place with Jesus, whose human nature and earthly career seem to require it.

There have, of course, been persons and groups who have minimized the human element in Jesus. They [[30]] have resolutely set themselves not "to know Christ after the flesh." Metaphysical speculation and controversy about him such as resulted in the creeds largely succeeded in dehumanizing Jesus. Already for Paul his human personality is unimportant except in certain directions. In the gospel of John with all its lifelike humanity he moves and speaks like the poet's "conscious god," self-consciously. In such circles the charge of modernizing Jesus can scarcely be brought, simply because he is not felt to be human at all. An upbringing in such an environment must have been the reason why a student, when asked of a certain narrative in the gospels what Jesus probably had in mind, replied simply that Jesus had no mind. The meaning of this startling reply to an innocent question was probably something like this. Since Jesus was very God his human life was not a series of acts and words humanly originated through the ordinary processes of mind. God need not think or consider or infer or intend or propose, and to assign such human processes to Jesus was erroneous, perhaps blasphemous. So far are God's thoughts from our thoughts.

With such thoroughgoing deification, Jesus is not identified with ourselves and modernization does not take place. But in the reaction from the purely theological Jesus which modern study of the life of Christ has brought about, the modernization of Jesus has [[31]] been abundant. A psychology of God, if that is what Jesus was, is not available, but in so far as he was man, he has been studied as a man and it is here that the distinction between the ancient and modern habits of mind must be observed. Liberal theology with its liberal portrait of Jesus has reveled in the emancipation of his figure from superhuman perversion. It has rightly claimed for him the reality of a personal historical existence, but in this recovery of his humanity the glaring defects of a dehumanizing theology naturally made the liberal mind less careful about its own methodological errors. In aiming to make him real and human it unconsciously made him real and modern. Complete modernization was, of course, impossible. The gospels now as ever have kept something of the ancient historical nexus between Jesus and his times. But where the evidence has been ambiguous or lacking, and sometimes almost in the face of clear evidence to the contrary, a modernized Jesus has been substituted for what was often intended to be an historical Christ. In this way the eager escape from a dehumanized Christ has been responsible for too little fidelity to the genuine first century elements which a truly historical portrait requires.

The overlooking of the errors of modernization is rendered the more easy by a common feeling that human nature has always been much the same. There [[32]] is much confirmation of this feeling even when one conscientiously attempts to study and differentiate the ancient mind. Perhaps the likenesses of the ancient world appeal to us. We seem to see for example in the Old Testament and in other ancient records the very same situations as we know in modern times. The psalmists, the prophets, and others who reveal their inner lives often sound what we like to call "a very modern note." We are astonished at the identities, and probably we attend to them more easily, so that we fail to appreciate the differences. The utter confidence in God which we find in the Psalms is so similar to our own piety that we extend it like our own to a life after death, though such a life is often explicitly denied and never really asserted in the whole psalter. The insistence on social justice by the prophets is easily accepted as akin to our humanitarian and democratic ideals, and their predictions of international war are treated as though they were political weather prophets writing like skilful foreign correspondents for the Jerusalem newspapers. Even the best of scholars often forget that the earliest prophets were never writing at all. It requires real skill and a disciplined historical imagination to appreciate the fundamental difference which exists between situations ancient and modern in which individuals apparently act and think alike. Comments that are similar in general purport [[33]] grow out of quite different mentality in different times, and it is easy to ignore the unexpressed difference. The very words of the Old Testament have a different meaning in their time. Its "holy" is often merely physical taboo, and so is its word "unclean." Its dietary laws were probably never even unconsciously due to sanitary reasons, and its objection to adultery belongs in the category of property rights. Even spirit is in it more material than with us. The heart is the seat of thought, not feeling, in the Bible, while the soul is frequently the physical life or nothing more than the reflexive pronoun.

These facts are generally known by scholars and so are the corresponding phenomena in the New Testament. But their lesson is often forgotten in the natural tendency to find the modern or universal in the ancient and particular.

In the case of Jesus a universality of character seems proved by subsequent history. A Galilean Jew of the first century who has become the object of devotion of so many persons of all lands, races and times would seem to have been particularly free from the limitations of age or race. If he was more than a Galilean Jew of the first century—in any sense whether human or divine—it seems to become *a priori* probable that the fullness of humanity as much as of godhead was summed up in him.

[[34]] But was such unusual universality, such permanent timelessness, really there in the historical Jesus? Was his appeal to his first followers and his offense to his first foes to be found in any special aloofness from the conditions of his time? Was he not a child of his own environment like most men, both great and small? And is it not precisely the process of unhistorical modernization beginning, as we know it did, immediately after his death, that is largely responsible for the feeling of kinship or contemporaneousness which successive generations have felt for him?[1] In that case *his* permanent timelessness is merely a euphemism for *our* perpetual anachronism.

---

1. The frequent claims of eternal contemporaneity for Jesus may be illustrated by a single quotation:

> One of the world's greatest stories is that of *The Wandering Jew*. It is a story which symbolizes a profound truth of Christian history. The hero of this medieval tale is one who is posed to be condemned by Jesus to immortality on earth. He can never

These questions must not be hastily answered either in the affirmative or in the negative. One wonders further whether with the deification of Jesus men have not somehow taken up the ancient and unmodern elements unmistakably present in the gospels into the divine aspect of his personality, so as to infer that in so far as he is like us today he is human, in so far as he is unlike us today he is divine. This would have been a curious development, but one not altogether improbable in an uncritical attitude to Jesus. We recall, for example, how the very Greek dialect of the New Testament was at one time regarded by serious philologists as the language of the Holy Ghost, because when its grammar was examined no ordinary [[35]] writings in the same idiom were known to exist. Jesus' parabolic teaching was long thought to be unique and hence a mark of somewhat superhuman ingenuity. Of course, now, through fuller information we know that the language of the gospels approximates the ordinary Greek of the age, and that a parabolic method, in form at least identical with the gospel examples, was precisely the method of contemporary rabbis. But the confusion of archaic and unique doubtless continues in all our popular Biblical thinking, and the quaint or unfamiliar, even the quaintness of a revered English version, easily becomes a mark of sanctity. So the hyphenated definition of Jesus' personality as both man and God, which so long in more or less distinct terms has been the background of Christian thought, has made it possible to accept the modern or universal in the gospels as human, and to assign what was unmodern and temporary not to ancient historical conditioning but to the Divine.

The modernization of Jesus is due, as we have already said, to lack of interest or trained imagination necessary to reconstruct an ancient scene. Every historian knows how great effort is required to orient oneself in an ancient age, how continuing study of contemporary materials more and more discloses the nuances and motifs of past scenes which are too subtle to be caught by the more superficial student. Even the [[36]] historical novelist, who perhaps more than the historian, aims at imaginative reconstruction of the past, rarely escapes making some kind of anachronistic error. But the general thought about Jesus has not been produced by trained historians. Theologians and apologists have been the official interpreters, and their interests have not been primarily historical accuracy. We do not accuse them of wilful perversion of truth when we say that their aims have made perversion inevitable if unconscious. To prefer abstract ideas to historical fact, to use history in order to defend a religious movement, or even, as with the preacher, in order to edify the believer or to illustrate modern situations and opinions—these purposes are not compatible with single-minded historical reconstruction.

---

retire completely from the human scene, but reappears in each new generation as its contemporary. In a high and reverent sense Jesus is the Wandering Jew. He does not come upon the scene in each new century as a Rip Van Winkle, but as the contemporary of each new age, the one in whom its highest aspirations find fulfillment. When the age of democracy came on the world's calendar, it found in Jesus its highest exponent and leader. So it is with many other characteristics of our time (H. E. Luccock, *Jesus and the American Mind*, Abingdon Press, 1930, 49f.).

But today our thought of Jesus is not dependent so much as in the past on apologist, theologian and preacher. He is the concern of laymen, sociologists, historians, novelists, scientists. The ordinary educated man has the gospels in his hands and he feels himself qualified to make his own portrait of their central figure. No doubt these exponents have set us free from much that was perverted in the older schools of thought, but they are subject to other biases. In part they, no less than the older apologists, wish to recommend him to their own age, in part they read into him their own thoughts and standards. The alienness [[37]] of Jesus is neither a subject they would emphasize, nor a feeling that they wish to cultivate. They are more quick to see likenesses than differences, and where the motive of Jesus is only to be conjectured or the fundamental principle is unexpressed they unconsciously read into his mind according to their own ways of thinking.

The unconscious process behind our claiming Jesus as one of ourselves is easily understood. There is usually even in the most emancipated minds a feeling that Jesus was probably right. In few circles would a proposal be damaged if shown to be in accordance with the mind of Christ. Everyone likes to find his own sentiment independently and unexpectedly sponsored by others. The agreement guarantees, if guarantee is necessary, the correctness of one's own opinion. One always especially endorses those parts of an address or an article of which he can say, "It is very good, I have always felt just the same way about the matter myself."

Now the gospels are books with varied content and permit of even more varied construction. Without effort, without dishonesty, and even without realizing what is happening, one can read into them and out of them one's own ideas. In fact such a process is almost unavoidable if one has any respect for the person of Jesus. We so easily assume that our own approach is [[38]] the right one, and therefore that a person of Jesus' insight must have shared it. Whether we assign to him omniscience, or only a more human degree of perception, we tend to think of that knowledge of his as coinciding with what we ourselves apprehend to be true.

There is something strangely naïve in this widespread appreciation for Jesus. For, aside from its genuine recognition of his real worth, it contains so often a quite unintentional self-flattery. Nearly every word of enthusiastic praise for truths we think we find in him is really only a claim of his support for our own viewpoint. When we say that in spite of apparently unmodern, unethical, unscientific, or impractical elements in Jesus' teaching, he must have meant such and such modern, ethical, scientific or practical truths we are calmly assuming that knowledge is with us, and that in so far as he was right he must agree with our standards. And if thereupon we can argue that he does agree with our standards then we can claim—ostensibly to his honor, but really to our own—that Jesus saw ahead of his time and has been gloriously vindicated by modern experience and knowledge.[2]

---

2. The legitimate citation of Jesus for our own ideas is well described in contrast with the illegitimate in a review written by S. J. Case, "Rival Efforts to Modernize Jesus," dealing

The real relation between Jesus and modern standards is not to be drawn by such easy methods. The bearing of his actual historical viewpoint on the questions we ask in a very different setting must be patiently determined by more complicated methods. [[39]] Intuitional understanding and spiritual sympathy do not guarantee for the modern Christian a secure grasp upon the "mind of Christ" in any real historical sense.

This is not the place to apply or even to describe the alternative method, to indicate how without haste to secure immediate application, without short cuts to the edifying results, the study of Jesus must first be made in his own setting before he can be used for our own.[3] It is worth while to consider the kind of argument or rather of unexpressed feeling that meets any effort to present Jesus in terms that do not appeal to the hearer. The objection may be expressed somewhat bluntly thus: "But if Jesus was like that, how do you account for Christianity?"

This appeal from Christianity to Christ is a familiar feature of ecclesiastical apologetic. One recalls how the early martyrs' fidelity was used as an argument for the historicity of the miracles in the gospels. In its present form the fallacy lies in the assumption that the Christian movement could have been given its great impetus only by such qualities in its founder as would give impetus to a movement today. When analyzed the fallacy is apparent. Early Christianity was no more modern than Jesus was, and a modernized Jesus would by no means help to account for the ancient church. To be sure, recourse will doubtless be had again to the argument of universality. Many will claim that unless there [[40]] was in Jesus a universally valid appeal his followers would never have perpetuated his memory, and efforts are made to define the nature of his influence which range all the way from mere human magnetism to the august assurance of the incarnate Son of God.

---

with a Ritschlian and a Barthian example (*The Journal of Religion*, 15, 1935, 82ff.). I quote from the beginning and the end:

> The attempt to capture the historical Jesus for one or another type of later Christian opinion is a time-honored quest. The chase still goes merrily on. . . . One who reads these two books side by side will easily perceive that both authors attempt to give vital reality to Jesus by depicting him in the religious imagery that accords most nearly with their respective tastes. It is the privilege, indeed the duty of the religious man of today to express his opinions and ideals in terms of the deepest realities of his own experience within his specific environment. . . . He is also entitled to draw support for his views from as wide a range of historical data as may be available to him, whether be resorts to Jesus, Paul, the evangelists, or any other notable persons of the past. As a selective and interpretative procedure, if so understood, his performance need not cause offense to anyone. But if he assumes that his presentation represents the totality of any given historical phenomenon, like the life and teaching of Jesus, or that his interpretation is the only justifiable one, then his readers have the right to demur.

3. See my article, "The Social Translation of the Gospel," in the *Harvard Theological Review*, 15, 1922, 1ff. The more objective method is not likely to be popular and the easygoing present day modernization of Jesus will continue until it is discarded for a more modern modernization of a succeeding generation.

Now the ultimate success of early Christianity in winning a wide and devoted adherence rests not exclusively on the life and teaching of Jesus. How
far success was due to this influence, personally, directly and accurately transmitted to the first and succeeding generations of his followers, and how far
to a religious propaganda in which there was an idealized Jesus who was the
future Messiah, or the present Lord, or the actual deity of an attractive cult,
we find it at this late day extremely difficult to tell. In such circumstances the
proverb is usually cited, that there can be no smoke without some fire. But
the ratio of smoke and fire varies enormously and the smoke often is misleading as to the exact location of the fire. I am not disposed to join those
who deny entirely the historicity of Jesus, but one must be prepared to admit
that the religion which became the Christianity of the Roman Empire may
have had but slight relation to the historical actuality of its founder. In any
case the things preached about Jesus which, whether historically accurate or
not, appealed to the mentality of the ancient world (like the guarantee of immortality, or protection from [[41]] the power of demons) are not the things
which we moderns find so significant in our restoration of him (like moral
originality, or perfect spiritual or mystical harmony with God). It is instructive in this connection to contrast Harnack's careful historical summary in his
Mission of Christianity of what appealed in Christianity's first dissemination
with the same author's (I think much less historical) portrait of Jesus which
he offers the modern world in his popular book *What Is Christianity?*[4] Even if
we should regard Jesus as entirely freed from the limitations of his environment, we can hardly extend the miracle to the whole medley which constituted his early followers. They were not moderns and if Jesus was modern it
would have been in spite of, not because of, his modernness that they believed in him.

In speaking thus of the modernizing of Jesus, I have spoken rather generally. Concrete illustrations will be found, I hope, sufficiently in the subsequent chapters to illustrate what I mean. I have not intended to condemn
those of us who are guilty—and who is not?—by standards which the guilty
had no reason to think of, or responsibility to observe. The tendency is natural and inevitable. One may take as symbolic the ancient story of the mocking
of Jesus as told in Matthew's gospel when "the soldiers of Pilate took Jesus
[[42]] into the praetorium and stripped him and put on him a scarlet military
cloak . . . and mocked him . . . and when they had mocked him they took the
cloak off him and put on him his own raiment."[5] The soldiers put on Jesus
their own kind of clothes and we all tend to clothe him with our own
thoughts.

4. One does not have to share the Roman standpoint of Father Tyrrell to sympathize
with his criticism of *What Is Christianity?* He says: "The Christ that Harnack sees, looking
back through nineteen centuries of Catholic darkness, is only the reflection of a Liberal Protestant face, seen at the bottom of a deep well" (*Christianity at the Cross Roads*, Longmans,
London, 1909, 44).

5. Matt 27:27–31.

In a self-conscious or self-critical age like ours unbridled modernization of Jesus is neither honorable nor profitable. Historical science—for better or for worse—is here with us and religion must conform to its demands in areas where religion itself claims historical foundation or validation. That history has its proper limits in religious thinking is true, but that does not justify the unhistorical modernization of Jesus in the name of either science or religion.

The tendency to modernize Jesus is not a new phenomenon in Christianity. It has always existed. The history of the study of the life of Christ, such as Schweitzer made for the last century and a half, is largely a study of this reading into Jesus the thought patterns of the age or group. In our own time different groups tend to make him in their own different images. If we were able to predict the mental atmosphere of a future generation we should be able to predict as clearly their understanding of Jesus.

The tendency is inevitable, and probably not entirely curable. To attempt to offset it is surely a reasonable [[43]] ambition. The means for doing so are fairly obvious. First, the realization of our own prejudices and presuppositions. We may try to look at ourselves objectively, to realize that we, like other generations or other groups, take our own mentality for granted and quietly read it into alien figures of the past, largely because we do not make the mental exertion of trying to understand them as they were. In the case of Jesus we are anxious (often quite unconsciously and without any formal Christian acceptance of him) to secure his authority for our own point of view. We flatter ourselves by praising his universality, his modernness, his insight, since we mean by these things merely our own judgment in the areas where we are quoting him. The first necessity is to know ourselves, to allow for this tendency and to discount it and to attempt to neutralize it. These pages are intended to contribute a little to this auto-psychoanalysis.

A second method of attempting to rectify our thought of Jesus is the effort to learn the mentality of his environment. There is much to be said for a knowledge of Moslem or oriental mentality as a corrective, though I suspect that the claims of orientalists to understand Jesus more truly are often overdone, as indeed are the claims of all specialists. I recall for example the characteristic behavior of three specialists who, meeting at my home one evening, happened (perhaps [[44]] at my instigation) to fall into a conversation on the historical character of Jesus. One was the late Professor G. F. Moore, who naturally emphasized Jesus' likeness to the Jewish rabbis; one was Professor F. G. Peabody, who stressed the practical ethical aspects of Jesus' character; the third was Professor Otto of Marburg, an expert in Western and oriental mysticism, for whom Jesus was very much of an old Jewish holy man. Nevertheless, within limits, a specialized knowledge of Semitic antiquity in general and of late Judaism in particular is quite valuable. Beyond that a feeling and an imagination for the ancient world, whether Semitic or Aryan, is a most useful corrective.

The third and most tangible corrective is the gospel records. They are a standing enemy as well as a standing ally to the modernization of Jesus. Their assistance to the movement consists in their own multiform suggestion, which allows us to find by selection, somewhere within their varied contents, proof-text support for almost any reconstruction of Jesus that we desire. They also leave so many gaps to be filled, so much outward material for our own psychological interpretation that, without actively suggesting each new portraiture of the master, they coöperate with any nuclear prejudice we may have by giving us pliable historical material for our purpose. How such simple biographies can be so variously understood is truly remarkable. [[45]] It would seem incredible if we did not know sane people who have held such varying views. But a knowledge of present day human nature and a new appreciation of the endless ambiguity and non-committal quality of the records will enable one to see how easily such opposite conclusions can be drawn.

But even more the gospels recall us to the Jesus of history. One shudders to think what would have happened to him in successive generations of oral tradition and Christian idealization if tradition and idealization had not been held in check by such written records. Some measure of what might have taken place we can sometimes draw from other purely oral religions and traditions. In Christianity itself before the gospel story was written and wherever it has been ignored, invention and imagination have had a free course. By putting down in writing this material the evangelists set a bound to change. Still today, as in the past, every imaginative portrait of Jesus must somehow square itself with these persistent standards.[6]

---

6. Of course a great deal depends on *how* the gospels are used or studied. Practical considerations have only too often led to ignoring the ancient Jewish character of the material, and the whole science may be regarded as a series of successive modernizations, since it is supposed that the results must have validity for the student's own day. Even some of the most modern and critical German studies are plainly tinged with Barthianism just as the earlier American books were a naïve reading back to Jesus of our "social gospel." There is some reason to hope that certain of the styles of gospel criticism *Formgeschichte* (form criticism) and the social or environmental interpretation of the evangelic material, by recalling us to the early influences contemporary with Jesus or evangelists, will obviate some temptations towards modernization. See the article by D. W. Riddle on "The Bearing of Recent Gospel Research upon the Study of the Teaching of Jesus" in *The Journal of Religion*, 14, 1934, 150f.

While speaking of method I cannot refrain from quoting some of the excellent words of C. H. Dodd in his recent inaugural lecture in which he meets the easy going assumption that one can find the permanent in Jesus by ignoring temporary or contemporary. He says:

> Our study is in the first place historical, for it aims at the interpretation of that significant phenomenon in history which is early Christianity. Such study is peculiarly relevant to a religion which so emphatically announces itself as an historical revelation. But the interpreter I have in mind will be one who, having penetrated to the historical actuality of the first-century Christianity, has received an impression of the truth in it which lies beyond the flux of time, and demands to be restated in terms intelligible to the mind of our own age. It is not that the thought of the twentieth century is, as such, superior in validity to that of the first century, but that no truth can be communicated, or even fully grasped, until it can be naturalized, in any age whatever.
>
> The problem of interpretation has not been fully comprehended, to my mind, if it be conceived as an attempt to disengage (according to a popular formula) the

Many might suppose that in a book like this which aims at recovering the historical Jesus much attention would be given to an evaluation of the gospel evidence, both in general and in detail. This is a familiar exercise to New Testament scholars which I do not intend to indulge in. I can avoid it partly because I can say in a general way that I accept the findings of modern [[46]] criticism. I shall be especially cautious about using the Fourth Gospel as history at all and I shall assume that the other three, and the oral tradition which preceded them, have been already affected by the interests of the early church; that is, as I have illustrated in the previous chapter, they have already been modernized. To distinguish in these books the historical and the unhistorical is a delicate task. Here there is more agreement in principle among scholars than there is in application. Subjective criteria are too easily accepted, and an item which is suspected by one scholar has for another the authentic marks of historicity. It has often happened that the stone which the critics rejected has become for a new school of critics the head of the corner. Nearly every idealization of Jesus makes of the evangelists its convenient scapegoat and each critic regards Jesus, i.e., his own particular Jesus, as, in the phrase of Matthew Arnold, "far above the heads of his reporters."

But I the more gladly avoid the sifting of gospel evidence since that would put the emphasis in quite the wrong place. I agree that for historical study the scrutinizing of the gospel material is essential, and I am prepared to engage in it at another time; but now I would direct attention to the defects in our own makeup. When I read a life of Christ that in the most careful approved fashion describes at length the [[47]] unhistorical character of the gospels and the aspects of their viewpoint which are to be rejected as late and secondary, but then proceeds to construct a portrait of the Master shot through with modern standards of value, I feel like saying, "Why beholdest thou the mote that is in thy brother's eye, but considerest not the beam that is in thine own eye?" In other words, a principal obstacle to the accurate recovery of Jesus is not so much the untrustworthiness of the evangelists, as the prejudices and presuppositions of our own minds, what the psychologist used to call "the apperceptive mass." To recognize the defect in the evangelists, and even in others of our own age with whose conclusions we do not agree, is easy. What we need is—if I may correct the poet slightly—to see ourselves as we see others.

In comparing ourselves with the evangelists we often note how loosely they and, indeed, all the New Testament writers quote the Old Testament.

"permanent" element in the New Testament from its "temporary" setting. No attempt to extract particular elements from it, and to exhibit these as "permanent" in isolation from the rest, can be other than superficial.

The ideal interpreter would be one who has entered into that strange first-century world, has felt its whole strangeness, has sojourned in it until he has lived himself into it, thinking and feeling as one of those to whom the Gospel first came; and who will then return into our world, and give to the truth he has discerned a body out of the stuff of our own thought (*The Present Task in New Testament Studies,* Macmillan; Cambridge Univ. Press, 1936, 37ff.).

Short passages are taken completely out of their context and given a force
which has only the slightest verbal likeness to the matter in hand. We almost
laugh at the naïveté of the early Christians. They seem never to have tried to
recover the actual historical context of the passages they are reading or quoting. Had they done so they would scarcely have found their quotations relevant or opposite. But this well known defect of Old Testament [[48]] citation in
the New is quite analogous to our own treatment of the latter. The twentieth
century is often more meticulous than the first in its respect for the literary
and historical context of the Bible that it quotes; our shortcoming is more often to ignore what I think we may call the "psychological context" of scripture.

In thus girding at modernists I do not wish to be understood as urging a
return to the theological Jesus of earlier and less critical schools. Still less do
I want to claim that I am immune from other temptations.

In particular, the aim of this book is to minimize the modernness of
Jesus. Yet it would be an error to write down as exclusively genuine everything archaic, obsolete, alien, uncongenial, grotesque or difficult for us in the
gospels or in their interpretation. I suppose that is the risk in our present approach. The reverse of modernization tends to over-archaize him.

Probably the real difficulty on each side is the unwillingness to leave
Jesus unknown and unexplained. The gaps in our knowledge of him are
many. Both Jesus and his reporters are often silent just when we should like
to know. Some of the most significant questions about him, not only external
details like the year of his birth and of his death, but inward questions like his
real attitude to Messiahship, are left to us unsolved problems. Let us recall
the words of the inscrutable Jesus himself, "No one knows the Son, save the
Father." He promises no further exception.

The Impossibility of a Biography of Jesus

[[46]] I regard the entire Life-of-Jesus movement as a blind alley. A blind alley usually has something alluring about it, or no one would enter it in the first place. It usually appears to be a section of the right road, or no one would hit upon it at all. In other words, we cannot reject this movement without understanding what is legitimate in it.

The Life-of-Jesus movement is completely in the right insofar as it sets the Bible against an abstract dogmatism. It becomes illegitimate as soon as it begins to rend and dissect the Bible without having acquired a clear understanding of the special nature of the problem and the peculiar significance of Scripture for such understanding. In other cases the problem is simply historical; here that is not so. The justification for the movement can be expressed in Luther's statement that we can never draw God's Son deep enough into our flesh, into our humanity.[1] Every truly evangelical movement shares this point of view in reflecting upon our Savior—ever since John 1 and 1 John 1:1ff. were written. But Luther's statement makes sense only if Christ is more than a mere man. It has no meaning at all for those who wish to maintain [[47]] and demonstrate that he is of no more importance to us than any other significant figure of the past. This was not Luther's view, nor can it be ours, so long as we agree with the apostle that "if you confess with your lips that Jesus is Lord, you will be saved" (Rom 10:9). If we believe with Christian dogmatics in the Christ who is more than a mere man in his essence, his mission, and his

---

Reprinted, with permission, from Martin Kähler, *The So-Called Historical Jesus and the Historic Biblical Christ* (trans. and ed. C. E. Braaten; Fortress Texts in Modern Theology; Philadelphia: Fortress, 1964) 46–71.

    1. Cited in I. A. Dorner, *Entwicklungsgeschichte der Lehre von der Person Christi* (2nd ed.; Berlin: Gustav Schlawitz, 1853), Part 2, p. 544. [Trans. W. D. Simon, *History of the Development of the Doctrine of the Person of Christ* (Edinburgh: T. and T. Clark, 1862).]

present function—i.e., if we believe in the supra-historical[2] Savior—then the
historical Jesus acquires for us that incomparable worth that moves us to confess before the biblical picture[3] of Jesus,

> My soul it shall refresh, my ear
> Can apprehend no tale more dear.[4]

Every detail that we can learn about him becomes precious and meaningful
for us. The tradition about him cannot be studied diligently and faithfully
enough. Hence a person may immerse himself in Jesus' actions, trying to understand them and to trace them to their presuppositions. So he plumbs the
depths of Jesus' consciousness and development before his public ministry;
he accompanies the boy Jesus through ravines and fields, from his mother's
bosom to his father's workshop and into the synagogue—and then he is most
certainly heading up a blind alley!

For the cardinal virtue of genuine historical research is modesty. Modesty is born of knowledge,[5] and he who knows the historical facts and sources
acquires modesty in knowledge as well as in understanding. But such modesty is unpopular with many because [[48]] their imaginations, sick of the field
of speculation, have now projected themselves onto another field, onto the
green pastures of alleged reality and into the business of historiography by
conjecture or of so-called positive criticism. On this field people are running
wild; they paint images with as much lust for novelty and as much self-confi-
dence as was ever exhibited in the *a priori* metaphysics of the philosophers or
the speculations of the theosophists, confident (with Richard Rothe)[6] that pious thinking can dissect God as the anatomist can dissect a frog. As far as the
efforts of positive criticism are concerned, I can very often recognize no difference between the "positive" and the "negative" theologians, to use the
common labels.

2. This is a term coined to designate what, to be sure, would not even exist apart from
history but whose significance is not exhausted in the historical effects of a particular link in
the chain of history or in the beginnings of a new historical movement, because in the supra-
historical what is universally valid is joined to the historical to become an effective presence.
Cf. my *Die Wissenschaf der christlichen Lehre* (2nd rev. ed.; Leipzig: A. Deichert, 1893), par. 13.
Cf. also pars. 8f., 365, 397, 404f.

3. [The German word *Bild* has been translated as "picture" or "biblical picture," or, occasionally, as "image" or "portrait."]

4. [From the first stanza of the hymn by Christian Renatus Graf von Zinzendorf (1727–
52), *Marter Gottes, Wer kann dein vergessen.*]

5. [Kähler is punning here on *Bescheidenheit* (modesty) and *Bescheid wissen* (to know).]

6. [Richard Rothe (1799–1867) developed a speculative theological system uniting
faith and knowledge, Christianity and culture. Kähler began his theological studies under
Rothe's guidance and was first stirred to an interest in the question of the historicity of revelation by his teacher's lectures on the life of Jesus. Kähler's assessment of Rothe is given on
pages 103–18 of the recently published edition of Kähler's classroom lectures on Protestant
theology in the nineteenth century, *Geschichte der protestantischen Dogmatik im 19. Jahrhundert,*
ed. Ernst Kähler (Munich: Christian Kaiser Verlag, 1962).]

To substantiate such a negative verdict some scientific assertions must now be made which at first sight may seem startling: we do not possess any sources for a "Life of Jesus" which a historian can accept as reliable and adequate. I repeat: we have no sources for a biography of Jesus of Nazareth which measure up to the standards of contemporary historical science. A trustworthy picture of the Savior for believers is a very different thing, and of this more will be said later. Our sources, that is, the Gospels, exist in such isolation that without them we would know nothing at all about Jesus, although the time and setting of his life are otherwise entirely clear to historians. He could be taken for a product of the church's fantasy around the year A.D. 100. Furthermore, these sources cannot be traced with certainty to eyewitnesses. In addition to this, they tell us only about the shortest and last period of [[49]] his life. And finally, these sources appear in two basic forms whose variations must—in view of the proximity of the alleged or probable time of origin of these forms—awaken serious doubts about the faithfulness of the recollections.[7] Consequently the "unbiased" critic finds himself confronted by a vast field strewn with the fragments of various traditions.[8] From these fragments he is called upon to conjure up a new shape if his task is to compose, according to modern requirements, a biography of this figure who looms up out of the mist. Even the task of establishing the external course of his life is fraught

7. This summary will scarcely meet with any serious objection. [In the 1896 edition Kähler added that he was mistaken in this belief—"we are not inclined to draw the final consequences from a view that turns out to be unfavorable to us and to our purposes." He refers the reader to the third essay in the 1896 edition in which he replies to the charges of "morbid skepticism" that had been leveled at him.] The exclusiveness with which we are referred to Christian sources must certainly arouse suspicion outside the Christian circle of vision. The way that the Gospel materials would be handled if we possessed some other sources can be indicated, for example, by the fate of the canonical Acts of the Apostles at the hands of current writers of "histories of New Testament times." In their preoccupation with F. C. Baur and with Strauss's revised edition of his life of Jesus *(Das Leben Jesu für das deutsche Volk,* 1864), people have almost forgotten the earlier edition of Strauss's work, with its interpretation of Jesus' life in terms of myth. But already Strauss's idea is emerging again—very understandably.

The uniqueness of the sources must be evaluated, of course, in accordance with one's view of their general nature. Above all, the relation between the Fourth Gospel and the Synoptics is important for the question of the reliability of the records. I must call attention especially to P. Ewald's work, *Das Hauptproblem der Evangelienfrage* (Leipzig: J. C. Hinrichs, 1890). His reference to the unmistakable one-sidedness of the Synoptic reports (p. 5, cf. pp. 50ff.) is completely justified. The enigma cannot be solved by passing over the difficulty in silence. In any case, this insight prevents one from pursuing the convenient method of making a bias in favor of the Synoptics into a principle of historical research, and of arbitrarily inserting either a few or many details from the Fourth Gospel into the framework of the Synoptic narrative, or even of borrowing the framework of the Fourth Gospel and then continuing from there as if the presentation of the Synoptics were normative and adequate. Obviously, this essay cannot furnish the specific proofs for these assertions. However, this seems to me unnecessary, for the facts are clearly known and beyond doubt to anyone who has had some kind of theological training. Differences exist only with respect to the evaluation and utilization of these facts.

8. On the discourses of Jesus cf., e.g., E. Haupt, *Die eschatologischen Aussagen Jesu in den synoptischen Evangelien* (Berlin: Reuther und Reichard, 1895) 5f.

with serious difficulties—leaving us [[50]] often with mere probabilities.[9] The
biographers, however, set themselves even more difficult tasks. Not all of
them refrain from discussing certain questions which titillate one's curiosity
but the answers to which still remain irrelevant to the main issue. To cite
some examples, there are discussions about how handsome or homely Jesus
was, or about his early life at home and at his work. Inquiries into his temper-
ament or his individuality I would put into the same category. We could go
on to mention others.

The biographers may refrain from such dubious inquiries, however. The
more recent ones, for example, are strong on psychological analysis. They
seek to show the variety and sequence of causes that would account for the
life and ministry of Jesus. Does the true humanity of Jesus not demand that
we understand how he grew, his gradual development as a religious genius,
the breakthrough of his moral independence, the dawning and illumination
of his messianic consciousness? The sources, however, contain nothing of all
that, absolutely nothing! At best only the short story of the twelve-year-old
Jesus can pass muster as a historical report; from the standpoint of literary
criticism, however, it is sheer caprice to sever it from the infancy narrative of
Luke's Gospel. And is there any section of this whole literature that has been
treated with more suspicion than precisely this one?[10] To be able to say [[51]]

9. We have in mind, for example, the question of the day of the month on which the
crucifixion occurred. But even apart from such secondary matters, how meager the prospects of harmonizing just the passion narratives, even when one puts the Fourth Gospel to
one side. Of course, if a person assumes the impartiality and objectivity of the records in
general, then the questions are not so painful. The materials agree on the whole. It is only
the details that we can no longer know. There are many times when historians must accept
such restrictions. However, here there is something special to bear in mind that should make
one especially cautious. The last week of Jesus' life is the period reported in greatest detail;
yet, its actual course impressed itself upon the memory of the eyewitnesses so indefinitely
that the later narrators took pains again and again to harmonize the various events and reports—but in vain—and almost each one did it differently from his predecessor. This hardly
encourages us to assume such a reliability of the given materials that further conclusions can
be drawn with confidence about matters which are not even recorded in the Gospels.

10. I am, of course, not unaware that it is common for historians to demonstrate from
the Gospels the development of Jesus' messianic consciousness during his public ministry.
Yet it will surely be generally conceded that such a development is outside the purview of the
sources themselves, or of those who reported in them. Therefore, here too the reconstructions are based on what the scholars profess to discover *behind* the sources. I cannot escape
the notion, however, that historical research must adhere strictly to the sources. As soon as
one disregards the task of evaluating the sources themselves and begins to appraise the materials without paying any attention to their origins and the question of their historicity, one
moves merely in the realm of uncertain conjecture. Negative judgments bearing some degree of certainty may be possible; but regarding the actual course of events, one cannot be
sure of anything. Otherwise the flawless fiction of a novel would constitute a proof of the
reality of its contents. It seems to me that in the work of the critics great unclarity reigns regarding the distinction between psychological (i.e., poetic) truth and the proper reproduc-
tion of reality in its often incomprehensible paradoxicality. Whereas present-day artists
[*Künstler*] are trying to refrain from purely imaginative effort and pride themselves on faithful reproductions of reality, historians [*die "historische Kunst"*] are pouring their energies into

anything more about Jesus requires recourse to *a posteriori* conclusions, and to make them cogent calls for extreme caution in one's approach, thoroughly reliable evidence, and a careful appraisal of the significance of one's findings. If we follow this reliable procedure, we shall scarcely achieve lavish results. That this is especially true of the Gospel materials I shall now show through a critique of the current methods used in writing the biographies.

The New Testament presentations were not written for the purpose of describing how Jesus developed. They show him manifesting himself and playing an active role, but not making confessions about his inner life, certainly not unpremeditated ones, except perhaps for a few sighs and ejaculations (e.g., Mark 9:19; John 12:27; Mark 14:36; 15:34).[11] An unprejudiced reader or scholar will hardly deny this. Therefore, the Gospels do not invite the drawing of *a posteriori* conclusions concerning the exact nature of Jesus' earlier development. It is, of course, undeniable that the Old Testament and Hebrew thought-forms have conditioned Jesus' outlook [[52]] on things.[12] Yet such obvious remarks gain us almost nothing. To assert anything more one must, in view of the silence of the sources, use as a means of research the principle of analogy with other human events—thus contradicting the whole tenor of the Gospel portrayals of Jesus.

First, there is the attempt to use psychology for the purpose of analyzing or supplementing data. Is such an attempt justified in this area? We will admit the validity of psychology only insofar as it rests demonstrably upon experience. A certain trustworthiness may be claimed for it where it deals with the *forms* of our inner experience, and undoubtedly they were the same for Jesus as for the rest of us. But here this is a matter of complete indifference. The dubious studies I have in mind always deal with the *content* of the inner life that developed and manifested itself in Jesus, and with the roots, the development, and the ramifications of his moral and religious consciousness (to use the going terms). Modern scientific psychology, however, no longer busies itself with the content of the inner life. That falls more in the province of other sciences. The poet, too, is accustomed to observe and depict that content. Where does the poet get his information? It is well known that in his poetry Goethe was describing mainly himself and his own experiences. He is such a great man because his observations "penetrated into the depths of human existence." Likewise, sensitive observers are generally impressive painters. Jeremias Gotthelf was as shunned in the region of Berne as Wildermuth was in Swabia—people were afraid of seeing an image of the haunted house

---

conjuring up before us a past reality from some "psychological law" that seems to be valid for the moment.

11. Matt 11:25f., with its solemn cadence, does not bear the marks of a confession forced out half unwillingly. To me it seems to be a public prayer, like John 17, with conscious reference to the disciples (cf. John 11:41, 42). The other view is supported neither by what follows (vv. 28f.) nor by the context (Luke 10:17–23).

12. Cf. my essay, *Jesus und das Alte Testament* (2nd ed.; Leipzig: A. Deichert, 1896).

in print.[13] Here, too, the person who employs the principle of analogy will have to seek his materials in the manifoldness [[53]] of reality. Therefore I ask once again, Is this method justified in writing about Jesus? Will anyone who has had the impression of being encountered by that unique sinless person, that unique Son of Adam endowed with a vigorous consciousness of God, still venture to use the principle of analogy here once he has thoroughly assessed the situation? We must not think that we can solve the problem with a pantograph, reproducing the general outlines of our own nature but with larger dimensions. The distinction between Jesus Christ and ourselves is not one of degree but of kind. We all know that poets create unreal and impossible figures insofar as they idealize them and cease to portray them with mixed qualities. Such idealization usually means simply the elimination of all the displeasing traits. We cannot, however, deal with Jesus merely by removing the blemishes from our own nature—that would merely leave us with a blank tablet. Sinlessness is not merely a negative concept. The inner development of a sinless person is as inconceivable to us as life on the Sandwich Islands is to a Laplander.[14] In the depths of our being we are different from him, so different in fact that we could become like him only through a new birth, a new creation. How then can we hope to analyze and explain Jesus' development, its stages and changes, in analogy with the common experience of humanity? Indeed, if we look deeper we encounter the objection, How could he have been sinless in the midst of a world, a family, and a people so full of offense? How could the boy Jesus develop in a pure and positive way when in his years of infancy, filial dependence, and immaturity he was surrounded by bad influences, and when his whole education, however well meant, must have been on the whole distorted? All this is a miracle which cannot be explained merely in terms of an innocent disposition. It is conceivable [[54]] only because this infant entered upon his earthly existence with a prior endowment quite different from our own, because in all the forms and stages of his inner life an absolutely independent will was expressing itself, because God's grace and truth became incarnate in him. In view of this fact we would all do well to refrain from depicting his inner life by the principle of analogy.

There remains the historical analogy. Here one goes back to the conditions and the thought world of Jesus' environment and to the historical records and Jewish literature which still survive from that period. Perhaps an examination of the history of such attempts will place them in proper perspective. Long before Baur, Semler had discovered the Judaistic tendencies[15]

---

13. [Under the pseudonym of Jeremias Gotthelf, the Swiss pastor Albert Bizius (1797–1854) penned numerous novels set in the Canton of Berne. Ottilie Wildermuth (1817–77) is known for her narratives of life in Swabia. Both writers' use of clearly recognizable characters and settings in their writings did not endear them to their friends and acquaintances.]

14. With good reason Dorner preferred the expression "sinless perfection," although he too did not think of Jesus as fully developed right from the beginning.

15. [Das "*Judenzen*," the term Semler used; see M. Kähler, *Geschichte der protestantischen Dogmatik im 19. Jahrhundert*, op. cit., 34.]

of the early Christian writers. Yet Semler's school exempted Jesus from any such attachment to Judaism. Was this mere prejudice or was it the result of observation, of a correct insight? David Strauss found Hellenistic influences in Jesus, or in any case something totally unrelated to late Judaism. If we compare the Jesus of our Gospels with Saul of Tarsus, we do in fact see a great difference between the disciple of the Pharisees and the Master. On the one hand we see the true Jew, so profoundly and indelibly influenced by the cultural forces of his people and epoch; on the other hand we see the Son of Man, whose person and work convey the impression of one who lived, as it were, in the timeless age of the patriarchs. Thus a return to the first century does not appear to be very promising.

Obviously we would not deny that historical research can help to explain and clarify particular features of Jesus' actions and attitudes as well as many aspects of his teaching. Nor will I exaggerate the issue by casting doubt on the historian's capacity to trace the broad outlines of the historical institutions and forces which influenced the human development of our Lord. But it is [[55]] common knowledge that all this is wholly insufficient for a biographical work in the modern sense. Such a work is never content with a modest retrospective analysis, for in reconstructing an obscure event in the past it also wishes to convince us that its *a posteriori* conclusions are accurate. The biographical method likes to treat that period in Jesus' life for which we have no sources[16] and in particular seeks to explain the course of his spiritual development during his public ministry. To accomplish that something other than cautious analysis is required. Some outside force must rework the fragments of the tradition. This force is nothing other than the theologian's imagination—an imagination that has been shaped and nourished by the analogy of his own life and of human life in general. If, in other areas, the historian's muse often paints pictures which lack every breath of the past and its distinctive characteristics, what will it make of this unique material?

The Gospels confront each of us with an Either/Or. The question is whether the historian will humble himself before the unique sinless Person— the only proper attitude in the presence of the norm of all morality. What a difference it must make in a person's interpretation whether he confesses the sinlessness of the Redeemer whom he is portraying or whether he charges Jesus with a catalog of sins, whether, with Jesus, he reckons every sinner as lost or whether he regards the boundaries as so fluid that moral errors are viewed as exaggerated virtues![17]

---

16. Bernard Weiss, however, does not do this.

17. Thus Theodor Keim, *Geschichte Jesu* (3rd ed.; 1873) [Zurich: Füssli, 1875] 372 [368]. Keim perceives a lack of harmony in the moral development of Jesus at several points. He noticed in Jesus the "scars" of a person refined through conflict, which David Strauss was not able to discover, although Strauss maintained that it was necessary and therefore self-evident to assume "individual perturbations and defects" in Jesus' development. Those who know the literature will recall the disgusting tirades of Renan, for example, in connection with the Gethsemane episode.

It is plainly evident that the imagination which thus orders and shapes the Gospel materials is being guided by still another force, [[56]] namely, by a preconceived view of religious and ethical matters. In other words, the biographer who portrays Jesus is always something of a dogmatician in the derogatory[18] sense of the word. At best he shares the point of view of the dogmatics of the Bible; most modern biographers, however, do so only to a very limited degree. Indeed, quite a few place themselves in conscious opposition to the "primitive world-view of the New Testament."

With this observation, however, we have made a very important discovery. There is no more effective method for securing the gradual triumph of a political party than to write a history of one's country like that of Macaulay.[19] Stripped of its historical dress, the bare thesis of the "historian" would arouse too many suspicions. Disguised as history, the historian's theory passes imperceptibly into our thought and convictions as an authentic piece of reality, as a law emanating therefrom. Thus Rotteck's "history" of the world was in reality a party pamphlet, which, through its wide distribution, shaped the political thinking of large numbers of the German middle class.[20] The same is true of dogmatics. Today everyone is on his guard when a dogma is frankly presented as such. But when Christology appears in the form of a "Life of Jesus," there are not many who will perceive the stage manager behind the scenes, manipulating, according to his own dogmatic script, the fascinating spectacle of a colorful biography. Yet no one can detect the hidden dogmatician so well as a person who is himself a dogmatician, whose job it is to pursue consciously and intentionally the implications of basic ideas in all [[57]] their specific nuances. Therefore, the dogmatician has the right to set up a warning sign before the allegedly presuppositionless historical research that ceases to do real research and turns instead to a fanciful reshaping of the data.

We all enjoy it when a gifted writer interprets a significant figure or event of the past in a play or novel. By freeing his portrayal from the requirements of historical accuracy and by giving his imagination freer rein, he can sometimes better reveal the true character of the event or figure. In biblically oriented circles, however, epics about the Messiah and dramas about Christ have always been viewed with some uneasiness; and, for the most part, we certainly share these reservations and these qualms. How many authors of the "Lives" blithely compose epics and dramas without being aware that this is what they are doing! And because this is done in prose, perhaps even from the pulpit, people think that this is merely a presentation of the historic, biblical picture

18. Naturally those who think of themselves simply as historians and claim to be completely without bias will view the dogmatician in this way.

19. [Thomas Babington Macaulay (1800–1859), whose *History of England from the Accession of James 11* was a best-seller in its day, was politically a Whig and has often been accused of partiality in his treatment of the rise of the Whig party and in his writing of history generally.]

20. [Karl W. R. von Rotteck (1775–1840) was a leading member of the liberal party and a writer of history. Kähler is here referring to his *Allgemeine Weltgeschichte*, a four-volume world history.]

of Christ. Far from it! What is usually happening is that the image of Jesus is being refracted through the spirit of these gentlemen themselves. This makes considerably more difference here than in any other field. For here we are dealing with the source from which the outpouring of the purifying Spirit is to proceed now as it has in the past. How can the Spirit perform his purifying work if he is not permitted to reach our ears and hearts without obstruction?

The Real Christ of Faith and History

Let us take a good look at this matter. What is the Life-of-Jesus research really searching for? In going behind Jesus Christ as he is portrayed in the church's tradition—and this means also behind the New Testament picture of Christ— it wants to get at the *real* Jesus, as he actually existed in all those respects that all, or some, might consider important or indispensable, or often only [[58]] desirable or titillating ("How interesting!").[21] Although the attempt to answer concerns such as these encounters the various kinds of difficulties we have pointed out, it is important that we capitalize on the opportunity they offer to seek out the legitimate element in such self-imposed quests. We shall find the answer when we succeed in isolating the real and ultimate reason behind the attempt—legitimate and indeed unavoidable as it is—to present the historic figure of Jesus, in its full reality, to our inner perception.

This brings us to the crux of the matter: *Why* do we seek to know the figure of Jesus? I rather think it is because we believe him when he says, "He who has seen me has seen the Father" (John 14:9), because we see in him the revelation of the invisible God. Now if the Word became flesh in Jesus, which is the revelation, the flesh or the Word?[22] Which is the more important for us, that wherein Jesus is like us, or that wherein he was and is totally different from us? Is it not the latter, namely, that which he offers us, not from our own hearts, but from the heart of the living God? I do not want to be misunderstood.

21. Even a serious theologian has been known to go astray by speculating on Mary's relation to Jesus on such a matter as his laundry! In the case of Schiller, students try to conclude from his financial state of affairs at a given point in his life—as ascertained from his notebooks—his incentives for public activity or his state of mind. If a theologian lacks a comparable basis for such imaginative additions to the tradition about Jesus, then these embellishments are merely a piece of phantasy, which is the exact counterpart, on another level, to the Moravians' playful intimacy with the Savior. This shows lack of taste even from the aesthetic point of view. For even the keenest aesthetic sensitivity can show a lack of delicacy in treating sacred subjects.

22. The person well versed in Scripture will not answer that it is the flesh which reveals and the Word which is revealed, for precisely the Word itself is the revelation. Cf. the quotation from Luther, cited by W. Herrmann [p. 240 in *Der Verkehr des Christen mit Gott* (4th ed; Stuttgart and Berlin: J. G. Cotta'sche Buchhandlung Nachfolger, 1903) 220 in the translation of the 2nd rev. ed. (1892) by J. Sandys Stanyon, *The Communion of the Christian with God* (London: Williams and Norgate, 1895)]: "We must let the humanity of Christ be a way, a sign, a work of God, through which we come to God" (*Erlanger Ausgabe*, 7,73) [*Church Postil, Sermon on Romans 15:4–13* (Second Sunday in Advent); Lenker Edition, VII, 54; *Weimar Ausgabe*, $10^{1,2}$, p. 84, lines 26–27].

That [[59]] he was like us is, of course, incomparably significant for us and is treasured by us; Scripture always emphasizes it, too, but hardly ever without adding expressions like "without sin," "by grace," "in humility and perfect obedience," etc. (Heb 4:15; 7:26, 27; 2 Cor 8:9; Phil 2:6f.). How he was like us is self-evident. It is also fairly obvious why the evidence of his likeness to us is to be found on every page of the Gospels. And yet how we have to search to muster such a biblical proof from statements which deliberately emphasize that likeness. Does this not explain why we recognize the emphasis on Jesus' moral achievement [*die sittliche Arbeit*] as a distinguishing peculiarity of the Epistle to the Hebrews? (cf. 2:17, 18; 4:15; 5:7f., perhaps also 12:2, 3).[23] If a person really asks himself what he is looking for when he reads the Gospels, he will admit to himself, "I am not seeking someone like myself, but rather my opposite, my fulfillment, my Savior." When a person reflects on what he finds when reading the Gospels, he will say, "No man has ever spoken or acted thus; never has such a man existed." He will not say that no one has ever said the same things Jesus said. For Jesus repeated many things which religious thinkers had written and said prior to him—things which become different, however, when he says them.[24] Nor will a reader of the Gospels maintain that everything Jesus did was unique, for he stands surrounded by a cloud of witnesses. And yet, there is something unique in the *way* he did things, for there has never been a man like him.[25]

Why, in the final analysis, do we commune with the Jesus of our Gospels? What does he offer us? "In him we have redemption [[60]] through his blood, the forgiveness of our trespasses"[26] (Eph 1:7). Do I really need to know more of him than what Paul "delivered to [the Corinthians] as of first importance, what [he] also received, that Christ died for our sins in accordance with the Scriptures, that he was buried, that he was raised on the third day in accordance with the Scriptures, and that he appeared" (1 Cor 15:3f.)? This is the good news brought in the name of God (1 Cor 15:12f.; Rom 1:1f.; 2 Cor 5:18f.; Gal 1:6f.). This is the witness and confession of faith which has overcome the world (1 John 5:4). If I have all this I do not need additional information on the precise details of Jesus' life and death.

Then why the Gospels? Why do we need that kind of preaching the content of which is, so often, what Jesus did and taught? We have redemption

---

23. These are passages that emphasize how important his moral achievement is for us, but also that it is important only because it appears striking in the light of his *total* person.

24. One might compare, for example, the Lord's Prayer with the Jewish prayers which in fact bear a resemblance to it. (See August Tholuck, *Die Bergrede Christi* [5th rev. ed.; Gotha: F. A. Perthes, 1872].) One also ought to note Jesus' use of Scripture. Cf. also the writing by Haupt cited earlier.

25. On pp. 53f. [[72f. in this volume]] we indicated in part what we mean by the "uniqueness" of Jesus. More will be said about this subject toward the end of our discussion.

26. I adduce this quotation of course only to summarize the answer, not as an adequate proof. That is hardly necessary; the New Testament and the catechisms are clear enough in this respect.

through *him.*[27] "Who is to condemn? Is it Christ Jesus, who died, yes, who was raised from the dead, who is at the right hand of God, who indeed intercedes for us?" (Rom 8:34). "We have an advocate with the Father, Jesus Christ the righteous" (1 John 2:1). "For we have not a high priest who is unable to sympathize with our weaknesses, but one who in every respect has been tempted as we are, yet without sinning" (Heb 4:15). We need, we have, and we believe in the living Christ. We believe in him because we know him; we have him as we know him; we know him because he dwelt among us, full of grace and truth, and chose for himself witnesses through whose word we are to believe in him (John 1:13, 14; cf. 1 John 1:1f.; John 15:27; 17:20).

Therefore, the reason we commune with the Jesus of our Gospels [[61]] is because it is through them that we learn to know that same Jesus whom, with the eyes of faith and in our prayers, we meet at the right hand of God, because we know, with Luther, that God cannot be found except in his beloved Son,[28] because he is God's revelation to us, or, more accurately and specifically, because he who once walked on earth and now is exalted is the incarnate Word of God, the image of the invisible God—because he is for us God revealed.

That is what the believer seeks. That is what the church celebrates.

How important, therefore, the least little feature becomes! How indispensable the removal of every optical illusion created by the prism of tradition, the removal of every obscurity in the interpretation of his first witnesses! How inexpressibly important the reality of Jesus, down to the minutest detail! It would be serious if this were really the case. Just suppose that the art of modern historiography were able to carry out a spectral analysis on the Sun of our salvation. Suppose that we today were able to remove those obscurities in the tradition. What would that imply with respect to our fellow Christians in the early period? If their contemplation and worship of the Jesus of the Gospels were distorted and deflected by those obscurities which the critic professes to find in their writings and feels bound to remove, then indeed they would not have known their Savior. And the same would be true of all subsequent Christians, including ourselves. Yes, gentlemen and brethren, what about ourselves? What would our situation be? Where do we come to know this Jesus? Only a very few can carry on the work of historical science, and only a few are sufficiently trained to evaluate such work. To be sure, such work would relieve us of the authority of the Bible, but it would in turn subject [[62]] us to the authority, not of an empirical science, but of the alleged results

---

27. I place this emphasis on these words from Eph 1:17 [7] and Col 1:14 in order to bring out the contemporary significance of Christ's *person* for all generations instead of only asserting Christ's work in the past. (Cf. my *Wissenschaft der christlichen Lehre*, op. cit., 397, 411f., 432f.) We are speaking here—as will surely be recognized—not of conversion to Christianity but of the ongoing life of the Christian.

28. Theodosius Harnack, *Luthers Theologie* (Erlangen, 1862–86) 2.81f.; cf. also ibid., 1.111f.; Gottfried Thonsasius, *Christi Person* (2nd ed.; Erlangen, 1857) 2.210f.; Julius Köstlin, *Luthers Theologie* (Stuttgart, 1863) 2.155, 300f., 383.

produced by this science. Meanwhile there is no one who can answer our question, Where is that fifth evangelist[29] capable of providing us with the picture of the exalted Christ, the picture of God revealed?[30] Which of the biographers can do this? We have our choice in a series from Hess and Zündel, through David Strauss, right up to Renan and Noack, to say nothing of the Social-Democratic pamphlets.[31]

If someone should object at this point, "Our situation with respect to dogmatics is the same as that with respect to historical science, for in relation to dogmatics we are dependent upon theologians," the comparison would be erroneous. Dogmatics is a matter of judging data that are accessible to every Christian, so long as it does not deal with detailed theological propositions that are not really essential in understanding the Christian faith. Historical research, on the other hand, requires the mastery of a sophisticated technique and a massive erudition. In this field no lay judgment is possible, except perhaps the kind made by inflated dilettantes.

Therefore, either we must do without the revealed God, or the reality of Christ as our Savior must be something quite different from the scarcely accessible, or even inaccessible, reality of those [[63]] clear and transparent details of his personal life and development which are generally deemed essential in the writing of a modern biography. There must be another way to reach the historic Christ than that of scientific reconstructions which employ source criticism and historical analogy.

Consider for a moment. What is a truly "historic figure," that is, a person who has been influential in molding posterity, as measured by his contribution to history? Is it not the person who originates and bequeaths a permanent influence? He is one of those dynamic individuals who intervene in the course of events. What they are in themselves produces effects, and through these effects their influence persists. In the case of thousands of people whose traces in the history of their contemporaries and of posterity are obliterated slowly or not at all, their earlier development remains for scholarship just so many roots hidden underground, and the particulars of their activity

29. Assuming, that is, that one cannot be satisfied with Renan's fifth gospel, namely, with a geography and ethnography of modern Palestine. [Cf. the introduction to Renan's *Life of Jesus.*]

30. [At this point Kähler inserted a long footnote replying to the charge by his colleague at Halle, Willibald Beyschlag, that Kähler expected from the biographers of Jesus something they had never claimed to do: "to paint 'a picture of the exalted Christ,' insofar as such a picture is distinct from that of the earthly Jesus" (Beyschlag, *Das Leben Jesu*; 3rd ed., Halle: Strien, 1893; 1.xix). "Just the opposite is the heart of my argument," says Kähler. "Otherwise why would I concern myself at all with the biographers? The discussion that follows concerning the preached Christ surely makes that clear. . . . For me, the connection between the earthly and the exalted Christ is expressed in the term 'suprahistorical' (see above, p. 47 [[p. 68 in this volume]]). . . ."]

31. [For a description of the place of these biographers in the Life-of-Jesus movement, see Albert Schweitzer, *The Quest of the Historical Jesus.* Some of the pamphlets of the German Social Democratic party in the nineteenth century pitted the socialist teachings of a "proletarian" Jesus against the "bourgeois" Jesus of ecclesiastical Christianity.]

are forever forgotten. The person whom history remembers lives on through his work, to which, in unforgettable words and personal characteristics, a direct impression of his dynamic essence often attaches itself. And the effect left by that impression is necessarily conditioned by the material on which it leaves its mark and by the environment upon which it had to and was able to work.[32] Thus, from a purely historical point of view the truly historic element in any great figure is the discernible personal influence which he exercises upon later generations. But what is the decisive influence that Jesus had upon posterity? According to the Bible and church history it consisted in nothing else but the faith of his disciples, their conviction that in Jesus they had found the conqueror of guilt, sin, temptation, and death. From this one influence all others emanate; it is the [[64]] criterion by which all the others stand or fall. This conviction of the disciples is summed up in the single affirmation, "Christ is Lord."

Contemporary history contributed nothing to this affirmation, and Jewish theology still less. The contemporary historical accounts in Josephus mention John, the son of Zechariah, but not a word about Jesus of Nazareth. Indeed, contemporary history counted him among the dead. After he died as a sacrifice for the sake of the nation (John 11:49f.), the Jews went raving and racing to their political destruction, without taking any notice of him. The small band of Nazarenes was of no importance to them. The rest of the world would have ignored him, had not Saul of Tarsus gathered a community in his name, the giant tree growing out of the mustard seed, under whose leaves the birds of the heaven build their nests. So much for contemporary history.

But what about Jewish theology and eschatology? We surely know how vigorously the unpretentious Rabbi had to contend with the terrestrial hopes for a splendiferous Son of David who was to lay the kingdoms of this world, in all their glory, at the feet of his people. Those images and metaphors from Jewish eschatology which Christians drew upon in painting their vivid pictures of the Christian hope still constitute the stumbling block which is apt to betray the hope of faith into denial of itself.

"Christ is Lord"—this certainty neither flesh nor blood can attain, sustain, or impart. Jesus himself said as much to Peter after his confession (Matt 16:17), and he said it also in reproach of the unbelieving Jews (John 6:43f.); it was confirmed by Peter's denial in the outer court of the High Priest and later by Paul, who could say it to his congregations in full expectation of their assent (1 Cor 12:3). Yet, wherever this certainty has arisen and exerted an influence, it has been bound up demonstrably with another conviction—that Jesus is the crucified, risen, and living Lord. And when we ask at what point in their discussions the historians [[65]] deal with this certainty, we find that they begin not with the much disputed and disconnected final narratives of the

---

32. The solitary figures who left only a written legacy, but left no mark on their contemporary world, are not historic figures. Jesus, however, the ministering friend of men, is as different as is conceivable from this sort of "eyeing" of posterity that reckons on being counted among "the class of people that are still to come."

evangelists but with the experience of Paul. They ascertain the unwavering faith of the early church as far as they can determine the testimonies and the traces left by those early witnesses. The risen Lord is not the historical Jesus *behind* the Gospels, but the Christ of the apostolic preaching, of the *whole* New Testament. To designate this Lord as "Christ" (Messiah) is to confess his historical mission, or as we say today, his vocation, or as our forefathers said, meaning essentially the same thing, his "threefold office." That is to say, to confess him as Christ is to confess his unique, supra-historical significance for the whole of humanity. Christians became certain that Jesus was the Messiah, the Christ, in total opposition to public opinion, not only with regard to the idea of the Messiah (that is, the way one conceived of the Messiah and what one expected of him), but also with regard to the person of this Jesus of Nazareth. This was as true then as it is today. When Christians tried to make the Messiahship of Jesus credible in their sermons and then in epistles and gospels, they always made use of two kinds of evidence: personal testimony to his resurrection, based on experience, and the witness of the Scriptures. As the living Lord he was for them the Messiah of the Old Covenant.

Therefore we, too, speak of the *historic Christ of the Bible.* It is clear that the historical Jesus, as we see him in his earthly ministry, did not win from his disciples a faith with power to witness to him, but only a very shaky loyalty susceptible to panic and betrayal.[33] It is clear that they were all reborn, with Peter, unto a [[66]] living hope only through the resurrection of Jesus from the dead (1 Pet 1:3) and that they needed the gift of the Spirit to "bring to their remembrance" what Jesus had said, before they were able to understand what he had already given them and to grasp what they had been unable to bear (John 14:26; 16:12, 13). It is clear that they did not later go forth into the world to make Jesus the head of a "school" by propagating his teachings, but to witness to his person and his imperishable significance for every man. If all this is clear and certain, it is equally certain that Jesus' followers were capable of understanding his person and mission, his deeds and his word as the offer of God's grace and faithfulness only after he appeared to them in his state of fulfillment—in which he was himself the fruit and the eternal bearer of his own work of universal and lasting significance, a work (to be exact) whose most difficult and decisive part was the *end* of the historical Jesus. Even though we once knew the Messiah according to the flesh, now we regard him thus no longer (2 Cor 5:16).

This is the first characteristic of Christ's enduring influence, that he evoked faith from his disciples. And the second is that this faith was *confessed.* His promise depends upon such confession (Rom 10:9–10), as does also the

---

33. Jesus' statement in Matt 16:15f. does not mean that his person and ministry have produced this confession. Rather, he ascribes this confession to God's revelation. He is not speaking about faith at all; hence, faith is not the "rock." The faith in question had so little power to endure of itself that it needed an explicit prayer to God, whose revelation evoked the confession in the first place (Luke 22:32). The *biblical* Jesus expected that the disciples' witness to him would be with power only after the Spirit had been sent (Luke 24:48f.; John 15:26; Acts 1:4, 8).

history of Christianity and our own decision of faith. The real Christ, that is, the Christ who has exercised an influence in history, with whom millions have communed in childlike faith, and with whom the great witnesses of faith have been in communion—while striving, apprehending, triumphing, and proclaiming—*this real Christ is the Christ who is preached.* The Christ who is preached, however, is precisely the Christ of faith. He is the Jesus whom the eyes of faith behold at every step he takes and through every syllable he utters—the Jesus whose image we impress upon our minds because we both would and do commune with him, our risen, living Lord. The person of our living Savior, the person of the Word incarnate, of God revealed, gazes upon us from the features of that image which has deeply impressed itself on the memory of his followers—here in bold outlines, there in single strokes—and which was finally disclosed and perfected through the illumination of his Spirit.

This is no reassuring sermon. It is the result of a painstaking consideration of the data at hand. It is the result achieved by a dogmatics[34] which sorts and sifts the evidence and states the conclusions in biblical language only because they happen to agree with the word of Scripture. Ought such a conformity to Scripture really provide a reason for looking with suspicion on this kind of dogmatics, especially among those who base their criticisms on Reformation (!) theology?

In popular usage the word "dogmatics" has come to connote arbitrary assertions, whereas "historical study" of a subject is regarded as always laying hold of reality. The latter is unfortunately not always the case, since historical science does not always observe its limitations or fulfill its obligations, nor is it always in a position to do so. It is equally true that the popular assumption about dogmatics is basically unfounded, though understandable in view of the dogmaticians' aberrations. Dogmatics also has a "given" with which it works, although this is not merely a past reality. Dogmatics is in a very real sense the mediator between past and present; it puts what is genuine and indispensable in the past at the service of the present. This task of mediation, then, belongs to dogmatics, after it has made a thorough and serious study of what historical study can accomplish and has learned from [[68]] history what is important enough to warrant consideration by dogmatics. The task of dogmatics is to provide an inventory of our assets.

The "data at hand" to which we referred above are not the individual events reported in the Gospels about the life of Jesus. In this whole discussion we are trying to explain how inadvisable and indeed impossible it is to

---

34. It is surely plain that I am here contrasting dogmatics with preaching, and scientific statement with untested interpretations. In the context the farthest thing from my mind is the arrogant assertion of the superiority of dogmatics to historical study, or a "tutelage" of historical study by dogmatics, Nevertheless this is the way Dr. Beyschlag interprets my sentence (see his *Leben Jesu*, xx); and by putting a colon before the words "This is," rather than indicating that they begin a new paragraph, he leaves readers with the impression that such an assertion was made by me. He also omits everything which makes clear that I am here referring to the portrayal of Jesus in the Gospels, interpreted of course from the viewpoint of the faith one encounters there as well as in the rest of the New Testament.

reach a Christian understanding of Jesus when one deviates from the *total* biblical proclamation about him—his life as well as its significance. The factual data which have led me to this judgment have to do with the nature of the tradition at our disposal. I have in mind especially two far-reaching facts: first, the impossibility of extracting from the sources a "genesis" of Jesus the Messiah and, second, the knowledge of what Christ has always meant to his church and still means to every believer today. These facts are, of course, a distillation of a series of other facts, as I have tried to indicate and as I intend to elaborate more fully. As far as the second is concerned, it is quite unwarranted to demand that the significance of Christ for Christianity be measured by what he means to those whose devotion to Christ has all but ceased. We must remind ourselves again and again that in trying to arrive at an understanding of man we must of course take into account the stages of his development, his existence as a fetus and as an adolescent, as well as his possible degeneration to the level of a cripple or an imbecile; nevertheless our conception of man will, in the last analysis, have to rest on a mature and healthy specimen of noble attributes. We may, if we wish, keep our christological formulae to the barest possible minimum; yet for Christians Christ must always be the object of faith in the "strictly religious sense of the word," to use an expression in vogue today. Otherwise we fall outside the bounds of his church. For this reason Christian language about Christ must always take the form of a confession or a dogma.

Those are the limits of the circle within which I would expect [[69]] the validity of these arguments to be acknowledged or at least to receive sympathetic consideration.

I can appreciate fully how a person will necessarily reach a totally different position if he denies or depreciates what we have called the second fact. If revelation is only an erroneous name for religious consciousness in its historically conditioned development, and if Jesus is merely a religious genius surpassing the rest of us only in degree, then doubtless the New Testament confession of faith, which also inspired the evangelists in their portrayal of Jesus, can only result in an obscuring of the facts. Then we must look with suspicion on everything, or almost everything, in that portrayal. Then we can only resort to the attempt to explain, at all costs, the mystery of this man in terms of the thought and life of his day, a man who not only wanted to be called the Messiah, but also was confessed and proclaimed as such by an astonishing number of people. Given these presuppositions, I do not look for widespread support of the affirmative side of my criticism. On the other hand, I expect the negative side of my criticism to be generally conceded, so far as it concerns the evaluation of the sources. At any rate, my arguments deal only with those theologians who wish to write a "Life of Jesus" in the service of the confession of Christ, and who think (at least some of them) that their work can do more to strengthen this confession than can dogmatics. I am concerned with a correct evaluation of what the constructive historical method can accomplish, particularly what it can contribute toward the right attitude to Christ within the church, the bearer of the gospel.

The rest of this essay will emphasize why we have the right to be sensitive to, and on guard against, all later embellishments of the biblical picture of Christ. Such imaginative reconstructions cannot stand without criticism, not even as specialized theological research. I think I can explain its popularity and influence in wide circles, especially in the younger generation. Often we do not [[70]] sufficiently appreciate to what extent the moods regarding the criterion and aim of knowledge change with the times. I say "moods" advisedly. I believe I can observe such a mood at the present time. Historical detail is very much in vogue today, despite widespread skepticism. Historical novels have contributed much to the blurring of the boundaries. Even Christian readers have been spoiled. Instead of approaching the early witnesses sympathetically, searching for the truth in their writings, they prefer to be stimulated and excited by the curiosity of one who was a contemporary, of one who was enflamed into passionate involvement, of one who delighted in the victory of the controversial orator. Although the psychological novel presented in the form of letters may have declined in popularity, we have in its place biographies consisting almost wholly of diaries and fragments of letters. People like to view the remote past in a modern refraction. *Homo sum*—man in every time and place is one and the same, today as always, as is illustrated by the sensation which a short story can create. In spite of these objections one might be able to put up with such attempts in the area of theology if they held themselves in check and heeded admonition. To accommodate a current mood one might conceal his displeasure at such bold manipulations of the noble elements of Jesus' picture.

However, it is another matter when—pardon my bluntness—the Christ-novels ascend to the pulpit. Lengthy discourses about first century history, seemingly profound insights into Jesus' inner life (supported by observations on the differences in outlook between then and now), poetic descriptions of the countryside—all this keeps the listener preoccupied with things which, after all, are merely the vehicles of the events in the Gospels and keeps him from the real thing, or better, from the Person who alone is worthy of our attention, from the one Person in his incomparable uniqueness. Certainly no age should be prevented from speaking its own language and from remaining true to its own character. [[71]] However, the restraint and sobriety of the first witnesses should remain the criterion for the message which the evangelical preacher has to deliver. We should attempt to do only *one* thing in our pulpits, namely, to present to our hearers these old, often heard, "outdated" stories— just as they stand, yet freshly and as if heard for the first time. Each listener should receive an indelible impression of what these accounts mean for him. If we immerse ourselves in our Gospels and consider them from every angle without a slavish and lazy adherence to the appointed lessons of the church year, there will be no danger of monotony—unless by monotony one means the repetition of the one keynote, which indeed is unavoidable. This, after all, is the obligation and final aim of every evangelical preacher (Phil 1:18).

It is a mistaken notion to think that it is enough simply to draw the attention of people to Jesus. The "interest" that is aroused here might easily become an obstacle to genuine attentiveness. That is to say, an interest in antiquity or in a modern psychological interpretation of some well-known event may become an obstacle to a true estimate of Christ's worth for our day. It is as noxious for outsiders as it is for "Christian" circles when Christ and the gospel become mere topics of conversation. A preacher must always be scrutinizing his sermons to see whether he is entertaining his congregation instead of witnessing to the gospel, whether he is engaging their intellect and judgment instead of reinforcing (with appropriate means) their inner stirrings in the direction of radical decision and providing their spiritual life with lasting nourishment. Even under the pretence of promoting biblical knowledge it is possible to do nothing more than "beat the air."

Part 2

Methodology

Introduction

JAMES D. G. DUNN

Anyone setting out on a quest needs to make proper preparations—deciding goal, directions, and means of getting there. So with "the quest of the historical Jesus," if there is to be any hope of progress, some preliminary attention must be given to methodology: how to go about such a quest. The history of the "quest" has been the history of a sequence of methods, and a steady refinement in the methods, moving on beyond some and sharpening others.

For the first phase (or two phases) of the "quest," the focus was on *sources*. The methodological assumption was that the source of a writer's portrayal of a historical figure would provide more valuable historical information than the writer who used the source (because it would show whether the writer had been faithful to his source, had made only tendentious use of it, or had improperly embellished it). In the case of "the quest of the historical Jesus," the solution reached by the end of the nineteenth century was the "two-source hypothesis." The conclusion reached from a close study of the Synoptic Gospels (Matthew, Mark, and Luke) was that they were interdependent at the literary level, that Mark was the earliest of the three, and that Matthew and Luke had been able to use both Mark and another source consisting of sayings of Jesus (known conveniently as *Logia* = sayings, or Q = *Quelle* = source). In consequence, the tendency at the end of the nineteenth century was to assume that Mark, as the earliest Gospel, was the most reliable historically.

The twentieth century was characterized, in contrast, with the conviction that all the Gospels, Mark included, could not properly be regarded as straightforward history. They gave too much evidence of the subsequent faith of the first and second generations of Christians. A study by William Wrede proved to be particularly influential in German scholarship at this point. The result was a reassessing of methodological tools. To identify the earliest written sources was no longer sufficient. It was now necessary to press behind the earliest sources to the still-earlier *tradition*. The quest for the right methods to penetrate back *behind* the Gospels became the necessary preliminary to the "quest" proper.

87

The main breakthrough, in the 1920s, is associated once again with the name of Rudolf Bultmann, though credit has to be given also to Martin Dibelius. *Form criticism* was the answer to the failure or inadequacy of source criticism as a way of penetrating behind the written Gospels. K. L. Schmidt had pointed the way forward by observing that Mark's narrative consisted of units that could be distinguished from his editorial framework—like pearls attached to the thread of narrative that could be detached from the thread to be examined, and appreciated, on their own. The form critics proceeded to scrutinize the Synoptic tradition and to classify all such units: individual sayings and parables of Jesus, episodes from Jesus' ministry that regularly climaxed in a profound dictum, and stories of Jesus' doings, particularly miracles and exorcisms. These were identifiable and fairly consistent "forms." The extract from Bultmann (below, pp. 90–106) gives a good example of one of the principal "forms" that he identified.

Form criticism itself soon came to be more valuable in providing evidence of how the forms of the traditions about Jesus were used and manipulated. But the possibility of penetrating behind our written sources to catch echoes of the authentic voice of Jesus continued to fascinate questers. I say "echoes," because the language of the Gospels (Greek) is already at least one remove from Jesus' own vernacular (Aramaic). It was Joachim Jeremias in particular who claimed that even through the Greek we can detect the rhythm and tones that must have been distinctive of Jesus himself. And Bruce Chilton has been able to draw on our knowledge of the transition in the (Jewish) Scriptures, from Hebrew texts to Aramaic translation (or interpretations), that is, targums, to inform us of how such a crucial category as "the kingdom of God" must have been heard and understood by Jesus' contemporaries.

In the period following Bultmann, "the quest of the historical Jesus" was revived by pursuing the possibility of using form criticism as a positive tool in sifting the Gospel traditions for evidence of what is best explained as going back to Jesus himself. The methodological quest was now redefined as the quest for *criteria*, criteria by which it could be determined what within the Jesus tradition can be attributed with confidence to Jesus himself. John Meier's discussion well represents the sort of broad consensus that had been reached on the subject by the 1990s, both the strengths and the weaknesses of the various criteria proposed.

One of the most positive contributions using the form-critical method was Heinz Schürmann's investigation of "the pre-Easter beginnings of the Logia tradition," which demonstrates how much of the actual content of the Q material gives no sign of having been reworked or created in a post-Easter setting. Regrettably, this seminal essay has never been translated into English. But Eugene Lemcio makes a similar contribution. Building on the insights of his doctoral supervisor, C. F. D. Moule, he observed that the Synoptic Evangelists retain a clear sense of the before and after Easter in their own retelling of the story of Jesus. Even if the *context* of their telling evinces a post-Easter perspective, the *content* of what they tell can often be shown to be unaffected by that perspective.

The latest turn in the quest for methodological credibility and viability of the "quest" has been the reopening of the question of how we access the Jesus tradition during its prewritten stage, when it was still in *oral form*. We know that there was a high level of illiteracy in the ancient world, Galilean peasants and fishermen not excepted (according to Acts 4:13, Peter and John were "unlettered" = unable to write). And we lack evidence of Jesus tradition put into writing prior to the 50s or 60s at the earliest. So, it is entirely probable that the teaching and stories about Jesus circulated only in oral form for some 20 or 30 years at least. One of the most plausible models for such oral transmission has been provided by Kenneth Bailey, on the basis of some 30 years' experience of Middle Eastern oral village culture. Taking up his insights, James Dunn argues that the combination of stability of substance and variation in detail that so characterizes the Jesus tradition, as we still have it in the Synoptic Gospels, is often best explained on Bailey's model. He envisages the practice of oral teaching in the earliest disciple groups and churches as going back in many cases to pre-Easter "performances" of that tradition, as Schürmann's work has also suggested.

Bibliography

Bailey, K. E.
   1991   Informal Controlled Oral Tradition and the Synoptic Gospels. *Asia Journal of Theology* 5: 34–54.
   1995   Middle Eastern Oral Tradition and the Synoptic Gospels. *Expository Times* 106: 363–67.
Dibelius, M.
   1934   *From Tradition to Gospel.* London: Nicholson & Watson, 1934. [original pub., 1919]
Moule, C. F. D.
   1967   The Intention of the Evangelists [original pub., 1959]. Pp. 100–114 in *The Phenomenon of the New Testament.* London: SCM.
Schmidt, K. L.
   1919   *Der Rahmen der Geschichte Jesus: Literarkritische Untersuchungen zur ältesten Jesusüberlieferung.* Berlin: Trowitzsch & Sohn.
Schürmann, H.
   1961   Die vorösterlichen Anfänge der Logientradition: Versuch eines formgeschichtlichen Zugangs zum Leben Jesu. Pp. 342–70 in *Der historische Jesus und der kerygmatische Christus*, ed. H. Ristow and K. Matthiae. Berlin: Evangelische.
Wrede, W.
   1971   *The Messianic Secret.* Cambridge: Clarke. [original pub., 1901]

RUDOLF BULTMANN

"I"-Sayings

[[150]] Our previous enquiry has shown that a reference to the person of Jesus is frequently a secondary introduction into the sayings. It is often done without changes or new formulations, and quite simply when a saying is put into a particular *content*. This applies to the blessing of the eyewitnesses in Matt 13:16f. par. (p. 109), for the sayings about the Queen of the South and the Ninevites Luke 11:31 par. (pp. 112f.), the Gentiles in the kingdom Matt 8:11f. par. (p. 116), the hundredfold reward Mark 10:29 (pp. 110f.), disciple and master Luke 6:40 par. (p. 99). As the "I" in the proverb in Matt 12:30 (ὁ μὴ ὢν μετ' ἐμοῦ κτλ [['whoever is not with me is against me']]) is interpreted of Jesus, so is the Son of Man in the sayings about discipleship, blasphemy against the Spirit, forgiveness, and the Lordship over the Sabbath Matt 8:20 par., 12:31f. par.; Mark 2:10, 28 and everywhere where apocalyptic sayings refer to the Son of Man, or parables to the householder.

Elsewhere the reference to the person of Jesus is effected by small alterations or additions. We can detect such alterations in the sayings about what is hidden Matt 10:27 (p. 95), confessing the words of Jesus Matt 20:32f. (p. 112), the reward of kindness to children Mark 9:37, 41 par. (p. 142), and being gathered in the name of Jesus Matt 18:20 (pp. 141f.). Jesus is introduced under the title "Son of Man" into the saying about the coming of the Kingdom Matt 16:28 (p. 121) and also, surely, in the description of the Last Judgement [[151]] Matt 25:31–46 (pp. 123f.). By addition the person of Jesus is referred to in the saying about losing and gaining life Mark 8:35 (p. 93). Similar additions are found in the Beatitudes in Luke 6:22f.; Matt 5:10–12 (p. 110), in the saying about greatness in service Luke 22:27 (p. 144), the warning against high sounding titles Matt 23:10 (pp. 144f.), and the saying about the time of the Parousia Mark 13:32 (p. 123).

Reprinted, with permission, from Rudolf Bultmann, *The History of the Synoptic Tradition* (trans. John Marsh; New York: Harper & Row, 1963) 150–66. Page numbers given in parentheses in the text are cross-references to other places in Bultmann's *History of the Synoptic Tradition*.

Additions which refer to the passion, death or resurrection of Jesus are to be found in the sayings about fasting Mark 2:19b, 20 (p. 92), the Sign of Jonah Matt 12:40 (p. 118), the return of Elijah Matt 17:12 (pp. 124f.); while Luke 17:25 (p. 121) inserts one in the eschatological discourse; to this corresponds the alteration which Mark 10:45 (p. 144) has taken from his source (Luke 22:27).

It is distinctive how Matt 23:34–35 (pp. 113f.) has made a Wisdom saying into one of Jesus' "I" sayings by omitting the introductory formula. In this connection we have *specifically Christian formulations*, of which Mark 13:23, 37 is relatively harmless (ὑμεῖς δὲ βλέπετε· προείρηκα ὑμῖν πάντα [['But be alert; I have already told you everything']] and ὃ δὲ ὑμῖν λέγω, πᾶσιν λέγω, γρηγορεῖτε) [['And what I say to you I say to all: keep awake']]. More important are the sayings about the certainty of Jesus' sayings Mark 13:31 (p. 123), and the rejection of false disciples Matt 7:22f. par. (p. 117). Here too we must mention the woes over the Galilean cities Matt 11:21–24 par. (pp. 117f.) with its indirect reference to the person of Jesus, and further the allegory of the Ten Virgins Matt 25:1–13 (p. 119) and the question about the Son of David Mark 12:35–37 (pp. 136f.). Finally we must remember that in numerous legal sayings and Church rules the risen Lord is conceived of as the speaker.

This review shows that in all these secondary formulations Jesus appears not only as the prophet sent by God at the decisive hour, but he is the *Messiah and Judge* of the world. References to his death and its effect and to the resurrection are also beginning to appear. His ὄνομα has a religious meaning (Mark 9:37, 41; Matt 7:22; 18:20), as in the sayings which are put into the mouth of the risen Lord Matt 28:19;[1] Luke 24:47. In distinction from these the sayings Matt 11:6 par. (. . . μακάριός ἐστιν ὃς ἐὰν μὴ σκανδαλισθῇ ἐν ἐμοί [['blessed is anyone who takes no offense at me']]); Mark 8:38 cp. Luke 12:8f. (confession of the sayings of Jesus) and also the rejection of those who say "Lord, Lord" Luke 6:46 par. in all probability belong to the primary tradition. In them the prophetic self-consciousness of Jesus speaks, and they have no specifically Christian ring at all. Here again we must emphasize that some sayings about the Son of Man [[152]] are manifestly not Christian formulations at all, but belong to the primary tradition, such as the saying just mentioned Mark 8:38 or Luke 12:8f. and further Luke 17:23f. par. These sayings could come from Jesus. Much the same applies to Matt 24:37–39 par., 43f. par.; yet these sayings could also have been taken from Jewish tradition, as we can certainly suppose Mark 13:24–27 was. If one could ascribe other sayings of this kind to Jesus, if one could hold, say, that Jesus himself quoted the Wisdom Saying (Luke 11:49–51 and 13:34f., p. 119), in no circumstances could one follow the evangelist's idea, which holds that the identity of Jesus and the Son of Man is self-evident, but one must first prove the point.

---

1. Did εἰς τὸ ὄνομά μου [['in my name']] stand alone in the original text of Mark? According to Loisy and others the whole passage from βαπτίζοντες [['baptizing']] to πνεύματος [['Spirit']] is an ancient interpolation. Cp. E. Klostermann, [[*Commentary on Matthew*,]] ad loc.

After such considerations we may pass on to the sayings as yet unexamined, where the person of Jesus plays a substantial part, and these I call I-sayings *a parte potiori* [['proportional']]. Nevertheless I shall spend much time on the predictions of the passion and resurrection, which have long been recognized as secondary constructions of the Church: Mark 8:31, 9:31, 10:33f. par. and their deposits Mark 9:9 (12b), 14:21, 41; Matt 17:12, 26:2; Luke 17:25, 24:7.[2]

The first sayings to come into question are those in which Jesus speaks of his coming.

Mark 2:17: . . . οὐκ ἦλθον καλέσαι δικαίους ἀλλὰ ἁμαρτωλούς.
[['I have come to call not the righteous but sinners']]

Luke 19:10 (in some MSS also Luke 9:56 and Matt 18:11):
ἦλθεν γὰρ ὁ υἱὸς τοῦ ἀνθρώπου ζητῆσαι καὶ σῶσαι τὸ ἀπολωλός.
[['For the Son of Man came to seek out and to save the lost']]

Luke 12:49–50: πῦρ ἦλθον βαλεῖν ἐπὶ τὴν γῆν, καὶ τί θέλω εἰ ἤδη ἀνήφθη,
βάπισμα δὲ ἔχω βαπτισθῆναι, καὶ πῶς συνέχομαι ἕως ὅτου τελεσθῇ.
[['I came to bring fire to the earth, and how I wish it were already
kindled! I have a baptism with which to be baptized, and what stress
I am under until it is completed!']]

Matt 10:34–36: μὴ νομίσητε ὅτι ἦλθον βαλεῖν εἰρήνην ἐπὶ τὴν γῆν·	Luke 12:51–53: δοκεῖτε ὅτι εἰρήνην παρεγενόμην δοῦναι ἐν τῇ γῃ; οὐχὶ λέγω ὑμῖν ἀλλ᾽ ἢ διαμερισμόν.

2. What W. Wrede advanced about these predictions of the passion and resurrection in *Das Messiasgeheimnis in den Evangelien* [[Göttingen, 1901,]] 82–92, still holds: they are an expression of the faith of the early Christians. But one may very well ask how far the (gnostic) myth of the Son of Man has affected the development of this faith or its formulation to which Reitzenstein has ascribed a normative influence [[Reitzenstein, *Das mand. Buch d. Herrn. d. Gr.*, 45; *Das iran. Erlösungsmyst*, 117–31; *Z.N.W.*, 20, 1921, 1–23]]. The question merits further enquiry. I cannot meanwhile persuade myself that the Synoptic sayings about the Son of Man come direct from the gnostic myth, but think that they have been mediated through Jewish apocalyptic (which has taken over parts only of the myth), and that it is in line with it that Christian faith has identified Jesus with the Son of Man, modifying it *ex eventu* [['after the fact']]. In Q there are no sayings at all which speak of the Son of Man as the divine envoy walking in humility on earth. When Jesus is referred to as the Son of Man in Q, we are dealing with a misunderstanding (on Matt 8:20 par., cp. [[Bultmann, *History of the Synoptic Tradition*,]] 28 and 97f.; on Matt 11:19 par. see below; on Matt 12:32 par., cp. [[Bultmann, *History*,]] 131; and the same for Mark 2:10, 28). For the rest Q speaks of the coming of the Son of Man as does Jewish apocalyptic (Matt 24:27, 37, 44 par.; further the sayings which can with all probability be ascribed to Q Luke 11:30, 12:8f., 17:30; Matt 10:23, 19:28). Mark 8:38, 13:26, 14:62 also share this meaning. Next we have the passages in Mark on the suffering, dying Son of Man 8:31, 9:9 [12] 31, 10:33f., 45, 14:21, 41 (all the component items are not used in each of these passages!), to which we must add Matt 17:12, 26:2; Luke 17:25, 24:7. But these sayings lack the following motifs characteristic of the myth: (1) The preexistence of the Son of Man (contrariwise John 3:13, 6:62); (2) his exaltation (contrariwise John 3:14, 8:28, 12:34); (3) his judicial office (contrariwise John 5:27); (4) the connection of his destiny with that of the redeemed (contrariwise John 12:32).

[[153]]
οὐκ ἦλθον βαλεῖν εἰρήνην ἀλλὰ
  μάχαιραν.

ἦλθον γὰρ διχάσαι
ἄνθρωπον κατὰ τοῦ πατρὸς αὐτοῦ
καὶ θυγατέρα κατὰ τῆς μητρὸς αὐτῆς
καὶ νύμφην κατὰ τῆς πενθερᾶς αὐτῆς

καὶ ἐχθροὶ τοῦ ἀνθρώπου οἱ
  οἰκιακοὶ αὐτοῦ.

ἔσονται γὰρ ἀπὸ τοῦ νῦν πέντε ἐν
  ἑνὶ οἴκῳ διαμεμερισμένοι.
τρεῖς ἐπὶ δυσὶν καὶ δύο ἐπὶ τρισὶν
  διαμερισθήσονται,
πατὴρ ἐπὶ υἱῷ καὶ υἱὸς ἐπὶ πατρί,
μήτηρ ἐπὶ θυγατέρα καὶ θυγάτηρ ἐπὶ
  μητέρα,
πενθερὰ ἐπὶ τὴν νύμφην καὶ νυμφη
  ἐπὶ τὴν πενθεράν.

[['Do not think that I have come
to bring peace to the earth;
I have not come to bring peace
but a sword.

For I have come to set a man
against his father,
and a daughter against her
mother, and a daughter-in-law
against her mother-in-law;

and one's foes will be members
of one's own household'.]]

[['Do you think that I have come
to bring peace to the earth?
No, I tell you, but rather division!

From now on five in one household
will be divided,
three against two and two against
three; they will be divided:
father against son and son against
father, mother against daughter
and daughter against mother,
mother-in-law against her
daughter-in-law and daughter-in-law
against mother-in-law'.]]

Matt 5:17: μὴ νομίσητε ὅτι ἦλθον καταλῦσαι . . .
  οὐκ ἦλθον καταλῦσαι ἀλλὰ πληρῶσαι.
  [['Do not think that I have come to abolish the law or the prophets;
  I have come not to abolish but to fulfill'.]]

Mark 10:45: καὶ γὰρ ὁ υἱὸς τοῦ ἀνθρώπου οὐκ ἦλθεν διακονηθῆναι, ἀλλὰ
  διακονῆσαι καὶ δοῦναι τὴν ψυχὴν αὐτοῦ λύτρον ἀντὶ πολλῶν.
  [['For the Son of Man came not to be served but to serve, and
  to give his life a ransom for many']]

Matt 11:18–19//Luke 7:33–34: ἦλθεν γὰρ Ἰωάννης . . .
  ἦλθεν ὁ υἱὸς τοῦ ἀνθρώπου ἐσθίων καὶ πίνων . . .
  [['For John came . . . ;
  the Son of Man came eating and drinking. . . '.]]

Mark 1:38 par.: ἄγωμεν ἀλλαχοῦ . . . ἵνα κἀκεῖ κηρύξω· εἰς τοῦτο γὰρ
  ἐξῆλθον.
  [['Let us go on . . . to proclaim the message; for that is what I came
  out to do']]

Matt 15:24: οὐκ ἀπεστάλην εἰ μὴ εἰς τὰ πρόβατα τὰ ἀπολωλότα οἴκου Ἰσραήλ.
[['I was sent only to the lost sheep of the house of Israel']]

Luke 10:16: ὁ ἀκούων ὑμῶν ἐμοῦ ἀκούει, καὶ ὁ ἀθετῶν ὑμᾶς ἐμὲ ἀθετεῖ·
ὁ δὲ ἐμὲ ἀθετῶν ἀθετεῖ τὸν ἀποστείλαντά με.
[['Whoever listens to you listens to me, and whoever rejects you
rejects me, and whoever rejects me rejects the one who sent me']]

Mark 9:37: . . . καὶ ὃς ἂν ἐμὲ δέχηται, οὐκ ἐμὲ δέχεται ἀλλὰ τὸν
ἀποστείλαντά με.
[['. . . and whoever welcomes me welcomes not me but the one who
sent me']]

Matt 10:40: ὁ δεχόμενος ὑμᾶς ἐμὲ δέχεται, καὶ ὁ ἐμὲ δεχόμενος δέχεται
τὸν ἀποστείλαντά με.
[['Whoever welcomes you welcomes me, and whoever welcomes me
welcomes the one who sent me']]

There are no possible grounds for objecting to the idea that Jesus could
have spoken in the first person about himself and his coming; that need be
no more than what befits his prophetic self-consciousness. Yet as individual
sayings they rouse a number of suspicions. If we want to understand Luke
12:49f. as simply a natural expression of Jesus' consciousness of his vocation—can we understand the "baptism" as anything else than his martyrdom,
as in Mark 10:38? and if that be so, must we not take the sayings as a *vaticinium ex eventu* [['prophecy after the fact']], like Mark 10:38 and other vaticinia? Nevertheless it is possible to look on v. 50 as a secondary development of
v. 49; for these sentences in [[154]] parallel do not really match each other
properly, since v. 49 is clearly referring to the aims of Jesus' ministry, while
v. 50 speaks of "a passing personal experience"[3] (Wellhausen).

So perhaps we can take v. 49 as a genuine saying of Jesus. But what would
it mean, if so? The suggestion is that πῦρ [['fire']] in v. 49 is not to be interpreted as the purification and preparation for the coming of the Kingdom
through repentance, but much rather as a final state; only so does τί θέλω κτλ
[['how I wish']] have its right and proper sense. Neither can the reference be
to the fire of judgement. So can the fire be anything else than the Christian
Church or the spirit which works in it? If so, v. 49 is a construction of the
Church. There would be a completely different picture if we could interpret
Luke 12:49f. in terms of the gnostic myth of salvation. The baptism would
then be the consecration by the spirit which the "envoy" receives on his as-
cent into the heavenly world, as is depicted in *Odes Sol.* 24:1 (applied to the re-

3. J. Weiss (*Arch. f. Rel. Wiss.*, 16, 1913, 441) thinks that the genuineness of the saying
in Luke 12:49 and 12:50 is hidden because "here the death of Jesus appears as a consequence of an immense discord and conflict which he must inflame," and this does not lead
us to think of trial and crucifixion, but of something like fighting in the streets. I cannot read
this out of the saying. J. Weiss: (1) interprets v. 49 in terms of vv. 51–53 and (2) he constructs
a connection between v. 49 and v. 50 which is not even hinted at.

deemed soul in 28:1f. and 35:1). The fire would be the judgement in which
the earth perishes, as is foretold in *Odes Sol.* 24:2ff. though, admittedly, without using the metaphor of fire. And then too, τί θέλω κτλ [['how I wish']] can
be made to refer to the judgement; moreover vv. 49 and 50 have an intelligible parallelism; cosmic catastrophe corresponds to the saviour's ascension.
In this case πῶς συνέχομαι [['what stress I am under']] refers to the frequently
depicted anxiety of the one who has been sent, which he feels because he is a
stranger in this world (cp. John 12:27 and *Z.N.W.* 24, 1925, 123–26). If this interpretation could be adopted there would be no genuine dominical saying as
the source of Luke 12:49f. but a section (a quotation?) of the myth would
have been transferred to his lips.

We are also faced with difficulties in considering Luke 22:51–53; Matt
10:34–36. The prophecy in Luke 12:52f. par. is the well-known prediction of
the troubles of the end from Mic 7:6, which is also the source behind Mark
13:12. Cp. *1 En.* 100:2; *b. Sanh.* 97a: "In that age, when the son of David comes
. . . the daughter will rise against her mother and the daughter-in-law against
her mother-in-law."[4] That this prophecy now appears in Matt 10:35 in the
form ἦλθον γὰρ διχάσαι κτλ [['for I have come to set']] is obviously a secondary
transposition. The Church, putting Jesus in God's place as the ruler of history,
has made him proclaim that he will bring the time of terror, and had obviously [[155]] experienced the fulfilment of the prophecy in its own life. But
then it is clear, that the previous saying Matt 10:34 = Luke 12:51 has the same
meaning: in the experience of the Church can be seen the fulfilment of that
eschatological prophecy, and in it all the Church knows, to its comfort in suffering, that Jesus himself has both willed it and brought it to pass. There is express defence against doubting his person and work in μὴ νομίσητε [['do not
think']] (or the questioning δοκεῖτε [['do you think?']]), which also introduces
the saying in Matt 5:17 which comes from the debates of the Church.

Formal considerations have already been seen to cast doubts on Mark
2:17b ([[see Bultmann, *History of the Synoptic Tradition,*]] 92). This is now
matched by the suspicion underlying all sayings about the coming of Jesus.
The variant in Luke 19:10 is certainly a late formulation which by turning the
apocalyptic title Son of Man on to the earthly Jesus shows that it is an Hellenistic product. This applies also to Matt 11:18f.//Luke 7:33f., though here
some older saying might have provided the source, in which the Son of Man
was not an apocalyptic figure, but like Mark 2:10, 28; Matt 8:20 par., simply
meant 'man.'

Matt 5:17 and Mark 10:45 have already been shown ([[Bultmann, *History,*]]
138f., 144) on other grounds to be secondary formulations of a later stage.
The same can be said of Mark 9:37 and Luke 10:16 and the saying they have
both influenced (pp. 192f.). If Matt 15:24 be originally an independent logion
(see p. 38), it would most probably, in view of its formulation of a principle,

---

4. Cp. Strack-B. [[= L. H. Strack and P. Billerbeck, *Kommentar zum NT aus Talmud und
Midrasch* (6 vols.; Munich: Beck, 1922–61; referred to by Bultmann as Strack-B.)]] 2.585f.

have derived from the missionary debates of the Palestinian Church, like Matt 10:5f. Finally Mark 1:38 manifestly does not belong to any old piece of tradition, but to an editorial section Mark 1:35–39, a passage which in contrast to the character of the old tradition gives us no particular scene and no particular saying, but describes a transition, or the motive and general character, of Jesus' ministry.

Since such serious considerations arise against so many of these sayings, one can have but little confidence even in regard to those which do not come under positive suspicion, such as Luke 12:49; Mark 2:17b; Matt 15:24. We must now add that all these sayings which speak of the ἐλθεῖν [['coming']] (or ἀποσταλῆναι [['being sent']] cp. esp. Luke 4:43 with Mark 1:38) of Jesus, are also under suspicion of being Church products because this terminology seems to be the means of its looking back to the historical appearance of Jesus as a whole. This is certainly the case in looking back on the Baptist— ἦλθεν in Matt 11:18 (ἐλήλυθεν [['has come']] Luke 7:33) and Matt 21:32; the same applies to the Baptist as Elijah—ἐλήλυθεν Mark 9:13 and ἦλθεν [['came']] Matt 17:12. Later developments confirm this impression. The Fourth Gospel shows how ἐλθεῖν and ἀποσταλῆναι [[156]] (or πεμφθῆναι [['being sent']]) are typical of the terminology of a later time (cp. esp. John 18:37, 8:42, 16:28, 3:19). 1 Tim 1:15 says: πιστὸς ὁ λόγος καὶ πάσης ἀποδοχῆς ἄξιος, ὅτι Χριστὸς Ἰησοῦς ἦλθεν εἰς τὸν κόσμον ἁμαρτωλοὺς σῶσαι [['The saying is sure and worthy of full acceptance, that Christ Jesus came into the world to save sinners']]. The history of the Text and the apocryphal tradition provide further evidence: At Luke 9:55f., etc., read: . . . ὁ υἱὸς τοῦ ἀνθρώπου οὐκ ἦλθεν ψυχὰς (ανθρώπων) ἀπολέσαι ἀλλὰ σῶσαι [['The Son of Man did not come to destroy the souls (of men) but to save']]. In Luke 22:27 D reads: ἐγὼ γὰρ ἐν μέσῳ ὑμῶν ἦλθον (instead of εἰμί!) οὐχ ὡς ὁ ἀνακείμενος ἀλλ' ὡς ὁ διακονῶν [['for I came among you not as one who is at the table but as one who serves']]. In *Strom.* 3.9.63 Clem. Alex. quotes the *Gospel to the Egyptians*: ἦλθον καταλῦσαι τὰ ἔργα τῆς θηλείας [['I came to release the works of the goddess']]. Jerome constructed a dominical saying: ἦλθον καταλῦσαι τὰς θυσίας [['I came to release the sacrifices']] (see [[Bultmann, *History,*]] 147).

The situation would not be altered if one had to suppose that in the supposed Aramaic source ἦλθον [['I came']] were to be represented by "I come" or "I am there."[5] For even if that be true of Matt 5:17 as a saying in all probability deriving from the primitive Church (see [[Bultmann,]] 138f.) and of other not necessarily Hellenistic-Christian Sayings, a phrase such as "I come" or "I am there" only serves to gather up the significance of the appearance of Jesus as a whole. Naturally it is always possible to ask whether such a phrase were possible to Jesus himself. And little as I am against that *a priori*, I am yet doubtful about proceeding by taking other sayings out of the complex of ἦλθον-sayings, where there are certainly community products and making genuine sayings of Jesus out of them, even though they may well be appro-

5. So C. G. Montefiore, *The Synoptic Gospels* [[2 vols.; 2nd ed.; London: Macmillan, 1927]] 2.47 on Matt 5:17.

priate expressions for his consciousness of his calling.[6] My scepticism is reinforced by considering that on the one hand Jesus was reckoned by the earliest faith to be the "Coming One," i.e., "the future one" (ὁ ἐρχόμενος) in the eschatological sense, and that on the other hand the O.T. nowhere speaks of a prophet's coming or having come. My conjecture is that the assertion of Jesus having come derives from a quite different sphere.[7]

Next comes a series of other sayings in which Jesus speaks of his [[157]] person. It is useful, before considering them, to quote some "I-sayings" that have no independent character but are woven into a narrative. They are to be found in part in the apophthegms already considered and in part in other narrative sources.

Mark 1:17: . . . ποιήσω ὑμᾶς γενέσθαι ἁλεεῖς ἀνθρώπων. [['. . . I will make you fish for people']].

Matt 8:10//Luke 7:9: ἀμὴν λέγω ὑμῖν, οὐδὲ ἐν τῷ Ἰσραὴλ τοσαύτην πίστιν εὗρον [['Truly I tell you, in no one in Israel have I found such faith']]. To these sayings, to which Matt 15:24 cited above may be added, we may say the same as we did about the character of the corresponding apophthegms ([[Bultmann, *History*,]] 27f., 38).

---

6. It is the inadmissible isolation of these sayings, both in their general and individual examination that is, in my view, Harnack's error ("ich bin gekommen," *Z.Th.K.*, 22, 1912, 1–30). A. Froevig has no appreciation of the problem at all, *Das Selbstbewusstsein Jesu*, 1918, 115–18. W. Wrede, *Das Messiahgeheimnis*, 222.2 rightly puts the Synoptic and Johannine ἦλθον-sayings [['I came']] together and asks: "Does this constitute a looking back on the life of Jesus?" W. Bousset, *Kyrios Christos*, [[Göttingen, 1921]] 6 establishes "that especially the frequently recurring formula ἦλθον ὁ υἱὸς τοῦ ἀνθρώπου [['the Son of Man came']] gives the impression from the first that it is a specifically hieratic stylization." L. v. Sybel, *T.S.K.*, 100, 1927/8, 382f. attempts to treat them as "I-sayings."

7. The O.T. never speaks of the prophets coming or having come in the technical sense, much less does any prophet say, "I am come." The O.T. frequently speaks of God's coming, and this is partly in reference to a theophany Gen 33:2; Exod 19:9; Hab 3:3. Mostly the eschatological coming of God is meant, both for salvation (Isa 40:10, 59:19f.; Zech 14:5, cp. Isa 60:1, 62:11) and for judgement (Isa 13:9?; Mal 3:1f.; Ps 96:13); and this is also true of the N.T. Heb 10:37; Jude 14. Parallel to this the N.T. speaks of the eschatological coming of Christ 2 Thess 1:10; Rev 1:7; 2:5, 25; 22:17, 20. Ὁ ἐρχόμενος [['the coming one']] in Matt 11:3//Luke 7:19 had evidently become a secret Messianic title in Judaism on the basis of O.T. passages; cp. Klostermann on Matt 11:3. (The title is found among the Mandaeans: GR, V, 4, p. 193.10 Lidzb[[arski, *Ginzā, der Schatz, oder das Grosse buch der Mandäer übersetzt und erklärt* (Göttingen, 1925)]]; Lit. p. 131.1 = Lidzb[[arski, *Mandäische Liturgien*; Berlin, 1920]].) We meet the phrase "I am come" in Egypt when the God addresses Thutmosis III at the beginning of each of the ten verses in which the God promises the king his support (A. Erman, *Die Literatur der Aegypter* [[Leipzig: Hinrichs, 1923]] 320–22; H. Gressmann (ed.), [[*Altorientalische Texte zum Alten Testament* [2nd ed.; Berlin, 1926]]] 18f.). Among the Mandaeans the divine envoy uses the phrase, Joh-Buch 57, 14; 94, 23ff.; 132, 11; 165, 31; cp. further *Z.N.W.*, 24, 1925, 106f. In Orig. *Contra Celsum* the Hellenistic prophet also says, ἥκω [['I have come']] 7.9, pp. 161, 6ff. Solon, p. 1 rests on the tradition of the prophetic style:

αὐτὸς κήρυξ ἦλθον ἀφ' ἱμερτῆς Σαλαμῖνος [['I am a herald come from beloved Salamis']],

κόσμον ἐπέων ᾠδὴν ἀντ' ἀγορῆς θέμενος [['My news from there my verses will reveal']].

The pleonastic use of "coming" has nothing whatever to do with thus usage examined here,

Mark 9:19 par: . . . ὦ γενεὰ ἄπιστος, ἕως πότε πρὸς ὑμᾶς ἔσομαι; ἕως πότε ἀνέξομαι ὑμῶν [['You faithless generation, how much longer must I be among you? How much longer must I put up with you?']]. We shall deal later on with the legendary character of Mark 9:14–29, but here it is already apparent, that it is a God of an epiphany who is speaking, "who appears in human form only for a time, and will soon return to heaven."[8]

Luke 22:32: ἐγὼ δὲ ἐδεήθην περὶ σοῦ, ἵνα μὴ ἐκλέπῃ ἡ πίστις σου [['but I have prayed for you that your own faith may not fail']].

Luke 23:43: ἀμήν σοι λέγω, σήμερον μετ' ἐμοῦ ἔσῃ ἐν τῷ παραδείσῳ [['Truly I tell you, today you will be with me in Paradise']]. The legendary character of both passages, in which the sayings occur, is beyond question (see below).

Finally, I add the sayings in which the *risen Lord speaks of his person*, though they could in part have been ante-dated by the evangelists into the lifetime of Jesus.

Matt 28:18–20: . . . ἐδόθη μοι πᾶσα ἐξουσία ἐν οὐρανῷ καὶ ἐπὶ γῆς. πορευ-θέντες μαθητεύσατε πάντα τὰ ἔθνη . . . καὶ ἰδοὺ ἐγὼ μεθ' ὑμῶν εἰμι πάσας τὰς ἡμέρας ἕως τῆς συντελείας τοῦ αἰῶνος [['. . . All authority in heaven and on earth has been given to me. Go therefore and make disciples of all nations . . . teaching them to obey everything that I have commanded you. And remember, I am with you always, to the end of the age']].

Luke 24:49: (after the missionary command has been previously given in direct speech) κἀγὼ ἐξαποστέλλω τὴν ἐπαγγελίαν τοῦ πατρός μου ἐφ' ὑμᾶς [['And see, I am sending upon you what my Father promised']].

Matt 16:18f.: κἀγὼ δέ σοι λέγω ὅτι σὺ εἶ Πέτρος, καὶ ἐπὶ ταύτῃ τῇ πέτρα οἰκοδομήσω μου τὴν ἐκκλησίαν . . . δώσω σοι τὰς κλεῖδας τῆς βασιλείας τῶν οὐρανῶν . . . [['And I tell you, you are Peter, and on this rock I will build my church. . . . I will give you the keys of the kingdom of heaven . . .']]. [[158]]

Matt 18:20: οὗ γάρ εἰσιν δύο ἢ τρεῖς συνηγμένοι εἰς τὸ ἐμὸν ὄνομα, ἐκεῖ εἰμι ἐν μέσῳ αὐτῶν [['For where two or three are gathered in my name, I am there among them']].

Without more ado I add to such sayings the following:

Matt 10:16a//Luke 10:3: ἰδοὺ ἐγὼ ἀποστέλλω ὑμᾶς ὡς πρόβατα ἐν μέσῳ λύκων [['See, I am sending you out like sheep into the midst of wolves']]. Here too the risen Lord is giving the missionary command; and besides the passages named we may further compare Matt 23:34, where by omitting the introductory formula a quotation is made into a dominical saying, to read: ἰδοὺ ἐγὼ ἀποστέλλω πρὸς ὑμᾶς . . . [['See, I am sending to you']].

Luke 10:19–20: ἰδοὺ δέδωκα ὑμιν τὴν ἐξουσίαν τοῦ πατεῖν ἐπάνω ὄφεων καὶ σκορπίων κτλ [['See, I have given you authority to tread on snakes and scorpions']].[9] Clearly v. 19 did not originally go with v. 18; and even the original

though P. Fiebig (*Jesu Bergpredigt* [[Göttingen, Vandenhoeck & Ruprecht, 1924]] 27, nos. 74–77) on Matt 5:17 gives pointless examples. Cp. John 1:39, 46.

8. M. Dibelius, *Die Formgeschichte* [[*des Evangeliums* (2nd ed., 1933)]] 87; also Windisch, *Theologisch Tijdskrift* 52, 1918, 214–16.

9. The reading δέδωκα [['I have given']] is original; for Luke has purposely placed the saying after the mission and has used v. 17, which he made himself, and v. 18, which he took

conjunction of vv. 19 and 20 is not certain. It is possible that v. 19 was originally an isolated promise of the exalted Lord (for he speaks here no less than
in the apocryphal ending to Mark 16:17f.) to the missionary, or to the Church
at large, much as in Luke 12:32: μὴ φοβοῦ, τὸ μικρὸν ποιμνίον; ὅτι εὐδόκησεν ὁ
πατὴρ ὑμῶν δοῦναι ὑμῖν τὴν βασιλείαν [['Do not be afraid, little flock, for it is
your Father's good pleasure to give you the kingdom']]. V. 20 could also have
circulated originally as a detached saying, as the apocryphal saying of Jesus in
Makarius Äg. Hom. 12, p. 17 shows: τί θαυμάζετε τὰ σημεῖα; κληρονομίαν μεγά-
λην δίδωμι ὑμῖν, ἣν οὐκ ἔχει ὁ κόσμος ὅλος [['Why are you amazed at the signs? I
give to you a great inheritance, which the whole world does not have']]. Actually the joining of v. 19 and v. 20 with πλήν [['however']] makes a characteristically Lucan impression. The exalted Lord also speaks in v. 20, and the saying
comes from a time when the Church was in danger of overrating miracle.[10]

Luke 22:28–30//Matt 19:28: ὑμεῖς δέ ἐστε οἱ διαμεμενηκότες μετ᾽ ἐμοῦ ...
κἀγὼ διατίθεμαι ὑμῖν, καθὼς διέθετό μοι ὁ πατήρ μου βασιλείαν, ἵνα ἔσθητε καὶ πίνητε
... καὶ καθήσεσθε ἐπὶ θρόνων τὰς δώδεκα φυλὰς κρίνοντες τοῦ Ἰσραήλ [['You are
those who have stood by me in trials; and I confer on you, just as my Father
has conferred on me, a kingdom, so that you may eat and drink at my table in
my kingdom, and you will sit on thrones judging the twelve tribes of Israel']].
Here too it is unquestionably the risen Lord who speaks. V. 28 is a connecting
verse supplied by Luke to put the saying into this particular setting, but the
original beginning of the saying was incorporated into it, for οἱ διαμεμενηκότες
[['those who have stood . . . in trials']] is parallel to οἱ ἀκολουθήσαντες [['(you)
who have followed']] in Matt 19:28. Otherwise it is not [[159]] easy to reconstruct the original form of the saying.[11] The analogies suggest that Luke's "I-
form" is secondary, and perhaps Luke uses διατίθεμαι [['I confer']] because it
makes the saying into a testamentary disposition, which makes it fit the context extremely well. The analogies also suggest that the distinction between
the Son of Man and the Jesus who was speaking was primary in Matthew,[12]
though such a distinction in a saying of the risen Lord cannot be seriously
meant. Matt 16:13 shows that the identity of Jesus and the Son of Man goes

---

from the tradition, to introduce it. So the saying is intended to explain the success which the
disciples have enjoyed: δέδωκα fits that. The reading δίδωμι [['I give']] (Dsyrr, etc.) is however
highly characteristic, for it gives expression to the special character of the verse as a promise
to the Christian missionary. There is no need to think of the influence of Hellenistic motifs
(as Frz. Boll, *Aus der Offenbarung Johannes*, 1914, 116f.). Ps. 91:13 and Jewish linguistic usage
(cp. Strack-B. 2.168f.) account for the construction of the saying.

10. Cp. A. Fridrichsen, *Le Problème du Miracle*, [[Strasbourg: Istra, 1925]] 94–96. Fridrichsen thinks vv. 19, 20 come from the Church; the relationship of the clauses in v. 20, formally a contradiction (not this . . . but that), is conceived in Semitic fashion as a comparative
(less this . . . than that). That does not sound convincing to me, any more than the reproof
of "joy," which was also a characteristic of ancient Hellenistic Christianity.

11. Loisy thinks that Matt 19:28 was the original answer to the disciples' question in
Mark 10:28, which Mark replaced with vv. 29f. for anti-Judaistic reasons (see [[Bultmann, *History*,]] 22).

12. Cp. Mark 10:32f. with Luke 12:8f.; Matt 16:21 with Mark 8:31 and Matt 5:11 with
Luke 6:22. The "I" in Matt 26:24 Syr^sin is also an emendation.

without question, so that he can substitute the pronoun "I" for the title. He could have done this here.[13] He means to say: "When I as the Son of Man. . . ." In any event we are dealing with a formulation deriving from the early Church, for it was there that the Twelve were first held to be the judges of Israel in the time of the end.[14]

Matt 11:25–30//Luke 10:21–22: ἐξομολογοῦμαί σοι πάτερ . . . ὅτι ἔκρυψας ταῦτα . . . πάντα μοι παρεδόθη ὑπὸ τοῦ πατρός μου καὶ οὐδεὶς ἐπιγινώσκει τὸν πατέρα εἰ μὴ ὁ υἱὸς καὶ ᾧ ἐὰν βούληται ὁ υἱὸς ἀποκαλύψαι. Δεῦτε πρός με πάντες οἱ κοπιῶντες κτλ [['I thank you, Father, . . . because you have hidden these things. . . . All things have been handed over to me by my Father; and no one knows the Son except the Father, and no one knows the Father except the Son and anyone to whom the Son chooses to reveal him. Come to me, all you that are weary']].[15] I am convinced that the three "strophes" of this saying did not originally belong together. That the last (δευτε κτλ [['come']]) did not go with the first two is shown, in my view, by its absence from Luke, but above all for its quite different character from Matt 11:27 (πάντα μοι παρεδόθη κτλ [['All things have been handed over to me']]). While v. 27 promises revelation, in vv. 28–30 the teacher makes his appeal and promises a reward for obeying his commands. While v. 27 sounds like a Hellenistic revelation saying, vv. 28–30 throughout resembles Wisdom literature, and Sir 51:23ff., 24:19ff.; Prov 1:20ff., 8:1ff. are the corresponding parallels, and not Corp-Herm. 1.27f., 7.1f.; Philo, *De Sacrif. Ab. et Caini* 70; *Odes Sol.* 33.[16] For in vv. 28–30 the sinner is not called from the path of destruction to repentance, but the man who cares and strives in vain is shown a more profitable way. The dualism, which is presupposed in the cited Hellenistic parallels is completely lacking. It seems to me that [[160]] Matt 11:28–30 is a quotation from Jewish Wisdom literature put into the mouth of Jesus. By contrast v. 27 is specifically an Hellenistic Revelation saying, as Dibelius has rightly characterized it.[17] The similarity of the

13. Cp. Matt 26:2.
14. W. Bousset (in his Commentary on Revelation [[*Die Offenbarung Johannis* [Göttingen: Vandenhoeck & Ruprecht, 1906]]) thinks it possible that Rev 3:21 is a more original form of this saying: ὁ νικῶν, δώσω αὐτῷ καθίσαι μετ᾽ ἐμοῦ ἐν τῷ θρόνῳ μου, ὡς κἀγώ ἐνίκησα καὶ ἐκάθισα μετὰ τοῦ οατπαρός [['To the one who conquers I will give a place with me on my throne, just as I myself conquered and sat down with my Father on his throne']]. W. Hadorn agrees, while E. Lohmeyer simply asks whether Rev 3:21 used another form of the dominical saying as its source. The connection of Rev 3:21 with 3:20 makes it highly probable that it belongs to the same tradition. But I am inclined to think that Rev 3:21 is the universalizing of a saying which applied originally only to the Twelve.
15. I refrain from going into the basis for the above version of v. 27 here.
16. Dibelius, *Formgeschichte*, 90. It seems probable to me that the *Odes of Solomon* was in its turn influenced by the style of Wisdom literature.
17. Cp. further W. Bousset, *Kyrios Chr.*², 45–50. Among the parallels from Hellenistic mysticism should also be included the ancient parallel from Akhnaton's Hymn to the Sun:

No other knows thee save thy Son Akhnaton.
Thou has initiated him into thy plans and thy power.

(Gressmann, *Altorient. Texte zum AT*², 18; cp. A. Erman, *Die Literatur der Aegypter*, 361; G. Roeder, *Urkunden zur Religion des alten Aegypten* [[Jena: Diederichs, 1923]] 65). I believe that

beginning with Matt 28:18 makes it easy to suppose that in the tradition Matt 11:27 was originally handed down as a saying of the risen Lord. Matt 11:25f.// Luke 10:21 is further, in my opinion, a saying originally Aramaic.[18] I also think it possible that it comes from a lost Jewish writing; it seems to be torn out of some context (to what does ταῦτα [['these things']] refer?). It cannot remain among the sayings of Jesus; yet, on the other hand, I see no compelling reason for denying it to him.

It is more difficult to reach a conclusion in the following instance: Luke 14:26//Matt 10:37: εἴ τις ἔρχεται πρός με καὶ οὐ μισεῖ τὸν πατέρα αὐτοῦ . . . οὐ δύναται εἶναί μου μαθητής [['Whoever comes to me and does not hate his father . . . cannot be my disciple']]. We can be certain that οὐ μισεῖ [['does not hate']] in Luke is more original than Matthew's φιλῶν . . . ὑπὲρ ἐμέ [['loves . . . more than me']]; for the former could hardly have developed from the latter. Moreover the reference to the Person of Jesus is strengthened by the phrase ὑπὲρ ἐμέ [['more than me']], and the analogies show that to be secondary. Finally Luke's εἶναι μαθητής [['be (my) disciple']] is more primary than Matthew's ἄξιός μου [['worthy of me']]; it is somewhat more concrete than "being worthy of Jesus," which cannot very well be other than Christian terminology.[19] This receives confirmation, as I believe, when Luke uses the same expression in making his application of the parable in v. 33; but this application, which narrows the parable's meaning, is his own, and it is therefore probable that he had some example in front of him, namely v. 26 (and 27); in the same way, in the form in which Luke gives them, v. 26 (and 27) are in the precise form to make them more easily understandable as an introduction to the parables in vv. 28–32. In addition Luke has altered the list of relatives by doing away with the parallelism and by some pedantic additions.

Luke 14:27//Matt 10:38 or Mark 8:34b par.: *Discipleship in bearing the Cross.* Once more Luke seems to have retained the Q form better than Matthew. Moreover the negative version of Q seems more original [[161]] than Mark, where "discipleship" is no longer a condition required but has already attained a lustre of its own.

The question has now to be asked, whether these two sayings are to be taken as Church formulations. They do not seem to me to come under suspicion in the way that "I-sayings" usually do, for it is not necessary to think that they were spoken originally by the risen Lord. That would be the case, of course, if the figure of cross-bearing in Luke 14:27 were to presuppose the martyr death of Jesus. But that is not proven in my opinion. If σταυρός [['cross']] had already become a Christian symbol of martyrdom, would we not expect to find simply τὸν σταυρόν [['the cross']] (without ἑαυτοῦ [['his']])? If

---

a close examination of the concept of revelation and knowledge (of God), which J. Schniewind *(Th.R.,* n.s.[2], 1930, 196f.) rightly desires, would confirm this judgement.

18. Cp. Strack-B. 1.606f.; Klostermann, ad loc.; A. von Schlatter, *Der Evangelist Matthaeus* [[Stuttgart: Calwer, 1933]] 380–83; also P. Fiebig, *Der Erzaehlungsstil der Evangelien* [[Leipzig: Hinrichs, 1925]] 137f.

19. Cp. G. Kittel, *Die Probleme des palaest. Spaetjudentums,* 1926, 54f.

so, then could not σταυρός [['cross']] have been at an earlier stage a traditional figure for suffering and sacrifice?[20] If that may be assumed, it seems clear to me that 14:27 no more than 14:26 really refers to anything beyond a sense of vocation, as do sayings like Matt 11:5f.; Luke 6:46, 12:8f. But a confident judgement as to whether they are genuine sayings of our Lord is prevented by the fact that they are obviously variants.

Mark 3:35 par.: *The True Kinsmen*. This saying must be mentioned here once again. We have already seen, on [[Bultmann, *History*,]] 143, that it is probably a Church formulation.

Luke 10:18: ἐθεώρουν τὸν σατανᾶν ὡς ἀστραπὴν ἐκ τοῦ οὐρανοῦ πεσόντα [['I watched Satan fall from heaven like a flash of lightning']]. Almost nothing can be said about the originality of this saying, since its meaning is almost lost to us. It gives a strong impression of being a fragment.[21] [[162]]

Matt 12:27//Luke 11:19: (καὶ) εἰ ἐγὼ ἐν Βεελζεβοὺλ ἐκβάλλω τὰ δαιμόνια, οἱ υἱοὶ ὑμῶν ἐν τίνι ἐκβάλλουσιν; κτλ [['If I cast out demons by Beelzebul, by whom do your own exorcists cast them out?']].

Matt 12:28//Luke 11:20: εἰ (δὲ) ἐν δακτύλῳ θεοῦ ἐγὼ ἐκβάλλω τὰ δαιμόνια, ἆρα ἔφθασεν ἐφ᾽ ὑμᾶς ἡ βασιλεία τοῦ θεοῦ [['But if it is by the Spirit of God that I cast out demons, then the kingdom of God has come to you']].

The two sayings placed together in Q have nothing to do with each other originally (cp. [[Bultmann, *History*,]] 14). The former looks very much like Church polemic, though without supplying the basis for anything to be said

---

20. It is of no significance for this present use of the word "cross" that Ps 22:17 (?) and Plato, *Resp.*, 362a refer to the crucifixion of the righteous (though both instances fail to use the actual words σταυρός [['cross']] or σταυρωθῆναι [['to be crucified']]). According to Strack-B. 2.587 the older Rabbinic literature did not know the phrase "to take up one's cross," but used the phrase "take up one's sufferings" (קַבֵּל יִסּוּרִין) instead. Yet Strack-B. cites *Gen. Rab.* 56 (36c), on which A. Meyer had already said (*Jesu Muttersprache*, 1896, 78): "Abraham took the wood for the burnt offering and laid it on his son Isaac (Gen 22:6). Just as one does who carries his cross on his shoulder." Schlatter (*Der Evangelist Matthaeus*, 350f.) who also quotes this passage, thinks it possible that the idiom grew up among the Zealots, whose followers would have to reckon with the cross, and from them passed on to the disciples of Jesus. The expression ἔρχεσθαι [['to come']] (Luke, ἀκολουθεῖν [['carry']]; Matthew, ὀπίσω [['take up']]) is also semitic; the form ἀπαρνεῖσθαι ἑαυτόν [['to deny himself']], which is foreign to semitic usage, is first introduced into Mark's version. Cp. Schlatter, *Der Evangelist Matthaeus*, 519; G. Dalman, *Jesus Jeschua*, 1922, 172f. When Dalman says that the expression "follow" in metaphorical usage is not paralleled in Rabbinic literature that can only be sustained if following means taking on the same fate; for the Rabbis not only talk of the following of disciples in the sense that they actually follow the Rabbis as they walk, but also use the derived meaning of learning from and imitating their mode of life (Strack-B. 1.187f., 528f.), and this meaning is adequate for Luke 14:27.

21. Conjectures are easy enough. First, naturally, that the saying refers to a vision of Jesus. Hence H. Windisch (e.g., "Jesus und der Geist," *Studies in Early Christianity*, 1928, 235) is inclined to suppose that Jesus' "apocalyptic announcements were fertilized in greater degree by ecstatic experiences, than the cannonical tradition hints"—which is by no means impossible; cp. [[Bultmann, *History*,]] 108f. We can be sure of this only: that the saying foretells the end of the Kingdom of Satan, even if it does not carry with it the special form of that idea which we have in Rev 12:8f.

confidently about it. But the latter can, in my view, claim the highest degree of authenticity which we can make for any saying of Jesus: it is full of that feeling of eschatological power which must have characterized the activity of Jesus.[22]

Confidence in the antiquity of the "I-sayings" is in the last resort considerably lessened by observing how such sayings multiply more and more in later tradition. Among such are sayings which look back on the work of Jesus as Orig. *Comm. Matth. tom* 13:2: διὰ τοὺς ἀσθενοῦντας ἠσθένουν καὶ διὰ τοὺς πεινῶντας ἐπείνων καὶ διὰ τοὺς διψῶντας ἐδίψων [['Because of the weak, I was weak; and I was hungry because of the hungry; and I was thirsty because of the thirsty']] (cp. already pp. 155f. [[96 above]]). Further the saying of the risen Lord in the Freer Logion (*kl. Texte*, 31, p. 31): . . . καὶ ὑπὲρ ὧν ἐγὼ ἁμαρτησάντων παρεδόθην εἰς θάνατον, ἵνα . . . κληρονομήσωσιν [['And for those who sinned I was given in death, so that . . . they might inherit']]. Finally the saying which comes from Hellenistic piety, *Pap. Ox.*, I, 3 (*kl. Texte*, 8, p. 16): ἔστην ἐν μέσῳ τοῦ κόσμου καὶ ἐν σαρκὶ ὤφθην καὶ εὖρον πάντας μεθύοντας καὶ οὐδένα εὖρον διψῶντα ἐν αὐτοῖς. καὶ πονεῖ ἡ ψυχή μου ἐπὶ τοῖς υἱοῖς τῶν ἄνων ὅτι τυφλοί εἰσιν τῇ καρδίᾳ αὐτῶν. . . . [['I stood [was placed] in the middle of the world and was seen [appeared] in the flesh and found all the drunks and found no one thirsting among them. And my soul toiled for the sons of death because they are blind in their hearts'.]]

The heavenly judge uses different language, as in Matt 7:22f., or the variant of this saying in *2 Clem.* 4:5, which is very like the version found in the Nazarean edition of Matthew: ἐὰν ἦτε μετ' ἐμοῦ συνηγμένοι ἐν τῷ κόλπῳ μου καὶ μὴ ποιῆτε τὰς ἐντολάς μου, ἀποβαλῶ ὑμᾶς καὶ ἐρῶ ὑμῖν; ὑπάγετε ἀπ' ἐμοῦ, οὐκ οἶδα ὑμᾶς πόθεν ἐστέ, ἐργάται ἀνομίας [['Even if you were nestled close to my breast but did not do what I have commanded, I would cast you away and say to you, "Leave me! I do not know where you are from, you who do what is lawless"']]. In addition there is Rev 3:20, 16:15 and the logion cited on [[Bultmann, *History*,]] 127, which was quoted by Justin [*Dialogue* 47] and others, ἐν οἷς ἂν ὑμᾶς καταλάβω, ἐν τούτοις καὶ κρινῶ [['In whatever things I catch you, in these I will judge you']] (*kl. Texte*, 11, p. 1). Related to this is the saying in the Nazarean edition of Matthew, which rests on the idea of Matt 25:31–46: "I choose for myself those good ones whom my heavenly Father has given me." Further we may add the saying quoted by Orig. in *Jer. Hom. Lat.* 3:3 and Didym. in Ps 80:8: ὁ ἐγγύς μου ἐγγὺς τοῦ πυρός. ὁ δὲ μακρὰν ἀπ' ἐμοῦ μακρὰν ἀπὸ τῆς βασιλείας [['He who is near me is near the fire. He who is far from me is far from the kingdom']] and the saying in *Barn.* 7:11: οὕτως (φησὶν) οἱ θέλοντές με ἰδεῖν καὶ ἅψασθαί μου τῆς βασιλείας ὀφείλουσιν θλιβέντες καὶ παθόντες λαβεῖν με [['So (he says): those who wish to see me and touch my kingdom must take hold of me through pain and suffering'.]]

---

22. On the question whether ἐν πνεύματι [['by the Spirit']] (Matthew) or ἐν δακτύλῳ [['by the finger']] (Luke) is original see, e.g., Windisch, "Jesus und der Geist," 217f. I think H. Leisegang's assumption unfounded (cp. p. 131 n. 1) that the original wording was ἐν ὀνόματι θεοῦ [['in the name of God']].

[[163]] The motif of continual presence from Matt 18:20, 28:20 is rendered variously in other terms, as in *Pap. Ox.*, I, 4: ὅπου ἐὰν ὦσιν β' οὐκ εἰσὶν ἄθεοι, καὶ ὅπου εἷς ἐστιν μόνος, λέγω· ἐγώ εἰμι μετ' αὐτοῦ. ἔγειρον τὸν λίθον κἀκεῖ εὑρήσεις με· σχίσον τὸ ξύλον, κἀγὼ ἐκεῖ εἰμι [['Wherever there are [three] they are without God, and where there is one alone I say I am with him. Lift the stone and there you will find me; cleave the wood and I am there']] (Supplementations as in *kl. Texte*, 8, p. 16). Ephraem. Syr. *conc. exp.* 165 (ed. Moesinger): *ubi unus est, ibi et ego sum, et ubi duo sunt, ibi et ego ero* [['Where there is one, there I am also; and where there are two, there I also will be']]. The saying quoted by Clem. Alex. *Strom.* 5.10.63 is, finally, unique: μυστήριον ἐμὸν ἐμοὶ καὶ τοῖς υἱοῖς τοῦ οἴκου μου [['My mystery is for me and for the sons of my house']]. To conclude we may mention various sayings in the so-called *Odes of Solomon*, in which the exalted Lord speaks, or the Gospel according to St. John, where the sayings about his own self (particularly those which contain the form ἐγώ εἰμι [['I am']]) are in principle on the same level as those which are ascribed to the historical Jesus.

The "I-sayings" were predominantly the work of the *Hellenistic Churches*, though a beginning had already been made in the *Palestinian Church*. Here too Christian prophets filled by the Spirit spoke in the name of the ascended Lord sayings like Rev 16:15. The following Synoptic I-sayings can be considered as coming from the Palestinian Church. Matt 5:17 points directly to the legal debates of the early Church, and Matt 15:24 to discussions about the Gentile mission. Matt 10:16a (ἰδοὺ ἐγὼ ἀποστέλλω ὑμᾶς ὡς πρόβατα κτλ [['see, I am sending you out like sheep into the midst of wolves']]), Luke 10:16 (ὁ ἀκούων ὑμῶν κτλ [['whoever listens to you']]) and perhaps Luke 10:19-20 (ἰδοὺ δέδωκα ὑμῖν τήν ἐξουσίαν κτλ [['see, I have given you authority']]) also comes from the mission of the early Church. Matt 12:27 (εἰ ἐγὼ ἐν βεελζεβοὺλ ἐκβάλλω κτλ [['if I cast out demons by Beelzebul']]) has come from the conflict with the Jews. Matt 11:25f., 28–30 (ἐξομολογοῦμαι σοι . . . δεῦτε πρός με πάντες κτλ [['I thank you. . . . Come to me, all']]) perhaps circulated as a dominical saying in the early Church, and then came to give expression to the antithesis to the legal piety of the scribes, and Mark 2:17b (οὐκ ἦλθον καλέσαι κτλ [['I have come to call']]) is in all probability to be understood in the same way. In addition Mark 3:35 (the true kinsman), Luke 14:26 (εἴ τις ἔρχεται πρός με [['Whoever comes to me']]) and perhaps Luke 14:27 (discipleship in Cross-bearing) could well have come from the primitive Church. Luke 22:28–30 or Matt 19:28 (The Twelve on twelve thrones) is related to the inner life of the early Church; as are Luke 22:27 (. . . ἐγὼ δὲ ἐν μέσῳ ὑμῶν κτλ [['but I am among you']]), Mark 9:37, 41 or Matt 10:40, 42 (reward of kindness to children), and Matt 18:20 (οὗ γάρ εἰσιν δύο η τρεῖς κτλ [['For where two or three']]). Matt 10:34–36 or Luke 12:51–53 (μὴ νομίσητε ὅτι ἦλθον βαλεῖν εἰρήνην κτλ [['Do not think that I have come to bring peace']]) have come out of the bitter experiences of the primitive Church. It is less certain that Luke 10:18 (fall of Satan) and Luke 12:49f. (πῦρ ἦλθον βαλεῖν κτλ [['I have come to bring fire']]) derived therefrom. For all the rest, especially for the sayings about the coming of the Son of Man, we have to assume an Hellenistic origin.

Supplement

Two passages of a special character have not been discussed in what has gone before. I treat them now as an addition:

Matt 12:43–45//Luke 11:24–26: *The Return of the Exorcized Demons.* This section is different from the other sayings of Jesus in both form and content. In style it is more closely related to a parable, and may actually have originated as such, Matthew perhaps having preserved its application in his οὕτως ἔσται καὶ τῇ γενεᾷ ταύτῃ τῇ πονηρᾷ [['So it will be also with this evil generation']]. But its original meaning is hardly discernible, though it seems to me to be the same as in certain Arabic proverbs. Cp. Alb. Socin, *Arabische Sprichwoerter und Redensarten* (Tuebing. Universitaetschr., 1878), no. 73: "He went away; and then he returned bringing Mahmud and Gillo with him as well." No. 94: "He died like a dog, and set us free from his service; but he left behind a young dog that was worse than his father." On no. 73 Socin refers to J. L. Burckhardt, *Arabische Sprichwoerter oder die Sitten und Gebraeuche der neueren Aegypter*, 1875, no. 5. Matt 12:43–45 par. does not seem to be a community construction, as it entirely lacks any Christian features; perhaps it is taken from some Jewish writing. Its appearance in the Christian tradition is due to the demonological material. It is not intended to function as a criticism of exorcism, but rather to warn the person who is healed to be wary of demonic powers.[23]

Matt 11:7–19//Luke 7:24–35; Matt 21:32//Luke 16:16: *Sayings about the Baptist.* Matt 11:7–19 par. which had already achieved essentially the same unity in Q, is made up of various units.[24] The Christian attitude to John the Baptist is a divided one: while some passages make the Baptist appear as a confederate in Christian affairs, others emphasize his inferiority to Jesus. Understandably, for both points of view were occasioned by the anti-Baptist polemic. Matt 11:7–11a, 16–19, 21:32 give expression to the solidarity of Jesus with John the Baptist. Mark 11:27–30 is a piece of the same kind.[25] The rivalry between the Christian and the Baptist communities is exemplified in their each having their own prayer (Luke 11:1b, most probably from Q; v. 1a a construction by Luke) and an independent practice in regard to fasting (Mark 2:20). The relegation of the Baptist is seen most clearly in the Christian addition in Matt 11:11b par. (ὁ δὲ μικρότερος κτλ [['yet the least']]), and in Matt 11:12f. par., which is no longer patent of confident interpretation, but which at least seems to be saying that the Baptist [[165]] belongs to a bygone age.[26] Correspondingly the Christian tradition has applied the saying about the mightier one in Mark 1:7, or Matt 3:11b; Luke 3:16b; Acts 13:25 to Jesus, and in this way depicted the Baptist as unworthy to perform for Jesus even the

---

23. Cp. John 5:14; *Acts Thom.* 46. Klostermann refers to Dio Chrys., 5.32.

24. On this and the following cp. M. Dibelius, *Die urchristliche Ueberlieferung von Johannes dem Taeufer* (Forschungen 15), 1911; M. Goguel, *Jean-Baptiste*, 1928.

25. Do passages like Matt 12:38f., 41f. also belong here? Cp. [[Bultmann, *History*,]] 118 n. 2.

26. Cp. M. Goguel, op. cit., 65–69; H. Windisch, *Z.N.W.*, 1928, 168f.

lowliest duties of a slave. Thus it carried on its polemic against the view that
the Baptist was the Messiah (Luke 3:15), and subordinated his water baptism
to Christian baptism—Mark 1:8, or Matt 3:11a, c; Luke 3:16a, c; Acts 1:5,
11:16, 19:1ff. It is something of a compromise when the Baptist is given the
role of the Forerunner: Jesus makes his appearance in connection with John's
baptism, Mark 1:9ff. par.; Acts 1:22, 10:37; the Baptist (whose Messianic
preaching was reinterpreted thus) pointed to Jesus as the coming Messiah
Mark 1:7f. or Matt 3:11f.; Luke 3:16f.; Acts 13:24f., 19:4. This theory of John
as the Forerunner was eventually to be given expression in his being identified
as Elijah, the one to prepare the way of the Lord, Mark 9:12f. par.; Matt 11:14.

Nevertheless part of the material in the Synoptic tradition concerning this
matter derives from the early Palestinian Church. Perhaps a genuine saying of
Jesus is preserved in it at Matt 11:7–11a. The qualifying addition in Matt
11:11b was already in Q and could well have come from the early Church too,
but it is in any event Christian, as is the intrusive 11:10 par. If Matt 11:16f. is
also an ancient parable by Jesus, then the appended interpretation Matt
11:18f. is also in any case a community product, which owes its form (ἦλθεν ὁ
υἱὸς τ. ἀνθρ.! [['the Son of Man came'!]]) to the Hellenistic Church. Clearly Mark
11:27–30 (cp. [[Bultmann, *History*,]] 20f.) and possibly also the other passage
concerned with prayer and fasting (Mark 2:19b, 20; Luke 11:1b) are products
of the Palestinian Church. Similarly Matt 11:12 par., which is as early as Q, will
also have come from the primitive Church. The same must be said of Luke
7:29f. (the form in Matt 21:32 is secondary), which can hardly be claimed as a
genuine saying of Jesus; it is retrospective, and reads as though there were already a Christian baptism established (Wellhausen). Finally it is manifest that
in the early Church the Baptist's messianic preaching was applied to Jesus and
the saying about the mightier one correspondingly interpreted.

But the rivalry between the community of Jesus and that of the Baptist
also persisted, as Acts and John show, in certain circles of the Hellenistic
Church, and this means that we have to reckon with the possibility of this or
that questionable saying having an Hellenistic origin. In this category may
well belong the Elijah theory, which Matt 11:14 has even introduced into the
text of Q. Perhaps also we may include the opposition of the Johannine water
baptism to the Christian Spirit baptism; and in addition, everything, of
course, which has to be taken as the special editorial work of the evangelists,
as also the corresponding passages in Acts.

JOACHIM JEREMIAS

Characteristics of the Ipsissima Vox

[[29]] So far we have been discussing linguistic and stylistic phenomena which did not represent a completely new development, but appeared in the sayings of Jesus with unusual frequency. Now we turn to characteristics of Jesus' speech to which there is no analogy in contemporary literature and which may therefore be designated as characteristics of the *ipsissima vox Jesu* [['the very words of Jesus']].

The Parables of Jesus

We find nothing to be compared with the parables of Jesus, whether in the entire intertestamental literature of Judaism, the Essene writings, in Paul, or in Rabbinic literature. One immediate difference is that some of the types of parabolic speech are not to be found in the sayings of Jesus at all. Thus, for example, we read in the Essene *Genesis Apocryphon* a fable which depicts how the palm tree (Sarai) pleads for the cedar tree (Abram) to be spared (1QGenAp ar 19.14–17). This fable continues the series of Old Testament plant-fables in which cedar, olive, fig tree, vine, bramble bush and thistle behave like human beings.[1] We find no fables on the lips of Jesus; fig tree and vine do not speak in his sayings.[2] Also, in *Ethiopian Enoch* (chaps. 85–90) [[30]] we read an outline of the history of Israel in the form of a long-winded allegory involving various animals. Jesus indeed regularly uses the familiar metaphors, mostly drawn from the Old Testament and familiar to everyone at that time, but he does not construct allegories.[3] His parables take us, rather, into the midst of throbbing, everyday life. Their nearness to life, their simplicity and clarity, the masterly brevity with which they are told, the seriousness of their appeal to the conscience, their loving understanding of the outcasts of religion—all this

Reprinted, with permission, from J. Jeremias, *New Testament Theology: The Proclamation of Jesus* (New York: Scribner's, 1971) 29–37.

1. Judg 9:8–15; 2 Kgs 14:9; Ezek 17:3–8; 31:3–14. Cf. also *4 Ezra* 4:13–21: the trees and the waves hold councils of war because they want to fight each other.

2. M. D. Goulder, "Characteristics of the Parables in the Several Gospels," *JTS* 19, 1968, 51–69: 51.

3. Jeremias, *Parables*[2], 88f.

is without analogy. If we want to find anything comparable we have to go back
a long way, to the high-points of prophetic proclamation: the parable of
Nathan (2 Sam 12:1–7), the song of the vineyard (Isa 5:1–7) and perhaps the
comparison with father and son in Hosea 11 (though that is hardly a parable,
i.e., a "short story").[4] Even in these cases we have only a few, scattered examples, whereas the first three gospels give us no fewer than forty-one parables of Jesus. It is generally recognized today—despite the need for a critical
analysis of every single parable and the history of its tradition—that the parables belong to the bedrock of the tradition about him.

The Riddles

Among the sayings of Jesus there are a considerable number which are riddles.
Not only are they riddles for us today; they were even felt to be riddles, at
least by outsiders, at the time when Jesus uttered them. One might mention
the following: sayings about John the Baptist like Matt 11:11 par., where John
is described paradoxically as the greatest among those born of woman and
less than the least in the reign of God, or the strange saying about the forcing
of the *basileia* [['kingdom']] (Matt 11:12 par.);[5] sayings about the mission of
Jesus like 11:5f. par. with the juxtaposition of salvation and scandal; pictorial
sayings about the old and the new like Mark 2:21f. par. and about the coming
time of distress like Mark 14:58; Luke 11:49; Matt 10:34; Luke 22:36; sayings
about the fate of Jesus like the word-play in Mark 9:31, that God will deliver
up the man (sing.) to men (plur.); the saying about Elijah in Mark 9:11; sayings about the three days like [[31]] Luke 13:32f.; riddles like that of the three
kinds of eunuch in Matt 19:12. Indeed, Mark 4:11, detached from its present
secondary context,[6] says of the whole preaching of Jesus that it must be in riddles to those ἔξω [['outside']]. All this is quite unusual. Teachers of the time
did not teach in this way, and the early church did not invent riddles (*měšālīm*)
for Jesus; on the contrary, it clarified them, a tendency that can be studied,
for example, in the prophecies of the passion.[7]

The Reign of God

As a designation of God's reign, the term βασιλεία (τοῦ θεοῦ/τῶν οὐρανῶν)[8]
[['kingdom (of God/of heaven)']] occurs on the lips of Jesus in the following
way:

---

4. The expression was used by G. Eichholz, *Einführung in die Gleichnisse* (Biblische Studien 37), Neukirchen-Vluyn 1963, 18.

5. For a suggestion about the meaning, see [[Jeremias, *NT Theology*,]] 111f.

6. Jeremias, *Parables*[2], 13–18.

7. [[Jeremias, *NT Theology*,]] 277ff. The misunderstandings of ambiguous words or
phrases in the Fourth Gospel are not comparable with the synoptic *měšālīm* [['proverbs']].
Some of them are extremely crude (cf. John 2:20; 3:4; 4:15; 7:35; 8:22, 57) and are no more
than a stylistic means used, e.g., to give a decisive turn to the dialogue.

8. On the question which of the two forms is the original, see [[Jeremias, *NT Theology*,]]
97.

Mark   13 times[9]
Logia common to Matthew and Luke   9 times[10]
Additional instances in Matthew only   27 times[11]
Additional instances in Luke only   12 times[12]
John   2 times[13]

The explanation for the disproportionately high number in Matthew is that a group of his examples represents redactional activity: in five instances he has inserted the term in the Marcan text (Matt 13:19; 18:1; 20:21; 21:43; 24:14); two examples occur in the interpretation of the parable of the wheat and the tares (13:38, 43), where his editorial work is considerable,[14] and in eight further instances we have an introduction to parables ὁμοία ἐστὶν [or ὡμοιώθη, ὁμοιωθήσεται] ἡ βασιλεία τῶν οὐρανῶν [['the kingdom of heaven is like (or may be compared to)']] preferred by Matthew or his source (13:24, 44, 45, 47; 18:23; 20:1; 22:2; 25:1).[15] Luke has added the term to the Marcan text three times (Luke 4:43; 18:29; 21:31). [[32]] An investigation of Jewish literature produces a completely different picture.[16] The term "reign (of God)" occurs only rarely in the Apocrypha and Pseudepigrapha of the Old Testament,[17] in the Targums[18] and in Philo;[19] otherwise it occurs in pre-Christian times only in the Kaddish and a few prayers related to it;[20] Josephus mentions βασιλεία on only one occasion[21] in connection with God (he does not have the term "reign of God" itself). Instances begin to increase somewhat only when we come to the Rabbinic literature, but as a rule they are limited to stereotyped phrases like "take the reign of heaven upon oneself," i.e., "subject oneself to God," "repeat the *Shĕma*'," "become a proselyte."[22] This general picture has been amply confirmed by the Dead Sea Scrolls: the phrase "reign (of God)" occurs only three times in the whole of the Essene literature so far as it is at

9. Mark 1:15 par.; 4:11 par., 26, 30 par.; 9:1 par., 47; 10:14 par., 15 par., 23 par., 24, 25 par.; 12:34; 14:25 par.

10. Matt 5:3 (par. Luke 6:20); 6:10 (par. Luke 11:2), 33 (par. Luke 12:31); 8:11 (par. Luke 13:29); 10:7 (par. Luke 10:9); 11:11 (par. Luke 7:28), 12 (par. Luke 16:16); 12:28 (par. Luke 11:20); 13:33 (par. Luke 13:20).

11. Matt 5:10, 19a, b, 20; 7:21; 8:12; 13:19, 24, 38, 43, 44, 45, 47, 52; 16:19; 18:1, 3, 4, 23; 19:12; 20:1; 21:31, 43; 22:2; 23:13; 24:14; 25:1.

12. Luke 4:43; 9:60, 62; 10:11; 12:32; 13:28; 17:20a, b, 21; 18:29; 21:31; 22:16, 18.

13. John 3:3, 5.

14. Jeremias, *Parables*², 82–84.

15. Ibid., 101f.

16. Dalman, *Words of Jesus*, 91–147; see also *Worte Jesu*², 310–14, 361–63, 375–78; Billerbeck, 1.172–84, 418f.

17. Dan 3:54 LXX; 4:34Θ; Tob 13:2; *Pss. Sol.* 5:18; 17:3; *1 En.* 84:2; *As. Mos.* 10:1; Wis 6:4; 10:10; *Sib. Or.* 3:47, 766.

18. Examples in Dalman, *Words of Jesus*, 101; *Worte Jesu*², 312, 361.

19. Instances in K. L. Schmidt, βασιλεία κτλ, *TDNT* 1.571–93: 574f.

20. Dalman, *Words of Jesus*, 99f., 109; *Worte Jesu*², 311 361f.

21. *Ant.* 6.60: τὸν μὲν θεὸν ἀποξειροτονοῦσι τῆς βασιλείας [['they had been unmindful of His benefits and rejected His sovereignty']].

22. Dalman, *Words of Jesus*, 98; Billerbeck, 1.174ff.

present known to us.[23] If we compare the figures in the tables above with this sparse collection, we have to admit that the accumulation of instances in the synoptic gospels is unusual (even taking into account the part played by redaction, which is particularly evident in the Gospel of Matthew).

Still more remarkable than this purely numerical differentiation is the fact that in the sayings of Jesus which deal with the βασιλεία, a great many phrases appear which have *no parallels* (not even secular ones) in the language of Jesus' contemporaries. Even if we apply the strictest standards, the following phrases must be noted as new instances:

ἁρπάζειν τὴν βασιλείαν τῶν οὐρανῶν	(Matt 11:12)
[['take the kingdom of heaven by force']]	
βιάζεται ἡ β. τ. οὐ.	(ibid.)
[['the kingdom of heaven has suffered violence']]	
ἤγγικεν ἡ βασιλεία τοῦ θεοῦ	(Mark 1:15 par.; Matt 10:7
[['the kingdom of God has come near']]	par.; Luke 10:11, cf. 21:31
	ἐγγύς ἐστιν ἡ β.τ.θ.) [[33]]
εἰσέρχεσθαι εἰς τὴν β.τ.θ.	(Mark 9:47; 10:15 par.; 10:23
[['for you to enter the kingdom of God']]	par., 24, 25 par.; Matt 5:20;
	7:21; 18:3; 23:13; John 3:5;
	there is a New Testament
	echo in Acts 14:22)
ἐλάχιστος ἐν τῇ β.τ.οὐ.	(Matt 5:19)
[['least in the the kingdom of heaven']]	
ἡ β.τ.θ.ἐντός τινός ἐστιν	
[['the kingdom of God is among you']]	(Luke 17:21)
ἔρχεται ἡ β.τ.θ.	(Mark 9:1; Matt 6:10 par.
[['the kingdom of God has come']]	Luke 11:2; Luke 17:20;
	22:18)[24]

23. *mĕlūkā* (of God): 1QM 6:6: "And the reign shall be to the God of Israel" (a free quotation of Obad 21).—*malkūt* (of God) 1QM 12:7: "terrible in the glory of thy reign" (cf. Ps 144:11ff.); 1QSb 4:25f.: "in the temple of the reign."

24. The phrase has no analogy in the Old Testament or in Jewish literature, cf. M. Burrows, "Thy Kingdom Come," *JBL* 74, 1955, 1–8. For the only comparable passage, Mic 4:8 (". . . the former dominion shall come, the kingdom to the daughter of Jerusalem"), together with the paraphrase in the Targum (". . . to you [the Messiah] will the kingdom come") does not speak of the reign of God, but of the reign of Jerusalem, or the Messiah. Furthermore, it should be noted that both in the original text and in the Targum the "coming" is bound up with the preposition *lĕ*; i.e., it is said that the reign will "be granted to" Jerusalem or the Messiah, whereas when Jesus speaks of the "coming" of the reign of God, he says that it will be revealed. (The difference can be made clear by a comparison between Rev 11:15 ἐγένετο ἡ βασιλεία . . . τοῦ κυρίου ἡμῶν [['the kingdom . . . has become . . . of our Lord']] and Luke 19:11: μέλλει ἡ βασιλεία ἀποφαίνεσθαι [['the kingdom was to appear immediately']].) The fact that in Luke 17:20a the Pharisees ask πότε ἔρχεται ἡ βασιλεία τοῦ θεοῦ [['when the kingdom of God was coming']] might be claimed as better evidence that Judaism spoke of the coming of the reign of God, but in view of v. 20b we have to ask whether in this case a formula from Jesus has not been placed on their lips. Mark 11:10 (εὐλογημένη ἡ ἐρχομένη βασιλεία τοῦ πατρὸς ἡμῶν Δαυίδ [['Blessed is the coming kingdom of our ancestor David!']]) is a secondary explanation of the preceding quotation from the Psalms (118:25f.); moreover, it speaks of the reign of David,

ἡ ἡτοιμασμένη βασιλεία	(Matt 25:34)
[['inherit the kingdom']]	
εὐνούχισαν ἑαυτους διὰ τὴν β.τ.οὐ.	(Matt 19:12)
[['eunuchs for the sake of the kingdom of heaven']]	
ζητεῖν τὴν β. αὐτοῦ	(God's: Matt 6:33 par.
[['the kingdom of God and his righteousness']]	Luke 12:31)
αἱ κλεῖδες τῆς β.τ.οὐ.	(Matt 16:19)
[['the keys of the kingdom of heaven']]	
κλείειν τὴν β.τ.οὐ.	(Matt 23:13)
[['lock people out of the kingdom of heaven']]	
οὐ μακρὰν εἶναι ἀπὸ τῆς β.τ.θ.	(Mark 12:34)
[['not far from the kingdom of God']]	

μέγας [['most']] (Matt 5:19), μείζθν [['greatest']] (18:1, 4), μικρότερος [['least']] (11:11) ἐν τῇ β.τ.οὐ. [['in the kingdom of heaven']]

τὸ μυστήριον τῆς β.τ.θ.	(Mark 4:11 par.)
[['secret of the kingdom of God']]	
ὁμοιοῦν την β.τ.θ., ὁμοία ἐστιν ἡ β.τ.θ.	(Mark 4:26, 30 par.; Matt
[['the kingdom of God is as']]	13:33 par. Luke 13:20 and eight special instances in Matthew: see p. [[109]])
προάγειν εἰς τὴν β.τ.θ. [[34]]	(Matt 21:31)
[['going into the kingdom of God']]	
ἔφθασεν ἐφ ὑμᾶς ἡ β.τ.θ.	(Matt 12:28 par. Luke 11:20)
[['the kingdom of God has come to you']]	

nominem intemptatum regna caelestia consecutivum [['no one can attain the heavenly kingdom who does not go through temptations']] (*agraphon* in Tertullian, *De baptismo* 20.2).[25]

Despite the lack of exact Jewish parallels, the following instances have not been included in the list given above:

a. all phrases for which there are secular parallels (e.g., οἱ υἱοὶ τῆς β. [['heirs of the kingdom']] Matt 8:12; 13:38; cf. *bĕnē malkūtā* [['sons of the kingdom']] *Tg. Qoh.* 5:8; εὔθετος εἶναι τῇ β.τ.θ. [['fit for the kingdom of God']] Luke 9:62; cf. *kāšēr lĕmalkūt* [['fit for the kingdom']] *Mek. Exod.* on 12:1, Venice 1545, 2b 5);

b. ἀνακλίνεσθαι ἐν τῇ β.τ.οὐ. [['heirs of the kingdom of heaven']] (Matt 8:11 par.) and πίνειν ἐν τῇ β.τ.θ. [['drink in the kingdom of God']] (Mark 14:25 par.), because in Luke 14:15 the related phrase φάγεται ἄρτον ἐν τῇ β.τ.θ. [['eat in the kingdom of God']] appears on the lips of a table-companion of Jesus;

---

not that of God. In the absence of any other evidence, it is of decisive importance to note that, as shown by the Kaddish (*yamlēk* [*v.l. yimlōk*] *malkūtēh*; text in Dalman, *Worte Jesu*[1], 305 n. 3, unfortunately not repeated in the second edition), Palestinian Judaism did not speak of the "coming" but of the "reigning" of the reign of God.

25. See Jeremias, *Unknown Sayings of Jesus*, London [2]1964, 73–75.

c. phrases added by Matthew and Luke to the sayings of Jesus in their version of Mark, which are therefore redactional: e.g., ὁ λόγος τῆς β. [['the word of the kingdom']] (Matt 13:19 contrast Mark 4:15); τὸ εὐαγγέλιον τῆς β. [['the good news of the kingdom']] (Matt 24:14 contrast Mark 13:10); εὐαγγελίζεσθαι τὴν β. [['the good news of the kingdom']] (Luke 4:43 contrast Mark 1:38); to these should be added on grounds of language[26] and content the passive εὐαγγελίζεται ἡ β.τ.θ. [['the good news of the kingdom is proclaimed']] (Luke 16:16 contrast Matt 11:12); διαγγέλειν τὴν β.τ.θ. [['proclaim the kingdom of God']] (Luke 9:60 contrast Matt 8:22) and μαθητεύεσθαι τῇ β.τ.οὐ [['trained for the kingdom of heaven']] (Matt 13:52).

The early church hardly had a share in the process of the creation of the new language which is reflected in this list. The phrases about the βασιλεία which it coined are of a different kind; they represent a secondary transformation of eschatological terminology into missionary language;[27] furthermore, the term "reign of God" becomes less frequent outside the synoptic tradition of the sayings of Jesus. It is already rare in Paul, and it occurs only twice in the Gospel of John (3:3, 5).[28] This power to create new eschatological language, which shows its effect in the numerous new phrases of our list, thus comes from Jesus himself. It is, of course, no coincidence that this process of new creation is concentrated on the βασιλεία; we shall see later that [[35]] Jesus not only made the term the central theme of his proclamation, but in addition filled it with a new content which is without analogy.

Amen

A new use of the word *’āmēn* emerges in the sayings of Jesus in the four gospels, which is without any parallel in the whole of Jewish literature and the rest of the New Testament.[29] The Hebrew word *’āmēn*, taken over by Aramaic, means "certainly."[30] It is a solemn formula with which already the Is-

---

26. Cf. Dalman, *Words of Jesus*, 104f., 140.

27. διαγγέλειν τὴν β.τ.θ. [['proclaim the kingdom of God']] (Luke 9:60); διαμαρτύρεσθαι τὴν β.τ.θ. [['testifying to the kingdom of God']] (Acts 28:23); εὐαγγελίζεσθαι τὴν β.τ.θ. [['the good news of the kingdom of God']] (Luke 4:43; 8:1) or περὶ τῆς β.τ.θ. [['about the kingdom of God']] (Acts 8:12); εὐαγγελίζεται ἡ β.τ.θ. [['the good news of the kingdom of God']] (Luke 16:16); τὸ εὐαγγέλιον τῆς β. [['the good news of the kingdom']] (Matt 4:23; 9:35; 24:14); κηρύσσειν τὴν β. [['proclaiming the kingdom']] (Acts 20:25; τοῦ θεοῦ [['of God']] Luke 9:2; Acts 28:31); λαλεῖν περὶ τῆς β.τ.θ. [['spoke to them about the kingdom of God']] (Luke 9:11); λέγειν τὰ περὶ τῆς β.τ.θ. [['speaking about the kingdom of God']] (Acts 1:3); ὁ λόγος τῆς β. [['the word of the kingdom']] (Matt 13:19); μαθητεύεσθαι τῇ β.τ.οὐ. [['trained for the kingdom of heaven']] (Matt 13:52); πείθειν περὶ τῆς β.τ.θ. [['argued persuasively about the kingdom of God']] (Acts 19:8); συνεργοὶ εἰς τὴν β.τ.θ. [['co-workers for the kingdom of God']] (Col 4:11); οἱ υἱοὶ τῆς β. [['children of the kingdom']] (Matt 13:38, given a Christian form in comparison with 8:12).

28. Outside the gospels there are only ten instances in the whole of the Pauline corpus of letters, eight in Acts, one each in Hebrews and James and two in Revelation.

29. Jeremias, "Characteristics," 112–15 = *Abba* 148–51 [[not reprinted here]].

30. W. Baumgartner, *Hebräisches und aramäisches Lexikon zum Alten Testaments*[3], Lieferung 1, Leiden 1967, 62b.

raelite of Old Testament times took up a doxology, an oath, a blessing, a curse or an execration.[31] Without exception it is used in answers assenting to the words of another, as also in 1 Cor 14:16; 2 Cor 1:20; Rev 5:14; 7:12; 19:4; 22:20. In the gospels, on the other hand, *'āmēn* is used, also without exception, to introduce and to strengthen a person's own words; in this unprecedented usage it is strictly confined to the words of Jesus. This introductory *'āmēn* occurs there as follows:

Mark	13 times[32]
Logia common to Matthew and Luke	9 times[33]
Matthew only	9 times[34]
Luke only	3 times[35]
John (here always in the form *'āmēn*, *'āmēn*)	25 times[36]

[[36]] The retention of this alien word shows how strongly the tradition felt that the way of speaking was new and unusual. An explanation of its meaning must start from the fact that in the words of Jesus *'āmēn* is always followed by λέγω ὑμῖν (σοι) [['I say unto (you)']]. The only substantial analogy to ἀμὴν λέγω ὑμῖν that can be produced is the messenger-formula "Thus says the Lord,"[37] which is used by the prophets to show that their words are not their own wisdom, but a divine message. In a similar way, the ἀμὴν λέγω ὑμῖν [['verily I say unto']] that introduces the sayings of Jesus expresses his authority. The novelty of the usage, the way in which it is strictly confined to the sayings of Jesus, and the unanimous testimony by all the strata of tradition in the gospels show that here we have the creation of a new expression by Jesus.[38]

31. Dalman, *Words of Jesus*, 226–29; Billerbeck, 1.242–44; 3.456–61.

32. Mark 3:28; 8:12; 9:1, 41; 10:15, 29; 11:23; 12:43; 13:30; 14:9, 18, 25, 30.

33. Matt 5:18, 26; 8:10; 10:15; 11:11; 13:17; 18:13; 23:36; 24:47. ἀμὴν [['verily, certainly']] does not occur in any of the nine passages in the Lucan version; in the Lucan version its place is taken by δέ [['but']] (Luke 10:12, contrast Matt 10:15), γάρ [['for']] (Luke 10:24, contrast Matt 13:17), ναί [['yes']] (Luke 11:51, contrast Matt 23:36), ἀληθῶς [['truly']] (Luke 12:44, contrast Matt 24:47); in the remaining five cases the ἀμήν is omitted in Luke without any replacement.

34. Matt 6:2, 5, 16; 10:23; 18:18; 21:31; 25:12, 40, 45 (also 18:19, as a variant).

35. Luke 4:24; 12:37; 23:43.

36. John 1:51; 3:3, 5, 11; 5:19, 24, 25; 6:26, 32, 47, 53; 8:34, 51, 58; 10:1, 7; 12:24; 13:16, 20, 21, 38; 14:12; 16:20, 23; 21:18. The duplication derives from Jewish liturgical usage; it is attested (only with *'āmēn* as a response!) in the Old Testament, in Qumran, in Pseudo-Philo, in the Talmud, in prayers, on inscriptions and in magical texts (cf. the instances in *TLZ* 83, 1958, col. 504).

37. Manson, *Teaching*[2], 207.

38. V. Hasler, *Amen. Redaktionsgeschichtliche Untersuchung zur Einführungsformel der Herrenworte 'Wahrlich, ich sage euch,'* Zurich-Stuttgart 1969, puts forward the hypothesis that the formula "Truly, I say to you" arose in the liturgy of the Hellenistic communities and was only secondarily placed on the lips of Jesus. He justifies his view with the assertion that even in Judaism *'āmēn* had lost the character of a response and was used to strengthen a man's subsequent statement (p. 173). He attempts to demonstrate this from four Rabbinic texts and

from Rev 7:12; 22:20. The four Rabbinic texts are, however, really a single text with parallels (the second reference of which has been wrongly copied from Billerbeck, 1.243, while the two most important versions, of which Billerbeck gives the wording, are not mentioned), and this text says exactly the opposite to what Hasler reads out of it: it attests that *ʾāmēn* has the character of a response. In Rev 7:12 the *ʾāmēn* is a response to the benediction in v. 10, and in Rev 22:20b to the promise of Jesus' imminent return in v. 20a. That means that in the sphere of Judaism and the primitive Christian liturgy *ʾāmēn* always and without exception has the character of a response; the new terminology of the gospels is without analogy. (In other respects, too, the work lacks the necessary care. On p. 173 the following should be noted: Neh 5:13 is not a doxological conclusion; anyone who lists Tob 14:25 as an instance of *ʾāmēn* despite its doubtful authenticity ought also to include Jdt 16:25; for Rev 7:11 read Rev 7:12; the reference Deut 27:33 is wrong, as the chapter has only 26 verses; in n. 148 all the Hexaplaric material is ignored—all this on one page!)

BRUCE CHILTON

Regnum Dei Deus Est

[[261]] "The Kingdom of God" is central in the proclamation of Jesus, the reality to which his preaching points and which the parables are designed to explicate;[1] the student of the New Testament must understand this concept if he is to appreciate dominical theology, and the ecclesial theology which developed from it. Since Albert Schweitzer's well-known study, it has been taken as a matter of course that Jesus' kingdom concept was "apocalyptic."[2] Yet just this assumption has necessitated crucial qualifications. To take two notable examples of this, Rudolf Bultmann assserted that Jesus rejected "the *whole content* of apocalyptic *speculation*,"[3] and Norman Perrin went a step or two further by saying that "the difference between Jesus and ancient Jewish apocalyptic is much greater than Bultmann will allow."[4] At this point, the term "apocalyptic," as applied to Jesus' preaching, is practically evacuated of content. On purely logical grounds, the propriety of its continued usage in this connexion is seriously to be questioned.

A serious historical objection to the consensus was voiced in 1964, when T. F. Glasson challenged the presupposition that the "kingdom" is of apocalyptic provenience by pointing to "the striking fact that while the apocalypses and pseudepigrapha often deal with the end-time and Messianic age they do not make use of the precise phrase 'the kingdom of God.'"[5] Glasson followed

Reprinted, with permission, from *Scottish Journal of Theology* 31 (1978) 261–70 (courtesy of University of Aberdeen).

1. This is an *opinio communis* [['common opinion']], shared by, e.g., Norman Perrin, "The Kingdom of God," in *Rediscovering the Teaching of Jesus* (New York, 1967).

2. (Tr. W. Montgomery), *The Quest of the Historical Jesus* (London, 1910, 1963 from the 1906 German edition), see p. 365, "The eschatology of Jesus can therefore only be interpreted by the aid of the curiously intermittent Jewish apocalyptic literature of the period between Daniel and the Bar-Cochba rising."

3. (Tr. L. H. Smith and E. H. Lantero), *Jesus and the Word* (New York, 1934, 1958 from the 1926 German edition) 36; the italics are not my own.

4. Cf. *Jesus and the Language of the Kingdom* (London, 1976) 77.

5. "The Kingdom as Cosmic Catastrophe," in F. L. Cross (ed.), *Studia Evangelica*, 3/2: *Texte und Untersuchungen* 88, pp. 187–88. In fairness, it should be noted that *Pss. Sol.* 17:3 ("The kingdom of our God is eternal . . .') provides a near equivalent to our phrase, but the

the lead of T. W. Manson by turning to the Rabbinic phrase, "the kingdom of the heavens"; here the kingdom [[262]] can refer to the divine authority which one takes on oneself by obedience.[6] But this position had already been undermined by Norman Perrin who, in a critique of Manson and Gustav Dalman, observed that these references in classical Rabbinic literature could not be used to establish first-century diction.[7] Effectively, the present situation is one of stalemate: apocalyptic usage fails to provide sufficiently exact parallels to dominical kingdom diction, while the Rabbinic passages in question come too late in the day for their parallels to be conclusive. Strangely enough, then, a dearth of evidence is the principal obstacle to our understanding Jesus' preaching, and this nearly a century after Johannes Weiss.

Further evidence is presently available and, at the outset, the possibility presents itself that some of it at least represents first-century diction. I refer to exegeses contained in the Latter Prophets Targums; these Aramaic documents are paraphrases of the prophetic books occasioned by the decline in the ability of some Jews (even some of those resident in Palestine) to understand classical Hebrew. The Targums incorporate the exegetical understanding and vocabulary of the communities in which they were used, and they appear to be the products of centuries of translation, discussion and selection.[8] In his magisterial study of the prophetic Targums, P. Churgin found allusions to circumstances in the period ranging from before the destruction of the Temple to the persecution of the Jews in Sassanian Babylon much later.[9] This suggests that the [[263]] Targums achieved their present form as part of the same process which gave us Mishnah, Midrash, and Talmud, a process dedicated to the preservation and evaluation of tradition. It is therefore possible that Jesus was familiar with diction presently contained in these documents, and even that he came to know it in association with the biblical

---

passage in question could not be called apocalyptic. Cf. the *T. Mos.* 10:1, where the noun may mean no mere than "rule," despite its usage within an eschatological scenario.

6. Glasson, p. 190; Manson, *The Teaching of Jesus* (Cambridge, 1931) 130–32.

7. Cf. *The Kingdom of God in the Teaching of Jesus* (London, 1963, 1966) 95, 24–27.

8. Two readable introductions to this subject: J. W. Bowker, *The Targums and Rabbinic Literature* (Cambridge, 1969); R. Le Déaut, *Introduction à la littérature targumique* (Rome, 1966). All citations from the prophetic Targums are taken from the Aramaic text of Alexander Sperber (Leiden, 1962). The *Isaiah Targum* has been translated into English by J. F. Stenning (Oxford, 1949); cf. the seventeenth-century translation of all the prophetic Targums by Bishop Brian Walton in his monumental *Biblia Sacra Polyglotta*.

9. Cf. *Targum Jonathan to the Prophets* (New Haven, 1927); he cites *Tg. Isa.* 28:1, where reference is made to a wicked high priest (p. 23), and 21:9, where a second judgment on Babylon is predicted (p. 28). S. H. Levey, "The Date of Targum Jonathan to the Prophets," *Vetus Testamentum* 21 (1971) 186–96 argues for a tenth-century *terminus ad quem*. While he does show a continuing interest in the prophetic Targums in the period of the Geonim, his argument is vitiated by the fact that his most convincing datum (the "Romulus" cipher for Rome at 11:4 which Saadia also used) is only a variant reading (see Sperber's critical apparatus). Since, however, the line between editorial redaction and textual transmission in Targum studies has not yet been clearly drawn, his contribution is a useful warning against assuming the antiquity of any reading.

passages which it presently explicates. How can we know if this is in fact, or even probably, the case?

For two reasons, our approach to this question must be circumspect. In the first place, these Targums are, as extant, too late to permit us to interpret Jesus' preaching as if he were directly and intimately familiar with them. Indeed, so far as the date of a given reading is concerned, the balance of probability must be tipped in favour of the view that it is later, rather than earlier, than a given New Testament passage, simply because these Targums had centuries of development in front of them by the time the Church's canon had achieved a fixed form. In the second place, Targumic renderings do not have the names of Rabbis attached to them, as is commonly the case in classical Rabbinic literature. Since this labelling is usually taken as a guide (however rough and ready) to the dating of Rabbinic traditions, Targumic passages cannot be dated by means of the standard procedure.

A different procedure is called for, one which can operate on the basis of the diction of the Targums alone, because this is the only evidence which they present. To speak of the date of an extant Targum, it would be necessary to place its characteristic exegeses in the context of other, datable Rabbinic pronouncements. In this way, the theology of a Targum, or a section thereof, would reasonably be associated with the Rabbinic circle to which it has the greatest affinity. The systematic application of such a method is clearly desirable, but it would constitute a major project and results should not be expected in the near future.[10] Fortunately, the student of the New Testament need not await the conclusive dating of extant Targums and their traditions; he is concerned only with those exegeses which display positive [[264]] coherence with the New Testament passages with which he is concerned, because the Targums may on occasion provide evidence of the vocabulary and thought on which the canonical tradition is built. I have said "*positive* coherence" because a merely notional connection would not be enough to suggest that a Targumic rendering underlies a New Testament reading. After all, both bodies of literature take the Old Testament as read. Positive coherence may only be posited where there is a strong similarity in language which is not explicable on the supposition that the Hebrew and Greek Old Testaments have influenced the diction of the New Testament. If that is the case, further analysis is warranted. If the same thought is expressed by this similar language, coherence is established, but the possibility that the Targum represents pre-Christian diction must be weighed against the possibility that it is a deliberate riposte to Christian teaching. That is, the substance, as well as the language, of a rendering must be evaluated in order to determine its pedigree in relation to the New Testament. Only such methodological evaluation can avoid

---

10. A recent contribution to this field which is very important, if preliminary, is offered by M. Aberbach and B. Grossfeld, *Targum Onkelos on Genesis 49*: Society of Biblical Literature Aramaic Studies 1 (Missoula, 1976). For the treatment of renderings which appear to cohere with New Testament passages, see M. McNamara, *The New Testament and the Palestinian Targum to the Pentateuch* (Rome, 1966) and *Targum and Testament* (Shannon, 1972).

the Charybdis of interpreting Jesus' preaching in terms of later developments and the Scylla of discounting prematurely a potentially significant body of evidence.

So far as mere language is concerned, on eight occasions the Prophetic Targums make use of the precise phrase "kingdom of God" or "of the Lord."[11] This means that we are on to much harder linguistic parallels to dominical usage than we would be if we were to limit ourselves to apocalyptic material. Moreover, the Targumic usage is nearer to Jesus' phrase than the periphrasis, "the kingdom of the heavens," which both the Gospel according to Matthew and classical Rabbinic literature prefer. Given the principles of investigation set out in the previous paragraph, the identity between Targumic and dominical diction requires us to look more closely at those passages in the Prophetic Targums in which the usage occurs. To set out the evidence, I have translated first the Masoretic Text (MT) counterpart of the Targumic passage in question, and then the Targum (Tg) reference itself, underscoring its *differentiae* so that they are apparent at a glance.

[[265]] It is convenient to begin with *Tg. Zech.* 14:9, because the use of kingdom diction in connexion with this verse can be dated with reasonable accuracy:

MT   and the LORD will be king upon all the earth
Tg.   and *the kingdom of* the LORD will be *revealed* upon all *the dwellers of* the earth

"Kingdom" (*mlkwt'*) appears in place of the corresponding MT term (*mlk*) and it takes the predicate "will be *revealed*" (from *gl'*, which is familiar from Rabbinic usage)[12] to convey an emphasis on disclosure. It is not just that the LORD will reign: his kingdom, already a reality, will be manifest. At the same time, there is no question of the kingdom being separate from God because the clause as a whole renders an assertion in MT of what God himself will be. An allusion to Zech 14:9 in association with a statement about the kingdom is contained in material ascribed to the first-century Rabbi Eliezer ben Hyrcanos.[13] This Rabbi was the student of Rabbi Yohanan ben Zakkai, who according to Jacob Neusner was active in Galilee at about the same time Jesus was.[14] It is therefore conceivable (but no more than that) that Jesus and Yohanan shared a then current kingdom vocabulary which has been preserved in both the New Testament and the Targums. Be that as it may, R. Eliezer's

---

11. Isa 24:23; 31:4; 40:9; 52:7; Ezek 7:7, 10; Obad 21; Mic 4:7, 8; Zech 14:9; cf. the Masoretic Text and Septuagint.

12. See, e.g., G. Dalman (tr. D. M. Kay), *The Words of Jesus* (Edinburgh, 1902) 97, and G. F. Moore, *Judaism* (Cambridge, Mass., 1946) 2.374.

13. *Mekilta Exodus* 17:14 (p. 186, lines 4–7, of the Horovitz and Rabin edition [Jerusalem, 1960]: "and the Place will be alone in eternity and his kingdom will be forever"; a citation of Zech 14:9 follows).

14. Cf. *A Life of Rabban Yohanan ben Zakkai* (Leiden, 1962) 27–32.

statement forces us seriously to consider the possibility that Targumic references akin to *Tg. Zech.* 14:9 reflect a first-century conception.

So far we have considered only the first *differentia* in *Tg. Zech.* 14:9 (the
kingdom of, revealed), and not the second (*the dwellers of*). In itself, the latter
addition does not alter the meaning of the Hebrew text. It tells in favour of
the relative antiquity of this reading, however, that it is reproduced verbatim
at *Tg. Obad.* 21:

> MT   and the kingdom will be the LORD's
> Tg.   and *the kingdom of* the LORD will be *revealed upon all the dwellers
>   of the earth*

[[266]] This suggests that the rendering at Zech 14:9 was practically a catchword for the interpreter of Obad 21. Of course, the rather universalistic
"dwellers" reading (which had no part in R. Eliezer's statement) might well
have been introduced after the kingdom diction was already established; I
only wish to suggest that *Tg. Obad.* 21 shows that *Tg. Zech.* 14:9 was considered
to be a conventional assertion of the divine kingship.

To recapitulate: the exegesis preserved in our passages accords with a
first-century conception of the kingdom. We have also seen that "the kingdom of God" refers to God himself, as it were, personally. This pattern is also
evident at *Tg. Isa.* 31:4:

> MT   so the LORD of hosts will descend to fight upon Mount Zion
> Tg.   so *the kingdom of* the LORD of hosts will be *revealed* to *dwell* upon
>   Mount Zion

What we have called a personal reference to God is especially evident here because "kingdom" does not represent a *mlk*-root word. This makes it undeniable that we must see more in "kingdom" than slavish translation; it
refers in context to God's activity on behalf of his people. The question now
is, does such a view of the kingdom coincide with that of Jesus? Recent research indicates not only that the understanding of the kingdom as God himself is consistent with Jesus' preaching, but that in the interpretation of
certain parables it is difficult to see what Jesus meant if he did not have such
an understanding (Matt 18:23–35; 22:1–14; Mark 4:26–29).[15] In other words,
the Targumic kingdom passages are substantively, as well as linguistically, coherent with Jesus' preaching of the kingdom.

The case for coherence could be rested here, because the evidence already indicates that Jesus' language and thought is similar to that of the Targums in the matter of kingdom diction, and there is not a whisper of anti-
Christian apologetic in the Targumic passages so far discussed. The evidence,
however, will bring us a bit further: *Jesus used* "the kingdom" in *contexts* [[267]]

---

15. See Perrin, *The Kingdom*, 184, and Joachim Jeremias (tr. S. H. Hooke), *The Parables
of Jesus* (London, 1972) 210–14; 176–80; 151–53. Chapter 3 of Perrin's *Jesus and the Language*
updates Jeremias with a competent review of the recent discussion (and see pp. 195, 196).

similar to those in which it appears in the Isaiah Targum. Jesus applied festal imagery to the gathering of many from east and west in the kingdom (Matt 8:11, 12 / Luke 13:28, 29), and this imagery is reminiscent of the LORD's banquet in Isa 25:6–8. The connexion becomes more than a reminiscence when we read an explicit reference to the kingdom in *Tg. Isa.* 24:23:

MT   because the LORD of hosts reigns on Mount Zion
Tg.   because *the kingdom of* the LORD of hosts *will be revealed* on
        Mount Zion.

Since the connexion between this passage and Jesus' preaching is linguistic, substantive, and contextual, it is worth noting that it is virtually repeated at 31:4 (with the addition of "*to dwell*," representing MT "to fight," and with "upon," again following MT, instead of "on"), and worth repeating that "kingdom" in the latter passage represents the very activity of God. This is also the case in the next passage to be cited. It is one of two in the *Isaiah Targum* in which kingdom usages occur as announcements; their contexts indicate that they are to be proclaimed (40:9; 52:7):

MT   behold your God
Tg.   *the kingdom of* your God is *revealed*
MT   your God reigns
Tg.   *the kingdom of* your God is *revealed*

Since Jesus is also described as consistently preaching the kingdom (Mark 1:14, 15; Matt 4:17, 23; 9:35; Luke 4:43; 8:1) and as sending others to do so (Matt 10:7; Luke 9:2, 60; 10:9, 11), we have another contextual link between his view and that represented in *Tg. Isaiah*. The near identity of the above two Targumic passages, despite variation in the Hebrew, again suggests that the interpreter's kingdom vocabulary was somewhat stereotyped, and therefore that it is part of a definite view, we might almost say a theology, and not an ad hoc translation. Finally, *Tg. Isa.* 40:9 is of particular interest because it is followed by a clause which says that God reveals himself "in power" (*btqwp*). It is not likely a coincidence that, in a unique phrase in Mark's Gospel, Jesus speaks of the kingdom of God "in power" (*en dunamei*, 9:1).[16]

[[268]] There is kingdom diction in other prophetic Targums, but it appears to reflect later locutions, and such positive associations with dominical logia as we have seen are not evident. Since this is the case, it seems convenient to summarise our findings for *Tg. Isaiah* before proceeding. The kingdom here is not separable from God, nor again is it simply a periphrasis for the verb *mlk*: it is neither an autonomous regime nor does it merely refer to the LORD's assertion of sovereignty. What is at issue is God's action, his very being as God. It is permissible at this stage to suggest that the dominical "kingdom" ought also to be seen as inalienable from God. Seen in this way, the

---

16. In "An Evangelical and Critical Approach to the Sayings of Jesus," *Themelios* 3 (1978) 78–85, the verse is analysed in detail.

"kingdom of God" is not a distinct entity which arrives apart from God, so that one need not pose what Johannes Weiss already called "die unfruchtbare Fragestellung" [['fruitless question']] concerning the time of the kingdom.[17] Jesus' eschatology has been variously described as, e.g., "consistent," "realised," "self-realising" and "inaugurated,"[18] but the evidence from *Tg. Isaiah* shows that all the time we have been talking about aspects of God's activity, which cannot be limited by time. Because the kingdom is the self-revelation of God, it can be taken as having various temporal dimensions, but none of these can be taken to be the exclusive domain of the kingdom. Jesus announced to his hearers the self-disclosure of the King; for him, as in *Tg. Isaiah*, *regnum dei deus est* [['the kingdom of God is God']].

For the sake of completeness, we may now turn to Targumic passages which apparently stem from a later period. Once the full phrase, "the kingdom of God," is familiar, one is inclined to use the term "kingdom" alone by way of abbreviation (as in the present paper). Such a usage occurs in the Gospel according to Matthew (see especially the summary statements 4:23; 9:35) and also in *Tg. Ezek.* 7:7(10):

MT   the crown(?) has come to you
Tg.   the *kingdom* is *revealed upon* you

The usage in the Targum need not have any connexion with that in Matthew; we are speaking here of a natural development in the use of vocabulary in which dependence need not be postulatd. There is a further usage in *Tg. Micah* which reflects a highly systematised theology (4:7b, 8): [[269]]

MT   and the LORD will reign upon them in Mount Zion from now
        and forever, and you, tower of the flock, hill of the daughter of
        Zion, to you it will come, even the former dominion will come,
        the kingdom of the daughter of Jerusalem
Tg.   and *the kingdom* of the LORD will *be revealed* upon them in Mount
        Zion from now and forever, and you *Messiah of Israel that is
        hidden from before the sins of the congregation of Zion*, to you *the
        kingdom* is about to come, even the former dominion will come
        to the kingdom of the *congregation* of Jerusalem.

The Mount Zion–kingdom connexion is already familiar to us from *Tg. Isa.* 24:23; 31:4; Obad 21, but there is a startling departure here in the progressive narrowing of the kingdom concept. The first use of the term simply replaces the root verb: the interpreter does not seem concerned substantially to alter the meaning of this clause. What does consume his interest is the scope of the revelation. The Targum announces that the kingdom is about to come to the messiah addressed, and this kingdom is subsequently associated with the "former dominion." This practical equation between God's kingdom

17. In the preface of the 1900 edition of *Die Predigt Jesu*.
18. For a handy review of this controversy, see O. Knoch, "Die eschatologische Frage," *Biblische Zeitschrift* 6 (1962) 112–20.

and Jerusalem's autonomy is underlined in the last clause, in which the "congregation" (not presently a national unit) becomes the recipient of the blessing. Such a limited kingdom conception is not that of the New Testament, and it even disagrees with *Tg. Zech.* 14:9. Relatively speaking, then, this passage appears to be a late-comer to the Targumic tradition which corrects earlier notions. The idea that the Messiah is hidden because of "the sins of the congregation" may permit us to date this passage. Generally speaking, the repeated use of "congregation" presupposes the Jewish loss of national status; more specifically, the rendering coheres with the fourth-century dictum that one day of Israelite repentance would bring the Messiah.[19]

Targumic kingdom diction, then, is a rich seam for students of Christian and Jewish origins. These passages provide specimens of a turn of phrase of which Jesus availed himself, [[270]] and they illustrate that Rabbinic theology was not monolithic, but developed markedly after the formation of the New Testament. Historically speaking, Jesus' proclamation is an important event in the development of Judaism which cannot be appreciated until it is placed in its proper context. Once that is done, it appears that the dominical "kingdom of God" was no cipher in an esoteric view of history. Rather, a contemporary catch-phrase which referred to God was taken up by Jesus to serve as the key term in his vivid assertion that God is active among us.

19. H. L. Strack and P. Billerbeck, *Kommentar zum Neuen Testament aus Talmud und Midrasch* (München, 1926) 1.164, citing the Jerusalem Talmud, *y. Ta'an.* 1.1.

JOHN P. MEIER

Criteria: How Do We Decide What Comes from Jesus?

[[167]] In the previous chapters we have seen that, in our quest for the historical Jesus, we are dependent, for the most part, on the four canonical Gospels. Since these Gospels are suffused with the Easter faith of the early Church and were written from forty to seventy years after the events narrated, we are left asking: How can we distinguish what comes from Jesus (Stage I, roughly A.D. 28–30) from what was created by the oral tradition of the early Church (Stage II, roughly A.D. 30–70) and what was produced by the editorial work (redaction) of the evangelists (Stage III, roughly A.D. 70–100)?[1] All too often, popular books on Jesus pick and choose among the Gospel stories in a haphazard way, the authors deciding at any given moment that what strikes them as reasonable or plausible is therefore historical.[2] More technical books usually enunciate rules for judging the Gospel material ("criteria of historicity"), but the rules sometimes seem to be forgotten when the Gospel pericopes are treated in detail.[3] In this chapter, I will spell out which rules of judgment

Reprinted, with permission, from John P. Meier, *A Marginal Jew: Rethinking the Historical Jesus*, vol. 1: *The Roots of the Problem and the Person* (ABRL; New York: Doubleday, 1991) 167–95, 185–95.

1. This is a schematic statement of the problem. The actual situation was naturally much more complex: e.g., some disciples of Jesus may have begun to collect and arrange sayings of Jesus even before his death (Stage I), and the oral tradition continued to develop during the period of the redaction of the Gospels (Stage III).

2. Even the fine book by the historian Michael Grant does not entirely escape this tendency; see his *Jesus. An Historian's Review of the Gospels* (New York: Scribner's, 1977); the appendix outlining his approach to criteria (pp. 197–204) is disappointing. Still weaker in the area of criteria is James Breech's *The Silence of Jesus. The Authentic Voice of the Historical Man* (Philadelphia: Fortress, 1983). While the book does at times use familiar criteria (embarrassment, discontinuity), the argument largely depends on scholarly consensus combined with aesthetic intuition about literature. The results cannot help but be highly subjective.

3. This is even the case with the judicious work of [[B. F.]] Meyer, *The Aims of Jesus* [[Pittsburgh Theological Monograph Series; San Jose: Pickwick, 2002]]. The first part of the book (pp. 23–113) spells out method and "indices" of judgment with great care; but, as the

(i.e., "criteria") are helpful in reaching a decision about what material comes from the historical Jesus.[4]

Granted the nature of ancient history in general and the nature of the Gospels in particular, the criteria of historicity will usually produce judgments that are only more or less probable; certainty is rarely to be had.[5] Indeed, since in the quest for the historical Jesus almost anything is possible, the function of the criteria is to pass from the merely possible to the really probable, to inspect various probabilities, and to decide [[168]] which candidate is most probable. Ordinarily, the criteria cannot hope to do more.[6]

Scholars seem to vie with one another to see who can compile the longest list of criteria.[7] Sometimes a subtle apologetic motive may be at work: so

---

book proceeds, more and more of the redactional theology of the evangelists is declared to come from the historical Jesus, leaving one wondering how useful the indices really are.

4. René Latourelle ("Critères d'authenticité historique des Evangiles," *Greg* 55 [1974] 609–37, esp. 618) rightly warns against confusing criteria with proof. Criteria are rules or norms that are applied to the Gospel material to arrive at a judgment.

5. In the quest for the historical Jesus, sometimes certainty is more easily had about "secondary" circumstances than about the words and deeds of Jesus himself. For example, the converging evidence of the Four Gospels and the Acts of the Apostles, Josephus, Philo, Tacitus, and the Caesarea Maritima inscription (found in 1961) makes it at least morally, if not physically, certain that Pontius Pilate was the Roman governor of Judea in A.D. 28–30. Even here, though, moral certitude is really just a very high degree of probability. The fact of Pilate's governorship is not absolutely or metaphysically certain, for it is not theoretically or metaphysically impossible that Josephus is mistaken or that the references to Pilate in Philo are Christian interpolations or that the Caesarea Mantima inscription is a fraud. But since any of these possibilities (not to mention all of them together) is so extremely unlikely, we are justified in considering our conclusion morally certain, especially since, in daily life, we constantly make firm theoretical judgments and practical decisions on the basis of high probability. Any talk about "proof" of authentic Jesus material must be understood within this context of a range of probabilities.

6. Sometimes scholars seek to distinguish between "criteria" and "indices" or even to substitute the word "index" for "criterion"; see, e.g., Latourelle, "Critères d'authenticité historique des Evangiles"; Meyer, *The Aims of Jesus*, 86; and Rainer Riesner, *Jesus als Lehrer* (WUNT, 2nd series, 7; Tübingen: Mohr [Siebeck], 1981) 86–96, esp. 86–87; Francesco Lambiasi, *L'autenticità storica dei vangeli* (Studi biblici 4; 2nd ed.; Bologna: EDB, 1986) 189–90. However, scholars favoring some sort of distinction do not always agree among themselves as to what constitutes the distinction. Sometimes "criterion" indicates what allows a fairly certain judgment, while "index" suggests a lower level of probability (so Latourelle; Lambiasi adds a third category, namely "motive," an argument that indicates verisimilitude). Others use indices for individual observations relevant to the question of authenticity, while criteria refer to more general rules (so Riesner). Meyer prefers to drop the language of "criteria" in favor of "indices." Personally, I see no great value in the various distinctions or changes in terminology. My own view is that our judgments about authenticity deal for the most part with a range of probabilities; I do not claim that the use of the criteria I propose will generate absolute certitude. Hence, I see no need to distinguish "criteria" from "indices"; the former term will be used throughout what follows.

7. The reader who follows up the bibliographical references will soon discover a wearisome repetition in much of the literature. I have therefore restricted the bibliography to a

many criteria surely guarantee the results of our quest! More sober scholars, instead, are no doubt seeking as many controls as possible over the difficult material. Often, however, what is naturally a single criterion is "chopped up" to create a number of criteria; and what are at best secondary, if not dubious, criteria are mixed in with truly useful ones. I agree with Occam that categories are not to be multiplied without necessity. Hence I prefer to distill five "primary" criteria from the many suggested. After we have looked at these five, we will consider five "secondary" (some would say "dubious") criteria; some of these secondary criteria may at times offer post-factum confirmation of decisions we have already reached on the basis of the five primary critera.

few contributions that say all that need be said on the issue. In addition to the works of Latourelle, Riesner, and Meyer, see Charles E. Carlston, "A *Positive* Criterion of Authenticity," *BR* 7 (1962) 33–44; Harvey K. McArthur, "A Survey of Recent Gospel Research," *Int* 18 (1964) 39–55, esp. 47–51; idem, "The Burden of Proof in Historical Jesus Research," *Exp Tim* 82 (1970–71) 116–19; William O. Walker, "The Quest for the Historical Jesus: A Discussion of Methodology," *ATR* 51(1969) 38–56; Morna D. Hooker, "Christology and Methodology," *NTS* 17 (1970–71) 480–87; idem, "On Using the Wrong Tool," *Theology* 75 (1972) 570–81; Rudolf Pesch, *Jesu Ureigene Taten?* (QD *52;* Freiburg/Basel/Vienna: Herder, 1970) esp. pp. 135–58; D. G. A. Calvert, "An Examination of the Criteria for Distinguishing the Authentic Words of Jesus," *NTS* 18 (1971–72) 209–19; Fritzleo Lentzen-Deis, "Kriterien für die historische Beurteilung der Jesusüberlieferung in den Evangelien," *Rückfrage nach Jesus* (QD 63; Freiburg/Basel/Vienna: Herder, 1974) 78–117; Neil J. McEleney, "Authenticating Criteria and Mark 7:1–23," *CBQ* 34 (1972) 431–60; Francesco Lambiasi, *Criteri di autenticità storica dei Vangeli sinottici. Rassegna storica e tentativo di sistematizzazione dei contributi di criteriologia degli ultimi venti anni (1954–1974)* (dissertation; Rome: Gregorian University, 1974); idem, *L'autenticità storica dei vangeli. Studio di criteriologia* (Studi biblici; 2nd ed.; Bologna: EDB, 1986); idem, *Gesù di Nazaret. Una verifica storica* (Fame della Parola; Monferrato: Marietti, 1983) 63–68; Schillebeeckx, *Jesus*, 81–100; Joseph A. Fitzmyer, "Methodology in the Study of the Aramaic Substratum of Jesus' Sayings in the New Testament," *Jésus aux origines de la christologie* (BETL 40; ed. J. Dupont; Leuven: Leuven University; Gembloux: Duculot, 1975) 73–102; Ernst Käsemann, "Die neue Jesus-Frage," *Jésus aux origines de la christologie* (BETL 40; ed. J. Dupont; Leuven: Leuven University; Gembloux: Duculot, 1975) 47–57; D. Lührmann, "Die Frage nach Kriterien für ursprüngliche Jesusworte—eine Problemskizze," *Jésus aux origines de la christologie* (BETL 40; ed. J. Dupont; Leuven: Leuven University; Gembloux: Duculot, 1975) 59–72; David L. Mealand, "The Dissimilarity Test," *SJT* 31 (1978) 41–50; Helge Kjaer Nielsen, "Kriterien zur Bestimmung authentischer Jesusworte," *Studien zum Neuen Testament und seiner Umwelt* 4 (1979) 5–26; Robert H. Stein, "The 'Criteria' for Authenticity," *Gospel Perspectives. Vol. I*, ed. R. France and D. Wenham (Sheffield: JSOT, 1980) 225–63; Reginald Fuller, "The Criterion of Dissimilarity: The Wrong Tool?" *Christological Perspectives* (H. K. McArthur Festschrift; ed. R. Berkey and S. Edwards; New York: Pilgrim, 1982) 42–48; Giuseppe Ghiberti, "Überlegungen zum neueren Stand der Leben-Jesu-Forschung," *MTZ* 33 (1982) 99–115; E. Earle Ellis, "Gospels Criticism: A Perspective on the State of the Art," *Das Evangelium und die Evangelien* (WUNT 28; ed. P. Stuhlmacher; Tübingen: Mohr [Siebeck], 1983) 27–54; Breech, *The Silence of Jesus*, 9, 22–26, 66–85; Dennis Polkow, "Method and Criteria for Historical Jesus Research," *Society of Biblical Literature Seminar Papers* 26 (1987) 336–56; M. Eugene Boring, "The Historical-Critical Method's 'Criteria of Authenticity': The Beatitudes in Q and Thomas as a Test Case," *The Historical Jesus and the Rejected Gospels* (Semeia 44; ed. Charles W. Hedrick; Atlanta: Scholars, 1988) 9–44. For a history of the development of thought about the criteria, see Lambiasi, *L'autenticità storica dei vangeli*, 19–110.

Primary Criteria

1. *The Criterion of Embarrassment*

The criterion of "embarrassment" (so Schillebeeckx) or "contradiction" (so Meyer) focuses on actions or sayings[8] of Jesus that would have embarrassed or created difficulty for the early Church. The point of the criterion is that the early Church would hardly have gone out of its way to create material that only embarrassed its creator or weakened its position in arguments with opponents. Rather, embarrassing material coming from Jesus would naturally be either suppressed or softened in later stages of the Gospel tradition, and often such progressive suppression or softening can be traced through the Four Gospels.[9]

A prime example is the baptism of the supposedly superior and sinless Jesus by his supposed inferior, John the Baptist, who proclaimed "a baptism of repentance for the forgiveness of sins."[10] Mysterious, laconic, stark Mark recounts the event with no theological explanation as to why the superior sinless one submits to a baptism meant for sinners (Mark 1:4–11). Matthew introduces a dialogue between the Baptist and Jesus prior to the baptism; the Baptist openly confesses his unworthiness to [[169]] baptize his superior and gives way only when Jesus commands him to do so in order that God's saving plan may be fulfilled (Matt 3:13–17, a passage marked by language typical of the evangelist). Luke finds a striking solution to the problem by narrating the Baptist's imprisonment by Herod before relating the baptism of Jesus; Luke's version never tells us who baptized Jesus (Luke 3:19–22). The radical Fourth Evangelist, John, locked as he is in a struggle with latter-day disciples of the Baptist who refuse to recognize Jesus as the Messiah, takes the radical expedient of suppressing the baptism of Jesus by the Baptist altogether; the event simply never occurs in John's Gospel. We still hear of the Father's witness to Jesus and the Spirit's descent upon Jesus, but we are never told when this theophany occurs (John 1:29–34). Quite plainly, the early Church was "stuck with" an event in Jesus' life that it found increasingly embarrassing, that it

---

8. While the criteria are usually aimed at the sayings of Jesus in particular, it must be remembered that they can also be applied to the actions of Jesus. In some forms of the quest, the actions of Jesus and their relation to his sayings are almost ignored. Morton Smith (*Jesus the Magician*), E. P. Sanders (*Jesus and Judaism*), and Joseph A. Fitzmyer ("Methodology," 73) rightly protest against this one-sided emphasis. As Nielsen ("Kriterien," 21) notes, the tradition of words and the tradition of works can act as a reciprocal check. For one reason why the sayings tradition tends to be emphasized, see D. Lührmann, "Die Frage," 64–65.

9. This phenomenon is sometimes listed as the separate criterion of either "modification" or "tendencies of the developing Synoptic tradition." What I think valid in these two suggested criteria I have subsumed under the criterion of embarrassment. For the criterion of modification, see Walker, "The Quest for the Historical Jesus," 48; Boring, "The Historical-Critical Method's 'Criteria of Authenticity,'" 21. The criterion is usually attributed to Ernst Käsemann, "The Problem of the Historical Jesus," *Essays on New Testament Themes* (SBT 41; London: SCM, 1964) 15–47, esp. 37.

10. On the baptism of Jesus as a test case for the criterion of embarrassment, see Breech, *The Silence of Jesus*, 22–24.

tried to explain away by various means, and that John the Evangelist finally erased from his Gospel. It is highly unlikely that the Church went out of its way to create the cause of its own embarrassment.

A similar case is the affirmation by Jesus that, despite the Gospels' claim that he is the Son who can predict the events at the end of time, including his own coming on the clouds of heaven, he does not know the exact day or hour of the end. Almost at the conclusion of the eschatological discourse in Mark 13, Jesus says: "But concerning that day or hour no one knows, neither the angels in heaven, nor the Son, but only the Father" (Mark 13:32). It is not surprising that a few later Greek manuscripts simply dropped the words "nor the Son" from the saying in Mark.[11] A significantly larger number of manuscripts omit "nor the Son" in the parallel verse in Matthew (Matt 24:36), which was more widely used in the patristic Church than Mark—hence the desire to suppress the embarrassing phrase especially in Matthew.[12] The saying is simply not taken over by Luke. In John, not only is there nothing similar, but the Fourth Evangelist goes out of his way to stress that Jesus knows all things present and future and is never taken by surprise (see, e.g., John 5:6; 6:6; 8:14; 9:3; 11:11–15; 13:1–3, 11). Once again, it is highly unlikely that the Church would have taken pains to invent a saying that emphasized the ignorance of its risen Lord, only to turn around and seek to suppress it.

An intriguing corollary arises from these cases of "embarrassment." All too often the oral tradition of the early Church is depicted as a game of "anything goes," with charismatic prophets uttering anything or everything as the words of the Lord Jesus and storytellers creating [[170]] accounts of miracles and exorcisms according to Jewish and pagan models. The evangelists would simply have crowned this wildly creative process by molding the oral tradition according to their own redactional theology. One would get the impression that throughout the first Christian generation there were no eyewitnesses to act as a check on fertile imaginations, no original-disciples-now-become-leaders who might exercise some control over the developing tradition, and no striking deeds and sayings of Jesus that stuck willy-nilly in people's memories. The fact that embarrassing material is found as late as the redaction of the Gospels reminds us that beside a creative thrust there was also a conservative force in the Gospel tradition.[13] Indeed, so conservative was this force that a

11. The few manuscripts that omit "nor the Son" in Mark include codex X (10th century).

12. The manuscripts that drop "nor the Son" in the Matthean version of the saying include the codices K, L, W, and the vast majority of later texts; the first scribe who sought to correct this text in codex Sinaiticus also omitted the phrase.

13. As Stein ("The 'Criteria' for Authenticity," 227) notes, another indication of the conservative force of the Jesus tradition is that several of the major problems that the early Church encountered never show up in the sayings of Jesus; a glaring case is the absence of any explicit pronouncement of Jesus on the question of circumcision for Gentiles. In a letter to me dated Oct. 13, 1990, David Noel Freedman points out an OT analogy. From the viewpoint of the Deuteronomistic Historian(s), Hezekiah and Josiah were the two best kings of Judah after David. Their military defeats, which raise questions about Yahweh's rewarding of the just, are not denied but rather explained theologically in somewhat contorted fashion.

string of embarrassing events (e.g., baptism by John, betrayal by Judas, denial by Peter, crucifixion by the Romans) called forth agonized and varied theological reflection, but not, in most cases, convenient amnesia.[14] In this sense, the criterion of embarrassment has an importance for the historian far beyond the individual data it may help verify.

Like all the criteria we will examine, however, the criterion of embarrassment has its limitations and must always be used in concert with the other criteria. One built-in limitation to the criterion of embarrassment is that clearcut cases of such embarrassment are not numerous in the Gospel tradition; and a full portrait of Jesus could never be drawn with so few strokes. Another limitation stems from the fact that what we today might consider an embarrassment to the early Church was not necessarily an embarrassment in its own eyes. A prime example is Jesus' "cry of dereliction" from the cross: "My God, my God, why have you forsaken me?" (Mark 15:34; Matt 27:46; the words are a citation of Ps 22:1). At first glance, this seems a clear case of embarrassment; the unedifying groan is replaced in Luke by Christ's trustful commendation of his spirit to the Father (Luke 23:46) and in John by a cry of triumph, "It is accomplished!" (John 19:30).

But the matter is not so simple. True, the cry of dereliction does not fit the later theological agendas of Luke or John. But form-critical studies of the Passion Narrative show that the earliest stages of the passion tradition used the OT psalms of lamentation, especially the psalms of the suffering just man, as a primary tool for theological interpretation of the narrative.[15] By telling the story of Jesus' passion in the words of these psalms, the narrative presented Jesus as the one who fulfilled the OT pattern of the just man afflicted and put to death by evildoers, but vindicated and raised up by God. Allusions to, rather than direct quotations [[171]] of, these psalms are woven throughout the Passion Narrative. A good example is the dividing of Jesus' garments. The words of Ps 22:19 are made part of the narrative in Mark 15:24, Matt 27:35, and Luke 23:34; only John marks off the words as a citation of Scripture (John 19:24).

---

14. My proviso "in most cases" takes cognizance of the Fourth Gospel's suppression of the baptism of Jesus.

15. See, e.g., C. H. Dodd, *According to the Scriptures* (London: Collins, Fontana, 1965) 96–103. Eduard Schweizer (*Lordship and Discipleship* [SBT 28; Naperville, IL: Allenson, 1960] 34) holds that "to the early Church the first book of the Passion of Jesus was formed by the Psalms of the suffering of the Righteous One. This is even true of the Gospel according to John. . . ." While Lothar Ruppert criticizes Schweizer for an undifferentiated, homogenized treatment of OT, pseudepigraphic, and rabbinic texts, his own thesis supports the basic point I am making. See Ruppert's *Jesus als der leidende Gerechte?* (SBS 59; Stuttgart: KBW, 1972) 58: ". . . the motif of the suffering just man is dominant in the older form of the Passion Narrative. . . . The motif points us . . . to the tradition of the primitive community." This monograph is in turn an expanded form of the last chapter of another work by Ruppert, *Der leidende Gerechte* (FB 5; Würzburg: Echter/KBW, 1972). Rudolf Pesch has accepted this theory in his treatment of the Passion Narrative in Mark; see his *Das Markusevangelium*, vol. 2 (HTKNT 2/2; Freiburg/Basel/Vienna: Herder, 1977) 25.

Therefore, it is not very surprising, from a form-critical point of view, that the dramatic first words of Psalm 22 supply the climax of the crucifixion and Jesus' last words in Mark's Gospel. The cry is by no means so unedifying or even scandalous as moderns might think. The OT psalms of lamentation regularly direct forceful complaints to God; their strong—to our ears, irreverent—address to God expresses neither doubt nor despair, but the pain of one who fully trusts that a strangely silent God can act to save if he so chooses. The very bitterness of the complaint paradoxically reaffirms the closeness the petitioner feels to this God he dares confront with such boldness. From the Babylonian exile to Auschwitz, pious Jews have used the words of Psalm 22 and other laments without being accused by their fellow religionists of impiety or despair.

Granted the roots of the Passion Narrative in the psalms of lamentation, as well as the bold address to God in those psalms—well understood by early Christian Jews but often misunderstood since—there is no reason for thinking that the earliest Christians (Jews who knew their Scriptures well) would have found the "cry of dereliction" at all embarrassing. Whether or not Jesus actually spoke Ps 22:1 on the cross, the criterion of embarrassment, taken in isolation, cannot establish the historicity of those words. It is not impossible that all of the "seven last words"—including the "cry of dereliction"—represent the theological interpretation of the early Church and the evangelists. But that is a question we will have to face later. The point here is that the criterion of embarrassment—like any other criterion—must not be invoked facilely or in isolation.

2. *The Criterion of Discontinuity*

Closely allied to the criterion of embarrassment,[16] the criterion of discontinuity (also labeled dissimilarity, originality, or dual irreducibility) focuses on words or deeds of Jesus that cannot be derived either from Judaism at the time of Jesus or from the early Church after him.[17] Examples often given are his sweeping prohibition of all oaths [[172]] (Matt 5:34, 37; but cf. Jas 5:12), his rejection of voluntary fasting for his disciples (Mark 2:18–22 pars.), and possibly his total prohibition of divorce (Mark 10:2–12 par.; Luke 16:18 par.).

This criterion is at once the most promising and the most troublesome. Norman Perrin hails it as the fundamental criterion, the basis of all reconstructions, since it gives us an assured minimum of material to work with.[18] But the criterion is not without its detractors. Morna Hooker complains that the criterion presupposes what we do not possess: a sure and full knowledge

16. Allied, but not reducible to discontinuity; in this I disagree with Polkow, "Method and Criteria," 341.

17. In his masterful essay ("The Historical-Critical Method's 'Criteria of Authenticity,'" 17–21), Boring highlights the methodological problem of whether we should speak of material that *can* be derived from Judaism or Christianity or material that *must* be so derived. I think it is preferable to speak in terms of "can."

18. Perrin, *Rediscovering the Teaching of Jesus*, 39–43.

of what Judaism at the time of Jesus and Christianity right after him were like, and what they could or would not say.[19]

Her objection does remind us of the healthy modesty required of any historian delving into the religious scene of 1st-century Palestine. Yet historical-critical work of the last two centuries has made notable advances in our understanding of 1st-century Judaism and Christianity. Moreover, one cannot overlook the glaring difference between knowledge about Jesus on the one hand and knowledge about 1st-century Judaism and Christianity on the other. We do have 1st-century documents coming directly from the latter movements—Qumran, Josephus, and Philo for Judaism, most of the NT for Christianity—to say nothing of important archaeological finds. We have no such documents coming directly from Jesus. Indeed, Professor Hooker's own work on the Son of Man title presupposes that we know something about early Judaism and Christianity and can apply such knowledge to outstanding problems. No doubt our present-day judgments will need correction by future generations of scholars. But if we were to wait until we possessed a fullness of knowledge that excluded later revision, we would postpone all NT scholarship until the parousia.[20]

A more serious objection is that the criterion of discontinuity, instead of giving us an assured minimum about Jesus, winds up giving us a caricature by divorcing Jesus from the Judaism that influenced him and from the Church that he influenced. Jesus was a 1st-century Jew whose deeds and sayings the early Church revered and handed on.[21] A complete rupture with religious history just before or just after him is a priori unlikely. Indeed, if he had been so "discontinuous," unique, cut off from the flow of history before and after him, he would have been unintelligible to practically everyone. To be an effective teacher (which Jesus seems to have been by almost every scholar's admission) means adapting oneself to the concepts and positions of one's audience, even if one's purpose is to change those concepts and positions. No matter how [[173]] original Jesus was, to be a successful teacher and communicator he would have had to submit himself to the constraints of communication,

19. Hooker, "Christology and Methodology," 480–87; idem, "On Using the Wrong Tool," 570–81. Ellis ("Gospels Criticism," 31) complains that the criterion of discontinuity assumes "that a Gospel traditioner or a Christian prophetic oracle could not have used a unique idea or expression. . . ."

20. For critiques of Hooker's position, see Mealand, "The Dissimilarity Test," 41–50; Nielsen, "Kriterien," 10–11.

21. The emphasis on Jesus' connections with the Judaism of his time is common in scholarship today and is well documented by Daniel J. Harrington, "The Jewishness of Jesus: Facing Some Problems," *CBQ* 49 (1987) 1–13.—It is curious that even skeptical scholars use the language of "handing on the Jesus tradition" and engage in tradition criticism. Yet if there really was a complete rupture in history between Jesus and the earliest Christians, there can be no talk of handing on tradition. However one defines the exact relationship between Jesus and the early Church, it is a fact of history, disputed by almost no scholar, that shortly after the death of Jesus some Jews, including people who had been his closest followers during his public ministry, gathered together to revere and celebrate him as Messiah and Lord, to recall and hand on his teachings, and to spread his teachings among other Jews.

the constraints of his historical situation.[22] To paint a portrait of Jesus completely divorced from or opposed to 1st-century Judaism and Christianity is simply to place him outside of history.

Imagine, for the sake of argument, that in the 16th century Martin Luther had delivered all his teachings orally and that they had been written down only later on by his disciples. If we excluded from the record of Luther's words and deeds everything that could be paralleled in late medieval Catholic authors before him or in 17th-century Lutheran theologians after him, how much would remain—and would it give anything like a representative portrait of Luther?

Hence, while the criterion of discontinuity is useful, we must guard against the presupposition that it will automatically give us what was central to or at least fairly representative of Jesus' teaching. By focusing narrowly upon what may have been Jesus' "idiosyncrasies," it is always in danger of highlighting what was striking but possibly peripheral in his message.[23] Especially with this criterion, complementary and balancing insights from other criteria are vital.

Of course, the same need for balance and correction holds true for the emphasis on Jesus' historical continuity with Judaism and early Christianity. In the case of Judaism in particular, we always have to pose the question: With what sort or branch or tendency of Judaism was Jesus "continuous" in a given saying or action? Moreover, just as we are not to decide that Jesus *must* have been discontinuous with the Judaism of his day in this or that matter, so we cannot decide a priori that he *must* have been in agreement with Judaism in all things. History does have its Luthers and Spinozas. One is surprised, for instance, to read E. P. Sanders's summary judgment on the historicity of Jesus' statement that all foods are clean (Mark 7:15). Without going into detailed arguments, Sanders simply declares: "In this case the saying attributed to Jesus . . . appears to me to be too revolutionary to have been said by Jesus himself."[24] In a sense, Sanders simply takes Perrin's view of the primacy of the criterion of discontinuity and stands it on its head. Instead of "if it is discontinuous, it must be from Jesus," we now have "if it is discontinuous, it cannot be from Jesus." Obviously, dogmatism in either direction must give way to a careful testing of claims in each case.

A further problem that often bedevils the criterion of discontinuity is a terminological one. Scholars will claim that this criterion isolates what is "unique" to Jesus. "Uniqueness" is a slippery concept in historical [[174]]

---

22. This point is argued at length by A. E. Harvey, *Jesus and the Constraints of History* (Philadelphia: Westminster, 1982); see in particular pp. 1–10. The failure to appreciate this point is one of the weaknesses of Breech's *The Silence of Jesus* (see, e.g., p. 10).

23. So rightly Walker, "The Quest for the Historical Jesus," 48: "Unique features are not necessarily the most characteristic features . . ."; cf. Boring, "The Historical-Critical Method's 'Criteria of Authenticity,'" 21. We might add that even what was strikingly characteristic about Jesus' message may not have been at the very heart of his message.

24. E. P. Sanders, *Jewish Law from Jesus to the Mishnah. Five Studies* (London: SCM; Philadelphia: Trinity, 1990) 28.

investigation. In some sense, Beethoven may be hailed as a "unique genius" in music, but that hardly means that individual aspects of his music cannot be found in composers like Bach before him or Mahler after him. Indeed, while it is hard enough for an individual like Beethoven to be "uniquely" different from anyone who has preceded him, it is asking far too much to require as well that he be "uniquely" different from all who follow. The gifted individual could hardly control that, and the more outstanding he was, the more likely he would be to have imitators.[25] Perhaps Beethoven's uniqueness is to be located instead in the special configuration of his personality, talent, production, and career, seen as a whole in a particular historical context, rather than in any one aspect of his work, seen in isolation.

Something similar might be said of the uniqueness of Jesus. When dealing with an individual saying or deed of Jesus, perhaps it is better to speak of what is "strikingly characteristic" or "unusual" in Jesus' style of speaking or acting, instead of claiming uniqueness at every turn. This distinction is especially important when we treat such characteristic phrases as "Amen, I say to you" or "Abba" addressed to God in prayer. Since we are not terribly well informed about popular Jewish-Aramaic religious practices and vocabulary in early 1st-century Galilee, modesty in advancing claims is advisable. Similarly, when we deal with the public actions of Jesus, it may be wiser to speak of "the sort of things Jesus did" (e.g., exorcisms, faith healings) instead of asserting that a particular story tells us precisely what Jesus did on one particular occasion. The same distinction can be applied to the sayings tradition taken as a whole. We can have some hope of learning the basic message of Jesus, the "kind of thing" he usually or typically said (the *ipsissima vox*).[26] Rarely if ever can we claim to recover his exact words (the *ipsissima verba*).

3. The Criterion of Multiple Attestation

The criterion of multiple attestation (or "the cross section") focuses on those sayings or deeds of Jesus that are attested in more than one independent literary source (e.g., Mark, Q, Paul, John) and/or in more than one literary form or genre (e.g., parable, dispute story, miracle story, prophecy, aphorism).[27] The force of this criterion is increased if a given motif or theme is found in

25. This problem was pointed out to me in a letter by David Noel Freedman, dated Oct. 15, 1990. For Freedman, to be unique, "it would be enough to be markedly different from those who preceded. What happened afterwards would not affect that status."

26. See Stein, "The 'Criteria' for Authenticity," 228–29.

27. The qualification "independent" is important. The mere fact that Peter's confession that Jesus is the Messiah is recorded in Mark, Matthew, and Luke does not satisfy the criterion of multiple attestation, since both Matthew and Luke are dependent on Mark for the basic narrative (though Matthew may be relying on a separate tradition for Jesus' praise and commission of Peter in 16:17–19). There is only one *independent* source for the core of the story. If the focus were broadened to "some sort of confession that Peter addresses to Jesus at a critical moment in the public ministry," then John 6:66–71 could be used; but we could no longer speak of Peter's confession of faith in Jesus precisely as the Messiah; both the location and the content of the confession in John's Gospel are different.

both different literary sources and different literary forms.[28] One reason that critics so readily affirm that Jesus did speak in some sense of the kingdom of God (or kingdom of [[175]] heaven) is that the phrase is found in Mark, Q, special Matthean tradition, special Lucan tradition, and John,[29] with echoes in Paul, despite the fact that "kingdom of God" is not Paul's preferred way of speaking.[30] At the same time, the phrase is found in various literary genres (e.g., parable, beatitude, prayer, aphorism, miracle story). Granted this wide sweep of witnesses in different sources and genres, coming largely from the first Christian generation, it becomes extremely difficult to claim that such material is simply the creation of the Church.[31]

When one moves from general motifs and phrases to precise sayings and deeds, one cannot usually expect such a broad range of attestation. Still, such key sayings as Jesus' words over the bread and wine at the Last Supper (Mark 14:22–25; 1 Cor 11:23–26; cf. John 6:51–58) and his prohibition of divorce (Mark 10:11–12; Luke 16:18 [= Q]; 1 Cor 7:10–11) are found in two or three independent sources.[32] Then, too, we may find "cross-referencing" between sayings dealing with a particular topic and actions of Jesus that also touch on that topic—e.g., sayings about the destruction of the Jerusalem temple and Jesus' prophetic "cleansing" of the temple. The example of the destruction of the temple is all the more forceful when we notice that both sayings and dramatic action are witnessed in more than one source and context (e.g., Mark 13:2; 14:58; John 2:14–22, esp. v. 19).

---

28. Some count multiple attestation in sources and multiple attestation in forms as two different criteria. Like Polkow ("Method and Criteria," 341), I think that they are better dealt with together under one criterion.

29. Once again I must stress that I do not accept the a priori exclusion of John from consideration as a possible source for knowledge of the historical Jesus; see Walker, "The Quest for the Historical Jesus," 54.

30. Those who accept the Coptic *Gospel of Thomas* as another independent source would naturally add it to this list (so Boring, "The Historical-Critical Method's 'Criteria of Authenticity,'" 13, 25–28; more cautiously, McArthur, "The Burden of Proof," 118). For my skepticism on this subject, see my remarks on the *Gospel of Thomas* under my treatment of the Nag Hammadi material as a source of knowledge of the historical Jesus ([[*The Roots of the Problem,*]] chap. 5, section 3).

31. McArthur ("The Burden of Proof," 118) claims that the following motifs are witnessed to by all four strands of the Synoptic tradition (i.e., Mark, Q, M, and L): Jesus' proclamation of the kingdom of God, the presence of disciples around Jesus, healing miracles, a link with John the Baptist, use of parables, concern for outcasts, especially tax collectors and sinners, a radical ethic, emphasis on the love commandment, a demand that the disciples practice forgiveness, clashes with his contemporaries over Sabbath observance, sayings about the Son of Man, and the Hebrew word "Amen" used to introduce Jesus' sayings.

32. I do not bother to list the "peeling away" of additions and modifications made by the oral tradition and the final redactor, since I consider such judgments a necessary part of the use of the criterion of multiple attestation. One would like to say that such judgments are simply "preliminary criteria" that precede the use of the "primary criteria" (so Polkow, "Method and Criteria," 342–45). But actual practice of the historical-critical method shows that all the way through the process one is constantly testing and revising one's judgments about modifications made by the oral tradition and the redactor.

Harvey K. McArthur was so taken with the force of the criterion of multiple attestation that he asserted that it was "the most objective" criterion and should be given first place.[33] Yet even McArthur admitted that multiple attestation was not an infallible indicator of historicity. In an individual case it is not a priori impossible that a saying invented early on by a Christian community or prophet met the needs of the Church so perfectly that it rapidly entered into a number of different strands of tradition.[34] Then, too, the mere fact that a saying occurs only in one source is no proof that it was not spoken by Jesus.[35] For example, the Aramaic invocation *Abba* ("my own dear Father") occurs on the lips of Jesus only once in all four Gospels (Mark 14:36), yet many critics ascribe it on other grounds to the historical Jesus. Once again, we are reminded that no criterion can be used mechanically and in isolation; a convergence of different criteria is the best indicator of historicity.

4. *The Criterion of Coherence*

[[176]] The criterion of coherence (or consistency or conformity) can be brought into play only after a certain amount of historical material has been isolated by the previous criteria. The criterion of coherence holds that other sayings and deeds of Jesus that fit in well with the preliminary "data base" established by using our first three criteria have a good chance of being historical (e.g., sayings concerning the coming of the kingdom of God or disputes with adversaries over legal observance). As can be readily seen, this criterion, by its very nature, is less probative than the three on which it depends.[36]

33. McArthur, "A Survey of Recent Gospel Research," 48; idem, "The Burden of Proof," 118. He makes the statement about giving it first place in conscious opposition to Perrin's emphasis on the criterion of discontinuity. In agreement with McArthur's view is Stein, "Criteria," 230.

34. G. Petzke puts it quite bluntly in his article, "Die historische Frage nach den Wundertaten Jesu," *NTS* 22 (1975–76) 180–204, esp. 183: there is no reason to think that something is more reliable historically because it is reported "a number of times" (*mehrfach*). Petzke's use of phrases like "a number of times" and "multiple appearances in early Christian tradition" points to a weakness in his argument. Petzke does not seem to take seriously enough the weight of a plurality of early *independent* literary sources and a plurality of literary genres, all acting as vehicles of a single given tradition. At one point, with a rhetorical wave of the hand, he dismisses the question of attestation in a number of independent traditions by observing that we cannot be certain about which early Christian sources were independent. Yet he himself proceeds to analyze the story of the cure of the "lunatic boy" (Mark 9:14–29 pars.) with the tool of the two-source theory.

35. So rightly Polkow, "Method and Criteria," 351.

36. Obviously, the conclusions drawn by the criterion of coherence are as good as the data base on which they depend. Carlston, a great proponent of the positive use of this criterion, uses it to discern authentic parables of Jesus: they will fit reasonably well into the eschatologically based demand for repentance that was characteristic of Jesus' message ("A *Positive* Criterion," 33–34). That is fine, provided one does not agree with revisionist exegetes who claim that Jesus' basic message was not essentially eschatological (e.g., Marcus J. Borg) or that repentance did not play a large role in Jesus' preaching (e.g., E. P. Sanders). Thus, one sees the vital importance of being as certain as possible about the data base created by the first three criteria before one proceeds to the criterion of coherence.

Since we should not conceive of the earliest Christians as totally cut off or different from Jesus himself, there is no reason why they could not have created sayings that echoed faithfully his own "authentic" words. In a loose sense such derived sayings could be considered "authentic" insofar as they convey the message of the historical Jesus;[37] but they cannot be considered "authentic" in the technical sense, i.e., actually coming from Jesus himself.[38]

Despite this limitation, the criterion of coherence has a certain positive use, namely, broadening an already established data base. One must, however, be wary of using it negatively, i.e., declaring a saying or action inauthentic because it does not seem to be consistent with words or deeds of Jesus already declared authentic on other grounds. Jesus would hardly be unique among the great thinkers or leaders of world history if his sayings and actions did not always seem totally consistent to us.[39] Moreover, we must remember that ancient Semitic thought, much more than our Western tradition of Aristotelian logic, delighted in paradoxical statements that held opposites in tension. (Even in our own day, American and European professors are often befuddled when they find out that students from Asia, while fiercely intelligent, may not subscribe to the Western philosophical principle of noncontradiction.) Then, too, Jesus was a popular preacher addressing a wide range of audiences on particular occasions with great oral skill; we should hardly seek in the various expressions of his teaching the type of systematic presentation expected of a written treatise.[40] Hence the debate between those scholars who stress the eschatological nature of Jesus' core message and those who portray Jesus teaching a wisdom tradition bereft of any eschatological slant may be misplaced. There is no reason why the preaching of Jesus may not have contained elements of both apocalyptic eschatology [[177]] and traditional Israelite wisdom. Both Jesus and his contemporaries might have been surprised by the charge (a very modern academic one) that such a message would be inconsistent or incoherent. In short, the criterion of coherence has a certain positive value; but its negative use, to exclude material as inauthentic, must be approached very cautiously.

37. Nielsen, "Kriterien," 14.

38. I should make clear that it is in this technical and restricted sense that I use the word "authentic" when discussing criteria of historicity; cf. Stein, "The 'Criteria' for Authenticity," 228. The word must not be taken to mean that, from the viewpoint of faith, what the oral tradition or final redaction contributed to our Gospels is any less inspired, normative, or true.

39. Cf. Hooker, "Christology and Methodology," 483; Stein, "The 'Criteria' for Authenticity," 250.

40. These considerations should make one wary about declaring a priori that Jesus could not possibly have spoken of the kingdom of God as both present and future or that he could not possibly have prophesied both a coming kingdom and a coming Son of Man. It is a matter of fact that the evangelists, and probably the gospel traditions before them, did just that. Nor are Paul's authentic letters totally devoid of paradoxes that strike some as blatant contradictions.

5. *The Criterion of Rejection and Execution*

The criterion of Jesus' rejection and execution is notably different from the first four criteria.[41] It does not directly indicate whether an individual saying or deed of Jesus is authentic. Rather, it directs our attention to the historical fact that Jesus met a violent end at the hands of Jewish and Roman officials and then asks us what historical words and deeds of Jesus can explain his trial and crucifixion as "King of the Jews."[42] While I do not agree with those who turn Jesus into a violent revolutionary or political agitator, scholars who favor a revolutionary Jesus do have a point. A tweedy poetaster who spent his time spinning out parables and Japanese koans, a literary aesthete who toyed with 1st-century deconstructionism, or a bland Jesus who simply told people to look at the lilies of the field—such a Jesus would threaten no one, just as the university professors who create him threaten no one. The historical Jesus did threaten, disturb, and infuriate people—from interpreters of the Law through the Jerusalem priestly aristocracy to the Roman prefect who finally tried and crucified him. This emphasis on Jesus' violent end is not simply a focus imposed on the data by Christian theology. To outsiders like Josephus, Tacitus, and Lucian of Samosata,[43] one of the most striking things about Jesus was his crucifixion or execution by Rome. A Jesus whose words and deeds would not alienate people, especially powerful people, is not the historical Jesus.

Secondary (or Dubious) Criteria

6. *The Criterion of Traces of Aramaic*

[[178]] Joachim Jeremias and many of his disciples point to traces of Aramaic vocabulary, grammar, syntax, rhythm, and rhyme in the Greek version of the sayings of Jesus as signs of an authentic saying. Used negatively, this criterion would cast doubt on a saying that could not be easily retroverted from Greek into Aramaic.[44] At first glance, this criterion seems scientific, since it rests on

41. Hence I would not say that it is simply "the resultant historical data shown by Dissimilarity . . . , Modification . . . , Embarrassment . . . , Incongruity . . . , and Hermeneutical Potential . . ." (Polkow, "Method and Criteria," 340). On p. 341, Polkow finally lists execution as merely a variation of discontinuity (or dissimilarity); cf. Lührmann, "Die Frage," 68.

42. On this criterion, see Schillebeeckx, *Jesus*, 97; cf. Walker, "The Quest for the Historical Jesus," 55.

43. See the treatment of their statements in [[Meier, *Roots of the Problem*,]] Chapters 3 and 4.

44. While Jesus may have known and even used some Greek (e.g., during his trial before Pilate), there is no indication that the sayings tradition in our Gospels was rooted, even in part, in sayings spoken by Jesus in Greek (so rightly Fitzmyer, "Methodology," 87). For a general overview of languages used in Palestine at the time of Jesus, see Joseph A. Fitzmyer, "The Languages of Palestine in the First Century A.D.," *A Wandering Aramean. Collected Aramaic Essays* (SBLMS 25; Missoula, MT: Scholars, 1979) 29–56; cf. [[Meier, *Roots of the Problem*,]] 255–68.

a vast fund of philological data developed in the 20th century by such experts in Aramaic as Jeremias, Matthew Black, Geza Vermes, and Joseph Fitzmyer.

Yet this criterion is not without serious problems. First of all, a good number of the earliest Christians were Palestinian Jews whose native tongue was the same Aramaic Jesus spoke. These Aramaic-speaking Christian Jews continued to exist in Palestine throughout the 1st century. Presumably, if Christians elsewhere in the Mediterranean world developed and sometimes created words of Jesus, Aramaic-speaking Jews in Palestine did the same.[45] Suppose, then, that some scholars are trying to discover an Aramaic substratum beneath a particular Greek saying in our Gospels. Even if they succeed, how—simply on the grounds of the Aramaic—are they to distinguish a saying first spoken in Aramaic by Jesus in A.D. 29 from a saying first spoken in Aramaic by a Christian Jew in A.D. 33? The mere fact that the saying has an Aramaic substratum gives no criterion for making such a distinction. The problem is complicated still further by the fact that the Jerusalem church was both Aramaic- and Greek-speaking from its beginning (cf. the Hellenists in Acts 6). The translation of Jesus' sayings into Greek is therefore not something that happened only at a later stage of the tradition.[46]

Secondly, the mere fact that a particular Greek saying can be retroverted into Aramaic with ease—or, on the other hand, only with great difficulty—does not give us a sure indication that the saying existed originally in Aramaic or originally in Greek. One Aramaic saying might be translated with great skill into elegant Greek, the translator aiming at sense-equivalence rather than a word-for-word rendering.[47] [[179]] Another Aramaic saying might be translated by another translator in a very literalistic, wooden fashion. The ease with which the two sayings could be retroverted into Aramaic might lead the unwary critic to judge quite wrongly that the first saying did not exist in Aramaic while the second did. Compounding the problem is that many Greek-speaking Christians knew very well the Greek translation of the Old Testament, the Septuagint, and could imitate the biblical Greek of the Septuagint, thus giving their original Greek composition a Semitic tone. This may have been the case with the Gospel of Luke.[48] Confusing the situation still further is the fact that scholars have become increasingly aware in recent decades that usages in the NT that we once considered "Semitisms" (i.e., vocabulary or grammar showing

45. For a similar observation, see Walker, "The Quest for the Historical Jesus," 43.

46. Riesner, *Jesus als Lehrer*, 93.

47. One must be especially sensitive to this possibility in the case of a saying that occurs only in Matthew or Luke. It is not impossible that an Aramaic saying was first translated into rough, Semitic Greek during the oral stage of the special Lukan tradition and then was given a more elegant Greek form when Luke incorporated it into his Gospel; cf. Riesner, *Jesus als Lehrer*, 93.

48. While not claiming to decide all instances once and for all, Fitzmyer seems to lean in the direction of explaining Luke's "Semitisms," especially his "Hebraisms," by reckoning "with a great deal of influence from the LXX" (Joseph A. Fitzmyer, *The Gospel According to Luke (I–IX)* [AB 28; Garden City, NY: Doubleday, 1981] 125).

Hebrew or Aramaic influence) may actually reflect the normal koine Greek of the less educated level of the population.[49]

Jeremias tries to mount a particular form of the "Aramaic argument" by pointing out that Jesus tended to deliver his teaching in Aramaic sayings that had a distinctive rhythm, that employed rhetorical tools like antithetic parallelism, alliteration, assonance, and paronomasia, and that employed the passive voice to avoid the frequent mention of God's name ("the divine passive").[50] While all this may be true, we again run into methodological problems. First, Jeremias' argument cannot entirely avoid being circular. He can tell us what is characteristic of Jesus' sayings only if from the start he can presume that a certain amount of sayings are authentic and then proceed to abstract from them the characteristics he lists. To be sure, such a list could legitimately arise from a lengthy process of isolating, collating, and examining authentic sayings of Jesus from a stylistic viewpoint. But such a list cannot be the starting point for deciding which sayings are authentic, for it would be presuming what is to be proven.[51] Second, if the list does reflect striking characteristics of Jesus' speech, would it be all that unusual if early Christian Jewish teachers and preachers in Palestine imitated the style of their master? Or did Jesus have a monopoly on rhythmic speech and antithetic parallelism in 1st-century Palestine? Was Jesus the only gifted and imaginative teacher among Jews and Christian Jews during this period? The same sort of questions may be asked about the supposed "poetic" quality of Jesus' Aramaic, all the more so since we are poorly informed about what 1st-century Palestinian Aramaic poetry looked like.[52]

At best, then, this criterion of Aramaic traces can provide additional support for an argument for historicity—but only when the material in [[180]]

---

49. So Walker, "The Quest for the Historical Jesus," 44; cf. Fitzmyer, "Methodology," 95 (citing R. M. Grant, *A Historical Introduction to the New Testament* [New York: Harper & Row, 1963] 41); idem, "The Study of the Aramaic Background of the New Testament," *A Wandering Aramean* (SBLMS 25; Missoula, MT: Scholars, 1979) 1–27, esp. 10–15. The question of the existence and extent of Semitisms (both Hebrew and Aramaic) in the NT is hotly debated today. For a short history of the debate, see Elliott C. Maloney, *Semitic Interference in Marcan Syntax* (SBLDS 51; Chico, CA: Scholars, 1981) 1–25. Maloney's conclusions, summarized on pp. 244–45, show how complex and varied Semitic influence may be. In particular, he notes "that much grammatical usage in Marcan Greek which various authors have claimed to be the result of Semitic interference is, in fact, quite possible in Hellenistic Greek. . . . On the other hand, certain constructions which various authors have argued are acceptable in Greek have been shown to be quite abnormal, or even totally unattested in Hellenistic Greek, whereas their appearance in Semitic is normal (sometimes only possible). These are true Semitisms" (pp. 244–45).

50. Joachim Jeremias, *New Testament Theology. Part One. The Proclamation of Jesus* (London: SCM, 1971) 3–29.

51. If these linguistic characteristics were first abstracted from sayings that had been declared authentic on other grounds, and if these characteristics were then applied to a new group of sayings to judge their authenticity, we would have a form of the criterion of coherence. Even then, however, the second methodological problem I indicate in the text would remain.

52. Fitzmyer, "Methodology," 97–98.

question has already given indications of being authentic on the grounds of other criteria.

7. *The Criterion of Palestinian Environment*

A criterion much like the Aramaic one, this criterion of Palestinian environment affirms that sayings of Jesus that reflect concrete customs, beliefs, judicial procedures, commercial and agricultural practices, or social and political conditions in 1st-century Palestine have a good chance of being authentic. Put negatively, a saying that reflects social, political, economic, or religious conditions that existed only outside Palestine or only after the death of Jesus is to be considered inauthentic. This criterion is much more useful in its negative guise. To take a well-known example that applies the criterion theologically rather than socially: parables that reflect concern about the delay of Jesus' parousia, the mission of the Church to the Gentiles, or rules for Church leadership and discipline are post-Easter creations, at least in their final, Gospel form.[53]

The positive use of this criterion is more problematic, for the same reasons mentioned under the Aramaic criterion. The Palestine inhabited by Christian Jews in A.D. 33 was not all that different from the Palestine inhabited by Jesus in A.D. 29. Pilate remained prefect in Judea until A.D. 36, Herod remained tetrarch in Galilee until A.D. 39, and Caiaphas remained high priest until A.D. 36 or 37. Basic commercial, social, and religious conditions naturally remained much longer. Hence, the Palestine reflected in sayings created by Christian Jews in A.D. 33 would hardly differ from the Palestine reflected in the sayings of Jesus in A.D. 29.[54]

8. *The Criterion of Vividness of Narration*

In the narratives of the Gospels, liveliness and concrete details—especially when the details are not relevant to the main point of the story—are sometimes taken to be indicators of an eyewitness report. Although he was not as uncritical in using this criterion as some of his followers, Vincent Taylor inclined to accept vivid, concrete details in Mark's Gospel as signs of high historical value.[55] Faithful to the early oral tradition, Mark had the special advantage of hearing Peter's [[181]] preaching.[56] Taylor himself is aware of the basic objection to this criterion:

---

53. See, e.g., the treatment of Joachim Jeremias, *The Parables of Jesus* (rev. ed.; London: SCM, 1969) 48–66. Of course, it is possible that behind the final form of such Gospel parables a scholar might discover, by means of form criticism, an earlier form without these ecclesiastical interests.

54. See also the observations of Walker ("The Quest for the Historical Jesus," 44), who adds: "Many apparent reflections of Palestinian life, however, may be derived from the Old Testament or other Jewish literature or reflect merely an acquaintance of sorts with the area on the part of a writer or transmitter of the tradition."

55. Vincent Taylor, *The Gospel According to St. Mark* (2nd ed.; London: Macmillan; New York: St. Martin's, 1966) 135–49.

56. Ibid., 148. Other conservative commentators take a similar tack; see, e.g., William L. Lane, *The Gospel According to Mark* (NICNT; Grand Rapids: Eerdmans, 1974) 10–12. Mark's

any skilled narrator can confer vividness on any story, however unhistorical. If liveliness and concrete details were in themselves proofs of historicity, many great novels would have to be declared history books.[57]

In reply to this objection, Taylor first admits that some concrete details may indeed be the result of Marcan redaction. But Taylor goes on to make two points: (1) Some of the details seem to serve no point in the narrative and apparently are included by Mark simply because they were in the tradition. (2) More importantly, a number of key episodes in the Gospel, episodes ripe for dramatic exploitation, are surprisingly jejune and bereft of concrete details: e.g., the choice of the Twelve (3:13–19b), the suspicion held by Jesus' family that he has gone insane (3:21), the plot by the priests (14:1–2), and the treachery of Judas (14:10–11). Taylor argues that the presence of these terse though important narratives shows that Mark did not indulge in massive creative rewriting; on the whole, some narratives are laconic and others detailed because that is the way they were in the early oral tradition that Mark has faithfully followed.[58]

Taylor's arguments do not seem as strong today as they might have appeared in the early fifties. Redaction criticism and contemporary narrative criticism have taught us to appreciate Mark as a talented author who may have his own theological and artistic reasons for alternating sparse and detailed narratives.[59] Moreover, not all critics would concede Mark's direct dependence on the preaching of Peter. If instead Mark is simply passing on oral traditions that come to him from many sources, can we not attribute the liveliness of some pericopes to the skill of certain early Christian preachers or storytellers, with the irrelevant details being explained by the untidy nature of oral as opposed to written composition? *Perhaps* the vividness of narration gets us behind Mark to his oral tradition. But does it get us back to Jesus himself?

A further problem arises from the succinct narratives that Taylor also finds in Mark. The terse, streamlined nature of particular dispute stories, miracle stories, and pronouncement stories may result, not from their unhis-

---

dependence on Peter is also defended by Martin Hengel, *Studies in the Gospel of Mark* (Philadelphia: Fortress, 1985) 50–53.

57. What makes the question even more complex is that what we consider a key sign of a historical novel—the creation of dialogue or the use of nonhistorical characters—was permissible in ancient historical writings. Hence the lines between what we would consider history and the historical novel are blurred in ancient literature.

58. This image of Mark as a conservative redactor of large amounts of early tradition has been revivified and pushed to the extreme by Rudolf Pesch, *Das Markusevangelium* (HTKNT 2/1–2; Freiburg/Basel/Vienna: Herder, 1976, 1977); see, e.g., 1.63–67; 2.1–25.

59. In sharp opposition to the picture of Mark as a conservative redactor are the redaction-critical approaches represented by most of the authors in Werner H. Kelber, ed., *The Passion in Mark* (Philadelphia: Fortress, 1976), and the rhetorical, narrative, and structural approaches represented by, e.g., Joanna Dewey, *Markan Public Debate* (SBLDS 48; Chico, CA: Scholars, 1980); Robert M. Fowler, *Loaves and Fishes* (SBLDS 54; Chico, CA: Scholars, 1981); Jack Dean Kingsbury, *The Christology of Mark's Gospel* (Philadelphia: Fortress, 1983); Vernon K. Robbins, *Jesus the Teacher* (Philadelphia: Fortress, 1984); and Elizabeth Struthers Malbon, *Narrative Space and Mythic Meaning in Mark* (San Francisco: Harper & Row, 1986).

torical nature, but from the very fact that they fit well into a particular form or genre. This neat "fit" may have caused some historical events to have been "slimmed down" to the "bare bones" of a particular genre in the oral tradition. In short, just as vividness in itself does not prove historicity, so too a pale skeletal narrative is not necessarily unhistorical.

Thus, as with the other secondary criteria we have seen so far, this [[182]] criterion can never serve as the main argument for historicity. At best, it may support the impression already created by one or more of the primary criteria.

9. The Criterion of the Tendencies of the Developing Synoptic Tradition

At this point we begin to consider criteria that, in my view, are highly questionable. The form critics like Bultmann thought they could isolate the laws of development within the Synoptic tradition. For instance, as the Synoptic tradition developed from Mark to Matthew and Luke, there supposedly was a tendency to make details more concrete, to add proper names to the narrative, to turn indirect discourse into direct quotation, and to eliminate Aramaic words and constructions. Bultmann suggested that, once these laws governing the transmission of tradition were discovered by analyzing changes in the Synoptic Gospels, they could be applied to the development of the tradition redacted by Mark and Q.[60] By extension, some critics have suggested, these laws might help us reconstruct original events or sayings coming from Jesus.

However, the whole attempt to formulate laws of the developing Synoptic tradition and then to apply them to the earlier oral tradition is dubious. First of all, one cannot establish that such firm laws exist. As E. P. Sanders has pointed out, we can find examples of the tradition becoming longer and shorter, of discourse becoming both direct and indirect, and of proper names being dropped as well as added. The tendencies run in both directions.[61] Moreover, even if we could discover firm laws among the Synoptic Gospels, we would still be dealing with redaction of the written Gospel of Mark by two other writers, Matthew and Luke. Whether and to what degree such laws would apply to the pre-Marcan oral stage of the gospel tradition is by no means clear.[62] In my opinion, the one negative use that can be made of a criterion based on "tendencies" is to discern the redactional tendency of each evangelist and to exclude from consideration those sayings or narratives which are massively suffused with the characteristic vocabulary and theology of the evangelist.

60. Rudolf Bultmann, "The New Approach to the Synoptic Problem," *Existence and Faith* (Meridian Books; Cleveland/New York: World, 1960) 34–54, esp. 41–42 (= *JR* 6 [1926] 337–62); similarly in his "The Study of the Synoptic Gospels," Rudolf Bultmann and Karl Kundsin, *Form Criticism* (New York: Harper & Row, 1962) 32–35; and in his *The History of the Synoptic Tradition*, 307–17 (= *Die Geschichte der synoptischen Tradition*, 335–46).

61. E. P. Sanders, *The Tendencies of the Synoptic Tradition* (SNTSMS 9; Cambridge: Cambridge University, 1969).

62. On the whole problem of the difference between oral and written tradition, see Werner H. Kelber, *The Oral and the Written Gospel* (Philadelphia: Fortress, 1983). I think, however, that Kelber exaggerates the gap between the oral and written forms of the Gospel.

10. *The Criterion of Historical Presumption*

[[183]] This criterion brings us squarely into the debate about where the "burden of proof" lies: on the side of the critic who denies historicity or on the side of the critic who affirms it? Critics who stress the decades between the original events and the writing of our Gospels, as well as the obvious cases of modifications or creations by the oral tradition or the evangelists, conclude that anyone claiming to isolate an authentic saying or action of Jesus must bear the burden of proof.[63] On the opposite side, critics who stress that eyewitnesses of Jesus' ministry were the leaders in the early Church and that in any historical investigation credence is given to early historical reports until the opposite is proven conclude that the burden of proof is on those who wish to discredit a particular saying or event as inauthentic ("in dubio pro tradito"). This is called by Neil J. McEleney the criterion of historical presumption.[64] If accepted, it could cut the Gordian knot in cases where the arguments are finely balanced and the final result seems to be permanent doubt.

However, common sense and the rules of logical argument seem to be on the side of critics like Willi Marxsen and Ben Meyer, who state the obvious: the burden of proof is simply on anyone who tries to prove anything.[65] In effect, this means that critics must allow a galling but realistic third column for a vote of "not clear" (*non liquet*). There will always be some difficult cases in which no criterion applies or in which different criteria apply but point in opposite directions. Such conundrums cannot be resolved by the *deus ex machina* of the criterion of historical presumption. In the convoluted case of the canonical Gospels, such a criterion simply does not exist.[66]

63. So Perrin, *Rediscovering the Teaching of Jesus*, 39: ". . . the nature of the synoptic tradition is such that the burden of proof will be upon the claim to authenticity" (this statement is set entirely in italics in Perrin's book). McArthur ("The Burden of Proof," 118–19) attempts a compromise stance: Initially the burden is on the person affirming historicity; but if a particular motif is supported by three or four Synoptic sources (multiple attestation), then the burden shifts to the person denying historicity.

64. McEleney, "Authenticating Criteria," 445–48; cf. Ellis, "Gospels Criticism," 32. McEleney's easy and undifferentiated use of the terms "reporter" and "history" (pp. 446–47) while discussing the Gospels does not inspire confidence. As Latourelle correctly observes ("Critères d'authenticité," 618), this "criterion" actually expresses an attitude of the exegete vis-à-vis the text rather than a criterion; similarly, Lambiasi, *L'autenticità storica dei vangeli*, 101, 137–38.

65. See Meyer, *The Aims of Jesus*, 83 and 277 n. 8, where he quotes Willi Marxsen, *The Beginnings of Christology: A Study of Its Problems* (Philadelphia: Fortress, 1969) 8. Hooker ("Christology," 485) expresses herself in a similar fashion, though she tends to dismiss the whole problem as not very profitable. This commonsense approach seems preferable to the subtle distinction Lambiasi tries to make between skeptical-systematic doubt and methodological-dynamic doubt *(L'autenticità storica dei vangeli*, 229).

66. Latourelle ("Critères d'authenticité," 628) claims that the most important of the fundamental criteria, though often ignored, is the criterion of "necessary explanation" (*explication nécessaire*). Actually, instead of being a precise criterion for judging the special material of the Four Gospels, this "criterion" is more like the "argument to the best explanation," which is one of the basic forms of all historical argumentation (McCullagh, *Justifying Historical*

Conclusion

Our survey indicates that five suggested criteria of historicity or authenticity are really valuable and deserve to be ranked as primary criteria: embarrassment, discontinuity, multiple attestation in sources or forms, coherence, and Jesus' rejection and execution. I have stressed the limitations and problems inherent in each criterion lest any single criterion [[184]] seem a magic key unlocking all doors. Only a careful use of a number of criteria in tandem, with allowances for mutual correction, can produce convincing results.[67]

Descriptions, 15–44). In a similar vein, Lambiasi *(L'authenticità storica dei vangeli*, 140) considers the criterion of necessary explanation to be basically the principle of the sufficient reason, a transcendent philosophical principle. But even if one accepts Latourelle's conception of this criterion of necessary explanation, the criterion is not of much use for the project that lies immediately ahead of us in this book [[Meier, *Roots of the Problem*]]: (1) The criterion of necessary explanation seeks to give a coherent and sufficient explanation of a considerable ensemble of facts or data. But most of this book will consist of sifting bit by bit through individual sayings, deeds, and motifs contained in the Gospels. One hopes bit that a moderate amount of fairly certain data will emerge; but the criterion, if useful at all, will be useful only at the end of this process. (2) The criterion seeks to group all the facts into a harmonious whole. This goal, however, presumes a coherence among the data that may be verified at the end of the process, but methodologically cannot be presumed at the beginning. (3) A review of a representative sample of books on the historical Jesus shows that exegetes of every stripe claim that they have found the true coherent explanation that illuminates all the facts about Jesus: he was an apocalyptic fanatic (Albert Schweitzer), a rabbi and prophet who issued the call to existential decision (Rudolf Bultmann), a gay antinomian magician (Morton Smith), a catalyst of nonviolent social revolution (Richard A. Horsely), or a charismatic man of the Spirit who founded a revitalization movement (Marcus J. Borg)—to name but a few "necessary explanations." Every author just named would claim that he has provided a coherent explanation to cover all the data he considers historical. If one is to argue with the varied explanations of these authors, one must first move back to their judgments about the historicity of individual pieces of the Jesus tradition, about the interpretation of the individual pieces, and only then move on to debate the meaning of the whole. (4) When Latourelle applies the criterion of necessary explanation, he seems to be already operating as a theologian in the area of fundamental theology or apologetics. That is a legitimate undertaking, but it must follow upon, not precede, the tedious work of the historian and exegete. We are all attracted by calls to a "holistic" approach (so Walker, "The Quest for the Historical Jesus," 54–56). But until we have at least a vague idea of what parts might qualify as belonging to the historical whole, a "holistic" approach remains a distant ideal.

67. I have omitted from consideration two further criteria suggested by Boring ("The Historical-Critical Method's 'Criteria of Authenticity,'" 23–24): (1) plausible *Traditionsgeschichte* [['history of tradition']] and (2) hermeneutical potential. (1) The criterion of plausible *Traditionsgeschichte* seeks to draw up a genealogy of the various forms of a saying. While this is a laudable goal, I do not think it a practical one for many of the sayings in the Jesus tradition. Even when attempted, the reconstruction of the tradition history must remain very hypothetical. (2) The criterion of hermeneutical potential looks at the variety of forms generated by the original form and asks what this original must have been in order to generate such variety. Again, the quest is a valid and laudable one; but, granted the paucity of data, I feel that the results must be highly subjective and hardly probative.

Despite their exaltation in some quarters, the criteria of Aramaic traces, Palestinian environment, and vividness of narrative cannot yield probative arguments on their own, even when all three are taken together. They can act as secondary, supportive criteria, reinforcing the impressions gained from one or more of the primary criteria. Finally, the criteria of the tendencies of the Synoptic tradition and historical presumption are, for all practical purposes, useless.[68]

As many a weary quester has remarked before, the use of the valid criteria is more an art than a science, requiring sensitivity to the individual case rather than mechanical implementation.[69] It can never be said too many times that such an art usually yields only varying degrees of probability, not absolute certitude. But, as we have already seen, such judgments of probability are common in any investigation of ancient history, and the quest for the historical Jesus cannot apply for a special exemption. Since moral certitude is nothing but a very high degree of probability, and since we run most of our lives and make many of our theoretical and practical judgments on the basis of moral certitude, we need not feel that the results of our quest will be unusually fragile or uncertain. They are no more fragile or uncertain than many other parts of our lives.[70]

68. The one exception here is the negative use of the criterion of an evangelist's redactional tendencies.

69. So, e.g., McArthur, "A Survey," 47; Walker, "The Quest for the Historical Jesus," 53 (who extends the observation to historiography in general); and Boring, "The Historical-Critical Method's 'Criteria of Authenticity,'" 35–36.

70. I might add here that, naturally, any scholar must be in dialogue with his or her peers and be respectfully attentive to their consensus on the authenticity of various Gospel material. However, I would not be willing, as Polkow is ("Method and Criteria," 355), to elevate scholarly consensus to another criterion. It should be noted in fairness to Polkow that he stresses that scholarly consensus can only be a corroborative criterion and can be used only when all else is said and done. I wonder, though, whether it is properly a criterion at all. A scholar must be prepared at any moment, because of the force of data and arguments, to go against a scholarly consensus on any issue. The heavy reliance on scholarly consensus from the very start weakens the whole approach of Breech (*The Silence of Jesus*, 9).

Introduction:
Faith, Kerygma, Gospels

[[1]] It would not be melodramatic to say that gospel study has entered a period of heady upheaval. The reigning though tenuous consensus among redaction critics has been dissolving without a newer one to take its place. Methods tried and true have been found wanting by a new generation of critics. The promise of redaction criticism to treat the gospels as wholes has finally been fulfilled by the appropriation of insights outside of biblical studies per se, from literary criticism. In the wake, some intriguing crossovers have occurred. At least one leading critic in the maturity of his career has moved from one discipline to the other.

An opportunist, observing this profusion of many and diverse techniques, might be tempted to ignore standard approaches. Of course a completely idiosyncratic method ought to be viewed with suspicion. But given the "state of the art," a reasoned fruitful approach sensitive to the gospels themselves and open to debate with opponents should not be turned aside. Such is the apologia offered for what follows. In this chapter, I shall state the thesis of the entire work, describe the method which confirms it, and then anticipate how both might fare among the various "schools" of criticism that dominate academic study of the gospels. However, I shall not merely report what potential objections might be. They will be analyzed and evaluated according to the "logic" and procedure characteristic of each. Of course, such engagement will not end here. In the chapters that follow, I shall attempt to provide further evidence and argument, gospel-by-gospel, beginning with Mark [[not reprinted here]], the fountainhead of the written tradition.

Reprinted, with permission, from E. E. Lemcio, *The Past of Jesus in the Gospels* (Cambridge: Cambridge University Press, 1991) 1–5, 74–90, and (the notes) 132, 150–54.

Thesis

I intend to show that the Evangelists, to an extent heretofore unrecognized, produced narratives distinguishing Jesus' time from their own. This effort transcended merely putting verbs in past tenses and [[2]] dividing the account into pre- and post-resurrection periods. Rather, they took care that terminology appropriate to the Christian era does not appear beforehand. Vocabulary characteristic prior to Easter falls by the wayside afterwards. Words common to both bear a different nuance in each. Idiom suits the time. And these are not routine or incidental expressions. They reveal what Jesus the protagonist and the Evangelists as narrators believe about the gospel, the Christ, the messianic task, the nature of salvation, etc.

This much is apparent from the study of internal evidence. Evidence outside of the gospels provides something of a control and enables one to know how to interpret the significance of these results. The gospels are not essentially or primarily expansions of Christian oral proclamation represented elsewhere in the New Testament. Kerygmatic expressions of "faith" found outside of the gospels were *not* projected back onto the narrative. None of the Evangelists writes with such explicit self-consciousness. Furthermore, expectations for idiomatic and linguistic verisimilitude in Greco-Roman historical and biographical writing *were* met and often exceeded by the Evangelists. Such data may prove useful in separate efforts to reconstruct the course of Jesus' life. And the literary critic can employ them to describe more fully the literary art of the narrators. Attempts to inhibit these two enterprises by calling them impossible, irrelevant, or illegitimate cannot be justified.

Method

In the confusing state of affairs alluded to above and evaluated recently by Robert Morgan,[1] some scholars are quite ready to rank the gifts bequeathed by generations of critics according to "a more excellent way." For example, in a welcome revision of Stephen Neill's much admired survey of NT research, Tom Wright has all but called for a reversing of steps in the critical process:

> I would . . . propose that work on the Gospels should be undertaken in the reverse order to that which is usually imagined to be normal or correct. Historical criticism, along the lines begun by the Third Quest, and literary criticism, taking the Gospels in the first instance as wholes and using all the tools currently available [including comparative religions], are the primary disciplines. Form-criticism and Source-criticism are essentially secondary, as can be seen by [[3]] their tacit, and thoroughly-warranted, neglect by modern students of history and literature.[2]

1. R. Morgan (with J. Barton), *Biblical Interpretation* (Oxford, University Press, 1988). See also A. E. Harvey (ed.), *Alternative Approaches to New Testament Study* (London, SPCK, 1985).

2. S. Neill and T. Wright, *The Interpretation of the New Testament 1861–1986* (Oxford,

However, neglect by non-specialists cannot itself be a reason. Rather, the very possibility of form criticism can be called into question if the logic of a thoroughgoing redaction criticism is pressed. Wright is on surer ground when he observes, "If the evangelists' work of redaction was as heavy as some would claim, our chances of recovering early forms, let alone sources, are at the mercy of so much speculation and so many unverifiable hypotheses that we are in a bad state indeed. How can we advance?"[3] Although one might wish to wait for a "super-method" that would embrace and integrate all legitimate ones, the presses continue to roll.

Without presuming a definitive answer to so important a query, I suggest that the way forward lies in beginning with the firmest data available, i.e., working from the best- to the lesser-known to the unknown: literary criticism, redaction criticism, comparative religions (Judaism, hellenism), historical criticism (life-of-Jesus research). Despite the caveats leveled later against certain versions of redaction criticism, 1 have not rejected either the premises or practices of the method *in toto*. Rather, I want to claim a place to stand between two disciplines. Because I affirm the redaction-critical commitment to treat the gospels as intentional compositions with purpose and plan, I have conducted the analysis at the literary level (i.e., the redactional product) without resorting to the past of Jesus or to the "present" of the Evangelists' communities. The literary investigation can and should be conducted before either of these historical operations is done. Each will be enhanced and enriched as a result.[4]

Yet I will not perform a full-scale literary-critical analysis. My goal is more specific. It fits more nearly with the attempt to determine voice(s) and tone(s).[5] However, in this case it will be various levels of theological tonality expressed throughout the gospel narratives. In practice, terms will always be examined within the range of meanings supplied by various historical contexts. But the ultimate objective will be to ascertain meanings from *within the text*. Their shades and gradations will depend upon the point being made by the narrator either directly or through the characters in the story.[6] Such is the burden of this monograph. A more specific account of the procedure is now in order.

University Press, 1988) 403. G. N. Stanton advocates starting "with the top layer, with the gospels as we have them," in *The Gospels and Jesus* (Oxford, University Press, 1989) 152.

3. Neill and Wright, *Interpretation*, 401–2.

4. L. Chouinard cites R. M. Frye in this connection in "Gospel Christology: A Study of Methodology," *JSNT* 30 (1987) 24. Although the likelihood is great that the original recipients of the gospels knew other oral and perhaps even written traditions, one must be constantly reminded that they did not examine them in the form of a *Synopsis Quattuor Evangeliorum* [['Fourth Synoptic Gospel']].

5. Tone is among the aspects of literary investigation that R. Alter lists, Chouinard, "Methodology," 24–25.

6. Ibid., 25, 30.

My approach takes its cue from two studies conducted by C. F. D. Moule (the second is summarized in chap. 2 [[not reprinted here]]). In "The Christology of Acts," [[4]] he investigated the use ὁ κύριος [['the Lord']] in Luke's writings and discovered that the Third Evangelist rarely allows the *dramatis personae* of the gospel to employ this title in the fully confessional sense that became so common after Easter. Moule then suggested that the Evangelists might not be as guilty of reading other post-resurrection convictions into the narrative as is often alleged.[7] To confirm his suspicion required other examinations along broader fronts. Otherwise, it might be deemed idiosyncratic or exceptional. In other words, did Luke and his colleagues show the same restraint with other christologies that refer to Jesus' status? And what about the nature of the messianic task? Might the same be found with soteriology and mission, too?

Even though I have been able to answer these questions affirmatively, I do not go further and posit historicity. That requires a separate step. All that emerges is a profound reluctance on the part of the gospel writers to recount the story of Jesus in their own terms. Strictly speaking, one has achieved only a fuller understanding of the narrators' representation of the past. However, their commitment to preserve its content and idiom give one confidence to pursue the historical task. Historians, accustomed to analyzing unpromising and prejudicial data anyway, may find the effort in the case of the gospels more rewarding.

In conducting the search for evidence, I appealed to the most obvious expressions of each Evangelist's beliefs. A necessary but often overlooked step examines the hardest surface information before proceeding to the softer strata below. One should read the lines ahead of the spaces between them. Consequently, I turned first to the resurrection appearances. (In the case of Mark, of course, there was none to investigate; but his title proved useful.) Here was vocabulary by which to determine both the precise "Easter faith" of each Evangelist and the extent to which it was or was not imposed on the preceding narrative.

Often, the gospel writer's point of view appears in obvious editorial comments on the scene: "The Lord chose seventy others" (Luke 10:1). Here one can test the use of ὁ κύριος [['the Lord']] as Moule did. Matthew's concept of Scripture's fulfillment in Jesus belongs to the editorial framework of the narrative. Mark 1:1 is also such an instance: "the beginning of the gospel about Jesus Christ [God's Son]."

The next places to detect post-Easter beliefs were those instances where Jesus (usually in private and to the disciples) speaks of the future—either near or remote—but after his death. [[5]] Examples are: "Many will come in my name" (Mark 13:6), and "Whoever receives one of these little ones in my name" (Mark 9:37). Occasionally such future reference points appear in introductions (the birth narratives of Matthew 1–2, Luke 1–2). Preludes some-

---

7. C. F. D. Moule, *The Phenomenon of the New Testament* (London, SCM, 1967) 56–59.

times parallel postludes. Once again, the vocabulary here can be used to determine how much, if any, has been injected into the narrative.

On a different level, perhaps the subtlest task of all (and therefore the most contestable) is the search for clues provided by teaching given before the resurrection to various audiences. Especially distinctive are the public and private phases of Jesus' ministry. While one cannot claim in advance that the latter usually reflects an Evangelist's convictions, nevertheless the very fact that some topics are reserved for more restricted consumption makes one curious. Why were certain things not said to the crowds?

Once these data were gathered (including allied vocabulary, cognates, and ideas that naturally clustered together), I examined them according to various (alleged) sources, oral or written. Could the distinctions observed be maintained in the regions of text demarcated as triple tradition, Q, M, and L? Such an approach enabled the test to be conducted on a *number* of fronts using *several* key categories. Thus, even if half had to be ruled out as inappropriate or insufficient, then the case might still be capable of standing on three legs rather than six.

This appeal primarily to internal evidence need not otherwise be justified. However, the pressure from some redaction critics to view the results in such a way as to deny an historical or literary reading required attention to external data. This represents the most promising way of breaking the impasse between those who make opposing assertions. Consequently, I ranged beyond the gospels but within the NT to determine whether or not they may be regarded as written expansions of the oral Christian proclamation. The appendix provides the evidence and arguments against the connection.

Finally, the results of study based upon internal evidence were compared with literature outside of the NT altogether: biographical and historical writing in the ancient world. The aim was not to make a case for the gospels as history or biography. Instead, the task was more specific: to see how the Evangelists' attention to preserving earlier and other idiom squares with ancient efforts to do so. If they compared favorably, then here was another criterion by which to evaluate the claims of some redaction critics that such data might only be accounted for as expressions of rival Christian points of view.

. . . .

Luke

Introduction

[[74]] With Luke, the contrasts which I have been underscoring could be made more easily by an appeal to Acts. Here, the post-Easter life of the church as he interpreted it meets us with clarity and force. However, I shall avoid this natural move, since the point of the entire exercise has been to rely upon internal evidence exclusively. And an abundance of it exists in chap. 24: except for John, the most extensive account of Jesus' post-resurrection activity in the gospels. As with Matthew [[not reprinted here]], I shall use this material to provide the major sections and sub-categories for the data. Finally, the Prologue will contribute its special brand of evidence to the argument.

Post-resurrection Narrative (Luke 24:13–53)

On the Road to Emmaus.   The two men whom Jesus joined on the journey are otherwise unknown, belonging to the outer circle of disciples (πᾶσιν τοῖς λοιποῖς [['all the rest']] of v. 9; cf. v. 33b). Yet Cleopas and his partner are inside enough to refer to "some of our women" who brought them the startling reports of the risen Jesus (v. 22). Likewise, the contingent of men who subsequently inspected the site are called "some of those with us." Their reactions afford a further insight into the pre-Easter mindset among the band of disciples. Through his miracles and preaching, Jesus had reminded them of Yahweh's historic spokesmen.

A man, a mighty prophet. (v. 19)

Not yet enlightened with the supreme estimate of the risen Lord, these two reflect what the earthly Jesus had said of himself. The proverb of prophets unappreciated on home ground applied to him, too (4:24), [[75]] a contention recorded by Matthew (13:57) and Mark (6:4). However, Luke alone relates a more direct association. In 13:33, to the Pharisees, Jesus claims that his agenda will be completed or perfected (τελειοῦν) according to the prophetic precedent: it is unthinkable for a prophet to perish outside of Jerusalem (13:32–33). The prophetic model appears again but along different lines and without even the hint of death. Luke seems to be avoiding the connection at 11:29–32. Matthew has Jesus appeal in public to the sign of Jonah as prototypical of his three days and nights in the whale's belly (12:38–42). But Luke makes Jonah's significance lie in his preaching of repentance to the Ninevites. While for him and Matthew Jesus is greater than Jonah (and Solomon), the precise understanding of that greatness is not spelled out by the Third Evangelist.

Could such a self-consciousness have fed popular perceptions as recorded in 7:16? In the wake of Jesus' restoring the widow's son to life, the crowd glorified God saying, " 'a great prophet has been raised up among us, and God has visited his people.' " This fits closely both the opinion of Herod and of the general populace (9:18, 19 paralleled in Matt 14:1–2; 16:14, and Mark 6:14–16; 8:28; see also Luke 9:7–8). One will have to wait until Luke's second volume to find a testimonium to the specifically Christian understanding of Jesus as the eschatological prophet spoken of by Deut 18:15 (3:22–23; cf. 7:37).[8]

But the violent actions of their leaders had dashed all expectations:

---

8. C. F. D. Moule, "The Christology of Acts," *Studies in Luke–Acts*, ed. L. E. Keck and J. L. Martyn (New York, Abingdon, 1966) 162–63 where a similar point is differently made.

We were hoping him to be the one to redeem Israel shortly. (v. 21)

The poignancy of this statement exceeds even that of the imprisoned Baptizer whose apocalyptic agenda Jesus had failed to fulfill (11:2–3//7:18–20). Although it is true that the hopes expressed here are not necessarily erroneous or canceled,[9] they were clearly misplaced as to the time and mode of fulfillment. Luke has a broader vision, to be sure, which may include and transcend any particularism suggested by the statement;[10] but the point is that he allows the report of its inadequacy to stand in its prima-facie sense. Thus, there appears to be no "advance" over the Spirit-inspired prophecy of Zechariah, who blesses God for visiting his people and making redemption for them (1:68). Anna's talk about the infant Jesus bears the same quality. She blesses God in the presence of all those who were expecting the redemption of Jerusalem (2:38). No further uses of this word group occur in the gospel or Acts. Luke lacks the λύτρον [['ransom']] saying about the Son of Man in Matt 20:28 and Mark 10:45 (and found only here in [[76]] the gospels). Although such vocabulary can be given greater or other meaning by the reader, the specific language maintains its integrity within the narrative.

In his critical rejoinder, Jesus calls them "foolish men and slow of heart to believe all that the prophets had spoken" (v. 25). Such references to prophetic witness will subsequently occur five more times (vv. 27, 44–46), illustrating the importance of biblical attestation for Luke. Nevertheless, its significance does not emerge in the same way prior to Easter. Here, the christological content of that witness takes on different features.

Was it not necessary for the Christ to suffer these things and enter into his glory? (v. 26)

With ὁ χριστός [['the Christ']] on the risen Lord's lips, there is dramatic evidence of christological precision which Luke, along with the other synoptists, has maintained to the end. In the L material, the title is an exalted one, indeed. The angels announce to the shepherds the birth of "a savior who is Christ the Lord" (2:11). Simeon had been promised that he would live until he had seen "the Lord's Christ" (2:26). Yet the settings are private, and the reference is to Jesus' ultimate, eschatological significance rather than to anything that he will achieve prior to Easter. Furthermore, John the Baptist stimulates messianic expectations among certain groups (3:15). Luke joins the other synoptists in relating that, during the public ministry, Jesus avoids using the title of himself in any way. And he forbids its usage by the disciples

---

9. R. J. Dillon, *From Eye-Witnesses to Ministers of the Word* (Rome, Pontifical Biblical Institute, 1978) 129.

10. Ibid., 130. Dillon's study shares the same approach as Hubbard's and Schaberg's on Matthew. The redaction-critical penchant for finding connections throughout a gospel tends to ignore the discontinuities. Of course, searches for the latter run the opposite risk. R. Tannehill's work, while full of fine observations about the total achievement of the Third Evangelist, tends either to minimize differences or to by-pass their significance. See, for example, *The Narrative Unity of Luke–Acts* (Philadelphia, Fortress, 1986) 200, 284, 295–96.

(16:20//8:30//9:21). The point about the Messiah's relation to David is, as in the other gospels, an academic question with no application made (22:41–45//12:35–37//20:41–44). No new instance in Q or L is introduced. After the resurrection, however, the phenomenon changes drastically. It is the only title that Jesus employs in his two post-resurrection appearances. (See also v. 46.)

Furthermore, prior to the resurrection, Jesus never speaks of the Messiah's suffering (ἔδει παθεῖν τὸν χριστόν [['it is necessary for the Christ to suffer']]). In keeping with the Marcan tradition, this theme remains confined to the Son of Man, δεῖ τὸν υἱὸν τοῦ ἀνθρώπου πολλὰ παθεῖν [['the Son of Man must undergo great suffering']] (e.g., Mark 8:31//9:22; cf. 17:24–25, and 22:37).[11] So it goes with scriptural fulfillment, here spoken of as "necessity." Although the risen Jesus maintains that the Messiah's suffering had been predicted by the prophets, the earthly Jesus cites a particular text in public which suggests that the accomplishment of the messianic task lies in a different direction. True, the noun χριστός [['Christ' or 'Messiah']] does not occur; the verb does: the Spirit anointed Jesus [[77]] (i.e., made him Christ: ἐχρισέν με) to fulfill the agenda set by Isa 61:1–2: to announce good news to the poor, release to the oppressed and captive and to cure the blind (4:16–21). Later, Jesus informs the disciples that journeying to Jerusalem will complete (τελεσθήσεται) "all the writings through the prophets regarding (τῷ) the Son of Man" (18:31–32). This is never said of the Messiah until after Easter.

Thus, to the Pharisees, Jesus anticipates death in keeping with prophetic precedent (as described in Scripture). To the disciples before the resurrection, he refers to it as the agenda set by scripture for the Son of Man. Only on this side of the resurrection, however, does Jesus instruct them about the *messianic* significance of these prophesied events. Can this be merely fortuitous? Or, do we have here a conspicuous effort to match idiom with audience and time? Could it be that controlling Luke's narrative is the conviction expressed by Peter that it was *at the resurrection* that "God made . . . [Jesus] both Lord and Christ"? (Acts 2:36; cf. 13:33 and Rom 1:3–4).

Such alleged carefulness about titles might risk the charge of splitting hairs or quibbling, especially since "Son of God" and "Christ" seem to be equivalents at 4:41. Yet this is an editorial comment, indicating a conjunction of the two in Luke's mind. In the narrative of the trial, the two terms are separated (22:67–70) in a way that they are not in Matthew and Mark (26:63//14:61). So far as Jesus' public ministry is concerned, the Third Evangelist does not multiply the occasions when he is addressed as ὁ υἱὸς τοῦ θεοῦ [['the Son of God']]. And no novel use is introduced. Jesus' attitude towards it remains constant: suppression when demons recognize him thus.

---

11. I. H. Marshall acknowledges the particular point without making the more comprehensive one: "what was said earlier about the Son of man is now predicated of the Messiah. Thereby the identification of the Son of man in Jesus' teaching with the Messiah in the church's teaching is established." See *The Gospel of Luke,* NIGTC (Grand Rapids, MI, Eerdmans, 1978) 905.

In private settings, Luke takes only one opportunity to increase the instances in the L material (the Annunciation to Mary in 1:35). Nothing new is added to Q in the Temptation narrative (4:3, 9), where Jesus' special status undergoes relentless testing. He is supremely the Son because he knows that a person's needs transcend the physical (v. 4), worships and serves God alone (v. 8), and refuses to put him to the test (v. 11).[12] Yet Luke will surpass even this level of care by a startling substitution. In Matthew and Mark (27:54// 15:39), the centurion's acclamation of Jesus as God's son forms the climax to the narrative. Finally, what only supernatural beings (divine and demonic) know and what the Jews have not perceived, a Gentile "confesses." Surely, Luke would be expected to follow suit; but he reports the soldier's glorifying *God* and acknowledging that Jesus was truly δίκαιος [['righteous' or 'innocent']] (23:47), a quality predicated of Simeon (2:25) and Joseph of Arimathea (23:50). Admittedly, the term could suggest υἱὸς θεοῦ [['son of God']] [[78]], since the two are equivalents in the Wisdom of Solomon 2:13, 16, 18.[13] Or, it might simply mean "innocent."[14] Either way, Luke requires his reader to infer what the other Evangelists have spelled out. And before Easter, he avoided associating suffering and "the Son of God" with the same care that he refused to link suffering with the "Christ."

It is not enough for Jesus to criticize the disciples' failure to trust the prophets' witness. Rather, he adopts a positive and more comprehensive approach.

> Beginning from Moses and from all the prophets he explained to them in all of the scriptures the things concerning himself. (v. 27)

The language of Jesus here is Lucan, to be sure. In the parable about "Dives" and Lazarus, Abraham uses the expression "Moses and the prophets" twice (16:29, 31). These, if obeyed, will enable one to avoid the torments of Hades, says the patriarch. However, the absence of a christological component is made even more stark in Abraham's insisting that a warning to errant brothers delivered by one risen from the dead (!) would have no effect (v. 31).

Furthermore, the term "the scriptures" (γραφή in the plural) does not appear earlier than chap. 24. The singular may be found exclusively at 4:21.

---

12. See C. H. Talbert for the view that Luke's altering the order of the second and third temptations enables him to refer the reader to Genesis 3 and conclude that Jesus as second Adam succeeded where the first Son of God (3:3–8) failed: *Literary Patterns, Theological Themes and the Genre of Luke–Acts*, SBLMS 20 (Missoula, MT, Scholars, 1974) 47.

13. E. Lövestam, *Son and Saviour: A Study of Acts 13:32–37; with an Appendix: "Son of God" in the Synoptic Gospels* (Lund, Gleerup, 1961) 104 n. 2.

14. F. Danker, who serves the reader a rich feast of classical allusions pertaining to Luke's Gospel, notes that the centurion's verdict "echoes what the Hellenistic world values most, namely excellence of the highest order, featuring especially magnanimity and integrity, the marks of a truly great benefactor." See his subtle and elegant study, *Luke*, 2nd edn (Philadelphia, Fortress, 1987) 106. Luke's skill could net both kinds of readers: the hellenistic Jew familiar with the Wisdom of Solomon and the pagan not acquainted with Jewish literature.

Otherwise, Jesus uses only the singular and plural participles (τὰ γεγραμμένα [['is written']], and τὸ γεγραμμένον [['the writing']]: 18:31, 20:17, 22:37) in the citation of scripture. And merely twice before does Luke report Jesus' reference to it in direct connection to himself (18:31, 22:37). Nothing like this sort of explanation (διερμηνεύειν) occurs beforehand. Jesus does not carefully and systematically interpret his mission. The reader is tempted to wonder why, given the disciples' penchant for dull-wittedness and misunderstanding, the Master Teacher waited so long to provide this much-needed information. (And, of course, the crowds are less informed still.) Luke even avoids informing the readers about the significance of Jesus' words and actions in the way that Matthew does: such and such was done/said in fulfillment of what the scriptures prophesied.

To the Band of Disciples. The same points may be made about the second resurrection monologue, though its particular features merit special attention. What occurred in the first encounter was not accidental. Once again, Luke maintains the distinctions between before and after with the [[79]] same care. It is a matter of deliberate narrative technique based upon theological convictions.

On returning to Jerusalem, after perceiving that the stranger is none other than Jesus himself, the two disciples are greeted with corroborating news.

> The Lord is risen indeed . . .

This way of referring to Jesus in the absolute occurs only here, in the wake of the resurrection (Luke makes an editorial reference in v. 3 to "the Lord Jesus"). Earlier, no one from the public had used the title. In private, it cannot be found on the disciples' lips. The two potential exceptions are contestable. Elizabeth greeting Mary as "the mother of my Lord" could mean "Master" (1:43); Zechariah's "before the Lord" (v. 76) more naturally refers to God.[15] So, rarely, if ever, does Jesus or anyone within the narrative before Easter use ὁ κύριος [['the Christ' or 'Messiah']] in the fully fledged Christian sense.[16]

To the Eleven and others assembled in secret, Jesus appeals first to his customary practice.

> These are my words which I spoke to you while I was with you. (v. 44)

However, one searches in vain for what follows, both in the statement's form and content.

---

15. Moule, "Christology," 160–61. The exclusion of honorific address, κύριε [['Lord']], is as appropriate here as it was for Mark and Matthew.

16. Although he makes some of these distinctions, J. Fitzmyer's failure to recognize the greater complexity of Luke's usage leads him to make the common claim that "Luke has time and again retrojected this title into the phase of Jesus' earthly ministry." Has Luke thereby been extremely careless when he reports Peter's assertion that God made Jesus Lord in the resurrection (Acts 2:36)? See *The Gospel according to Luke I–IX*, AB 28 (Garden City, NY, Doubleday, 1981) 1.202–3.

It was necessary for all things written in the Law of Moses, and the prophets and in the psalms concerning me to be fulfilled. (v. 44)

This appeal to a tripartite "canonical" witness is as unprecedented in Luke as the "Trinitarian" baptismal formula is in Matthew. Each component (or a near equivalent) is cited separately throughout the narrative,[17] but never collectively. How much of this discrimination occurred self-consciously, one cannot know. If it belongs to an unconscious phenomenon, then the distinction becomes more noteworthy.

Furthermore, so far as content is concerned, Jesus did not previously appeal to texts from the writings of Moses or the psalms to substantiate the messianic agenda which he outlines subsequently, according to the Evangelist. Moreover, neither alleged earlier instruction nor that which is to follow stems from a plain reading of the biblical texts. In other words, the scriptures do not speak for themselves. A special act by the Risen Lord is required to read them aright:

He opened their minds to understand the scriptures. (v. 45)

[[80]] Luke thus implies that the disciples could not have made sense of them beforehand. This inference finds support earlier on. In the one clear instance where the appeal to prophetic scriptures did occur regarding the Son of Man's fate (18:31–33), Luke reports that the disciples "did not understand any of these things, and this word was hidden from them; and they did not know what was being said" (v. 34; see 9:44–45 for the same statement except for the prophetic reference). Now enlightened, the disciples may receive Jesus' instruction without obstacles:

Thus it has been written: the Christ is to suffer and rise on the third day. (v. 46)

In this statement, the necessity of the Messiah's suffering has been defined as *scriptural* necessity: events have proceeded according to the sacred texts (however obscure to us their precise location may be). Divine will, prophetic precedent, and now biblical warrant converge as determinators of the drama. As before (v. 26), the christology is "messianic" in the strict sense. The passion figures in both. In the earlier text, entry into glory followed suffering; here the commoner reference to resurrection occurs. Twice now, the risen Jesus speaks in a manner atypical of the prior narrative. If he here uses the vocabulary of the early church, then it has not been imposed previously.

And repentance leading to forgiveness of sins is to be proclaimed. (v. 47)

---

17. κατὰ τὸν νόμον Μωϋσέως [['according to the law of Moses']] (2:22), οἱ προφῆται [['the prophets']] (16:16, 29, 31), ἐν βιβλίῳ ψαλμῶν [['in the book of Psalms']] (20:42), Μωϋσῆς καὶ οἱ προφῆται [['Moses and the prophets']] (16:29, 31).

The language of this clause sets forth the preaching agenda for the church, without a doubt. How does it square with prior terminology? Will its program have been anticipated by Jesus? An uncritical comparison will answer affirmatively. One can appeal to the typically Lucan stress upon repentance. Both μετανοία [['repentance']] and μετανοεῖν [['to repent']] occur more frequently (fourteen times) in this gospel than in Matthew and Mark combined (ten times). In Luke alone, Jesus describes his vocation as calling sinners to repent (5:32). And he joins Matthew in recounting Jesus' rebuke of entire cities for refusing to do so (11:20–21//10:13).

Furthermore, the church's proclamation of forgiveness could be linked to Jesus' granting forgiveness during his ministry. All of the synoptists relate how this belonged to the authority of the Son of Man upon the earth (9:6//2:10//5:24). All three recount the incident of [[81]] Jesus' anointing by a woman (26:6–13//14:3–9//7:37–49). But Luke identifies her as Mary Magdalene whose sins Jesus forgives in consequence of her saving faith (v. 50).[18] The Third Evangelist includes the Lord's Prayer from Q, with its petition to God (without any christological mediation) for release from sins, linked to forgiving other sinners for wrongs incurred (6:12//11:4). And the sinning brother must enjoy unlimited forgiveness (18:21–22//17:3–4). But these are hardly characteristically Lucan. Neither he nor the other synoptists report that Jesus forgave the disciples. Nor does he bestow forgiveness with every cure or to every sinner. And no connection whatever is made with Jesus' death.

The task given to Christians of proclaiming repentance that leads to forgiveness (v. 47) does not fall within the description of Jesus' role. Instead, it characterizes the ministry of John the Baptist which Mark and Luke together report (1:4//3:3; see 1:77). The vocabulary is quite remarkably similar:

κηρυχθῆναι ἐν τῷ ὀνόματι αὐτοῦ μετανοίαν εἰς ἄφεσιν ἁμαρτιῶν πᾶσιν τοῖς ἔθνεσιν
[['repentance and forgiveness of sins is to be proclaimed in his name to all nations']]
κηρυσσων   βάπτισμα   μετανοίας εἰς ἄφεσιν ἁμαρτιῶν
[['proclaiming . . . baptism . . . repentance for the forgiveness of sins']]

Of course, the differences are patent enough. John required baptism of Israel. The church was to mediate forgiveness arising from repentance through Jesus' name to the nations. Yet, though mode and scope differ, the offer remains the same. (One could argue that the similarity in this instance is the more awkward feature.)

But the real distinction lies between the church's task as given by the Risen Lord and that of Jesus' self-proclaimed mission at Nazareth. Indeed,

---

18. All nine instances of πίστις [['faith']] also follow the pattern established for Mark and Matthew earlier. The eleven examples of πιστεύω [['to have faith']] conform to the general pattern, no matter what the source or setting. Never is Jesus himself explicitly the subject of faith. Furthermore, as in the other synoptists, "receiving" language characterizes the post-Easter relation to Jesus rather than "believing" or "following."

the ministry of John and the church seem closer to each other than that of the church and Jesus (at 4:18):

<u>κηρυχθῆναι</u> ἐν τῷ ὀνόματι αὐτοῦ μετανοίαν εἰς <u>ἄφεσιν</u> ἁμαρτιῶν πᾶσιν τοῖς
   ἔθνεσιν
[['that repentance and forgiveness of sins is to be proclaimed in his
   name to all nations']]
<u>κηρύξαι</u>   αἰχμαλώτοις   <u>ἄφεσιν</u>
[['to proclaim release to the captives']]

What makes these two statements so important for inspection is that both refer to the Messiah's (ἔχρισεν) and the church's charge to preach (κηρύσσειν); both are descriptions of a fundamental agenda; and both are functions of a Spirit-endowed ministry (see 24:48). Consequently, their disjunction becomes all the more impressive. Proclaiming release to captives has little or nothing to do in an obvious sense with announcing repentance that leads to forgiveness. So, when it comes to describing what lay at the heart of Jesus' and the church's mission, Luke refuses to justify the Christian blueprint by making it a carbon copy of Jesus' sense of calling.[19] Although at some [[82]] extra-textual level, continuity might well be identified, the point is that Luke refused to achieve it within the text.[20] Past and present, before and after retain their (sometimes awkward and painful) integrity.[21]

Further evidence of such restraint comes from two accounts of mission conducted by the Twelve (9:1–6, 10) and by the Seventy ([-two] 10:1–17), the latter unique to Luke. Jesus' instructions to both groups bear clear similarities in seven categories.[22] But each differs from those in chap. 24 along several notable lines. The subject preached is the Kingdom of God (9:2; 10:9, 11) rather than forgiveness of sins. In chap. 10, it is quite specifically the Kingdom's drawing near (ἤγγικεν [ἐφ' ὑμᾶς]).[23] The focus is theocentric. Whatever christology there is belongs to the "ambassadorial" type, whose

19. Such distinctions tend to counter the claim of J. Fitzmyer that the Lucan presentation of Jesus and his preaching "obviously reflects an early Christian understanding of the kerygma in which the herald is already being presented as the one heralded. Luke, in making use of this in the programmatic Nazareth synagogue scene, may be retrojecting back into the ministry and preaching of Jesus a developed understanding of him." See *Luke I–IX*, 153–54.

20. E. E. Ellis, in my view, overstates the point (with most commentators): "The post-resurrection mission is still the mission of Jesus (Ac. 1:1, 'began'; 9:4). In it the same message is proclaimed and the Spirit and the 'name' of Jesus still have the same function. Cf. 4:18; 10:21; Ac. 1:8; 3:16. . . ." See *The Gospel of Luke*, NCBC (Grand Rapids, MI, Eerdmans, 1974) 15. The "name" of Jesus and endowment with the Spirit are discussed below.

21. It may well be correct to say that Jesus' fellowship at table with sinners implies forgiveness; but that only proves the point. One must infer for the ministry what became only explicit later.

22. A summary of the event, the content of their preaching, the healing ministry, impediments to be avoided, establishing a "base of operation," responses to rejection, a report of their return.

23. Although occasionally the Kingdom of God is the subject of preaching in Acts, it is never that God's Rule has drawn near.

ultimate reference is God, not Jesus or his name: "Whoever hears you, hears me; and whoever ignores you [ἀθετεῖν], ignores me; but [ὁ δέ] the one ignoring me ignores him who sent me" (10:16). Finally, without denying that Luke anticipated the Gentile mission in the Seventy (a number, with Seventy-two, which stands for the nations of the world in Jewish reckoning),[24] it must be borne in mind that they extend *Jesus'* message and activity, confining their itinerary to those places where he would *subsequently* visit (10:1).

Somewhat less dramatic, but no less important, stands the related topic of the Lucan "soteriology." The cognates belonging to the vocabulary of salvation retain several distinctions among them. In the celebrations of Jesus' birth, salvation is theocentric and nationalistic. Thus, Mary rejoices in *God* her Savior (1:47), while angelic hosts declare to shepherds that a Savior has been born for all the people (of *God*, παντὶ τῷ λαῷ, 2:10). Earlier, Zechariah had praised God for providing salvation from David's line which includes national liberation from Israel's enemies (1:69, 71).[25] Gentiles are to be embraced, to be sure. Simeon blesses God for allowing him to see in Jesus salvation for all (2:30–32). This is the promise of the Old Testament (Isa 40:3–5) quoted in 3:6. But it is their *future,* post-Easter inclusion. Nothing on this order occurs in what follows.[26] Until eschatological fulfillment begins in earnest, John the Baptist will give knowledge of salvation through the forgiveness of sins (1:77). Although angels hail Jesus as Savior, no one in the narrative does. (Yet he brings *immediate* salvation to Zaccheus because he is a son of Abraham, 19:9.) Thus, while the prelude and postlude of the Third Gospel roughly correspond in outlook, the narrative in between differs both in point of view and idiom. Again, there need not be conflict [[83]] among them; but Luke has not constructed an obvious harmonization.[27] If it is to occur at all, it must be done by others and at another level of interpretation.

24. F. W. Beare, *The Earliest Records of Jesus* (New York, Abingdon, 1962) 156. Beare notes A. Farrer's observation that Luke found typology in Numbers where Moses chose Twelve to represent the Twelve Tribes (1:4–6) and Seventy of the Elders to share his responsibility (chap. 11).

25. E. Schweizer tends to "spiritualize" these statements. Regarding "salvation from our enemies" (v. 71), he says that "Luke probably has in mind temptations." He acknowledges that "[v. 74] The ultimate purpose of God's salvation presupposes deliverance from the enemy [v. 75] but is in fact undisturbed worship": *The Good News according to Luke* (Atlanta, John Knox, 1984) 43. Yet, the point is that such worship depends upon political liberation. This calls to mind God's demand of Pharaoh, "Let my son go so that he may serve me . . ." (Exod 4:23). Schweizer does acknowledge such a level or meaning but apparently ascribes it to a previous tradent, "a Jewish Christian" (p. 44).

26. H. Conzelmann, famous for his theory about Luke's periodizing the ministries of Jesus and the church, acknowledges this disparity: "The introductory chapters of the Gospel present a special problem. It is strange that the characteristic features they contain do not occur again either in the Gospel or in Acts." See *The Theology of St. Luke* (London, Faber, 1960) 172.

27. When these distinctions are not observed, then such overstatements become possible: "the infancy narrative sounds initially many of the motifs to be orchestrated later on in the Gospel and Acts. Many of the chords of the Lucan composition are first struck in it:

Before concluding this section on what must now be regarded as a much more complexly wrought Lucan soteriology, I shall include two related subjects. Besides the granting of forgiveness and the mediation of salvation by his presence, Jesus teaches the way to eternal life by applying what has already been established by Moses and recognized in Judaism.[28] Unlike Matthew and Mark, Luke does not report that Jesus taught that love for God and neighbor lay at the heart and head of Torah (22:35–40//12:28–33). Rather, to the lawyer's question about inheriting eternal life, he responds with another: "What does the Law say?" This prompts the νόμικος [['lawyer']] himself to join Deut 6:5 and Lev 18:5. Jesus then urges him to "do this and live" (10:25–28), just as Moses, speaking for God, had said (Lev 18:5). Jesus' only role here lies in lending his authoritative support to what had already been revealed. Nothing is made of the fact or the significance of his person or role.

The same may be claimed for righteousness. Already, Zechariah and Elizabeth have this standing before God (1:6), as does Joseph of Arimathea (23:50). The publican, by virtue of his acknowledgment of sin and appeal to the mercy of God, returns home justified (18:14). Again, the christological component in the process is entirely absent. That Jesus underscored and confirmed the tax collectors' attitude before God seems adequate for Luke. How then does Jesus fit in the proclamation of the Church? How is repentance leading to forgiveness to be preached?

In his name

Up to this point neither repentance, nor forgiveness, nor preaching of any kind has been done in the name of Jesus. The disciples have invoked it to subject the demons (10:17);[29] but neither their proclamation nor his ever has a contemporary christological referent of any sort. Of course, as in the case of Matthew and Mark, Jesus does teach the disciples about activities done in his name: receiving a child (9:48), the coming of impostors (21:8), and enduring opposition (vv. 12, 17). But these clearly point to the era of his absence introduced by the Easter event which, as chap. 24 shows, changes everything.

Striking here is the absence of any reference to the cross, even though the risen Jesus cites scripture predicting the Son of Man's suffering and death. Neither before nor after Easter do these pointers [[84]] to Calvary ever indicate what his death was to achieve. Nor is it ever described as *pro nobis* [['for us']]. The closest hint comes in Luke's account of the Last Supper which by its association with Passover implies deliverance and explicitly claims covenant

---

for instance, John as the precursor of Jesus, Jesus as the Savior, Messiah, and Lord." See Fitzmyer, *Luke I–IX*, 163. Yet little if anything of what these saints sing has to do with the life of Jesus as Luke recounts it. John the Baptist's query in Q (11:3//7:19–20) fits the situation exactly. Nothing that he knew, whether by scripture, the expectation of his parents and kin, or direct revelation, had prepared him for what Jesus was doing—or not doing.

28. *T. Iss.* 5:2, *T. Dan* 5:3.

29. Mark and Luke report the success of the "free-lance" exorcist using Jesus' name (9:38–40//9:49–50).

bonding (for many [= all] in Matthew and Mark, 26:28//14:24; for the disciples in Luke 22:20, *si vera lectio* [['if this is a true reading']]).

Could it be then, that repentance leading to forgiveness in his Name suggests that, for Luke, it is the entire career of Jesus (i.e., his history, past and present) which saves rather than a particular segment or moment of it?[30] Does Luke mean to say that what Jesus granted to Israel during his life now by virtue of his death and resurrection becomes a universal legacy?

   To all the nations

Jesus did not demand repentance from and offer forgiveness to Gentiles. This is an astonishing fact, though it and related data are nearly always overlooked in studies of the gospel for the Gentiles. Consequently, a more detailed analysis must be conducted among various sources.

   The Double and Triple Tradition.   One might have expected Luke to increase the number of contacts with non-Jews. Yet, this is not the case. He does not, for example, reproduce Jesus' exorcism of the Syrophoenician woman's daughter (15:21–28//7:24–30). Strangely, the Evangelist fails to mention as Mark 5:20 does that the former demoniac reported his cure by Jesus in the Decapolis, cities established on a hellenistic model. Instead, he simply announces it throughout the whole city (Luke 8:39). And the "backlash" to the event takes on larger proportions: "the entire multitude of the region of the Gerasenes" asks Jesus to leave (v. 37).

   When Luke relates the final passion prediction, his description of what Jesus is to suffer at the hands of the Gentiles is fuller than in the other synoptics (20:19//Mark 10:33–34//18:32). Nor does Luke soften Jesus' description about the power by which Gentiles rule (20:25//10:24//22:25). Unlike Matthew, he does not take the opportunity to name "the others" who will inherit the vineyard seized by murderous tenants as another "nation" (21:41–43//12:9//20:16). At 21:24, Luke alone aggravates the role of the Gentiles during the attack on Jerusalem: taking people into exile and trampling the Holy City during its prescribed occupation. How noteworthy, too, [[85]] is Luke's omission in the Olivet Discourse of witness-bearing or gospel proclamation before the nations and their rulers (10:18//13:10//21:12–13).

   At the crucifixion, while Matthew and Luke report the centurion's confession of Jesus as God's son (which may perhaps carry less christological weight if "Colwell's Rule" cannot be invoked), Luke has him declare that Jesus was δίκαιος [['righteous']] (22:54//15:39//23:47). This designation may, of

---

   30. Fitzmyer, *Luke I–IX*, 224, puts it this way: "He has, by all that he was and did, cancelled the debt of guilt incurred by their evil conduct." G. Caird has described the connection another way: "the death of Christ was only the inevitable outcome of the life he had lived. If at the end *he was reckoned with transgressors* (22:37), it was because he had always chosen to be numbered with them. This was the price of friendship with tax gatherers and sinners." See *Saint Luke* (Philadelphia, Westminster, 1963) 39. Seeing Jesus' entire life as redemptive has now become a "commonplace" view according to E. Richard in "Luke—writer, theologian, historian: research and orientation of the 1970's," *BTB* 13 (1983) 6.

course, carry its own christologieal freight; but it may also be saying something less; or at least the Gentile centurion is not being credited with a confession made rather frequently in Acts.[31]

Q. Luke retains the pericope relating Jesus' cure of the centurion (7:1–10) but takes special pains to describe the favor that he already enjoyed among the Jews (vv. 3–5) and the humility that prevented him from appealing to Jesus directly (vv. 6–7). Otherwise, the point about faith was the same: unexampled in Israel (v. 10) and not, strictly speaking, "in" Jesus. Also one might have expected Luke to omit the unfavorable comment about the Gentiles anxiously seeking material security (6:32//12:30) since he seems to have done so at 6:33 (//Matt 5:47). But this can hardly be called a tendency or pattern.

Given such a less-than-thoroughgoing redactional program, one cannot read Luke's version of the parable of the Great Supper as most critics tend to. On seeing the hall not filled by the needy from the city, the host commands his servants to complement their number with people from the "highways and hedges" (14:21–23). Yet, even if the city here refers to the Jerusalem of the Christian mission, outside still lies all of Judean and Samaritan territory (Acts 1:8) before one sets foot on "Galilee of the Gentiles" and beyond. Volume 2 of Luke's work should help to prevent such eisegesis. But even within the pericope itself, the distinction is being made among Jews themselves.[32]

L. In the examination above "salvation" had been anticipated by Simeon as enlightenment for the Gentiles (2:32). Indeed, one may also cite Luke's genealogy, whose range extends behind Abraham (the first Jew) to Adam, who was God's son (3:23–38). But the point could be as much a christological one: Jesus successfully resisting Satan's [[86]] temptation makes him God's *obedient* son. Be that as it may, nothing specific is made of the family tree per se.

One might be tempted to refer next to Jesus' inaugural sermon at Nazareth. To be sure, references to Gentiles are not part of the sermon proper, nor are they explicit. Only when the crowd illustrates the proverb about prophets being honored by others rather than their own does Jesus cite the experiences of Elijah and Elisha. The point, however, is extended. Because these men of God were not honored by their own people, they honored others: they channeled the power of God to a widow of Zerephath and Naaman the Syrian (4:25–27).

Although scholars routinely claim that Jesus' journey through Samaria is really a prefigurement of the church's subsequent Gentile mission there, Luke's treatment is rather mixed. The only thankful one of ten lepers cleansed is a Samaritan, also called a foreigner by Jesus (ἀλλογένης, 17:16–18). And a Samaritan becomes a Jew's savior, not vice versa (10:29–37). But

31. Modern students of *narrative* are more inclined to see the use of titles as being true to *character* than are redaction critics, who see them as true to the alleged *reader's* interests. See the helpful, but not comprehensive, study by J. M. Dawsey, "What's in a name? Characterization in Luke," *BTB* 16 (1986) 146. I mention Acts here only because of the tendency to claim parallel themes for the two volumes.

32. For a fuller treatment of this point, see my study, "Supper and Wedding," 8–9, 13–15.

earlier an entire village refuses to receive Jesus and his company (9:52–56). This is quite unlike the uniformly positive response of Acts 8. And, although apostolic confirmation suggests a certain reluctance or reserve about Samaritan conversions, this is certainly a long way from the disciples' earlier desire to call down heavenly fire upon the inhospitable villages (9:54).[33] Such a mentality will eventually be overcome as the gospel becomes launched from Jerusalem where they are to receive a divine gift.

> I will send the promise of my father upon you. (v. 49)

With this word, Luke implies that Jesus had earlier spoken of this event in these terms. Yet, such is not the case. In fact, the only vocabulary occurring beforehand is ἀποστέλλειν [['apostles']] and ἐπαγγελίαν [['announcers']]. Otherwise, it is John the Baptist who deflects messianic acclaim by predicting that the coming Stronger One will baptize the people in the Holy Spirit and fire (3:16), an expectation reported by Matthew and Mark, too (3:1//1:8).[34] Yet Luke does not make Jesus in the narrative reinforce either John's pre-Easter or his own post-Easter convictions.

Such restraint appears in a gospel which all recognize to be especially devoted to documenting the operation of the Spirit. Jesus in particular, conceived by the Spirit, is led and motivated by him, as the "L" material makes especially clear (1:35; 4:1, 14, 18; cf. 10:21 and Matt 11:25). However, that same "source" shows that others are said to be led and filled by the Holy Spirit: Elizabeth, Zechariah, John the Baptist, and Simeon (1:15, 41, 67; 2:25–27). Already, these choice servants share in the experience of God's revelatory Spirit. Yet, a day is coming when Jesus' followers will encounter him in another capacity.

> You will be empowered from on high.

If "promise of the Father" is an exceptional concept in Luke's gospel, then the promise of heavenly power is, too. Previously, Jesus had given them authority (ἐξουσία) over serpents and scorpions and even over the power (δύναμις) of the Enemy himself, enabling them to subject unclean spirits in his own name (10:17–20, L). Acts shows that such power was not retracted. But something else needed complementing. Just as a special act of the risen Jesus made the Scriptures' witness to him intelligible (v. 45), so now their own witness (v. 47) becomes empowered, as Acts 1:8 will bear out. Although the designation of Jesus' followers as μάρτυρες [['martyrs']] is exceptional in the gospel here, it will become standard in volume 2.

---

33. J. Jervell, although making a different point, notes the different treatment: "In Luke 9:51ff. the Samaritans reject Jesus because of his connections with Jerusalem." See *Luke and the People of God* (Minneapolis, Augsburg, 1972) 126.

34. Conzelmann, *Theology*, 179 n. 2 acknowledges that the two epochs of salvation distinguished by different manifestations and roles attributed to the Spirit.

With this promise, the logia of Jesus come to an end. Luke concludes his account thus: leading the disciples out towards Bethany, he lifted his hands in blessing.

> And he departed from them, and was being borne up into heaven. (v. 51)

Even if the second clause did not appear in the autograph, both the event of ascension and the means of referring to it are exceptional. (Διιστῆναι [['to withdraw']] occurs only once before [22:59], in a reference to the passing of time;[35] ἀναφέρειν [['to be carried up']] is found here alone.) Luke's reference to Jesus' ἀναλήμψις [['being taken up']] at 9:51 is unclear. Interpretations of this hapax oscillate between the ascension itself (see ἀνελήμφθη [['taken up']] in Acts 1:2) and all of those moments (τὰς ἡμέρας) belonging to his ἔξοδός [['exodus']] (9:31).[36] There is no stock terminology in Luke[37] and certainly little if any prior notice of such an occurrence.

> And they worshiped him. . . . (v. 52)

The Third Evangelist is perhaps the most careful of the synoptists in restricting the worship of Jesus to this point. Not even the sense of προσκυνεῖν as "obeisance/reverence" precedes the resurrection. Luke 4:7–8 relates Jesus' insistence that the worship desired by Satan belongs to *God alone*. And fitting though the worship of Jesus is from here on, the disciples' Temple service is conducted as *divine* liturgy. [[88]]

> Praising God (v. 53)[38]

Whether or not the "non-interpolations" of vv. 50b–53 are genuine, they display Lucan sensibilities seen elsewhere. Perhaps this datum from internal evidence lends weight to the massive external evidence in favor of the longer readings.[39]

The Prologue

Besides joining the other synoptists in distinguishing between the idioms of pre- and post-resurrection eras, Luke goes a step farther. Unlike them, he betrays yet a third—another post-Easter "dialect." It occurs in the much-examined

---

35. A careless reading of Marshall, *Luke*, 909 might lead one to infer that διιστῆναι [['go away']] is the means by which "Luke often describes the departure of supernatural visitors." The conclusion could be drawn that Jesus' divinity is suggested by the use here of a quasi-technical term.

36. Fitzmyer, *Luke I–IX*, 827–28.

37. In Acts 1:9–11 the range of vocabulary also includes ἐπήρθη [['he was lifted up']], ὑπέλαβεν [['(a cloud) took (him)']], and πορευομένου [['while he was going']].

38. The pattern reminds one of Phil 2:11 where the confession of Jesus as "Lord" is to the glory of *God the Father*.

39. B. M. Metzger, *A Textual Commentary on the Greek New Testament*, 3rd edn (New York, United Bible Societies, 1971) 189–91 for a full discussion of the variants.

Prologue (1:1–4) where the Evangelist clearly states his purpose in writing. In thus revealing his intent, Luke resembles the author of the Fourth Gospel at 20:30–31. But whereas John's statement corresponds in its essential idiom with that of the preceding narrative . . . , Luke's does not. It stands apart from what follows in vocabulary and theme. A moment's glance at the two passages set side-by-side discloses striking similarities between eleven categories in each.

Luke 1:1–4	John 20:30–31
(a) διήγησις [['orderly account']]	(a) τῷ βιβλίῳ [['(in) the book']]
(b) τῶν πληροφορημένων [['that have been fulfilled']]	(b) πολλὰ . . . ἐποίησεν Ἰησοῦς [['many . . . Jesus did']]
(c) πραγμάτων [['events']]	(c) σημεῖα [['signs']]
(d) αὐτόπται [['eyewitnesses']]	(d) ἐνώπιον [['in the presence of']]
(e) ὑπηρέται[40] [['servants']]	(e) τῶν μαθητῶν [['the disciples']]
(f) γράψαι [['to write']]	(f) γέγραπται [['are written']]
(g) ἵνα [['in order that']]	(g) ἵνα [['in order that']]
(h) ἐπιγνῷς [['you may know']]	(h) πιστεύ [σ] ητε [['you may believe']]
(i) περὶ ὧν λόγων [['concerning the things']]	(i) ὅτι Ἰησοῦς ἐστιν ὁ Χριστὸς ὁ Υἱὸς τοῦ Θεοῦ [['that Jesus is the Christ the Son of God']]
(j) κατηχήθῆς [['you have been instructed']]	(j) ἔχητε [['you might have']]
(k) ἀσφάλειαν [['truth']]	(k) ζωήν [['life']]

But the differences within the Third Gospel are even more evident. Nothing that Luke wants to do for Theophilus corresponds to what Jesus sought to accomplish with his disciples *before* Easter. At this level, there is no evidence to support the dominant redaction-critical claim. Nor do the Evangelist's efforts on Theophilus' behalf mirror anything that Jesus said to his disciples *after* the resurrection. Again, the classical assertion of redaction critics is vitiated when examined from this perspective. The language of the Prologue has lent [[89]] nothing to the *patois* of those eras; nor have they contributed to the idiom of the Prologue.[41]

---

40. It is not necessary to settle the debate as to whether αὐτόπται [['eyewitnesses']] and ὑπρέται [['servants (of the word)']] are synonyms or references to separate groups. The main point is that the former term shares with ἐνώποιν [['presence']] in John a root that pertains to vision: -ωπ- and -οπ.- Both refer to persons with firsthand acquaintance.

41. Although they cannot be part of the main argument, the linguistic phenomena of Acts corroborate this contention. Some of the Prologue's language occurs in volume 2. Of Apollos, Luke says that "he had been instructed [κατηχηένος] in the way of the Lord and with zealous spirit spoke and taught accurately [ἀκριβῶς] the things concerning Jesus, although he knew only John's baptism" (18:25). It was up to Prisca and Aquila to set forth the way of God more accurately (ἀκριβέστερον, v. 26). (Might the description of Apollos provide clues about Theophilus, both in what each possessed and lacked?) Felix himself wanted more precise knowledge about the Way (24:22). Πράγμα [['deeds']] shows up only here and at Acts 5:4 (in the singular). Ἐπιγινώσκω [['to know']] will appear six more times in the gospel,

Conclusions about Luke's διήγησις [['orderly account']]

Now with the analysis of Luke complete, I must reiterate the point that at no instance has my aim been to vindicate him as an historian. Instead, the goal has been to study the Evangelist's narrative art. I say "narrative" because there exist estimates of his work as *art* which are much too general and exclusive. For example, N. Q. King pits art against history in a treatment of the Gentile mission as if these were the only possible categories, and antithetical ones at that.

> Clearly St. Luke was universalistic in his outlook in that he envisaged the Gospel's being carried to the non-Jews. But in his gospel, with consummate skill, he does not obtrude this. Rather, there is a partial κρύψις of his universalism while he is writing the Gospel. He indicates that the preaching to the gentiles is to come after the Jews have done their worst to the Messiah and he has triumphed in the power of God. One would like to suggest that he is too good an historian to commit the anachronism of inserting a fully fledged gentile mission into the Lord's own ministry, but of course, that is thinking in the categories of a modern historian. Rather, one may say it is the sure touch of an artistic genius. The theme which he played over earlier and had repeated now and then, has to wait until the second part of the work (that is, Acts) for its crescendo.[42]

One can concur, for the most part. But why bring in "the modern historian" (as if there were not historians of various "schools") at all? Luke at least ought to be credited with sensitivity to the historical, something lacking in medieval art that represents scenes from the gospels in the costume and architecture of the painter's age. (Are some redaction critics accusing him of a literary version of this?) And why make the avoidance of anachronism a virtue of modern historiography? The ancient Greek tradition held to the ideal, whatever the lapses in practice.

John Drury makes the point more adequately:

> He simply knows that Jesus' ministry was at a particular time; not in his own time or the time of the Old Testament, but the link between them. It was yesterday—not today, or the [[90]] day before yesterday. He is, for example at pains to keep the gentiles off stage in his gospel. Mark's Syrophoenician woman disappears and Matthew's centurion is kept off the scene by hectic stage management. For Luke knew that the mission of the

---

all in the narrator's comments but none with the sense of deepening previous understanding (1:22; 5:22; 7:37; 23:7; 24:16, 31). The same is true of thirteen instances in Acts, although 24:8, 11 and 25:10 belong to the narrative. Ἀσφάλεια [['certain, certainty']] and its cognates will surface again only in Acts three times with γινώσκω [['to know']] (2:36; 21:34; 22:30) and once with γράφω [['to write']] (25:26, in Festus' conundrum of what to say to Caesar about Paul).

42. N. Q. King, "The 'Universalism' of the Third Gospel," in *SE*, ed. K. Aland, F. L. Cross, J. Daniélou, H. Riesenfeld, and W. C. van Unnik, TU 73/18 (Berlin, Akademie-Verlag, 1959) 204–5.

gentiles was later and avoids the anachronism. This finer sense of time distinguishes Luke.[43]

My contentions go further (without begging the question of historicity). Once the narrative is analyzed on several fronts (so as to avoid all suspicion of idiosyncrasy), the conclusion must follow that Luke, perhaps more than Matthew and Mark, maintained an almost severe standard in portraying Jesus' past. Neither the Jewishness of the infancy narratives nor the obviously Christian character of chap. 24, nor the narrator's arrangement and adaptation of what lies between has intruded decisively upon the Jesus story. Of course there is a Lucan redaction. But detection of its character and scope must take into account the clear evidence that he resisted the pervasive encroachment of post-Easter convictions within the story of "all that Jesus began to do and teach."[44] As a result there now exist data to describe more adequately the nature of that διήγησις [['orderly account']] which the Evangelist ordered for the most excellent Theophilus (1:1–4).[45]

43. J. Drury, *Tradition and Design in Luke's Gospel* (Atlanta, John Knox, 1977) 13. The author goes on to say, "He has the historian's nose. Above all he shows the need of a community for strong, historical roots, how a talented writer went about providing them, and the problems which such an achievement solves and raises."

44. In treating the phases of Luke's salvation-historical schema, Fitzmyer acknowledges the Evangelist's dividing it into periods that nonetheless maintain a high level of continuity: "What Jesus proclaimed about himself and the kingdom is now continued in the apostolic kerygma and in Luke's own kerygma." See *Luke I–IX*, 181–87, esp. 186. While acknowledging the temporal demarcation, Fitzmyer takes no notice of the kind of ideological and terminological distinctives that I have identified between the phases of Jesus' career and Luke's narrating of them.

45. J. M. Dawsey, *The Lukan Voice. Confusion and Irony in the Gospel of Luke* (Atlanta, Mercer, 1986) applies well-known studies of Lucan language to categories commonly employed by literary critics. Supplementing them with his own analyses, he claims to be able to distinguish the language and style of speech assigned to Jesus, various characters, and the Narrator himself, who is yet different from Luke the Author/Evangelist (pp. 157–83, 13–16). Dawsey concludes that Luke thereby created a narrative full of irony wherein the narrator's exalted prose (e.g., in the Prologue) and glorified *christ*ology contrast sharply with the peasant dialect and reversal *theo*logy of the earthly Jesus (pp. 143–56). Although much of Dawsey's work is congenial to mine, I feel that his case could have been made stronger by a more comprehensive coverage of theologically significant terms. Furthermore, I do not believe that the evidence marshaled necessarily leads to his ironic reading of the Third Gospel.

Jesus the Founder of Christianity

[[174]] We have already noted the irony that for most of its existence, the "quest of the historical Jesus" was not historical enough in that it attempted to distance Jesus, by one means or another, from his historical context as a Jew. As many of the rationalists, savaged by Strauss, had attempted to "save" the miracle-working Jesus by allowing a little bit of miracle, so most of the Liberals had attempted to "save" the real Jesus by "inoculating" the quest with a little bit of history. At the same time, the other strand in "life of Jesus" research, from Reimarus to the neo-Liberals, has attempted to "save" Jesus from Christian dogma by distancing him from the movement which followed his death and which became Christianity. In the most common scenario, it was Paul who counts (or is to be blamed!) as the real founder of Christianity. This has been one of the real peculiarities of the quest, that it has attempted to find a Jesus who was neither a Jew nor founder of Christianity, or who was contingently one but not the other. But in seeking to avoid the Christianized Jesus as well as the Jewish Jesus, all that remained, all that could remain, was the idiosyncratic Jesus, who could hardly be other than an enigma to Jew and Christian alike, and who reflected little more than the quester's own idiosyncrasies.

In fact, the obvious way forward is simply to reverse the logic. If the starting assumption of a fair degree of continuity between Jesus and his native religion has a priori persuasiveness, then it can hardly make less sense to assume a fair degree of continuity between Jesus and what followed. The initial considerations here are straightforward.

Reprinted, with permission, from J. D. G. Dunn, *Jesus Remembered* (Christianity in the Making 1; Grand Rapids, Michigan: Eerdmans, 2003) 174–86, 238–54. Most footnotes have been omitted.

The Sociological Logic

Several indicators have long been familiar. For one thing, it has long been recognized that the historian needs to envisage a Jesus who is "big" enough to explain the beginnings of Christianity. For another, the first followers of Jesus were [[175]] known as "Nazarenes" (Acts 24:5), which can be explained only by the fact that they saw themselves and were seen as followers of "Jesus the Nazarene"; and then as "Christians" (Acts 11:26), which again must be because they were known to be followers of the one they called the "Christ." Moreover, Jesus is explicitly referred to once or twice in the early tradition as the "foundation" (*themelion*), which Paul laid (including Jesus tradition?), and on which the Corinthians were to build their discipleship (1 Cor 3:10–14); or as the "corner stone" (*akrogōniaios*) which began the building and established its orientation (Eph 2:20; 1 Pet 2:6).

Sociological reflection on what this self-identification on the part of the Christians would have involved yields further fruit. Here, after all, were small house groups who designated themselves by reference to Jesus the Christ, or Christ Jesus. Sociology and social anthropology teach us that such groups would almost certainly have required a foundation story (or stories) to explain, to themselves as well as to others, why they had formed distinct social groupings, why they were designated as "Nazarenes" and "Christians." It is hardly likely that a bare kerygmatic formula like 1 Cor 15:3–8 would have provided sufficient material for self-identification. Even the initiatory myths of the mystery cults told more elaborate stories. Stories of such diverse figures as Jeremiah and Diogenes were preserved by their disciples as part of the legitimation for their own commitment. And if Moses is to be regarded as the nearest equivalent (as founder of the religion of Israel), then we need simply recall that Exodus to Deuteronomy are framed and interspersed by the story of Moses' life. Of course, counter-examples can be named: we know very little of Qumran's Teacher of Righteousness. On the other hand, the Teacher of Righteousness never gave his [[176]] name to the movement he initiated, whereas the first Christians could explain themselves only by referenced to him whom they called "(the) Christ." But if the Gospels tell us anything they surely tell us that the first Christians felt the need to explain themselves by telling stories about Jesus, what he said and what he did.

Teachers and Tradition

This a priori logic is supported by the evidence that the passing on of *tradition* was part of church founding from the first. Paul was careful to refer his churches back to such foundation traditions on several occasions; the evidence is hardly to be explained as references solely to kerygmatic or confessional formulae. Rather, we find that it includes community tradition (1 Cor 11:2, 23), teaching on how the new converts should live (e.g., Phil 4:9; 1 Thess 4:1; 2 Thess 3:6), and traditions of Jesus in accordance with which they should conduct their lives (Col 2:6–7; *kata Christon* [['according to Christ']] in 2:8).

If further confirmation is needed, it is provided by the prominence of *teachers* within the earliest Christian churches. Teachers, indeed, seem to have been the first regularly paid ministry within the earliest Christian movement (Gal 6:6; *Did.*13:2). Why teachers? Why else than to serve as the congregation's repository of oral tradition? What else would Christian teachers teach? A Christian interpretation of the Scriptures, no doubt. But also, we can surely safely assume, the traditions which distinguished house churches from local house synagogues or other religious, trade, or burial societies.

We should pause at this point to recall just how crucial teachers were to ancient communities. All who read these pages will have been bred to a society [[177]] long accustomed to being able to rely on textbooks, encyclopaedias, and other reference works. But an ancient oral society had few if any such resources and had to rely instead on individuals whose role in their community was to function as what Jan Vansina describes as "a walking reference library."

Nor should it be forgotten that, at least according to the tradition, Jesus himself was regarded as a 'teacher' (*didaskalos*), and was so regarded by his disciples. Jesus may even have regarded himself as such (Matt 10:24–25/Luke 6:40). That the disciples of Jesus are consistently called 'disciples', that is 'those taught, learners' (Hebrew *talmidim*; Greek *mathētai*), should also be included. The relation between Jesus and his disciples was remembered as one between teacher and taught, with the implication that, as such, the disciples understood themselves to be committed to remember their teacher's teaching.

Witnessing and Remembering

Two important motifs in the NT also confirm the importance for the first Christians of retelling the story of Jesus and of taking steps actively to recall what Jesus said and did.

One is the motif of "*bearing witness.*" The motif is particularly prominent in Acts and John. In Acts it is stressed that the role of the first disciples (or apostles in particular) was to be 'witnesses' (*martyres*) of Jesus (1:8). Particularly in mind were the events of Jesus' crucifixion and resurrection (2:32; 3:15; 5:32; 10:41; 13:31). But it is clear from 1:22 and 10:37–39 that Luke understood the witnessing to include Jesus' ministry "beginning from the baptism of John." Paul preeminently is presented as a "witness" of Jesus (22:15, 18; 23:11; 26:16). In John's Gospel the importance of witness-bearing to Jesus is equally stressed. [[178]] John the Baptist is the model witness (John 1:7–8, 15, 19, 32, 34; 3:26, 28; 5:32) but also the woman at the well (4:39) and the crowd (12:17). The immediate disciples have a special responsibility to bear witness (*martyreō*) to Jesus, assisted by the Spirit (15:26–27), a responsibility which the Evangelist was deemed to be carrying out by means of his Gospel (19:35; 21:24).

The motif runs over into the Johannine epistles (1 John 1:2; 4:14), where it is strengthened by two complementary motifs. One is the 'from the beginning' (*ap' archēs*) theme: what is borne witness to is "that which was from the beginning" (1:1), what the witnesses heard "from the beginning" (2:24), particularly the command to love one another (2:7; 3:11; 2 John 5–6); in John 15:26–27 it is made clear that "from the beginning" embraces the whole of the original disciples' time with Jesus (as with Acts 1:22). Luke had the same concern when he promised to narrate what had been "delivered to us by those who from the beginning were eyewitnesses and ministers of the word" (Luke 1:1–2; cf. Mark 1:1).

The other complementary theme emphasizes the importance of a continuity of "hearing" from first disciples to converts, and of the converts both retaining what they had "heard" and living in accord with it—again not only in the Johannine epistles, but also in Heb 2:1, 3 and in the later Paulines. All this indicates a strong sense within first-century Christianity of the need to ensure a continuity of tradition from first witnesses to subsequent disciples and of a life lived in consistency with that tradition.

More striking still is the motif of *"remembering,"* also important for identity formation. Already Paul stresses the importance of his converts remembering him and the "traditions" which he taught them (1 Cor 11:2; 2 Thess 2:5). And close to the heart of the Lord's Supper tradition which Paul passed on was the exhortation to remember Christ—'Do this in remembrance of me' (*eis tēn emēn anamnēsin*) (1 Cor 11:24–25; Luke 22:19)—by no means a merely cognitive act of recollection. 2 Timothy retains the motif with reference to well-established [[179]] traditions (2:8, 14), the first (2:8) echoing the (presumably well-known) formula with which Paul reassured the Roman believers regarding his own gospel (Rom 1:3–4). The importance of post-Easter believers remembering Jesus' words is a repeated theme in Luke–Acts and John; the equivalence of John 14:26 and 15:27 indicates that "remembering all I have said to you," and "witnesses with me from the beginning," are two sides of the same coin. 2 Peter confirms that remembering the teaching first given was a central concern in early Christianity (1:15; 3:2); similarly Rev 3:3. *1 Clement* uses the phrase "remember(ing) the words of the Lord Jesus" to introduce a brief catena of Jesus' sayings on two occasions (13:1–2; 46:7–8), as does Polycarp with a similar introductory formula, "remembering what the Lord taught when he said" (*Phil.* 2.3). Here we should also simply note the famous Papias tradition, which repeatedly emphasises the importance of "remembering" in the transmission of the earliest traditions stemming from the first disciples (Eusebius, *HE* 3.39.3–4, 15; 6.14.6), and Justin's concern to "bring to remembrance" teachings of Jesus (*Dial.* 18.1; *1 Apol.* 14.4).

Cameron argues that "the formulaic employment of this term ('remembering') to introduce collections of sayings of Jesus is a practice which began with the relatively free production of sayings traditions. . . ."[1] And it is certainly true that the motif includes some freedom in the transmission of the sayings in view. But the idea of remembering Jesus tradition is as early as our earliest references to such tradition (Paul). And it is notable that John, de-

---

1. R. Cameron, *Sayings Traditions in the Apocryphon of James* (Philadelphia: Fortress, 1984) chap. 3.

spite his freedom in producing dialogues of Jesus, seems for the most part to have restricted the remembering motif to sayings which have clear Synoptic parallels, that is, which were well rooted in Jesus tradition. It is more likely, then, that the use of the motif in the [[180]] *Apocryphon of James* (Cameron's main focus) was an attempt to manipulate a well-established and deeply rooted concern (to remember Jesus' teaching) by using it to commend a sayings tradition laced with "secret" (Gnostic) elements).

In short, the witnessing and remembering motifs strengthen the impression that more or less from the first those who established new churches would have taken care to provide and build a foundation of Jesus tradition. Particularly important for Gentiles taking on a wholly new life-style and social identity would be guidelines and models for the different character of conduct now expected from them. Such guidelines and models were evidently provided by a solid basis of Jesus tradition which they were expected to remember, to take in and live out.

Apostolic Custodians

The idea of the "apostles" as themselves the foundation of the church, or of the new Jerusalem, appears already in Eph 2:20 and Rev 21:14. More striking is the fact that a clear emphasis of the early chapters of Acts is the role of the apostles as ensuring continuity between what Jesus had taught and the expanding mission of the movement reinvigorated afresh at Pentecost. The implication of the opening words is that Acts is a continuation of "all that Jesus began to do and teach" as recorded in "the first part of his work," the Gospel of Luke (Acts 1:1). The instruction given to the apostles (1:2), the implication continues, had just the same continuity in view. Hence, when the traitor Judas is replaced by a new twelfth apostle, the criterion for his election is that he should have been one of their number throughout the ministry of Jesus, "beginning from the baptism of John" (1:21–22). Hence also the emphasis in 2:42, where the first mark of the new post-Pentecost community is its continuation in and firm attachment to (*proskartereō*) "the teaching of the apostles."

Such an emphasis might be regarded as a late perspective, when, arguably, continuity questions would have become (more) important. But there are indications that such continuity was seen as important from the first. These indications focus on the importance of Peter, James, and John to which our texts testify. They were evidently reckoned as the first men among the leaders of the initial Jerusalem community (Acts 1:13)—Peter certainly (1:15; 2:14; 5:1–10, 15, 29), [[181]] with John as his faithful shadow (3:1–11; 4:13, 19; 8:14), and James by implication (12:2). Fortunately for any concerned at such over-dependence on Acts, Paul's testimony confirms that a Jerusalem triumvirate (with James the brother of Jesus replacing James the executed brother of John) were generally accounted "pillars" (Gal 2:9). The imagery clearly implies that already, within twenty years of the beginnings of the new movement, these three were seen as strong supports on which the new community (temple?) was being built. This correlates well with the remembrance of the Jesus tradition that Peter and the brothers Zebedee had been closest to Jesus and thus were accounted principal witnesses to and custodians of Jesus' heritage.

Paul's concept of apostleship is somewhat different from Luke's. But it coheres to the extent that Paul regarded his apostolic role to consist particularly in founding churches (Rom 15:20; 1 Cor 3:10; 9:1–2). And, as we have seen, a fundamental part of that role was to pass on foundation tradition (above, pp. 168–169).

How the Jesus Tradition Was Used

The circumstantial and cumulative evidence cited above is not usually given the weight I am placing upon it, because Paul in particular seems to show so little interest in the ministry of Jesus and so little knowledge of Jesus tradition. We cannot assume that he ever encountered Jesus personally or had been in Jerusalem during the time of Jesus' mission. On the other hand, Paul would surely have used the two weeks spent in Peter's company (three years after his conversion) to fill out his knowledge of Jesus and of the traditions of Jesus' mission and teaching from Jesus' leading disciple (Gal 1:18). Nevertheless, the fact remains that Paul cites Jesus explicitly on only three occasions, all curiously in 1 Corinthians (7:10–11; 9:14; 11:23–25), though he also implies that had he known Jesus tradition relevant to other issues of community discipline he would [[182]] have cited it (1 Cor 7:25; 14:37). At the same time, there are various echoes of Synoptic tradition in Paul's letters, but none which he refers explicitly to Jesus; nor does he cite Jesus' authority to give the teaching more weight.

Does this evidence suggest Paul's own lack of interest in "remembering" what Jesus said and that it was Jesus who said it? Those who argue for an affirmative answer seem to forget that the pattern we find in Paul's letters is repeated elsewhere within earliest Christianity, particularly in the letters of James and 1 Peter. [[183]] Only occasionally is Jesus cited as the authority for the sayings quoted. Usually the teaching which echoes the Jesus tradition is simply part of more extensive paraenesis, without explicit attribution to Jesus.

What are we to make of this? Given that James and 1 Peter probably take us into the second generation of Christianity, when the Synoptic tradition and the Synoptic Gospels themselves would be becoming known, it is very unlikely that in every case the authors were unaware that the teaching originated with Jesus. More plausible is the suggestion I have made elsewhere, that we see in these data one of the ways the Jesus tradition was remembered and used. It is generally recognized that when groups become established over a lengthy period they develop in effect their own identity- and boundary-forming language, that is, at the very least, the use of abbreviations, a kind of shorthand and code words which help bond them as a group and distinguish insiders from outsiders (who do not know the language). The whole point is that in in-group dialogue such inferences are *not* explained; on the contrary, it is the recognition of the code word or allusion which gives the insider-language its bonding effect; to unpack the reference or allusion (for a stranger) in effect breaks the bond and lets the outsider into the group's inner world. My suggestion, then, is that the Jesus tradition formed such an insider's language among the earliest Christian communities; Paul's use of it in Romans (to a church he had never visited) implies his confidence that this language was a language common to all Christian churches, given by the founding apostle when he/she passed on the Jesus tradition to the new foundation (pp. 168–171 above). In terms of the argument to be developed [[184]] below, we have to assume a wider knowledge of the Jesus story among the recipients of Paul's letters, which his auditors would be able to draw upon to bridge the "gaps of indeterminacy" in his letters.

In short, the fact that almost all the references to Jesus tradition in the writings of earliest Christianity are in the form of allusion and echo should be taken to confirm (1) that such letters were not regarded as the medium of initial instruction on Jesus tradition to new churches, and (2) that churches could be assumed to have a relatively extensive knowledge of Jesus tradition, presumably passed on to them when they were first established.

The Gospels as Biographies

Bultmann led questers up another false trail by his strong assertion that "There is no historical-biographical interest in the Gospels."[2] The influence of this view, that the Gospels are not biographies of Jesus, persists to the present day. However, it is too little recalled that on this point Bultmann was reacting against the Liberal questers' confidence that they could penetrate back into Jesus' self-consciousness and could trace the development of his self-understanding as Messiah (messianic self-consciousness). Kähler had already responded to the Liberal questers by observing that the real sources for such attempts were the questers' own imaginations, an unfortunate extension of the historical principle [[185]] of analogy (§6.3c). The point was, as Kähler makes clear, that the original questers were attempting to write biographies on the model of the nineteenth-century biography, with its interest in the personal life and development of the biographical subject.[3] So what Bultmann was actually decrying was the attempt to write a *modern* biography of Jesus.

Since the 1970s, however, the question of the Gospels' genre has come under increasingly close scrutiny, and it has become much clearer that the Gospels are in fact very similar in type to *ancient* biographies (Greek *bioi*; Latin *vitae*). That is, their interest was not the modern one of analysing the subject's inner life and tracing how an individual's character developed over time. Rather, the ancient view was that character was fixed and unchanging; and the biographer's concern was to portray the chosen subject's character by narrating his words and deeds. Which is just what we find in the Synoptic (indeed all the canonical) Gospels, though not, it should be noted, in the other

2. R. Bultmann, *History of the Synoptic Tradition* (Oxford: Blackwell, 1963) 372.
3. M. Kähler, *So-Called Historical Jesus and the Historic Biblical Christ* (Philadelphia: Fortress, 1964) 55, 63.

Gospels now frequently drawn into the neo-Liberal quest. Moreover, it is clear that common purposes of ancient *bioi* were to provide examples for their readers to emulate, to give information about their subject, to preserve his memory, and to defend and promote his reputation. Here again the Gospels fit the broad genre remarkably well. Of course, it remains true that the Gospels were never simply biographical; they were propaganda; they were kerygma. But then neither were ancient biographies wholly dispassionate and objective (any more than modern biographies). In other words, the overlap between Gospel and ancient biography remains substantial and significant.

In short, the genre itself tells us at once that there was a considerable historical interest in the formulating, retelling, and collecting into Gospel format of the material which now comprises the Synoptic Gospels. This should hardly [[186]] surprise us. As Richard Burridge points out: "biography is a type of writing which occurs naturally among groups of people who have formed around a certain charismatic teacher or leader, seeking to follow after him." And later on he quotes Momigliano's comment that "The educated man of the Hellenistic world was curious about the lives of famous people."[4] Which brings us back more or less to where we started (*Jesus Remembered*, §6.2).

To sum up, there is substantial circumstantial evidence on two points. First, that the earliest churches would have wanted to remember and actually did remember and refer to Jesus tradition, provided for them as foundational tradition by their founding apostle(s). And second, that the Gospels attest to a lively interest among the first Christians in knowing about Jesus, in preserving, promoting, and defending the memory of his mission and in learning from his example.

. . . .

Oral Transmission

[[238]] In the light of the above we can begin to sketch in the likely process of traditioning in the case of the Jesus tradition. The fact that it coheres so well with the "in principle" sketch of [[*Jesus Remembered*]] §6.5 and a priori considerations of §§8.1–2 [[partially reprinted above, pp. 167–174]] is significant.

In the Beginning

[[239]] In the beginning, already during Jesus' own ministry, as soon as disciples began to gather round him, we can envisage initial impressions and memories being shared among the group. "Do you remember what he did/ said when he . . . ?" must have been a question often asked as the embryonic community began to feel and express its distinctiveness. No doubt in similar ways their village communities had celebrated their identity and history in

---

4. R. A. Burridge, *What Are the Gospels? A Comparison with Graeco-Roman Biography* (SNTMS 70; Cambridge: Cambridge University Press, 1992) 80–81, 150–51.

regular, even nightly gatherings. And as soon as the disciples of Jesus began to perceive themselves as (a) distinctive group(s) we may assume that the same impulse characteristic of oral and village culture would have asserted itself. As Jesus' immediate group moved around Galilee, encountering potential and then resident groups of disciples or sympathisers in various villages, the natural impulse would be the same. We can assume, of course, that Jesus was giving fresh teaching (as well as repeat teaching) all the while. But in more reflective gatherings, or when Jesus was absent, the impulse to tell again what had made the greatest impact on them would presumably reassert itself.

Three features of this initial stage of the process are worth noting. First, if Bailey's anecdotal accounts bring us closer than any other to the oral culture of Galilee in the second quarter of the first century C.E., then we may assume that the traditioning process *began* with the initiating word and/or act of Jesus.[5] That is to say, the impact made by Jesus would not be something which was only put into traditional form (days, months, or years) later. The impact would *include* the formation of the tradition to recall what had made that impact. In making its impact the impacting word or event *became* the tradition of that word or event. The stimulus of some word/story, the excitement (wonder, surprise) of some event would be expressed in the initial shared reaction; the structure, the identifying elements and the key words (core or climax) would be articulated in oral form in [[240]] the immediate recognition of the significance of what had been said or happened. Thus established more or less immediately, these features would then be the constants, the stable themes which successive retellings could elaborate and round which different performances could build their variations, as judged appropriate in the different circumstances. Subsequently we may imagine a group of disciples meeting and requesting, for example, to hear again about the centurion of Capernaum, or about the widow and the treasury, or about the brother who sins. In response to which a senior disciple would tell again the appropriate story or teaching in whatever variant words and detail he or she judged appropriate for the occasion, with sufficient corporate memory ready to protest if one of the key elements was missed out or varied too much. All this is wholly consistent with the character of the data reviewed above.

It also follows, second, that those accustomed to the prevalent individualism of contemporary culture (and faith) need to make a conscious effort to appreciate that the impact made by Jesus in the beginning was not a series of disparate reactions of independent individuals. Were that so we might well wonder how any commonality of tradition could emerge as individuals began to share their memories, perhaps only after a lengthy period. Postmodern pluralism would have been rampant from the first! But tradition-forming is a *communal* process, [[241]] not least because such tradition is often constitutive of the community as community. As it was a shared experience of the impact

---

5. See K. E. Bailey, *Poet and Peasant: A Literary-Cultural Approach to the Parables in Luke* (Grand Rapids: Eerdmans, 1976); idem, *Through Peasant Eyes* (Grand Rapids: Eerdmans, 1980).

made by Jesus which first drew individuals into discipleship, so it was the formulation of these impacts in shared words which no doubt helped bond
them together as a community of disciples. "Already the pre-Easter circle of
disciples was a 'confessing community' (*Bekenntnisgemeinschaft*) of committed
disciples (*nachfolgenden Jüngern*), who confessed Jesus as the final revealer and
interpreter of the word of God."[6]

At the same time, the points made in [[*Jesus Remembered*]] §6.5 should not
be forgotten. The character of the tradition as shared memory means that in
many instances we do not know precisely what it was that Jesus did or said.
What we have in the Jesus tradition is the consistent and coherent features of
the shared impact made by his deeds and words, not the objective deeds
and words of Jesus as such. What we have are examples of oral retelling of
that shared tradition, retellings which evince the flexibility and elaboration of
oral performances. There is surely a Jesus who made such impact, the remembered Jesus, but not an original pure form, not a single original impact to
which the historian has to try to reach [[242]] back in each case. The remembered Jesus may be a synthesis of the several impacts made on and disciple responses made by Jesus' earliest witnesses, but the synthesis was already firm
in the first flowering of the tradition.

Third, it follows also and is perhaps worth repeating that the traditioning
process should not be conceived of as initially casual and only taken seriously
by the first disciples in the post-Easter situation. As just implied, community
formation was already at an embryonic stage from the first call of Jesus' immediate circle of disciples; "formative tradition" would have had an indispensable part in that process. To the extent that the shared impact of Jesus,
the shared disciple-response, bonded into groups of disciples or adherents
those thus responsive to Jesus' mission, to that extent the dynamics of group
formation would be operative. In that process it is scarcely conceivable that
the shared memories of what Jesus had said and done (already "Jesus tradition"!) did not play an important part, both in constituting the groups' identity (what other distinguishing features had they?), and in outlining the
boundaries which marked them off as groups (however informal) from their
fellow Jews (here, no doubt, the pronouncement and controversy stories had
an early, even pre-Easter role; why not?).

Nor should we forget the continuing role of eyewitness tradents, of those
recognized [[243]] from the first as apostles or otherwise authoritative bearers
of the Jesus tradition (see p. 171 above). Such indications as there are from
the pre-Pauline and early Pauline period suggest already fairly extensive out-
reach by such figures, both establishing and linking new churches, and a general concern to ensure that a foundation of authoritative tradition was well
laid in each case. In focusing particular attention on the communal character
of the early traditioning process we should not discount the more traditional
emphasis on the individual figure of authority respected for his or her own
association with Jesus during the days of his mission.

---

6. H. Schürmann, *Jesus: Gestalt und Geheimnis* (Paderborn: Bonifatius, 1994) 429.

Within the Jesus tradition itself we should recall the clear memory that Jesus sent out his disciples as an extension of his own mission (Mark 6:7–13 pars.). Mark tells us that the twelve were chosen "to be with him and that he might send them out to preach . . ." (Mark 3:14). What would they have said when they preached? The implication of the text is clear, and the inference from the fact of a shared mission hard to avoid, that their preaching would have at least included teaching which Jesus had given them. Also that Jesus would have taught them what to say—not in a verbatim mode, but in a mode which would convey the disciple-effecting impact which they themselves had experienced. We may be confident that a good deal at least of the retellings of Jesus tradition now in the Synoptic Gospels were already beginning to take shape in that early pre-Easter preaching of the first disciples.

[[244]] This is *not* to accept Theissen's thesis that the Jesus tradition was the preserve of wandering charismatics, and that they were primarily responsible for maintaining and circulating it. As already observed, community formation and tradition formation go hand in hand. And the Q material, on which the thesis is principally based, itself betrays settings for the tradition in towns and villages. In this particular phase of discussion, there is a danger of thinking of the tradition in effect simply as "gospel" and of its transmission simply in terms of evangelistic preaching. But as early form critics recognized, the Jesus traditions are traditions which have come down to us because they were in regular and repeated use. That is, the principal conduit for their transmission was not a single, once-only proclamation by evangelists in missionary situations, but the communities which had been called into existence by such preaching, which identified themselves by reference to such tradition, and which referred to the tradition in their regular gatherings to inform and guide their common life and in relation to their neighbours. It was this breadth of tradition which provided the context of reception for individual performances of items of the tradition, shaping the congregation's "horizon of expectation" and enabling them to fill in the "gaps of indeterminacy." This I believe is a fair statement of what must have been the case, which remains persuasive even if we do not know how extensive was the body of Jesus tradition held by individual communities; the influx of new converts, the reception of further tradition and the creative reworking of the tradition already received need not modify the basic picture to any significant extent.

Did Easter and the transition from Galilean village to Hellenistic city, from [[245]] Aramaic to Greek not make any difference, then? Yes, of course it did. Easter shaped the perspective within which this first tradition was remembered. The transition from village to city shaped the tradition for changing circumstances. The transition from Aramaic to Greek (already implied by the description of "Hellenists" = Greek-speakers in Acts 6:1) would introduce the shifts in nuance which any translation involves. But the oral Jesus tradition itself provided the continuity, the living link back to the ministry of Jesus, and it was no doubt treasured for that very reason; the very character of the tradition, retaining as it does so many of its Galilean village and pre-Easter themes, not to mention its Aramaic resonances (*Jesus Remembered*, §8.5a),

makes that point clear enough. Here again we may learn from postmodern-
ism's emphasis on the reception rather than the composition of text. If it is
indeed the case that the hearer fills in the "gaps in signification" from the tradition (Iser), that an audience interprets a particular performance from their
shared knowledge (Foley),[7] then we can be fairly confident that the Jesus tradition was an essential part of that shared knowledge, enabling the hearers in
church gatherings to "plug in" to particular performances of the oral tradition and to exercise some control over its development. We see this happening, I have already suggested, in the variations Paul plays upon several
elements in the Jesus tradition which he echoes in his letters (p. 172 above).

Tradition Sequences

Another questionable assumption which has dominated the discussion since
the early form critics is that in the initial stage of the traditioning process the
tradition consisted of individual units. That may indeed have been the case
for the [[246]] very beginning of the process, and the *Gospel of Thomas* gives it
some credibility for the continuing tradition. But editorial fingerprints on collections of Jesus tradition in the present Synoptics do not constitute sufficient
evidence that each of the collections was first composed by those who thus
handled them. There is also good evidence of sayings being grouped and stories linked from what may have been a very early stage of the transmission
process—even, in some cases, that Jesus may have taught in connected sequences which have been preserved. To group similar teachings and episodes
would be an obvious mnemonic and didactic device for both teachers and
taught, storytellers and regular hearers, more or less from the beginning.

We may think, for example, of the sequence of beatitudes brought together in oral tradition or Q (Matt 5:3, 4, 6, 11, 12/Luke 6:20b, 21b, 21a, 22,
23), and elaborated differently by Matthew and Luke (Matt 5:3–12, Luke
6:20b–26). Or Jesus' responses to would-be disciples (Matt 8:19–22/Luke
9:57–62). Or the sequence of mini-parables (the wedding guests, new and old
cloth, new and old wineskins) in Mark 2:18–22 (followed by Matt 9:14–17
and Luke 5:33–39). Or the sequence of teaching on the cost of discipleship
and danger of loss (Mark 8:34–38; again followed by Matt 16:24–27 and Luke
9:23–26), where Q/oral tradition has also preserved the sayings separately.
Similarly with the sequence of sayings about light and judgment in Mark
4:21–25 (followed by Luke 8:16–18), with equivalents scattered in Q and the
Gospel of Thomas.

We will have occasion to analyse some of the most fascinating of the sequences later on: the "parables of crisis" in Matt 24:42–25:13 pars., Jesus and
the Baptist in Matt 11:2–19 par., and Jesus' teaching on his exorcisms [[247]]
in Matt 12:24–45 pars. (*Jesus Remembered,* §§12.4g, 12.5c, 12.5d). Even more
fascinating, but almost impossible to set out in tabular form, is the tradition
of the sending out of the disciples on mission, where it is evident from Mark

7. J. M. Foley, *Immanent Art: From Structure to Meaning in Traditional Oral Epic* (Bloom-
ington: Indiana University Press, 1991).

6:7–13 and the parallels in Matt 9:37–10:1, 7–16 and Luke 9:1–6; 10:1–12 that there were at least two variations, one used by Mark and another oral (Q?) version. The variations make it probable that the material was used and re-used, probably beginning with Jesus' own instructions for mission, but developed and elaborated in terms of subsequent experience of early Christian mission.

As for Q itself, we may recall the earlier observation that it is almost impossible to devise a secure method for distinguishing redaction from (initial) composition in a hypothetically reconstructed document (*Jesus Remembered*, §7.4c). The point can be pushed further by arguing that Q was itself composed as a sequence of discourses. But Kloppenborg's findings that Q's sayings have been gathered into "coherent or topical groupings" is also to the point.[8] And the composition of Mark itself can be understood as setting in appropriate sequence a number of groupings already familiar in the oral traditioning process:

24 hours in the ministry of Jesus	Mark 1:21–38
Jesus in controversy (in Galilee)	Mark 2:1–3:6
Parables of Jesus	Mark 4:2–33
Miracles of Jesus round the lake	Mark 4:35–5:43; 6:32–52
Marriage, children, and discipleship	Mark 10:2–31
Jesus in controversy (in Jerusalem)	Mark 12:13–37
The little apocalypse	Mark 13:1–32
The passion narrative	Mark 14:1–15:47

Of course most of this is unavoidably speculative, even more so if we were to guess at whether and how passages like Mark 4:2–33 (parables of Jesus) and Mark 13:1–32 (the little apocalypse) grew by a process of aggregation from earlier, [[248]] smaller groupings. The point is that we should not assume that such compositional procedures came into the process only at a later stage of the process or only when the tradition was written down.

Not Layers but Performances

One of the most important conclusions to emerge from this review of the oral character of so much of the Jesus tradition, and of the likely processes of oral transmission, is that the perspective which has dominated the study of the history of Synoptic tradition is simply wrong-headed. Bultmann laid out the playing field by conceiving of the Jesus tradition as "composed of a series of layers."[9] The consequence of this literary paradigm was that each retelling of episodes or parts of the Jesus tradition was bound to be conceived on the analogy of an editor editing a literary text. Each retelling was like a new (edited) edition. And so the impression of each retelling as another layer superimposed upon earlier layers became almost inescapable, especially

---

8. J. S. Kloppenborg, *Formation of Q* (Philadelphia: Fortress, 1987) 90–92; *Excavating Q: The History and Setting of the Sayings Gospel* (Minneapolis: Fortress, 2000) 168–69, 206–9.

9. R. Bultmann, *Jesus and the Word* (New York: Scribner's, 1935) 12–13.

when the literary imagery was integrated with the archaeological image of the ancient tell, where research proceeds by digging down through the historical layers. The consequence has been widespread disillusion at the prospect of ever being able successfully to strip off the successive layers of editing to leave some primary layer exposed clearly to view. Equally inevitable from such a perspective were the suspicion and scepticism met by any bold enough to claim that they had been successful in their literary archaeology and had actually uncovered a large area of Jesus' bedrock teaching.

But the imagery is simply inappropriate. An oral retelling of a tradition is not at all like a new literary edition. It has not worked on or from a previous retelling. How could it? The previous retelling was not "there" as a text to be consulted. And in the retelling the retold tradition did not come into existence as a kind of artefact, to be examined as by an editor and re-edited for the next retelling. [[249]] In oral transmission a tradition is performed, not edited. And as we have seen, performance includes both elements of stability and elements of variability—stability of subject and theme, of key details or core exchanges, variability in the supporting details and the particular emphases to be drawn out. This is a very different perspective. And it allows, indeed requires, rather different conclusions. These include the likelihood that the stabilities of the tradition were sufficiently maintained and the variabilities of the retellings subject to sufficient control for the substance of the tradition, and often actual words of Jesus which made the first tradition-forming impact, to continue as integral parts of the living tradition, for at least as long as it took for the Synoptic tradition to be written down. In other words, whereas the concept of literary *layers* implies increasing remoteness from an "original," "pure," or "authentic" layer, the concept of *performance* allows a directness, even an immediacy of interaction, with a living theme and core even when variously embroidered in various retellings.

The concept of oral transmission, as illustrated from the Synoptic tradition itself, therefore, does not encourage either the scepticism which has come to afflict the "quest of the historical Jesus" or the lopsided findings of the neo-Liberal questers. Rather it points a clear middle way between a model of memorization by rote on the one hand and any impression of oral transmission as a series of evanescent reminiscences of some or several retellings on the other. It encourages neither those who are content with nothing short of the historicity of every detail and word of the text nor those who can see and hear nothing other than the faith of the early churches. It encourages us rather to see and hear the Synoptic tradition as the repertoire of the early churches when they recalled the Jesus who had called their first leaders and predecessors to discipleship and celebrated again the powerful impact of his life and teaching.

Oral Tradition to Written Gospel

We need not follow the course of oral transmission beyond the transition from oral tradition to written Gospel. The significance of that transition can be exaggerated, as we noted above in reviewing the work of Kelber (*Jesus Re-*

membered, §8.3f): Jesus tradition [[250]] did not cease to circulate in oral form simply because it had been written down; hearings of a Gospel being read would be part of the oral/aural transmission, to be retold in further circles of orality; the written text was still fluid, still living tradition. But there are two other aspects, misleading impressions or unexamined assumptions, which have encouraged false perspectives on the subject and which should be highlighted here.

One is the impression that the oral Jesus tradition was like two (or several) narrow streams which were wholly absorbed into the written Gospels through their sources. So much of the focus in Gospel research has been on the question of sources for the Gospels that it has been natural, I suppose, for oral tradition to be conceived simply as source material for the Gospels, without any real attempt being made to conceptualize what oral communities were like and how the oral tradition functioned prior to and independently of written collections and Gospels. As already noted, some narrative criticism and some discussions of Synoptic pericopes at times almost seem to assume that when a copy of Mark or Matthew or Luke was initially received by any church, that was the first time the church had heard the Jesus tradition contained therein. But this is to ignore or forget one of the key insights of form criticism in the beginning, namely the recognition that the tradition took various forms because the forms reflected the way the tradition was being used in the first churches. In fact, it is almost self-evident that the Synoptists proceeded by gathering and ordering Jesus tradition which had already been in circulation, that is, had already been well enough known to various churches, for at least some years if not decades. Where else did the Evangelists find the tradition? Stored up, unused, in an old box at the back of some teacher's house? Stored up, unrehearsed, in the failing memory of an old apostle? Hardly! On the contrary, it is much more likely that when the Synoptic Gospels were first received by various churches, these churches *already* possessed (in communal oral memory or in written form) their own versions of much of the material. They would be able to compare the Evangelist's version of much of the tradition with their own versions. This conclusion ties in well with the considerations adduced above (pp. 167–174). And as we have seen above, the divergences between different versions of the Synoptic tradition imply a lively and flexible oral tradition known to the Evangelists and presumably also to the churches with which they were associated.

This line of thought links in with the other assumption which has become debilitatingly pervasive: that each document belongs to and represents the views [[251]] of only one community, and that the tensions within and among documents indicate rival camps and already different Christianities. The assumption derives again from the first insights of form criticism: that the forms of the tradition reflect the interests of the churches which used them. This was reinforced by the sociological perspective of the final quarter of the twentieth century: literature as the expression not so much of a single mind as of a social context. But these insights have been narrowed (and distorted) in a quite extraordinary way, to claim in effect that each text was written by and for a particular community—a Q community, a Mark community, a Matthean community, and so on. I have already challenged this assumption with regard to Q (*Jesus Remembered*, §7.4b), and by implication for the Gospels generally. But the assumption covers also the streams of tradition which entered into the Gospels. The assumption, in other words, is of different and conflicting streams of tradition more or less from the first, celebrating in effect different Jesuses—a prophetic and/or apocalyptic Jesus, Jesus the wisdom teacher, the Jesus of aretalogies (divine man), and so on.

[[252]] Richard Bauckham has recently challenged this assumption with regard to the written Gospels. His counter-thesis is that "the Gospels were written for general circulation around the churches and so envisaged a very general Christian audience. Their implied readership is not specific but indefinite: any and every Christian community in the late first-century Roman Empire."[10] The claim may be stated in an exaggerated form (for *all* Christians?), but we should not discount the likelihood that Evangelists wrote out of their more local experience primarily with a view to a much larger circle of churches, in Syria–Cilicia, for example. And Bauckham needs to give more weight to the likelihood that particular communities were the Evangelist's *source* for Jesus tradition, as distinct from communities as the Evangelist's *target* in writing his Gospel. But he is justified in dismissing the idea that the Evangelist would have written his Gospel for the community in which he lived.[11] And he rightly challenges any suggestion that the tradition-stock available to any one Evangelist was limited to his own community or circle of churches.[12]

The point here is that Bauckham is certainly correct to highlight the evidence that the first churches were by no means as isolated from one another and at odds with one another as has been so often assumed. If Paul's letters (and Acts) are any guide, the first churches consisted rather of "a network of communities in constant communication," linked by messengers, letters, and visits by leading figures in the new movement.[13] This ties in with what was noted above, that church founding included the initial communication of foundation tradition and that Paul could assume common tradition, including knowledge of Jesus tradition, even in a church which he had never previously visited (Rome). And though there were indeed severe tensions between Paul and the Jerusalem leadership, Paul still regarded the lines of continuity between the churches in Judea and those of the Gentile mission as a matter of first importance. In short, the suggestion that there were churches who knew only one stream of tradition—Jesus only as a miracle worker, or only as a wisdom teacher, etc.—has been given far [[253]] too much uncritical credence in scholarly discussions on the Gospels and ought to have been dismissed a lot sooner.

---

10. R. Bauckham, "For Whom Were the Gospels Written?" in *The Gospels for All Christians* (ed. R. Bauckham; Grand Rapids: Eerdmans, 1998) 1.
    11. Ibid., 28–30.
    12. Private correspondence.
    13. Bauckham, "For Whom?" 30–44.

In Summary

This has been a lengthy chapter, so let me sum up what has emerged about the Jesus tradition prior to its being written down.

First (pp. 167–174 above), I noted the strong circumstantial case for the view that, from the beginning, new converts would have wanted to know about Jesus, that no church would have been established without its store of foundation (including Jesus) tradition, and that the churches were organised to maintain and to pass on that tradition. The importance of remembering Jesus and learning about him and of responsible teachers is attested as early as we can reach back into earliest Christianity, in Jewish as well as Gentile churches. The apparent silence of Paul and the character of the Gospels themselves provide no substantive counter-argument.

Second (*Jesus Remembered*, §8.2), the assumption that prophecy within the earliest churches would have added substantial material to the Jesus tradition has been misleading. It is not borne out to any great extent by what we know of early church prophetic activity. On the contrary, recognition of the danger of *false* prophecy would almost certainly have been as widespread as prophecy itself, and the first churches would probably have been alert to the danger of accepting any prophetic utterance which was out of harmony with the Jesus tradition already received.

When we turned, third (*Jesus Remembered*, §8.3), to examine the relevance of oral tradition to our quest, we noted the widespread recognition among specialists in orality of the character of oral transmission as a mix of stable themes and flexibility, of fixed and variable elements in oral retelling. But we also noted that such insights have hardly begun to be exploited adequately in the treatment of Jesus tradition as oral tradition. However, Bailey's observations, drawn from his experience of oral traditioning processes in Middle Eastern village life, have highlighted points of potential importance, particularly the rationale which, in the cases in point, determined the distinction between the more fixed elements and constant themes on the one hand, and the flexible and variable elements on the other. Where stories or teaching was important for the community's identity and life there would be a concern to maintain the core or key features, however varied other details (less important to the story's or teaching's point) in successive retellings.

Our own examination, fourth (*Jesus Remembered*, §§8.4, 8.5), of the Jesus tradition itself confirmed the relevance of the oral paradigm and the danger of assuming (consciously or otherwise) the literary paradigm. The findings did not call into serious question the priority of Mark or the existence of a document Q. But, in each of the examples marshalled, the degree of variation between clearly parallel traditions [[254]] and the inconsequential character of so much of the variations have hardly encouraged an explanation in terms of literary dependence (on Mark or Q) or of literary editing. Rather, the combination of stability and flexibility positively cried out to be recognized as typically oral in character. That probably implies in at least some cases that the variation was due to knowledge and use of the same tradition in oral mode, as part of the community tradition familiar to Matthew and Luke. And even if a pericope was derived from Mark or Q, the retelling by Matthew or Luke is itself better described as in oral mode, maintaining the character of an oral retelling more than of a literary editing.

In both cases (narrative and teachings) we also noted (1) a concern to remember the things Jesus had done and said. The discipleship and embryonic communities which had been formed and shaped by the impact of Jesus' life and message would naturally have celebrated that tradition as central to their own identity as disciples and churches. We noted also (2) that the memories consisted in stories and teachings whose own identity was focused in particular themes and/or particular words and phrases—usually those said by Jesus himself. And (3) that the variations and developments were not linear or cumulative in character, but the variations of oral performance. The material examined indicated neither concern to preserve some kind of literalistic historicity of detail, nor any readiness to flood the tradition with Jewish wisdom or prophetic utterance.

Finally (pp. 174–182 above), we have observed that the pattern of the oral traditioning process was probably established more or less from the beginning (before the first Easter) and was probably maintained in character through to (and beyond) the writing down of the tradition. The first impact (sequence of impacts) made by Jesus resulted in the formation of tradition, which was itself formative and constitutive of community/church through Easter, beyond Galilee and into Greek, and was preserved and celebrated through regular performance (whether in communal or specifically liturgical gatherings) or reviewed for apologetic or catechetical purposes. In other words, what we today are confronted with in the Gospels is not the top layer (last edition) of a series of increasingly impenetrable layers, but the living tradition of Christian celebration which takes us with surprising immediacy to the heart of the first memories of Jesus.

On the basis of all this we can begin to build a portrayal of the remembered Jesus, of the impact made by his words and deeds on the first disciples as that impact was "translated" into oral tradition and as it was passed down in oral performance within the earliest circles of disciples and the churches, to be enshrined in due course in the written Synoptic tradition.

Part 3

Teachings of Jesus:
God, Kingdom, Ethics, Parables,
and Old Testament

Introduction

JAMES D. G. DUNN

The teachings of Jesus became a main focus of interest among those involved in "the quest of the historical Jesus" during the second half of the nineteenth century. This was partly a reflection of the preoccupations of the times, typically on questions of morality and the sources and warrants for ethical conduct; and partly a corollary of the recognition that one of the two earliest sources for the Synoptic Gospel tradition was the Q (= *Quelle* = source) material common to Matthew and Luke. Because this material consists almost exclusively of sayings, that is, teachings of Jesus, the "discovery" of Q naturally aroused interest in Jesus the Teacher.

It did not take much effort to deduce from the Synoptic tradition that a prominent subject in Jesus' preaching and teaching was "the kingdom of God." (One of the curiosities of the four-Gospel tradition is the fact that the importance of the kingdom motif in Matthew, Mark, and Luke is hardly shared by John.) In the cultural context of the late-nineteenth-century "quest," it was almost inevitable that this Synoptic emphasis was read in terms of morality: the kingdom of God proclaimed by Jesus was understood in terms of the community of the disciples, ethical in character and motivated by love—thus the most prominent of the "Liberal Protestant" theologians, Albrecht Ritschl. The temptation to identify the kingdom of God on earth with the Church was hard to avoid. But Johannes Weiss (ironically, Ritschl's son-in-law) upset the applecart by pointing out that "the kingdom of God" was an apocalyptic motif and that in Jesus' teaching the primary reference is to the final, end-time (eschatological) inbreaking of God's rule in the near future. This gave Albert Schweitzer the key to his own portrayal of Jesus as an eschatological prophet (above, pp. 6–49) and ensured that the eschatological character of the kingdom of God became the dominant preoccupation of the "quest" for most of the twentieth century.

The extract from Werner Kümmel (below, pp. 190–200) gives a very good flavor of the consequent discussion. Did Jesus teach that the kingdom of God was imminent? And if so, how imminent? Others had argued that primary emphasis should be given to the passages in the Jesus tradition where

187

Jesus seems to envisage the (eschatological) kingdom as already present (notably, C. H. Dodd). But Kümmel's essay is a reminder of how hard it was to escape from the shadow cast by Weiss and Schweitzer through the middle decades of the twentieth century.

The extract from Tom Wright (below, pp. 207–224), however, indicates something of the transformation in discussion of Jesus' talk of the kingdom of God that took place toward the end of the twentieth century, particularly in the 1990s. In some cases it has meant dressing Jesus' kingdom message once more in the older Liberal clothes but with a more dashingly contemporary cut. Jesus' message was that of a social rebel, concerned about political issues and the reformation of society (Dominic Crossan, and the extract from Richard Horsley, pp. 288–301 below). Wright's disillusion with the Schweitzer-paradigm takes a different expression. The apocalyptic framework is reinterpreted in the light of the ongoing story of Israel; narrative rather than apocalypse becomes the decisive clue. Jesus' proclamation of the kingdom is to be seen rather as the climax of Israel's story and the fulfillment of Israel's hitherto unfulfilled hope of return from exile.

This interest in the relation between Jesus' teaching and the teachings that he inherited as a Jew, that is, the teachings of the Jewish Scriptures (= the Christian Old Testament) and their post-OT interpretation, has provided the other principal focus of the "quest" for the authentic voice of Jesus the Teacher. Joachim Jeremias famously concentrated on Jesus' prayer to God as "Abba" (below, pp. 201–206) and made a very persuasive case for the view that the degree of intimacy expressed in that prayer-style is without real precedent in Jewish tradition. Given that Paul reflects the importance of the "Abba"-prayer for the first Christians (Rom 8:15; Gal 4:6), this is a finding of lasting significance.

More typical of the discussion of whether and to what extent Jesus was influenced by or overrode the teachings he inherited has been the issue of Jesus and the law. For many it has been almost an article of faith that Jesus (must have) reacted against the law of Moses and "broken" with it. This finding was in part at least a spillover from a characteristically Lutheran setting of "law" and "gospel" in sharp and irreconcilable antithesis. A typical piece from E. P. Sanders, however, calls into radical question that whole perspective on Jesus' teaching. There is no evidence that Jesus disregarded or opposed the law—in the essay reproduced here (below, pp. 225–237), the laws governing relations between God and humans. Rather, Jesus' teaching shows him to have participated in a debate within Judaism, not on whether these laws should be obeyed, but on how they should be obeyed.

In a more recent discussion, Dale Allison (pp. 238–247) illustrates that the question of the use made by Jesus of the (Jewish) Scriptures and of their influence on his teaching is not a simple one of straightforward quotation. The Q material provides many examples of allusive reference and of allusions that (were we more attuned to what Jesus' hearers would take for granted) should catch us by surprise. Such studies help us toward a very elusive goal, that is, of hearing Jesus' teaching with the overtones and echoes that his teaching must have often prompted in first-century Palestine.

The other highly characteristic feature of Jesus' teaching is his parables. So characteristic are they, and so distinctive of his teaching in the regularity with which he used them (see Mark 4:33–34!), that Jesus can fairly be called a "parabolist" (Birger Gerhardsson). These too have been a staple element in the "quest," with endless discussion on what they tell us about Jesus and his teaching—their meaning being so dependent on how they were/are heard and what reaction they provoke(d). Klyne Snodgrass has long specialized in the study of the parables of Jesus, and thus that his essay on the history of their interpretation provides as valuable an overview of the subject as one could wish for (below, pp. 248–268).

Bibliography

Crossan, J. D.
    1991   *The Historical Jesus: The Life of a Mediterranean Jewish Peasant.* San
            Francisco: Harper.
Dodd, C. H.
    1935   *The Parables of the Kingdom.* London: Religious Book Club.
Gerhardsson, B.
    1979   *The Origins of the Gospel Traditions.* Philadelphia: Fortress.
Ritschl, A.
    1999   *Instruction in the Christian Religion,* §§5–25 [original pub., 1875]. Con-
            veniently reprinted, pp. 154–71 in *The Historical Jesus Quest: Land-
            marks in the Search for the Jesus of History,* ed. G. W. Dawes. Leiderdorp:
            Deo.
Weiss, J.
    1971   *Jesus' Proclamation of the Kingdom of God.* Philadelphia: Fortress / Lon-
            don: SCM. [original pub., 1892]

W. G. KÜMMEL

The Pressing Imminence of the End

[[54]] Before we can clarify this question further [[how the promised Kingdom could already be fulfilled in some way and also still be expected]], the meaning of Jesus' message about the future appearing of the Kingdom of God must be elucidated further. . . . Jesus predicted its coming to be near, indeed to be arriving within the lifetime of his generation. Can this statement be confirmed or defined more precisely? That Jesus felt the end to be critically near is seen also in the calls for watchfulness. We are concerned here with a very intricate complex of the tradition from the literary point of view. On the one hand are found general calls for watchfulness (βλέπετε, ἀγρυπνεῖτε, οὐκ οἴδατε γὰρ πότε ὁ καιρός ἐστιν [['Beware, keep alert; for you do not kow when the time will come']] Mark 13:33, 37; "let your loins be girded and your lamps burning" Luke 12:35); on the other hand the tradition contains in several variations the parable of the absent householder, for whose return the servants are to wait (Mark 13:34–36; Luke 12:36–38; Matt 24:42, 45–51 = Luke 12:42–46); then there is the parable of the master of the house who would have watched, had he known when the thief was coming, with the application "be ye ready, for in the hour that ye think not the Son of Man cometh" (Matt 24:43f. = Luke 12:39f.); finally the parable of the ten virgins admonishes: "watch therefore, for ye know not the day nor the hour" (Matt 25:1–13). Without going into all the literary problems posed by these texts, the following may yet be said: the first-named general calls to watchfulness are passages of transition about which nothing certain as to their independent traditional origin can be said.[1] The parable of the absent householder is [[55]] handed down in its essen-

---

Reprinted, with permission, from W. G. Kümmel, *Promise and Fulfilment: The Eschatological Message of Jesus* (trans. D. M. Barton; London: SCM, 1957) 54–64 and portions of (bibliography) 9–14.

1. In Mark 13:33 we meet with the term χαιρός which only occurs again as a designation of the eschatological date in Luke 21:8 in a secondary Lucan addition. As the term in the Septuagint renders the most varied ideas of time in the original text (see G. Delling, *Th. Wb. z. N.T.* 3, 459f.) and besides has no specific Aramaic equivalent, it hardly goes back to an old tradition. In Luke 12:35 the exhortation "let your lamps be burning" can be interpreted as

tials in two forms (in Luke 12:36–38 the servants are to be found watching by their lord when he returns from the marriage feast; in Matt 24:42, 45–51 = Luke 12:42–46 the lord has given the servants definite tasks for the period of his absence and when he returns unexpectedly he will ask about their performance). Both forms are characterized by a strong predominance of metaphorical features which are meant to suggest the application of the picture language to the relationship of the returning Jesus to his disciples. But there is no ground for denying on principle that these allegorizing features were Jesus' own.[2] The undoubted meaning of this imagery is that the disciples must at all times be ready for the arrival of the Lord. Indeed the term ἔρχεσθαι [['to come, to arrive']] points already, as we have seen, to the expectation of the coming eschatological day, and the "coming" of the man Jesus who is now still living on earth cannot be mentioned at all except with the "futurist" eschatological expectation in mind. So there is no doubt that these parables are intended to urge preparedness for the day of the appearance of the parousia which may occur at any time and is therefore pressing.[3] The parable of the master of the house who would have watched for the thief, had he known when he was coming (Matt 24:43f. = Luke 12:39f.) cannot be understood in any other way. For the deduction drawn from the imagery with its application by [[56]] contrast: "therefore be ye also ready" is associated unambiguously with the expectation of the parousia by the reason given in Matt 24:44b = Luke 12:40b "for in the hour that ye think not the Son of Man cometh"; moreover the imagery of the coming of the thief can hardly admit of any interpretation other than the *coming* of the Son of Man.[4] Thus this parable also stresses the ignorance of the date and at the same time the pressing imminence of the expected *eschaton*.

---

an allusion to the parable in Matt 25:1ff. (thus in my first edition); but this is by no means necessary and so this saying may belong to the original tradition.

2. It is not correct that the texts present as a problem the failure of the parousia to appear and thereby are shown to be framed by the Church (thus Bultmann, *Tradition*, 125). Michaelis, *Verheissung*, 5ff. has proved that the references to the different night-watches in which the lord may come and the reflection of the servant "my lord tarrieth" belong to the imagery of the parable and are not due to the problem arising out of the delay of the parousia. W. Foerster, *Herr ist Jesus*, 1924, 231f., 268ff. has emphasized rightly that the parables under discussion do not speak fortuitously of the coming of the lord, but are proved just by this metaphorical trait to be parables of the parousia, which undoubtedly originated with Jesus himself. Yet in no case should the imagery be turned so far into allegory as to explain the servants to be the apostles under the leadership of Peter. (Thus A. Feuillet, *R.B.* 56, 1949, 89; and 57, 1950, 66.)

3. The parables lose all real meaning if the wakefulness for the unexpected coming of the lord is interpreted as readiness for the judgment which is always in process (Duncan, *Jesus*, 181; C. W. F. Smith, *Jesus*, 251ff.; Glasson, *Advent*, 95) or the coming of the lord as the return of Jesus at the end of the life of each apostle, and the waking and watching as the preservation of the first ardour (A. Feuillet, loc. cit. in [[n. 2]]).

4. Here too all meaning is taken from the imagery if it is given the interpretation that the unexpected character of the Kingdom of God demands constant readiness (C. W. F. Smith, *Jesus*, 248).

The parable in Luke 12:58f. also probably points in the same direction. This instruction to be reconciled with one's adversary before the beginning of legal proceedings, because one might otherwise be obliged to pay the last mite, is clearly added in Matt 5:25f., attracted by a catchword, to the exhortation to be reconciled before offering a gift, and in this position cannot be understood as anything but a prudential maxim. But Luke, by placing 12:57 "Why even yourselves judge ye not what is right?" in front of it, clearly understood the text as a parabolic exhortation: as one should be reconciled on the way to the judge even at the last moment, so one should know that it is a matter of importance to be ready now at the last moment for the coming judgment. Since this interpretation yields a meaning free from objection, it corresponds undoubtedly with the original meaning of this text, which must therefore be understood as a pointer to the necessity of preparedness in view of the pressing imminence of the end.[5]

This applies finally also to the parable of the ten virgins (Matt 25:1ff.). The proceedings at a rural wedding assumed here obviously cannot be interpreted with certainty as to detail,[6] but there is no doubt that the parable enjoins readiness for an event of which the time is not known, but is certainly very near. That it is intended to point to the parousia of the Son of Man appears quite certainly from the metaphorical words of the bridegroom (= the judge of the world): "I know you not" (25:12) and in the appended exhortation to await the day and the hour. This explanatory exhortation (25:13) was presumably added by the evangelist, as it emphasizes wrongly watchfulness instead of [[56]] preparedness.[7] But the parable does not receive an allegorical colour by this addition alone; and it is erroneous to regard it as a summons not to desist from preparedness although the parousia has not yet arrived, which would show the parable, at any rate in the form handed down to us, to have been formulated by the Church.[8] Owing to the allegorical features of the parable (Jesus is the bridegroom, the speech of the bridegroom is that of the world's judge, etc.) others have conjectured that a simpler parabolic story underlies the traditional form, but that this can no longer be reconstructed.[9] Now it is not absolutely necessary to consider the figure of the bridegroom in this parable to be a metaphor and to apply it to Jesus as the messianic bridegroom; but since the messianic age is often described as a

---

5. Thus Bultmann, *Tradition*, 101, 185f.; Klostermann, *Matthäus*, 44f.; Hauck, *Lukas*, 177; especially Jeremias, *Parables*, 31f., 126f. (in German 28f., 129f.).

6. Cf. the plausible explanation of Michaelis, *Sämann*, 162ff. for the details.

7. See [[Kümmel, *Promise and Fulfillment*,]] pp. 39f.

8. Thus Klostermann, *Matthäus*, 199f.; Bultmann, *Tradition*, 125, 190f.; G. Bornkamm, "Die Verzögerung der Parusie," *In memoriam B. Lohmeyer*, 1951, 120ff. Also J. Jeremias, *Th. Wb z. N.T.* 4, 1098 and *Parables*, 41 (in German 39) also considers 25:13 to be a postscript of the evangelist and that the parable originally had no allegorical features.

9. Thus Jülicher, *Gleichnisreden* 2, 456f.; T. W. Manson, *Mission and Message*, 535ff.; similarly J. Wellhausen, *Das Evangelium Matthaei*, [2]1914, 121ff.—According to C. W. F. Smith, *Jesus*, 165f. the parable ended originally with 25:10 (thus also Sharman, *Son of Man*, 38f., who wishes to show that the parable thus shortened was even a reshaping of Mark 13:35–37 par. Luke 12:35, 38; 13:25!).

wedding feast,[10] the metaphorical meaning of the bridegroom in the parable is very likely.[11] Yet this metaphor no more turns it into "a formation by the Church completely overgrown with allegory" (Bultmann) than do the metaphorical words of the bridegroom which are paralleled in the metaphorical conclusions of the parables in Mark 4:29; [[58]] Matt 22:13a; 24:51a = Luke 12:46b; Matt 25:30a and which are thereby seen to be customary in Jesus' style. On the contrary it is rather a question of a parable urgently directing the hearer by means of its metaphorical features to a correct interpretation: the eschatological coming of the Son of Man is completely incalculable, but is very near; therefore it is important to hold oneself in readiness for it. It follows from this that the problem of the delayed parousia is in no way suggested in the parable, since the trait "while the bridegroom tarried" (25:5) belongs only to the vivid embellishment of the picture half. It follows equally that the parable by means of its metaphorical features enforces the interpretation to be prepared for the eschatological coming of the Son of Man. It is therefore completely mistaken for Dodd[12] to interpret the parables just discussed (the waiting servants, the faithful and unfaithful servant, the thief in the night and the ten virgins) not as summons to be prepared for the future coming of the Son of Man, but as an exhortation to be on the alert for possible developments in the supreme crisis of history introduced by Jesus' coming. For this interpretation does not only necessarily water down the parables to general truths,[13] but even in Matt 25:1ff. pushes to one side those metaphorical

10. Jeremias, *Weltvollender*, 22ff.

11. J. Jeremias, *Th. Wb. z. N.T.* 4, 1094ff. and *Parables*, 41f. (in German 39f.) has disputed that Jesus designated himself allegorically as the messianic bridegroom. But even though Jeremias is probably right in saying that late Judaism does not know the messianic title of "bridegroom," yet Mark 2:19a "Can the sons of the bridechamber fast while the bridegroom is with them?" can hardly be weakened so much as to mean only: can the friends of the bridegroom fast during the wedding celebrations? (Bultmann, *Tradition*, 107 n. 1; Dodd, *Parables*, 116 n. 2; B. T. D. Smith, *Parables*, 95 also interpret it similarly.) For in connexion with the accusation against the disciples that they do not fast, the words about the bridegroom and his friends can only be applied metaphorically to Jesus and the disciples. So the designation "bridegroom" can hardly be only for Mark "a name with a messianic sound" (W. Wrede, *Das Messiasgeheimnis in den Evangelien*, [2]1913, 19). On the contrary, Jesus is here making an affirmation concerning himself in terms which veil his meaning (thus recently Taylor, *Mark*, 210) and perhaps first grew out of the picture of the messianic marriage feast, and which may therefore very likely be intended as well in Matt 25:1ff.

12. Dodd, *Parables*, 154ff. in agreement with J. Jeremias, *Th. Wb. z. N.T.* 4, 1097. Quite similarly for the parable of the ten virgins Glasson, *Advent*, 93; C. W. F. Smith, *Jesus*, 169ff.— A. Feuillet, *R.B.* 57, 1950, 71ff. wishes to refer it to the last judgment at the end of each human life and to identify the bride with the virgins and the Church!

13. For this purpose Dodd must, e.g., in Matt 24:45ff. set aside the departure and return of the master as unimportant and interpret the parable as intending to pillory the leaders of the Jews as God's unfaithful servants. In the parable of the waiting servants (Luke 12:35ff. = Mark 13:33ff.) the waiting for the return of the master is watered down to the "idea . . . of alertness and preparedness for any emergency." The exhortation deduced from the parable of the thief at night to be prepared for a coming event (Matt 24:43f.) is directed towards preparedness for the imminent persecution of Jesus and his disciples, the destruction of Jerusalem and the Jewish nation. The parable of the ten virgins also is only intended to

passages which demand the interpretation that the parousia is to be expected; thus no explanation is given why in all these parables the "coming" of the master, the bridegroom, the thief is constantly mentioned. On the contrary it [[59]] follows also from all these exhortations to be on the alert and to be prepared that Jesus describes the coming of the Son of Man and therewith the entry of the Kingdom of God as possibly very imminent, and in any case pressingly near, although its actual date was completely unknown.

Finally this fact is confirmed by some other detached sayings. To the parable of the widow who importunes the unjust judge (Luke 18:1–6), by means of an introduction undoubtedly formulated by himself (Luke 18:6 εἶπεν δὲ ὁ κύριος [['and the Lord said']]), Luke appends an interpretation which promises that God will listen to the elect who pray without ceasing: λέγω ὑμῖν ὅτι ποιήσει τὴν ἐκδίκησιν αὐτῶν ἐν τάχει [['I tell you, he will quickly grant justice to them']] (18:8a). The parable appears to emphasize only the efficacy of continuous prayer and therefore many consider that its application, namely that the prayer for justification on the last day will be answered, is a secondary addition to the parable.[14] But this assumption is not in the least necessary.[15] For on the one hand the interpretation 18:6–8a is in no way a re-interpretation, since the parable, as a metaphor, can bear a particular as well as a general application and can scarcely do without one altogether; on the other hand the decision of the judge "to avenge" the woman is probably a metaphorical feature which is intended to suggest an application to the justification procured by God for the elect. But if there is no necessity to detach 18:6–8a from the original parable, there need also be no hesitation in recognizing the promise that God will avenge ἐν τάχει [['quickly']] as original. In that case this text also shows the expectation of the eschatological judgment and the coming of the Kingdom of God after a short delay.

Two further texts indicate that this short delay was understood by Jesus to have a definite limit. In Mark 13:30 par. Matt 24:34; Luke 21:32 there is appended to the parable of the fig tree, which has already been discussed and which illustrates the proximity of the end, the saying: ἀμὴν λέγω ὑμῖν ὅτι οὐ μὴ

give warning against the consequences of not being prepared for the imminent events during Jesus' ministry. Similarly Glasson, *Advent*, 93 wishes to apply the parable of the ten virgins to the blindness of the Jews who do not recognize the crisis in their history, and C. W. F. Smith, *Jesus*, 169 to a situation in which some could see what the occasion demanded and others could not see it! C. J. Cadoux, *Mission*, 313ff. rightly turns away from these weakening interpretations.

14. Thus Jülicher, *Gleichnisreden* 2, 284ff.; Bultmann, *Tradition*, 189; B. T. D. Smith, *Parables*, 152f.; C. J. Cadoux, *Mission*, 303; Glasson, *Advent*, 90f.; Sharman, *Son of Man*, 64f. That 18:8b is a secondary addition is probably correct (thus recently Jeremias, *Parables*, 84 [in German 84f.]; Guy, *Last Things*, 37). E. Fuchs also, *Verkünd. u. Forsch.* 1947/48, 77 wants to ascribe the whole passage 18:1–8a to the primitive Church.

15. Cf. Hauck, *Lukas*, 219; W. Michaelis, *Das hochzeitliche Kleid*, 1939, 256ff.; Liechtenhan, *Mission*, 15, 18.—The idea of K. Weiss, *Irrtumslosigkeit*, 220 that in Luke 18:8a "speedily" applies to help after the final distress and the prayer during that time is quite impossible!

παρέλθῃ ἡ γενεὰ αὕτη μέχρις οὗ ταῦτα πάντα γένηται [['Truly I tell you, this generation will not pass away until all these things have taken place']]. It appears from the [[60]] introduction to the saying and the catchword-link with the next verse that this is a detached saying fitted on to ταῦτα γινόμενα [['these things come about']] 13:29 by the catchword ταῦτα γένηται [['these things have taken place']]. In this parable the meaning of ἡ γενεὰ αὕτη [['this generation']] and ταῦτα πάντα [['all these things']] is much debated. In the context of Mark ταῦτα πάντα [['all these things']] designates clearly the whole of the eschatological happenings including the final parousia (Mark 13:26); this meaning can in any case be given to the original detached saying, since πάντα [['all']] refers most readily to the eschatological happenings as a whole. Michaelis has indeed asserted[16] that ταῦτα πάντα refers back to ταῦτα in 13:29 where ταῦτα indicates events *before* the end; in that case the limited proximity of the *end* would certainly not be clearly mentioned in 13:30. But this exegesis overlooks the fact that according to Mark also ταῦτα πάντα need not necessarily take up the ταῦτα in 13:29, and moreover it is wrong to attempt to derive the exegesis of the saying from the *immediate* context given by Mark, which the original independence of the saying does not justify. Finally it would be a remarkable statement that *definite* events *previous* to the end will be limited to the period of this γενεά [['generation']], without making a pronouncement about the actual moment of the end which alone is of importance. There can therefore be no doubt that Mark 13:30 is intended to mean: the events leading up to the end will occur before the period of this γενεά has ended.[17] This is usually understood without more ado as a prediction that the end will come during the lifetime of the present generation. But this natural explanation has been disputed and two other translations [[61]] have been proposed. According to one of them γενεά here, denotes "nation," as "in all other sayings of Jesus in which the expression occurs"; then the saying would mean that the Jewish nation would not perish till the end had come.[18] According to

16. Michaelis, *Verheissung*, 30ff.—In a letter Michaelis raised the question whether ταῦτα πάντα [['all these things']] could not also be referred back to 13:4, i.e., to the destruction of Jerusalem; but a logion with such a limited meaning could scarcely have been handed down in isolation, and the destruction of Jerusalem is of course in Jesus' thought also a strictly eschatological event. That Mark 13:30 was originally identical with Mark 9:1 and only developed away from it secondarily is a completely arbitrary assumption (against C. Lindeskog, "Logia-Studien," *Studia Theologica* 4, 1950/52, 181).

17. Sharman, *Son of Man*, 98f., wishes to refer ταῦτα πάντα [['all these things']] to 13:5–23, to the events before the destruction of Jerusalem, K. Weiss, *Irrtumslosigkeit*, 109ff. and A. Feuillet, *R.B.* 56, 1949, 84 to the destruction of Jerusalem, which will take place during the lifetime of this generation; Walter, *Kommen*, 83 wishes to interpret it as the destruction of Jerusalem *and* the final judgment, and Taylor, *Mark*, 521 assumes that ταῦτα πάντα has secondarily "replaced a reference to some definite event, probably the destruction of the Temple and the fall of Jerusalem." But quite apart from the question whether this would even catch the meaning of the saying in Mark's context, the detached saying does not admit of such a limitation (cf. also n. [[17]] and T. W. Manson, *Mission and Message*, 625f.).

18. Thus Schniewind, *Markus*, 167; Busch, *Eschatologie*, 133f.; H. Bietenhard, *Das tausendjährige Reich*, Diss. Bern, 1944, 121; Meinertz, *Theologie* 1, 61.

the other translation γενεά here denotes "the type" and the saying declares that "this type, namely the perverse and faithless . . . nature of man will continue to the last day."[19]

But in the other passages in the synoptists where this word occurs it usually indicates distinctly the men of Jesus' generation (Matt 11:16 = Luke 7:31; Mark 8:12 par. Luke 11:29; especially Matt 23:36 = Luke 11:51) and also in Matt 12:39, 45; 16:4 this meaning is by no means excluded. So ἡ γενεὰ αὕτη in Mark 13:30 can hardly be rightly understood otherwise than as referring to "this generation."[20] In that case the coming of the end during the lifetime of this generation is predicted unambiguously in Mark 13:30 which signifies, as in Mark 9:1, that at any rate some of the men alive at present will witness the *eschaton* in their lifetime.

Thus Mark 13:30 corroborates what has already been concluded from Mark 9:1; but the meaning of Matt 10:23 is essentially more difficult to determine. The connexion of the saying is very loose. In the missionary charge to the disciples in 10:17–25 Matthew includes a prediction that they will be persecuted. First 10:17–22 deals with their accusation before councils, and these verses correspond largely with Mark 13:9–13, which section Matthew has left out in chap. 24. To the prediction that the disciples will be hated for Jesus' sake there is attached in 10:23a the instruction preserved only in Matthew: "But when they persecute you in this city, flee into the next." According to the context this can only indicate that the disciples must endure persecution in their missionary work, that they should not expose themselves to this danger, but should flee to another city, of course to continue their mission there (cf. Matt 10:14). Now to this is attached Matt 10:23b ἀμὴν γὰρ λέγω ὑμῖν, οὐ μὴ τελέσητε τὰς πόλεις τοῦ Ἰσραὴλ ἕως ἔλθῃ ὁ υἱὸς τοῦ ἀνθρώπου [['truly I tell you, you will not have gone through all the towns of Israel before the Son of Man comes']]. After v. 23a this can only mean: in your flight you will not reach all the cities of Israel before [[62]] the Son of Man appears in glory. But τελέσητε can hardly signify "to come to the end of anything"; it connotes the completion of a task ("to bring to an end, to discharge," cf. Luke 12:50). The saying therefore probably deals with the completion of the missionary task and declares that the disciples cannot fulfil it with regard to their nation before the parousia appears.[21] As 10:23b is by no means smoothly attached to 10:23a, we must ask whether 23a in fact represents the original introduction to 23b, especially since 10:24f. deals with the relation between master and disciples; according to 10:25b this probably means that the disciple is not to fare better than his master. Since this saying occurs in Luke 6:40 in a quite different connexion in which it is certainly not applied to suffering like the master, it follows that 10:23b was also not originally connected with 10:24f. These considerations prove, in spite of all objections, that the logion 10:23b is a de-

19. Michaelis, *Verheissung*, 30ff.

20. Thus also Cullmann, *Hoffnung*, 36f.; Cullmann, *Retour*, 24; G. Schrenk, *Die Weissagung über Israel im Neuen Testament*, 1951, 65 n. 4; M. Albertz, *Die Botschaft des Neuen Testamentes* 1, 1, 1947, 79; Walter, *Kommen*, 81.

21. See Michaelis, *Matthäus* 2, 94f.; G. Schrenk, op. cit. in n. [[20]], 14f.

tached saying which in its essentials fits very well into the missionary charge, but has no firm connexion with its surroundings. Now, as we know, A. Schweitzer[22] interpreted 10:23 in its place in the missionary charge to mean that Jesus "did not expect his disciples back in this age," and that, as this prediction was not fulfilled because the disciples did after all return to Jesus, "the non-fulfilment of Matt 10:23 signifies the first postponement of the parousia"; "the missionary charge is historical as a whole and down to the smallest detail." After the return of the disciples Jesus' endeavours are now according to Schweitzer directed to escaping from the people (Mark 6:30ff.); in his view Jesus wishes to go to Jerusalem at once in order to take upon himself there the remaining final tribulation through his death at the hand of the authorities, and thereby to compel the coming of the Kingdom of God. M. Werner[23] has taken up Schweitzer's exegesis and declares it to be its merit that "it alone . . . makes it intelligible to us that Jesus on the occasion of sending out his disciples should really have pronounced this discourse essentially as Matthew's gospel records it." Now it is of course correct that it is possible for Schweitzer to explain Matt 10:23 strictly within the situation when the discourse sending out the disciples was held as recorded by Matthew. But he makes this possible only by tacitly combining the circumstances of Matthew 10 with those of Mark 6. Thus Matthew does [[63]] indeed presume as the occasion for his missionary charge the dispatch of the disciples on a mission (10:5ff.), but Schweitzer then transfers the charge at once to the situation described in Mark 6:6ff., so that now the return of the disciples and Jesus' endeavour to separate himself from the crowd (Mark 6:30ff.) appear as the sequel in time to the mission, although Matt 14:13 paralleled in Mark 6:30 in fact omits the return of the disciples. This combination produces therefore an *artificial* connexion between the missionary discourse and the disciples' return; and to this it must be added that nothing in the sources affords grounds for the assertion that Jesus was disappointed that the disciples came back without the end of the world having appeared. Matt 20:23b must rather be interpreted, contrary to Schweitzer's exegesis, as an isolated logion.[24] Then the meaning of the saying appears clearly to be: the parousia of the Son of Man will arrive before the disciples have finished proclaiming the Kingdom of God in Israel.[25] Thereby the coming of the Kingdom of God is transferred here also to the lifetime of Jesus' disciples, and moreover it is presumed as

22. Schweitzer, *Quest*, 357ff. (in German *Leben Jesu*, 10, 405ff.).

23. Werner, *Dogma*, 71ff.; Werner, *Schweiz. Theol. Umschau* 12, 1942, 49ff.

24. Werner's demand that the problem of the missionary charge as a whole must be solved if objections are raised to Schweitzer's exegesis *(Umschau,* 51), overlooks completely the literary results of the analysis of the discourse as to the composite character of the tradition recorded there.

25. The assertion that the saying could not go back to Jesus (Duncan, *Jesus*, 182; Sharman, *Son of Man*, 29; K. Kundsin, *Das Urchristentum in Lichte der Evangeliumforschung*, 1929, 15; Glasson, *Advent*, 103f.; C. J. Cadoux, *Mission*, 95, 143; T. W. Manson, *Mission and Message*, 474; probably also Wilder, *Eschatology*, 39f.; against this V. Taylor, *Exp. T.* 58, 1946/47, 14), can be proved only by arguing very unconvincingly that the experience of the primitive Church shows itself here or that Jesus made no such temporal predictions.

well that this coming may happen at any time and suddenly within this period. But how is it to be explained in the face of this prediction that the disciples nevertheless return to Jesus (Mark 6:30 par. Luke 9:10, cf. also Luke
10:17)? It is very open to question whether we ought to ask this. For firstly it
does indeed seem within the frame of the Marcan account that the return to
Jesus of the commissioned disciples was final; but it is by no means certain
that the information used by Mark does not presuppose that the disciples, or
some of them, set out again to proclaim their message anew. And then Matt
10:23b in no way assumes that the expectation of an early coming of the Son
of Man excludes the return of the disciples to Jesus in the course of their missionary activity. Therefore the information that [[64]] Jesus sent out disciples
on a missionary errand and that these disciples returned to him again does
not in anyway contradict the assumption that Jesus promised his disciples
that the Kingdom of God would come before the *complete* discharge of their
missionary commission. So Matt 10:23 confirms the conclusion already obtained that Jesus reckoned on the coming of the Kingdom of God and of the
Son of Man in glory within the lifetime of the generation of his hearers.[26]
This may conclude the discussion of all the relevant texts which show that
Jesus proclaimed the proximity of the *eschaton* (within a limited time) or at
least its coming *in the future*.[27]

26. It is not possible to prove the assertion that for Jesus the coming of the Son of Man
was not identical with the coming of the Kingdom, but only with the last act of God's royal
rule in history (thus Flew, *Church*, 32). Equally impossible is the assertion that "the coming
of the Son of Man" did not concern the world, but Israel alone, and that the prediction was
fulfilled by the destruction of Jerusalem in the year 70 (thus P. Benoit, *L'évangile selon Saint
Matthieu*, 1950, 74).

27. J. Jeremias quotes as a further authority for Jesus' imminent expectation Mark 9:13;
par. Matt 17:12, where the Baptist is designated as Elias who has already come and in whom
the predicted suffering has been fulfilled *(Th. Bl.* 20, 1941, 216; *Th. Wb. z. N.T.* 2, 938). This
text is today usually regarded as a formulation by the Church (cf. Bultmann, *Tradition*, 131f.;
Dibelius, *Tradition*, 226f. (in German *Formgeschichte*, 228f.); Klostermann and Lohmeyer,
Markus ad loc.). But at least as regards 9:11, 13 there is no compelling need for this (see Taylor, *Mark*, 394f.; that Jesus argues here from an apocryphal quotation, as 9:13 presumes, does
not refute the assumption that the tradition is primitive, see E. Stauffer, *Theologie des Neuen
Testaments*, [4,5]1948, n. 267). But neither does the text prove that Jesus also supported the rab-
binical dogma that Elias would come *immediately* before the Messiah, so this text had better
be omitted as an authority for Jesus' imminent expectation (he certainly does not say that the
Messiah and the day of Jahve have already appeared, thus Guy, *Last Things*, 48).

Bibliography

[[Albertz, *Die Botschaft*   M. Albertz. *Die Entstehung der Botschaft*. Vol. 1 of *Die Botschaft des
des Neuen Testa-   Neuen Testamentes. In memoriam Ernst Lohmeyer*. Zurich: Evan-
mentes   gelischer Verlag, 1947.]]
[[Benoit, *L'évangile*   P. Benoit. *L'évangile selon Saint Matthieu*. Paris: Cerf, 1950.]]
selon Saint Matthieu

[[Bornkamm, "Die Verzögerung der Parusie" G. Bornkamm. "Die Verzögerung der Parusie." Pp. 120ff. in *In memoriam Ernst Lohmeyer*. Edited by W. Schmauch. Stuttgart: Evangelische Verlagswerk, 1951.]]

Bultmann, *Tradition* R. Bultmann. *Die Geschichte der synoptischen Tradition*. 2nd ed. [[Göttingen: Vandenhoeck & Ruprecht,]] 1931.

Busch, *Eschatologie* F. Busch. *Zum Verständnis der synoptischen Eschatologie: Markus 13 neu untersucht*. [[Gütersloh: Bertelsmann,]] 1938.

Cadoux, *Mission* C. J. Cadoux. *The Historic Mission of Jesus: A Constructive Reexamination of the Eschatological Teaching in the Synoptic Gospels*. [[London: Lutterworth,]] 1941.

Cullmann, *Hoffnung* O. Cullmann. *Die Hoffnung der Kirche auf die Wiederkunft Christi*. Verhandlungen des schweizerischen reformierten Pfarrvereins 83. 1942.

Cullmann, *Retour* O. Cullmann. *Le retour de Christ, espérance de l'Eglise selon le Nouveau Testament*. [[Neuchâtel: Delachaux & Niestle,]] 1943.

Dibelius, *Tradition* (in German *Formgeschichte*) M. Dibelius. *From Tradition to Gospel*. [[London: Nicholson & Watson,]] 1934. [German: *Die Formgeschichte des Evangeliums*. 2nd ed. 1933]

Dodd, *Parables* C. H. Dodd. *The Parables of the Kingdom*. 3rd ed. [[London: Nisbet,]] 1935.

Duncan, *Jesus* G. S. Duncan. *Jesus, Son of Man*. [[London: Nisbet,]] 1947.

Flew, *Church* R. N. Flew. *Jesus and His Church: A Study of the Idea of the Ecclesia in the New Testament*. 2nd ed. [[London: Epworth,]] 1943.

[[Fuchs, *Verkündigung und Forschung* E. Fuchs, in *Verkündigung und Forschung: Theologischer Jahresbericht* 4. Evangelische Theologie Beihefte. Munich: Chr. Kaiser, 1947–48.]]

Glasson, *Advent* T. F. Glasson. *The Second Advent: The Origin of the New Testament Doctrine*. 2nd ed. 1947.

Guy, *Last Things* H. A. Guy. *The New Testament Doctrine of the "Last Things."* [[Oxford: Oxford University Press,]] 1948.

Hauck, *Lukas* F. Hauck. *Das Evangelium des Lukas*. Theologischer Handkommentar zum Neuen Testament 3. [[Leipzig: Deichert,]] 1934.

Jeremias, *Parables* J. Jeremias. *The Parables of Jesus*. [[London: SCM,]] 1954 [trans. from German 3rd ed., 1954].

Jeremias, *Weltvollender* J. Jeremias. *Jesus als Weltvollender*. [[Gütersloh,]] 1930.

Jülicher, *Gleichnisreden* A. Jülicher. *Die Gleichnisreden Jesus*. Vol. 1, 2nd ed. Vol. 2, 1910. [[Repr. BZNW 103. Berlin: de Gruyter, 1999.]]

Klostermann, *Markus* E. Klostermann. *Das Markusevangelium*. Handbuch zum Neuen Testament 3. 3rd ed. [[Tübingen: Mohr Siebeck,]] 1936 (= 4th ed. 1950).

Klostermann, *Matthäus* E. Klostermann. *Das Matthäusevangelium*. Handbuch zum Neuen Testament 4. 2nd ed. [[Tübingen: Mohr,]] 1927.

Liechtenhan, *Mission* R. Liechtenhan, *Die urchristliche Mission: Voraussetzungen, Motive und Methoden*. [[Zurich: Zwingli,]] 1946.

Lohmeyer, *Markus* E. Lohmeyer. *Das Evangelium des Markus*. Kritischexegetischer Kommentar über das N.T., begründet von H. A. W. Meyer, 1/2. 10th ed. [[Göttingen: Vandenhoeck & Ruprecht,]] 1937 (= 11th ed., 1951).

Major, *Mission and Message*

H. D. A. Major, T. W. Manson, and C. J. Wright. *The Mission and Message of Jesus: An Exposition of the Gospels in the Light of Modern Research.* [[No place: Nicholson & Watson,]] 1937.

Manson, *Sayings*

Part 2 of H. D. A. Major, T. W. Manson, and C. J. Wright. *The Mission and Message of Jesus: An Exposition of the Gospels in the Light of Modern Research.* [[New York: Dutton,]] 1949.

Meinertz, *Theologie*

M. Meinertz. *Theologie des Neues Testamentes.* 2 vols. [[Bonn: Hanstein,]] 1950.

Michaelis, *Sämann*

W. Michaelis. *Es ging ein Sämann aus zu säen . . . : Eine Einführung in die Gleichnisse Jesu über das Reich Gottes und die Kirche.* [[Berlin: Furche,]] 1938.

Michaelis, *Verheissung*

W. Michaelis. *Der Herr verzieht nicht die Verheissung: Die Aussagen Jesu über die Nähe des Jüngsten Tages.* 1942.

Schniewind, *Markus*

J. Schniewind. *Das Evangelium nach Markus.* Das Neue Testament Deutsch. Neues Göttinger Bibelwerk 1. [[Göttingen: Vandenhoeck & Ruprecht,]] 1933.

[[Schrenk, *Die Weissagung über Israel im Neuen Testament*

G. Schrenk. *Die Weissagung über Israel im Neuen Testament.* Zurich: Gotthelf, 1951.]]

Schweitzer, *Quest* (in German *Leben Jesu*)

A. Schweitzer. *The Quest of the Historical Jesus.* 3rd ed. [[London: SCM,]] 1954 [German: *Geschichte der Leben-Jesus-Forschung.* 6th ed. 1951]].

Sharman, *Son of Man*

H. B. Sharman. *Son of Man and Kingdom of God.* 2nd ed. [[New York: Harper,]] 1943.

B. T. D. Smith, *Parables*

B. T. D. Smith. *Parables of the Synoptic Gospels: A Critical Study.* [[Cambridge: Cambridge University Press,]] 1937.

C. W. F. Smith, *Jesus*

C. W. F. Smith. *The Jesus of the Parables.* [[Philadelphia: Westminster,]] 1948.

Stauffer, *NT*

E. Stauffer. *New Testament Theology.* [[London: SCM,]] 1955 [German: *Die Theologie des Neuen Testaments.* 4th–5th eds., 1948].

Taylor, *Mark*

V. Taylor. *The Gospel according to St. Mark.* [[London: Macmillan,]] 1952.

Walter, *Kommen*

E. Walter. *Die Eschatologische Situation nach den synoptischen Evangelien.* Vol. 2 of *Das kommen des Herrn* [[Freiburg im Breisgau: Herder,]] 1947.

Weiss, *Irrtumslosigheit*

K. Weiss. *Exegetisches zur Irrtumslosigkeit und Eschatologie Jesu Christi.* [[Münster i. W.: Aschendorff,]] 1916.

[[Wellhausen, *Das Evangelium Matthaei*

J. Wellhausen. *Das Evangelium Matthaei.* 2nd ed. Berlin: Reimer, 1914.]]

Wilder, *Eschatology*

A. N. Wilder. *Eschatology and Ethics in the Teaching of Jesus.* 2nd ed. [New York: Harper,]] 1950.

[[Wrede, *Das Messiasgeheimnis in den Evangelien*

W. Wrede. *Das Messiasgeheimnis in den Evangelien: Zugleich ein Beitrag zum Verständnis des Markusevangeliums.* 2nd ed. Göttingen: Vandenhoeck & Ruprecht, 1913.]]

JOACHIM JEREMIAS

'Abba *as an Address to God*

The Sources

[[62]] All five strata of tradition in our gospels (Mark, *logia* material, Matthaean special material, Lucan special material, John) are unanimous in affirming that Jesus addressed God as "my Father."[1] The instances are distributed as follows (parallels are only counted once):

Mark	1[2]
Material common to Matthew and Luke	3[3]
Additional instances in Luke only	2[4]
Additional instances in Matthew only	1[5]
John	9[6]

Not only do the five strata agree that Jesus used "Father" as a form of address; it is also their unanimous witness that Jesus used this address in *all* his prayers. (The one exception is Mark 15:34 par. Matt 27:46, the cry from the cross: "My God, my God, why hast thou forsaken me?" and here Ps 22:2 already provided the form of address.)[7] The essential point of this assertion is the unanimity of the tradition.

Reprinted, with permission, from J. Jeremias, *New Testament Theology: The Proclamation of Jesus* (New York: Scribner's, 1971) 62–68.

    1. A distinction must be made between "my Father" as an *address* to God and the *designation* of God as Father on the lips of Jesus (cf. J. Jeremias, [["Abba," in *The Prayers of Jesus*; SBT 2/6; London, 1967]], 35–59). This section is concerned only with the address.

    2. 14:36.

    3. Matt 6:9 (par. Luke 11:2); 11:25f. (par. Luke 10:21, twice).

    4. 23:34, 46.

    5. 26:42.

    6. 11:41; 12:27f.; 17:1, 5, 11, 21, 24f.

    7. See [[Jeremias, *NT Theology*,]] 5 n. 2.

Quite apart from the question of the authenticity of individual prayers, this shows that "Father" as an address to God was firmly rooted in the tradition about Jesus.

Furthermore, in the Gethsemane story Mark records that when Jesus addressed God as "my Father," he used the Aramaic form 'Abbā:[8] καὶ ἔλεγεν· Ἀββὰ ὁ πατήρ, πάντα δυνατά σοι· παρένεγκε τὸ ποτήριον τοῦτο ἀπ᾽ ἐμοῦ [['And he said, "Abba, Father, for you all things are possible; remove this cup from me; yet not what I want, but what you want" ']] (14:36).

The Uniqueness of 'Abbā as an Address to God

[[63]] Judaism had a great wealth of forms of address to God at its disposal. For example, the "Prayer" *(Těphilla,* later called the Eighteen Benedictions), which was already prayed three times a day in the New Testament period,[9] ends each benediction with a new form of address to God. In what is presumably its earliest form, the first benediction runs as follows:[10]

> Blessed art thou, Yahweh,
> God of Abraham, God of Isaac and God of Jacob (cf. Mark 12:26 par.),
> the most high God,
> Master[11] of heaven and earth (cf. Matt 11:25 par.),
> our shield and the shield of our fathers.
> Blessed art thou, Yahweh, the shield of Abraham.

It can be seen here that one form of address to God is put after another. If we were to collect together all the forms of address that appear in early Jewish prayer literature, we would find ourselves with a very extensive list.

Nowhere, however, in the Old Testament do we find God addressed as "Father." The cry of despair *'ābīnū 'attā* [['you are our father']][12] or *'ābī 'attā* [['you are my father']][13] and the king's privilege of saying *'ābī 'attā* to God[14] certainly come very near to it, but they are statements and not addresses to God using the name "Father." In post-canonical Jewish literature there are isolated examples of the use of πάτερ [['father']] as an address to God;[15] these,

---

8. Accent on the closing syllable. In what follows, *'Abbā* is capitalized where it is an address to God, otherwise written lower case.

9. J. Jeremias, "Daily Prayer in the Life of Jesus and the Primitive Church," *The Prayers of Jesus,* 66–81: 70–72.

10. Following Dalman, *Worte Jesu*[1], Leipzig 1898, 299 (unfortunately not in the second edition). What are probably additions have been omitted.

11. For this translation of *qōnē,* see Jeremias, "Daily Prayer," 74 n. 33.

12. Isa 63:16 (twice); 64:7.

13. Jer 3:4.

14. Ps 89:27, taken up in Sir 51:10 (Hebrew).

15. Sir 23:1, 4 LXX; *3 Macc* 6:3, 8; *Apoc. Ezek.* Fragm. 3 (ed. K. Holl, in: *Gesammelte Aufsätze zur Kirchengeschichte II, Der Osten,* Tübingen 1928, 36); Wis 14:3.

however, come from Diaspora Judaism, which is here following the influence of the Greek world. In Palestine, it is only in the early Christian period that we come across two prayers which use "Father" as an address to God, both in the form *'ābīnū malkēnū* [['our father, our king']].[16] But it should be [[64]] noted that these are liturgical prayers in which God is addressed as the Father of the community, that the language used is Hebrew, and that *'ābīnū* is associated with *malkēnū*: the Father to whom the community calls is the heavenly king of the people of God. On the other hand, we look in vain for the personal address "my Father." It occurs for the first and only time in *Seder Eliyyahu Rabbah*, a writing which originated in Southern Italy about A.D. 974, in the form *'ābī šebbaššāmayīm* (i.e., in Hebrew and with the addition of "who art in heaven")[17]—the original text of Sir 23:1, 4 to be inferred from a Hebrew paraphrase ran *'el 'ābī* and therefore is to be translated "God of my Father," and not "God, my Father."[18] That means that in the literature of Palestinian Judaism *no evidence has yet been found* of "my Father" being used by an individual as an address to God. It first appears in the Middle Ages, in Southern Italy.

It is quite unusual that Jesus should have addressed God as "my Father"; it is even more so that he should have used the Aramaic form *'Abbā*. True, the actual word has only been handed on in Mark 14:36 but two things suggest that Jesus used this *'Abbā* as an address to God elsewhere in his prayers. First, there is a remarkable variation of forms in the tradition of "Father" as an address to God. On the one hand, we find the correct Greek vocative form πάτερ,[19] which Matthew provides with a personal pronoun πάτερ μου;[20] on the other hand, we find the nominative with the article (ὁ πατήρ) as a vocative.[21] It is particularly striking that we find πάτερ and the vocative ὁ πατήρ side by side in one and the same prayer (Matt 11:25f. par. Luke 20:21). This remarkable variation points to an underlying *'abbā* which, in the time of Jesus, was used in colloquial language at the same time as an address, for the emphatic state ("the Father") and for the form with the first person suffix ("my, our Father").[22] Second, we learn from [[65]] Rom 8:15 and Gal 4:6 that the cry Ἀββὰ ὁ πατήρ, uttered in the spirit, was widespread in the early church. Indeed, Paul presupposes that it is not only to be heard in his own congregations (Gal 4:6) but that it also rings out as cry of prayer in congregations which he has not founded, like that in Rome (Rom 8:25). The unusual character of this

16. Jeremias, [["Abba,"]] 27–29; the prayers are the *'ăhābā rabbā* (the second of the two benedictions which introduced the *Shĕma'* in the morning and which probably even belonged to the ancient priestly liturgy of temple worship) and the New Year Litany (the basic elements of which are already attested by R. Akiba, died after A.D. 135).

17. I have listed the instances [["Abba"]], 28 n. 65.

18. [["Abba"]], 28f.

19. Matt 11:25 par. Luke 10:21a; Luke 11:2; 22:42; 23:34, 46; John 11:41; 12:27f.; 17:1, 5, 11, 24f.

20. Matt 26:39, 42.

21. Mark 14:36; Matt 11:26 par. Luke 10:21b (Rom 8:15; Gal 4:6). πατήρ without the article as a vocative, which has been transmitted by some witnesses at John 17:5, 11, 21, 24f., is an inner-Greek variation (vulgarism).

22. Jeremias, [["Abba,"]] 59f.

form of address (see below) shows that it is an echo of the prayer of Jesus. Thus we have every reason to suppose that an *'Abbā* underlies every instance of πάτηρ (μου) or ὁ πατήρ in his words of prayer.

There may be a few sparse instances of πάτερ as a form of address to God in the milieu of Hellenistic Judaism[23]—probably under Greek influence—but it can certainly be said that there is no instance of the use of *'Abbā* as an address to God in all the extensive prayer-literature of Judaism, whether in liturgical or in private prayers.[24]

As we can learn from the Targum, Jews deliberately avoided applying the word *'abbā* to God even outside prayers. In the three passages of the Old Testament where God is called *'ābī* [['my father']], the Targum twice renders the word *ribbūnī* ("my Lord") (Jer 3:4, 19); only in the *Tg. Ps.* 89:27 did the translator feel himself compelled by the sense to translate *'ābī* as *'abbā*. Otherwise, *'abbā* is applied to God elsewhere in the Targum only at Mal 2:20 (Hebrew *'āb*); here, too, the translator saw no other possible rendering in view of the content. Outside the Targum there is only a single passage in Rabbinic literature in which *'abbā* is used with reference to God. It is a story which was told of Ḥanin ha-Neḥba, famous for his prayers for rain, who lived about the end of the first century B.C.:

> Ḥanin ha-Neḥba was the son of the daughter of Onias the Circledrawer.[25] When the world needed rain, our teachers used to send schoolchildren to him, who seized the hem of his coat[26] and said to him, *'abbā, 'abbā, hab lan miṭrā* ('Daddy, [[66]] daddy, give us rain!'). He said to Him (God): "Master of the world, grant it for the sake of these who are not yet able to distinguish between an *'Abbā* who has the power to give rain and an *'abbā* who has not."[27]

Ḥanin appeals to God's mercy by using the trustful *'abbā, 'abbā* which the school-children cry out to him and describes God—in contrast to himself—as the "*'Abbā* who has the power to give rain." The little story can be regarded as a prelude to Matt 5:45, where God is described as the heavenly Father who grants the gift of rain without discrimination to both righteous and unrighteous—but it does not provide the missing Jewish example of *'Abbā* used as an

---

23. See above, p. 202 n. 15.

24. Nor can E. Haenchen, *Der Weg Jesu*, Berlin 1966, 492–94 n. 7a produce any evidence. Neither of the two passages to which he refers contains *'Abbā* as an address to God. His next remarks, "It is quite clear that the form *'Abbā*, which occurs only in Aramaic, is not to be found in the Mishnah (c. A.D. 200), which is written in pure Hebrew," betray an inadequate conception of Mishnah Hebrew. For the situation is precisely the opposite. The Hebrew form *'ābī* does not stand for 'my father' in any passage in the Mishnah; without exception the Aramaic form *'abbā* is used, more than fifty times. (All these passages are instances of secular usage; 'my father' does not occur at all in the Mishnah as an address to God or a designation of God.)

25. See Jeremias, [["Abba,"]] 61.

26. A gesture of urgent request, cf. Mark 5:27.

27. *b. Ta'an.* 23b.

address to God. For we must remember that Ḥanin does not in any way address God himself as ’*Abbā*; his address is "Master of the world."

All this confronts us with a fact of fundamental importance. *We do not have a single example* of God being addressed as ’*Abbā* in Judaism, but Jesus *always* addressed God in this way in his prayers. The only exception is the cry from the cross (Mark 15:34 par. Matt 27:46), and the reason for that is its character as a quotation.

There is a linguistic explanation for the striking silence of the Jewish prayer literature. In origin, ’*abbā* is a babbling sound, so it is not inflected and takes no suffix. "When a child experiences the taste of wheat (i.e., when it is weaned), it learns to say ’*abbā* and ’*immā* [['mother, mamma']] (i.e., these are the first sounds that it prattles)."[28] Originally an exclamatory form, ’*abbā* had gained considerable ground in Palestinian Aramaic even before the New Testament period. It suppressed the "Imperial Aramaic" and biblical-Hebraic form of address ’*ābī* all along the line, and even took its place in statements; in addition, it took the place of the emphatic ’*ābā* and largely established itself as an expression for 'his father' and 'our father'.[29] By the time of Jesus, ’*abbā* had long had a wider use than in the talk of small children. Even grown-up children, sons as well as daughters, now addressed their father as ’*abbā*.[30] The story of Ḥanin ha-Neḥba (see above, pp. 204f.), which is set in pre-Christian times, is an example of the way in which older, respected people other than fathers might be addressed as ’*abbā*. A newly-discovered Jewish-Christian source[31] says that it is a peculiarity of the [[67]] Hebrew language that 'son' can designate a true and upright slave and 'father' the lord and master.[32] The Midrash confirms this: "as the disciples are called sons, so is the master called father."[33] In the house of R. Gamaliel II (c. A.D. 90), even the slave Ṭabi was called "’*abba* Ṭabi."[34]

If we keep in mind this setting for ’*abbā*, it will be clear why Palestinian Judaism does not use ’*abbā* as a form of address to God. ’*Abbā* was a children's word, used in everyday talk, an expression of courtesy. It would have seemed disrespectful, indeed unthinkable, to the sensibilities of Jesus' contemporaries to address God with this familiar word.[35]

28. *b. Ber.* 40a Bar. par. *b. Sanh.* 70b Bar.

29. Instances are collected in Jeremias, [["Abba,"]] 58ff.

30. Ibid., 58 n. 32, 60 n. 43.

31. Worked over in ‘Abd el-Jabbār, *Erweis der Prophetenschaft unseres Herrn Mohammed*, preserved in Istanbul, Sammlung Shehid Ali Pasha, no. 1575 (cf. S. Pines, *The Jewish Christians of the Early Centuries of Christianity according to a New Source*, The Israel Academy of Sciences and Humanities, Proceedings, 2/13, Jerusalem 1966).

32. f.55b–56a (according to Pines, *The Jewish Christians*, 8).

33. *Sipre Deut.* 34 on 6:7.

34. *y. Nid.* 49b 42f. Bar.

35. G. Kittel, [["ἀββα," *TDNT* 1]], 5. E. Haenchen's objection against Kittel (*Der Weg Jesu*, 59 n. 19), "It is pure supposition that Jesus' way of expressing himself caused offence to his contemporaries," is not to the point, as is shown by what is said on p. [[204]] above about the terminology of the Targum; cf. also *Ta‘an.* 3.8 (familiarity towards God which is expressed in childlike urgency deserves to be punished by the ban).

Jesus dared to use *'Abbā* as a form of address to God. This *'Abbā* is the *ipsissima vox Jesu* [['very voice of Jesus']].

The Significance of *'Abbā as an Address to God*

The complete novelty and uniqueness of *'Abbā* as an address to God in the prayers of Jesus shows that it expresses the heart of Jesus' relationship to God. He spoke to God as a child to its father: confidently and securely, and yet at the same time reverently and obediently.

At this point it is necessary to issue a warning against two possible misunderstandings. First, the fact that *'abbā* was originally a child's exclamatory word has occasionally led to the mistaken assumption that Jesus adopted the language of a tiny child when he addressed God as "Father"; even I myself believed this earlier. However, the discovery that even in the period before the New Testament, grownup sons and daughters addressed their fathers as *'abbā*, stands in the way of any such limitation. Secondly, the fact that the address *'Abbā* expresses a consciousness of sonship should not mislead us into ascribing to Jesus himself in detail the "Son of God" christology, e.g., the idea of pre-existence, which developed very early in [[68]] the primitive church. This over-interpretation of the address *'Abbā* is prohibited by the everyday sound of the word.

Jesus regarded *'Abbā* as a sacred word. When he instructs the disciples to "Call no man your father on earth, for you have one Father, who is in heaven" (Matt 23:9),[36] he certainly does not mean to prohibit them from addressing their physical fathers as "father." He is thinking, rather, of the custom of addressing distinguished people, especially older men, as *'abbā*. The disciples are not to do this, because that would be a misuse of the word. He wanted to reserve the honour of the name "father" for God alone. This prohibition shows the degree to which Jesus felt that the address *'Abbā* should be revered.

'Abbā as a form of address to God expresses the ultimate mystery of the mission of Jesus. He was conscious of being authorized to communicate God's revelation, because God had made himself known to him as Father (Matt 11:27 par.).

36. On the passage, see Jeremias, [["Abba,"]] 41f.

N. T. WRIGHT

Kingdom Redefined:
The Announcement

Introduction:
Summary Announcements

[[226]] . . . [T]he obvious features of Jesus' work, to any casual observer, would be certain styles of action and teaching that marked him out as a prophet. We are now in a position to see that the crucial element in his prophetic activity was the story, both implicit and explicit, that he was telling and acting out. It was Israel's story reaching its climax: the long-awaited moment has arrived! The kingdom has come! These statements, repeated (especially by Matthew) as summaries of what Jesus was saying, can only be understood as statements-in-context. They are like saying "Frodo and Sam have reached Mount Doom," or "They're coming into the home straight," or "Jayne has had her baby": the hearer is assumed to know the context, the previous acts in the drama. To say "the kingdom of god is at hand" makes sense only when the hearers know "the story so far" and are waiting for it to be completed.

This recognition of the nature of the kingdom-announcement as part of an assumed larger *story* enables us to make a preliminary assessment of historicity. We may remind ourselves that if Jesus' announcement of the kingdom is to make historical sense it must make sense *both* as something that would be clearly understood within its Jewish context *and* as the presupposition for the significantly different resonances of "kingdom" in the early church. At the same time it would clearly *both* challenge some prevailing assumptions within that Jewish context *and* retain a special focus which would be characteristic only of Jesus' career, not of the work of his post-Easter followers. It must be set within Judaism, but as a challenge; it must be the presupposition for the church, but not the blueprint. As we argued earlier [[not reprinted

Reprinted with permission from N. T. Wright, *Jesus and the Victory of God* (Christian Origins and the Question of God 2; Minneapolis: Fortress, 1992) 226–43 and portions of (bibliography) 674–700.

here]], double similarity and double dissimilarity must characterize any analysis that claims historicity.

How does this affect our reading of the opening statement of Jesus' public career reported in Matthew and Mark?

> From then on Jesus began to make an announcement, saying, "Repent! For the kingdom of heaven is at hand."
>
> Jesus came, announcing the good news of god, and saying, "The time is fulfilled; the kingdom of god is at hand. Repent, and believe in the good news."[1]

[[227]] No one in Judaism had said quite that before,[2] but the sayings make no sense except in a firmly Jewish context. Equally, the early church, venturing beyond the borders of Judaism, did not announce the kingdom in these terms—they would have meant nothing to Gentiles—and yet the announcement they made, and the life they led, are unthinkable without this kingdom being believed to have come in a still very Jewish sense. They were not, after all, offering "a different religious option" to a world already sated with such things. They were announcing that the one true god, the creator, had fulfilled his purpose for Israel and was now, in consequence, addressing the whole world. That is why the evangelists stressed Jesus' announcement of the kingdom. They were not simply reading their own communities' preaching back into an imagined "history"; recent studies have shown that part of what they wanted to convey, as their message to their own communities, was the fact that in the unique and unrepeatable career of Jesus Israel's history had reached its climactic moment.[3] Thus, without as yet going into the finer detail of the sayings, the preliminary indications are that we have substantial historical ground under our feet in saying that Jesus' characteristic message was the announcement of the kingdom. This conclusion, indeed, is not particularly controversial except where dogma has gained total control over history.

This sort of announcement is presumably what Matthew means when he refers, later, to Jesus "preaching the gospel of the kingdom."[4] It is also presumably what Luke has in mind when he has Jesus refer to "preaching the good news of the kingdom of god."[5] The disciples, too, are sent out with the same message, both as a group[6] and as individuals.[7] We must stress, again,

---

1. Matt 4:17/Mark 1:15.

2. Apart, perhaps, from John the Baptist: Matt 3:2, cf. Matt 11:11–12/Luke 16:16, on which see below. John, in any case, would be the exception that proved the rule. No doubt other prophetic and revolutionary movements had announced the coming of the kingdom, but we have no reason for thinking they produced the same combined message as Jesus had done; in particular, we have no record of them calling Israel to *repent* at the same time as announcing the kingdom.

3. Cf. esp. *NTPG* chap. 13, with details of secondary discussions.

4. Matt 4:23; 9:35.

5. Luke 4:43; 8:1.

6. Matt 10:7/Luke 9:2/Luke 10:9, 11.

7. Luke 9:60.

that this message is *part of a story*, and only makes sense as such. And there is only one story that will do. Israel would at last "return from exile"; evil would be defeated; YHWH would at last return to "visit" his people. Anyone wishing to evoke and affirm all this at once, in first-century Palestine, could not have chosen a more appropriate and ready-made slogan than "kingdom of god."

[[228]] This means, of course, that the announcement of the kingdom of god could never, in the nature of the case, be heard as a "timeless" message, an incidental example or occurrence of some general truth.[8] The whole point of it was that Israel's dream was coming true *right now*. Equally important, it could never be divorced from the person and deeds of the proclaimer. This will have been as true for John the Baptist as for Jesus. *This* baptism is the "getting-ready-for-the-kingdom" baptism; *this* proclamation is the one that is actually inaugurating the kingdom. The two are, it seems, very closely linked; Jesus regarded the work of John as the launching-pad for his own work, and it is historically probable that he saw John's arrest as the appropriate time to begin his own independent career of kingdom-proclamation.[9] The link of message and messenger is, of course, part of the scandal: the scandal of particularity (that YHWH should act *here and now* rather than at other times and places); the scandal that *this* was how the kingdom was coming; the scandal, too, of just who it was that YHWH was using, and the methods that he was employing. Like Salieri in Shaffer's *Amadeus,* scandalized that his god should choose the disreputable Mozart as the vehicle for divine music, Jesus' hearers could not but be struck, if they realized what was going on, at his extraordinary and shocking implicit claim.[10]

The significance of the kingdom-announcement, as reported in the short synoptic summaries, is strongly reinforced by certain elements of Jesus' praxis which we studied in the previous chapter. In particular, the exorcisms carry with them the haunting word: "If I by the finger of god cast out demons, then the kingdom of god has come upon you."[11] This evokes the same implicit narrative: Israel's god will one day become king; the establishment of this kingdom will involve the defeat of the enemy that has held Israel captive; there are clear signs that this is now happening; therefore the kingdom is indeed breaking in. YHWH really is becoming king; Israel really is being liberated.

If the short summary kingdom-announcements, even by themselves, evoke the entire story of Israel, the parables do so even more. Many of them

---

8. By "timeless" truth I do not mean necessarily a lofty philosophical abstraction. I mean something conceived to be a generally valid principle—e.g., "God is love" or "oppressors must be overthrown" or "brokered empires are bad for you"—which could lead to political and/or revolutionary activity, and could indeed suggest some theological underpinnings for such activity, but which, crucially, would not carry the sense that the story of Israel was reaching its climax.

9. John 3:22–26; 4:1f.; Matt 4:12, 17/Mark 1:14. Cf. esp. Cleary 1988; Murphy-O'Connor 1990, 371f.; Meyer 1992, 30–33.

10. See Shaffer 1985 [1980] 27, etc. Cf. chap. 13 [[in Wright, *Jesus and the Victory of God*]].

11. Luke 11:20/Matt 12:28. See ibid., 193–95.

are best understood as the retelling of precisely that story which is implicit in the [[229]] summaries. We shall look at some crucial ones here, under the first of the three headings suggested by our analysis of the Jewish context of kingdom-meanings: "return from exile," happening at last, but not in the expected way. . . .

Stories of Israel's Paradoxical History

Introduction

Several of the best-known parables find an obvious setting in the context we have sketched, as miniature stories which evoke the underlying narrative of Israel, and which show, in their different ways, how it is coming to a highly paradoxical resolution.[12] The collections of parables in Mark 4 and Matthew 13 are the obvious place to begin. These collections are clearly designed to characterize Jesus' preaching as a whole. This, the evangelists seem to be saying, is the sort of thing you would have heard Jesus say in a typical Galilean village at some stage (perhaps early on?) during his public career. These parables are the fuller tellings of the story which is implicit in the briefer kingdom-announcements.

Moreover, in explicitly describing what the kingdom is like, the parables in that very act inaugurate it, by inviting people to come and share the secret, to make this strange story their own, and to join Jesus in his new way of being Israel. The hearers are summoned to understand that their own present story—the story of Israel's dream of national liberation—is being subverted and changed into the dangerous and revolutionary story Jesus is telling. The parables offer not only information, but challenge; they are stories designed to evoke fresh praxis, to reorder the symbolic world, to break open current understandings and inculcate fresh ones.

The subversive nature of these stories, telling the story of Israel and giving it a devastating new twist, results again and again in the evocative challenge: "If you have ears, then hear!" To add that to a public utterance implies that what has been said is cryptic, and suggests that a certain secrecy is necessary in the present circumstances.[13] This saying, which is firmly [[230]] established in the tradition, reinforces the reading of the parables which I am

---

12. On the parables, cf. *NTPG* 433f., and [[Wright, *Jesus and the Victory of God*,]] 174–82 and [[pp. 210f. here]].

13. Matt 11:15 (after declaring that John is Elijah); Matt 13:9/Mark 4:9/Luke 8:8 (after the parable of the sower); Matt 13:43 (after the explanation of the "weeds"); Mark 4:23 (secret things will come to light); 7:16 (what comes out of the heart is what defiles; this verse is omitted by some good MSS); Luke 14:35 (useless salt will be thrown out). A parallel to this cryptic communication, at the level of the evangelists' own writing, is in Matt 24:15/Mark 13:14, "Let the reader understand"; in other words, one cannot speak about these things openly just now. Cf. *NTPG* 390–96. See too Rev 13:9, 18; *Gos. Thom.* 8:2 (the dragnet); 21:5 (seed growing secretly); 24:2 (light and darkness); 63:2 (the rich fool); 65:2 (the wicked tenants); 96:2 (leaven).

proposing. Their frequent apocalyptic imagery reflects, of course, a characteristically Jewish mode of communicating a subversive new reading of the hope of Israel."[14] They are stories which both affirm the Jewish expectation and declare that it is being fulfilled in a radically new fashion.

The Sower[15]

Of all the oddities about the parable of the sower, perhaps the strangest is this: there is still no agreement on what it was originally supposed to mean.[16] Considering the important place it occupies in all three synoptic gospels, and by common consent in the teaching of Jesus himself, this should be regarded as an indication that historians have not yet caught up with something fairly central in Jesus' career. Leaving aside at this stage the vexed question of what the parable meant to each of the synoptic evangelists, let alone to *Thomas*, I suggest that the context of the kingdom-announcement, in the form we have been studying it, provides a way forward.

I propose that, in Jesus' use of it, the parable of the sower (or whatever else it should be called; various names have been tried, and all disputed[17]) does two closely related things. Using imagery and structure which evoked "apocalyptic" retellings of Israel's story, the parable *tells the story of Israel, particularly the return from exile, with a paradoxical conclusion,* and it *tells the story of Jesus' ministry, as the fulfilment of that larger story, with a paradoxical outcome.* Various indications point in this double direction.

[[231]] First, the parable as it stands in all three synoptic versions exhibits, both in form and in content, that narrative mode which we know as "apocalyptic," and which is used in such writings to tell the cryptic story of the creator's dealings with the world and/or Israel, and to show how that story is reaching its dramatic and surprising climax.[18] An obvious example is Dan 2:31–45, in which the great statue has a head of gold, a chest of silver, a belly of bronze, and feet of clay. This is interpreted, in that allegorical style so typical of apocalyptic visions, to refer, not (as one might perhaps have supposed)

14. On the apocalyptic background of the Mark 4 parables in particular, cf. *4 Ezra* 4:26–32; 8:41–45; 9:26–37. These are discussed by, e.g., Boucher 1977, 45–53; Drury 1985, 26f., 53; and cf. *NTPG* 433f.

15. Matt 13:1–23/Mark 4:1–20/Luke 8:4–15/*Gospel of Thomas* 9; cf. *Ap. Jas.* 6:11; 8:1f.; *1 Clem.* 24:5; Justin, *Dial.* 125:1–2. In *Inf. Gos. Thom.* 12:1–2 the parable has become a miracle, performed by Jesus as a boy. On this parable see . . . Garnet 1983; Chilton 1984, 90–98; Marcus 1986; and other bibliography in Guelich 1989, 186f., 198f., 215f.; Davies and Allison 1988–91, 2.403–6.

16. So Boucher 1977, 47; Hooker 1991, 124; and, behind much of the modem tradition, Bultmann 1968 [1921] 199f.: "the original meaning of many similitudes has become irrecoverable"—citing this parable as an example.

17. E.g., "soils," "seeds," etc.; Matthew at least refers to it as the "parable of the sower" (13:18). Garnet (1983, 41) suggests "the parable of the fortunes of the seed." In K. Aland's *Synopsis* [[*of the Four Gospels* (Stuttgart, 1972)]], 174 (para. 122), the Latin and English titles refer to the "sower," but the German one to the "soils."

18. See *NTPG* 393f., 433; and pp. 212–221 here.

to different features of a contemporaneous kingdom, but to successive stages, different kingdoms, in ongoing world history. At the end of the succession there will come a stone, cut from a mountain, which will smash the statue on its feet and destroy it; the stone will then become a mountain, filling the whole earth. This represents the kingdom which shall never be destroyed, which the creator god will establish in those days.

The parallel between Daniel 2 and Mark 4 is instructive. The vision in Daniel 2 concerns the kingdom of god and its triumph over the kingdoms of the world. The revelation of this vision is described as the unveiling of a "mystery" which could not be made known any other way.[19] The "stone" which smashed the clay feet and which then became a huge mountain was fairly certainly read as messianic by some groups in the first century, not least, perhaps, because of the well-known play between 'stone' (*eben* in Hebrew) and 'son' (*ben*),[20] and the passage offers a natural link to Daniel 7, with its four kingdoms and its "son of man."[21] The themes of the Daniel passage clearly have a good deal in common with themes in Mark, not least chap. 4. It will not do to object pedantically that statues and seeds (or soils) are like apples and elephants, or that Daniel sketches a chronological sequence while the parable describes different things that happen simultaneously. The point is that, just as the *form* of Mark 4:1–20 and its parallels resembles that of an apocalypse (its cryptic story, its transition passage about the revealing of mysteries, and its point-by-point interpretation), so here the *content* is so close (the failed sowings, and the kingdom of the creator god successfully set up, seen as the unveiling of the mysterious divine plan and, as we shall see, as the revelation of the Messiah) that it gives the lie to any suggestion of either forcing the evidence or mere coincidence. When we read it in its first-century Jewish context, the parable of the sower, [[232]] like the vision of the statue, asks to be understood as a retelling of Israel's controlling narrative about the kingdoms of the world and the kingdom of god.

The second indication that the sower is a retelling of the story of Israel is found in the fairly close parallel with the wicked tenants (Mark 12:1–12 and parallels).[22] There should be no doubt that this parable narrates the history of Israel in terms of YHWH's sending of prophets, and finally of his son. The prophets are looking for "fruit," which is of course what the unsuccessful seeds fail to produce and what the successful seed produces in abundance.[23] They come in sequence: the first is beaten, the second wounded in the head,

---

19. Dan 2:17–23: in vv. 18, 19 the key word is *raz* [['secret']], translated *mysterion* [['mystery']] in LXX.

20. Cf. Snodgrass 1983, 113–18; and recently Gundry 1993, 689–91, citing, e.g., Exod 28:9f., Isa 54:11–13, and other passages. Rabbinic texts identifying the rejected stone of Ps 118:22f. with Abraham, David and the Messiah are collected in SB 1.875f. Cf. [[*Jesus and the Victory of God*,]] 501.

21. Cf. *NTPG* 313–17, and [[*Jesus and the Victory of God*,]] 500f.

22. Cf. [[ibid.,]] 497, 501.

23. Cf. Mark 12:2/Matt 21:34/Luke 20:10; Matt 21:41.

the third killed.[24] Finally he sends his "son," who, in being rejected, nevertheless becomes the "stone" spoken of in Ps 118:22. Three sendings with no fruit; then a final sending with apparent failure but actual success, both in that the owner eventually gets the fruit and in that the son, the "stone," though rejected, becomes the head of the corner. This is Jesus' subversive retelling of the story of Israel, which as we shall see belongs exactly with his action in the Temple.[25] It evokes Daniel 2 in various ways; I suggest that it also describes something very similar to what is going on in the parable of the sower.

The third indication that the parable is retelling the story of Israel—and this is also an indication of where, within the story, the teller and hearers belong—lies at the heart of the narrative, in the idea of the "seed" itself. Within second-Temple Judaism, the idea of "seed" is capable of functioning as a shorthand for the "remnant" who will return when the exile is finally over. The "seed" is a metaphor for the true Israel, who will be vindicated when her god finally acts, "sown" again in her own land.[26] For someone [[233]] announcing the kingdom to tell a story about the seed being sown, then, would be to say: the remnant is now returning. The exile is over. Your god is at last sowing the good seed, creating his true Israel. It will not do to object that, in the parable's interpretation, the "seed" is the "word."[27] That is precisely what we should expect, granted one of the central and classic prophecies of return from exile:

24. The reference to "many others" being sent after this (Mark 12:5/Matt 21:36, missing from Luke and the *Gospel of Thomas*) is regarded by some as an interpolation, spoiling the neat patterning of the story (cf. Gundry 1993, 685f.). But the narrative is governed more by its cryptic reference to Israel's history, in which multitudes of prophets were sent and rejected (cp. Jer 7:25; 25:3, and frequently) than by formal laws of story-structure. It is far more likely that it has been smoothed down to regulation size in Luke and the *Gospel of Thomas* than that it has been untidily "expanded" in Mark and Matthew.

25. [[Wright, *Jesus and the Victory of God*,]] 497–501.

26. The usage goes back at least to Isa 6:13c ("the holy seed is its stump"), referring to the tree of Israel, felled in the exile. Behind that, of course, are the promises to Abraham and his "seed" (Gen 12:7; 13:15, etc.), reflected in, e.g., Tob 4:12. For the idea of return from exile as a "sowing," and/or the returnees as "seed"; cf. Ezra 9:2 (cp. 1 Esd 8:70, 88); Ps 126:6; Isa 1:9 (quoted in this sense in Rom 9:29); Isa 31:9 LXX; 37:31f. ("the remnant that is escaped of the house of Judah shall again take root downward, and bear fruit [LXX *sperma*, "seed"] upward; for out of Jerusalem shall go forth a remnant, and out of Mount Zion those who escape"); Isa 43:5 ("I will bring your seed from the east, and from the west I will gather you"); Isa 44:3; 45:26; 53:10; 54:3; 60:21; 61:9; 65:23; 66:22; Jer 24:6; 31:27; 32:41; 46:27 ("I will save you from afar, and your seed from the land of captivity; and Jacob shall return, and shall be quiet and at rest, and none shall make him afraid"); Ezek 17:22f.; 36:8–12 (n.b. the whole context); Hos 2:23; Amos 9:15; Zech 10:8f.; Mal 2:15. In post-biblical material, cf. *Jub.* 1:15–18; 21:24; *Pss. Sol.* 14:2f.; *1 En.* 62:8; *4 Ezra* 8:41 (a simile very like the parable under discussion); 1QM 13:7; 1QH 8:4–26; 17:14. See esp. Garnet 1983, whose suggestive piece helped me bring this already-germinating suggestion to fruition, though I have pruned some of his ideas and grafted in others.

27. Mark 4:14/Luke 8:11; Mark 4:15/Matt 13:19/Luke 8:12; etc.

> For as the rain and the snow come down from heaven,
>> and do not return there until they have watered the earth,
> making it bring forth and sprout,
>> giving seed to the sower and bread to the eater,
> so shall my word be that goes out from my mouth;
>> it shall not return to me empty,
> but it shall accomplish that which I purpose,
>> and succeed in the thing for which I sent it.
> For you shall go out in joy,
>> and be led back in peace;
> the mountains and the hills before you shall burst into song,
>> and all the trees of the field shall clap their hands.
> Instead of the thorn shall come up the cypress;
>> instead of the brier shall come up the myrtle;
> and it shall be to YHWH for a memorial,
>> for an everlasting sign that shall not be cut off.[28]

The close thematic links between several aspects of the parable (and its interpretation) and this passage suggest strongly that we are on the right lines. The sowing of seed, resulting in a crop that defies the thorns and briers, is a picture of YHWH's sowing of his word, and the result is the return from exile and, indeed, the consequent renewal of all creation. At the heart of the story is the cryptic announcement that the time foretold by the prophets is at last coming to birth.

But if the parable informs Jesus' hearers that they are living in the days of the return, it also warns them that the final harvest will not come about in the way they had imagined. It will not simply be the case that, following previous unsuccessful "sowings," there is now to be a thoroughly successful one. The parable does not describe a chronological sequence, but different [[234]] results from simultaneous sowings. Israel's god is acting, sowing his prophetic word with a view to restoring his people, but much of the seed will go to waste, will remain in the "exilic" condition, being eaten by birds (satanic forces, or perhaps predatory Gentiles), or lost among the rocks and thorns of the exilic wilderness.[29] The eventual harvest, though, will be great. We are here not far from Jesus' story about the great banquet. The party will go ahead, and the house will be full, but the original guests will not be there.[30] Judgment and mercy are taking place simultaneously.

The parable, therefore, not only informs, but, as has been pointed out often enough, it *acts*. It creates the situation where having ears to hear is itself one of the marks of the true remnant. Israel as she stands may look as though

28. Isa 55:10–13.
29. Birds = Gentiles: Ezek 17:23; 31:6, 13; Dan 4:12; = satanic enemies, *Jub.* 11:11; *Apoc. Abr.* 13:1–15; with Guelich 1989, 202. Thorns = exilic judgment: Isa 5:5f.; 7:23–25; 32:13; Ezek 28:24; Hos 9:6; 10:8; and, behind these, of course, Gen 3:18. Sowing among thorns is forbidden in Jer 4:3, as part of the prophetic warning of coming judgment; cf. too Jer 12:13.
30. Matt 22:1–14/Luke 14:15–24/*Gospel of Thomas* 64.

she had returned from exile; she may want to consider herself automatically and inalienably the true people of YHWH; but only those who hear the word as it is now proclaimed, and hold it fast, will form the remnant that Israel's god is creating. Those who do not are like those who reject the prophetic summons in the "wicked tenants." They are calling down judgment upon themselves.

These considerations tell strongly in favour of the "sower" being a story about the return from exile, as it is taking place in Jesus' own work. His telling of the story forms a cryptic warning and invitation. Israel will not be re-affirmed as she stands when her god acts, as he is now doing. The parable is, obviously, self-referential; it describes its own effect.

One recent writer who came close, in outline at least, to this view, was Robert Guelich. The parable of the sower, he wrote, is about

> the outcome of God's eschatological activity in history, an outcome that is more complex than the common Jewish expectation of a final harvest . . . God's eschatological activity . . . , like scattered seed, encounters opposition and failure but also produces an abundant harvest.[31]

This, I suggest, is on the right lines, and can now be sharpened up. The parable, as I said, tells two closely related stories—or rather, the same story from two different points of view.

[[235]] On the one hand, it tells the long and puzzling story of Israel, and says cryptically, but plainly for those with ears to hear, that now at last the story is reaching its goal. To say this is already to launch a stupendous claim. Jesus is implying that *his own career and kingdom-announcement* is the moment towards which all Israel's history has been leading. If we fail to see how profoundly subversive, how almost suicidally dangerous, such a claim was, it is perhaps because we have forgotten that there was another would-be king of the Jews, Herod Antipas, not too far away. People who attempted to set themselves up against that family tended to come to a bad end.

On the other hand, precisely because it is telling the story of Israel, the parable also tells the story of Jesus' own ministry as the *encapsulation,* not merely the *climax,* of that story. Jesus, as himself first and foremost a prophet, was to suffer the fate of the prophets. He was the prophetic agent through whom the recreative word of YHWH was being sown; but, like Isaiah, he would sow that seed on the path, on the rock, and among the thorns—just as he would come as a prophet to the vineyard-tenants, and himself be rejected. But (and here is the mystery indeed, . . . in this very rejection, in this very failure, there was to be seen the god-given plan for the establishment of the kingdom. The rejected stone would become the head corner-stone. The vineyard would be given to others, who would give the owner his fruit. Some seed would fall on good soil, and produce an abundant harvest.

---

31. Guelich 1989, 197. Cf. too Dodd 1961 [1935], 135 (expounding the secret seed): "The parable in effect says, Can you not see that the long history of God's dealings with His people has reached its climax?" On the paradoxical results (Israel expected harvest, not seed-time; the kingdom should be manifest, not hidden) cf. Evans 1990, 374.

Observe how the matter then unfolds. Jesus tells a story about a sower sowing seed in a field. Scholars have argued as to whether or not the picture fits with contemporary Palestinian farming methods,[32] but this is really beside the point. In the narrative logic of the parable (as opposed to a historicizing what-would-really-have-happened sort of reading), the sower sows in three unsuccessful places, and finally succeeds with the fourth. In the tradition of cryptic second-Temple Jewish stories, the assumption should be, until we have firm evidence otherwise, that the sower is YHWH himself, and that his desire (as the sower's desire is to plant successful seed) is to establish his kingdom. The other plantings will bear no fruit, but there will be one that will yield a large and satisfying crop.[33]

Jesus, then, in telling this story, indicates that his own work is at one and the same time the climax and the recapitulation of the story of Israel. [[236]] Climax: as Matthew and Luke record in a different context, the law and the prophets were until John, but since then—that is, in Jesus' own ministry—the good news of the kingdom has been proclaimed.[34] Israel's long wait is over; YHWH is at last sowing good seed which will bring forth fruit. As with the wicked tenants, the previous sowings represent the unfruitful work of the prophets, longing to bring Israel back to her god. Jesus is also rejected—by some; but ultimately he succeeds where the prophets had failed. Recapitulation: if Jesus is a prophet like the prophets of old, then the reaction they provoked—and received—will be his as well. His message will be rejected by most, and judgment will result; but YHWH's strange purposes of salvation will not thereby be thwarted, but rather fulfilled. The story is, then, about Jesus' own ministry, but not entirely in the way sometimes supposed.[35]

We are now in a position to understand the quotation from Isa 6:9–10 in Mark 4:12, Matt 13:13–15, and Luke 8:10, that has given exegetes and theologians so much trouble down the years.[36] Isaiah's prophetic commission summoned him to a strange ministry which would bring Israel *through* devastating judgment to mercy. The hardening process ("keep looking, but do not see; keep listening, but do not comprehend") will lead the people to judgment:

---

32. Cf. Fitzmyer 1981, 703 for discussion and bibliography. Among the chief protagonists are Jeremias 1963 [1947] 11f. (the parable fits with the culture) and Drury 1985, 55–58 (the parable mysteriously controverts the culture). Jeremias was following Dalman 1926.

33. Another debate should be regarded as settled: thirtyfold, sixtyfold and a hundredfold indicate a substantial return; much better than average, but not wildly exaggerated or miraculous. Cf. Meyer 1979, 41; Guelich 1989, 195; Davies and Allison 1988–91, 2.385.

34. Luke 16:16/Matt 11:12f., on which see [[Wright, *Jesus and the Victory of God*,]] 468f.; cf. Meyer 1992a, chap. 2.

35. For the view that the parable is simply about Jesus' ministry and the varied response it produces, cf., e.g., Guelich 1989, 192; Nolland 1989, 376; Hooker 1991, 122f.

36. See, e.g., the recent discussions in Guelich 1989, 198–215; Hooker 1991, 125–29; Gundry 1993, 195–204. Cf. too John 12:40f.; Acts 28:26f.; and cp. Rom 11:8.

until cities lie waste without inhabitants, and houses without people. . . .
Even if a tenth part remain in it, it will be burned again, like a terebinth
or an oak whose stump remains standing when it is felled.[37]

—but there will be mercy beyond the judgment. And the sign of mercy will
be, of course, the "seed," hidden within the charred stump: "the holy seed is
its stump."[38] Just as the parable of the wicked tenants evokes Isaiah 5, so, I
suggest, the sower evokes Isaiah 6—not accidentally, or obliquely, but by way
of *telling the story of Israel as the story of rejected prophets, consequent judgment,
and renewal the other side of judgment,* and by way of describing Jesus' own ministry as the culmination, and hence encapsulation or recapitulation, of that
prophetic heritage. For Jesus, Isaiah was *both* an earlier part of the story, one
of his predecessors in the long line, one (moreover) whose own commission
contained a most striking statement of the inevitable [[237]] rejection of his
message—*and* one whose ministry, and its results, were being climactically recapitulated in his own work.

This suggests a way through the puzzle of the apparently predestinarian
passage in Mark 4:10–12, which seems to say that Jesus told parables *so that*
people would not understand him. The problem only arises, in fact, when the
historical context is not taken seriously, and when the vacuum thus created is
filled with a generalized "theology" in which Jesus is either the teacher of
timeless truths or the announcer of impenetrable enigmas. Parables are neither of these. "If you have ears, then hear"; if too many understand too well,
the prophet's liberty of movement, and perhaps life, may be cut short. Jesus
knew his kingdom-announcement was subversive. It would be drastically un-
welcome, for different reasons, to the Romans, to Herod, and also to zealous
Jews and their leaders, whether official or not. He must therefore speak in
parables, "so that they may look and look but never see." It was the only safe
course. Only those in the know must be allowed to glimpse what Jesus believed was going on.[39] These stories would get past the censor—for the moment. There would come a time for more open revelation. The parable of the
wicked tenants did not need an explanation. "They perceived that he had
told this parable against them," and took appropriate action.

The second-order offence of the parable then emerges into the open.
Not only was Jesus making the risky claim that the story of Israel was coming
to its climax in his own work. He was claiming that this climax, so far from

37. Isa 6:11–13.

38. This last phrase of Isa 6:13, missing from LXX, is present in 1QIs[a]. This link between Isaiah 6 and Mark 4 is explored suggestively by Bowker 1974; Evans 1981, 1985.

39. The parable, as is often seen, thus asks to be closely correlated with the final paragraph of Mark 3 (Mark 3:31–35/Matt 12:46–50/*Gospel of Thomas* 99/*Gospel of the Ebionites* 5),
in which Jesus coolly redefines his "family": "Who are my mother and brothers? Those who
hear the word of god and do it." There are "insiders" who are outside, and vice versa. For
other cryptic and deeply subversive sayings which can only be explained when away from the
crowds, cf., e.g., Mark 7:17; 10:10.

underwriting Israel's present life and ambitions, was radically challenging them—so much so that his proclamation would simply harden them in their ways. The son would come to the vineyard, and the tenants would reject him. They would look and look, but never see.

This insight is a "mystery": not a "puzzle," something merely opaque or confusing, but the secret plan of YHWH, now cryptically unveiled.[40] The disciples stand to Jesus as the seer to the angel in, for example, *4 Ezra* 10:29–58, where 10:38 assures Ezra that the Most High has revealed "many [[238]] mysteries" to him[41]—mysteries concerning precisely the strange judgment that has fallen on Jerusalem. The "mystery," the whole secret plan of Israel's god, is that *this* was how his purpose for Israel is to be worked out. He would come to rescue his people, not in a blaze of triumphant glory, but in the sowing of seed, the long-promised prophetic "word," the god-sent agency through which Israel and the world would be renewed. (The "word" was, after all, one of the ways in which second-Temple Jewish thought was able to express YHWH's active involvement in the world, and in Israel's history, without transgressing her basic monotheism.[42]) The method of YHWH's return, and of Israel's release from bondage, would therefore itself involve a hiddenness and a secret revelation. What was revealed was not only what the mystery was but also that the plan was indeed a mystery. It was a plan of judgment and mercy; a plan to be put into operation, not through the Herodian dynasty, nor through the Pharisaic movement, nor through high-priestly activity in the Temple, nor yet in the plottings of holy revolutionaries, but in Jesus' own proclamation and activity. As Mark indicates, this parable is thus itself *about* parables.[43]

The "explanation" of the parable at last falls into place.[44] The paradoxical prophetic "sowings" of the "word" were being recapitulated in Jesus' own

---

40. Mark 4:11 and pars. speak of Israel's god *giving* a mystery to the disciples; this is rare in Jewish literature, and some have quite reasonably doubted whether Jesus would have spoken thus (so Harvey 1980, 335f.). The passive, "it has been given," clearly refers to divine action. But the form of words is not unknown, and in any case may well represent an attempt to express in Greek a more natural Aramaic idiom: so Gundry 1993, 197, citing *1 En.* 51:3; 68:1.

41. The Latin is *mysteria multa* [['many mysteries']], no doubt reflecting an underlying Greek *mysteria polla* [['many mysteries']]. The Ethiopic version has "a hidden secret," and the first Arabic version "a mighty secret." On "mystery" in *4 Ezra*, see above all Stone 1990, 332–34.

42. Cf. *NTPG* 256–59. The other ways are of course Torah, Shekinah, Wisdom and Spirit.

43. Mark 4:13: "Do you not understand this parable? How then will you understand all the parables?"

44. Among those who have stood against the tide on the matter of the explanation's belonging intrinsically with the parable are Moule 1969; Bowker 1974; Payne 1980a and b; and now Gundry 1993, 204–11. Caird's objection, that an explained parable is about as interesting as an explained joke (1980, 165f.), misses the point: explanation is not for the particularly obtuse, but for those who are to be allowed into the deeper secret. Caird, however, does go on to allow for the possibility that the content of the interpretation represents Jesus' intention.

ministry. The satan was at work to snatch away the seed.[45] Many were called, but few chosen; many sown, few harvested—though the harvest itself would be abundant. The explanation functioned as a challenge to "those inside," who had been grasped by Jesus' words. They must persevere, and become those that bear fruit. In them the destiny of Israel would be realized.

The evangelists are therefore correct, I suggest, to treat the sower as the classic parable of Jesus' kingdom-announcement. It claimed that Israel's history had reached its great climactic moment with the work of Jesus himself. The end of exile was at hand; the time of lost seed was passing away, and the [[239]] time of fruit had dawned; the covenant was to be renewed; YHWH himself was returning to his people, to "sow" his word in their midst, as he promised, and so restore their fortunes at last. The parable of the sower tells the story of the kingdom.

Other Parables of Israel's Story

Space forbids a full treatment of all the parables which could be included here. We shall simply indicate the way in which some of them fall into the same pattern, of Israel's history reaching its paradoxical climax. We begin with the smaller parables in Mark 4:21–34.

The section begins with some short sayings which emphasize the same point as the sower. Mark has apparently collected them here from different places; they occur scattered in the parallels.[46] The lamp is made to be put on a lampstand, not under a cover;[47] the measure one gives is the measure one gets;[48] the one who already has will receive more, but the one who has not will lose what he has.[49] Commentators sometimes despair of being able to recover the original sense of these cryptic little sayings.[50] But the exposition of the sower offered above provides some clues. The question about the lamp is explained in v. 22:[51] "Nothing is hidden except to be revealed, nothing secret except to be publicized." This implies that something has already been covered up, so that the "lamp" saying in 4:21 retrospectively gains the force: "so, granted that the plan has been hidden, it cannot be the divine purpose to keep it so for ever." Do not be surprised, Jesus is saying, that at last the divine plan is being revealed. There had to come a time when this would happen, otherwise Israel's god would be like someone who kept the lamp permanently under the bed. At the same time, since the secret is still a mystery (in

---

45. See above, n. 31. I am grateful to Dr. Michael Knowles for letting me see an unpublished paper of his on this subject.

46. Guelich 1989, 227 speaks of a "vast consensus" on this point, which is rare enough in gospel interpretation.

47. Mark 4:21–23/Matt 5:15; Matt 10:26/Luke 8:16f.; Luke 11:33; Luke 12:2/*Gospel of Thomas* 33; cf. 5, 6/*P. Oxy.* 654.5.

48. Mark 4:24/Matt 7:2/Luke 6:38.

49. Mark 4:25/Matt 13:12; Matt 25:29/Luke 19:26/*Gospel of Thomas* 41.

50. E.g., Hooker 1991, 133: "It is impossible for us now to recover their original application."

51. Cf. Guelich 1989, 230.

the popular sense, i.e., a puzzle) to most of Jesus' contemporaries, this saying functions as a warning: complete disclosure is on the way, and will not long delay.[52] Mark, strangely, has Jesus speak of the light [[240]] as "coming."[53] The best explanation of this is in terms of a combination of themes: the coming of YHWH to his people,[54] the coming of the kingdom,[55] and of course the coming of Jesus himself, in the sense of the commencement of his public career.[56] Again, the saying itself is cryptic, as is indicated well enough in the warning of v. 23, repeating v. 9: "if you have ears, then hear!"

A similar warning to hear properly introduces the saying about measuring (v. 24). Since contemporary English does not use "to measure" with the metaphorical sense it clearly has here (and elsewhere in Jesus' world[57]), we may have to switch images, and say something like "The attention you give will be the attention you get," where the first "attention" picks up "look out how you hear" at the start of the verse, and the second "attention" alludes to the way in which Israel's god will care for those who are listening appropriately to the announcement of the kingdom. This then introduces the frequently repeated proverb about those who have and those who do not. Clearly, those who "have" are equated with those who hear aright, who in turn are identified as Jesus' true family, those to whom is revealed the mystery of the kingdom; those who "have not" are identified as "those outside" (4:11, compare 3:31–35).[58] Israel's story, now reaching its climax, will be marked (as in some other second-Temple thought) by a great divide between the true Israel and the renegades. Mark's bringing together of these sayings reflects a sure instinct for the meaning of Jesus' kingdom-announcement.

Mark's section continues with the short parable of the "seed growing secretly."[59] Having read the sower carefully, we should be on familiar territory here. Israel's god is not working in a sudden dramatic way. He will not bring in his kingdom in the manner that Jesus' contemporaries desired. He is work-

---

52. Contrast Gundry 1993, 212, who thinks the saying is explaining Jesus' practice of concealing things from the crowds and revealing them to the disciples. The immediacy of the explanation in Mark 4:13–20, he says (pp. 214f.), rules out the possibility of Jesus' ministry remaining a riddle until his death and resurrection. But (a) 4:13–20 is still somewhat cryptic (like Jesus' other explanation in 7:17–23, which Mark has had to supplement in 7:19b); (b) at this stage, the secret is only revealed to the disciples, not to outsiders.

53. Matthew, Luke, and the *Gospel of Thomas* speak of the lamp being "lit," though using different terms. (On the secondary nature of the *Gospel of Thomas* saying, cf. Fitzmyer 1985, 717.) It has been argued, however, that the underlying Aramaic for "come" may mean "to be brought": cf. Gundry 1993, 212, with refs.

54. For Israel's god as a "lamp," cf. 2 Sam 22:29; Job 29:3; Ps 27:1.

55. So Guelich 1989, 229, 231f.

56. With possible kingly overtones; cf. 2 Sam 21:17; 1 Kgs 11:36; 15:4; 2 Kgs 8:19.

57. Cf. Chilton 1984a, 123–25, noting esp. *Tg. Isa.* 27:8. He comments (p. 125) that, since this thought is part of common folk-wisdom developed by Jesus in a particular way, the gospels are probably correct to envisage him using the saying on a number of occasions. This point of method deserves wider application.

58. With Marcus 1986, 156f. Guelich 1989, 234 thinks it impossible to be precise here.

59. Mark 4:26–29, with some echoes at the end of *Gos. Thom.* 21:4 and in *Ap. Jas.* 8:1f.

ing in a way that is hidden and opaque, but which, nevertheless, [[241]] Israel *ought* to recognize. There is something strangely familiar about the secret seed. It sleeps and rises, just as the observer does, and yet he does not understand. There may be overtones here of resurrection: this is how the creator god raises the dead in the inauguration of the kingdom, by sowing seeds and letting them grow secretly so that only those with eyes to see can realize what is happening.[60] There are, too, clear overtones of the apocalyptic scenario that is to come: when harvest comes, he puts in the sickle. This refers directly to a passage in Joel (3:13) which speaks of the great coming judgment and harvest. Jesus is not abandoning the idea that there will be a great judgment in which Israel's destiny will at last be realized. He is reinterpreting it, declaring that, though there will come a day of clear vindication, at the moment, i.e., during Jesus' ministry, the seed is growing quietly in ways that Israel does not understand—though she should.

The parable of the mustard seed[61] is another redefinition of the kingdom. It will not appear all at once in its full splendour, but will begin inconspicuously. Those who expect Jesus to lead a march on a Roman garrison will be disappointed. Nevertheless, what he is offering remains a redefinition, not an abandonment, of the dream. YHWH has planted a small seed, which will grow into a great shrub. The ministry of Jesus, which does not look like the expected coming kingdom, is in fact its strange beginning. This time the apocalyptic image is of the birds of the air coming to nest in the tree:[62] this seems to be a hint that when the tree has grown to full height—when Israel becomes what her god intends her to become—others, presumably Gentiles, will come to share in her blessing. This was of course one part of some mainstream tellings of Israel's story;[63] but to announce it at a time of nationalist fervour was revolutionary indeed, directly cognate with the "Nazareth Manifesto" of Luke 4.

The leaven in the lump[64] similarly declares that the kingdom is not like a new loaf, appearing suddenly as a whole. It is more like the leaven which works its way quietly through a lump of dough. Once again, this parable was not originally about the influence of Christianity on the world, but about the effect of the kingdom's inauguration within Israel. The key word in the parable is "hidden." This was not the natural way to describe what the woman did with the leaven; but it coheres well with the theme of all these parables, namely, that what Israel's god was doing in the ministry of Jesus was veiled and cryptic. The leaven of Jesus' message is hidden within Israel, so that it [[242]] may work its way through the whole people. The parable is a warning not to look (yet) for sudden dramatic events; it is an invitation to see Israel's god at work in the secret workings of Jesus' paradoxical activity.

---

60. Cf. [[Wright, *Jesus and the Victory of God*,]] 128f.
61. Mark 4:30–32/Matt 13:31f./Luke 13:18f./*Gospel of Thomas* 20.
62. Cf. Dan 4:20–22.
63. Cf. *NTPG* 267f.
64. Matt 13:33/Luke 13:20f./*Gospel of Thomas* 96.

The same theme of hiddenness is the obvious characteristic, too, of the treasure and the pearl.[65] But a new twist is added. The hiddenness means that people can, and must, seek out the treasure, and then abandon everything else in favour of it. It is within their power to grasp it. What must be abandoned? Clearly, the cherished assumptions and expectations of Jesus' contemporaries. They are challenged to realize what is going on before their eyes, and so, dropping their other aspirations, to embrace this new possibility. They may appear foolish in the eyes of their contemporaries, who are building their hopes on a kingdom which will restore the national fortunes of Israel; but they will have found something far better, over which they will rejoice, for it is they who will be vindicated when God acts. This theme projects us forward towards the developed story which we will explore in the next two chapters [[not reproduced here]].

Matthew ends his particular parable-collection with the householder,[66] and, though it clearly reflects his own interests,[67] there is no very good reason for denying it to Jesus as well. The image presupposes that Israel is being reconstituted around Jesus, and goes on to suggest that those who are in on the secret ("scribes trained for the kingdom of heaven") will be like householders producing things new as well as things old. Jesus has introduced a radically new note into Israel's expectation. This does not mean a total break with the past, nor even an abandonment of the framework of Israel's hope; it means filling that framework with new content. The "therefore" with which the parable begins indicates that it functions, and that Matthew clearly intends it to function, as a statement of what happens when people respond to the other parables.

There are, of course, many other parables which fill out the announcement of the kingdom as the story of Israel's paradoxical history. The most obvious, perhaps, is the one we have already used as a case-study, namely the prodigal son.[68] There, most clearly (in my view), Jesus was retelling the story of Israel's return from exile, and doing so in a sharp and provocative manner. We should also note the way in which this whole theme dovetailed into one aspect of Jesus' praxis. . . . The acts of healing were understood by the evangelists, and most probably by Jesus himself, as [[243]] the fulfilment of prophecy; but not just any miscellaneous prophecy. They fulfilled the prophecies of *return from exile*. The time when the blind would see, the deaf hear, the lame walk, and the poor hear good news was the time when Israel would return at last from Babylon.[69] This gives further indication that our reading of these stories is on the right track.

---

65. Matt 13:44–46/*Gospel of Thomas* 109; 76. In the *Gospel of Thomas*, the purchaser of the field does not know about the treasure until after he has made the purchase.

66. Matt 13:51–52.

67. Cf. *NTPG* 384.

68. Luke 15:11–32: cf. chap. 4 [[in Wright, *Jesus and the Victory of God*]].

69. Isa 35:5, and the chap. as a whole; cf. Isa 29:18f.; 32:3; Matt 11:2–6/Luke 7:18–23.

Bibliography

Boucher, Madeleine
    1977   *The Mysterious Parable: A Literary Study.* Catholic Biblical Quarterly
            Monograph 6. Washington, D.C.: Catholic Biblical Association.
Bowker, John W.
    1974   Mystery and Parable: Mark iv.1–20. *Journal of Theolobical Studies* n.s.
            25: 300–317.
Bultmann, Rudolf
    1968   *The History of the Synoptic Tradition.* Translated by John Marsh. 2nd
    [1921] ed. Oxford: Blackwell.
Caird, George B.
    1980   *The Language and Imagery of the Bible.* London: Duckworth.
Chilton, Bruce D.
    1984   *A Galilean Rabbi and His Bible.* Wilmington, Delaware: Glazier.
Cleary, M.
    1988   The Baptist of History and Kerygma. *Irish Theological Quarterly* 54:
            211–27.
Dalman, Gustaf H.
    1926   Viererlei Acker. *Palästina-Jahrbuch* 22: 120–32.
Davies, W. D., and Allison, Dale C.
    1988–91 *A Critical and Exegetical Commentary on the Gospel according to Saint
            Matthew.* 2 vols. so far. Edinburgh: T. & T. Clark.
Dodd, C. H.
    1961   *The Parables of the Kingdom.* Revised ed. London: Nisbet / New York:
    [1935] Scribner's.
Drury, John
    1985   *The Parables in the Gospels: History and Allegory.* London: SPCK.
Evans, Christopher F.
    1990   *Saint Luke.* London: SCM.
Evans, Craig A.
    1981   A Note on the Function of Isaiah vi.9–10 in Mark iv. *Revue Biblique*
            88: 234–35.
    1985   On the Isaianic Background of the Sower Parable. *Catholic Biblical
            Quarterly* 47: 464–68.
Fitzmyer, J. A.
    1981   *The Gospel according to Luke (I–IX).* Anchor Bible 28a. New York:
            Doubleday.
Garnet, Paul
    1983   The Parable of the Sower: How the Multitudes Understood It. Pages
            39–54 in *Spirit within Structure: Essays in Honor of George Johnston on
            the Occasion of His Seventieth Birthday*, ed. E. J. Furcha. Pittsburgh
            Theological Monographs n.s. 3. Allison Park, Pennsylvania: Pickwick.
Guelich, Robert A.
    1989   *Mark 1–8:26.* Dallas: Word.
Gundry, Robert H.
    1993   *Mark: A Commentary on His Apology for the Cross.* Grand Rapids, Michi-
            gan: Eerdmans.

Harvey, Anthony E.
    1980   The Use of Mystery Language in the Bible. *Journal of Theological Sudies* n.s. 31: 320–36.
Hooker, M. D.
    1991   *A Commentary on the Gospel according to St Mark.* Black's New Testament Commentaries. London: Black.
Jeremias, Joachim
    1963   *The Parables of Jesus.* London: SCM / New York: Scribner's.
    [1947]
Marcus, Joel
    1986   *The Mystery of the Kingdom of God.* Society of Biblical Literature Dissertation Series 90. Atlanta: Scholars Press.
Meyer, Ben F.
    1979   *The Aims of Jesus.* London: SCM.
    1992   *Christus Faber: The Master-Builder and the House of God.* Allison Park, Pennsylvania: Pickwick.
Moule, C. F. D.
    1969   Mark 4:1–20 Yet Once More. Pages 95–113 in *Neotestamentica et Semitica: Studies in Honour of Matthew Black,* ed. E. E. Ellis and M. Wilcox. Edinburgh: T. & T. Clark.
Murphy-O'Connor, J.
    1990   John the Baptist and Jesus: History and Hypotheses. *New Testament Studies* 36: 359–74.
Nolland, John
    1989   *Luke 1–9:20.* Word Biblical Commentary 35a. Dallas: Word.
NTPG = Wright, N. T.
    1992   *The New Testament and the People of God.* Volume 1 of *Christian Origins and the Question of God.* London: SPCK / Minneapolis: Fortress.
Payne, Philip B.
    1980a   The Authenticity of the Parable of the Sower and Its Interpretation. Pages 163–207 in vol. 1 of *Studies of History and Tradition in the Four Gospels,* ed. R. T. France and David Wenham. Gospel Perspectives. Sheffield: JSOT Press.
    1980b   The Seeming Inconsistency of the Interpretation of the Parable of the Sower. *New Testament Studies* 26: 564–68.
SB = Strack, H. L., and Billerbeck, P.
    1926–56 *Kommentar zum Neuen Testament aus Talmud und Midrasch.* 2 volumes. Munich: Beck.
Shaffer, Peter
    1985   *Amadeus.* London: Penguin.
    [1980]
Snodgrass, Klyne
    1983   *The Parable of the Wicked Tenants.* Wissenschaftliche Untersuchungen zum Neuen Testament 27. Tübingen: Mohr.
Stone, Michael E.
    1990   *Fourth Ezra: A Commentary on the Book of Fourth Ezra.* Minneapolis: Augsburg Fortress.
Thomas (ed. A. Guillaumont et al.)
    1959   *The Gospel according to Thomas.* Leiden: Brill / London: Collins.

E. P. SANDERS

Jesus and the First Table of the Jewish Law

[[55]] The two pillars of Judaism are the election and the law: God called Abraham and his descendants to be his people; a few centuries later he gave them the law by the hand of Moses. If we are to discuss Jesus' Jewishness, we must address these two topics. Because these are short essays, however, each can deal with only some of the most crucial points. . . . I shall explain the basic division of the law and shall discuss the first half.

The Two Tables

The Jewish law falls naturally into two parts, often called "tables." The first table consists of the commandments that govern relations between humans and God, and the second table contains commandments governing relations among humans. The division can be seen, for example, in the Ten Commandments [[56]] (Exod 20:2–17; Deut 5:7–21): "You shall have no other gods before me" begins the first table; "You shall not kill" begins the second. It is probable that, in Jesus' day, all learned Jews knew this division into tables and the contents of each. How many Jews were learned? I think that most of them were educated enough to know about the division of the law and most of the principal laws in each table. Some, of course, were especially learned and were able to teach the law; the rest were fairly learned because they listened as it was taught in the synagogues. Philo of Alexandria, a very wealthy man who was as learned as he was rich, maintained that, on the Sabbath, Jews throughout the world gathered in "schools" where they learned what he calls their "ancestral philosophy." This "philosophy," he notes, falls under two headings: duty toward

Reprinted, with permission, from E. P. Sanders, "Jesus and the First Table of the Jewish Law," in *Jews and Christians Speak of Jesus* (ed. A. E. Zannoni; Minneapolis: Fortress, 1994) 55–73, 164–66.

God 'and duty toward other humans;[1] that is, the Jewish "philosophy" consisted of the two tables of the Jewish law.

When they wanted to summarize these two divisions of the law, Jews quoted two central passages from their Scripture (the Christian "Old Testament"). One is found in Deuteronomy 6, the famous passage called the *Shema*ʿ in Hebrew, from its first word, 'Hear'. These are the first two verses of the passage:

> Hear, O Israel: The Lord is our God, the Lord alone. You shall love the Lord your God with all your heart, and with all your soul, and with all your might. (Deut 6:4–5)[2]

The second passage enjoins, as Philo put it, fellowship with all humans and *philanthrōpia*, love of humanity.[3] It is "Love your neighbor as yourself" (Lev 19:18). Strictly speaking, Lev 19:18 requires Jews to love only their "neighbors," that is, fellow Jews. But a few verses later comes the requirement to "love the alien as yourself" (Lev 19:34). Philo, along with other thoughtful Jews, read these and other verses as divine commandments requiring love of all humanity. We see this especially clearly when we note that Philo and others sometimes used an epigram based on both Lev 19:18 and 19:34, [[57]] rather than quoting the passages. Three different sources offer us this epigrammatic summary (with only minor variations): "Do not do to anyone what you would hate that person to do to you."[4] "To anyone" shows that, whatever the original meaning of "neighbor" and "alien" in Leviticus 19, later Jews understood that God commanded them to show love to all humanity.

It is striking that two of the people to whom the epigram "Do not do" is attributed (Philo and Hillel) said that it summarized "the whole law." Logically, the epigram summarizes only the second table. If he were pressed on this point, probably Philo would have explained that loving treatment of others proves that one is devoted to God. In the decades after Jesus' time, some rabbis said that refusing to worship other gods was tantamount to obeying the whole law.[5] Logically (again), avoidance of idolatry shows only that one observes the commandments on the first table. But (these rabbis probably thought) people who worshiped only the true God would also keep his other commandments, including the commandments governing how to treat hu-

---

1. Philo, *Special Laws* 2.63. The two tables are often, here as elsewhere, indicated by such terms as "piety" and "holiness" (both indicating observance of commandments governing relations with God) and "justice," "righteousness," and "love of humans" (treatment of other people). See E. P. Sanders, *Judaism: Practice and Belief* (Philadelphia: Trinity International, 1992) 192–94, and, more fully, "The Question of Uniqueness in the Teaching of Jesus," The Ethel M. Wood Lecture, 1990 (London: University of London, 1990) 28f., n. 26.

2. I have quoted the New Revised Standard Version. For the first clause, the RSV has "The Lord our God is one Lord."

3. Philo, *Special Laws* 1.299f., 324.

4. Tob 4:15; Philo, *Hypothetica* 7.6; Hillel, according to *Shabbat* 31a.

5. *Sifre Deuteronomy* 54, end. For similar cases and discussion of the logic of this point, see E. P. Sanders, *Paul and Palestinian Judaism* (Philadelphia: Fortress, 1977) 134–38.

mans. Jews who used one saying as a summary of the whole law were not excluding other parts of the law; they regarded all the commandments as being implied by one of the great commandments.

Jesus and the Two Tables

Two passages in the Gospels indicate that Jesus agreed fully with the view of the law that I have exemplified by citing Philo and others. A scribe asked him, "Which commandment is the first of all?" Jesus answered:

> The first is, "Hear O Israel: The Lord our God, the Lord is one; and you shall love the Lord your God with all your heart, and with all your soul, and with all your mind, and with all your strength." The second is this, "You shall love your neighbor as yourself." There is no other commandment greater than these. (Mark 12:28–31)

[[58]] The scribe agreed fully (as we should expect), and Jesus said that he was not far from the kingdom of God (Mark 12:32–34).[6] We see that Jesus was among those who knew that the law was divided into two tables and who knew the main biblical passages that summarize each. Implicit, of course, is his agreement that people should obey the laws on both of the two tables.

As did Philo, Jesus also offered a one-sentence epigram to summarize the whole law: "So whatever you wish that people would do to you, do so to them; for this is the law and the prophets" (Matt 7:12). Logically, this statement summarizes only the second table. Yet Jesus called it "the law and the prophets." This does not imply that he wished to cancel the laws on the first table, such as the requirement to serve the Lord alone. Rather, for homiletical purposes, he, like others, could use a summary of the second table to stand for the whole law; by implication, the commandment concerning treatment of other people includes the requirement to love the God who commanded love of one's neighbor.

In all of these cases—the passages from Leviticus, Deuteronomy, Philo, the Talmud, Tobit, and the Gospels—"love" does not mean only, or even primarily, an emotion. In Leviticus 19, the general commandment to love one's neighbor includes several very specific actions that demonstrate love: leave some of the harvest for the poor and the sojourner; do not lie, cheat, or steal; do not oppress your neighbor; pay a servant's wages promptly; care for the deaf and the blind; be impartial in judgment; do not slander (Lev 19:9–16). You should, to be sure, love your neighbor "in your heart" (Lev 19:17), but love is expressed by just and honest treatment. The love commandment is a summary; in the second half of the Ten Commandments and elsewhere we find specific behavioral requirements: honor your father and mother; do not kill; do not commit adultery; and the like (Exod 20:12–17; Deut 5:16–21).

Similarly, in the first half of the Ten Commandments there are specifics: have no other gods; do not make graven images; do not [[59]] bow down to and worship idols; do not take God's name in vain; keep the Sabbath in

---

6. Matt 22:34–40 is very similar; see also Luke 10:25–28.

honor of God (Exod 20:2–11; Deut 5:6–15). Observing these specific commandments demonstrates "love."

Specific Aspects of the First Table

Today, when we read the second commandment, "You shall not bow down to [idols] or serve them" (Deut 5:9), we often do not consider the precise meaning of the word "serve" in Judaism and other ancient religions. It meant "serve by sacrificing to"; that is, "serve" refers to the cultic or ritual aspect of religion, the part having to do with priests, purification, and sacrificial slaughter. In the past few centuries, few terms have drawn as much censure in religious propaganda and polemic as "cult" and "ritual." Protestants have criticized Catholics for ritualism and externalism, and Protestants and Catholics have joined forces to criticize ancient Jews on the very same grounds. Propagandists usually assume that the targets of their attacks *substitute* external forms and rites for internal devotion, and then they regard the fact of ritual observances as proving a lack of correct inner piety. To many Protestants, the fact that Catholicism has a rite of penitence proves that Catholics do not truly repent in their hearts.

I do not doubt that, because human nature is what it is, there have always been some people who left their religion at the altar. It is not, however, the case that the rites of Catholicism destroy interior devotion, nor is it true that most Roman Catholics substitute cultic ritual for inner piety. It is just as indefensible to accuse ancient Judaism on this ground. Ancient Jews, in fact, recognized the danger and spent considerable time warning each other about it. Hosea depicted God as desiring love rather than sacrifice and knowledge of God rather than burnt offerings (Hos 6:6). Similarly, a few centuries later, Jesus ben Sira warned people not to say "He will consider the multitude of my gifts, and when I make an offering to the Most High [[60]] God he will accept it." God expects his worshipers to pray and to give alms to the poor (Sir 7:9f.). Several decades later, the pseudonymous author of the *Epistle of Aristeas* wrote that Jews "honor God not with gifts or sacrifices, but with purity of heart and of devout disposition."[7] These passages do not mean that Hosea, Ben Sira, and Pseudo-Aristeas were against sacrifice; they were, rather, against sacrifice without love, devotion, purity of heart, and charitable acts. In ancient Hebrew parlance (as we shall see more fully below), "desire mercy *and not* sacrifice" meant "desire mercy *more than* sacrifice." Pseudo-Aristeas and Ben Sira both favored sacrifice, provided that it was offered in the right spirit (for example, *Ep. Aristeas* 170–71; Sir 34:18–19; 35:12). These admonitions to put mercy, love, honesty, and interior devotion first did not stop with Ben Sira and Pseudo-Aristeas. In the centuries after Jesus, the rabbis endlessly urged the importance of "intention" and "directing the heart" when observing "external" practices.[8]

---

7. *Ep. Aristeas* 234.
8. For a few passages, see Sanders, *Paul and Palestinian Judaism*, 107–9 and subject index, under "Intention."

Now we shall turn our attention to the question of Jesus' attitude toward the first table of the Jewish law. Did he oppose any of its aspects? We start with sacrifice.

Jesus and Sacrifice

According to Matthew, Jesus quoted Hos 6:6, "I desire mercy and not sacrifice," in two cases when his critics seemed to be lacking in mercy (Matt 9:13; 12:7). In neither case is sacrifice actually an issue, and these passages offer no direct information about Jesus' view of sacrifice. According to Mark 12:33, however, when Jesus used this prophetic passage he said that love "is *much more than* all whole burnt offerings and sacrifices." Mark's version corresponds to the original meaning of Hosea; there is no objection to sacrifice.

Other passages reveal that Jesus shared the view of Philo, Pseudo-Aristeas, the rabbis, and other Jews. The teaching that mentions sacrifice most directly is this: [[60]]

> If you are offering your gift at the altar, and there remember that your brother has something against you, leave your gift there before the altar and go; first be reconciled to your brother, and then come and offer your gift. (Matt 5:23–24)

The "gift" here is probably a guilt offering, brought in order to complete the process of atonement for harming another person. The sacrifice did not count if the offender had not first compensated the person whom he had harmed and paid an additional twenty percent as a fine. This is clear in the biblical legislation itself (Lev 6:1–7), and we have already exemplified the general principle by citing Ben Sira and others. Philo put it this way:

> The lawgiver [Moses] orders that forgiveness be extended to [a wrongdoer] on condition that he verifies his repentance not by a mere promise but by his actions, by restoring the deposit or the property which he has seized . . . or in any way usurped from his neighbour, and further has paid an additional fifth as a solatium for the offense. And when he has thus propitiated the injured person he must follow it up, says the lawgiver, by proceeding to the temple to ask for remission of his sins. (Philo, *Special Laws* 1.236f.)

Philo continues by noting that the transgressor must not only repent but also sacrifice a ram (ibid.).

Thus, although sacrifice is not a major topic of the teaching attributed to Jesus, Matt 5:23–24 indicates that his views on it were precisely the same as those held by other Jewish thinkers and teachers.

Sacrifice is alluded to indirectly, but nevertheless positively, in another passage. Jesus healed a leper and then commanded him, "show yourself to the priest, and offer for your cleansing what Moses commanded, for a proof to the people" (Mark 1:40–44). "What Moses commanded" turns out to be sacrificial birds and lambs (Lev 14:1–32). Here again a saying attributed to Jesus presupposes acceptance of the Jewish sacrificial system. [[62]]

Jesus and the Sabbath

The fourth of the Ten Commandments is the requirement to do no work on the seventh day of the week (Exod 20:8–11). The Sabbath loomed quite large in Jewish life in the first century. Despite its prominence in the Ten Commandments and the creation story (Gen 2:2–3), the Sabbath plays a very small role in most of the Hebrew Bible. We do not read, for example, that David or Hezekiah had to change his plans because of the Sabbath, nor is the Sabbath a major topic of the preexilic prophets. It appears that it became an important and distinctive feature of Jewish life during and after the Babylonian captivity.[9] From the time of the Hasmoneans (Maccabees) on, Jews agreed that it was illegal to wage war on the Sabbath unless they were directly attacked.[10] The major pious groups, the Pharisees and the Essenes, elaborated Sabbath law in various ways,[11] which shows that defining what was and was not permitted on the Sabbath was a topic of major concern during Jesus' lifetime. Everyone, even the most radical Essene or Pharisee, agreed that saving life overrides the Sabbath. This sounds precise, but in fact it is not. Can one work on the Sabbath in order to prevent life-threatening situations from arising? Pompey, the Roman general, knew of the Jewish Sabbath law, and when he besieged Jerusalem he built earth-works and brought up his engines of war on the Sabbath, when the Jews would not fire on his men.[12] We may well imagine that some Jews were arguing that moving catapults into range and bringing up a battering ram were *tantamount* to a direct assault, and that therefore they should attack the Romans on the Sabbath. This argument, if it was made, did not prevail; the Jews allowed the Romans to bring their heavy weapons up to the wall, and eventually Jerusalem fell to Pompey.

The question of invasion is only a dramatic instance of a general problem. Once appeals to *mitigating circumstances* are allowed, it is hard to know where to stop. I shall stay with Pompey's invasion [[63]] in order to give hypothetical examples. The principle, to repeat, is that work is permitted in order to save life. Perhaps, then, the Jews should have attacked Pompey's men on the Sabbath while they were building the earthworks that would allow them to bring catapults and battering rams up to the wall. Perhaps the Jewish defenders should have attacked on a previous Sabbath, before the Romans reached Jerusalem. That is, possibly the Sabbath should be violated in order to keep danger more than an arm's length away.

This same argument can be applied to medical treatment. I shall give an example that depends on modern knowledge of infection. Should the application of antibiotic ointment be allowed on the Sabbath if someone cuts his

9. See, e.g., Ezek 20:12–24; Neh 10:31; 13:15–22.

10. See 1 Macc 2:29–42; Josephus, *J.W.* 1.57–60; 1.145–47; 2.147; *Ant.* 13.252; 14.202; 14.237; *Covenant of Damascus* (CD) 10:14–11:18. For discussion of these and other passages, see E. P. Sanders, *Jewish Law from Jesus to the Mishnah* (Philadelphia: Trinity International, 1990) 6–8.

11. [[Ibid.,]] 8–14.

12. Josephus, *J.W.* 1.145–47.

hand? It is a long step from cutting one's hand to being in danger of death, but infection is potentially life-threatening, and an argument could be made that minor cures should be allowed in order to be safe; conceivably, a small cut could become infected, and a minor wound might turn into a major illness. Ancient Jews did not know about bacteria and infection, and consequently causes and effects in medical matters were by no means clear to them. Some people had minor injuries or illnesses that escalated in ways that were not at all visible. Who knew which illness or injury would lead to death? Therefore, possibly cures of even minor problems should be allowed.

These examples are hypothetical, but the general point is not. Both the early rabbis and one wing of the Essene party discussed minor cures on the Sabbath;[13] if the most pious discussed this topic, it is highly probable that many ordinary Jews were willing to attempt to heal even minor injuries or illnesses on the Sabbath. They could have had an argument: "We do not know for sure which accidents or illnesses will turn out to be fatal."

This gives us, I hope, enough perspective to understand the Sabbath passages in the Gospels. Although not all of them bear on healing, those that do not nevertheless require us to understand the question of "mitigating circumstances": when is a problem serious [[64]] enough to justify transgression of the Sabbath? There are several passages about the Sabbath in the Gospels, and I shall discuss the major ones.

Plucking Grain on the Sabbath (Matt 12:1–8; Mark 2:23–28; Luke 6:1–5). According to this passage, Jesus and his disciples were going through a grain field and were hungry. The disciples, not Jesus, picked grain and started to eat it. The Pharisees (who, quite surprisingly, were looking on) asked Jesus why he allowed his disciples to break the law. In Mark's version, Jesus appealed to the precedent of David, who, when he and his men were hungry, ate holy bread, ordinarily forbidden to laymen. The passage concludes with two sayings: "The Sabbath was made for man, not man for the Sabbath"; "The Son of man is lord of the Sabbath." According to Matthew, Jesus advanced still another argument: on the Sabbath the priests in the temple work (by sacrificing) but are considered innocent.

In this passage, Jesus argues that there were mitigating circumstances that excuse the violation: the disciples were hungry. A modern analogy to this argument would be defending driving over the speed limit by explaining that a passenger is ill. Moreover, Jesus offers a precedent (in Matthew, two precedents). This is like arguing that, previously, a driver who sped because of an emergency was not fined. Appealing to mitigating circumstances (hunger) and precedent (David) shows fundamental respect for the law. There is nothing in this passage to indicate that Jesus wished to oppose the Sabbath law. On the contrary, the implication is that he and his disciples ordinarily kept it. He was prepared to argue that a minor breach was justified by hunger, and

---

13. See CD 11:10, accepting the interpretation of *sam* as referring to medicine. See Chaim Rabin, *The Zadokite Documents* (2nd ed.; Oxford: Clarendon, 1958) 56. For the rabbis, see Mishnah tractate *Shabbat*.

for this argument he appealed to biblical precedent. It follows that he did not reject the Sabbath law as such.

The Man with the Withered Hand (Matt 12:9–14; Mark 3:1–6; Luke 6:6–11). In this story, Jesus heals a man on the Sabbath by telling him to stretch out his hand. Apparently he did no work; [[65]] talking is not work. Even in the strictest legal documents from first-century Judaism, the *Covenant of Damascus* and the Qumran *Community Rule,* there is no hint that talking on the Sabbath was regarded as a transgression. Moreover, we again note that Jesus offers an argument to justify his action: "Is it lawful on the Sabbath to do good or to do harm, to save life or to kill?" (Mark 3:6). This justification seems to imply that Jesus accepted the argument that was sketched above: One cannot know for sure when an apparently minor illness will lead to death; therefore, minor cures are permitted. We also note that, as in the previous case, Jesus' appeal to mitigating circumstances shows that he did not oppose the Sabbath law in principle. Thus, although (according to Mark) the scribes who looked on took grave exception to the cure of the man's hand, the reader of the passage cannot say that Jesus opposed the Sabbath law.

Further Passages in Luke. Luke contains two other passages that deserve comment: 13:10–17 and 14:1–6. According to the first, Jesus healed a woman on the Sabbath by laying his hands on her and telling her that she was healed. According to the second, he "took" a man and healed him on the Sabbath. "Taking" seems to mean that he put his hands on the man in connection with the healing. Both these cases probably would have been regarded as transgressions by members of the pietist parties. As we noted above, the early rabbis discussed minor cures on the Sabbath, and they generally regarded work done on these occasions as wrong. For example, in one case they discussed whether a person with a sore tooth could put vinegar on it. The answer was that this should not be done, but that the sufferer could eat something with vinegar on it, and thus avoid transgression.[14] We cannot know whether Galilean Pharisees in Jesus' day would have held the same opinion, but it is reasonable to assume that they would not have disagreed very much.

I think it probable that the most pious groups in Judaism in Jesus' day would either have opposed or looked askance at performing [[66]] minor cures on the Sabbath if they required work. But the discussions in the *Covenant of Damascus* (presumably reflecting one wing of the Essene party) and Mishnah *Shabbat* (which stems from the rabbinic successors of the Pharisees) reveal, by their tone and content, that most Jews did not agree. The rabbis even disagreed among themselves about the status of minor cures. It is historically conceivable that Jesus performed one or more minor cures on the Sabbath by laying his hands on the injured or afflicted person, and that some pietists objected. This would not have been, however, a major issue; it was one about which reasonable people could agree to disagree. Some people would do no work on the Sabbath unless there was an obvious and immediate threat to life. Some took a more lenient view, and Jesus appears to have

14. *M. Shabbat* 14:4.

belonged to the latter group—which was, in all probability, a large one. It is most dubious that minor cures on the Sabbath were a major item of disagreement between Jesus and other pious Jews.

Jesus and Food Laws

Two major passages in the Hebrew Bible (Leviticus 11; Deuternomy 14) prohibit various foods. The two most famous are pork and shellfish, but the exclusions also cover birds of prey, rodents, insects, donkeys, carnivorous animals, and numerous other potential foods—many of which have been and are as objectionable to non-Jews as to Jews. These laws were very important to first-century Jews, who clung to them despite the fact that Gentiles ridiculed them for avoiding the most succulent meat, pork. The significance of the food laws was in some ways much greater outside of Palestine than in Palestine. A Jew who lived in Jerusalem would have found it quite difficult to break the food laws. Pigs were not kept anywhere near Jerusalem, and the closest source of shellfish was many miles away. Apart from the problems of transporting forbidden foods to Jewish cities and villages in Palestine, moral suasion would have been very strong. The vendors [[67]] and the consumers of pork or shellfish would both have been reported to the authorities, and the populace would have expressed its disfavor in very strong ways. There were, of course, Gentile cities in geographical Galilee, and there it would be easy for a Palestinian Jew to disobey the food laws. Had he wished to flaunt these laws, Jesus could have gone to Scythopolis (for example), where pork surely could be had. As far as we know, he did not do this.

For Jews who lived in Gentile surroundings (such as Paul), the issue was quite different. Pork was readily available (it was probably the most common meat), and shellfish could be obtained in any town that was close to the Mediterranean. In the Gentile cities of Asia Minor and Greece, the markets, managed by civic officers, offered what the managers decreed. Some market managers were not especially friendly to Jews, but after the Jews aided Julius Caesar, he showed his appreciation in various ways, some direct and some indirect. One of the results was that the Greek-speaking cities of Asia Minor began passing decrees in favor of the Jews. Among the top three or four items was the right to have their own food.[15] The managers of the markets were forced to supply the Jews with their "ancestral food." It appears that previously the Jews did not always have food that Moses allowed. That is, in Palestine, nothing was easier than to observe the Mosaic food laws: they were hard to disobey. Outside Palestine, the situation was reversed: obedience to Moses sometimes left Jews in very grave difficulties. Some, no doubt, transgressed rather than go hungry. Julius Caesar corrected this situation, but we do not know how long this more favorable climate lasted.

---

15. Josephus, *Ant.* 14.226, 261. See discussion of this and other rights sought by diaspora Jews in Sanders, *Judaism: Practice and Belief*, 211f.

It Is Not What Goes In (Matt 15:10–20; Mark 7:14–23). According to Mark (7:1–8), Jesus fell into a dispute with some Pharisees and scribes about handwashing. This argument led to his pronouncement that "there is nothing outside a person which by going into him can defile, but the things which come out of a person are [[68]] what defile" (Mark 7:15). After the crowd departed, Jesus explained his view to the disciples: "Do you not see that whatever goes into a person from outside cannot defile him, since it enters, not his heart but his stomach, and so passes on?" (Mark 7:18–19). The author of the Gospel then adds: "Thus he declared all food clean."

If the author of Mark correctly states Jesus' own view, we have here an explicit statement that the law of Moses need not be observed. That is, if Jesus "declared all food clean," he opposed both Leviticus 11 and Deuteronomy 14. It is, however, dubious that the author's comment in Mark 7:19 reflects Jesus' own view. This is potentially a long argument, one that I have made in more detail elsewhere,[16] and I shall here merely outline the points.

1. The passage appears in both Matthew and Mark, but only Mark states that Jesus declared all foods clean. In Matthew, Jesus neither here nor elsewhere counsels his followers to break the law.

2. The saying in Mark 7:15 does not necessarily mean that Jesus intended to denounce the food laws. For the sake of emphasis, I shall quote it again: "There is nothing outside a person which by going into him can defile, but the things which come out of a person are what defile him." The construction *not . . . but* quite frequently means "not only this, but much more that."[17] When Moses told the Israelites that their murmurings were *not* against Aaron and himself, *but* against the Lord, they had just been complaining to *him* (Exod 16:2–8). The sentence means, "Your murmurings directed against us are in reality against the Lord, since we do his will." When the author of the *Epistle of Aristeas* wrote that Jews "honor God" *not* with gifts or sacrifices, *but* with purity of heart and of devout disposition" (*Ep. Arist.* 234), he did not mean that sacrifices were not brought, nor that he was against them (see, e.g., *Ep. Arist.* 170–71), but rather that what really matters is what they symbolize. Similarly, Mark 9:37, "Whoever receives me, receives *not* me *but* the one who sent me," means "receiving me is tantamount to receiving God." "*Not* what goes in *but* what comes out" in Mark 7:15, then, [[69]] probably means, "What comes out—the wickedness of a person's heart—is what really matters," leaving the food laws as such untouched. In this case there is no conflict with the law. This interpretation of the core saying in Mark 7:15 leads to the conclusion that the interpretation in 7:19 is incorrect.

3. After Jesus' death, his disciples did not know that he had told them to eat whatever food they liked. According to Acts 10, Peter three times saw a

---

16. Sanders, *Jewish Law from Jesus to the Mishnah,* 23–28.
17. See A. B. Du Toit, "Hyperbolical Contrasts: A Neglected Aspect of Paul's Style," *A South African Perspective on the New Testament: Essays Presented to Bruce Manning Metzger* (ed. J. H. Petzer and P. J. Martin [Leiden: Brill, 1986]) 178–86; Sanders, *Jewish Law from Jesus to the Mishnah,* 28.

vision of all sorts of animals, including "beasts of prey and reptiles," and a voice told him, "kill and eat."[18] These foods were, of course, forbidden by Moses. Even after seeing this vision and hearing the commandment three times, Peter remained puzzled as to the meaning (Acts 10:17). Had Jesus already explained to his disciples that they could disregard the food laws (Mark 7:19), Peter would probably have understood the vision more quickly. Later, Peter and James disputed several points of the Jewish law with Paul—especially circumcision but also food laws and the Sabbath. It appears that neither side could appeal to the teaching of Jesus for support.[19] The conclusion to be drawn, then, is that Mark's statement in 7:19, "he declared all foods clean," represents a possible interpretation of Jesus' words, but not a necessary one. Moreover, the other early Christians did not think that Jesus had canceled the food laws for his followers.

Other Legal Issues

A complete treatment of Jesus and the first table of the Jewish law would include more topics: purity, tithes, other offerings, blasphemy, fasting, and worship. Scholars usually regard the three that we have considered (sacrifice, Sabbath, and food) as the major areas where Jesus may have opposed the law. I shall not here attempt to analyze these other topics in detail, partly because of the preferred length of these essays, partly because I have discussed all these issues elsewhere.[20] I shall instead make a few comments. [[70]]

1. Purity. The major purity issue in the Gospels is leprosy. In a passage that we discussed under "sacrifice" (Mark 1:40–44), Jesus commands the leper to do what Moses commanded him; there is no opposition to the law.

Handwashing before meals (Mark 7:5) was a tradition followed by a few Jews, but it was not a law. The Hebrew Bible contains no commandment to wash hands before eating. In Jesus' day, some Jews probably washed their hands before eating, but some did not.[21]

2. Tithes, and so on. According to Matt 23:23, Jesus agreed that even minor herbs should be tithed.

3. Fasting. The Hebrew Bible requires only one fast, on the Day of Atonement. There is no indication that Jesus feasted on this day. Various groups, and sometimes an entire city or region, might fast for some special reason: to commemorate a day of destruction, to try to persuade God to send rain, and so on. According to Mark 2:18–22, Jesus and his followers did not fast on some occasion when the Pharisees and the disciples of John the Baptist were fasting. This was obviously an optional fast, because only members of two pietist groups were observing it. The law of Moses was not in question.

---

18. Acts 10:12 has "all kinds of animals and reptiles and birds of the air"; in Peter's retelling, the phrase is "animals and beasts of prey and reptiles and birds" (Acts 11:6).

19. Circumcision: Gal 2:3 and elsewhere; food: perhaps Gal 2:11–13; Sabbath: Gal 4:10.

20. Sanders, *Jewish Law from Jesus to the Mishnah*, part 1.

21. Handwashing: ibid., 260–63, and further pages listed in the index.

4. Worship. The gospel evidence is that, on Sabbaths, Jesus attended the synagogue (e.g., Mark 1:21). Unfortunately, we are not told much about Jesus' worship in the temple. We do know, however, that he observed at least one festival, which included eating an animal sacrificed in the temple (e.g., Mark 14:12). The Gospels omit most of the details of Jesus' life prior to his short ministry, and I assume that he had previously attended the temple during one or more festivals each year. In any case, there is no evidence that he refused to worship the God of Israel in the way that the Hebrew Bible commands.

5. Blasphemy. This is potentially a major issue; according to the trial scenes in the synoptic gospels, Jesus was accused of and executed for blasphemy. I hope that readers who accept this view will [[71]] take the time to study my earlier discussions.[22] In brief, the situation is this: According to Mark, the high priest cried, "Blasphemy!" when Jesus admitted that he was "the Christ, the Son of the Blessed" (Mark 14:61–64). According to Matthew and Luke, he did not give a clear answer. But we may stay with Mark. As the author presents the account, the high priest was determined to have Jesus executed. His first effort was to have Jesus accused of attacking the temple (Mark 14:55–60). This charge was thrown out. He then got Jesus to admit that he was "the son of the Blessed," and immediately cried "Blasphemy!" There is nothing intrinsically blasphemous in the claim to be son of God. All ancient Jews thought of themselves as sons of God. What we learn from this passage is *not* that Jesus held blasphemous views of himself (that he put himself on the same level as God), but that the high priest would take any admission as an excuse for the verdict that he desired. That is, the high priest had determined that Jesus should die. The question of the charge was only technical. If a group of Jewish legal authorities, either past or present, coolly examined what Jesus said (or is reported to have said), they would not conclude that he was a blasphemer.

Conclusion

Many Christians believe that Jesus opposed his native religion. If so, he should have spoken against either its theology or its ethics—that is, against the table of laws that govern relations between humans and God or those that apply to humans' relations with other humans. I cannot find the evidence that he attacked either table. His debates and arguments with his contemporaries fall within the parameters of disagreement in his place and time. With regard to his view of the laws on the first table, with which this essay concerns itself, we cannot say that Jesus was against monotheism, sacrifice, the Sabbath, or food laws. I have more briefly sketched other possible topics of disagreement. We find that Jesus did not oppose the [[72]] laws of purity, of support of the priesthood, of fasting, or of worship. We have also seen that he did not denigrate or blaspheme against God.

22. Sanders, *Jesus and Judaism* (Philadelphia: Fortress, 1985) 296–301; *Jewish Law from Jesus to the Mishnah*, 57–67; *The Historical Figure of Jesus* (London: Penguin, 1993) 270–73.

This does not mean that he did not have his own distinctive viewpoints. On the contrary, it is plain that he did so. (I have not discussed them in this essay.) I can well imagine that he rubbed some people the wrong way. Joseph Caiaphas, the high priest, clearly thought that Jesus should be done away with. But that was not because he and Jesus disagreed about Deuteronomy or Leviticus. I have elsewhere argued extensively that Caiaphas was afraid of civil turmoil and that Jesus posed a threat to peace and order. To understand the death of Jesus, we would have to change topics and discuss the politics of the day. With regard to our present subject, however, we should conclude that Jesus did not favor transgression of the laws on the first table of the law of Moses.

DALE C. ALLISON JR.

The Allusive Jesus

Jesus and the Scriptures

[[213]] Most of the Jewish literature that has survived from the period between the Maccabees and the destruction of the second temple is, in one way
or another, in constant dialogue with the Tanak. The same is true of primitive Christian literature, including the earliest written deposits of the Jesus
tradition known to us, Q and Mark. One might, then, employ the criterion of
dissimilarity to contend that the literary Jesus, who so regularly refers to
Scripture, cannot be identified with the historical Jesus of Nazareth, for the
former's references to the Bible do not distinguish him from characteristic
emphases of Judaism and the Church, both of which were intertextual facto-
ries. Gerd Theissen has written,

> We must remember that where the Christian sources attribute clearly
> identifiable scriptural quotations or allusions to biblical traditions to
> Jesus, it is by no means certain that these go back to him. For the biblical
> scriptures depict a perception and interpretation of reality which was com-
> mon to all Jews (and Christians). After Easter the story and message of
> Jesus were interpreted and continued to be told in the light of scripture.[1]

The criterion of dissimilarity, however, is an unwieldy and perilous tool, and
it has promised results that it cannot deliver, as Theissen himself has well argued.[2] In the present case, moreover, it seems more plausible that if most of

---

Reprinted, with permission, from Dale C. Allison Jr., *The Intertextual Jesus: Scripture in Q*
(Harrisburg, Pa.: Trinity Press International, 2000) 213–22.

    1. Gerd Theissen and Annette Merz, *The Historical Jesus: A Comprehensive Guide* (Min-
neapolis: Fortress, 1998) 357.

    2. Gerd Theissen and Dagmar Winter, *Die Kriterienfrage in der Jesusforschung: Vom Differ-
enzkriterium zum Plausibilitätskriterium* (NTOA 34; Freiburg/Göttingen: Universtitätsverlag/
Vandenhoeck & Ruprecht, 1997).

Palestinian Judaism was an intertextual Judaism, we might expect a Palestinian teacher such as Jesus to be an intertextual teacher. What Jewish teachers do we know of who did not feel constrained to relate their words continually to the Tanak?

The primitive Church's interest in the Bible, so far from weakening the inference from Judaism's fixation on Scripture, fortifies it, for if, as the sources lead us to believe, and as a critical sifting of them confirms, many of the first Christian disciples preoccupied themselves with the First Testament, what [[214]] reason do we have for imagining that such preoccupation emerged only after Easter? If, as it seems, early leaders of the Church turned immediately to biblical texts to interpret the passion and resurrection of Jesus,[3] surely it was only because some of them were already accustomed to using such texts to make sense of things.

But this is a big generalization, and it can only become fully persuasive through a careful examination of each individual unit in the Jesus tradition, canonical and noncanonical. Such an examination cannot be undertaken within the present volume [[referring to Allison's book]], which confines itself to the Sayings Source. One may nonetheless observe that many of the Q sayings that allusively refer to the Scriptures or recast them are taken by many competent scholars to belong to the original tradition. Consider the following seven examples, all of which John Dominic Crossan has attributed to Jesus.[4]

> Q 6:20–21, the first three beatitudes, draw upon the prophetic oracle in Isa 61:1–2.
>
> Q 9:58 informs a would-be follower, in language that ironically alludes to Psalm 8, that while foxes have holes and birds of the air have nests, the Son of man has nowhere to lay his head.
>
> Q 9:62, the call to put hand to the plow and not look at the things behind, alludes to both the call of Elisha in 1 Kings 19 and to the fatal error of Lot's wife in Genesis 19.
>
> Q 11:20, Jesus' declaration that he casts out demons by the finger of God, depends upon Exod 8:19 and traditions about the contest between Moses and the magicians of Egypt.
>
> Q 12:27 asks one to consider the lilies, how they grow yet neither toil nor spin, and how even Solomon in all his glory was not arrayed like one of these.
>
> Q 12:51–53 appends to the declaration that Jesus has come not to bring peace but a sword a paraphrase of Mic 7:6: "For the son treats the father with contempt, the daughter rises up against her mother, the daughter-in-law against her mother-in-law."

3. Cf. 1 Cor 15:3–4: κατὰ τὰς γραφάς, "according to the scriptures." See further Donald Juel, *Messianic Exegesis: Christological Interpretation of the Old Testament in Early Christianity* (Philadelphia: Fortress, 1988).

4. John Dominic Crossan, *The Historical Jesus: The Life of a Mediterranean Jewish Peasant* (San Francisco: HarperCollins, 1991).

Q 14:26 enjoins disciples to hate their own father and mother, an imperative that inevitably invites comparison with the fifth of the Ten Commandments, which requires love of father and mother.

A few might wish to contend that Crossan has not been skeptical enough,
that some of these sayings do not in fact go back to Jesus. Rudolf Bultmann
rejected the authenticity of Q 9:58, and the Jesus Seminar has printed [[215]]
Luke (Q) 9:62 in black, Luke (Q) 12:51–53 in gray. (The other five, however,
come in red or, in one case, pink.)[5] Some others might want to urge, especially in the case of Q 6:20–23, that the scriptural language is secondary.[6]
Certainly elsewhere, as in Q's story of Jesus' temptation, the biblical references come from the Church, not Jesus. Still others might query whether
each of the proposed allusions has been sufficiently established.

To all this one can only respond that most of the units just cited are regularly reckoned to Jesus; that, unlike Matthew's formula quotations and the
biblical citations added to 1QS,[7] most of the relevant scriptural language cannot be stripped off without destroying everything;[8] and that, in the seven
cases cited, the present volume makes the case for the proposed allusions, all
of which have been espied by others. So the way is cleared to entertain the
possibility that the intertextual Jesus of Q is not a misleading representative of
the historical Jesus. Indeed, those persuaded that many more than seven of
Q's allusive units derive from Jesus will necessarily believe that the consciously intertextual nature of Q corresponds to the consciously intertextual
nature of Jesus' speech, that he "evidently knew the Old Testament well"[9]
and presupposed an audience able to catch allusions to it.

Of late much work has been done on the intertextuality of both the First
and Second Testaments. We have learned about the numerous allusions to
Scripture in, for example, Deutero-Isaiah, Matthew, and Paul. What needs to
be remembered is that such intertextuality was at home in oral performances: Deutero-Isaiah, Matthew, and the Epistles of Paul were, like all other
writings in antiquity, intended to be read aloud. This means that their scriptural allusions were designed to be perceived by ears, not eyes. This matters
so much because Jesus' teaching was, from every indication, oral. We have no
evidence that he ever wrote anything. Indeed, we do not know what sort of

---

5. Bultmann, *History of the Synoptic Tradition*, 28; Robert W. Funk, Roy W. Hoover, and
the Jesus Seminar, *The Five Gospels: The Search for the Authentic Words of Jesus* (New York: Macmillan, 1993).

6. See [[Allison, *Intertextual Jesus*,]] 104–7.

7. 1QS contains explicit citations missing from 4QS[b] and 4Q5[d]; see Sarianna Metso,
"The Use of Old Testament Quotation in the Qumran Community Rule," in *Qumran between
the Old and New Testaments* (ed. Frederick H. Cryer and Thomas L. Thompson; JSOTSS 290/
Copenhagen International Seminar 6; Sheffield: Sheffield Academic Press, 1998) 217–31.

8. The exception is Q 6:20–21. See [[Allison, *Intertextual Jesus*,]] 104–7. On the originality of the allusion in Q 12:51–53 as opposed to the variant in *Gos. Thom.* 16, see Allison, "Q
12:51–53 and Mark 9:11–13 and the Messianic Woes," 295 n. 32.

9. C. K. Barrett, *Jesus and the Gospel Tradition* (Philadelphia: Fortress, 1968) 41.

education he might have had, nor even know for sure whether he could read, although this may be the best guess.[10] But our ignorance in [[216]] these particulars is no argument against Jesus' ability to allude. Even if he did not write anything, and even if he could not read at all, the evidence is that he and his hearers, whether formally educated or not, had heard Scripture recited often enough that large portions of it were quite familiar to them, sufficiently so that oblique and sometimes even subtle references to it could be appreciated. Q may not presuppose the sort of intertextual expertise on display in the Dead Sea Scrolls,[11] but it also does not presuppose the sort of religious ignorance people have so often associated with peasants of the Middle Ages. Q's Jesus rather takes for granted an oral literacy in the Scriptures.

The Eschatological, Mosaic Jesus

Q, in accord with its declaration that the kingdom of God has arrived and/or come near (10:9, 11; 11:20), reads the Scriptures from an eschatological perspective. It construes John the Baptist as the historical realization of the prophecy in Mal 3:1 (Q 7:27). It interprets Jesus as the fulfillment of oracles in the book of Isaiah, especially Isa 61:1–2 (Q 6:20–21; 7:22). It characterizes the present with the eschatological language of Mic 7:6: now is the time not of peace but of the sword, of the eschatological tribulation, when children rise up against their parents (Q 12:52–53). Q also borrows the language of Dan 7:13–14 in forecasting Jesus' imminent return (Q 12:8–9; 12:40; 22:30).

Q's eschatological perspective is congruent with the outlook of the historical Jesus, a millenarian prophet who longed for the fulfillment of Jewish eschatological expectations and so necessarily looked for the fulfillment of the scriptural texts that grounded those expectations.[12] Apart from the issue of which, if any, of the Q texts cited in the previous paragraph might be assigned in whole or in part to Jesus himself, their collective conviction that the present is the time of eschatology entering history faithfully represents the worldview of Jesus.

This fact should come as no surprise. Quite a few sources show us that certain religious Jews readily interpreted their own experiences with the aid

---

10. See Meier, *A Marginal Jew*, 1.268–78. On p. 276 Meier writes: "If we take into account that Jesus' adult life became fiercely focused on the Jewish religion, that he is presented by almost all the Gospel traditions as engaging in learned disputes over Scripture and halaka with students of the Law, that he was accorded the respectful—but at that time vague—title of rabbi or teacher, that more than one Gospel tradition presents him preaching or teaching in the synagogues . . . and that, even apart from formal disputes, his teaching was strongly imbued with the outlook and language of the sacred texts of Israel, it is reasonable to suppose that Jesus' religious formation in his family was intense and profound, and included instruction in reading biblical Hebrew."

11. Cf. what Josephus has to say about the Essenes in *J.W.* 2.136 ("They display an extraordinary interest in the writings of the ancients"), 159 (some "are versed from their early years in holy books").

12. Dale C. Allison Jr., *Jesus of Nazareth: Millenarian Prophet* (Minneapolis: Fortress, 1999).

of an eschatological scheme.[13] Even Josephus, who seems so distant from
[[217]] all apocalyptic expectation, "understood the prophecies in Numbers
23–24 and in Daniel (2 and 7–10) to be predictions referring to Josephus's
own lifetime, partly the catastrophe in the year 70 C.E. and partly the approaching eschatological redemption of the Jewish people."[14] That Jesus similarly thought of scriptural prophecies as fulfilled in his own day is only to be
expected of one whose outlook was so thoroughly eschatological.

One particular dimension of Q's eschatology merits further remark.
Chapter 2 sets forth the evidence that, in the Sayings Source, Jesus is like
Moses, rewrites parts of the Torah, and experiences a new exodus. One can
ask to what extent the typology created by these themes is a secondary imposition upon the tradition and to what extent it may reflect the self-conception
of the historical Jesus. On the one hand, the appearance of the new exodus
and new Moses motifs throughout the Jesus tradition as well as in Acts and
Paul shows us that these themes go back to an early time in the Church, and
certainly some of the things that go back so far do so because they were already there on the other side of Easter—opposition to divorce, for example,
and the emphasis upon loving one's neighbor. On the other hand, we know
from the temptation story, which surely does not preserve words of Jesus,
that the new exodus theme could be added at a secondary stage. We must
give the creativity of the post-Easter tradents its due.

In sorting through this problem, one needs to ask whether any of the
pertinent Q material has a decent chance of going back to Jesus. The answer
is that some of it does. Despite the skepticism of the Jesus Seminar, the
Lord's Prayer, with its request for daily bread that alludes to the tale of the
manna (Q 11:3), probably comes from Jesus.[15] So too Q 11:20, where Jesus
alludes to Exod 8:19 in claiming that he casts out demons by the finger of
God. Here the speaker is indicating "that he places himself alongside Moses
and Aaron, genuine messengers from God who were empowered by him to
perform symbolic miracles in connection with Israel's liberation from slavery."[16] Also pertinent are the sayings in Q 6:27ff. that revise Leviticus 19 as
well as Q 14:26, which daringly inverts the commandment to honor father
and mother: in these two places—where so many have not doubted that we
hear a pre-Easter voice—Jesus seemingly sets his words over against Moses.
And then there is Q 11:29–30, where Jesus' generation is spoken of with language characteristic of the generation of Moses ("This generation is an evil

---

13. For some examples, see Dale C. Allison Jr., *The End of the Ages Has Come: An Early
Interpretation of the Death and Resurrection of Jesus* (Philadelphia: Fortress, 1985) 6–14, 101–6.
See also now the provocative work of Michael O. Wise, *The First Messiah: Investigating the Sav-
ior before Jesus* (San Francisco: HarperSanFrancisco, 1999).

14. Per Bilde, "Josephus and Jewish Apocalypticism," in *Understanding Josephus: Seven
Perspectives* (ed. Steve Mason; JSPSS 32; Sheffield: Sheffield Academic Press, 1998) 54.

15. Cf. Meier, *A Marginal Jew*, 2.294.

16. Ibid., 411.

generation"; cf. Deut 1:35). This may reflect the idiom and perspective of Jesus.[17]

[[218]] Taken together, these several units strongly suggest that the eschatological Jesus, like Deutero-Isaiah long before him, conceived of the coming of the kingdom in his own day as a sort of new exodus. One might even speculate, as did Ben F. Meyer, that Jesus, who surely conceived of himself as an eschatological prophet (cf. Q 7:22), found the fulfillment of Deut 18:15, 18 (God will raise up a prophet like Moses) in his own ministry.[18] To this one could find a parallel in Dositheus, who appears to have been "an early first century A.D. eschatological figure among the Samaritans, who applied the 'Prophet like Moses' passage of Dt. 18 to himself. As the Prophet, he was, in all likelihood a miracle-worker and the author of new texts and/or interpretations of biblical law."[19] But however that particular issue is judged, the main point stands—and it is strengthened by other sources besides Q. Matthew's tradition, for example, preserves two parallel units (Matt 5:21–22, 27–28) in which "You have heard that it was said to those of old" (by Moses at Sinai) is the foil for "But I [Jesus] say to you." I have elsewhere argued that these two units rest upon words of Jesus,[20] and in them we have the same phenomenon as in Q 6:27ff. and Q 14:26: Jesus recalls Moses only in order to daringly go his own and different way. If Jesus really did speak these words, he must have been consciously relating himself in some profound way to the lawgiver.

Again, those of us who strongly suspect that behind the various versions of the two feedings of multitudes[21] lies a meal with a large crowd in a deserted place, a meal that was, in a way reminiscent of the Jewish sign prophets in Josephus,[22] intended to be an eschatological symbol, an anticipation of

17. Cf. Martin Hengel, "Kerygma oder Geschichte? Zur Problematik einer falschen Alternative in der Synoptikerforschung aufgezeigt an Hand einiger neuer Monographien," *ThQ* 101 (1971) 334.

18. Ben F. Meyer, "Appointed Deed, Appointed Doer: Jesus and the Scriptures," in Chilton and Evans, eds., *Activities of Jesus*, 171. Contrast Teeple, *Mosaic Eschatological Prophet*, 115–18. The term "scripture prophet," used by Michael Wise, *The First Messiah*, is appropriate for Jesus.

19. Stanley Jerome Isser, *The Dositheans: A Samaritan Sect in Late Antiquity* (SJLA 17; Leiden: Brill, 1976) 163.

20. Allison, *Jesus of Nazareth*, 185–87. Cf. Luz, *Matthew*, 1.276–79, 281, 291.

21. Matt 14:13–21; 15:32–39; Mark 6:30–44; 8:1–10; Luke 9:10–17; John 6:1–15.

22. See Josephus, *Ant.* 18.85–87 (the Samaritan who claimed he would recover the sacred vessels that Moses had deposited); *Ant.* 20.97–99 (Theudas, who tried to part the Jordan in imitation of Moses' successor, Joshua), 167–68 (unnamed "impostors and deceivers" who called upon people to follow them into the desert and who promised to show "unmistakable marvels and signs that would be wrought in harmony with God's design"; cf. *J.W.* 2.258–60), 188 (an unnamed "imposter" "who had promised them salvation and rest from troubles if they chose to follow him into the wilderness"); *J.W.* 2.261–63 (= *Ant.* 20.169–72: the would-be ruler from Egypt who led his followers from the desert to the Mount of Olives; cf. Acts 21:38).

the messianic feast, will probably feel that Jesus, like most of those sign prophets, was recalling memories of the exodus.[23] Commentators from patristic times on have certainly been put in mind of the manna in the [[219]] wilderness,[24] and John's probably independent account not only relates that the crowd regarded Jesus as "the (Mosaic?) prophet" (6:14) but further draws several parallels and contrasts between Jesus and Moses (6:25ff.). Maybe John here has it right.

And then there is the Last Supper. In both Mark 14:24 and Matt 26:28, where the Last Supper is a Passover meal, Jesus speaks of "my blood of the covenant" (τὸ αἷμά μου τῆσ διαθήκης). Similarly, in Luke 22:20 and 1 Cor 11:25 he uses the expression "the new covenant in my blood" (Luke: ἡ καινὴ διαθήκη ἐν τῷ αἵματί μου; Paul: ἡ καινὴ διαθήκη ἐστὶν ἐν τῷ ἐμῷ αἵματι). Both phrases function partly as allusions to Exod 24:8: "Moses took the blood and dashed it on the people and said, 'See the blood of the covenant (MT: דם הברית; LXX: τὸ αἷμα τῆς μου διαθήκης) that the Lord has made with you in accordance with all these words.'" As John Lightfoot commented,

> Moses sprinkled all the people with blood, and said, "This is the blood of the covenant which God hath made with you": and thus that old covenant or testimony was confirmed. In like manner, Christ having published all the articles of the new covenant, he takes the cup of wine, and gives them to drink, and saith, "This is the new testament in my blood": and thus the new covenant is established.[25]

Matthew clearly divined the allusion and enlarged it,[26] and the perception that the Lord's Supper should be connected with the exodus appears in John 6, where allusions to the Last Supper (e.g., 6:53–58) stand beside references to the miracle of the manna. There is also 1 Cor 10:1–5, where the Eucharist is likened to the supernatural food Israel ate in the wilderness. So we have

23. Allison, *New Moses*, 73–84; P. W. Barnett, "The Jewish Sign Prophets—A.D. 40–70: Their Intention and Origin," *NTS* 27 (1981) 679–97. But for caution in this matter, see Rebecca Gray, *Prophetic Figures in Late Second Temple Jewish Palestine: The Evidence from Josephus* (New York/Oxford: Oxford University Press, 1993) 112–44. She is confident of a connection with Moses and the exodus only for Theudas and the Egyptian: about the others we are, Gray thinks, insufficiently informed to draw such a conclusion.

24. E.g., Cyril of Alexandria, *Comm. Luke* 48 (citing Ps 78:24; CSCO Scriptores Syri 70, ed. J.-B. Chabot, p. 159); Eusebius, *Dem. ev.* 3.2 (92b–c) (GCS 23, ed. I. A. Heikel, p. 98).

25. John Lightfoot, *Commentary*, 2.353. Cf. Maldonatus, *Commentarii*, 1.406; Bengel, *Gnomon*, ad loc.; Gundry, *Old Testament*, 57–58. "Blood of the covenant" also appears in Zech 9:11, but (a) Zech 9:11 may itself be an allusion to Exod 24:8 (cf. the targum on Zech 9:11: "You also, for whom a covenant was made by blood, I have delivered you from bondage to the Egyptians"); (b) Exod 24:8 is the only place in the Tanak where blood-sprinkling for cleansing is connected with a meal, as in the Gospels; (c) the Peshitta as well as *Tg. Ps.-J.* and *Tg. Onq.* on Exod 24:8 use a demonstrative, which agrees with the NT's τοῦτο and (d) the Greek of Mark 14:24 = Matt 26:28 (τὸ αἷμα μου τῆς διαθήκης [['my blood of the covenant']]) is closer to LXX Exod 24:8 (τὸ αἷμα τῆς διαθήκης [[the blood of the covenant']]) than to LXX Zech 9:11 (ἐν αἵματι διαθήκης [['in the blood of the covenant']]).

26. Details in Allison, *New Moses*, 256–61.

here a very old tradition. How old? If one can think that "my blood of the covenant" or "the new covenant in my blood" represents something Jesus said,[27] one would have additional evidence that he himself drew a significant [[220]] analogy between himself and Moses and/or between his own time, that of the latter days, and the redemption from Egypt.

The Ironic Jesus

If Q's allusive, eschatological, Mosaic Jesus is not a misleading representative of the historical Jesus of Nazareth, what about that other prominent feature of Q's intertextuality, namely, the way it inverts subtexts to startle and generate irony? Here too Q seems to put us in touch with the originating tradition. Consider the following six passages or verses:

Q 6:27–45, which contains several imperatives that reverse commandments of Leviticus 19

Q 9:58, which offers a cynical reapplication of Ps 8:5

Q 12:22–31, which, against the spirit of Prov 6:6–11 and other Wisdom texts, encourages believers not to worry because God takes care of animals that do not work

Q 13:19, which describes the kingdom of God with imagery that Ezekiel and Daniel associate with ungodly powers

Q 14:26, which commands one not to honor father and mother but to hate father and mother

Q 16:18, which prohibits divorce despite the provision for it in Deut 24:1–4

In all these places Scripture is not appealed to as a supporting authority but is instead turned upside down and used as a foil for saying something different. This provocative use of the Tanak, as we have seen, has good parallels in Jewish tradition, especially in Deutero-Isaiah. So it cannot be classified as antinomian rhetoric, nor can we apply the criterion of dissimilarity and forthwith attribute the relevant units to the historical Jesus. There are, however, other means by which to argue that the historical Jesus was the ironically allusive Jesus.

One way is to decide, one by one, which of the sayings cited might in fact be plausibly attributed to Jesus. I forego that exercise here and content myself with an appeal to the Jesus Seminar, which many of us think is not optimistic enough about tracing synoptic sayings to Jesus. Its voting resulted in

---

27. I cannot here discuss the tradition history of the Lord's Supper or the question of a Semitic equivalent for "my blood of the covenant" or the origin of the tradition. Suffice it to say that one sympathizes with Strauss, *Jesus*, 634, who in view of Paul's testimony found it hard to doubt that the words of institution rest upon words of Jesus; and further that, despite the doubts of many, who have regarded an allusion to Exod 24:8 as secondary, a good case can be made for its belonging to the original tradition. See Rudolf Pesch, *Das Abendmahl und Jesu Todesverständnis* (QD 80; Freiburg/Basel/Vienna: Herder, 1978).

coloring eight of the verses in Q 6:27–41 and six of the verses in Q 12:22–31 red or pink, and it also prints Q 9:58; 13:19; and 14:26 in pink. Only 16:18, Jesus' prohibition of divorce, is not in red or pink. It gets gray—surely an idiosyncratic judgment. Few have doubted that the prohibition of divorce goes back to Jesus.

[[221]] A second way to confirm that Jesus liked to allude to biblical subtexts in a daring manner would be to observe that such a use of Scripture is not just a feature of Q. Matt 5:21–22 cites Exod 20:13 = Deut 5:17, the prohibition of murder, not in order to agree or disagree with it but in order to transcend it. Similarly, Matt 5:27–28 quotes Exod 20:14 = Deut 5:18, the command not to commit adultery, and then goes beyond it to demand more. In both of these places, whose authenticity can be reasonably maintained,[28] Scripture is not the last word but the first word only: Moses is not enough. Another intriguing passage for comparison is Mark 12:35–37, which has Jesus set Ps 110:1 against itself. If David (the author of the psalm according to the superscription) calls the Messiah "lord," how can the Messiah be his son? The question "represents a puzzling piece of christology that is at home neither in first-century Judaism, nor in first-century Christianity, nor in the flow of Mark's story."[29] This is at least some reason to ask whether Mark 12:35–37 preserves a memory.[30] Whatever one's judgment on that matter, Q is not the only source in which Jesus quotes the Tanak neither to illumine a point nor to support an argument but rather to provocatively transcend it.[31] We have here a teaching method that belongs to more than one strand of the Jesus tradition.

A third way of coming to the conclusion that Jesus himself, and not just the tradition about him, undid subtexts builds upon the fact that such a rhetorical strategy fits with what we otherwise know of him. Robert Funk has rightly remarked that Jesus'

> stories are laced with surprise. As with all good jokes and stories, one cannot anticipate the outcome. His listeners did not anticipate that everyone would be invited to the dinner party. They did not expect those hired last to be paid the same as those hired in the morning. They didn't believe things would turn out well for the shrewd manager. In other words, Jesus detypifies, he defamiliarizes common perceptions. He says the un-

28. See n. 20 on p. 243.
29. Joel Marcus, *The Way of the Lord: Christological Exegesis of the Old Testament in the Gospel of Mark* (Louisville: Westminster/John Knox, 1992) 140.
30. See further the survey of opinion and evaluation of arguments pro and con in Davies and Allison, *Matthew*, 3.250–51.
31. See further the interesting article of John A. T. Robinson, "Did Jesus Have a Distinctive Use of Scripture?" in *Christological Perspectives: Essays in Honor of Harvey K. McArthur* (ed. Robert F. Berkey and Sarah A. Edwards; New York: Pilgrim, 1982) 49–57. In this Robinson urges that Jesus sometimes used Scripture not to add an aura of authority or confirm a point or to offer exegesis but to turn it into a challenge—"using the Bible to pose rather than to prove" (p. 54).

expected. He confounds by contradicting what everybody already knows.[32]

[[222]] Surely few would disagree with what Funk says here, and his words apply equally well to Q 6:27–45; 9:58; 12:22–31; 13:19; 14:26; and 16:18 once their subtexts are exposed. In these places Jesus defamiliarizes common perceptions, says the unexpected, and contradicts what everyone knows. So once again we are encouraged to believe that Jesus liked referring to a text in order to say something not in that text. He appears to have been akin to Aristophanes, who quoted from Euripides precisely in order to give his predecessor's famous words a new twist and make them mean what they did not mean before, or maybe even a bit like so many contemporary journalists who habitually construct headlines out of familiar expressions. The allusive Jesus reformulated and in some cases we might say even deformed tradition in order to convey his urgent message. It was and remains an effective and memorable strategy. One understands why the tradition has people asking themselves, "What is this? A new teaching" (Mark 1:27), and even why some of Jesus' followers came to believe that something greater than the intertext is here.

32. Robert W. Funk, *Honest to Jesus: Jesus for a New Millennium* (San Francisco: HarperSanFrancisco, 1996) 153–54. Also relevant is Jesus' use of the aphorism, which so often makes its point by contradiction. See Crossan, *In Fragments*, esp. his discussion of proverb and aphorism on pp. 3–36.

KLYNE R. SNODGRASS

From Allegorizing to Allegorizing: A History of the Interpretation of the Parables of Jesus

[[3]] In no other area of New Testament study is a history of interpretation so crucial as it is with the parables of Jesus. Here a history of interpretation is virtually a prerequisite for understanding (1) the issues that must be addressed and (2) the tendencies that appear in many of today's treatments. It is a story that has been told repeatedly and in much greater detail by others than is possible here (see, for example, the works by Blomberg, Jones, Kissinger, Perrin, and Stein in the bibliography). Nonetheless, one cannot do a serious study of the parables without first setting out and interacting with such a history of interpretation. For these seemingly simple stories of Jesus, which are widely seen to be gems of articulation about life and God, have proven to be anything but simple.

Theological Allegorizing

The primary interpretive issue with regard to Jesus' parables has always been the extent to which the details of the stories are to be taken as relevant for a proper understanding. From the earliest days and throughout most of the church's history, Jesus' parables have been allegorized—that is people have read into them various features of the church's theology, [[4]] with many of those features often having little to do with Jesus' own intent.

The best-known example of such theological allegorization is Augustine's interpretation of the Parable of the Good Samaritan (Luke 10:30–37), where virtually every item is given a theological significance: (1) the man is Adam; (2) Jerusalem is the heavenly city; (3) Jericho is the moon, which stands for our

Reprinted, with permission, from Klyne R. Snodgrass, "From Allegorizing to Allegorizing: A History of the Interpretation of the Parables of Jesus," in *The Challenge of Jesus' Parables* (ed. R. N. Longenecker; McMaster New Testament Studies; Grand Rapids: Eerdmans, 2000) 3–29.

mortality; (4) the robbers are the devil and his angels, who strip the man of his immortality and beat him by persuading him to sin; (5) the priest and Levite are the priesthood and the ministry of the Old Testament; (6) the good Samaritan is Christ; (7) the binding of the wounds is the restraint of sin; (8) the oil and wine are the comfort of hope and the encouragement to work; (9) the donkey is the incarnation; (10) the inn is the church; (11) the next day is after the resurrection of Christ; (12) the innkeeper is the Apostle Paul; and (13) the two denarii are the two commandments of love, or the promise of this life and that which is to come (summary from *Quaestiones Evangeliorum* 2.19).

Such allegorizing of texts was not limited to the church. It is found frequently in the writings of the Jewish philosopher-theologian Philo, was used by various Hellenistic interpreters of Homer and Plato, and appears in some of the *pesharim* or interpretive treatments of Scripture found in the Dead Sea Scrolls at Qumran, like that of lQpHab 12:2–10 (on Hab 2:17). In the church this "Alexandrian exegesis" went hand in hand with the belief that Scripture could yield a fourfold meaning: a literal meaning; an allegorical-theological meaning; an ethical meaning; and a heavenly meaning, which reflected future bliss. So, for example, Thomas Aquinas took God's statement of Gen 1:3, "Let there be light," to refer literally to creation, but also allegorically to mean "Let Christ be born in the church," ethically to mean "May we be illumined in mind and inflamed in heart through Christ," and with regard to heaven to mean "May we be conducted to glory through Christ" (see his *Commentary on the Epistle to the Galatians* 4:7).

In the history of parable interpretation, therefore, it is not surprising to find commentators asserting with respect to the Parable of the Hidden Treasure (Matt 13:44) either that Christ is the treasure, who is hidden in the field of Scripture, or that the treasure is doctrine, which is hidden in the field of the church. Competing allegories could coexist without difficulty. Similarly, Gregory the Great understood the three times that the owner came looking for fruit in the Parable of the Barren [[5]] Fig Tree (Luke 13:6–9) to represent (1) God's coming before the law was given, (2) his coming at the time the law was written, and (3) his coming in grace and mercy in Christ. He also understood the vinedresser to represent those who rule the church, and the digging and dung to refer to the rebuke of unfruitful people and the remembrance of sins (see his *Forty Gospel Homilies*, 31). Allegorizing, in fact, was the primary method for the interpretation of Jesus' parables from at least the time of Irenaeus to the end of the nineteenth century (for numerous other examples, see Wailes, *Medieval Allegories*). Unfortunately, it still occurs all too often in modern preaching.

Some Church Fathers and Reformers, of course, protested such allegorizing. Tertullian and Luther did, at least to some degree. Likewise, John Chrysostom and John Calvin voiced opposition to allegorical exegesis—though, at times, allegorizing continued to creep into their own treatments (cf. D. Steinmetz, "Calvin and the Irrepressible Spirit," *Ex Auditu* 12 [1996] 94–107). Chrysostom's comment on the Parable of the Vineyard Workers is still good advice:

> The saying is a parable, wherefore neither is it right to inquire curiously
> into all things in parables word by word, but when we have learnt the ob-
> ject for which it was composed, to reap this, and not to busy one's self
> about anything further. (*The Gospel of Matthew*, Homily 64.3)

Some caution, however, needs to be exercised in our evaluations of those
who allegorized, for people like Augustine were not ignorant. Those who engaged in allegorical interpretation assumed (1) that life had a relation to the
text and (2) that the text had power to direct their lives. Such assumptions, of
course, are highly laudatory. Furthermore, they did not base their doctrinal
formulations on allegorical exegesis, but sought to establish controls in order
to prevent excesses by limiting those who could participate in such interpretations and by setting up boundaries within which that interpretation should
operate (cf. Steinmetz, "Calvin and the Irrepressible Spirit," 97).

Still, allegorizing is no legitimate means of interpretation. It obfuscates
the message of Jesus and replaces it with the teaching of the church. Such an
interpretive procedure assumes that one knows the truth before reading a
text, and then finds that truth paralleled by the text being read—even if the
text is about another subject. [[6]]

Historical, Non-allegorizing Approaches

Theological allegorizing of the parables came largely to an end in scholarly
circles during the latter part of the nineteenth century and throughout most
of the twentieth century, principally through the work of Adolf Jülicher, C. H.
Dodd, and Joachim Jeremias—even though, as we will see, they were not always consistent.

Adolf Jülicher

Although others before him had argued against the abuses of allegorizing,
Adolf Jülicher's two volumes on the parables of Jesus in 1888 and 1899
sounded the death knell for theological allegorizing as a legitimate hermeneutical tool and radically affected the interpretation of Jesus' parables thereafter. In his war against allegorizing, Jülicher denied that Jesus used allegory
at all (which he defined as a series of related metaphors) or incorporated any
allegorical traits into his stories (where a point in a story "stands for" something else in reality). Allegory was too complex for the simple Galilean
preacher. Rather, Jesus' stories contained self-evident comparisons that did
not need interpretation. All allegorizing interpretations of the parables,
therefore, must be viewed as being illegitimate.

Furthermore, Jülicher insisted, where allegory or allegorical traits do appear in the stories—such as in the Parable of the Sower or the Parable of the
Wicked Tenants—the evangelists are to blame. For the evangelists misunderstood the parables, assumed that they had a concealing function (e.g., Mark
4:10–12), and turned them into dark and mysterious sayings (*Gleichnisreden
Jesu*, 1.44–70 and 80–81). Paradoxically, however, Jülicher retained confidence

about the genuineness of the parable tradition, and he knew that parables in "Hellenistic scribal learning" were sometimes enigmatic (cf. ibid., 1.42).

In Jülicher's view, a parable is an expanded simile, whereas an allegory is an expanded metaphor. Simile and parable are features of literal speech, and so are easily understood. Metaphor and allegory, however, are non-literal; they say one thing and mean another. Therefore, they are to be seen as features of indirect speech, which hide meaning and need to be decoded. Jülicher allowed no mingling of parable and allegory, no "mixed forms."

[[7]] Furthermore, in Jülicher's understanding there could be no positing of several points of comparison between an image (*Bild*) and the object (*Sache*) portrayed, as happens with allegory. Jesus' parables had only one point of contact (one *tertium comparationis*) between an image and its object. His purpose was not to obscure, and so his parables cannot be viewed as allegories. Rather, Jesus' parables should be seen as enunciating only one somewhat general religious maxim—or, perhaps more accurately said, some pious moralism about God and the world.

Jülicher's impact on the study of parables was not limited to his discussion of allegory. He also distinguished between various types of parables: "similitudes" (as the Parable of the Leaven), "parables" proper, and "example stories" (as the Parable of the Good Samaritan). These distinctions—along with that of allegory—are still used today, though there is considerable debate about whether allegory and example story are, in fact, legitimate categories. Also, by arguing that the evangelists had altered Jesus' parables, Jülicher opened the door for attempts to reconstruct the original version of the parables (for his reconstruction of the Parable of the Banquet in Matt 22:1–14 and Luke 14:15–24, see *Gleichnisreden Jesu*, 2.431; note also his admission that this parable has numerous correspondences between image and object [ibid., 432]). Such reconstructions are fairly common among scholars today, even when those who make them complain about their hypothetical character.

Attacks on Jülicher's position came quickly and have continued right to the present. Among the first was Paul Fiebig, who argued that Jülicher had derived his understanding of Jesus' parables from Greek rhetoric rather than from the Hebrew world, where allegorical parables and mixed forms were common (*Altjüdische Gleichnisse und die Gleichnisse Jesu* [Tübingen: Mohr-Siebeck, 1904]; *Die Gleichnisreden Jesu im Lichte der rabbinischen Gleichnisse des neutestamentlichen Zeitalters* [Tübingen: Mohr-Siebeck, 1912]). And in contemporary treatments of the parables, as we will see, scholars who focus on a Jewish background for the parables object to Jülicher's reductionistic views and reject the idea that any literature is self-interpreting. In fact, it may fairly be said that the more attention one pays to Jewish parables, the less impressed one is with Jülicher's explanations.

Furthermore, many scholars have called attention to the confusion that exists between "allegory" and "allegorizing" in Jülicher's treatment of the issues. Hans-Josef Klauck (*Allegorie und Allegorese in synoptischen* [[8]] *Gleichnistexten* [Münster: Aschendorff, 1978]), for example, speaks of Jülicher as having thrown out allegory, which is a literary form, whereas the real problem is that of allegorizing, which is an interpretive procedure of reading into material a theology not originally intended. And others, particularly Madeleine Boucher (*The Mysterious Parable* [Washington: Catholic Biblical Association of America, 1977]) and John Sider (*Interpreting the Parables* [Grand Rapids: Zondervan, 1995]), have argued that allegory is not a literary genre at all, but a way of thinking that can be present in various genres.

Few today accept Jülicher's definition of parable, for most view a parable as an expansion of a metaphor and not a simile (e.g., H. Weder, *Die Gleichnisse Jesu als Metaphern* [Göttingen: Vandenhoeck & Ruprecht, 1978]). And virtually no one accepts his claim that the parables present us with only rather general religious maxims. Several scholars, in fact, have pointed out that Jülicher's reaction against allegory only reflects a nineteenth-century distaste for the allegories that were written during the sixteenth through the eighteenth centuries (e.g., Mary Ford, "Towards the Restoration of Allegory," *St. Vladimir's Theological Quarterly* 34 [1990] 162–63). And others have mounted frontal attacks against many of Jülicher's views (e.g., Maxime Hermaniuk, Matthew Black, Raymond Brown, John Drury, and Craig Blomberg), particularly against his treatments of metaphor and allegory (cf. esp. C. L. Blomberg, *Interpreting the Parables* [Downers Grove: InterVarsity, 1990]).

Even so, Jülicher's conclusions have had surprising staying power—continuing on in the scholarly and popular psyches right down to the present, despite the inadequacy of his views. People often still speak of a parable as having only one point and are suspicious of any feature that may have allegorical significance. And even when aware of the inadequacy of Jülicher's arguments, many scholars are still caught in the vortex of his procedures and conclusions. It is as if once the seeds of the attack on the allegorizing of the church were scattered, they cannot be collected again for reevaluation but must be allowed to germinate without hindrance.

C. H. Dodd and Joachim Jeremias

The Dodd and Jeremias era of parable studies extends from 1936, with the appearance of Dodd's *Parables of the Kingdom*, to roughly 1970—though [[9]] Jeremias's *Parables of Jesus* (1963) is still influential. Jeremias's work was an extension of Dodd's, and both were dependent on Jülicher. Both tried to understand the parables in their historical and eschatological contexts, even though they differed in their respective understandings of eschatology. Both viewed the parables as realistic first-century peasant stories and sought to explain the cultural setting of the individual parables. But in seeking to recover the original situations in which Jesus spoke, both Dodd and Jeremias also tried to remove the allegorical features found in the evangelists' presentations of the parables.

At least a third of Dodd's small book is not explicitly on the parables, but is concerned more generally with Jesus and the kingdom. Dodd understood Jesus' message in terms of "realized eschatology"—that is, that the kingdom of God had already arrived. His treatments of the parables are relatively brief and often quite straightforward. But Dodd believed that later Gospel tradition had, at certain points, obscured Jesus' original message by reorienting his original realized eschatology to ethical issues and a futuristic eschatology. For example, the Parable of the Talents (Matt 25:14–30//Luke 19:11–27) was originally about the conduct of the Pharisees, but was changed to address matters of moral responsibility and to speak about the second advent of Christ (*Parables*, 146–53). Likewise, parables about the end time, such as that of the Ten Virgins (Matt 25:1–13) and those regarding the harvest (Mark 4:26–29; Matt 13:24–30), were not originally about a coming end time, but about the crisis of Jesus' earthly ministry.

Jeremias extended Dodd's work in detail. He provided historical and cultural evidence for understanding the parables and, guided by the canons of form criticism, sought to ascertain a parable's original form by stripping away the allegorical features and other additions that had been supplied by the early church. Almost a third of his book discusses ten areas where changes made by the church need to be addressed and rectified in order to return to the original utterances of Jesus—these secondary, non-original matters having to do, invariably, with the contexts, introductions, conclusions, and interpretive comments connected with the stories as they now appear in the Synoptic Gospels. Such shortened, deallegorized versions of Jesus' parables are close to the versions of the parables found in the *Gospel of Thomas*, a collection of sayings of Jesus that probably dates from the second century (although the question of date is debated).

[[10]] While granting the presence of the kingdom in Jesus' ministry, Jeremias described Jesus' message as an eschatology that was in the process of realization. In his parables Jesus presented people with a crisis of decision and invited them to respond to God's mercy. Thus the parables are often viewed as a vindication of Jesus' offer of the gospel to the poor.

Jeremias's influence has been so strong that Norman Perrin once asserted that all future interpretations of the parables would have to be interpretations of them as Jeremias analyzed them (*Jesus and the Language of the Kingdom*, 101)! Few today, however, would make such a claim. Rather, many contemporary scholars hold that just as Jülicher's work was foundational, but aberrant, so Jeremias's work, while significant, is fatally flawed. At the very least, one must double-check all of Jeremias's claims, for some of them will not stand up to investigation.

One further point should also be made. While both Dodd and Jeremias attempted to remove allegory from Jesus' parables, both of them also brought allegorical interpretations back into consideration when they discussed the meaning of the parables. For example, Jeremias held that Jesus could not have uttered the Parable of the Banquet (Luke 14:7–14) as an allegory of the feast of salvation, but that he may, nonetheless, well have had it in mind (*Parables*, 69)! Such duplicity led Matthew Black to accuse Dodd of running with the allegorical hare and yet hunting with the Jülicher hounds ("The Parables as Allegory," *Bulletin of the John Rylands Library* 42 [1960] 283). Such inconsistency often occurs among those who overreact against allegory.

Existentialist, Artistic, and
Initial Literary Approaches

Since about 1970 a mood has prevailed among New Testament scholars that feels the historical, eschatological approaches of people like Dodd and Jeremias to be insufficient. The beauty and the power of Jesus' parables is considered to have been lost, or at least seriously curtailed. Attention has turned to hermeneutical and aesthetic concerns.

Several persons and movements have attempted to go beyond the work of Dodd and Jeremias. Yet while seeking something more than the merely historical, most of these approaches still follow their predecessors in method by first stripping off those features of the parables that are thought to be allegorical or interpretive additions.

Existentialist Approaches

[[11]] As part of the "New Hermeneutic," Ernst Fuchs, along with his students Eta Linnemann and Eberhard Jüngel, brought the concerns of existentialism and the insights of a particular understanding of language to bear on the interpretation of the parables. Fuchs and Jüngel, however, are not principally important in the study of the parables because of their exegesis of specific parables. Rather, they are significant because of their application of their understanding of language to the interpretation of the parables generally.

For Fuchs, existence is essentially linguistic. He argues for what he calls "the language-character of existence" (*Studies of the Historical Jesus*, 211), and he asserts that "the real content of language . . . is . . . being itself" (ibid., 222). Language does not merely describe. It enacts; it imparts! Language has the power to bring into being something that was not there before the words were spoken. To call someone a brother, for example, does not make him one, but it admits that person as a brother and establishes community (ibid., 209–10).

The parables are such "language events" (*Sprachereignisse*). This concept is similar to the idea of "performative utterances," which emphasizes the power of language to accomplish and enact. For Fuchs, parables are analogies, and in analogy lies the very language power of existence. The purpose of an analogy is not to increase the knowledge that one has. Rather, an analogy functions to shape one's attitude. Thus Jesus' parables have the power to bring to expression the reality to which they point. In his parables, Jesus' understanding of his own situation enters language in a special way so that his existence is available to his hearers. The parables, therefore, are a summons to this existence; and to respond, one must allow oneself to be laid hold of by Jesus' existence (ibid., 220).

Fuchs and his colleagues were also part of "the new quest for the historical Jesus," and so they placed heavy emphasis on understanding Jesus and his mission. The parables are verbalizations of Jesus' understanding of his situation in the world. Understandably, therefore, one of the main features of Linnemann's *Parables of Jesus* (London: SPCK, 1966), which stands as much in the Jeremias tradition as it does in the new hermeneutic, is her attempt to hear the parables as Jesus' original audience would have heard them.

Much can be said by way of evaluating the views of Fuchs, Linnemann, and Jüngel with respect to the parables of Jesus. Pertinent critiques [[12]] have been set forth by Jack Dean Kingsbury ("Ernst Fuchs' Existentialist Interpretation of the Parables," *Lutheran Quarterly* 2 [1970] 380–95; idem, "The Parables of Jesus in Current Research," *Dialog* 11 [1972] 101–7) and Anthony C. Thiselton ("The Parables as Language-Event," *Scottish Journal of Theology* 23 [1970] 437–68), as well as by Norman Perrin and Warren Kissinger (see bibliography). For my part, I believe the importance of their stance is in forcing people to consider language and its effect more seriously than before. For the parables of Jesus are, in fact, language events that create both new worlds and the possibility of a changed existence.

Artistic Approaches

If Fuchs and his colleagues were still concerned with the situation of the historical Jesus, the same cannot be said for those who today emphasize the artistic character of the parables. Existential concerns still rank high on the agenda of current artistic approaches. But a focus on the historical situation of Jesus has been deemphasized.

Many interpreters in the past have commented on the artistic character of the parables, including C. H. Dodd (cf. *Parables*, 195). But they had not made this a major factor for interpretation. Geraint Vaughn Jones in 1964, however, sought to widen the relevance of the parables by emphasizing their artistic and literary character and to highlight the way that they mirror human experience—that is, "to transpose them into the field of symbols of our permanent human experience" (*Art and Truth of the Parables*, xi). He attempted to distinguish between symbol and allegory, the former being present in the parables, and accepted that Jesus told allegorical stories. Yet despite seeking a wider relevance for the parables, he considered only eight of the fifty parables he studied to be candidates for a wider interpretation—viewing nineteen of them, in fact, to be strictly limited by their historical reference (ibid., 141–43).

Dan Via, who was heavily influenced by existentialist interpreters like Fuchs, argued in 1967 that the parables are not bound by their author's intent (cf. his *Parables*), and so expressed less interest in Jesus' original situation. The parables are aesthetic works that should be interpreted as texts in their own right. They must be viewed as being autonomous. They address the present because in their patterns is an understanding of existence that calls for decision. [[13]] Both Jones and Via sought to recover the humanity of the parables and to highlight their universal appeal to the human condition. Jones, however, was willing to say that some of Jesus' parables were allegories, whereas Via spent considerable effort (as many had before him) trying to distinguish parable and allegory. Yet even Via granted that parables may have allegorical correspondences and argued against a "one point" approach.

Via also emphasized that parables cannot be completely translated into another form (cf. *Parables*, 32–56). And this understanding, as we will see, has become increasingly important in more recent studies.

Via divided the parables of the Gospels into "tragic" and "comic" parables, with "comic" connoting a sense of positive movement. His procedure for the interpretation of the parables has three divisions: (1) historico-literary criticism; (2) literary existential analysis, which is usually the longest section; and (3) existential-theological interpretation. The lessons he draws from the parables sometimes seem strikingly similar to Jülicher's pious maxims, though with an existential twist. But are we really to believe that the Parable of the Wicked Tenants is only a parable of "unfaith" that teaches that sin is a person's self-centered effort to reject any and all limitations that God imposes (cf. *Parables*, 137)?

Initial Literary Approaches

Robert Funk's 1966 *Language, Hermeneutic, and Word of God* is perhaps the most influential work on the parables of the last few decades (though only pp. 124–222 deal directly with the parables themselves). He too was heavily influenced by the German existentialist theologians, but he brought a literary focus that they did not have. Adapting Dodd's definition of parable, he emphasized four basic points: (1) that a parable is a simile or metaphor, which may remain simple or be expanded; (2) that the metaphor or simile is drawn from common life; (3) that the metaphor arrests the hearer by its vividness or strangeness; and (4) that the application is left imprecise to tease the hearer into making his or her own application (ibid., 133).

Contrary to Jülicher, however, Funk understood a parable not as an extension of a simile, but as an extension of a metaphor. Furthermore, he did not view metaphors as inferior to similes in their communicative abilities. Quite the opposite: if similes illustrate, metaphors create meanings [[14]] (ibid., 137). Furthermore, a metaphor cannot be closed off to only one particular meaning, since it is incomplete until the hearer is drawn into it as a participant. Therefore, a parable cannot be reduced to a single meaning, as Jülicher claimed in reducing the lessons of the parables to pious moralisms or as Dodd and Jeremias did in distilling a single eschatological point. For since metaphors are hearers of the reality to which they refer, and a parable is an extended metaphor, parables cannot be reduced to ideas and are not expendable once their meaning has been derived.

Metaphors—and therefore parables—remain open-ended with a potential for new meanings. Even in their original contexts they were heard by diverse audiences, and so had the capacity for various ideas. In asserting a potential for new meanings in the parables, Funk, however, is not arguing for an unbridled creation of meaning. For in his understanding, the original telling had an intent that served as a control over every reinterpretation. Furthermore, Funk's emphases on "everydayness" and "vividness or strangeness"—which were the second and third points in Dodd's definition—may seem somewhat contradictory. But Funk shows that everydayness points to the ways that parables address human existence, whereas strangeness points to the ways in which parables shatter the familiar. Paradox, therefore, is intrinsic to Jesus' parables. And the *Gospel of Thomas*, as Funk views it, is to be seen as sometimes superior to the canonical Gospels.

Several of Funk's points have been well-received by scholars today. That parables are extended metaphors and that they cannot be translated into ideas and then discarded are commonplace themes among contemporary interpreters. Likewise, his focus on reader response and his insistence on paradox are accepted by many, as is also his high valuation of the *Gospel of Thomas*.

Following the direction of Funk's work is John Dominic Crossan's *In Parables: The Challenge of the Historical Jesus* (New York: Harper & Row, 1973). The stated purpose of Crossan's book is to render explicit all that is contained in a phrase drawn from Günther Bornkamm: that "the parables are the preaching itself and are not merely serving the purpose of a lesson quite independent of them" (cf. Bornkamm's *Jesus of Nazareth* [New York: Harper & Row, 1960] 69). Not surprisingly, Crossan, following Paul Ricoeur, distinguishes between an allegory and a parable—arguing that an allegory can always be translated into a text that can be understood by itself, which renders the allegory useless, whereas myth and metaphor cannot be reduced to "clear language" (*Parables*, 11).

[[15]] The metaphors that Crossan is interested in are not ones that simply illustrate information, but those in which participation precedes information. He argues against a linear view of time and for a permanent eschatology—that is, for an eschatology that emphasizes "the permanent presence of God as the one who challenges the world and shatters its complacency repeatedly" (ibid., 26). Furthermore, he believes there are three parables that provide us with a key to the understanding of all the others, for they show the deep structure of the kingdom: the Treasure (Matt 13:44); the Pearl (Matt 13:45); and the Great Fish (*Gospel of Thomas*, Logion 8). Also, he divides the parables into three categories that correspond to the "three modes of the kingdom's temporality": (1) parables of advent; (2) parables of reversal; and (3) parables of action.

Crossan offers detailed analyses of the parables, usually favoring the *Gospel of Thomas* and ending up with shortened versions, after eliminating the introductions, the interpretations, and the conclusions that he thinks were added by the church. The parables of reversal, for example, are understood to have been changed into example stories by the early church. Creative reinterpretation of Jesus' parables by the primitive church, in fact, is a stated presupposition of Crossan's work (cf. *Parables*, 5), and so necessitates the work of scholarly reconstruction. The meanings that Crossan assigns to the parables are sometimes creative and helpful, but at other times are quite unconvincing—for example, his suggestion that the Parable of the Wicked Tenants is an immoral story about people who acted quickly on an opportunity (ibid., 96).

In the decade between 1970 and 1980, "structuralist" approaches dominated the study of the parables, especially in the "Parables Seminar" of the

Society of Biblical Literature and the early issues of *Semeia* (which is appropriately subtitled *An Experimental Journal for Biblical Criticism* and published by
the SBL). Funk, Via, and Crossan were all participants in the Parables Seminar, and they have continued to be active in many of the later developments
of parables research as well.

A structuralist approach to the parables is not concerned with historical
meaning or the author's intent. Rather, structuralists seek to compare both
the surface and the deep structures of the texts themselves, highlighting matters having to do with movements, motives, functions, oppositions, and resolutions within those texts. At times structuralist analyses have been suggestive.
Most of the time, however, structuralist studies only dripped with technical
jargon and provided little additional insight. [[16]] Not surprisingly, structural-
ism quickly faded from the scene. Norman Perrin's negative assessment was
fully justified: "The contribution this [the literary-structuralist approach] may
make to the understanding and interpretation of this or any parable is by no
means either obvious or immediate" (*Jesus and the Language of the Kingdom*,
180, see also 181).

The work of Madeleine Boucher in *The Mysterious Parable* (1977), however, is quite unlike the mainstream of studies that take a literary approach.
In my estimation, this brief book is one of the most significant treatments of
the parables ever written. For from her expertise in literary criticism, she has
provided a devastating critique of Jülicher, sane discussions of parable and allegory, and a helpful treatment of Mark's supposed theory on the purpose of
parables in Mark 4.

Boucher argues, as does John Sider (see his *Interpreting the Parables*
[1995]) and a number of other literary specialists, that allegory is not a literary genre at all, but a way of thinking. In one fell swoop, therefore, she sets
aside all previous discussions that have attempted to distinguish between a
parable and an allegory. She finds, in fact, nothing inherently objectionable
about the presence of allegorical features in the parables of the Gospels, for
parables can be either simple or complex and are often mysterious. And her
explanation of the redactional shaping of Mark 4 and of the theology operative in that chapter is superb.

Other literary approaches today question the legitimacy of the distinction between an image and its object in the parables, as well as the search for
a *tertium comparationis* (cf., e.g., H. Weder, *Die Gleichnisse Jesu als Metaphern*
[Göttingen: Vandenhoeck & Ruprecht, 1978] 97). Such questioning is almost
a by-product of an emphasis on the irreducibility of metaphor and parable.
For if a metaphor cannot be reduced to non-metaphorical language, but
must be participated in, one cannot set aside an image to find its object.

Studies Emphasizing Palestinian Culture
and the Jewish Parables

From at least as early as C. A. Bugge (*Die Haupt-Parabeln Jesu* [Giessen: Ri-
cker'sche Verlagsbuchhandlung, 1903]) and Paul Fiebig (*Altjüdische Gleichnisse*

und die Gleichnisse Jesu [Tübingen: Mohr-Siebeck, 1904]; cf. also his *Gleichnisreden Jesu im Lichte der rabbinischen Gleichnisse des* [[17]] *neutestamentlichen Zeitalters* [Tübingen: Mohr-Siebeck, 1912]), some scholars had argued for the importance of recognizing the Jewish origin of Jesus' parables. And in the last three decades this focus has received major attention from several directions.

J. Duncan M. Derrett, a specialist in ancient oriental law, is one scholar who has drawn attention to the importance of Palestinian culture for interpreting Jesus' parables. Derrett has published a number of articles—many of them on the parables—which seek to show the significance of first-century Jewish culture for an understanding of the New Testament generally (see his *Law in the New Testament* [London: Darton, Longman and Todd, 1976]; also his *Studies in the New Testament*, 2 vols. [Leiden: Brill, 1977, 1978]). Derrett's studies are never boring. He brings information from the rabbinic material and from a variety of other ancient sources in order to display attitudes and presumptions of the ancient Jews about such things as contracts, ownership issues, employer-employee relations, and social relations—that is, about the everyday situations from which the parables were formed. The material he presents is always helpful, though, it needs to be also noted, the conclusions he draws sometimes stretch credulity. Few, for example, would accept his view that the Parable of the Wicked Tenants alludes to the story of the expulsion from the garden in Genesis 3 (cf. *Law*, 310–12) or that the Parable of the Banquet is an artistic midrash on Zeph 1:1–16 (cf. *Law*, 126–29). Nonetheless, so much background material for the parables is brought together by Derrett that his work should not be ignored.

Another scholar who draws attention to Palestinian cultural features is Kenneth Bailey, who also engages in a detailed analysis of the literary structure of each parable that he treats (cf. *Finding the Lost: Cultural Keys to Luke 15* [St. Louis: Concordia, 1992]; see also his *Poet and Peasant: A Literary Cultural Approach to the Parables in Luke* [Grand Rapids: Eerdmans, 1976], and his *Through Peasant Eyes: More Lucan Parables, Their Culture and Style* [Grand Rapids: Eerdmans, 1980]). Bailey interprets the parables not only from research in ancient Jewish sources, but also from what he learned of the Palestinian mindset as a missionary in Lebanon and from examining Arabic and Syriac translations of the parables. Unfortunately, one cannot always assume that the attitudes and practices of modern peasant life in either Lebanon or Palestinian are the same as they were in Jesus' day, or that such modern contexts should be taken as keys to the interpretation of Jesus' parables. Nonetheless, Bailey's work is valuable, even though it must be used with caution.

[[18]] Quite different in their focus on Jewish origins are several works that directly compare ancient Jewish parables with those of Jesus. Asher Feldman (*The Parables and Similes of the Rabbis* [Cambridge: Cambridge University Press, 1924]) and W. O. E. Oesterley (*The Gospel Parables in the Light of Their Jewish Background* [New York: Macmillan, 1936]), among others, did preliminary work in this area. To date, at least 1,500 rabbinic parables have been collected. And in the last two decades at least eight books have appeared that analyze these rabbinic parables and their relevance for an understanding of the parables of Jesus, with that of David Flusser (*Die rabbinischen Gleichnisse und der Gleichniserzähler Jesus*, Teil 1: *Das Wesen der Gleichnisse* [Bern: Peter Lang, 1981]) being the most significant.

Flusser's work, as well as that of the other scholars who focus on parables within Judaism, challenges the conclusions not only of Jülicher, but also of Jeremias, of reader-response approaches, and of much of contemporary New Testament scholarship. Flusser acknowledges that a thoroughgoing editing of Jesus' parables by the evangelists has taken place, but he is nonetheless optimistic about the reliability of the parables as they are set out in the Gospels. He argues (1) that the contexts of the parables are usually correct, and (2) that the introductions and conclusions to the parables are both necessary and usually derive from Jesus himself. He views the *Gospel of Thomas* as dependent on the Synoptic Gospels and as being unimportant for researching the words of Jesus. Furthermore, he asserts that the parables are not realistic, but pseudo-realistic—that is, that while Jesus' parables build on the features of everyday life, they go well beyond those everyday, realistic features in making their points.

Of the other studies that have recently been published analyzing Jewish parables vis-à-vis the parables of Jesus, the most important (in English) are those by Brad H. Young (*Jesus and His Jewish Parables* [New York: Paulist, 1989]), Harvey K. McArthur and Robert M. Johnston (*They Also Taught in Parables* [Grand Rapids: Zondervan, 1990]), and David Stern (*Parable in Midrash: Narrative and Exegesis in Rabbinic Literature* [Cambridge, MA: Harvard University Press, 1991]). Comparing the structure of Jesus' parables with the structure of the rabbinic parables reveals that explanations usually accompany not only the parables of Jesus but also those of the rabbis—which, of course, raises questions about the ease with which New Testament scholars have deleted the explanations in the Gospels. Stern, in fact, argues directly against Jülicher's notion, which has [[19]] often been adopted by others, that parables do not require an interpretation. He rightly insists that no literature is self-interpreting (cf. his "Jesus Parables from the Perspective of Rabbinic Literature," in *Parable and Story in Judaism*, ed. C. Thoma and M. Wyschogrod [New York: Paulist, 1989] 45–51).

Two words of caution, however, need to be expressed with regard to this "Jewish" approach to the study of the parables. The first has to do with some of the conclusions reached. Sometimes studies focusing on the Jewish parables find it necessary to go out of their way to defend against either an anti-Semitism or a disparagement of the Jewish parables, as if they were inferior. Given the insensitivity and hyperbole of some Christian scholars, this is not surprising and may be necessary.

A second word of caution regarding method needs also to be expressed. For while comparison with the rabbinic parables is absolutely necessary, numerous pitfalls exist in using the rabbinic materials. The most obvious problem, of course, is the late date of the rabbinic parables. Virtually no Jewish parables, other than those in the Old Testament and one found to date in the Dead Sea Scrolls, can be demonstrated to be older than the parables of Jesus, and so with rabbinic parables we are dealing with material that is later than the Gospels. Furthermore, while the rabbinic parables are similar in form and content to those of Jesus, unlike Jesus' parables they were used to support the rabbis' exegetical interpretations and explanations of Scripture. Suggestions of dependence between the rabbis and Jesus, or vice versa, should probably be ignored, for direct dependence in either direction is unlikely (see further the article by Craig A. Evans, "Parables in Early Judaism," in the present volume).

One other comment needs here also to be made. For while numerous studies exist on the relation of the Gospel parables to Jewish parables, relatively little has been done by way of studying Graeco-Roman parables and their relevance for our understanding of Jesus' parables. This is a serious lacuna that needs to be filled.

The Return of Allegory, Allegorizing, and Polyvalence

From approximately 1980 to the present, several discernible shifts have taken place in the study of the parables. Most of these have been influenced principally by literary criticism.

[[20]] Somewhat surprisingly, allegory has resurfaced in a much more positive light. Craig Blomberg in *Interpreting the Parables* (1990), for example, argues that we need to recognize that Jesus' parables are allegories, and that a parable may have more than one correspondence between an image and the reality depicted. A parable, in fact, can be expected to have at least as many correspondences as it has main characters. His argument is legitimate, if one accepts that allegory is a literary genre. In my opinion, however, it is better to view allegory as a literary mode rather than a genre, and so to view parables as proportional analogies (as argued by Mary Ford, "Towards the Restoration of Allegory' and John W. Sider, *Interpreting the Parables*). Nonetheless, I agree that parables may be allegorical and have more than one point.

In several of his later writings, John Dominic Crossan has radically altered his earlier views on the parables and advocated a much more positive view of allegory. His appreciation for the usefulness of allegory, however, is quite different from that of Blomberg. For Crossan's concern is less with the question of correspondences and more with issues having to do with reader-response, in which a text's meaning is determined by the interaction of the reader with the text (see his *Cliffs of Fall* [New York: Seabury, 1980], esp. 96–97; and "Parable, Allegory, and Paradox," in *Semiology and the Parables*, ed. D. Patte [Pittsburgh: Pickwick, 1976] 247–81, esp. 271–78).

Increasingly Crossan has emphasized that parables are paradoxes and that they are polyvalent, capable of multiple meanings. For since they can be read in multiple contexts, they possess the capability of multiple meanings. Polyvalent narration reveals the play of the various plots across many levels of reality. Thus an interpreter of parables must be one who plays with a narrative in its various contexts, and the possibilities are without limit. This emphasis on polyvalence, which has become popular in the last few decades, is the fruit of seeds planted by Robert Funk and Dan Via, as well as, to some degree, by G. V. Jones.

In _Perspectives on the Parables_ (Philadelphia: Fortress, 1979), Mary Ann Tolbert offers a defense of polyvalent interpretation that assists us in understanding the movement. For in that work she argues for multiple meanings on the basis of the fact that competent scholars, who use the same methods, have reached equally valid but different interpretations (ibid., 30). She admits that the specific contexts of the Gospel parables limit their interpretation, but also notes that sometimes the Gospel writers themselves place the same parable in different contexts (ibid., 52–55). She does not disparage [[21]] the allegorizing exegesis that existed prior to the Enlightenment; on the contrary, she calls attention to the challenge and excitement that it provided ancient preachers (ibid., 63–64). She views interpretation as a creative act, as an art rather than a skill. She also seeks to preserve the integrity of the parables, but at the same time to allow the interpreter to choose the particular context in which each of the parables is to be read (ibid., 68–71) in order to "exploit" the polyvalency of the parable (ibid., 93).

For example, on one reading, using the terms of Freudian psychology, Tolbert interprets the Parable of the Prodigal Son as speaking to the wish of every individual for harmony and unity within. The younger son corresponds to Freud's _id_, the elder brother to the _superego_, and the father to the _ego_ (ibid., 102–7). Alternatively, but still in line with Freud, she sees the parable as speaking about the painful nature of emotional ambivalence. The excessive love of the father betrays hostility toward the prodigal, while the anger of the elder brother is displaced onto the father. Both interpretations she views as being legitimate. Or to take another example, Daniel Patte offers three competing, but in his estimation equally valid, interpretations of the Parable of the Unforgiving Servant ("Bringing Out of the Gospel-Treasure What Is New and What Is Old: Two Parables in Matthew 18–23," _Quarterly Review_ 10 [1990] 79–108). Clearly we have moved a long way from Jülicher. While Augustine might not have understood the interpretive conclusions, he would certainly have enjoyed the process!

A word of caution is necessary, for people use "polyvalence" in different ways. Craig Blomberg uses the term to point to a depth of meaning that is present in the parables, but he means by it reading the parables from the multiple perspectives of the characters within the stories. He is not interested in reading the parables in contexts other than those provided by the Gospel writers (see his "Poetic Fiction, Subversive Speech, and Proportional Analogy in the Parables," _Horizons in Biblical Theology_ 18 [1996] 123). This is quite different from the way others, like Tolbert, use "polyvalence" to refer to multiple meanings the reader may assign parables from reading them in various contexts.

That Jesus' parables have depth, far-reaching implications, and are not reducible to simple explications are valid observations. But those who argue for polyvalent readings in various non-Gospel contexts have, it seems to me, not been reflective enough about their practice. For in adapting and retelling the parables in new contexts, they have ceased being hearers of the parables and have become tellers of the parables instead.

[[22]] Susan Wittig's advocacy of polyvalent readings reveals what really is happening. She grants that the original teller of the Gospel parables had a meaning system in mind and that from the sender's [i.e., the author's] perspective multiple signifieds are wrong. Still, she argues that what was originally signified by the parable becomes a secondary signifier, which leads to multiple meanings. Her argument is: "From another, more objective point of view [i.e., other than the author's], what is demonstrated here is the ability to semantically alter a parabolic sign by embedding it within another belief-system and validating the new significance by reference to those beliefs" ("A Theory of Polyvalent Reading" in *SBL 1975 Seminar Papers*, vol. 2, ed. G. MacRae [Missoula: Scholars, 1975] 169–83; quotation from p. 177).

Embedding parables in another belief system was exactly what Augustine was doing. When one does this, however, one is no longer interpreting the parables of Jesus. One is, rather, reflecting on the significance of his parables in another system, however close or far away. Meditating on the parables is perfectly legitimate. But it is far different from discerning the intent of Jesus. Part of the difficulty is, of course, our multiple uses of the word "meaning," And it is for this reason that I prefer to talk about the "function" of the parables in the teaching of Jesus and of the "significance" of that function for us today.

Reduction to Banality

The charge of banality against many modern treatments of the parables—that is, of reducing the parables of Jesus to worn-out conventions or simplistic statements, with their messages being drearily predictable—is not new. It was leveled against Jülicher's pious religious maxims, and Norman Perrin spoke of the surprising banality of Dan Via's conclusions (cf. Perrin, *Jesus and the Language of the Kingdom*, 154). Indeed, Jülicher himself claimed that Jesus' parables were originally about "trifling matters," and that they had only been given more theological meanings by the evangelists (see his "Parables," *Encyclopedia Biblica* [New York: Macmillan, 1902] 3.3566). And tendencies to reduce the parables to the level of banality continue today.

One such example is Bernard B. Scott's *Hear Then the Parable* (1989), which is one of the more comprehensive treatments of the parables of the [[23]] Synoptic Gospels in recent years. Scott stands in the Jeremias tradition of reducing the parables to an earlier form. Unlike Jeremias, however, he does not seek the original words or *ipsissima verba* of Jesus, but the original structures or *ipsissima structura* of the parables. In his opinion, people did not memorize words; rather, when first hearing the parables they memorized structures. Like Jeremias, he views the *Gospel of Thomas* as an early and often superior source of the Jesus tradition.

Scott accepts that the parables as originally given had a number of allegorical features, though he seeks to remove the allegorical additions that he believes have been inserted by tradition. Allegorical features in the parables, he asserts, open them up to polyvalence. His method is first to analyze the "performance" of a parable by each evangelist as he works back to the simplest form. Second, he analyzes how the originating structure effects meaning; and third, he analyzes the parable's juxtaposition to the kingdom to discover how the parable challenges conventional wisdom.

The first part of Scott's book offers a number of helpful insights regarding parables in general. His interpretations, however, regularly reduce the parables to rather simplistic statements, which are often reminiscent of Jülicher's reduction of the parables to pious moralisms. In the end, one wonders—if, indeed, the intent of the parables was so evasive and general—why the stories were ever remembered. Why, it must be asked, was the Parable of the Pharisee and the Toll Collector ever remembered? In Scott's view, it is not an example story and has no lesson. Rather, it subverts the system that sees the kingdom of God in terms of the temple, and so places the holy outside the kingdom and the unholy inside the kingdom (*Hear Then the Parable*, 97). Likewise, the Parable of the Prodigal Son subverts the idea that the kingdom decides between the chosen and rejected, for the father rejects no one and both are chosen (ibid., 125). And the Parable of the Wicked Tenants is understood to question whether the kingdom will go to the promised heirs, since "*in the plot the kingdom fails and the inheritance is in doubt*" (ibid., 253, italics his).

Like Jülicher, Charles Hedrick explicitly says that Jesus' parables were banal and that it was the evangelists who inserted theological and kingdom significance into them in an attempt to make them relevant (cf. his *Parables as Poetic Fictions* [Peabody: Hendrickson, 1994]). Hedrick's views on the parables run counter to virtually all previous works. He argues that parables are not metaphors/symbols, that they do not reference the kingdom of God, and that they were poetic fictions that Jesus taught to stimulate [[24]] thought. The specific circumstances of their original narration in the life of Jesus is irretrievably lost. The original stories were brief fictions that portrayed realistic aspects of first-century Palestinian life and were meant to be open to a range of possible meanings (ibid., 3–8, 27, 35). The parables, therefore, are "potentially radical poetic fictions that competed with Judaism's paradigmatic narrative rigidity" (ibid., 87).

With these assumptions, Hedrick proposes that the Parable of the Good Samaritan offers two responses to the injured man: the first, that of callous indifference; the second, outlandish benevolence. The first is wrong; the second is an impossible ideal. The parable is, in fact, a parody of the ideal of the righteous person in late Judaism (ibid., 113, 115–16). The Parable of the Rich Fool, he believes, is about the laughingly inappropriate action of a rich man who tears down his barns when he should be harvesting. The parable is ultimately nihilistic and offers no hope, meaning, or theology (ibid., 158–61). And with regard to the Parable of the Pharisee and the Toll Collector, the prayer of the toll collector assumes that one may rely on God's mercy without confession, repentance, or restitution. The reader is left with a frightening glimpse of two possible alternatives, neither of which is satisfying, and does not know in the end which person it is that God accepts (ibid., 233–35).

William Herzog's *Parables as Subversive Speech* (Louisville: Westminster/ John Knox, 1994) is quite different from the works of Scott and Hedrick, but the procedure and the results are much the same. Herzog assumes that the parables are not theological or moral stories, but political and economic ones. The scenes they present are codifications about how exploitation expressed itself in the ancient world. The work of Paulo Freire, the twentieth-century Brazilian pedagogue of the oppressed, is the lens that Herzog uses to read the New Testament parables. He sees Jesus using parables to present situations that were familiar to the rural poor and to encode the systems of oppression that controlled their lives and held them in bondage. The parables, therefore, were not a means of communicating theology and ethics, but of stimulating social analysis (ibid., 27–28). They were discussion starters, and that is why the "conclusions" are often unsatisfying (ibid., 259–61).

Since the parables are to be separated from their Gospel contexts, a new context must be found in which they are to be read. For Herzog it is the context of exploitation, a theory derived from his work on the Parable of the Vineyard Workers. The vineyard owner does not correspond to [[25]] God, but is a member of an oppressing elite class (ibid., 96). In the Parable of the Wicked Tenants, the tenants are not wicked; rather, they are the original landowners who lost their land through usurpation and their action is an attempt to reassert their honorable status as heirs. In the end the parable codifies the futility of violence (ibid., 112–13). The Parable of the Unforgiving Servant points to the hopelessness of looking for a messianic ruler and to the critical role played by "retainers" in an oppressive system. The parable proposes that neither the messianic hope nor the tradition of popular kingship can resolve the people's dilemma (ibid., 148–49).

Undeniably, a number of recent studies have made helpful methodological contributions to an understanding of Jesus' parables. Nonetheless, the extent to which many modern critical approaches and assumptions have caused problems for parable interpretation is displayed by some recent interpretations of the Parable of the Widow and the Judge—all of which are liable to the charge of banality. Dan Via, for example, taking a Jungian approach, views this parable as presenting a problem in male psychology: The male ego refuses to respond to the anima, the archetype of a woman in a man's unconscious ("The Parable of the Unjust Judge: A Metaphor of the Unrealized Self," in *Semiology and Parables*, ed. D. Patte [Pittsburgh: Pickwick, 1976] 1–32). Herman Hendrickx applies the parable to the red tape and bureaucracy of today's society and to the bribery and venality of judges, as a result of which Christians should seek justice (*The Parables of Jesus* [San Francisco: Harper & Row, 1986] 231–32). Bernard Scott focuses on the widow's continued wearing down of the judge, viewing it as a metaphor for the kingdom—that is, it teaches that the kingdom keeps coming, keeps battering down opposition regardless of honor or justice, and may even come under the guise of shamelessness (*Hear Then the Parable*, 175–87). And Charles Hedrick argues that the parable presents the judge as a thoroughly honest man who in the end compromises his integrity for his own comfort, which should lead readers to reflect on the integrity of their own compromises (*Parables as Poetic Fictions*, 187–207).

More radically, William Herzog interprets the scene as a clear violation of Jewish legal practice, since only one judge is present. The widow refuses to be silent, and by her shameless behavior she achieves a just verdict. Thus, Herzog concludes, the oppressed must collude in their oppression for the system to work—and, by implication, suggests that hey should refuse to accommodate to the system (*Parables as Subversive Speech*, 215–32). More radically still, Robert Price argues that this parable was originally an [[26]] exemplary story and that it has been adulterated by Luke to keep women in submission. The parable, in his view, attests the bitterness of widows who have been mistreated by church officials. The unjust judge is the pastor, and the parable advises widows to get justice by the terrorism of nuisance (*The Widow Traditions in Luke–Acts: A Feminist-Critical Scrutiny* [Atlanta: Scholars, 1997] 191–201).

What is obvious in all of these attempts to interpret the Parable of the Widow and the Judge is that the more one cuts a parable from its contexts in the Gospels, the life of Jesus, and the theology of Israel, the more there exists a lack of control and the more subjectivity reigns. With the removal of the theology of the evangelists there has been introduced the ideology or sociology of the interpreter. Herzog asserted that it is "naive to assume that the form of any parable found in the Gospels coincides with the parable spoken by Jesus" (*Parables as Subversive Speech*, 46). But while, undoubtedly, the Gospel parables have been redactionally shaped by the evangelists, it seems far more naive to think that interpreters can abandon the Gospel contexts and ever hope to find the message of Jesus—particularly when correspondences exist between the parables and the non-parabolic teachings of Jesus. If the message of the parables is what many modern studies suggest, one wonders why the stories were ever originally told and—even more—why they were ever remembered.

Concluding Reflections

We have come full circle. For if the patristic and medieval interpreters allegorized the parables by reading into them their own theologies, modern scholarship is no less guilty in reading into them its own agenda. We have gone from allegorizing to allegorizing—in some cases, straying today even further from hearing the voice of Jesus. In fact, if some of the assumptions of our contemporary, more radical interpreters are correct, the average person surely cannot read the parables and come to an understanding of them. This is not to castigate everything done by interpreters today, for in many ways much good work has been done and many insights have been achieved—particularly, we believe, by scholars who have paid attention to the context of Jesus' ministry and to parallels that exist in the Jewish parables.

We stand at a time when, for all our modern insights into how [[27]] figurative speech works, we need to readdress issues of method. Jülicher was certainly correct to react to the theological allegorizing of the church. A similar reaction, however, is needed against the sociological and ideological allegorizing of today. The blunder that Jülicher made in his assessment of allegory needs to be set aside. But also several questions of method deserve better answers than we have been given.

One of the important questions for current interpreters concerns the contexts in which the parables of Jesus have been placed by the evangelists. Clearly, many of Jesus' parables (but not all) would have been told several times. So we should probably not think of only one specific occasion for the telling of each of the parables. And to the degree that this is true, we should give up attempts to reconstruct a parable's original form.

The parables are stories with an intent in the context of Jesus' ministry, though they also have been framed by the evangelists to speak to the situations that they addressed. It is legitimate, therefore, to ask: To what degree in reading the parables do we see Jesus' intent and to what degree do we see the situation of the early church? But if the general contexts in which the evangelists have placed the parables are totally unreliable, I see little hope of finding the intent of Jesus.

Equally important are the explanations that often come at the conclusion of the parables. Is this common feature of Old Testament and Jewish parables true also of Jesus' parables, or were his parables left imprecise and without any clear indication of their intent? Do we hear in these explanations the voice of the church or the voice of Jesus?

Contemporary New Testament scholarship rightly resists the idea that the parables are reducible to abstract explanations, as if the stories could be distilled and then discarded. At the same time, the parables do point beyond themselves to other realities and can be explained in nonfigurative speech—which is what all scholars attempt to do in writing books and articles on the parables. How do we do justice to the "language event" character of the parables, retain their force, and yet understand the theology they express without reducing them to pious (or not so pious) moralisms? The parables have an unquestionable depth. How can we legitimately appreciate their "field of meaning" within the intent of Jesus without turning them into polyvalent modeling clay?

That the parables are artistic and poetic must never be denied. Equally important, however, is the conviction that they are also historically and contextually based. In 1977 Madeleine Boucher had the good sense to [[28]] say: "If the poetic structures in the parables became dominant, their power to achieve an effect in the hearer would then be lost" (*Mysterious Parable*, 16). Sadly, that has happened all too often. The parables derive their meaning from Jesus who told them, and they cannot legitimately be understood apart from the context of his ministry.

Can interpreters do justice to the variety of forms in Jesus' parabolic teaching? Frequently the category "parable" has been defined by a small number of examples. Such a practice, however, predetermines how other forms are assessed and interpreted. Peter Dschulnigg is correct to complain that previous parable theories have been shaped too little from the parables of Jesus themselves ("Positionen des Gleichnisverständnisses im 20. Jahrhundert," *Theologische Zeitschrift* 45 [1989] 347). Related to this is the question of realism: To what degree are the parables realistic, everyday occurrences, and to what degree are they pseudo-realistic, extravagant, or unrealistic? If predetermined to be realistic, any item not fitting the norm will be found offensive and excluded.

I am painfully aware of studies, both general and specialized, that have been omitted from our present survey—for example, the six volumes on the parables produced in 1835 by Edward Greswell (Jülicher was not the first to do a serious study of the parables), or modern studies by Jack Kingsbury, Charles Carlston, John Donahue, Jan Lambrecht, and numerous others. An enormous amount of work has been done on the parables. One might be tempted to say, as Geraint Jones did in 1964, "I doubt, moreover, if many further lines of interpretation can be explored than those which have already been established" (*Art and Truth of the Parables*, x). But that would be as wrong now as it was then, for work will and should continue. Perhaps, however, we have provided enough perspective so as not to repeat the errors of previous interpreters and to appreciate more fully something of the depth of Jesus' intent in these relentlessly engaging stories.

Selected Bibliography

Blomberg, Craig L. *Interpreting the Parables*. Downers Grove: InterVarsity, 1990.

_____. "The Parables of Jesus: Current Trends and Needs in Research," in *Studying the Historical Jesus: Evaluations of the State of the Current Research*, ed. B. D. Chilton and C. A. Evans. Leiden: Brill, 1994, 231–54.

Boucher, Madeleine. *The Mysterious Parable*. Washington: Catholic Biblical Association of America,1977.

Dodd, C. H. *The Parables of the Kingdom*. London: Nisbet, 1936.

Flusser, David. *Die rabbinischen Gleichnisse und der Gleichniserzähler Jesus*. Teil 1: *Das Wesen der Gleichnisse*. Bern: Peter Lang, 1981.

Fuchs, Ernst. *Studies of the Historical Jesus*. Naperville: Allenson, 1964.

Funk, Robert W. *Language, Hermeneutic, and Word of God*. New York: Harper & Row, 1966.

Jeremias, Joachim. *The Parables of Jesus*. London: SCM; New York: Scribner's, 1963.

Jones, Geraint Vaughn. *The Art and Truth of the Parables*. London: SPCK, 1964.

Jülicher, Adolf. *Die Gleichnisreden Jesu*, 2 vols. Freiburg: Akademische Verlagsbuchhandlung von J. C. B. Mohr, 1888, 1899.

Kissinger, Warren S. *The Parables of Jesus*. Metuchen, NJ: Scarecrow, 1979.

Perrin, Norman. *Jesus and the Language of the Kingdom*. Philadelphia: Fortress, 1976.

Scott, Bernard Brandon. *Hear Then the Parable: A Commentary on the Parables of Jesus*. Minneapolis: Fortress, 1989.

Stein, Robert H. *An Introduction to the Parables of Jesus*. Philadelphia: Westminster, 1981.

Via, Dan Otto, Jr. *The Parables*. Philadelphia: Fortress, 1967.

Wailes, Stephen L. *Medieval Allegories of Jesus' Parables*. Berkeley: University of California Press, 1987.

Part 4

Jesus: Who Was He?

Introduction

SCOT MCKNIGHT

At the end of the eighteenth century, Hermann Samuel Reimarus not only called into question the traditional orthodox view of Jesus Christ, the Second Person of the Trinity but offered an alternative understanding of that Jesus: a political enthusiast who thought the kingdom was about to appear and who called people to radical change in light of that imminent end of history (Jesus the Apocalyptist). As Albert Schweitzer, the major chronicler of the rise of the quest for the historical Jesus, says of Reimarus: "Seldom has there been a hate so eloquent, a scorn so lofty" (Schweitzer 2001: 16).

In the proposal of Reimarus the word *critical* received its definitive form: a "critical" Jesus would be one that offered an alternative to the orthodox understanding of Jesus Christ. The implications would be enormous, for the Jesus so presented would shape the faith of that person and anyone who cared to agree with him or her. At the least, one's historical reconstructions would be a challenge to orthodox Christology. The number of such proposal continues to "boggle."

One of the earliest proposals was that there should be no proposal: Martin Kähler and his student Rudolf Bultmann (along with his numerous students) argued that the biblical Christ was enough. Any other depiction of Jesus would not sustain faith. But behind them was the lurking shadow of Friedrich Schleiermacher, whose Jesus was unparalleled in communion with God, in fact was an existence of God in human nature. This liberal understanding of Jesus has had a lasting impact on the discussion and has never been able to avoid finding a winsome Jesus (see Borg below, pp. 302–314). Following in the yawning wake of Reimarus, plenty of Jesus portraits were attached to the walls in the halls of the academics that emphasized his revolutionary spirit, but none put it all together more forcefully than S. G. F. Brandon, whose work has now found itself in a more modified form in J. Dominic Crossan and R. A. Horsley. Reimarus touched on a theme that came to fruition in Schweitzer and continues to dot the academic landscape, as can be seen in E. P. Sanders and Dale Allison: Jesus was drawn into an eschatological vision of the imminent demise of the world. One of the more interesting, but least compelling, voices today is the work of Bruce Chilton, whose view of Jesus was that he was a thoroughly rabbinic kind of mystic.

All along there have been moderating voices: eschatological? Yes, but let's not overdo it. Political? Yes, but let's not make Jesus a Zealot. A religious genius? Indeed, but there is more to him than that. Major moderating voices include Hoskyns and Davey, Joachim Jeremias, B. F. Meyer, J. P. Meier, N. T. Wright, and J. D. G. Dunn.

The above setting explains what G. B. Caird, at the time a Senior Tutor at Mansfield College of Oxford, means when he begins his 1965 Ethel M. Wood Lecture with these words:

> Anyone who believes that in the life and teaching of Christ God has given a unique revelation of his character and purpose is committed by this belief, whether he likes it or not, whether he admits it or not, to the quest of the historical Jesus. (in this volume, p. 275)

Here is a formidable challenge to the Kähler-Bultmann proposal, but done in a manner so typical of English scholarship: instead of offering a tome drenched in methodology and laced together by an abundance of evidence and then conversant with every piece of scholarship, which has become the trademark of continental scholarship, Caird set forth his overall view of Jesus in an elegantly written and suggestive lecture. This piece answers the view that was first set forth by Reimarus and then exhaustively laid out in Albert Schweitzer's *Quest of the Historical Jesus*, but absorbs the understanding of Jesus' eschatology put forth by C. H. Dodd, beginning with his *Parables of the Kingdom*, and does so in such a way that Jesus is a "man of his times" and a prophet who addresses the nation of Israel (Jesus the Prophet). Caird's own views were never completely presented, but a posthumous composition of both what he said and where he was headed has been stitched together lovingly by Lincoln Hurst, in *New Testament Theology*. Caird set the agenda for what is now called the Third Quest, which focuses on Jesus as a Prophet to Israel.

Along a similar line of thought but with a thoroughgoing commitment to the use of social-scientific models, Richard Horsley, who follows up an earlier work that sought to explain Jesus by using major social types (bandits, prophets, messiahs), offers to understand Jesus in a way that extends the generic "prophet" label: Jesus is a political revolutionary with an egalitarian and even economic agenda, and Jesus should not be understood as a nonviolent apolitical figure. Horsley's study (below, pp. 288–301) avoids the simplicity of the older question (was Jesus a Zealot or not?) but nonetheless presents a Jesus who is thoroughly political and revolutionary in character and whose teachings lead into a spiral of violence. Jesus may have been a prophet, but his sort of prophetism was directed at political powers, and it called for a revolution (Jesus the Political Revolutionary).

One of the standard approaches to Jesus for nearly two centuries has focused on Jesus as a "spiritual genius," and this focus has spawned a variety of books and proposals, but none are any more suggestive and influential than

Marcus Borg's *Jesus: A New Vision*. Borg takes Jesus from the traditional model and dips Jesus into the inks of the spirit world of religious geniuses. Once again, the problem is the orthodox depiction of Jesus as the Son of God: for Borg, Jesus was a visionary, a man of prayer, and one who made a numinous impact on those around him (Jesus the Religious Genius).

In recent years, perhaps no scholar has brought the traditional Jesus more often to the table than has the German scholar Peter Stuhlmacher. If Germany's historical-critical method led historical Jesus scholars away from the orthodox model, Stuhlmacher is determined to show that Germany can lead it back to traditional questions with some refined, however traditional, answers. In particular, a vexing question is whether or not Jesus thought about himself in the terms of the Servant of God, the famous figure of Isaiah (esp. 52:13–53:12) and how this category can be of use in understanding the overall mission of Jesus (Jesus, Messiah, and Servant).

Son of Man scholarship requires occasional monographs that simply summarize the state of the discussion. No one has been more forceful of late about the Son of Man than Maurice Casey in his study of the development of early Christian Christology. Casey is known for exacting Aramaic-based analyses of the sayings of Jesus, and nothing is more central to his studies than what "Son of Man" meant to Jesus. In brief, Casey stands apart from scholars like Stuhlmacher who think it derives from Daniel 7 and argues that such a title stems from early Christian faith and not from Jesus, but that Jesus himself did use such an expression, but "son of man" meant little more than "man" and is used to say something about a person or about a group of persons including the speaker.

And this is but a sampling of what scholarship has said about a simple question: who was Jesus?

Bibliography

Borg, M.
    1987   *Jesus: A New Vision: Spirit, Culture, and the Life of Discipleship*. San Francisco: Harper & Row.

Bornkamm, G.
    1960   *Jesus of Nazareth*, trans. I. and F. McLuskey, with J. Robinson. New York: Harper & Row.

Brandon, S. G. F.
    1967   *Jesus and the Zealots*. Manchester: Manchester University Press.

Bultmann, R.
    1958   *Jesus Christ and Mythology*. New York: Scribner's.

Caird, G. B.
    1965   *Jesus and the Jewish Nation*. Ethel M. Wood Lecture 1965. London: Athlone.
    1994   *New Testament Theology*, ed. and completed by L. D. Hurst. Oxford: Clarendon.

Casey, P. M.
  1991 *From Jewish Prophet to Gentile God: The Origins and Development of New Testament Christology*. Edward Cadbury Lectures 1985–1986. Cambridge: Clarke.
Chilton, B. D.
  2000 *Rabbi Jesus*. New York: Doubleday.
Dodd, C. H.
  1935 *The Parables of the Kingdom*. London: Religious Book Club.
  1971 *The Founder of Christianity*. London: Collins.
Dunn, J. D. G.
  2003 *Jesus Remembered*. Christianity in the Making 1. Grand Rapids: Eerdmans.
Horsley, R. A.
  1987 *Jesus and the Spiral of Violence: Popular Jewish Resistance in Roman Palestine*. San Francisco: Harper & Row.
Horsley, R. A., and Hanson, J. S.
  1985 *Prophets, Bandits, and Messiahs*. Minneapolis: Winston-Seabury.
Hoskyns, E., and Davey, N.
  1931 *The Riddle of the New Testament*. London: Faber & Faber.
Jeremias, J.
  1971 *New Testament Theology: The Proclamation of Jesus*, trans. J. Bowden, New York: Scribner's.
Kähler, M.
  1964 *The So-Called Historical Jesus and the Historic Biblical Christ*. Foreword by P. Tillich; trans. and ed. C. E. Braaten. Philadelphia: Fortress.
Käsemann, E.
  1964 *Essays on New Testament Themes*, trans. W. J. Montague. Studies in Biblical Theology 41. London: SCM.
Meier, J. P.
  1994– *A Marginal Jew*. 3 vols. Anchor Bible Reference Library. New York:
  2000   Doubleday.
Meyer, B. F.
  1979 *The Aims of Jesus*. London: SCM.
Reimarus, H. S.
  1970 *Fragments*, ed. C. H. Talbert; trans. R. S. Fraser. Philadelphia: Fortress.
Schleiermacher, F.
  1975 *The Life of Jesus*, ed. J. C. Verheyden; trans. S. M. Gilmour. Philadelphia: Fortress.
Schweitzer, A.
  2001 *The Quest of the Historical Jesus*, ed. J. Bowden. Minneapolis: Fortress.
Stuhlmacher, P.
  forth- *Foundations*. Volume 1 of *Biblical Theology of the New Testament*, trans.
  coming D. P. Bailey. 4 vols. Grand Rapids: Eerdmans.
Wright, N. T.
  1996 *Jesus and the Victory of God*. Christian Origins and the Question of God 2. Minneapolis: Fortress.

G. B. CAIRD

Jesus and the Jewish Nation

[[3]] Anyone who believes that in the life and teaching of Christ God has given a unique revelation of his character and purpose is committed by this belief, whether he likes it or not, whether he admits it or not, to the quest of the historical Jesus. Without the Jesus of history the Christ of faith is merely a docetic figure, a figment of pious imagination. The Christian religion claims to be founded on historic fact, on events which happened *sub Pontio Pilato* [['under Pontius Pilate']]; and having appealed to history, by history it must be justified. But where in the Gospels, after a century or more of exposure to the corrosions of criticism, are we to find history, uncontaminated by the piety of those early generations whose needs and interests were unquestionably influential in determining the selection of the traditions about Jesus which have survived and the shape in which they came to be written down? This is the question which has rightly dominated the study of the Gospels for two generations, and to which I shall try to make a small contribution in this lecture, with due appreciation to Mrs. Ethel M. Wood and the University of London for giving me the opportunity to do so.

One answer to this question, which still finds a certain amount of support, is that associated for the past forty years with the name of Rudolf Bultmann. In 1926 Bultmann wrote: "Critical investigation shows that the whole tradition about Jesus which appears in the three synoptic gospels is [[4]] composed of a series of layers which can on the whole be clearly distinguished." Having stripped off the Hellenistic layer, which owes its origin to the Gentile communities in which the Gospels were actually written, we are left with Palestinian material, where again "different layers can be distinguished, in which whatever betrays the specific interests of the church . . . must be rejected as secondary." [1] In all this Bultmann was, however, by no means original. Twenty-five years

Reprinted from G. B. Caird, *Jesus and the Jewish Nation* (Ethel M. Wood Lecture, 9 March 1965; London: Athlone, 1965) 3–22.

1. *Jesus* (Deutsche Bibliothek, 1926; Eng. tr. by L. P. Smith and E. Huntress: *Jesus and the Word*, Charles Scribner's Sons, 1934) 12–13.

earlier Paul Schmiedel, in the massive essay on the Gospels which he contributed to the *Encyclopaedia Biblica,* had declared that five sayings only could be
regarded as authentic, on the grounds that they could not conceivably have
been invented by the early church. These he called the "foundation pillars for
a truly scientific life of Jesus"; and it is interesting to note that only two of them
have since gone unchallenged (Mark 10:17–"Why do you call me good?" and
Mark 3:21–"He is out of his mind"). In the same year Wilhelm Wrede was arguing in his work on the Messianic Secret[2] that so all-pervasive is the influence
of church theology in the Gospels that not even a kernel may be attributed to
Jesus, unless that kernel is so hard, so special, so incompatible with its context
that it could not conceivably be attributed to the church. It is the paradox of
synoptic studies that the most sceptical and devastating results have been
achieved by those who set out to provide a firm historical foundation on which
the superstructure of faith might with confidence be reared. *Absit omen* [['May
it not be an omen']].

I should perhaps make it plain at the outset that I do not subscribe to
this school of criticism. I have never been able to persuade myself that the interests of Jesus and those of the early church were so mutually exclusive that
what may be [[5]] ascribed to the one must be denied to the other. It is therefore interesting to discover that Bultmann himself declines to put his own
cardinal principle into practice with the ruthless logic of Schmiedel and
Wrede. It is essential to his conception of the gospel that two historical statements can be made about Jesus: that he was a messianic prophet who proclaimed the inbreaking of God's sovereign rule, and that he was a rabbi who
argued with other rabbis about the interpretation of the Jewish Law. He recognizes that both these elements in the tradition fall within the interests of
the early church, yet he defends their authenticity. Of the one he says: "The
certainty with which the Christian community puts the eschatological preaching into the mouth of Jesus is hard to understand if he did not really preach
it"–a conservative principle astonishingly at variance with his major premiss;
and of Jesus as rabbi he says: "The disputes between Jesus and the opponents
were now recounted and written down as models, and were naturally told in
such a way as to correspond to the interests of the church." In neither case is
he prepared to say: "Whatever betrays the specific interests of the church . . .
must be rejected as secondary."

Nevertheless Bultmann's principle has a certain negative validity. If we
find in the tradition something which corresponds to the interests of the
early church, it is false logic to suppose that it cannot therefore be a genuine
teaching of Jesus. But if we find in the tradition a large body of material
which has no direct relation to the life, needs, and interests of the primitive
church, then we have every right to assume that we are in touch with solid
historical fact. Now my contention is that the Gospels contain a very large
amount of material which links the ministry and teaching of Jesus with the
history, politics, aspirations, and destiny of the Jewish nation. Early in the his-

2. *Das Messiasgeheimnis in den Evangelien* (Vandenhoeck and Ruprecht, 1901).

tory of the church the gospel broke out from its Jewish cocoon to become a universal faith. The [[6]] Jewish nation was regarded as a persecuting opponent, against which the church had to defend itself; and the idea that this nation had once occupied the forefront of the gospel message, though it was never wholly forgotten, slipped into the background. The result is that the evangelists record the facts to which I shall draw your attention, but without evincing any special interest in them. They record, for example, that among the Twelve one was a member of the Jewish resistance movement and another belonged to the group of Quislings who had taken service under the government and were hated for fraternizing with the enemy; yet they never so much as hint at the personal strain that must have been generated when these two were thrown regularly into each other's company. They record the death of John the Baptist, but it is Josephus, not Mark, who gives us the political explanation of that tragic event. They tell us of the release of Barabbas, "who had committed murder in the insurrection," without any reference to that series of violent revolts, suppressed with a growing ruthlessness, which is the history of first-century Judaism. But if we admit that the evangelists were largely indifferent to Jewish politics, this does not mean that Jesus shared their indifference.

I

We begin, then, at the beginning. It is the consensus of all four Gospels, confirmed in the preaching tradition of the speeches in Acts, that the beginning of the gospel was the baptism proclaimed by John and the fact that Jesus went to be baptized. Now John announced the imminent arrival of a crisis, which he called "the wrath to come." The woodsman had his axe already poised to cut down the rotten tree, the farmer had his winnowing shovel in his hand, ready to separate the wheat from the chaff. John has sometimes been [[7]] portrayed as a prophet of sheer gloom, taking a ghoulish delight in the coming destruction of the ungodly; but this is to do less than justice to his imagery. The object of winnowing is not to collect enough chaff to have a glorious bonfire, but to gather the wheat into the granary; the bonfire is purely incidental. In other words, John's crisis was one which would determine who among the Jews belonged to the true Israel. "Don't start saying," he warned them, "'I am racially descended from Abraham'; for God can raise up children to Abraham from the stones of the desert." Descent from Abraham will not guarantee membership in the new Israel, nor will lack of it be a disqualification. In the coming crisis race will not count, only conduct. John accordingly summoned the Jews to a national movement of repentance, and his baptism was the proleptic symbol of admission to the Israel of the new age.

And Jesus went to be baptized. Why? The baptism of Jesus was early found to be an embarrassment to the church, both because it seemed to imply that he was John's subordinate, and because it suggested that he personally experienced the need for forgiveness. This embarrassment is further evidence in support of the point I have already made, that the early church showed all too little interest in the political background to the ministry of Jesus. For the simple explanation is that Jesus recognized the national character of John's summons to repentance and accepted his own involvement in the national life of his people. But this is to say that from the outset of his ministry Jesus was concerned with questions of national policy: What does it mean to be the Chosen Nation of God? How can Israel preserve her character as the holy nation in a world overrun and controlled by pagans? What must Israel do if at God's winnowing she is to prove wheat, and not chaff?

In the middle of his ministry Jesus sent his disciples out on a missionary tour. The instructions he gave them have [[8]] come down to us in several forms, drawn from at least four strands of tradition; and in details they differ. But in one essential respect they all agree. The mission was to be conducted with the utmost urgency. The missionaries were to travel light and travel fast. They were to greet nobody on the road; not that Jesus set a premium on bad manners, but because the endless civilities of oriental etiquette would consume more time than they could afford. They were to eat whatever was put before them, without pausing to enquire, as a good Pharisee would have done, whether their host had conformed with all the levitical food laws, which even Peter had observed from his youth. They were not to waste time in any place that was slow to give them a hearing. Why the desperate hurry? Albert Schweitzer had good reasons for picking on this question as the key to the understanding of Jesus' ministry. His answer was that Jesus expected the coming of the Son of Man, God's final and decisive intervention in the history of mankind, and that when this hope was frustrated he went to his death in order to force God's hand. Schweitzer's answer has long since been found inadequate, but his question remains. Why the hurry? The more probable answer is that Jesus was working against time to prevent the end of Israel's world, that the haste of the mission was directly connected with the many sayings which predict the fall of Jerusalem and the destruction of the temple. He believed that Israel was at the cross-roads, that she must choose between two conceptions of her national destiny, and that the time for choice was terrifyingly short. This explains why, in his instructions to his disciples, he speaks of "towns where they receive you" and "towns where they do not receive you." He seems to have expected not individual but mass response. "It shall be more tolerable for Sodom and Gomorrah in the judgment than for that town." The disciples were not evangelistic preachers, sent out to save individual souls for some unearthly paradise. They were [[9]] couriers proclaiming a national emergency and conducting a referendum on a question of national survival.

This reading of the gospel story receives strong confirmation from the criticisms which Jesus is recorded to have made against his contemporaries. I leave on one side the criticisms of the Pharisees, which are in a category of their own, and concentrate on those directed against "this generation" or Jerusalem. According to Mark (8:11–13) Jesus said: "An evil and adulterous generation asks for a sign, and no sign shall be given them." Matthew (12:38–40) and Luke (11:29–30) add "except the sign of Jonah," and each then supplies his own explanation of that enigmatic phrase. I think we may take Mark's word for it that Jesus met the demand for irrefragable proof of his credentials with a flat negative, for "except the sign of Jonah" does not constitute a serious qualification. Jonah was sent to Nineveh with a message of extreme urgency: "Within forty days Nineveh shall be destroyed"; and the Ninevites did not wait to examine his credentials. To those who were spiritually alive, who had any sort of love and loyalty to God, the urgent warning of Jesus should have needed no more authentication than Jonah had; and, because they failed to recognize the word of the God they claimed to serve, they were stamped as an irreligious and disloyal generation. To this saying both Matthew and Luke have added the twin sayings about the Queen of Sheba and the men of Nineveh, each of whom responded to the best revelation available in their day. In the great assize they will be called as witnesses, and their evidence will secure the condemnation of "this generation," because it has failed to respond to a fuller revelation.

In these sayings it is not at once clear what Jesus means by "this generation" or what form he expected their sentence to take. It is possible to assume that he was thinking of his contemporaries as individuals and envisaging them on trial at the last judgment. No such interpretation is possible in [[10]] the next example. "The Wisdom of God has said, 'I will send them prophets and messengers; and some of them they will persecute and kill, so that this generation will have to answer for the blood of all the prophets shed since the foundation of the world'" (Luke 11:49–51; cf. Matt 23:34–35). Here there can be no question of individual responsibility at the last judgment. It is the whole nation of the time of Jesus which, in the preaching of John and Jesus, has been given an opportunity to break with the past, and which, if it refuses this chance, must answer at the bar of history for the accumulated guilt of former generations. This generation is in imminent danger of being the last generation in Israel's history.

The impression we have received so far is further strengthened by the references Jesus makes to Jerusalem. In answer to a threat from Herod he retorts: "I must be on my way today, tomorrow, and the next day, for it cannot be that a prophet should meet his death outside Jerusalem" (Luke 13:33). Jesus feels perfectly safe in Herod's territory. As T. W. Manson has put it: "Herod must not be greedy: for Jerusalem has first claim on the blood of God's messengers."[3] Here, as in the previous passage and in the parable of the wicked tenants, Jerusalem is being treated as heir to a long national tradition. In Luke's Gospel this saying of savage irony is followed by another of deep pathos, in which God is the speaker: "Jerusalem, Jerusalem, the city that kills prophets and stones the messengers sent to her! How often have I wanted to gather your children as a hen gathers her brood under her wings, and you would not let me. Look how your temple is left deserted! I tell you, you shall not see me until the time comes when you say, 'Blessed is he who comes in the name of the Lord!'" Shortly before the destruction of Jerusalem by the Babylonians in 586 B.C. Ezekiel had a vision in which he saw the glory

---

3. *The Sayings of Jesus* (S.C.M., 1937) 277.

of the Lord [[11]] abandon the Holy of Holies, leaving temple and city deserted by the divine presence and exposed to enemy attack. Jesus has seen Jerusalem similarly deserted and similarly exposed, because she has not been prepared to welcome him who came in the name of the Lord. Not long afterwards Luke shows us Jesus weeping over Jerusalem, because she did not recognize the day in which God was visiting her (19:44).

To these passages we can add others: the picture of Jerusalem surrounded by avenging armies (Luke 21:20–24), the cleansing of the temple (Mark 11:15–19), the prediction that not one stone of it will be left on another (Mark 13:1–2), and the words to the weeping women (Luke 23:27–31)—if the Romans do this when the tree is green (when the victim is innocent of political offence), what will they do when the tree is dry (when all Israel is tinder, ready to be ignited by the first spark)? Not all these passages are generally agreed to be genuine sayings of Jesus, but they make a cumulative impression to which we may properly apply the more conservative of Bultmann's principles: the certainty with which the Christian community puts this preaching into the mouth of Jesus is hard to understand if he did not really preach it.

There can be no serious doubt that Jesus predicted the destruction of Jerusalem, and predicted it as the direct consequence of the rejection of his own preaching. But what is the logical connexion between the crucifixion and the fall of Jerusalem? It would be intolerable to suppose that Jesus regarded God as a vindictive tyrant, capable of inflicting an arbitrary retribution on a recalcitrant city. The truth must be that he regarded his own teaching, not just as religion for the individual or for a church within the nation, but as a national way of life which the nation could disregard only at its mortal peril. It is true that he never offered security to man or nation. But he pointed to the paradox that the whole Jewish nation, and the Pharisees in particular, were bending [[12]] every effort to maintain their national integrity, and that this was the one sure way of losing all they treasured. "He who saves his life shall lose it." If they wished to save their national life, they must lose it in the service of God's kingdom, offering to God a radical obedience in excess of anything contemplated by the Pharisees, and leaving the results in the hands of God.

II

Once we begin with this outline of the teaching of Jesus, other facts rapidly drop into position. There is for example the attitude of Jesus to the Gentiles. According to that indubitably pro-Gentile book, the Acts of the Apostles, the church in its very early years was devoid of all concern for the preaching of the gospel to the Gentiles. The Christians were assiduous in their attendance at temple and synagogue, and in all outward respects remained good Jews; and the Pharisees, led by Gamaliel, were content to have it so. When later, through Peter's experience with Cornelius, the church faced for the first time the prospect of having Gentiles among their numbers, they received the intimation, not indeed with reluctance, but certainly with unfeigned astonishment, "So then to the Gentiles also God has granted repentance leading to life" (Acts 11:18). Now this might be allowed to pass without remark, if it were not that in the Gospels we find Jesus so often saying and doing things which imply the universality of the gospel. Whenever he spoke of the Son of Man, whatever he may have meant by that much-debated title, he was calling up a picture of the symbolic figure whom Daniel had seen coming on the clouds of heaven, and to whom "was given dominion and glory and sovereignty, that all peoples, nations, and languages should be his subjects" (Dan 7:14). When he rode [[13]] into Jerusalem, he reminded the spectators of another prophet's vision:

> Rejoice greatly, daughter of Zion!
> Shout aloud, daughter of Jerusalem!
> See, your king comes to you;
> Triumphant and victorious is he,
> Humble and riding on an ass,
> On a colt, the foal of an ass . . .
> And he shall command peace to the nations.
> His dominion shall be from sea to sea,
> From the River to the ends of the earth.
>
> (Zech 9:9–10)

When he cleansed the temple court, he is reported to have justified his action by a quotation from Isa 56:7: "My house shall be called a house of prayer for all nations" (Mark 11:17). And he repeatedly compared Gentiles favourably with his fellow-Jews—the Queen of Sheba, the men of Nineveh, Naaman the Syrian, the widow of Zarephath, the people of Tyre and Sidon, even those of Sodom and Gomorrah.

How then are we to explain the discrepancy between this aspect of the teaching of Jesus and the practice of the early church? Are we to say that Jesus actually taught universalism, but that his disciples were slow to understand his meaning, until in the course of time events stimulated their comprehension? Or are we to say that this universalism was read back into the gospel tradition by the church of a later age? There is a third and much more plausible hypothesis, which has been offered to us by J. Munck of Aarhus and developed by J. Jeremias of Göttingen.[4] Although these two scholars do not see eye to eye on all details, they are [[14]] fully agreed that the answer to our question is to be sought in eschatology.

The Jews in the time of Jesus held a wide variety of beliefs and hopes about the ultimate destiny of the Gentile nations, but there was one school of thought, strongly represented in the Old Testament, particularly in the books

---

4. J. Munck, *Paulus und die Heilsgeschichte* (Universtets forlaget, Aarhus, 1954), Eng. tr. *Paul and the Salvation of Mankind* (S.C.M., 1959); J. Jeremias, *Jesus' Promise to the Nations* (S.C.M., 1958).

of Isaiah and Zechariah, which declared that the Gentiles would have a place in God's final kingdom. But their inclusion was not to be brought about by any missionary activity on the part of the Jews, not by any gradual process of making individual converts to Judaism, but rather by a great act of God in the last days. When the Day of the Lord arrived, first of all Israel would be restored to the righteousness and dignity proper to her calling as the holy people of God, and Jerusalem would become a truly holy city, in which God could be expected to dwell, and from which the voice of authority could issue to the world; then the redeemed nation would act as a beacon, drawing all nations to Jerusalem to join in the worship and service of the one true god.

> In the end the mountain of the Lord's house
> Shall be firmly set above all other mountains,
> Raised higher than the hills.
> All nations will come streaming to it,
> Many peoples will come and say:
> "Come! Let us go up to the mountain of the Lord,
> To the house of the God of Jacob,
> So that be may teach us his ways,
> And we may walk in his paths.
> For from Zion comes teaching with authority,
> And the Lord speaks his word from Jerusalem."
>   (Isa 2:2–3)

> In those days ten men out of nations speaking every language will seize hold of the robe of a single Jew and say: "We will go with you, for we have heard that God is with you." (Zech 8:23)

[[15]] When Jesus began preaching that the time foretold by the prophets had arrived and that the sovereign power of God was now breaking in upon human history, it might have appeared that this was the signal sent out from God to summon the nations from east and west, north and south, to sit down with Abraham, Isaac, and Jacob at the great banquet of the Kingdom. In fact, however, Jesus warned his disciples that this prophecy was not yet ripe for fulfilment. "Go nowhere among the Gentiles, and enter no town of the Samaritans, but go rather to the lost sheep of the house of Israel" (Matt 10:5–6). His task, which they were to share as they set out on their mission, was to seek and save these lost sheep, so that Israel, "ransomed, healed, restored, forgiven" might become the magnet nation, drawing all peoples into the service of God. It is interesting to find that this view of the mission of Jesus is preserved even in the Fourth Gospel. "The hour is coming when neither on this mountain nor in Jerusalem will you worship the Father. You worship what you do not know; we worship what we know, for salvation comes from the Jews" (John 4:21–22). In God's new order all earthly worship will be transcended and all earth's peoples will be one; but, until that time arrives, it remains true that "salvation comes from the Jews."

It is understandable, then, that after the death and resurrection of Jesus the members of the church in Jerusalem should have felt their immediate task to be the winning of Israel to an acceptance of her proper role as God's nation. "Repent therefore and return to God, so that your sins may be blotted out, that God may grant you a period of recovery, and that he may send the Messiah appointed for you, Jesus, who must remain in heaven until the time for the universal restoration of which God spoke through his holy prophets in days of old" (Acts 3:19–21). The winning of the Gentiles, so they believed, belonged to that universal restoration, which [[16]] would begin just as soon as Israel had accepted the demand and invitation of the gospel.

But how does this comparatively optimistic picture of the bringing in of the Gentile nations fit with our earlier and more gloomy picture of the Jewish nation facing its last grim crisis? We shall best solve that problem by asking another question: Did Jesus intend to found a church? In a book which still remains the classic treatment of this subject Dr. Newton Flew adduced a large volume of evidence which enabled him to give an affirmative answer.[5] But he made it quite plain that we can speak of Jesus and his church only if we give to the word *ecclesia* its proper biblical meaning. Jesus did not intend to found a new religious organization, nor even a new religious community. He intended to bring into existence the restored nation of Israel, promised in the Old Testament prophecies. It was to this end that he accepted baptism at the hands of John, to this end that he appointed the Twelve to be his intimate associates, instructing them that their number was a symbol of their relation to the twelve tribes of Israel. This was why he spoke of his followers as a "little flock"—a word already used in the Old Testament to denote the Israel of the messianic age (Mic 5:4; Isa 40:11; Ezek 34:12–24). This was why he predicted the raising up of a new temple made without hands, to take the place of the old hand-made temple, and why he interpreted his own forthcoming death as the sacrifice by which God was sealing his covenant with the renewed Israel. It was, I believe, integral to the purpose of Jesus that he should continue to the end to make his prophetic appeal to the nation as a whole; and the triumphal entry and the cleansing of the temple are best interpreted as symbolic preaching, like the symbolic acts of the ancient prophets, by which Jesus was making his last appeal to the city not to sign the death warrant which would be both his and hers. Yet the success of [[17]] his mission in no way depended on the acceptance of his preaching by the nation as a whole, for he had already brought into existence, in nucleus at least, the Israel of the new age. The very existence of this nucleus was a part of his appeal to the nation. Like the children of Isaiah in an earlier crisis, the "little ones" of Jesus were to be "a sign and a portent in Israel" (Isa 8:18). The rejection of his message might mean death to himself, persecution for his followers, and utter ruin for the heedless Jerusalem; but some at least of the bystanders would live to see the vindication of his words and of his life-work. "There are some standing by

5. *Jesus and His Church* (Epworth, 1938).

who shall not taste death until they have seen the reign of God established in power" (Mark 9:1).

III

This brings me to the main object of my lecture, which is to say something about New Testament eschatology, and particularly about the Day of the Son of Man. When the third volume of the *Oxford English Dictionary* was published in 1897, the only definition of eschatology recognized by Dr. Murray was as follows: "The department of theological science concerned with the four last things: death, judgment, heaven, and hell." Since then the word has come to be used in a widely different sense, to denote the Old Testament belief that God would one day intervene in the history of nations to introduce a new era of justice and peace. Let us distinguish the two senses by calling the one individual eschatology and the other historical or national eschatology. The second is almost the only kind of eschatology we find in the Old Testament, and this is hardly surprising, when we remember that almost all the books of the Old Testament were already written before the Jews achieved a belief in an afterlife. I am inclined, however, to regret that the one word [[18]] ever came to be used to cover two such divergent forms of future hope, for the use has almost inevitably led to the quite baseless assumption that the finality which attaches to death, judgment, heaven, and hell must be characteristic also of national eschatology, and therefore to an intolerable deal of literalism in the interpretation of the imagery used by prophet and apocalyptist to describe the Day of the Lord. There is not the slightest justification for describing the Day of the Lord as an *eschaton*, a final event beyond which nothing else could conceivably happen. It is final only in the sense in which the end of a nursery story is final: "and they all lived happily ever after." National eschatology has been well defined by Ernst Jenni of Basel in the *Interpreter's Dictionary of the Bible*: " 'Eschatology' in the broader sense refers to a future in which the circumstances of history are changed to such an extent that one can speak of a new, entirely different, state of things, without, in so doing, necessarily leaving the framework of history." Let me illustrate this from the Old Testament before we return to the New.

Jeremiah had a vision in which he saw the whole earth return to primeval chaos:

> I saw the earth—there it lay, waste and void,
> The sky, and its light was gone.
> I saw the mountains totter before my eyes,
> And all the hills rocking to and fro.
> I saw—and not a man was there,
> The very birds of the air had fled.
>
> (Jer 4:23–25)

Another prophet had a vision of paradise restored, the wolf keeping company with the lamb and the leopard with the kid (Isa 11:1–9). Yet neither of these visions has anything to do with the end of the world. The one is a vivid prediction of an invasion of Judah by foreign armies, the other an idealized picture of an earthly kingdom, in which justice still needs to be administered and the rights of the poor [[19]] protected. The classic description of the Day of the Lord, found in Isaiah 13, begins:

> The Day of the Lord is coming, cruel in its fury and fierce anger,
> To make the earth a desert and exterminate its sinners.
> The stars in the sky and their constellations shall withhold their light;
> The sun shall be dark at its rising, and the moon shall cease to shine.
> I will punish the world for its evil and the wicked for their sin.

This might appear to be both cosmic and final, yet, when we read on, we discover that what the prophet expects is the invasion and destruction of the Babylonian empire by the armies of the Medes. When we turn from prophecy to apocalyptic, there is a difference of literary convention, but no difference of theological content. The book of Daniel was written in time of persecution, and the only end its author was interested in was the one he refers to in his last chapter: "when the shattering of the power of the holy people comes to an end, all this will be completed" (Dan 12:7). The lesson of the book, which Nebuchadnezzar has to learn the hard way, is that "the Most High controls the kingdom of men and gives it to whom he chooses" (4:17, 25, 32). When the prophet sees the throne of judgment erected, this is not the end of the world, but a climax of history, in which world dominion is to pass from the bestial and tyrannical oppressor by whom it has been exercised into the hands of the saints of the Most High, represented by that symbolic figure, "one like a son of man" (7:9–27).

When we turn to the New Testament the situation is a little more complicated, because by this time both Jews and Christians hold a well-established belief in life after death. It is therefore not always easy to tell whether we are dealing with national or individual eschatology, and, as the church moved more and more away from its original Palestinian setting into the Gentile world, there must have been a tendency to reinterpret the national in terms of the individual. [[20]] Nevertheless, whatever we may say about the Parousia or Advent of Christ in the epistles, there is a strong case for saying that the Day of the Son of Man in the teaching of Jesus remained firmly in the sphere of national eschatology. Here, as in the book of Daniel, from which the imagery is drawn, the coming of the Son of Man on the clouds of heaven was never conceived as a primitive form of space travel, but as a symbol for a mighty reversal of fortunes within history and at the national level.

Was there, then, any connexion between this eschatological crisis and the other national crisis which, as we have seen, bulked so large in the teaching of Jesus? It would greatly simplify our problem if we could say that they were one and the same. T. W. Manson, who argued so persuasively that "Son of Man" on the lips of Jesus was not a title for the Messiah but a conventional ideogram for the Israel of the new age, dismissed out of hand the idea that the Day of the Son of Man might be an event in Israel's national history. "For the Fall of Jerusalem as a fulfilment of the prophecy there is simply nothing to be said. The ruthless suppression by a great military empire of an insane rebellion in an outlying part of its territory has as much—and as little—to do with the coming of the Kingdom of God in power as the suppression of the Indian Mutiny."[6] But can this theory be so easily discarded? There was in fact all the difference in the world between the Jewish revolt and the Indian Mutiny. Jesus believed that Israel was called by God to be the agent of his purpose, and that he himself had been sent to bring about that reformation without which Israel could not fulfil her national destiny. If the nation, so far from accepting that calling, rejected God's messenger and persecuted those who responded to his preaching, how could the assertion of God's sovereignty fail to include an open demonstration that Jesus was right and the nation was wrong? [[21]] How could it fail to include the vindication of the persecuted and the cause they lived and died for? "Shall not God vindicate his elect, he who listens patiently while they cry to him day and night? I tell you, he will vindicate them speedily. Nevertheless, when the Son of Man comes, will he find faith on the earth?" (Luke 18:7–8).

The fact is that in more than one strand of tradition the coming of the Son of Man and the fall of Jerusalem are inextricably interwoven. Luke has a passage about the Day of the Son of Man, usually thought to be derived from his source Q, which includes a piece of advice more useful to a refugee from military invasion than to a man caught unawares by the last trumpet. "On that day, a man who is on the roof, with his belongings indoors, must not go down to collect them; and similarly, the man who is in the field must not return home" (Luke 17:31). Exactly the same instructions are given to those who see Jerusalem surrounded by enemy armies (Luke 21:21). Again, Mark 13 begins with a prediction that the temple will be torn down stone from stone, and a question from the disciples as to when this will happen; but it continues with a prediction of a sequence of events leading up to the coming of the Son of Man on the clouds of heaven. How odd of Mark, say the critics, to append to a question about a historical crisis a discourse which is an answer to a question about an eschatological crisis! What a simpleton he must have been, a naive stitcher together of heterogeneous traditions which he most imperfectly understood! Matthew at least has had the wits to recognize Mark's ineptitude, and has altered the question to make it fit the answer; for he has turned Mark's question about the temple into a question about the Advent of Jesus and the end of the world. But supposing Mark was right! Supposing he actually understood what he was about! Supposing the prediction of the coming of the Son of Man on the clouds of heaven really was an answer to the disciples' [[22]] question about the date of the fall of Jerusalem! Is it indeed credible that Jesus, the heir to the linguistic and theological riches of the prophets, and himself a greater theologian and master of imagery than them all, should ever have turned their symbols into flat and literal prose?

6. *The Teaching of Jesus* (Cambridge, 1931) 281.

Here then, in conclusion, is the picture of the ministry of Jesus I have been trying to put before you. Jesus believed that Israel had been called to be God's saved and saving nation, the agent through whom God intended to assert his sovereignty over the rest of the world, and that the time had come when God was summoning the nation once for all to take its place in his economy as the Son of Man. His teaching was something more than individual piety and ethics, it was a national way of life through which alone God's purpose could be implemented. The nation must choose between the way of Jesus and all other possible alternatives, and on its choice depended its hope for a national future. For nothing but the thoroughgoing change of heart which Jesus demanded and made possible could in the end keep the nation out of disastrous conflict with Rome. If the nation would not listen to him, it must pay the consequences; but he at least, and anyone else who would share it with him, must fulfil the destiny of the Son of Man. But so deeply does he love his nation, so fully is he identified with its life, so bitterly does he regret what he sees coming upon it, that only death can silence his reiterated and disturbing appeal. He goes to his death at the hands of a Roman judge on a charge of which he was innocent and his accusers, as the event proved, were guilty. And so, not only in theological truth but in historic fact, the one bore the sins of the many, confident that in him the whole Jewish nation was being nailed to the cross, only to come to life again in a better resurrection, and that the Day of the Son of Man which would see the end of the old Israel would see also the vindication of the new.

RICHARD A. HORSLEY

Abandoning the Unhistorical Quest for an Apolitical Jesus

Toward a More Comprehensive and Concrete Approach

[[149]] The standard picture of Jesus the advocate of nonviolence, as presented in books and articles in biblical studies and religious ethics is no longer historically credible. This situation calls not only for a new and more critical examination of the gospel evidence for Jesus' practice and preaching, but for an equally critical reassessment of our own assumptions and approaches to Jesus through that evidence.

Of Foils and False Starts

The portrait of Jesus as a sober prophet of nonviolence has been sketched with the Zealots movement as a foil. "The Zealots," one of the four principal parties or sects of "Judaism" and a prominent force in the society motivated by a fanatical zeal for the Law, were busy advocating violent revolt, indeed a "messianic holy war" against the Romans. Diametrically and directly opposed to "the Zealots," Jesus, understood as an apolitical religious teacher addressing the individual, taught "love your enemies," understood as nonviolence, and "turn the other cheek," understood as nonresistance vis-à-vis the Romans. He even purposely associated with tax collectors, who were despised by the Jews generally as hopeless sinners, and whom the fanatical "Zealots" would avoid absolutely as collaborators with the alien enemy. The fact that Jesus was executed as a political criminal is explained away by the claim that the charges brought against him in his trial were false. He was innocent, it is said. After all, when asked about paying the Roman tribute, which was sharply opposed

---

Reprinted, with permission, from Richard A. Horsley, *Jesus and the Spiral of Violence: Popular Jewish Resistance in Roman Palestine* (San Francisco: Harper & Row, 1987) 149–66, 338–39.

by "the Zealots," he had declared "render unto Caesar." And what might have appeared as an attack on [[150]] the Temple was really just a "cleansing," a purification, or a final call for repentance in anticipation of the coming of the kingdom he had been proclaiming. Virtually all the components of this picture are historically invalid or inaccurate as they stand in most of the scholarly and popular literature, and the foil on which the whole picture depends is now known to be without historical basis. Thus it is necessary to reexamine these, along with many other aspects of Jesus' ministry, in order to understand how Jesus dealt with the reality of violence. Before proceeding with such a reexamination, however, it would be well critically to review some of the approaches and assumptions typical of standard biblical studies.

At the outset we must abandon an approach that asks "What does Jesus (or the Gospel) say about violence or nonviolence?" An examination of the theme of "love" or of "peace" in the gospel tradition might seem to offer an appropriate approach to Jesus' "teaching" with regard to violence. But neither of these themes is all that important in the gospel tradition. Although "love" is a prominent theme in John's Gospel, 1 John, and Paul's letters, the term occurs relatively infrequently in the synoptic tradition. The group of sayings headed by "love your enemies" in the Sermon on the Mount (Matthew) and Sermon on the Plain (Luke), of course, have been extensively used in connection with the issue of violence/nonviolence, as well as in connection with the historical question of the Jews' response to Roman rule. But there is no indication in the Gospels that loving one's enemies had any reference to the Romans or that turning the other cheek pertained to nonresistance to foreign political domination.[1] Among other occurrences of "love" in the synoptic tradition, the principal passage that might have some relevance, albeit indirect, is the redactional phrase in Mark 10:21 that Jesus "loved" the rich man who asked how to inherit eternal life (but was unable to relinquish his great wealth): i.e., Jesus loved the rich man whom he and others had reason to resent. Exploration of the "love" theme simply does not generate much direct illumination on the issue of Jesus and violence.

Examination of the theme of "peace" might produce more of relevance to the issue of violence, but only indirectly. Only rarely in its [[151]] relatively infrequent occurrences in the gospel tradition does the Greek term *eirene*, usually translated "peace," mean the absence of conflict, violence, or war. In the most significant of those occurrences, Matt 10:34 and Luke 12:51, Jesus declares that he came "not to bring peace but a sword." Otherwise *eirene* occurs primarily in Luke, where it means something like "salvation" in a comprehensive sense. Like the Hebrew term *shalom*, for example, in the later sections of Isaiah (e.g., 48:18; 52:7; 54:10; 59:8; 60:17–18), where "peace" is parallel to "justice" or "righteousness" and has the sense of liberation from imperial oppression, *eirene* bears a sense of justice and liberation in Luke. A passage in Josephus provides a sense of the connotations of "peace" as the

---

1. See R. A. Horsley, "Ethics and Exegesis: 'Love Your Enemies' and The Doctrine of Non-Violence," *JAAR* 54 (1986) 3–31.

absence of conflict or war, in contrast with the liberation for the lowly that
came with Jesus in Luke: Josephus says that in response to the sharply repres-
sive violence unleashed by the Roman governor Florus, the chief priests and
most powerful men, "being men of position and owners of property, were de-
sirous of peace" (*J.W.* 2.336–38). Unfortunately for the concern to find in
Jesus a teacher of "love of enemies" in the sense of a nonviolent stance toward political enemies and a preacher of peace in the sense of an absence of
conflict, thematic study of "love" or "peace" is not very fruitful. Besides being
far broader and more concrete, our approach must move beyond the quest
for what Jesus may have said about a particular issue.

Modern Assumptions versus Historical Realities

In broadening and concretizing our approach it will be necessary to take into
consideration and make critical allowances for some of our more determinative modern assumptions about reality. In post-Enlightenment Western culture
generally there is a strong bias toward individualism. This bias is unusually
determinative in philosophy, theology, and religious studies. It may well be legitimate to acquiesce in that individualism in our various apologetic hermeneutical attempts to make historical texts and events meaningful for modern
"individuals." But the concern for contemporarily relevant interpretation seriously affects the selection of data and methods of historical investigation. The
extensive influence and intensive resonance of Bultmann's [[152]] "demythologizing" and his existentialist interpretation in New Testament studies well illustrates this problem.[2] What in the discourse of Jesus or in Jewish apocalyptic
literature was an understanding of a whole life-world, of society and history
as the context of people's own personal and community life, became reduced
to "self-understanding." Jesus' message that the kingdom of God was at hand
became reduced in its implication to the necessity of individuals to *decide* (!)
about one's own "authentic existence." Correspondingly, the broader concerns
of Jesus and his followers for community life, as well as the historical context
of Jewish Palestine, were left relatively unexplored. The method of "form-
criticism," which ostensibly promised a genuine sociological investigation of
the historical context of gospel traditions, stopped short with contexts such as
preaching and teaching—interestingly enough, contexts more appropriate to
decision about individual existence. Far from existentialist interpretation's being a special problem, it is merely a symptom of an important underlying assumption that has strongly influenced our understanding of Jesus.

Integrally related to the modern individualistic focus is our assumption
that religion is an area of life separable from the more material or social areas
such as economics and politics. This is also part of modern Western culture,
in which there has been a tacit agreement since the Enlightenment ("strangle
the last king in the entrails of the last priest") that "religion" and "politics"

---

2. R. Bultmann, *Jesus Christ and Mythology* (New York: Scribners, 1958); *Jesus and the
Word* (New York: Scribners, 1958; orig. 1926).

should not interfere in each other's respective spheres. Indeed, in modern industrialized society we do in fact presuppose a considerable degree of institutionalized "structural differentiation" among the interrelated spheres of life. Of course this historical development has also tended to mean the reduction of "religion" to individual inner experience along with what takes place in churches or synagogues. Accordingly we have tended to read and interpret the Bible, particularly the New Testament, as if it dealt primarily or only with "religious" life. Of course, there was no such concept as "religion" when the materials in the Bible originated or were written.[3] More important, in traditional historical societies there was no separation of life into different areas such as "religion" and "politics" and "economics." Yet, in accordance with the modern [[153]] assumption that "religion" is a separate area of life, New Testament scholars often interpret Jesus as utterly apolitical.[4]

The Bible, however, whether Old or New Testament, whether we refer to the priestly writers of the Torah or Jesus and the gospel tradition, exhibits no separation of "religious" and "political" or other areas of life. In historical biblical narratives about early Israel, for example, it is unavoidably clear that Yahweh was understood as the king of Israel, so that Israel should not have any human king "like all the nations" (Judg 8:22–23; 1 Sam 8:4–7). In second Temple times, the income of the priestly aristocracy, and the basis of their wealth and power, was provided by the tithes and offerings given to "the god who is in Jerusalem" (Ezra 1:3; Neh 10:32–39; 12:44–47; 13:10–14). The high priest was simultaneously the political head of the society, a Persian or Hellenistic imperial official, and the principal beneficiary of the tithes and sacrifices owed to God. As Josephus says, following the reign of the Herodian client kings the "constitution" of Judea again "became an aristocracy, and the high priests were entrusted with the leadership of the nation" (*Ant.* 20.251). There is no reason to believe, no evidence that Jesus and his followers or the gospel tradition were only or even primarily "religious" in their concerns. The evidence in the gospel tradition—e.g., the political symbol of "the kingdom of God" as his central message, the healing of bodies as well as souls as the activity for which he was most renowned—rather confirms the opposite: that Jesus was concerned with the whole of life, in all its dimensions.

Besides our modern individualism and our assumption that "religion" is somehow separate from the other dimensions of life such as "politics," we must take into account our own idealist orientation toward reality. It is understandable that people focused on religion and other cultural expressions should have idealist assumptions. In biblical studies and theology we have been working primarily with words, symbols, ideas, stories, and, through it all, texts. Our primary task is to glean new or renewed meaning from those texts,

---

3. See W. C. Smith, *The Meaning and End of Religion* (New York: Mentor, 1964) chap. 2.

4. See, e.g., the influential books, G. Bornkamm, *Jesus of Nazareth* (New York: Harper, 1960, etc.), e.g., 66–67, 121–23; J. Jeremias, *New Testament Theology* (London: SCM, 1971), e.g., 71–72, 122–23, 228–29. Proclaimed explicitly by O. Cullmann, *Jesus and the Revolutionaries* (New York: Harper & Row, 1970) 1–10. More critical historical awareness, e.g., in W. D. Davies, *The Gospel and the Land* (Berkeley: University of California Press, 1974) 344.

symbols, or ideas. It is a fundamental conviction in biblical literature and a basic commitment of faith for Jews and Christians, however, that meaning is
[[154]] incarnate, as it were, in historical life: in material, personal, social particulars. Thus, simply in order to be faithful to the material we are investigating and interpreting we must become far more concrete than is our habit.
Serious commitment to becoming more concrete will have wide-ranging implications for historical inquiry into Jesus' practice, preaching, and effects.

For example, what if "Jesus of Nazareth" actually spent some of his formative years in Nazareth, which was a few miles from the small "city" of Sepphoris in Galilee. The Sepphoris area was the center of the popular movement
that had acclaimed Judas, son of the brigand-chief Hezekiah, as its "king" in
4 B.C.E. When the Romans reconquered the area they devastated Sepphoris itself and sold the people into slavery (Josephus, *J.W.* 2.56, 68; *Ant.* 17.271–72,
289). Sepphoris was then reconstructed as a Hellenistic city, with new, presumably Greek-speaking, inhabitants. If there was still sharp opposition between
the people of Sepphoris and the Galileans in the surrounding area in 66–67
(*J.W.* 2.511; 3.30–34, 59–62; *Life* 373–95), then there must have been a good
deal of conflict between Galilean villagers and the alien city in their midst earlier in the first-century as well. Thus memories of struggles to regain their autonomy and of renewed devastation and enslavement by the Romans, along
with continuing conflict with an alien city to which they were subordinated,
were probably important factors in the lives of Jewish villagers in the area.

In our idealist orientation and procedure we take seriously the importance of cultural factors such as the influence of foreign ideas, even when the
influence is supposedly operating in a situation centuries removed from the
original impulse. We "explain" images such as "one like a son of man" and
"the ancient of days" as derived from "Canaanite myth." Or we "explain"
apocalyptic dualism as "Iranian" influence. However, not only might those images no longer be expressions of a "mythic" view of reality; more importantly,
they may be rooted in the concrete social-historical situation of the people
responsible for the vision in Daniel 7. Or, not only might the dualism not be
derived from Iran; but even if borrowed it may be, more importantly, an expression of Palestinian Jews' sense of being caught in the intensely conflictual
situation of domination by foreign empires. Demon-possession may [[155]]
have more to do with the concrete political-economic-religious realities of the
then-current imperial situation than with the transmission of particular cultural content, such as ideas of dualism.

Further examples: the crucifixion, central religious symbol for Christians, was a form of execution that the Romans used for those who disrupted
the *pax Romana* [['peace of Rome']]. Compared with other issues, relatively
little attention has been given to why, concretely, Jesus may have been crucified. Finally, eating and hunger are important themes in the gospel tradition.
To be sure, people "do not live by bread alone." Considering the importance
of the imagery of debt in Jesus' parables, however, it should be considered
that sayings such as "blessed are you who hunger now, for you shall be satisfied" or "give us our bread for subsistence" had concrete as well as "spiritual"

reference in Jesus' ministry. Or, to remind ourselves of the wider dimensions of concrete considerations, Jesus and his followers are significantly portrayed as eating together in memory and anticipation of God's historical activity of liberation and renewal.

Closely related to the concern for becoming more concrete is the recognition of social diversity and class conflict. In this connection the problematic assumption to be taken into account is less our belief that there is no such conflict in our own social experience than our habit of generalizing from the written sources, on which we are so dependent, to the society in general that we are dealing with. We thus constantly deal in abstractions such as "Judaism" or "apocalypticism," and we tend to proceed as if *everyone* in ancient society thought in the way manifested in our sources. The latter, of course, were produced by a literate elite who were more than likely being supported by the rulers. The vast majority of people in any premodern agrarian society could not write and left no records other than artifacts that can be unearthed by archaeologists, or stories that have been edited by the elite. Biblical narratives and prophecies and the gospel traditions, of course, are highly unusual as historical documents because they contain so much from popular culture and express the concerns of ordinary, illiterate people—concerns that may well conflict with views expressed in other literary sources.

The Content and Orientation of the Gospel Tradition

Not Peace but Conflict

[[156]] The gospel tradition is full of conflict. Often the conflict is violent. All three synoptic Gospels begin and end with conflict, the most prominent being the crucifixion of Jesus by the Romans, followed by his vindication in the resurrection. The enemies of God and of the people are the authors of the conflict and violence in some cases. At the beginning of the story in Matthew stands Herod's massacre of the innocents (Matt 2:16). But God or Jesus himself also brings about or provokes conflict, sometimes violent. At the beginning of the story in Luke, Mary sings of God as "put[ting] down the mighty from their thrones and exalt[ing] those of low degree" (Luke 1:52). In Jesus' first action after calling some disciples in Mark, the unclean spirit cries out, "What have you to do with us, Jesus of Nazareth? Have you come to destroy us?" (Mark 1:24). Now it has become a standard generalization that our Gospels are, among other things, apologetic documents that have toned down the conflict, especially with the Romans. Yet the intensity and variety of conflict that runs through the gospel tradition is still overwhelming.

The situation in which Jesus heals and preaches is pervaded by conflict, some of it explicit, much of it implicit in stories and sayings. Most obvious, perhaps, is the conflict between rich and poor or between the rulers and the people. More particularly Herod Antipas arrests and then executes John the Baptist; the Pharisees keep Jesus under close surveillance; and finally the high priests and their governing council arrest him and hand him over to the Romans for execution.

Far from avoiding or transcending such conflicts, however, Jesus himself enters into them and even exacerbates or escalates them. He offers the kingdom of God to the poor and pronounces woes against the rich (Luke 6:20–24). Not only does he carry out actions that irritate the Pharisees, but he then criticizes them sharply and even pronounces judgmental woes against them as well (Luke 11:37–52). When certain villages do not respond to his message of the kingdom, he announces [[157]] their condemnation. When told that Herod Antipas wants to kill him, he declares that he will continue his objectionable activities (Luke 13:31–33). Finally, following what appears to have been a highly provocative "messianic demonstration" at his entry into Jerusalem, he disrupts business in the Temple courtyard and not only challenges the authority of the chief priests but tells a parable clearly indicating their imminent judgment by God (Mark 12:1–12 and parallels). It is difficult to imagine more provocative behavior from a popular prophet. The only prophets from the biblical tradition to match or outdo Jesus were Elijah and Elisha, who were busily engaged in fomenting popular revolution against Ahab's oppressive regime. In terms of the spiral of violence, it is clear in the gospel tradition that Jesus directly and sharply opposed the oppression of the ruling groups and that he virtually invited their action in suppressing him.

Was Jesus, however, simply another popular prophet engaged in resisting injustice and oppression? Or are there aspects of the gospel tradition indicating that Jesus engaged more fundamentally in a revolt against the powers controlling the imperial situation in Palestine? Further, did Jesus simply move into the fourth stage of the spiral of violence, or did he in some way transcend or avoid violence while still catalyzing a revolution against the established order? These are the overarching questions that will be pursued in the next several chapters. Prior to more detailed exploration of gospel traditions leading toward a more precise and concrete understanding of Jesus' practice and preaching, we can first determine more generally that Jesus and perhaps some of his Jewish contemporaries as well were engaged in more than resistance to oppression.

Jesus and the Revolutionary Perspective of Jewish Apocalypticism

Jesus' overall perspective was that God was bringing an end to the demonic and political powers dominating his society so that a renewal of individual and social life would be possible. This is a perspective he shared with and probably acquired from the contemporary Jewish apocalyptic orientation. Until recently such a statement might have seemed utterly ridiculous in the field of biblical studies, which has [[158]] viewed apocalypticism as alienated from history. Thus an explication of the statement should include an examination of how biblical studies have been decisively affected by the problematic modern assumptions mentioned above. If we can move beyond the previous understanding that has been limited by certain modern presuppositions, then it would be possible to discern that the "revelations" received by Jewish visionaries in late second Temple times were "revolutionary," at least in perspective.

Jesus preached that the kingdom of God was at hand. Since the turn of the century, beginning with the ground-breaking study of Johannes Weiss as popularized by Albert Schweitzer and especially through the pervasive influence of Rudolf Bultmann, Jesus' preaching of the kingdom of God has been understood against the background of Jewish apocalypticism.[5] "Jesus' message is connected with the hope . . . documented by the *apocalyptic* literature, a hope which awaits salvation not from a miraculous change in historical (i.e., political and social) conditions, but from a cosmic catastrophe which will do away with all conditions of the present world as it is."[6] "The Kingdom of God . . . is that *eschatological* deliverance which ends everything earthly. . . . It is wholly supernatural. . . . Whoever seeks it must realize that he cuts himself off from the world."[7] Now it is evident to anyone who sensitively or critically reads much of the synoptic Gospels and/or sections of the Book of Daniel or *1 Enoch* that such bizarre descriptions constitute a gross distortion of both Jesus' preaching and Jewish apocalyptic literature. How can we explain that precisely the supposedly supercritical biblical scholarship can have been dominated by such a view for a half century or more? Here, in fact, is a prime example of how our rather nonhistorical view of Jesus as well as of Jewish apocalyptic literature is rooted in certain distinctive presuppositions of modern religious scholarship that we are now only beginning to recognize and take into account.

It would seem fairly clear what happened. Reading literature that portrays God as dramatically effecting the replacement of an old order with a new order, but assuming that this "revelatory" literature is only or primarily religious and not political-economic, we have emphasized the cosmic and supernatural imagery in which that dramatic [[159]] replacement is portrayed. The effect is to divert attention from the social-political-economic dimensions in this literature and to find in Jesus' message not a hope for any "change in historical (i.e., political and social) conditions," but an end of the present world in "cosmic catastrophe." Correspondingly the discovery of the dramatic transformative aspects and implications of the kingdom of God in Jesus' preaching, far from challenging the individualism of ethical liberalism, in effect intensified it, particularly in Bultmann's demythologizing interpretation and nonethical existentialism. Since the kingdom of God was wholly superhistorical and supernatural, since it brought the End, people and their activities were no longer of any significance, but only God's power. Jesus' preaching of the kingdom brought people face to face with Eternity. The only

5. J. Weiss, *Jesus' Proclamation of the Kingdom of God* (Philadelphia: Fortress, 1971; orig. 1892); A. Schweitzer, *The Quest of the Historical Jesus* (New York: Macmillan, 1961; orig. 1906), esp. chap. 19.

6. R. Bultmann, *New Testament Theology*, 2 vols. (New York: Scribners, 1951–55) 1.4.

7. Bultmann, *Jesus and the Word*, 35–37.

appropriate response was decision about one's individual "authenticity." Ironic as it might seem, the understanding of Jesus' preaching of the kingdom in terms of cosmic catastrophe led to apolitical quietism.

What would appear as the overall thrust or perspective of apocalyptic literature and the preaching of Jesus, however, if we read them not only (a) less literally *but* with greater appreciation of the distinctive function of apocalyptic imagery, and (b) less doctrinally as a synthesis of theological ideas, but also (c) without imposing the modern separation between religion and social-political life? As was noted in the last chapter, recent studies of apocalyptic literature have provided us a sense of particular documents far more precise than that available a few decades ago.[8] Combining that more precise sense of particular documents with a more concrete sense of the referents of visionary imagery, we can take a more realistic look at the transformation portrayed in key apocalyptic texts. In Daniel 7, although some of the imagery had a background in Canaanite cosmogonic myth centuries earlier, it is used in a vision portraying a judgment scene in heaven, the point of which turns out to be that political dominion is about to be taken away from the oppressive Seleucid regime and the kingdom given to "the people of the saints of the Most High." In Daniel 10–12, the battles led by the heavenly prince Michael are clearly for the sake of the people caught in desperate historical circumstances. The language of the end refers not to the end of history or of creation but to the resolution of the historical [[160]] crisis, and the main hope is for the deliverance of the people by the (divine) defeat of the Seleucid imperial forces.[9]

In each of these sections from apocalyptic literature prior to the time of Jesus the focus is on the judgment or defeat of oppressive historical enemies and the vindication and restoration of the people in independence and righteousness under God's rule. The enemies, moreover, are easily identifiable as the regime of Antiochus Epiphanes or the Roman empire and/or the Jewish ruling group collaborating with the imperial regime. What earlier biblical scholarship labeled as expectations of "cosmic catastrophe" typical of Jewish apocalypticism would be called, in ordinary contemporary language, eager hopes for anti-imperial revolution to be effected by God.

Jesus' proclamation and practice of the kingdom of God indeed belonged in the milieu of Jewish apocalypticism. But far from being an expectation of an imminent cosmic catastrophe, it was the conviction that God was now driving Satan from control over personal and historical life, making pos-

8. See [[Horsley, *Jesus and the Spiral of Violence*,]] chap. 5, nn. 19 + 30.
9. Illustrations of such a less literalistic doctrinal and more concrete contextual reading of key apocalyptic texts could be multiplied. For example: in The Apocalypse of Weeks, *1 Enoch* 93 and 91, the "new heaven" of the tenth week seems subordinate to the real fulfillment, the perpetuation of "goodness and righteousness" (i.e., societal life the way God wills it) during "weeks without number forever"; in *Assumption of Moses* 10 the imagery of "cosmic catastrophe" and the elimination of Satan used in connection with God's kingdom appearing throughout all the creation serves as a vivid expression of how fantastic will be God's vindication and restoration of his people against their oppressive enemies, probably the Romans.

sible the renewal of the people Israel. The presence of the kingdom of God meant the termination of the old order.

The Charges against Jesus Not Totally False

Did Jesus' own activities match his revolutionary perspective? In being crucified, he was executed as a political agitator or criminal. The inscription on the cross, supposedly giving the reason for his execution, also indicates that the Roman and/or Jewish officials viewed him as an actual or potential revolutionary: "Jesus of Nazareth King of the Jews." Much standard interpretation of Jesus and the Gospels, however, understands the charges brought against Jesus as false, his crucifixion as resulting from the hostility of the Jewish rulers who manipulated both the crowds and the Roman governor Pilate, and Jesus himself as "innocent." Sometimes the latter claim is qualified to allow that Jesus' ministry was indeed a threat of some sort to the Jewish ruling groups, although by no means revolutionary, and that the Gospels, in attempting to have Jesus appear unthreatening to the Roman order (especially after the Jewish revolt of 66–70), wove apologetic themes and elements into their accounts, particularly the passion narratives.

[[161]] Claims that the charges against Jesus were totally false and that Jesus was innocent, however, do not hold up to closer reading of the gospel texts. Moreover, even though the Gospels themselves have, as commonly agreed, overlaid the earlier traditions with a clearly apologetic layer, they still present Jesus as proclaiming and symbolically acting out the judgmental termination of the old order and the inauguration of the new. This can be discerned very clearly both in Mark, the earliest Gospel, and in Luke, supposedly the most politically apologetic.

The Gospel of Mark may not be sophisticated literature. But the story Mark tells may be more complex and subtle than has often been allowed. A clearly awkward insertion or addition may indicate more than simply the author's editorial clumsiness. In his account of Jesus' trial before the Sanhedrin, the Jewish aristocratic governing council dominated by the high priests, Mark explains that although sought, incriminating testimony against Jesus could not be found; he then says that many bore false witness but their witness could not agree; he then again says that some bore false witness about his claim to destroy and rebuild the Temple, yet their testimony did not agree (Mark 14:55–59). Moreover, in citing Jesus' claim to destroy and rebuild the Temple, Mark adds the phrases "made with hands" and "not made with hands," which are neither in Matthew's parallel nor in the mockery against Jesus on the cross about having made this same threat against the Temple (Mark 14:58; cf. 15:29 and Matt 26:61). We are left wondering if the falsity of the witnesses lay in their duplicitous intention or in their testimony. And why the explanatory phrases about the Temple that soften the severity of the charge? Awkward editing, to be sure, but likely intended to indicate something to the reader.

Mark is almost certainly presenting the events as having more than one level of significance. Yes, Jesus was convicted on the charge of threatening

destruction of the Temple on testimony brought by "false witnesses." At a
deeper level, however, the charge was true, as can be discerned by seeing the
account of the trial in the context of the overall story.[10] Earlier in the narrative Jesus had dramatically disrupted activities in the Temple courtyard (Mark
11:15–19) and had predicted the destruction of the Temple (Mark 13:2).
Then, following his condemnation and execution for threatening destruction
of the Temple, the [[162]] curtain of the Temple's inner court is rent in two, a
clear sign of the impending destruction of the Temple. Mark intends the
reader to understand the charge as true in terms of what is ultimately happening in these events, despite the apparently trumped-up character of the
charge. Now, it would strain credibility to claim that Jesus originally was absolutely innocent of having said or done anything threatening to the Temple,
and that Mark (or pre-Marcan tradition) invented the idea of the false charge
as part of an apologetic strategy to place the blame for Jesus' crucifixion on
the Jews. Moreover, the original motivation for the apology would virtually
disappear on such a reconstruction. We must rather believe that it was firmly
embedded historical tradition that Jesus had threatened the Temple in some
way and that, although Mark provided an apologetic overlay of the "false witnesses" and ridiculous trial, he was also both transmitting and affirming that
Jesus' actions and words (including his death at the hands of the ruling powers) meant the end of the old order.

Luke both elaborates on the charge brought against Jesus and adds apologetic touches to further soften the apparent Roman responsibility for Jesus'
crucifixion. To Mark's brief account of the trial before Pilate, Luke adds the
further accusations that Jesus had been "perverting our nation" and "stirring
up the people," as well as "forbidding us to give tribute to Caesar" (Luke 23:2,
5). Luke then seemingly counters the accusations by having Pilate declare
three times that he finds no crime deserving death in Jesus (Luke 23:4, 14,
22). But this does not mean that in the Gospel as a whole Luke presents Jesus
as innocent of the charges against him. The usual "proof-text" that Jesus was
"innocent" (Luke 23:47) involves Luke's deliberate alteration of Mark and
thus provides no historical evidence about Jesus' ministry. It is not clear,
moreover, even at the Lucan level, how *dikaios* should be translated. Reading
it as "innocent" would make a certain amount of sense, considering that it is a
declaration by a Roman centurion. But the reading "surely this man was righteous" would fit well with Luke's overall interpretation of the historical-soteri-
ological significance of Jesus as the prophet-messiah sent to Israel and then,
although martyred, vindicated by God as "the righteous one." Might Luke
have intended a double meaning? [[163]] In any case, even if "innocent" was
the only sense intended, it would be Luke's own apologetic twist.

In the rest of the Gospel, however, Luke portrays Jesus in such a way that
at least two of the three principal charges brought against him in the trial before Pilate ring true. Unclear, without further investigation, is whether Jesus

---

10. See, e.g., D. Juel, *Messiah and Temple* (SBLDS 31; Missoula: Scholars, 1977) 122–23,
138, 212–13; J. R. Donahue, *Are You the Christ?* (Missoula: Scholars, 1973) 73–75.

was guilty of having forbidden the people to pay tribute. That Jesus was the annointed king, son of God, is clear at several points in Luke, including Jesus' baptism and "triumphal entry" (Luke 1:32; 3:21–22; 9:20; 19:37–38; cf. 23:36–37). Most prominent are Luke's portrayals of Jesus' "stirring up the people." From the beginning of his ministry in Galilee, the crowd "presse[s] upon him to hear the word of God" or "to be healed" (Luke 5:1–3, 15), while the scribes and Pharisees look on suspiciously. As Jesus moves toward Jerusalem, the crowds increase, as do the tensions between him and the Pharisees. Once in Jerusalem, he moves directly into the symbolic and material center of the society, the power base of the ruling aristocracy: "He was teaching daily in the Temple: The chief priests and the scribes and all the principal men of the society sought to destroy him; but they did not find anything they could do, for all the people hung upon his word" (Luke 19:47–48). The same opposition between Jesus and the people on the one side and the chief priests and other rulers on the other continues in a stand-off in the city until he is finally arrested (e.g., Luke 20:6, 19; 21:37–38; 22:2). Jesus was indeed, especially from the rulers' point of view, "perverting our nation." Far from blaming "the Jews" generally for the crucifixion of Jesus, Luke's Gospel portrays a virtual class conflict between Jesus and the people on the one side and the Jewish rulers on the other. Nor did Luke invent this conflict, which is deeply rooted in the earliest gospel traditions. If Luke was attempting to soften the responsibility of the Roman officials for Jesus' death, he would hardly have created the element of class conflict, which was just as threatening to the Roman order as a popular provincial agitator.

It should thus be clear that the synoptic Gospels do not portray Jesus as "innocent" and innocuous. In fact they indicate rather clearly that Jesus had threatened the Temple, that he was understood as an annointed king, and that he had "stirred up" the people. Given their clear [[164]] apologetic concerns vis-à-vis the Romans, it is difficult to imagine that the evangelists would have created such elements themselves. They must rather be presenting, with various adaptations and twists of their own, fundamental features of the ministry of Jesus. Indeed, the latter judgment is confirmed by the considerable amount of early or "authentic" material in the gospel tradition that has Jesus prophesying against the Temple, condemning the rulers, or lamenting over an imminently desolate Jerusalem. Such material will be examined more closely in the following chapters. At this point it is important simply to recognize that even our apologetic Gospels present a Jesus whose actions as well as perspective appear to have been revolutionary. Apparently he did not simply protest against or resist the oppressive features of the established order in Jewish Palestine; he articulated and acted upon his anticipation that God was now bringing an end to that order with the coming of the kingdom.

Procedure

Attempting to understand Jesus in concrete social-historical context and without abstracting a separate "religious" dimension from the whole fabric of historical life may involve a serious departure from much previous biblical scholarship. Yet there are many scholarly treatments that can be followed and built upon as we move toward more comprehensive approaches. For example, we can follow Wilder in appreciating the special symbolic character of apocalyptic imagery, although not those who forget the realities of the earthly circumstance.[11] We can follow Weiss in appreciating that God reigns, but not those who forget that the kingdom of God is concerned with people in society.[12] We can follow Yoder in appreciating Jesus' nonviolence, but not those who forget about the politics of Jesus.[13]

Our fundamental mode of procedure will be critical probing of the synoptic tradition of Jesus' practice and preaching. We will be presupposing the standard solution to the "synoptic problem" (the relationship between our Gospels), according to which Mark was the first Gospel written, while Matthew and Luke both followed Mark and drew on a common "sayings source," "Q," besides each having his own special material. In our critical probing of the Jesus traditions we will [[165]] be relying upon the method and results of form-criticism, as adapted by more recent reflection.[14] More particularly we will be attempting to explore the social context of both the origin and the transmission of Jesus' sayings and doings. It is virtually certain that Jesus did not speak and act in anticipation of his ministry's being "written up" into literature to be read. Rather, as the Gospels portray him, he moves from place to place speaking to people and acting in particular social contexts. Yet we must work through written texts to even begin to approach the origin and/or oral transmission of Jesus' sayings or reports of his actions. The analysis of such once-oral materials is hardly an exact science; criteria and techniques are hotly debated, and few are still under any illusions about reaching the precise words of Jesus. But in dealing with once-oral materials we are in a social situation, and this has certain implications that critics are only beginning to recognize.

We have been aware for some time that the words and deeds of Jesus (and other such figures) transmitted to us depend upon and involve the active role of people who heard and witnessed Jesus. More than that, however, what was remembered was remembered because it was significant for the people who remembered it. It is perhaps not too strong a statement to say that "what lives on in memory is what is necessary for present life."[15] Indeed, in contrast with the way in which we ordinarily experience the effect of the written word, "spoken words can produce the actuality of what they refer to

---

11. A. N. Wilder, "Eschatological Imagery and Earthly Circumstance," *NTS* 5 (1959) 229–45.

12. J. Weiss, *Jesus' Proclamation of the Kingdom of God.*

13. J. H. Yoder, *The Politics of Jesus* (Grand Rapids: Eerdmans, 1972).

14. Bultmann, *History of the Synoptic Tradition* (London: Blackwell, 1963); and more recently, see esp. E. Güttgemanns, *Candid Questions Concerning Gospel Form Criticism* (PTMS 26; Pittsburgh: Pickwick, 1979); W. H. Kelber, *The Oral and Written Gospel* (Philadelphia: Fortress, 1983); J. G. Gager, "The Gospel and Jesus: Some Doubts about Methods," *JR* 54 (1974) 244–72. Further references in Kelber.

15. Kelber, *The Oral and Written Gospel,* 15.

in the midst of people."[16] Recognition of this possible effect or function of the spoken word in concrete situations will be important not only in working our way through the transmissions of gospel materials, but in our assessing the point and effects of Jesus' ministry in certain important connections.

The transmission as well as the origin of sayings and doings in an oral culture also involves concrete social context. Bultmann and other early form-critics held that the tradition of Jesus' words and deeds really began after the dramatic break and creative impulse constituted by the Easter experience of Jesus' closest followers. But much of the Jesus material has hardly been affected by the experience of Jesus resurrected and exalted. Indeed it has been argued that much of what is now in the synoptic tradition was transmitted by followers of Jesus who were not involved in, effected by, or interested in the resurrection.[17] We [[166]] must take far more seriously than did Bultmann and early form-critics the concrete social context of oral transmission. Like the initial memory of sayings and doings, the continuing transmission of oral traditions depends upon social relevancy. This means, moreover, that the transmission of stories and sayings in the gospel tradition cannot be confined to a few leaders (disciples, teachers, or "itinerant charismatics"); the "common folk" cannot be ruled out.[18] In pursuit of the unfulfilled promise of "form-criticism"—assimilating much of the criticism of and adaptation of this method—we will be attempting throughout the explorations below to approach the context indicated in the content of reliable Jesus traditions.

16. Kelber, *The Oral and Written Gospel*, 19.

17. H. Koester, "One Jesus, Four Primitive Gospels," *HTR* 61 (1968) 203–47.

18. Kelber, *The Oral and Written Gospel*, 20–24; and contra G. Theissen, *The Sociology of Early Palestinian Christianity* (Philadelphia: Fortress, 1978) and "Itinerant Radicalism: The Tradition of Jesus' Sayings from the Perspective of the Sociology of Literature," *The Bible and Liberation: A Radical Religion Reader*, ed. N. Gottwald and A. C. Wire (Berkeley, 1976) 73–83.

MARCUS J. BORG

The Spirit-Filled Experience of Jesus

[[39]] Given the subsequent historical importance of Jesus, it is remarkable that his public activity was so brief. The synoptic gospels imply that his ministry lasted only a year, the gospel of John that it lasted three years, or a bit more. Which is correct, we can no longer know, but both agree that it was brief, extraordinarily so. The Buddha taught for forty-five years after his enlightenment, Muhammad for about twenty years. According to Jewish tradition, Moses led his people for forty years. But Jesus' ministry was brief, a light flashing momentarily but brilliantly like a meteor in the night sky. What was he like?

Jesus was born sometime during the waning years of Herod the Great, who died in 4 B.C. Nothing is known about his life prior to the beginning of his ministry as a mature adult, except by inference.[1] He grew up in Nazareth, a hill town in the northern province of Galilee, some twenty miles inland from the Mediterranean Sea, fifteen miles from the Sea of Galilee to the east, and roughly one hundred miles north of Jerusalem. Most of his neighbors would have been farmers who lived in the village and worked the fields nearby, or workers in the relatively small number of trades necessary to support agricultural life. He may or may not have been a carpenter; both "carpenter" and

Reprinted, with permission, from Marcus J. Borg, *Jesus: A New Vision—Spirit, Culture, and the Life of Discipleship* (San Francisco: Harper & Row, 1987) 39–56.

1. Two of the gospels, Mark and John, say nothing at all about Jesus before the ministry, not even about his birth. Matthew and Luke do include accounts of his birth and early childhood, though in somewhat different form from each other (see Matthew 1–2 and Luke 1–2). Moreover, the accounts contain many symbolic elements (for the meaning of the word *symbolic*, see [[Borg, *Jesus: A New Vision*,]] chap. 4, pp. 59–60). Symbolic elements can be based on actual historical occurrence, but how much is historical we can no longer know. For a compact treatment of the birth stories, see W. Barnes Tatum, *In Quest of Jesus* (Atlanta: John Knox, 1982) 108–12; for a full treatment, see Raymond Brown's authoritative *The Birth of the Messiah* (Garden City, New York: Doubleday, 1977).

"carpenter's son" were used metaphorically within Judaism to mean "scholar" or "teacher."[2]

We may surmise that he experienced the socialization of a typical boy in that culture. Growing up in a Jewish home, most likely he attended school from roughly age six to at least twelve or thirteen, as a system of "elementary education" was widespread in Palestinian Judaism. His "primer" would have been the book of Leviticus. Whether he had formal training as a teacher of the Torah[3] beyond [[40]] the schooling given to every boy, we do not know.

As a boy and young man, Jesus almost certainly attended the synagogue (a place of Scripture reading and prayer in local communities) every Sabbath, and perhaps on Mondays and Thursdays as well. As a faithful Jew, he would have recited the *Shema* upon rising and retiring each day, the heart of which affirmed: "Hear O Israel: The Lord our God is one Lord; and you shall love the Lord your God with all your heart, and with all your soul, and with all your might."[4] Presumably, he participated in the Jewish festivals and went on pilgrimages to Jerusalem. From the gospels, it is clear that he was very familiar with his Scriptures, the Hebrew Bible. He may have known it from memory, a feat not uncommon among the learned. The Psalms were probably his "prayer book."

That is about all we can know about Jesus prior to his emergence as a public figure, despite attempts to fill in the missing years in later apocryphal gospels and occasional scholarly speculations. Suggestions that Jesus lived among the Essenes,[5] or studied in Egypt, or traveled to India, or somehow came in contact with the teaching of the Buddha, are not only without historical foundation but also unnecessary. We need not go beyond the mainstream of the Jewish tradition to find a "home" for everything that is said about him.

The Source of Jesus' Ministry: The Descent of the Spirit

When Jesus does appear on the stage of history as an adult, the first episode reported about him places him directly in the charismatic stream of Judaism. His mission began with a vision from the other world and the descent of the Spirit upon him. At about the age of thirty, early in the governorship of Pontius

2. See Mark 6:3, Matt 13:55, and Geza Vermes, *Jesus the Jew* (New York: Macmillan, 1973) 21–22.

3. *Torah* in Hebrew means "divine teaching or instruction" and is most commonly translated "law." It has a range of meanings, sometimes referring to the first five books of the Bible (or "Pentateuch"), as in the phrase, "the *law* and the prophets." It can also refer to the 613 specific written laws contained in the Pentateuch, or, more broadly, to those laws plus the "oral law" which expands the written laws. To be trained in the Torah refers both to being familiar with the content of the law as well as with the methods of interpretation and argumentation.

4. Deut 6:4–5; included in the recitation were Deut 6:4–9, 11:2–21, and Num 15:37–41.

5. The Essenes were a Jewish monastic group; see [[Borg, *Jesus*,]] chap. 5, p. 88.

Pilate,[6] something impelled Jesus to go to a wilderness preacher of repentance named John and known ever since as "John the Baptist." All of the gospels (as well as Acts) connect the beginning of Jesus' ministry to his baptism by John.

Known to us both from the New Testament and from the Jewish [[41]] historian Josephus,[7] John stood in the charismatic stream of Judaism. His style of dress emulated Elijah, and his contemporaries compared him to a prophet.[8] Renowned for his eloquent and passionate call for repentance, John proclaimed that it was not sufficient to be "children of Abraham," but called the Jewish people to a more intense relationship to God sealed by a ritual of initiation.[9] Crowds flocked to this charismatic, some to be baptized.

Jesus was among them. As he was being baptized by John, he had a vision.[10] It is very tersely described: "He saw *the heavens opened* and *the Spirit*

6. According to Luke 3:23, he was "about thirty" when he began his ministry; according to John 8:57, Jesus was "not yet fifty." Though not being fifty is consistent with being about thirty, the former is an odd way of saying the latter. On other grounds, the younger age is to be preferred; the tradition that Jesus was born in the last years of Herod the Great (died in 4 B.C.) is reasonably strong. Thus, at the beginning of his ministry, Jesus was probably in his early to mid-thirties. Pilate was the Roman governor of Judea from A.D. 26 to 36; Jesus was probably crucified in A.D. 30, with his ministry beginning a year or a bit more before.

7. The writings of Josephus are one of our primary sources for first-century Jewish history. As a young man, Josephus was a Jewish general in the great war against Rome, which broke out in A.D. 66. Captured by the Romans in Galilee early in the war, he spent most of the rest of his life (perhaps another thirty-five years) in Rome, where he wrote his multi-volumed *Jewish Antiquities* and *History of the Jewish War*, as well as two more minor works. Though Josephus refers to John the Baptist, he apparently does not refer to the ministry of Jesus; the only direct reference is in a passage which is believed to be a Christian addition. The standard translation of Josephus is now the Loeb Classical Library edition, nine volumes, translated by H. St. J. Thackeray, R. Marcus, and A. Wikgrin (Cambridge: Harvard University Press, 1958–1965).

8. According to Mark 1:6, John wore "camel hair" (presumably a camel skin) and a leather girdle; for a similar description of Elijah, see 2 Kgs 1:8. For a "hairy coat" as the mark of a prophet, see Zech 13:4. For John as prophet, see Mark 11:32, Matt 11:9 = Luke 7:26.

9. Mark 1:4–6, Matt 3:7–10 = Luke 3:7–9. Ritual immersion in water (both in Judaism and other cultures) can have two different meanings. When repeated frequently (as it was among the Essenes), it has the meaning of a washing or purification. When it is a once-only ritual (as it apparently was for John) it may also be a purification, but its primary meaning is as an initiation ritual which symbolizes and confers a new identity. "Once-only" baptism was also known in Judaism; when a Gentile converted to Judaism, he or she was baptized (and if male, circumcised as well). But it is important to remember that John's baptism was intended for people who were already Jewish.

10. It is historically unlikely that John recognized Jesus at the time as an extraordinary or Messianic figure. According to Mark, Luke, and Q ("Q" is a designation used by scholars to refer to material found in very similar form in *both* Matthew and Luke, but not in Mark; "Q" is thus presumed to be an early collection of traditions about Jesus that predates both Matthew and Luke, and which may be earlier even than Mark), there is no such recognition. The common image in Christian circles of John as primarily a forerunner of Jesus who self-consciously knew himself to be such, and who recognized Jesus as "the coming one," is based on the gospels of John and Matthew. According to John 1, the Baptist proclaims Jesus as the Lamb of God, Son of God, even as one who preexisted him. But John's gospel cannot be taken historically, as already noted. Matt 3:14 reports a snippet of conversation between

descending upon him like a dove."[11] The language recalls earlier experiences of the other world in the Jewish tradition. Like Ezekiel some six centuries before, Jesus saw "the heavens opened," momentarily seeing into the other world, as if through a door or "tear." Through this door he saw "the Spirit descending upon him," echoing the words of an earlier Spirit-filled one: "The Spirit of the Lord is upon me."[12]

The vision was accompanied by a "heavenly voice" which declared Jesus' identity to him: "Thou art my beloved Son; with thee I am well-pleased." About the historicity of the baptism and the vision itself, there is little reason for doubt. Unless we think that visions simply do not happen, there is no reason to deny this experience to Jesus. However, about the "heavenly voice" there is some historical uncertainty, simply because the words so perfectly express the post-Easter perception of Jesus' identity. As such, they must be historically suspect as the product of the followers of Jesus in the years after Easter.

Yet how we interpret the words affects the historical judgment. If "beloved Son" is taken to mean "unique" Son of God in the sense in which the church uses that term, then the phrase must be viewed as historically suspect. But if it is given the meaning which similar expressions have in stories of other Jewish charismatic holy men, then it is historically possible to imagine this as part of the experience of Jesus. For they too had experiences in which a "heavenly voice" declared them to be God's "son."[13] If read in this way, the words not only become historically credible but are a further link to charismatic Judaism.

[[42]] Whatever the historical judgment concerning the "heavenly voice," the story of Jesus' vision places him in the Spirit-filled heart of Judaism. It reflects the multi-layered understanding of reality which was part of the belief system and actual experience of his predecessors in his own tradition. Indeed, standing as it does at the beginning of his ministry, the vision is reminiscent of the "call narratives" of the prophets. Like them, his ministry began with an intense experience of the Spirit of God.

Jesus and John; John says, "I need to be baptized by you, and do you come to me?" However, this (and Jesus' response) is almost certainly an insertion by Matthew into the story. Apart from these historically suspect references in John and Matthew, there is no reason to think that John believed Jesus to be "the coming one" at an early stage of the ministry. John's question from prison later in the ministry ("Are you he who is to come or shall we look for another?" Matt 11:3 = Luke 7:19, and thus "Q" material), is therefore to be read as the dawning of curiosity or hope, not as the beginning of doubt.

11. Mark 1:10. According to Mark, the experience was private to Jesus. There is no indication that the crowd or John saw anything; and the "heavenly voice" in the next verse is addressed to Jesus alone ("*Thou* art . . ."). Matthew and Luke both change the text slightly, apparently making the experience of Jesus more public. According to Matthew, the voice declared Jesus' identity to the crowd (3:17); according to Luke, the Spirit descended in "bodily form" (3:22). But Mark presents it as an internal experience of Jesus; it is not thereby less real.

12. See Ezek 1:1 and Isa 61:1. See also Isa 64:1 for the image of a "tear" or "rent" in the heavens: "O that thou wouldst *rend* the heavens and come down. . . ."

13. See [[Borg, *Jesus*,]] chap. 2, p. 31.

The Course of Jesus' Ministry:
A Person of Spirit

Jesus' ministry not only began with an experience of the Spirit, but was dominated throughout by intercourse with the other world.

Visions

The vision of the descent of the Spirit was followed immediately by another visionary experience or sequence of experiences. According to both Mark and the tradition behind Matthew and Luke, the Spirit "drove" or "led" Jesus out into the wilderness. Mark's account is very brief: "And Jesus was in the wilderness forty days, tempted by Satan; and he was with the wild beasts; and the angels ministered to him." [14]

Matthew and Luke agree that he spent a forty-day solitude in the wilderness, where he was tested by the lord of the evil spirits and nourished by beneficent spirits. They add that Jesus fasted and had a series of three closely related visions. [15] In the first, Jesus was tempted by Satan to use his powers to change stones into bread. In the second and third, Jesus and Satan traveled together in the spirit world. The devil took Jesus to the highest point of the temple in Jerusalem, and then "took him up and showed him all the kingdoms of the world in a moment of time." [16] Throughout, Satan tempted Jesus to use his charismatic powers in self-serving ways and to give his allegiance to him in exchange for all the kingdoms of the world.

[[43]] Both the setting and the content of the visions are noteworthy. Like Moses and Elijah and other Jewish holy men, Jesus journeyed into the wilderness, alone, beyond the domestication of reality provided by culture and human interchange. There, in a desolate desert area near the Dead Sea, he underwent a period of extended solitude and fasting, practices which produce changes in consciousness and perception, typical of what other traditions call a "vision quest." Indeed, the *sequence* of initiation into the world of Spirit (the baptism) followed by a testing or ordeal in the wilderness is strikingly similar to what is reported of charismatic figures cross-culturally. [17]

---

14. Mark 1:13.

15. Matt 4:1–11 = Luke 4:1–13.

16. Luke 4:5 = Matt 4:8. Such travel is found elsewhere in the Bible. Ezekiel, for example, reports, "The Spirit lifted me up between earth and heaven, and brought me in visions of God to Jerusalem" (Ezek 8:3; see 11:1–2). For Elijah's travels "in the Spirit," see 1 Kgs 18:12; cf. 2 Kgs 2:11–12, 16. In the New Testament, see Acts 8:39–40. J. R. Michaels, *Servant and Son* (Atlanta: John Knox, 1981) 50, comments, "Jesus' journeys to the Holy City and to the high mountain belong in the same category as the journeys of Ezekiel." The phenomenon is widely reported in traditional cultures. See, for example, John Neihardt, *Black Elk Speaks* (Lincoln: University of Nebraska Press, 1961), and the books of Carlos Castenada; even if Don Juan is regarded as a fictional character, as some have argued, his portrait is based on solid anthropological research. Such journeyings probably involve what are sometimes called "out-of-body" experiences.

17. Stephen Larsen, *The Shaman's Doorway* (New York: Harper & Row, 1976) 61–66. See also a section entitled "The Road of Trials" in Joseph Campbell, *Hero with a Thousand Faces*

The synoptic gospels report one more visionary experience of Jesus. According to Luke, in the middle of the ministry, a group of Jesus' followers exclaimed: "Lord, even the demons are subject to us in your name!" Jesus responded, "I *saw* Satan fall like lightning from heaven."[18] The passage uses language typically used to introduce a vision (*"I saw"*), though the passage could also be a metaphorical exclamation about the defeat of Satan.

We do not know if Jesus had other visions. The fact that none are reported may be without significance. Presumably, Jesus would not routinely report such, but would do so only if they served some purpose in his teaching.[19] The rest of the New Testament frequently reports visions, suggesting that the early church continued to experience reality in the same Spirit-filled way that Jesus did.[20]

Prayer

Among the reasons that we in the modern world have difficulty giving credence to the reality of Spirit is the disappearance of the deeper forms of prayer from our experience. Most of us are aware primarily of a form of prayer in which God is addressed with words, whether out loud in the context of public prayer, or internally in private prayer. Such "verbal prayer" is typically relatively brief, ordinarily no longer than a few minutes, perhaps sometimes longer in private devotion.

But verbal prayer is only one form of prayer in the Jewish-Christian tradition. Indeed, it is only the first stage of prayer; [[44]] beyond it are deeper levels of prayer characterized by internal silence and lengthy periods of time. In this state, one enters into deeper levels of consciousness; ordinary consciousness is stilled, and one sits quietly in the presence of God. Typically called contemplation or meditation, its deepest levels are described as a communion or union with God.[21] One enters the realm of Spirit and experiences God.

(Cleveland: World, 1956) 97–109. On shamanism more generally, see Mircea Eliade, *Shamanism: Archaic Techniques of Ecstasy* (New York: Pantheon, 1964); and W. A. Lessa and E. Z. Vogt, *Reader in Comparative Religion: An Anthropological Approach*, third edition (New York: Harper & Row, 1972) 381–412.

18. Luke 10:17–18.

19. The vision at his baptism may well have been his "call story" (the Old Testament prophets apparently thought it important to tell such stories), and the temptation narrative seems to have a teaching function in addition to reporting an experience.

20. This occurs very frequently in the book of Acts, and the whole of the book of Revelation is presented as a series of visions.

21. The difference between communion with God and union with God is subtle and perhaps not important. Both are mystical states, and both are known in the Jewish-Christian tradition. In union with God, all sense of separateness (including the awareness of being a separate self) momentarily disappears and one experiences only God; in communion with God, a sense of relationship remains. Communion is typically associated with Western mysticism and union with Eastern mysticism, though the contrast is not as sharp as the typical association suggests. See Peter Berger, ed., *The Other Side of God* (Garden City, New York: Anchor, 1981). For the "polarity" within Judaism, see especially the essay by Michael Fishbane,

For a variety of reasons, this form of prayer has become quite unfamiliar within the modern church. Though preserved in religious orders, by a few groups such as the Quakers, and by individuals scattered throughout Christian denominations, it has largely disappeared as part of the experience of most people in modern culture.

The tradition in which Jesus stood knew this mode of prayer. Moses and Elijah spent long periods of time in solitude and communion with God. Nearer the time of Jesus the Galilean holy men regularly spent an hour "stilling their minds" in order to direct their hearts toward heaven.[22] Meditation also is found in Jewish mysticism. Though most familiar to us from the medieval Kabbalah, Jewish mysticism stretches back to the *merkabah* ("throne") mysticism of Jesus' time and before.[23] For the *merkabah* mystics, contemplative prayer was the vehicle for ascending through the heavens to the ultimate vision of beholding the throne of God—that is, of experiencing the kingship of God.

The gospels portray Jesus as a man of prayer who practiced this form of prayer increasingly unknown in modern Western culture.[24] Like Moses and Elijah, he regularly withdrew into solitude for long hours of prayer: "In the morning, a great while before day, he rose and went out to a lonely place and there he prayed." Another time, "After he had taken leave of them, he went into the hills to pray."[25] Luke reports that Jesus on occasion prayed all night.[26] Such lengthy hours of prayer accompanied by solitude do not imply verbal prayer, but contemplation or meditation, the stilling of the mind and directing of the heart toward God reported of Hanina ben Dosa and others in the Jewish spiritual tradition. Jesus practiced one of the classic disciplines for becoming present to the world of Spirit.

"Israel and the Mothers," 28–47. For communion mysticism in the East, see the most popular form of Hinduism, *bhakti*.

22. *Mishnah Ber.* 5:1; see A. Büchler, *Types of Jewish Palestinian Piety* (New York: KTAV, 1968; first published in 1922) 106–7.

23. For a history of Jewish mysticism reaching back to the time of Jesus and earlier, see especially the work of Gershom Scholem, *Major Trends in Jewish Mysticism* (New York: Schocken Books, 1946), and *Jewish Gnosticism, Merkabah Mysticism, and Talmudic Tradition,* 2nd ed. (Hoboken: KTAV, 1965). A connection between apocalypticism and visions of or journeys into another world is increasingly affirmed in studies of Jewish apocalyptic. See, for example, John J. Collins, *The Apocalyptic Imagination* (New York: Crossroad, 1984), who speaks of two strands of tradition in Jewish apocalypses, one visionary and one involving otherworldly journeys.

24. For an excellent summary of Jesus and prayer, including bibliography, see Donald Goergen, *The Mission and Ministry of Jesus* (Wilmington: Michael Glazier, 1986) 129–45. Goergen's book arrived too late to be incorporated significantly into the present book, but I highly recommend it as one of the best recent works on the historical Jesus.

25. Mark 1:35, 6:46.

26. Luke 6:12. Luke emphasizes the role of prayer in Jesus' life more than the other evangelists; in addition to 6:12, see 3:21, 5:16, 9:18, 9:28–29, 11:1. However, the picture is not due simply to Lucan redaction, as is clear from the references to Jesus' prayer life in the other gospels.

[[45]] The intimacy of Jesus' experience of Spirit is pointed to by one of the distinctive features of his prayer life: his use of the word *Abba* to address God.[27] An Aramaic word used by very young children to address their father, *Abba* is like the English "Papa." Within Judaism, it was common to refer to God with the more formal "Father," but rare to call God *Abba*. The most plausible explanation of Jesus' departure from conventional usage is the intensity of his spiritual experience, a supposition supported by the parallel within Judaism. Namely, *Abba* is used as a term for God in traditions reported about Jewish charismatics contemporary with Jesus.[28] Thus at the heart of Jesus' prayer life was the experience of communion with God.

"The Spirit of the Lord Is upon Me"

The image of Jesus as a Spirit-filled person in the charismatic stream of Judaism is perfectly crystallized in the words with which, according to Luke, Jesus began his public ministry:

> The Spirit of the Lord is upon me, because he has anointed me to preach good news to the poor. He has sent me to proclaim release to the captives and recovering of sight to the blind, to set at liberty those who are oppressed, to proclaim the acceptable year of the Lord.

About these words, quoted from an earlier charismatic, Jesus said, "Today this scripture has been fulfilled in your hearing."[29] Though the passage as a whole is often attributed to Luke and not to Jesus himself,[30] the picture of Jesus as one "anointed by the Spirit" succinctly summarizes what we find in

27. See Mark 14:36. Though this is the only occurrence of the Aramaic *Abba* in the gospels (which were written in Greek), it may lie behind the unadorned "Father" in Luke's version of the Lord's Prayer (Luke 11:2). A consensus of scholarship affirms its authenticity. That it was also part of the prayer life of first-century Christians is indicated by the appearance of the word in Rom 8:15 and Gal 4:6, remarkable in letters composed in Greek for Greek-speaking audiences. It is reasonable to assume that early Christian usage derived from Jesus' own practice. The classic study of *Abba* is J. Jeremias, *The Prayers of Jesus* (Naperville, IL: Allenson, 1967), though Jeremias overemphasizes its distinctiveness, arguing that it was *unique* to Jesus (an argument perhaps motivated by theological considerations).

28. See Vermes, *Jesus the Jew*, 210–13.

29. Luke 4:18–21, quoting Isa 61:1–2; see also Isa 58:6.

30. Even by quite conservative scholars, Luke 4:18–30 is commonly attributed to Luke and categorized as "inauthentic" (that is, not among the actual words of Jesus). To a large extent, this is because the placement of the sermon is so obviously the product of Luke's compositional work: these verses replace Mark's account of Jesus' "inaugural address" (Mark 1:15: "The Kingdom of God is at hand"). Moreover, the verses identify one of Luke's central themes: Luke stresses the presence of the Spirit in Jesus more than the other gospels. Thus it seems to be Luke's advance summary of who Jesus was and the thrust of his ministry. However, the possibility remains that Jesus did use these words with reference to himself at some other time in his ministry (perhaps even in the context of a synagogue reading—there is nothing improbable about the scene); though Luke is responsible for inserting the story at this point in the narrative, it is not necessarily created by Luke. Moreover, even if Luke did create the story, it aptly describes what we have seen to be true on other grounds. Whether Luke was reporting or creating tradition, he has seen well.

the gospels. From his baptism onward, through his ordeal in the wilderness, and continuing throughout his ministry, his life and mission were marked by an intense experiential relationship to the Spirit.

Thus far we have been speaking about Jesus' *internal* life: his prayer life, the visions he experienced, his sense of intimacy with God. We also see his connection to the world of Spirit in central dimensions of his public life: in the impression he made on others, his claims to authority, and in the style of his speech.

The Impression Jesus Made on Others

[[46]] In his classic book about the experience of the holy or the *numinous*, Rudolf Otto describes the *numinous presence* that frequently is felt in charismatic figures by those around them. There is something uncanny about such figures which evokes awe and amazement and impresses people with the feeling of another world. There may be something authoritative about the way they speak, penetrating about the way they see, powerful about their presence.[31]

Such was true of Jesus. A verse in Mark vividly conveys the impression he made, the "cloud of the *numinous*" that was present around him: "And they were on the road, going up to Jerusalem, and Jesus was walking ahead of them; and they were amazed, and those who followed were filled with awe."[32]

As a teacher Jesus made a striking impression, very different from the official teachers: "They were astonished at his teaching, for he taught them as one who had *authority*, and not as the scribes."[33] Behind the Greek word for authority lies the rabbinic term for the power or might of God, the *Gevurah:* "He speaks from the mouth of the *Gevurah*,"[34] that is, from the mouth of power or Spirit.

Popular opinion associated him with earlier charismatic figures, with Elijah or the prophets or John the Baptist.[35] The aura of "otherness" around him may explain the reaction of his family on one occasion: "They went out to seize him, for they said, 'He is beside himself,'" that is, insane.[36] Even his

31. Rudolf Otto, *The Idea of the Holy* (New York: Oxford University Press, 1958; first published in German in 1917), especially 155–59. On p. 158, Otto writes, "The point is that the 'holy man' or the 'prophet' is from the outset, as regards the experience of the circle of his devotees, something more than a 'mere man.' He is the being of wonder and mystery, who somehow or other is felt to belong to the higher order of things, to the side of the numen itself. It is not that he himself teaches that he is such, but that he is *experienced* as such" (italics added). See also Otto's *The Kingdom of God and the Son of Man,* translated by F. V. Filson and B. L. Woolf (Grand Rapids, ca. 1938), especially pp. 162–69, 333–76.

32. Mark 10:32. As Otto puts it, in "these few masterly and pregnant words," Mark states "with supreme simplicity and force *the immediate impression of the numinous that issued from Jesus.*" *The Idea of the Holy,* 158; italics added.

33. Mark 1:22.

34. On *Gevurah*, see E. E. Urbach, *The Sages* (Jerusalem: Magnes, 1975) 80–96; for his interpretation of this verse, see pp. 85–86.

35. Mark 6:14–16, 8:28; Matt 21:11; Luke 7:12.

36. Mark 3:21. The Greek text means literally, "He is out of himself," that is, ecstatic, a nonordinary state often characteristic of holy men, easily mistaken as dementia.

opponents granted that there was a spiritual power at work in him, but interpreted it as coming from "Beelzebul, the prince of demons."[37]

Not surprisingly, he attracted crowds. "The whole city was gathered around the door," people "could not get near him because of the crowd," "a great crowd followed him and thronged about him."[38] Such language is only what we would expect in the early church's account of his ministry, but it also undoubtedly conveys the historical impression which he made. Jesus was widely known as a charismatic figure, and it was this reputation as a man of Spirit that drew the crowds which flocked around him.

Jesus' Own Sense of Authority

[[47]] Jesus himself was aware of this power or authority which others sensed in him. When some of the religious leaders in Jerusalem questioned him about his authority, Jesus responded with another question: "I will ask you a question; answer me, and I will tell you by what authority I do these things. Was the baptism of John from heaven or from men?"[39] Was the authority of John "from heaven," from the "other world," or from men? Though unexpressed, Jesus' own view is clear: implicitly he claimed the same authority as John, one grounded neither in institution nor tradition but in the Spirit.

Similarly, Jesus was aware of the power of the Spirit flowing through him. In the context of casting out a demon, he identified the power as the Spirit of God: "If it is by *the Spirit of God* that I cast out demons, then the Kingdom of God has come upon you."[40] On another occasion, after a woman had touched his garment in order to be healed, he perceived that *power* had gone out of him.[41]

The style of Jesus' teaching also shows an awareness of a *numinous* authority not derived from tradition. It is seen in his emphatic and unusual "I say unto you" statements, often prefaced in an unprecedented manner with "Amen" ("truly," "certainly"), a solemn formula which normally followed a statement.[42] Sometimes his emphatic "I say unto you" was incorporated into a contrast with the words of the tradition using the pattern, "You have heard that it was said . . . but I say to you."[43] Thus the language of Jesus indicates an

---

37. Mark 3:22–30, Matt 12:24–32, Luke 11:14–23.

38. Quoted phrases are from Mark 1:33, 2:4, and 5:24; the motif runs throughout the gospels.

39. Mark 11:27–33. The narrative, in which Jesus puts his opponents in a dilemma, is also an excellent example of Jesus' skillful repartee in debate.

40. Matt 12:28 = Luke 11:20. Matthew has "Spirit of God," Luke has "finger of God"; however, the two expressions are synonymous.

41. Mark 5:30.

42. On "Amen," see J. Jeremias, *New Testament Theology* (New York: Scribner, 1971) 35–36. According to his tables, it appears thirteen times in Mark, nine times in Q sayings, nine times in Matthew only, and three times in Luke, as well as twenty-five times in John. Thus all strata of the gospel tradition attest to it.

43. See the six antithetical statements found in the Sermon on the Mount, Matt 5:21–22, 27–28, 31–32, 33–34, 38–39, 43–44. Some scholars accept the antithetical formulation of

awareness of a tradition-transcending authority, one from the mouth of the Spirit.

Moreover, he called disciples, an action which points to his sense of charismatic authority even as it also testifies to the deep impression he made on people. Though it was relatively common for a teacher within Judaism to have devoted students, the phenomenon of discipleship is different and uncommon, involving an uprooting and a following after. The stories of the call of the disciples describe with compact vividness the imperative of Jesus' call, the immediacy of their response, and the radical rupture from their previous lives: [[48]]

> And passing along by the Sea of Galilee, Jesus saw Simon and Andrew casting a net in the sea. And Jesus said to them, "Follow me." And immediately they left their nets and followed him. And going on a little farther, he saw James the son of Zebedee and John his brother, who were in their boat mending the nets. And immediately he called them; and they left their father Zebedee in the boat with the hired servants and followed him.[44]

Later, one of them exclaimed: "Lo, we have *left everything* and followed you."[45] The phenomenon of discipleship is located within the charismatic stream of Judaism, occurring in response to a charismatic leader.[46]

Given all of the above, it is not surprising that Jesus had a prophetic consciousness. Not only did some of his contemporaries put him in the prophetic tradition, but he also twice referred to himself as one, albeit somewhat indirectly. In his home town, he said, "A prophet is not without honor, except in his own country." Later, he said, "It cannot be that a prophet should perish away from Jerusalem."[47] Identifying himself with the prophets, Jesus saw himself in the tradition of those who *knew* God.[48]

The Transfiguration

Some of his disciples reportedly experienced a strange episode which underlines the connection between Jesus and the world of Spirit. According to Mark, shortly before Jesus began his final journey to Jerusalem, the inner

---

only the first, second, and fourth as authentic (for example, Bultmann, *The History of the Synoptic Tradition* [New York: Harper & Row, 1963] 134–36). For a defense of the antithetical form as original to all six, see Jeremias, *New Testament Theology*, 251–53.

44. Mark 1:16–20; see also the call of Levi in Mark 2:13–14.

45. Mark 10:28.

46. See Martin Hengel, *The Charismatic Leader and His Followers* (New York: Crossroad, 1981; originally published in German in 1968). Hengel finds Matt 8:21–22 especially illuminating, and notes that it echoes the call of Elisha by Elijah in 1 Kgs 19:19–21.

47. Mark 6:4, Luke 13:33.

48. For a superb and passionate exposition of prophetic consciousness (including the prophet as one who knew God), see Abraham Heschel, *The Prophets* (New York: Harper & Row, 1962), especially volume 1.

core of the disciples momentarily saw him transformed, his form and clothing suffused with light. Jesus "led them up a high mountain apart by themselves; and he was transfigured before them, and his garments became glistening, intensely white. And there appeared to them Elijah with Moses; and they were talking to Jesus."[49]

The details link Jesus to the world of the charismatics. Like Moses before him, he momentarily "glowed" with the radiance of the Spirit (stories of "glowing" holy men are also reported elsewhere). With him were seen Elijah and Moses, the two great charismatic figures of the Jewish tradition.[50] Of course, it is very difficult to know what to make of the story historically. Did the [[49]] disciples actually have this experience, or is the whole narrative a symbolic statement of Jesus' identity? But even if the narrative is viewed as the creation of the church, it remains significant that the tradition associated Jesus with the two great men of Spirit of Israel's history.

Jesus' Own Sense of Identity

Jesus himself, his contemporaries, and the gospel writers all identified him with the charismatic stream of Judaism, as having a consciousness akin the prophets. Did he also think of himself with the exalted titles with which the early church proclaimed him after Easter? Did he think of himself as the Messiah (Christ)? Or as "the Son of God"? As already noted, historical scholarship has tended to give a negative answer.[51] But, as with the "heavenly voice" at his baptism, the historical judgment hinges in part upon the sense in which these terms are understood.

If "Son of God" is used in the special Christian sense which emerges in the rest of the New Testament (by the time of Paul and John, preexistent with God from before creation; by the time of Matthew and Luke, conceived by the Spirit and born of a virgin), then almost certainly Jesus did not think of himself as *the* Son of God. But if "son of God" is—given the meaning that it carried within Judaism at the time of Jesus, then it is possible he did. There, "son of God" was used in three different contexts to refer to three different entities, though with a common nuance of meaning. In the Hebrew Bible, it referred to Israel as a whole or to the king of Israel.[52] Contemporary with Jesus, the image of God as father and a particular person as God's son was used, as already noted, in stories about Jewish charismatic holy men. All three uses have one element in common. All designate a relationship of special intimacy with God—Israel as the chosen people, the king as the adopted son, the charismatic as one who knows and is known by God.

49. Mark 9:2–4, Matt 17:1–8, Luke 9:28–36. Matthew calls the experience a vision.

50. Moses and Elijah are significant *not* because they represent "the law and the prophets," as is often stated in commentaries, for they were *not* symbolic of the law and prophets in the time of Jesus. Rather, they were the two great holy men of the Jewish Scriptures.

51. See [[Borg, *Jesus*,]] chap. 1, pp. 10–11.

52. Examples of it referring to Israel as a whole: Hos 11:1, Exod 4:22–23; referring to the king of Israel in particular: Ps 2:7, 2 Sam 7:14.

In this Jewish sense, Jesus may have thought of himself as "son of God." He clearly was aware of a relationship of special intimacy. His use of the term *Abba* has as its corollary the term "son." There are also a number of passages which may plausibly be attributed to [[50]] him where he uses father-son imagery to speak at least indirectly of his relationship to God. Finally, the use of the image by other Jewish charismatics contemporary with him, with whom he shared much in common, provides a context in which the term is not only appropriate but virtually expected.

Moreover, there is a web of associations connecting this experiential awareness of intimacy with God with the term Messiah. "Messiah" (*Mashiah*) in the Jewish Scriptures means simply "anointed," that is, "smeared with oil." Such anointing was part of the coronation of the king of Israel, who thereby became God's "son." Jesus was aware of both "sonship" and being anointed by the Spirit, as we have seen. Thus the phrases "anointed by God," "son of God," and the term "Messiah" are all closely related.

We cannot know if Jesus made these associations himself; no saying which does this explicitly can be confidently attributed to him. Moreover, we may surmise that he did not spend a great deal of time thinking about who he was. Finally, of course, it does not matter whether he thought of himself as Messiah or Son of God, for whether or not he was does not depend on whether he thought so.[53] Yet our exploration of his life as a Spirit-filled person shows that the church's exalted designations of him were not an arbitrary imposition, but had roots in the historical experience of Jesus himself.

Jesus' intense relationship to the world of Spirit thus not only enables us to glimpse what he was like as a historical figure, but also enables us to understand the origin and appropriateness of the titles with which he was later proclaimed. Clearly, Easter played the major role in leading the followers of Jesus to describe him in the most glorious terms known in his culture. Yet the seeds of the church's proclamation lie in the experience of the historical Jesus, even if the full-grown plant needed the experience of Easter to allow it to burst forth.

The cumulative impression created by the synoptic gospels is very strong: Jesus stood in the charismatic tradition of Judaism which reached back to the beginnings of Israel. Matthew, Mark, and Luke all portray him as a Spirit-filled person through whom [[51]] the power of Spirit flowed. His relationship to Spirit was both the source and energy of the mission which he undertook. According to these earliest portraits, Jesus was one who knew the other world, who stood in a long line of mediators stretching back to Elijah and Moses. Indeed, according to them, he was the climax of that history of mediation. Moreover, as we shall see, Jesus' relationship to the world of Spirit is also the key for understanding the central dimensions of his ministry: as healer, sage, revitalization movement founder, and prophet.

---

53. This is an important point. To use a very mundane example, George Washington is legitimately referred to as "the father of his country" even though he presumably did not think of himself in those terms. Similarly, from a Christian point of view, Jesus is legitimately spoken of as the Messiah, *even if* he did not think of himself as such.

P. M. CASEY

Son of Man

[[46]] The term "son of man" is of fundamental importance for our under-standing both of Jesus himself and of the christology of the earliest church.[1] As the Gospels now stand it is much the commonest title of Jesus, and it is the term which he characteristically uses to refer to himself. It occurs 69 times in the synoptic Gospels, and 13 times in John. Our oldest Gospel has 14 ex-amples in the teaching of Jesus, and when all parallels are discounted, the three synoptic Gospels still produce 38 independent sayings. At least some of them must go back to Jesus, for the following reasons. The term occurs very

Reprinted, with permission, from P. M. Casey, *From Jewish Prophet to Gentile God: The Origins and Development of New Testament Christology* (Edward Cadbury Lectures at the University of Birmingham, 1985–86; Cambridge: James Clarke / Louisville: Westminster John Knox, 1991) 46–56.

1. For recent surveys, J. D. G. Dunn, [[*Christology in the Making: A New Testament Inquiry into the Origins of the Doctrine of the Incarnation* (1980)]], chap. 3; W. O. Walker, "The Son of Man: Some Recent Developments," *CBQ* 45, 1983, 584–607; J. R. Donahue, "Recent Studies on the Origin of 'Son of Man' in the Gospels," *CBQ* 48, 1986, 484–98. Of the massive second-ary literature, cf. especially G. Vermes, "The Use of *br nš/br nš'* in Jewish Aramaic," Appendix E in M. Black, *An Aramaic Approach to the Gospels and Acts* (3rd ed., 1967) 310–28; G. Vermes, *Post-Biblical Jewish Studies* (1975) 147–65; P. M. Casey, [[*Son of Man: The Interpretation and Influence of Daniel 7* (1979)]]; R. Kearns, *Vorfragen zur Christologie* (3 vols. 1978–82); B. Lindars, *Jesus Son of Man* (1983); M. Müller, *Der Menschensohn in den Evangelien* (1984); M. Müller, "The Ex-pression 'the Son of Man' as Used by Jesus," *StTh* 38, 1984, 47–64; O. Betz, *Jesus und das Danielbuch*. II. *Die Menschensohnworte Jesu und die Zukunftserwartung des Paulus (Daniel 7,13–14)* (1985); P. M. Casey, "The Jackals and the Son of Man," *JSNT* 23, 1985, 3–22; R. Kearns, *Das Traditionsgefüge um den Menschensohn*. Ursprünglicher Gehalt und älteste Veränderung im Urchristentum (1986); G. Schwarz, *Jesus, "der Menschensohn"* (1986); P. M. Casey, "General, Ge-neric and Indefinite. The Use of the Term 'Son of Man' in Aramaic Sources and in the Teach-ing of Jesus," *JSNT* 29, 1987, 21–56; A. Y. Collins, "The Origin of the Designation of Jesus as 'Son of Man,'" *HThR* 80, 1987, 391–407; R. Kearns, *Die Entchristologisierung des Menschensohn. Die Übertragung des Traditionsgefüges um den Menschensohn auf Jesus* (1988); V. Hampel, *Men-schensohn und historischer Jesus: Ein Rätselwort als Schlüssel zum messianischen selbstverständnis Jesu* (1990); P. M. Casey, "Method in Our Madness, and Madness in Their Methods: Some Ap-proaches to the Son of Man Problem in Recent Scholarship," *JSNT* (1991).

frequently; it is found in all Gospel sources—Mark, Q, the separate traditions of both Matthew [[47]] and Luke, John, and some non-canonical traditions; the early sources attribute it almost exclusively to Jesus himself; it is not normal Greek, a fact which we can explain only if it originated as a translation of the Aramaic expression *bar nash* or *bar nasha*; and the early church did not use it in any of its confessions nor in any New Testament epistle. This combination of reasons should be regarded as decisive: Jesus certainly used the term "son of man."

So far, so good, but we cannot go further without meeting serious problems. The Aramaic term *bar nash(a)*, "son of man," was a normal term for "man"; further, it now seems clear that it was not also a title in the Judaism of the time of Jesus.[2] The mere fact that it was a normal term for man means that sentences containing *bar nash(a)* would not have sufficient referring power to denote a single individual, unless the context made this reference clear. This means that *bar nash(a)* was a generally unlikely term for an author or a social group to select for use as a major title. The general improbability that *bar nash(a)* would be selected for use as a messianic title is supported by the empirical data: there is no satisfactory documentary evidence that any social group took this improbable step.

In the Gospels, however, the term "son of man" does not function as a normal term for "man" at all: it functions as a title, and it generally refers to Jesus alone. Jesus cannot have used the term like this. If it was not a title, he cannot have used it to refer to a known figure, "the Son of Man," whether he is supposed to have identified himself with such a figure or not. Nor can he have produced it as a title for the first time. The fact that it was a normal term for "man" means that he is unlikely to have wanted to use it as a title. Had he used it as a title, he would have had to make it clear from the context that he was doing so, but the "son of man" sayings in the Gospels do not do this. Had he been obscure enough to use it as a sort of title without making clear that he was doing so, his sentences would not have made proper sense or would have made the wrong sense, his disciples would have been puzzled, and we should have traces of this in the tradition.[3] In fact, some "son of man" sayings are not satisfactory sentences when they are reconstructed in the original Aramaic, but people appear to understand them without difficulty as references to Jesus alone.

Mark 8:31 illustrates several of these points: "And he began to teach them that the son of man must suffer many things, and be rejected by the elders and the chief priests and the scribes, and be killed, and after three days rise. And he spoke the word openly." This saying cannot be turned into a satisfactory Aramaic sentence. It contains a general term for man which does

---

2. This is still controversial, but the matter is too complicated to enter into here, and I have discussed it elsewhere: *Son of Man*, esp. chaps. 2 and 5. On the *Similitudes of Enoch*, [[see Casey, *From Jewish Prophet to Gentile God*, 87–88]].

3. For more detailed discussion of these effects, with reconstruction of possible and impossible Aramaic sentences, Casey, *JSNT* 29, 1987, 21–56, esp. 34–36, 47–50.

not refer clearly to Jesus, yet it makes precise reference to the elders and chief priests and scribes, that is, to the specific circumstances of Jesus' death and not to the death of men in general. Peter is none the less portrayed as understanding this saying very clearly. "And Peter took him on one side and began to rebuke him. But he turned and, seeing his disciples, rebuked Peter and said, 'Get behind me, Satan, for your mind is not set on the will of God but on the concerns of men.'" So serious a criticism of Peter would not be found in Mark's Gospel if it did not represent approximately what Jesus said. But if Peter's reaction is authentic, he must have had something like Mark 8:31 to react to. There are, therefore, good [[48]] reasons why Mark 8:31 must be authentic, and good reasons why it cannot be. This is how the "son of man" problem has appeared insoluble, with the straightforward application of apparently firm criteria leading to opposite conclusions from the equally straightforward application of other apparently firm criteria.

The key to a solution was provided by Vermes in his seminal paper, first published in 1967.[4] Vermes argued that, in addition to being a normal term for "man," the Aramaic *bar nasha*, "son of man," was also a conventional substitute for the first person pronoun, "I." This would, in a sense, solve the problem, in that it would explain why Jesus used the term "son of man" to refer to himself. Vermes' interpretation of the Aramaic evidence has not, however, convinced most scholars who can read the Aramaic sources. Also, if this were no more than a well-established Aramaic idiom, we might reasonably have expected bilingual translators to render *bar nash(a)* with the Greek word for "I," but there are only two known examples of this (Matt 10:32–33) to set against all the "son of man" sayings in the Gospels. I have therefore proposed a more complex theory which is partly based on the evidence which Vermes collected and presented.[5] The rest of this discussion is an updated summary of this theory.

Genuine sayings will be examined first. These belong to an Aramaic idiom, in accordance with which a speaker might use a general statement primarily in order to say something about himself. In general, he might do this in order to avoid sounding arrogant, self-centred, unusual or humiliated. We have similar idioms in English, using "a man," "we," "you," "one," "everyone" and other terms of this kind. Aramaic examples include a saying of R. Simeon ben Yohai, who lived in a cave for 13 years at the end of the Bar-Cochba revolt. When he was wondering whether it was safe to come out, he saw birds being hunted. Some were captured, others escaped, and he declared, "A bird is not caught without the will of heaven; how much less the soul of a son of man" (*Gen. Rab.* 79:6). R. Simeon then emerged from the cave. It follows that he intended to apply the statement to himself, but it does not follow that it is nothing more than a substitute for the first person pronoun. On the contrary, the first sentence, "A bird is not caught without the will of heaven," is quite clearly a general statement: the second must be interpreted in the same way,

4. Vermes, op. cit.
5. Casey, op. cit.; cf. especially Lindars, op. cit.; Müller, op. cit.

because we already know that "son of man" was a general term for "man," and this ensures that "how much less the soul of a son of man" balances and follows from the general statement about birds. The general statement may be used to refer to more people than the speaker. In this version of the story, R. Simeon has his son with him, and since they both emerge from the cave, the general statement is clearly intended to refer to them both. The idiom may therefore be defined as follows: In Aramaic, a speaker might use a general statement, in which the general term was *bar nash(a)*, "son of man," in order to say something about himself or a group of people including himself. He would normally do so in order to avoid being and sounding unduly arrogant, self-centred or humiliated.

Aramaic examples of this idiom may use either the indefinite state, *bar nash*, or the definite state, *bar nasha*. Examples translated into Greek in the Gospels consequently use the Greek definite article, which may be either genuinely [[49]] definite, the equivalent of the English definite article "the," or it may be generic. Owing to differences in the structure of Greek and Aramaic, this results in two articles in Greek, one before "son" and one before "man." In the following examples from the Gospels, I use the indefinite English article "a" to make the point that the original sayings were general statements: there is no way that they can be translated without some distortion of this kind.[6] The conventional use of "the" for the first article, before "son," is merely a conventional distortion. I follow the convention of omitting the second article, before "man," for this is clearly generic.

This idiom accounts for about a dozen sayings in the synoptic Gospels. One of the more straightforward examples is Mark 2:28, which concludes a dispute between Jesus and the Pharisees.[7] Some of Jesus' disciples had been going along a path through the fields, plucking the grains of corn, an action to be expected of poor and hungry people taking *peah*. Jesus' disciples were however doing this on the sabbath, and for this reason the Pharisees objected. Jesus warded off the Pharisees' criticism with two arguments, the second of which may be rendered, "The Sabbath was created for man, not man for the Sabbath. So, you see, a son of man is master even of the Sabbath!" The general nature of Mark 2:28 is guaranteed by the general statement of 2:27. This idiom, in which a general statement is deliberately used to divert attention from the speaker, is the only use of "son of man" that makes proper sense of both sentences. Otherwise, the statement that a son of man, or the Son of Man, is lord or master of the sabbath does not follow from the obviously general declaration that the sabbath was created for man, not man for the sabbath. This declaration looks back to God's purpose at creation, when he made man effectively lord of the creation, provided that he remains obedient to God (cf. Gen 1:26, 28; Ps 8:6–9; 2 Esd 6:54; *2 Bar* 14:18). Thus the general statement of Mark 2:28 includes the disciples, who as masters of the sabbath

6. For detailed discussion, *JSNT* 29, 1987, 27–34.
7. For detailed discussion of this pericope, P. M. Casey, "Culture and Historicity: The Plucking of the Grain (Mark 2:23–28)," *NTS* 23, 1988, 1–23.

were entitled to take *peah* on it. It is an indirect way of making clear that Jesus did have the authority to take the halakhic decision that they were entitled to take *peah* on the sabbath. Jesus' general statement is a dramatic one, but no more dramatic than that of Rabbi Aqiba, who settled another small point of sabbath law with the declaration "Profane the Sabbath, and don't depend on people" (*b. Šabb.* 118a / *b. Pesaḥ.* 112a). Thus at Mark 2:28 Jesus declared his right to fend off unwanted sabbath *halakhah*, indirectly claiming his prophetic ability to interpret the will of God, but not using any christological title.

A more serious conflict with orthodox Jews arose over Jesus' healing ministry. Scribes who came from Jerusalem accused him of casting out demons by means of Beelzebub. Jesus replied in a number of sharp sayings, one of which may be reconstructed from the differing versions in Mark and Q, the strongest possible combination of sources for a dispute which followed inevitably from the differing life-stances of Jesus and the most orthodox Jews: "Everyone who speaks a word against a son of man shall be forgiven, and everyone who speaks a word against the Spirit of holiness shall not be forgiven" (cf. Mark 3:28, Matt 12:32/Luke 12:10).[8]

Jesus was famous for his preaching of forgiveness to sinners, and the first part [[50]] of this saying, "Everyone who speaks a word against a son of man shall be forgiven," has a straightforward general level of meaning. At the same time, this part of the saying was spoken with reference to Jesus himself, and therefore appears to offer forgiveness even to his most vigorous opponents. In fact it sets up the second part, in which the orthodox attack on his healing ministry is repudiated in the strongest possible terms, yet without directly mentioning it. "Everyone who speaks a word against the Spirit of holiness" refers to anyone who criticizes God in action. This is precisely what Jesus believed that orthodox Jews were doing when they accused him of casting out demons by means of Beelzebub. Jesus effectively told them that they had committed an unforgivable sin. His use of indirect expressions, "everyone" instead of "you" or "scribes and Pharisees," "son of man" instead of "me," "the Spirit of holiness" instead of "God, who has given me power to cast out these demons," all are due to the highly charged nature of the situation, which led Jesus to eschew direct polemic, and to make a statement which would have commanded widespread agreement at its general level. Its application to him will not have been in doubt, and, as at Mark 2:28, there is an implicit claim that Jesus, unlike his orthodox opponents, was acting with divine authority, a fundamental claim made without the use of any christological title.

Another saying which can be reconstructed from varying forms in Mark and Q also dealt with commitment and opposition to Jesus' ministry. "Everyone who confesses me before men, a son of man will confess him before the angels of God, and everyone who denies me before men, a son of man will deny him before the angels of God" (cf. Luke 12:8–9/Matt 10:32–33, Mark

---

8. For an Aramaic reconstruction and discussion, Casey, *Son of Man*, 230–31; Lindars, op. cit., 34–38, 178–81; Casey, *JSNT* 29, 1987, 36–37. For an explanation of the conflict between Jesus and orthodox Jews, [[see Casey, *From Jewish Prophet to Gentile God*, 62–64]].

8:38).[9] This saying uses the imagery of the divine court. It was conceived in terms modelled on a human court, so it assumes that individual people stand up and testify for or against anyone who is judged. The saying is more direct than the previous example, in that Jesus uses the first person pronoun for himself as the object of witness, but he uses a general statement to say indirectly that he will respond to earthly witness now by speaking for or against people when the divine court meets. Thus the saying indirectly assumes, without using any title, that Jesus will soon be one of the most powerful people in the universe, but he avoided saying this directly by making a general statement, which assimilates his position in the divine court to that of a witness like everyone else.

One of the Q examples of this idiom belongs to a more mundane level of experience: "Jackals have holes, and the birds of the air have roosts, but a son of man has nowhere to lay his head" (Matt 8:20/Luke 9:58).[10] This saying belongs to the migratory phase of Jesus' ministry, and contrasts the divine provision of natural haunts for animals with the lack of such provision for men, who have to build houses to live in. The reference will have been in the first place to Jesus himself, for he had nowhere to go as he moved about, and he could not provide for his disciples. This would be a humiliating thing to say, and consequently Jesus used an indirect way of saying it. The general level of the saying also takes in the disciples, especially the one who had just declared that he would follow Jesus wherever he went (Matt 8:19/Luke 9:57).

These four examples illustrate Jesus' use of this idiom. He used it in the same [[51]] way as such idioms generally are used, to declare his own exalted status and function only indirectly, and to avoid direct mention of a humiliating situation. Both these feelings were involved in his predictions of his death and resurrection.[11] It is simplest to start at the Last Supper, where Mark 14:21 goes straight back into Aramaic without much modification: "A son of man goes as it is written of him, but woe to that man by whom a son of man is betrayed: it would be good for that man if he had not been born." The first general statement, "a son of man goes as it is written of him" depends on the universal fact that people die, recorded in scriptural passages such as Gen 3:19 and Isa 40:6. At this general level, the "son of man" statement is obviously true, and the function of its being obviously true was to make it easier for his disciples to accept the application of it to Jesus himself. At a second level, the saying is a prediction of Jesus' forthcoming death. There should be no doubt that Jesus did interpret scriptural passages of himself and his ministry, though we do not have much reliable evidence as to which ones. It is not difficult to suggest some possible interpretations.[12] For example, Mark 14:18

9. For an Aramaic reconstruction and discussion, Casey, *Son of Man*, 161–64; Lindars, op. cit., 48–56, 181–84; Casey, *ExpT* 96, 1985, 235–36.

10. For an Aramaic reconstruction, with full critical discussion, Casey, *JSNT* 23, 1985, 3–22.

11. For detailed discussion, including reconstruction of Aramaic originals, Casey, *JSNT* 29, 1987, 40–49.

12. Cf. Casey, *JSNT* 29, 1987, 41.

implies the use of Psalm 41, and Jesus might have seen God's support and vindication of him in this understanding of the Hebrew text of Ps 118:14–17: "The Lord is my strength and song, and he is for me, for Jesus. . . . The right hand of the Lord raises up. . . . I shall not die because I shall live." This was one of the psalms set for singing at Passover (cf. Mark 14:26).

The first part of Mark 14:21 also helps to set up the condemnation of Judas Iscariot. This begins with a second "son of man" saying: "Woe to that man by whom a son of man is betrayed." This can be understood as a general condemnation of traitors, a highly functional level of meaning because it would command almost universal assent. The application of this saying to Jesus himself will however have been perfectly clear. The verse ends with a quite indirect condemnation of Judas: "it would be good for him if that man had not been born." This is also perfectly comprehensible in the general terms of the previous sentence—it is generally accepted that traitors should come to a sticky end. Throughout this verse, the general level of meaning functions to enable the vigorous condemnation of Judas Iscariot to be accepted without objection, and the references to Jesus' own death are made easier to mention by means of the two idiomatic uses of the term "son of man."

We can now return to Mark 8:31. It is not possible to reconstruct a satisfactory Aramaic version of this. The editing of the predictions by Matthew and Luke shows a pronounced tendency to expand them with reminiscences of the passion, and we may suspect the same tendency in some of the other predictions in Mark, notably 10:33–34. We must therefore see whether we can reconstruct an original general statement which could have been modified in the same way to produce Mark 8:31. I have suggested something on the following lines: "A son of man will die, and after three days he will rise." This is a sound general statement. The first part of it is obviously true, because we all die, and this is the key to its function. It is because we all know that all of us die that Jesus' first effort to tell the disciples that he intended to die is couched in such a general form. In this situation, reference to resurrection was essential. Death might be [[52]] interpreted as rejection by God: resurrection was the culturally relevant form of vindication. "After three days" is both a general term for a short interval, and long enough, in a literal sense, to ensure that he was really dead.[13] When this prediction was translated into Greek, "die" was rendered as "be killed" because Jesus was killed. The rest of Mark 8:31 consists of details added from the events themselves, or from scripture.

A third authentic prediction of Jesus' death is to be found at Mark 10:45: "a son of man comes not to be served but to serve, that is, to give his life as a ransom for many."[14] In Aramaic, "come" was used with reference to the purpose of life, and "give one's life" could cover devoting or risking one's life, not only being killed. The saying has a general level of meaning which fits well into its context: the purpose of life is service, even to the point of death.

13. See further [[in Casey, *From Jewish Prophet to Gentile God*, 64–68]].
14. For an Aramaic reconstruction, with critical discussion, Casey, *JSNT* 29, 1987, 42–43.

The application to Jesus will also have been clear, the idiomatic use of "son of man" being set up in the context. Jesus had just predicted his death indirectly at Mark 10:38, when he challenged the sons of Zebedee, "Can you drink the cup which I drink, or be baptised with the baptism with which I am baptised?" Since they accepted this challenge, the "son of man" saying necessarily includes a reference to them as well, but this in no way undermines its clarity as a prediction of Jesus' death.

This gives us three authentic "son of man" predictions from which Mark 9:31 and 10:33–34 have been formed. This mixing in the tradition is understandable, for the clarification of sayings by means of scripture, tradition and the actual events was natural in a culture accustomed to midrashic expansion. Mark needed to record predictions of Jesus' death. It was a drastic event which could have been interpreted as God's condemnation of him: the only alternative to that view was the positive evaluation of it that we find in the early church. We must deduce from the arrangement of Jesus' teaching in Mark's Gospel that Mark did not know when most of the teaching was given. He therefore placed the predictions which he had, and perhaps developed and clarified, at regular stages in the build-up towards the final events. Thus the additional and clarified predictions have an excellent *Sitz im Leben* in the post-Easter church, which needed their content, and in the composition of Mark's Gospel, which needed the dramatic build-up of the series. The "son of man" passion predictions therefore give us two insights. They show us part of the origin of christology in Jesus' declaration of his forthcoming death, its significance as an atoning sacrifice, and his confidence in his vindication by God. The second insight is into the work of the early church, who took up the predictions in the light of scripture and subsequent events, expanding them in the manner of Jewish *midrash* to make their meaning clearer, and arranging them in a feasible sequence in the structure of our earliest Gospel.

The predictions of the parousia give us more insight into the work of the early church. Some are patently not authentic. For example, Luke 17:24 cannot be reconstructed in feasible Aramaic. There are however predictions of the parousia which make use of Dan 7:13, and the authenticity of some of them must be seriously considered. Mark 14:62 is usually regarded as the outstanding example. In response to the High Priest's question, Jesus replied, "I am, and you will see the Son of Man sitting on the right of Power and coming with the clouds [[53]] of heaven." Here Dan 7:13 is combined with Ps 110:1, and perhaps with Zech 12:10. While the Aramaic is not that of the idiom which we have largely been considering, it is feasible Aramaic. A virtual quotation from a scriptural text referred by a speaker to himself cannot be excluded as unidiomatic in a culture where it was relatively normal to apply scriptural texts to contemporary and future events. The saying should none the less be regarded as the midrashic work of the early church, for reasons which I have set out at length elsewhere and summarize now.[15]

---

15. Casey, *Son of Man*, chap. 8, esp. pp. 182–83, 213–18. A hypothetical Aramaic reconstruction is given on p. 178.

Firstly, this is one of a small group of sayings which speak of the "Son of Man coming." Only this group of parousia sayings can be authentic, because only if there is a clear reference to the scriptural text (Dan 7:13) can the Aramaic be regarded as feasible. Further, if a large group of such sayings are regarded as authentic, we cannot explain why the expectation of the kingdom of God and the parousia of the Son of Man are always separate, except in the editorial work of Matthew (Matt 13:41; 16:28). On this ground also, therefore, the group of authentic sayings must be small. Furthermore, half of this small group of sayings must be secondary for quite separate reasons. Matt 16:28 is one such saying: "Amen, I tell you, there are some of those standing here who will not taste death until they see the Son of Man coming in his kingdom." This is an edited version of Mark 9:1. The earlier Marcan saying does not contain the term "son of man," and Matthew's editorial work has produced the combination of son of man and kingdom that we would expect in the teaching of Jesus if this group of sayings were authentic. When other sayings are removed for detailed reasons of this kind,[16] we are left with only four (Mark 13:26, 14:62; Matt 24:44/Luke 12:40; Matt 10:23).

The next peculiarity is the purely scriptural basis of Jesus' references. Several New Testament writers refer to the second coming of Jesus in a variety of ways, but in the synoptic Gospels, where the influence of Dan 7:13 is clearly found (Mark 13:26/Matt 24:30, Mark 14:62/Matt 26:64), this event is almost invariably referred to in terms of "the Son of Man" coming. This consistency is striking, and can be explained only by the influence of this text. But we cannot explain why the Jesus of history should depart from his normal practice of teaching clearly with authority, whether openly to the crowds or in private to the disciples, in favour of indirect references to a scriptural text which he is never said to have quoted. We should not connect this with any motif of secrecy, because the Gospel writers do not treat these sayings as in any way ambiguous. Further, in Aramaic as in Greek and English, these sayings could not easily be understood as references to Jesus, who would have had to explain at some stage that it was his own coming to which he was referring. But of confusion and explanation there is no trace. Two of these sayings are not just references to one biblical text: Mark 13:26 and 14:62 lie in combinations of Old Testament allusions, a mode of preaching not generally characteristic of our records of the teaching of Jesus. Nor can we explain why the predictions of Jesus' second coming are never associated with the predictions of his resurrection. Both sets of predictions declare God's forthcoming vindication of him—why does the Son of Man never rise from the dead *and* come on the clouds of heaven?

[[54]] On the other hand, all these sayings have an excellent *Sitz im Leben* in the early church. We know from Acts and the epistles that they eagerly awaited his return, and that they searched the scriptures for evidence and interpretation of the events of salvation history. We have seen that there is

---

16. Mark 8:38c; Matt 25:31; Luke 18:8; Casey, *Son of Man*, 161–64, 190–91, 196–97, 201–2.

other evidence that they produced some sayings of this group. For example, the same evidence which shows that Matt 16:28 is not in its present form an authentic saying of Jesus, also demonstrates that it was produced by Matthew. The group of parousia sayings which cannot be reconstructed in feasible Aramaic are important again here too. The evidence which shows that Luke 17:24 is not an authentic saying of Jesus, also shows that the early church secondarily attributed to Jesus a "son of man" saying which predicts his parousia. The same goes for all sayings in this group.

There are additional reasons for doubting the authenticity of Mark 14:62, the saying most frequently defended, and containing perhaps the clearest reference to Dan 7:13. It occurs in the context of equally unsatisfactory use of the terms "messiah" and "son of the Blessed," and it does not give grounds for conviction on the legal charge of blasphemy indicated at Mark 14:63–64. It has also a particularly good *Sitz im Leben* in the Gospel of Mark. It brings the messianic secret to an end, declaring Jesus' future vindication with all three of the major christological titles used by St. Mark.[17] It explains that Jesus was wickedly condemned because he said who he really was and how God would vindicate him, and it thereby condemns his judges. We must conclude that Mark 14:62 and the other "son of man" parousia sayings were produced by the early church. In these sayings, "son of man" is a title. A Greek-speaking audience would understand it as indicating that Jesus was the outstanding member of mankind, and with "son of God" in the tradition, the understanding of "son of man" as a reference to Christ's human nature could not fail to occur eventually. Christians who did not speak Aramaic would be likely to assume that the term "son of man" was a title in the translated versions of authentic sayings too.

17. Cf. [[Casey, *From Jewish Prophet to Gentile God,*]] 43.

PETER STUHLMACHER

The Messianic Son of Man: Jesus' Claim to Deity

Literature: J. Becker, *Jesus of Nazareth* (ET 1998) 186–224; **K. Berger**, *Theologiegeschichte des Urchristentums* (1995²); **O. Betz**, *What Do We Know about Jesus?* (ET 1967) 83–118; rev. ed., *Was wissen wir von Jesus?* (1991²) 101ff.; **M. Bockmuehl**, *This Jesus: Martyr, Lord, Messiah* (1994); **G. Bornkamm**, *Jesus of Nazareth* (ET 1960) 169–78; **H. Braun**, *Jesus—der Mann aus Nazareth und seine Zeit* (1989²); **R. Bultmann**, *Jesus and the Word* (ET 1934); **D. Burkett**, *The Son of Man Debate: A History and Evaluation* (1999); **C. C. Caragounis**, *The Son of Man* (1986); **J. J. Collins**, "The Son of Man in First-Century Judaism," *NTS* 38 (1992) 448–66; *The Scepter and the Star* (1995); **N. A. Dahl**, "The Crucified Messiah," in idem, *The Crucified Messiah and Other Essays* (1974) 10–36, 167–69; **J. D. G. Dunn**, *Christology in the Making* (1989²); *Jesus Remembered* (2003) 615–762; **C. A. Evans**, "Jesus' Self-Designation 'the Son of Man' and the Recognition of His Divinity," in *The Trinity: An Interdisciplinary Symposium on the Trinity*, ed. S. T. Davis, D. Kendall, and G. O'Collins (1999) 29–47; **H. Gese**, "The Messiah," in idem, *Essays on Biblical Theology* (ET 1981) 141–66; **J. Gnilka**, *Jesus of Nazareth* (ET 1997) 248–65; **W. Grimm**, *Die Verkündigung Jesu und Deuterojesaja* (1981²); **F. Hahn**, *The Titles of Jesus in Christology* (ET 1969); **V. Hampel**, *Menschensohn und historischer Jesus* (1990); **M. Hengel** and **A. M. Schwemer**, *Der messianische Anspruch Jesu und die Anfänge der Christologie* (2001); **T. Holtz**, *Jesus von Nazareth* (1979) 84ff.; **W. Horbury**, *Jewish Messianism and the Cult of Christ* (1998); **M. de Jonge**, *Jesus, the Servant-Messiah* (1991); **M. Karrer**, *Der Gesalbte* (1991); *Jesus Christus im Neuen Testament* (1998); **E. Käsemann**, "Das Problem des historischen Jesus," in idem, *Exegetische Versuche und Besinnungen*, vol. 1 (1960) 187–214 = ET, "The Problem of the Historical Jesus," in idem, *Essays on New Testament Themes* (1964) 15–47; **S. Kim**, *The "Son of Man" as the Son of God* (1983); **W. Manson**, *Jesus the Messiah: The Synoptic Tradition of the Revelation of God in Christ* (London, 1943, repr. 1956, 200 pp./Philadelphia, 1946, 267 pp.) chap. 6, pp. 94–120 (London) = 134–68 (Philadelphia); **H. Merklein**, "Jesus, Künder des Reiches Gottes," in idem, *Studien zu Jesus und Paulus* (1987) 127–56; **B. F. Meyer**, *The Aims of Jesus* (1979) 174ff.; **G. S. Oegema**, *The Anointed and His People: Messianic Expectations from the Maccabees to Bar Kochba* (1998); **E. P. Sanders**, *Jesus and Judaism*

Reprinted, with permission, from Peter Stuhlmacher, *Biblical Theology of the New Testament* (trans. D. P. Bailey; Grand Rapids, Michigan: Eerdmans, forthcoming) chap. 9; because this printing precedes the official publication by Eerdmans, minor differences may exist, and the page numbers of that printing are not cited. Translated from *Biblische Theologie des Neuen Testaments*, vol. 1 (3rd ed.; Göttingen: Vandenhoeck & Ruprecht, 2005) 107–24.

(1985); **A. Schlatter**, "Der Zweifel an der Messianität Jesu," in idem, *Zur Theologie des Neuen Testaments und zur Dogmatik*, ed. U. Luck (1969) 151–202; **E. Schweizer**, *Jesus* (ET 1971) 13ff.; **P. Stuhlmacher**, *Jesus of Nazareth–Christ of Faith* (ET 1993); "Der messianische Gottesknecht," in idem, *Biblische Theologie und Evangelium* (2002) 119–40; **G. Theissen** and **A. Merz**, *The Historical Jesus: A Comprehensive Guide* (ET 1998) 523–53; **J. C. VanderKam**, "Righteous One, Messiah, Chosen One, and Son of Man in 1 Enoch 37–71," in *The Messiah: Developments in Earliest Judaism and Christianity*, ed. J. H. Charlesworth (1992) 169–91; **P. Vielhauer**, "Gottesreich und Menschensohn in der Verkündigung Jesu," in idem, *Aufsätze zum Neuen Testament* (1965) 55–91; **A. Vögtle**, "Exegetische Erwägungen über das Wissen und Selbstbewußtsein Jesu," in idem, *Das Evangelium und die Evangelien* (1971) 296–344; **B. Witherington**, *The Christology of Jesus* (1990); **W. Wrede**, *The Messianic Secret* (ET 1971) 209–52.

Jesus' public ministry and proclamation were provocative even in his own day, and novel enough to raise questions among friend and foe alike about who this man actually was (cf. Mark 8:27–30 par.; Matt 11:2–3/Luke 7:18–19; Mark 11:27–33 par.). Historically this is an unavoidable question, and therefore it is also necessary theologically to consider the much-discussed question of Jesus' personal claim to deity.

1. If one approaches Jesus as his contemporaries did, from the perspective of the Old Testament and early Judaism, then there are several possible ways of understanding him. Mark 8:27–30 par. records that people could see Jesus as John the Baptist risen from the dead after his martyrdom, as the prophet Elijah who was to come again before the final judgment (cf. Mal 3:23 [ET 4:5]), as one of the prophets of the end times, or as the Messiah. The same tendency is evident in the Baptist's question of whether Jesus was the expected "coming one," ὁ ἐρχόμενος (Matt 11:2–3 par.). The proclamation of Jesus Christ in Acts 10:34–43, which provides the framework for our theological work, looks back to the story of Jesus from Easter. It stresses that in Jesus' destiny God's word of promise has become historical reality and presents Jesus as the one anointed with the Holy Spirit, that is, as Lord and Messiah (cf. Acts 2:36).

If one works in both directions, moving forward from the Old Testament and early Judaism as well as backward from the post-Easter proclamation about Christ, the *theological significance* of the question about Jesus' mission consciousness becomes clear. *The answer to this question determines the historical justification of the early Christian gospel proclamation. This speaks of Jesus as the "only begotten" Son of God and Messiah and testifies that the one God who created the world and chose Israel as his own people has made atonement in and through Jesus for the salvation of all people even before they came to faith* (cf. Rom 5:6–8).

2. The question of Jesus' claim to messianic authority has been answered in extremely different ways and remains controversial today. Following W. Wrede, R. Bultmann and H. Braun hold that the earthly Jesus lived merely as a rabbi and end-time prophet and was designated Messiah and Lord only after Easter. On the other side of the question, scholars including O. Betz, L. Goppelt, J. Jeremias, M. Hengel, and A. M. Schwemer follow A. Schlatter by assuming

that Jesus knew himself to be the Messiah already during his earthly life and that together with the Twelve he gathered the end-time people of God. A third group of researchers, including H. Conzelmann, G. Bornkamm, E. Käsemann, and E. Lohse, take a middle position. They posit a unique relationship with God and a virtually messianic self-consciousness of the earthly Jesus, but nevertheless think that all christological titles applied to Jesus in the Synoptics, the early Christian kerygma, and the Gospel of John are of post-Easter origin. These highly diverse positions point to great aporias in research. They can be held together theologically only as long as the exegetes agree that Jesus' message and destiny represents a historically unique and unrepeatable act of God, deciding between salvation and disaster for all people, Jews and Gentiles.

3. If we wish to make progress, we will do well to follow E. Schweizer's way of thinking. In his 1968 book on Christology, *Jesus* (ET 1971), he placed the question of Jesus' proclamation and divine consciousness with good reason under the heading, "Jesus: The Man Who Fits No Formula" (p. 13). It can in fact be shown that Jesus saw himself as God's representative on earth and that he simultaneously lived as a truly obedient human being before God, even dying on a cross. Yet he did so in a completely novel way over against the Old Testament–Jewish expectation of the Son of Man and Messiah. Among Roman Catholic exegetes a very similar view is held for example by H. Merklein. He assumes that while Jesus lacked a "titular self-understanding," he possessed a "*unique, immediate relationship with God.*" Merklein adds that "in the unique event (also when considered from the history of religion) that Jesus proclaims, none of the traditional messianic or eschatological titles can adequately express the specific role of Jesus" ("Jesus, Künder des Reiches Gottes," 150, 151). In 1987 Schweizer decided to speak about Jesus with E. Jüngel as a "parable of God," while Merklein says that Jesus was "not the proclaimer but the representative of the kingdom of God" (ibid., 152). This language also makes good sense. For Jesus' word and work in fact reveal who God is for people, and what people are for and before God.

3.1 The approach of Schweizer and Merklein can be made exegetically more precise and the question of Jesus' divine consciousness can also be answered historically if we once again follow our earlier thesis: *As the completely obedient "Son," Jesus identified himself with the "stronger one" heralded by John the Baptist, the messianic Son of Man and Judge of the World.*
    This view is unavoidable if we follow the *narrative plan* of the Synoptic Gospels. After Jesus' baptism by John and his temptation, the "initial choosing of the ways" (F. Neugebauer), the Synoptics present him as beginning his public ministry in Galilee. Not until after Peter's confession in Caesarea Philippi does Jesus make his way to Jerusalem to seek his decisive movement. After his "final choosing of the ways" in Gethsemane and his confession before the Sanhedrin, Jesus meets his death on the cross (cf. Mark 15:24ff. par.). As Jesus makes his way from Galilee to Jerusalem, Jewish opposition to him grows with his messianic claim. This claim then becomes the scarlet thread

running through the report of his final ministry in Jerusalem and his passion (Mark 11:1–16:8). The gospel narrative is therefore held together by the confession of Jesus as the messianic Son of God. In our view this confession is in keeping with historical reality: *Jesus lived, ministered, and suffered as the very Christ that Christian faith confesses him to be.*

3.2 If one examines the first three titles applied to Jesus in Mark 8:27–30—"John the Baptist; Elijah; one of the prophets"—it quickly becomes apparent that he transcends them.

3.2.1 It is understandable that people found in Jesus, the "master student" of John the Baptist, the fresh embodiment of the spirit and voice of the Baptist whom Herod Antipas had executed. Nevertheless Matt 11:2–6/Luke 7:18–23 as well as Jesus' own testimony about the Baptist in Matt 11:7–19/Luke 7:24–35 document that *Jesus was more than the Baptist.*

3.2.2 Although his arrival on the scene had unmistakable prophetic features (cf. Luke 13:33), Jesus also transcends the designations "Elijah" and "one of the prophets." To be sure, Jesus called his disciples to follow him as Elijah had called Elisha (cf. 1 Kgs 19:19–21), and he made the same radical demand that they renounce all previous ties (cf. Mark 1:16–20 par.; Luke 9:59–62/Matt 8:21–22; Mark 8:34 par.) in favor of fellowship with the homeless Son of Man (Luke 9:58/Matt 8:20). Jesus applied the prophetic promise of Isa 61:1–3 to himself and his ministry (cf. Luke 4:16–30; Matt 11:2–6 par.), and he even saw his death as an analogy to the death of the prophets (cf. Luke 13:31–33). Nevertheless, his claim far exceeds that of an eschatological prophet as they used to appear in the first century in Palestine. The clearest sign of this is Jesus' choosing of the twelve disciples, by which he laid claim to the end-time people of the twelve tribes. Jesus saw John the Baptist as the returning "Elijah" (Matt 11:14), yet *Jesus himself with his own call to repentance was "more than Jonah"* (Matt 12:41). In the transfiguration scene in Mark 9:7 par., Jesus' disciples are commanded to "listen to him"; this suggests that Jesus is the messianic prophet of Deut 18:15 to whom the people must also "listen" (cf. Acts 7:37).

3.2.3 When we recall that Jesus was also not a Jewish rabbi educated in a rabbinic house of instruction, and that as a teacher of the alternative wisdom God had given him (Matt 11:25–30 par.) he was "more than Solomon" (Luke 11:31/Matt 12:42), then the only remaining possibility is to understand Jesus' mission *messianically* (cf. Mark 8:29 par.).

4. As we have already seen, a whole line of exegetes until today holds that all christological titles applied to Jesus in the Gospels, including Messiah, Son of Man, Son of God, etc., originated only after Easter.

   "I consider all passages in which any kind of Messianic predicate [ET incorrectly 'prediction'] occurs to be kerygma shaped by the community," writes E. Käsemann ("Das Problem des historischen Jesus," 211 = "The Problem of the Historical Jesus," 43). G. Bornkamm holds the same view in his book on Jesus (*Jesus of Nazareth*, 226–31), while in E. Lohse's *Grundriß der neutestamentlichen Theologie* it says: "Jesus did not apply any of the messianic titles of Judaism to himself, but he spoke and acted with incomparable authority" (p. 43).

Three historical considerations tell against this view: (1) A Jesus who avoided any self-designation is a historically unreal abstraction, which has only grown up out of the aporias of current Gospel research. This view assumes that despite his highly conspicuous and provocative behavior, Jesus placed no value on being understood by his contemporaries, not even by his own disciples. (2) The synoptic tradition rests upon a traditional and personal continuum stretching from the circle of Jesus' disciples to the early Jerusalem church, and from the church to the "teaching of the apostles" (Acts 2:42) which was foundational to the Gospels. Therefore the synoptic presentation of Jesus cannot be rejected outright as unreliable. (3) *This blanket criticism takes the easy way out with the messianic texts and the Son of Man sayings.* Both general historical considerations and the findings of the synoptic tradition speak against this widespread thesis of a "lack of a titular self-understanding with Jesus" (H. Merklein).

5. We have seen that Jesus was more than a Jewish teacher of the law and wisdom, but also more than an eschatological prophet or a student of John the Baptist. It remains to examine *Peter's confession* in Mark 8:29 par., "You are the Christ" (σὺ εἶ ὁ χριστός) and to relate this to Jesus' own confession in Mark 14:61–62 par.

In order to understand Peter's confession and the self-confession of Jesus, we must first understand how a claim that Jesus is the Messiah could arise in the circle of Jesus' followers and be opposed by his enemies.

5.1 According to the messianic prophecies of the Old Testament, the Messiah is above all the royal Davidide sent by God. As the bearer of the wisdom, righteousness, and power of God he is supposed to establish the time of salvation for Israel (cf. Isa 9:1–6; 11:1–8; Psalm 72, etc.). His origin goes back to prehistory (Mic 5:1 [ET 5:2]) and he is promised to stand before God in the special relationship of the "Son" (2 Sam 7:14; Ps 2:7; 89:27). 2 Sam 7:10–14 and Ps 1:1; 2:1–2 are interpreted messianically in 4Q174 (4Q*Florilegium*) and applied to the "branch of David" (4Q174 frags. 1 col. I + 21 + 2, line 11 = *DSSSE* 1:352), while in 1Q28a II 12, 14, 20 he is called "the Messiah of Israel" (*DSSSE* 1:102). The expectation of the Davidic Messiah was current in early Judaism and had full-blown national and political implications. According to the *Psalms of Solomon* (first century B.C.) the Messiah will gather the people of Israel, redeem them from foreign domination by the Gentiles, purify them, and rule over them in righteousness as God's people (*Pss. Sol.* 17 and 18). Very similarly it says in the fourteenth of the Eighteen Benedictions (according to the older Palestinian recension):

Be merciful, Lord our God, with thy great mercies, to Israel thy people and to Jerusalem thy city; and to Zion, the dwelling-place of thy glory; and to thy Temple and thy habitation; and to the kingship of the house of David, thy righteous Messiah. Blessed art thou, Lord, God of David, who buildest Jerusalem. (trans. Schürer, Vermes, Millar, *History of the Jewish People*, 2:461)

Finally *4 Ezra* 13 speaks of the work of the Messiah. The *filius dei* [['son of God']] will walk atop Mount Zion in the end time, execute judgment, gather the people of the twelve tribes, and protect them forevermore.

5.2 With respect to this dominant form of the messianic expectation one must however not forget that *the picture of the Messiah in the Old Testament and early Judaism was extraordinarily diverse.* Zech 9:9–10 presents the Messiah as the humble prince of peace, whereas in Zech 12:10 he appears as the martyr who has fallen in the end-time battle. Moreover, the term "anointed one" (χριστός) is not reserved for the Davidide alone. Already in Isa 45:1 the Persian king *Cyrus* is called Yahweh's "anointed," and according to 1 Kgs 19:16; Isa 61:1–2; Sir 48:8 and CD II 12 Elijah and other *prophets* counted as anointed ones. The same is true according to Lev 4:3, 5, 16 and Sir 45:15 of the high priest. Therefore in a few early Jewish texts the messianic high priest or the *Messiah from the house of Aaron* enters beside the Davidic Messiah. He appears partly alone (*Testament of Levi* 18), partly together with the Davidic Messiah (1QS IX 11; 1Q28a II 12, 20; CD XX 1), and according to 4Q540–541 he can even display traces of a suffering figure (from Isaiah 53). In 11Q13 (11QMelch) the messenger of peace of Isa 52:7 and the one anointed by the Spirit in Isa 61:1–2 are both referred to *Melchizedek* as the heavenly redeemer. In *1 Enoch* the *Son of Man* appears as the anointed one (48:10; 52:4) and simultaneously as the chosen Servant (45:3–4; 49:2; 61:5, 8). According to *1 En.* 61:8; 62:2 he is set upon the end-time judgment throne by God in keeping with Ps 110:1 and is given the Spirit of truth and righteousness (from Isa 11:1–5). His appearance will astonish the powerful upon earth (cf. *1 En.* 46:4; 62:3; 63:11 with Isa 52:13). Finally, the late Armenian text of *T. Benj.* 3:8 as well as rabbinic texts speak of the *Messiah ben Joseph* who is warlike and dies for the godless.

According to M. Karrer, *Der Gesalbte* (1991), the early Christian confession Χριστὸς ἀπέθανεν [['Christ died']] (1 Cor 15:3) first arose as an "immediate response to the death of Jesus" (p. 406). It is indebted to a specific early Jewish idea of anointing centered on the Jerusalem temple cult and the Holy of Holies: "In the popular consciousness the Holy of Holies was until its destruction in A.D. 70 the anointed place, 'the anointed thing' *par excellence*: τὸ χριστόν (Dan 9:26b LXX)" (p. 176; cf. also 161 n. 84). Jesus as the Christ supposedly takes the place of the Holy of Holies in early Christianity from Easter onward: "As God's sphere of blessing radiated from the Holy of Holies according to the inherited belief about the cult, so now it radiates in the new faith experience from Jesus, the Anointed One who is the focus of Christian faith" (p. 406). Nevertheless, three considerations tell against Karrer's view: (1) The abstract equation of Jesus Christ with the Holy of Holies is unknown in early Christianity; passages such as Mark 15:38 par.; Rom 3:25; Heb 9:1–28 and John 2:18–22 formulate the matter differently and in more detail. (2) According to general Greek usage the substantive τὸ χριστόν denotes an "ointment" (W. Grundmann, *TDNT* 9:495 item 2). It is therefore no accident that τὸ χριστόν is never used as a technical term for the anointed Holy of Holies in early Jewish and Christian literature. (3) In the LXX version of Dan 9:26, the genitive μετά τοῦ χριστοῦ [['with the anointed one']] on which Karrer builds his case is not the neuter τὸ χριστόν as he supposes (p. 161 n. 84; 176 with n. 15; cf. *TDNT* 9:510 n. 74) but rather the masculine ὁ χριστός. The whole phrase βασιλεία ἐθνῶν φθερεῖ τὴν πόλιν καὶ τὸ ἅγιον μετὰ τοῦ χριστοῦ (Dan 9:26 LXX) therefore concludes with a reference to an anointed person rather than an anointed object: "A kingdom of the Gentiles will destroy the city and the Holy Place [i.e., the temple] with the *Anointed One*," where the Anointed One refers to the Messiah or the messianic high priest. The LXX version arrives at this rendering by reading the Hebrew not as the MT's עַם נָגִיד, "the city and the sanctuary (direct object) *they* will destroy, [namely] *the people* (עַ) of the prince who is to come," but rather as עִם נָגִיד "they will destroy the city . . . *with the prince*" (see *BHS* apparatus at Dan 9:26). The LXX translates this appropriately as μετὰ τοῦ χριστοῦ, "*with* the Messiah" (Theodotion's version similarly has σὺν τῷ ἡγουμένῳ, "*with* the ruler"). Therefore Karrer's thesis cannot be supported either exegetically or philologically and tradition historically. In the meantime he has slightly modified his thesis (cf. M. Karrer, *Jesus Christus im Neuen Testament*, 136–37).

5.3 The question whether messianic expectations could be associated with Jesus' ministry is to be answered in the affirmative. Jesus' saving deeds on behalf of "the poor," including his table fellowship and healing miracles, already bore messianic traits from Isa 61:1–2. But above all the claim upon the people of the twelve tribes which he raised by creating the circle of the Twelve, his demonstrative entrance into Jerusalem (Mark 11:1–10 par.), and the cleansing of the temple must have appeared as messianic signs not only to Jesus' disciples but also to his Jewish contemporaries. Jesus' Davidic descent, his ministry as "messianic teacher of righteousness," and his sovereign interpretation of the Torah of Sinai also come together with this. It therefore lay historically near at hand to see Jesus as the Messiah or to suspect him of messianic claims. The title on the cross, which alluded critically to Jesus' kingdom and was formulated in a Roman rather than Christian manner, and the admission of the disciples on the road to Emmaus after Jesus' crucifixion that they had hoped that Jesus would "redeem" Israel (Luke 24:21) provide the documentation that Jesus was in fact seen this way.

5.4 Examining Peter's confession in *Mark 8:27–33 par.* against the background of these findings yields important results.

From a literary standpoint the text is composed of three elements: (1) the actual confession scene, which has a precise geographic location and concludes with a command of silence (vv. 27–30). (2) Jesus' passion prediction, beginning with "And he began" (καὶ ἤρξατο) and concluding with "And he was stating the matter plainly" (καὶ παρρησίᾳ τὸν λόγον ἐλάλει) (vv. 31–32a). (3) Peter's rebuke of Jesus and its sharp rebuttal by Jesus (vv. 32b–33).

The command of silence in Mark 8:30 makes good historical sense in the context of the story. Here the verb ἐπιτιμάω means (as in Mark 3:12) to "command" or "sternly order," whereas in vv. 32–33 it is to be translated "rebuke" (cf. Mark 4:39; 9:25). But judging by this word choice in v. 30 and comparing with Mark 9:9, where a similar command of silence is given at the Transfiguration (though using a different verb, διαστέλλω), v. 30 could also be a remark first added redactionally by the evangelist. The introductory phrase in v. 31, "And he began to teach" (καὶ ἤρξατο διδάσκειν), is one of Mark's favorite expressions (cf. 4:1; 6:2, 34). However, παρρησίᾳ ("plainly, openly") and προσλαμβάνω ("to take aside") in v. 32 occur only here in the Gospel of Mark. The mention of "his disciples," οἱ μαθηταὶ αὐτοῦ, in v. 33 is common in Mark (cf. 2:15, 16, 23; 3:7, 9, etc.), whereas the equation of Peter with Satan is extraordinary both linguistically and materially. Assuming that the evangelist has not already taken over vv. 27–33 as a unit but has created the context himself, the decisive connecting thread lies between v. 30 and v. 31, with vv. 32–33 securely tied to v. 31. A direct connection between v. 33 and v. 29 can be established only by artificially and violently removing vv. 30–32 from the context (so, e.g., E. Dinkler, "Petrusbekenntnis und Satanswort," in idem, *Signum Crucis* [1967] 283–312 or F. Hahn, *The Titles of Jesus in Christology*, 223–28).

None of the three compositional elements of this text originates first and foremost from the reflection of the church. The text rather suggests that people's opinions about Jesus were divided and that the disciples nourished the hope that Jesus was the Messiah. Peter was their spokesman. His viewpoint was not simply rejected by Jesus nor rebuked as a tempting request (cf. v. 33). It was rather accepted, but subjected to the command of silence. Jesus apparently did not put any stock in being prematurely and publicly hailed as the Messiah in order to direct the people's widespread political hopes of redemption to himself. He therefore immediately supplements Peter's confession by his first lesson to the disciples about his coming suffering. This instruction as well should not be judged indiscriminately as a secondary "passion summary." Although Mark 8:31 is clearly intended to have a literary effect as the first passion prediction in Mark's Gospel, the statement as such need not fall historically by the wayside. It is rather to be judged (from the perspective of Mark 9:31) as historically authentic at its core. Peter's rebuke of Jesus is directed against this passion prediction, and Jesus' exceptionally sharply formulated (and therefore also pre-Easter) counter-rebuke is directed against Peter's unwillingness to face up to this teaching about Jesus' passion (and *not* against his confession of Jesus as Messiah).

The text as a whole leads to a clear result that was highly unusual in the realm of Jewish tradition: *According to Mark 8:27–33 Jesus did not wish to be publicly hailed as the Messiah by his disciples; he wanted to be the Messiah only as the suffering Son of Man.* Jesus' attitude transcended the current early Jewish picture of the Messiah as well as the expectation of the Son of Man that the Baptist had placed upon him. Early Judaism merely hinted at the suffering of the Messiah in a few texts (Zech 12:10; 4Q540–541; *T. Benj.* 3:8; see above) and knew nothing of a suffering Son of Man. E. Schweizer's observation that Jesus "fits no formula" (*Jesus*, 13) also holds true for the titles "Messiah" and "Son of Man," which can be applied to Jesus only with modification.

5.5 In *Matt 16:13–20*, the Matthean parallel to Mark 8:27–30, Peter's confession is supplemented in two ways. In v. 16 Jesus "the Christ" (ὁ χριστός) is further identified as ὁ υἱὸς τοῦ θεοῦ τοῦ ζῶντος, "the son of the living God" (see below). Verses 17–18 add the famous saying about Peter as the rock from Matthew's special material:

> And Jesus answered him, "Blessed are you, Simon son of Jonah! For flesh and blood has not revealed this to you, but my Father in heaven. And I tell you, you are Peter, and on this rock I will build my church, and the gates of Hades will not prevail against it." (Matt 16:17–18)

These verses can easily be translated back into Aramaic. The formulations have close parallels in the Qumran texts, where we read for example that the Teacher of Righteousness was installed "to found the congregation" (4Q171 [4QpPs^a] III 16; *DSSSE* 1:344–45); similar expressions include "you [God] place the foundation upon rock" (1QH XIV 25–27; *DSSSE* 1:176–77) and the plea "establish for them a rock from of old" (4Q160 frags. 3–5 II 3; *DSSSE* 1:312–13). In this sense Matt 16:18 also resembles Isa 51:1–2, "Look to the rock from which you were hewn. . . . Look to Abraham. . . ." Peter is given the name "Cephas" (from the Aramaic כֵּיפָא, "rock"). He is the foundation stone of Jesus' "church" (ἐκκλησία). The Semitic equivalent for ἐκκλησία is probably קָהָל, "assembly, convocation, congregation," though it could also be עֵדָה, denoting the assembly or "cultic congregation." The saying speaks of the structure of the messianic people of God to which Jesus saw himself called and for which Peter was supposed to play his literally foundational role. After Easter Matt 16:17–19 was applied to the founding of the early church through this "rock man," Cephas (cf. 1 Cor 15:5). The future tense "*I will build* (οἰκοδομήσω) my church" points beyond Jesus' lifetime but does not exceed the bounds of Jesus' own immanent expectation of the future. Linguistically and materially there is no reason to deny Jesus this logion.

6. A complement to Peter's confession is found in Jesus' own confession of himself as Messiah in *Mark 14:61–62 par.* In his judicial hearing before the Sanhedrin, Jesus is asked by Caiaphas the high priest whether he is ὁ χριστὸς ὁ υἱὸς τοῦ εὐλογητοῦ, "the Messiah, the Son of the Blessed One." This Jesus affirms, expanding as follows:

> ἐγώ εἰμι, καὶ ὄψεσθε τὸν υἱὸν τοῦ ἀνθρώπου ἐκ δεξιῶν καθήμενον τῆς δυνάμεως καὶ ἐρχόμενον μετὰ τῶν νεφελῶν τοῦ οὐρανοῦ.
> I am; and "you will see the Son of Man seated at the right hand of the Power" [= God] and "coming with the clouds of heaven." (NRSV)

As the NRSV indicates by its use of quotation marks, Jesus' answer involves literal borrowing from the Old Testament. In his decisive hour before the Jewish authorities Jesus confessed his messianic mission and announced to them that they would soon have to answer to him as the Son of Man and Judge of the World whom God will exalt to his right hand according to Ps 110:1 and who will return with the clouds of heaven according to Dan 7:13. This clear appropriation of divine prerogatives earned Jesus the accusation of blasphemy and ultimately cost him his life.

6.1 Before we investigate Jesus' answer to the Sanhedrin in more detail, we must first assess the *historical value of Mark 14:61–62 par.* This is usually denied today. Hence E. Lohse writes:

> The possibility that the Jewish high priest should have spoken in one breath of the Messiah and the Son of God can be excluded in view of the great restraint that Judaism exercised regarding the title Son of God. On the other hand the formulations of both the high priest's question and Jesus' answer, which combines the two scriptural sayings from Ps 110:1 and Dan 7:13, are completely understandable from the confession of the Christian church. (*Grundriß der neutestamentlichen Theologie* [1989⁴] 45)

H. Conzelmann and A. Lindemann express a very similar opinion about Mark 14:61–62 in their workbook *Interpreting the New Testament*:

> It is clear that this scene is devoid of a historical core, for the presentation of the trial is altogether determined christologically. The question of the high priest presupposes that the designations Messiah and Son of God are ultimately identical—a linguistic usage that is foreign to Judaism. The passage Mk 14:61f. was very obviously drawn up as a compendium of the community's Christology; it is intended to show that all of the messianic titles—Messiah, Son of God, Son of Man—are of equal value. (*Interpreting the New Testament* [ET 1988] 323–24 [translation modified])

On the other hand A. Strobel in his study *Die Stunde der Wahrheit* (1980) emphasizes the conspicuous congruence of Mark 14:61–62 with Jewish formulations. About 14:62 he writes:

> We stand before a tradition that is peculiar to its core. Its content, which is probably largely accurate, is Jesus' own expectation of exaltation, expressed even before the highest court of the Jewish people. At issue here is the historical core of Jesus' expectation and mission. (p. 75)

6.1.1 The following considerations make it necessary to temper the wholesale criticism of Mark 14:61–62: (1) Jesus' public ministry, including his entrance into Jerusalem and his temple cleansing, must have awakened messianic expectations. Therefore the Sanhedrin could indeed have discussed whether and how to hand over Jesus as a pseudo-Messiah. (2) Early Jewish texts like

11Q13 (11QMelch), *1 Enoch* 45–50, 61–64 and *4 Ezra* 13 show that messianic titles were used not exclusively but functionally and *cumulatively* in early Judaism (so already R. Bultmann, *Theology of the New Testament*, 52–53). (3) According to 2 Sam 7:14; Ps 2:7; 89:27 the Davidic Messiah stands over against Yahweh as his "Son." Already from this perspective the accumulation of titles in Mark 14:61–62 appears completely plausible in the context of early Judaism. The publication of the fragments of the Aramaic Daniel Apocalypse 4Q246 (4Q*Aramaic Apocalypse*) has led still further. In the interpretation of a text from Daniel the designations "son of God" (ברה די אל) and "son of the Most High" (בר עליון) occur in parallel in a single line and applied to a single ruler figure with divine claim (4Q246 II 1 = *DSSSE* 1:494). This figure has been identified with the end-time opponent of God (cf. 4Q175 [4Q*Testimonia*] 23–30), but it is even better to relate him to the Son of Man of Dan 7:13. The designations "son of God" (cf. Matt 16:16) and "son of the Most High" and their relationship to the book of Daniel are therefore attested in this original Essene text of the pre-Christian period; people from that time could have used such ideas to expose Jesus as a pseudo-Messiah. (4) From the Talmud it can be seen that well into the third century A.D. the rabbis debated the manner of the Messiah's coming. Without recognizable Christian influence they inquired whether the Messiah would come majestically with the clouds of heaven according to Dan 7:13, or humbly on a donkey according to Zech 9:9:

> R. Alexandri said: R. Joshua opposed two verses: it is written, *And behold, one like the son of man came with the clouds of heaven*; whilst [elsewhere] it is written, [*behold, thy king cometh unto thee . . .*] *lowly, and riding upon an ass!*—If they are meritorious, [he will come] *with the clouds of heaven;* if not, *lowly and riding upon an ass.* (*b. Sanh.* 48a, Soncino)

This text shows that the messianic exegesis of Dan 7:13 was a Jewish interpretive tradition that as such need not bear any specifically Christian stamp. (The two rabbis mentioned were active ca. A.D. 270 and 250, respectively.) (5) Finally *1 En.* 61:8 and 62:2 show that Ps 110:1 was already at home in the early Jewish Son of Man tradition (for the Jesus tradition, cf. Mark 12:35–37 par.).

6.1.2 It follows from the above that *the high priest's question and Jesus's answer in Mark 14:61–62 were completely possible linguistically and conceptually in Jewish tradition before Easter.* Provided that one thinks Jesus and his opponents capable of any messianic reflection at all—which can hardly be doubted in light of the Roman formulation of the title on the cross in Mark 15:26 par.—A. Strobel takes the correct view of Mark 14:61–62 against E. Lohse and H. Conzelmann–A. Lindemann.

6.2 The following interpretation results for Jesus' self-testimony in Mark 14:61–62 par. The Jewish trial against Jesus was above all about the question of the Messiah. Jesus allowed the use of the title Messiah in his circle of disciples, but he did not claim it publicly for himself. He performed messianic signs up to and including his cleansing of the temple, and finally at the insistence of the high priest who questioned him on the night before his execution, *he confessed his messianic mission openly.* This confession then served to incriminate Jesus before Pilate and is the historical basis for the Roman title on the cross. Jesus placed his messianic mission in the light of the Son of Man tradition both with his disciples and before the Sanhedrin.

This result for Jesus' self-testimony in Mark 14:61–62 par. confirms what we learned from Peter's testimony in Mark 8:27–33 par.: *Jesus identified himself in his own independent way with the "coming one" announced by John the Baptist and saw himself as the messianic Son of Man. With this identification he not only reformulated early Jewish expectations of the Davidic Messiah, but also gave decisively new features to the early Jewish picture of the Son of Man.*

7. Familiarity with the Old Testament–Jewish background is also essential for understanding the *Son of Man tradition* in the New Testament.

7.1 The Hebrew and Aramaic equivalents to the Greek expression for the "son of man," ὁ υἱὸς τοῦ ἀνθρώπου, are respectively בֶּן־אָדָם (found 107 times in the Hebrew OT, e.g., Num 23:19) and בַּר אֱנָשׁ (Dan 7:13) or בַּר (אֱ)נָשָׁא. They mean the person as a member of the human race, a human being. The terms בֶּן and בַּר are therefore used to single out a member of this group (K. Koch, *Das Buch Daniel*, 217). Both expressions may be translated as a mortal "person" (= generic "man" in older English usage) or "individual human." This generic usage is common in the Old Testament and is particularly evident in the pairing of "man (human being)" (אֱנוֹשׁ) with the "son of man" (בֶּן־אָדָם) (Job 25:6; Ps 8:5; Isa 51:12; 56:2). We also find an individual expression for a "man" (a male, אִישׁ) paired with a "son of man" (Num 23:19; Job 35:8; Ps 80:17; Jer 49:18, 33; 50:40; 51:43). In the book of Ezekiel "son of man" (NRSV: "mortal") occurs conspicuously 93 times as a designation of the prophet himself (cf. Ezek 2:1, 3, 6, 8; 3:1, 3, 4, 10, 17, 25; 4:1, 16; 5:1; 6:2, etc.). In part of the Old Testament–Jewish tradition, however, the generic "son of man" as a human being grows into a special designation for a person who *represents* others. Hence in Ps 80:18 Israel's king is called the "son of man" (בֶּן־אָדָם). Similarly in Dan 7:13 the בַּר אֱנָשׁ is the representative of the Zion-βασιλεία [['kingdom']]. The scene is as follows: In the vision of the four world kingdoms in Daniel 7, four terrifying beasts first appear to symbolize the sequence of the four kingdoms of Babylon, Media, Persia, and Macedonia (Dan 7:1–8). Verses 9–14 then present the final judgment: the four beasts are deprived of their power and the end-time kingdom of God is established. This is signaled by a new symbolic figure, the "son of man," who stands over against the four beasts:

> I saw one like a son of man [NRSV/NJPS: human being] coming with the clouds of heaven. And he came to the Ancient of Days and was presented

before him. To him was given dominion and glory and kingship, that all peoples, nations, and languages should serve him. His dominion is an everlasting dominion that shall not pass away, and his kingship is one that shall never be destroyed. (Dan 7:13–14)

Comparison of Dan 7:13–14 with 7:27 proves crucial. The son of man's kingship and dominion from 7:14 are given to "the people of the holy ones of the Most High" in 7:27. Therefore, just as Israel's king represents Israel as the son of man in Ps 80:18, so also the son of man in Dan 7:13 is the representative of God's people, Israel. However, "son of man" does not yet function as a divine title in Daniel 7. But Dan 7:13 is also interpreted further in the Similitudes, i.e., chaps. 37–71 of the book of *1 Enoch* (first century B.C. or A.D.). Here the "Son of Man" (also called God's "Elect One" or "Chosen One") is a preexistent *end-time ruler figure* who will exercise judgment in God's name and so will establish salvation and righteousness (*1 En.* 45:3ff.; 46:1ff.; 48:2ff.; 49:1ff.; 61:5–62:16; 71:13ff.). This salvation is described among other things as eternal table fellowship of the righteous and chosen ones with the Son of Man: "The Lord of the Spirits will abide over them; they shall eat and rest and rise with that Son of Man forever and ever" (*1 En.* 62:14). In the book of *1 Enoch*, Enoch, the God-pleasing descendant in the seventh generation from Adam (cf. Gen 5:22–24; Sir 44:16; 49:14; Jude 1:14), is taken up to heaven and installed in the "office" of the preexistent Son of Man (cf. *1 En.* 71:5–17 and cf. *OTP* 1:50 note "*s*" on the language of *1 En.* 71:14). Moreover, the Son of Man is identified with the Messiah (e.g., *1 En.* 48:10) and God's Chosen One (i.e., the Servant). Yet hints of the *suffering* of this Son of Man are completely absent in *1 Enoch*, as in Daniel 7. John the Baptist's announcement concerning the coming "stronger one," the Son of Man and Judge of the World, similarly makes no suggestion about his suffering.

7.2 *The Son of Man tradition in the New Testament is almost completely concentrated in the four Gospels* (82 occurrences), *where the expression occurs only in the sayings of Jesus.* The expression does occur four times in the New Testament outside the Gospels, yet three of these borrow from the Old Testament: Heb 2:6 cites Ps 8:5–7 while Rev 1:13 and 14:14 allude to Dan 7:13. Only in Acts 7:56 is there an independent post-Easter logion: Stephen see the heavens opened and the Son of Man standing at the right hand of God (cf. Dan 7:13 and Ps 110:1). The fact that we have only this single independently formulated post-Easter Son of Man logion contradicts the assumption that "Son of Man" is a divine title applied to Jesus only after Easter. It is much more likely that the Gospel tradition has preserved a historical fact: *The title "Son of Man" was characteristic of the proclamation and teaching of Jesus, and for this very reason it seems very rarely to have been used independently after Easter.*

7.3 It has long been customary to divide the many synoptic Son of Man passages (69 occurrences) into three groups: sayings about *the present ministering, the suffering,* and *the coming Son of Man.*

7.3.1 The sayings about the *presently ministering Son of Man* occur in the following passages: Mark 2:10, 28 par.; Luke 9:58/Matt 8:20; Luke 7:34/Matt 11:19 and Luke 12:10/Matt 12:32. On earth the Son of Man has authority to forgive sins, is Lord of the Sabbath, has no place to lay his head, eats and drinks with tax collectors and sinners, and forgives those who speak a word against him.

According to the shared opinion of R. Bultmann (*Theology of the New Testament*, 30), J. Jeremias (*New Testament Theology*, 261–62) and C. Colpe (*TDNT* 8:430–32) these sayings are indebted to the translation (or mistranslation, according to Bultmann) of the originally generic sense of בַּר (אֱ)נָשָׁא as a human being into Greek, where the designation ὁ υἱὸς τοῦ ἀνθρώπου [['son of man']] was supposedly misunderstood as a christological title. The Christology of the Greek-speaking church possibly (Jeremias and Colpe) or certainly (Bultmann) stood behind this (mis)translation. But historical investigation shows that even these apparently non-christological statements about Jesus' present ministry as the Son of Man were characteristic of his messianic self-understanding. They include for example the statements, "For John came neither eating nor drinking, and they say, 'He has a demon'; the Son of Man came eating and drinking, and they say, 'Look, a man who is a glutton and a drunkard (ἄνθρωπος φάγος καὶ οἰνοπότης)'" (Matt 11:18–19/Luke 7:33–34) and "Foxes have holes, and birds of the air have nests; but the Son of Man has nowhere to lay his head" (Matt 8:20/Luke 9:58). This vivid third-person reference to the "human being" or "son of man" corresponds to the parabolic language of prophets (cf., e.g., Ezek 33:1–9; Jer 3:1–5; 8:4–7; 2 Cor 12:2–5). We are therefore faced with riddles of Jesus, which force readers and listeners to ask and answer for themselves who the "man" or human being in these sayings actually is.

As E. Schweizer showed long ago (*The Good News according to Mark* [ET 1970] 166–71), the sayings about the presently ministering Son of Man are characteristic of Jesus' self-understanding to the extent that one may compare them to the Old Testament language of the prophet Ezekiel as "son of man." From this perspective Jesus' words show that he understood himself as the "man" singled out by God from among people as their comrade and representative. As such people called him a "glutton" and "drunkard," and during his public ministry he was less well housed than foxes and birds. But when Jesus designated himself as the (son of) "man" who heals and forgives sins by God's authority (Mark 2:10 par.) and is Lord of the Sabbath (Mark 2:28 par.), this points beyond the usage in Ezekiel: *the "man" who acts this way is not only the true human before God but also at the same time God's representative among people.*

One cannot obscure this double dimension of the son of man language by a linguistic theory of mistranslation of בַּר (אֱ)נָשָׁא into Greek. Compared with the Baptist's announcement of the coming "stronger one," Jesus' language appears as new and extraordinary: in Jesus, the true human, the coming "stronger one" (and through him the only true God) is already on the scene.

7.3.2 The sayings about the *suffering Son of Man* lead a decisive step further. They are found in the three synoptic passion predictions (Mark 8:31 par.; 9:31 par.; 10:33–34 par.) and in the ransom saying of Mark 10:45 par.

7.3.2.1 The three *passion predictions* have the literary function (especially in Mark) of preparing readers for Jesus' passion. They are "passion summaries" before the passion story (Mark 11:1–16:8) and are therefore usually judged as *vaticinia ex eventu*, put into Jesus' mouth after the fact. But here too we must be careful about jumping to conclusions. J. Jeremias has shown that at least one authentic riddle of Jesus lies behind these summaries (*New Testament Theology*, 281–82, 295–97): "God will (soon) deliver the man to men" (Mark 9:31; cf. with Luke 9:44). The logion contains an Aramaic wordplay and is formulated with an echo of Isa 43:4 and 53:12. Isa 43:3–5 contains the following saving promise of God to Israel:

> I am the LORD your God, the Holy One of Israel, your Savior. I give Egypt as your ransom, Ethiopia and Seba in exchange for you. Because you are precious in my sight, and honored, and I love you, I give people in return for you, nations in exchange for your life. Do not fear, for I am with you.

Moreover, in Isa 53:11–12 it says about the Suffering Servant:

> Out of his anguish he shall see light; he shall find satisfaction through his knowledge. The righteous one, my servant, shall make many righteous, and he shall bear their iniquities. Therefore I will allot him a portion with the great, and he shall divide the spoil with the strong; because he poured out himself to death, and was numbered with the transgressors; yet he bore the sin of many, and made intercession for the transgressors (LXX: and he was delivered up for their sins).

If one reads Mark 9:31 (Luke 9:44b) in the light of these two passages, Jesus appears as *the (Son of) Man whom God in his love delivers for Israel, in order to save his own people*. Or put differently: *Jesus (even as the Son of Man) is the vicariously suffering Servant for Israel*. Romans 4:25, with its clear allusion to Isa 53:12, shows that this logion of Jesus was in fact understood in this way.

7.3.2.2 The ransom saying in *Mark 10:45/Matt 20:28* leads to the same conclusion. Its origin with Jesus is hotly debated, and it is usually considered a creation of the church. But once again precise exegesis of the text leads to the opposite result.

In 1 Tim 2:5–6 the original ransom saying has been incorporated into an early Christian confessional formula and reworked linguistically for the better understanding of the Greek-speaking church. Hence the original "son of man" (ὁ υἱὸς τοῦ ἀνθρώπου) becomes simply "the man (Christ Jesus)," ἄνθρωπος Χριστὸς Ἰησοῦς; "to give his life" (δοῦναι τὴν ψυχὴν αὐτους) becomes simply "to give himself" (δοῦναι ἑαυτόν), while λύτρον ἀντὶ πολλῶν becomes ἀντίλυτρον ὑπὲρ πάντων (these last two hardly differ in English translation, outside the obvious variation of "many" and "all"). Mark 10:45 (Matt 20:28) is obviously a tradition from which early Christianity took its christological bearings.

The basic synoptic form of the logion is found in Mark 10:45/Matt 20:28. It is easy to translate back into Aramaic. (Luke 22:24–27 contains a variant tradition to Mark 10:42–45. It is redactionally fitted to the situation of Jesus' farewell discourse at the Last Supper and reflects terminologically the developed practice of the church. Compare the expressions of Luke 22:26–27 with the "younger men" or the "humble" of Acts 5:6; 1 Tim 5:1; Tit 2:6; 1 Pet 5:5 and Sir 32:1; with the "elders" and other "leaders" of Acts 14:12; 15:22; Heb 13:7, 17, 24; and with the idea of "serving" in Acts 6:1–2; 19:22; 1 Tim 3:10, 13.) The ransom saying moreover stands in marked contrast to the picture of the ruling and judging son of man in Dan 7:13–14, the Similitudes of *1 Enoch*, and the preaching of John the Baptist: instead of sitting on God's judgment throne, executing final judgment with the help of angels, and receiving the homage of the nations, this "Son of Man" sees himself sent by God to serve humanity and to be for them the λύτρον ἀντὶ πολλῶν or "ransom for many." In the background of the ransom text stand expressions not only from Isa 53:11–12 such as "the many" (οἱ πολλοί) and "to give one's life" (Mark's δοῦναι τὴν ψυχὴν αὐτοῦ, "to give his life," recalls Isaiah's παρεδόθη εἰς θάνατον ἡ ψυχὴ αὐτοῦ, "his life was given over to death"), but also and above all from Isa 43:3–4 (W. Grimm). For only in Isa 43:3–4 (and not in Isaiah 53) is there talk of a "ransom" (כֹּפֶר; LXX: ἄλλαγμα) which God gives "in your place" (תַּחְתֶּיךָ; LXX: ὑπὲρ σοῦ) and which moreover consists of other "people" (אָדָם sg.; LXX: ἀνθρώπου). Mark 10:45 with its expression λύτρον ἀντὶ πολλῶν, which is formulated independently of the Septuagint (cf. ἄλλαγμα, ὑπερ), as well as its idea of the Son of Man taking the place of other people corresponds more closely to the wording of Isa 43:3–4 than of Isa 53:11–12.

In its present form the ransom saying of Mark 10:45 (Matt 20:28) is not derivable either from early Jewish tradition, which has no knowledge of a suffering Son of Man, or from early church tradition, which rather built its confession in 1 Tim 2:5–6 upon the ransom saying. We are dealing with a *"non-derivable" or "dissimilar" saying* in the strict methodological sense of the word and therefore with an *original Jesus saying.*

The traditions of the second passion prediction in Mark 9:31 (Luke 9:44b) and the ransom saying in Mark 10:45 speak for themselves: both times the divine Son of Man tradition is reinterpreted in terms of a theology of suffering, with Isa 43:3–5 and 53:11–12 providing the leitmotifs. The possibility of a connection between the Son of Man and Servant traditions was already anticipated in *1 En.* 46:4; 62:3, but only in the Jesus tradition are the suffering features of the Servant brought into the Son of Man tradition. *During his earthly ministry Jesus wanted to be the God-sent messianic Servant by exchanging his existence for that of "the many," both Israel and the nations.*

7.3.3 The third group of synoptic passages consists of Jesus' sayings about the *coming Son of Man*. These include the need of believers not to be ashamed of the Son of Man in Mark 8:38/Luke 9:26 (cf. with Matt 10:32–33/Luke 12:8–9), the parable of the final judgment separating the sheep from the

goats in Matt 25:31–46, the already analyzed answer of Jesus before the Sanhedrin in Mark 14:62 par., the desire of the Son of Man to find faith on the
earth at his second coming in Luke 18:8, and the debate about David's Son or
David's Lord in Psalm 110 found in Mark 12:35–37 par.

Positions concerning this group of Son of Man sayings tend to fall into
one of three schemes: (1) The first position holds that these cannot be authentic Jesus sayings because the immediacy with which Jesus speaks of the
kingdom of God which dawns and comes with him leaves no room for him to
interject between himself and the βασιλεία [['kingdom']] yet another figure,
the coming Son of Man. This argumentation, adopted for example by P. Vielhauer and E. Käsemann, fails to recognize that in early Judaism the Son of
Man is not a competing figure to God but the messianic emissary of God. It
also fails to consider that according to Dan 7:13–14, 27 the end-time kingdom of God which is to be given the "holy ones of the Most High" is represented by the Son of Man himself. This first scheme therefore involves a
historically unconvincing modern critical construction. (2) Ever since J. Wellhausen and R. Bultmann, scholars in the second group have attributed several of the sayings about the coming Son of Man to the preaching of Jesus,
but have claimed that, like John the Baptist, Jesus expected the heavenly Son
of Man to be a judge figure differentiated from himself. But in view of the
analysis of the Jesus sayings about the presently ministering and the suffering
Son of Man, as well as the analysis of Jesus' self-testimony in Mark 14:62 par.,
this view is not very probable. Jesus' style of dividing the references to himself between the first and third person is already anticipated in prophetic
language about God (cf. Amos 5:4–12 and K. Berger, *Theologiegeschichte*, 2nd
ed., 665). Such variation is evident in Luke 12:8–9 (cf. with Mark 8:38): "And
I tell you, everyone who acknowledges me before others, the Son of Man also
will acknowledge before the angels of God; but whoever denies me before
others will be denied before the angels of God." The point of this passage is
precisely not that Jesus and the coming Son of Man are different, but that
they belong together. (3) The third scheme focuses precisely here and is represented for example by C. Colpe, L. Goppelt, J. Jeremias, and W. G. Kümmel. It assumes that *the earthly Jesus aligned himself in a considerably close
relationship to the coming Son of Man*, and it most fully does justice to the texts
under consideration.

In the *parable of the Growing Seed (Mark 4:26–29)* the present and future
ministry of Jesus as the Son of Man are connected exactly as in the third
scheme above. The parable speaks of the miracle of the seed of the word (of
Jesus) that ripens for the harvest by itself from inauspicious beginnings:

> He also said, "The kingdom of God is as if a 'man' [ἄνθρωπος: see below]
> would scatter seed on the ground, and would sleep and rise night and
> day, and the seed would sprout and grow, he does not know how. The
> earth produces of itself [αὐτομάτη], first the stalk, then the head, then the
> full grain in the head. But when the 'fruit' [καρπός, NRSV: grain] is ripe, at
> once he goes in with his sickle, because the harvest has come [cf. Joel
> 4:13]." (Mark 4:26–29)

Two motifs of the parable immediately stand out: (1) The carefree attitude concerning the growth of the seed, which is strange and almost ironic for a careful farmer (cf. Isa 28:23–26). (2) The identity of the sower and the reaper, who according to Joel 4:13 "puts in the sickle" (Mark 4:29). However, one should not separate v. 29 from the original text of the parable as a later allegorizing addition, as is sometimes suggested, for there is no support for this in the manuscript tradition. Moreover, the quotation of Joel 4:13 (ET 3:13) in Mark 4:29 is not based strictly on the Septuagint text. Against the Septuagint's plural δρέπανα Mark reads the singular δρέπανον, "sickle," following the MT and *Targum Jonathan*. Mark also reads θερισμός, "(grain) harvest" instead of the Septuagint's τρύγητος, "vintage." The parable's metaphors involve double entendre: "harvest" is a common metaphor for the final judgment (cf. Jer 51:33; Rev 14:15); "seed" is likewise common for the proclamation of the word (*4 Ezra* 8:6; 9:31, 36; cf. also Philo, *Somn.* 1.199; *Spec. leg.* 3.29 and the interpretation of the sowing in Isa 28:24 in terms of the prophetic proclamation and its reception in *The Isaiah Targum* [ed. B. D. Chilton, p. 56]). In an early Jewish context the language of "automatic" growth carries the connotation of the miraculous activity of God. For example, the αὐτόματα ἀναβαίνοντα or "spontaneous aftergrowths" in Lev 25:5, 11 are the plants that spring up of themselves without human effort during the years of Sabbath and Jubilee. Philo (*Opif. mund.* 167) and Josephus (*Ant.* 1.46) use the same word for the fruit available without labor to people in paradise. "Fruit" is a common picture for the produce of piety and obedience (cf., e.g., *Ep. Arist.* 232), while "when the fruit/grain is ripe" is a circumlocution for the date of the judgment set by God in his own time. Although the parable is not a full-blown allegory, its meaning depends upon its vivid language. The "man" (ἄνθρωπος) who sows can do his work in calm assurance because he is confident that growth and harvest are miraculously produced by God. The obvious question for Jesus' Jewish listeners confronted with such a metaphorical presentation heightened by the citation from Joel would be, Who is this ἄνθρωπος who so confidently goes about his work of sowing and puts in his sickle at the right time? The answer is found in the proclamation of Jesus: It is Jesus himself; he is the "man" who now proclaims and teaches the word but some day will judge the world; he is the presently working Son of Man of Dan 7:13 und *1 Enoch*. Finally, in Rev 14:14–16 the sickle and reaping of Joel 4:13 are combined with the one like a Son of Man seated on the cloud from Dan 7:13 (though Revelation cites both passages according to the original Hebrew or Aramaic rather than the LXX). The book of Revelation therefore confirms our proposed understanding of Mark 4:26–29: *The parable of the Growing Seed exhibits exactly the same mysterious connection between the "man" Jesus and the coming Son of Man and Judge of the World that is also characteristic of Mark 8:38 par., where the coming Son of Man will be ashamed in the judgment of those who have been ashamed of Jesus, and Luke 12:8 par., where the Son of Man will confess in the judgment those who have confessed Jesus.*

Jesus considered himself to be the Son of Man who serves and works secretly on earth, who will be exalted by God and appear at the world judgment. The verbs used reciprocally in Luke 12:8–9 and Mark 8:38, "confess," "deny," and "be ashamed of," point to the situation of the final judgment: the Son of Man, whom God will exalt to his right hand and entrust with the final judgment, will speak out as the eschatological judge on behalf of those who were faithful to him while he still worked secretly on earth. On the other hand he will reject those who denied or opposed him on earth. From this developed the early Christian expectation of the exalted Christ's intercession and advocacy for those who belong to him (cf. Rom 8:34; Heb 7:25; 9:24; 1 John 2:1–2).

Jesus' expectation of his own exaltation is attested not only by his self-testimony in Mark 14:61–62 par. (see above) but also in the debate about David's Son and David's Lord in the *controversy of Mark 12:35–37 par.* This passage deals with an exegetical antinomy: according to early Jewish expectation the Messiah is the Son of David, but in Ps 110:1 (LXX Ps 109:1) the psalmist, whom early Judaism identified with David, speaks of the coming Messiah as ὁ κύριός μου, i.e., David's Lord. How are these two related? The answer suggested by our text is that even though Jesus lived on earth as the serving Son of David, David's coming Lord is superior to the earthly Son of David. The one seated at the right hand of God in Psalm 110, to whom everything is subjected, must be identified with the "son of man" of Psalm 8, to whom God has likewise subjected everything: "you have subjected all things under his feet," πάντα ὑπέταξας ὑποκάτω τῶν ποδῶν αὐτοῦ (Ps 8:7 [ET 8:6]; cf. 1 Cor 15:27; Heb 2:8). In fact in the quotation of LXX Ps 109:1 in Mark 12:36 the last words of Ps 109:1, ὑποπόδιον τῶν ποδῶν σου, "a *footstool* for your feet," are replaced by ὑποκάτω τῶν ποδῶν σου, "*under* your feet," from Ps 8:7. This linking means that Ps 110 (LXX 109):1 has been interpreted from Ps 8:7 according to the rabbinic principle of analogy and therefore refers to the Son of Man. The controversy of Mark 12:35–37 testifies to both Jesus' consciousness of his messianic mission and his expectation of his exaltation; it also provides the perspective for the Jewish-Christian formula about the (earthly) Son of David and the (exalted) Son of God that Paul cites in Rom 1:3–4.

Jesus' sayings about the coming Son of Man therefore show that he lived in the expectation that after his earthly ministry, he would be exalted to the right hand of God according to Ps 110:1 and become the judge in the end times. Just as Jesus' task on earth was to proclaim the kingdom of God and to "serve the many" by vicariously surrendering his life, so his end-time "office" will be to establish God's kingdom through the final judgment. Paul connects directly with this tradition in 1 Cor 15:23–28.

8. If we consider all this together with Jesus' parable about the great world judgment in Matt 25:31–46 and our analyses of Peter's confession in Mark 8:27–33 par. and of Jesus' self-testimony in 14:61–62 par., the end result is clear: Jesus identified himself in a truly novel way with the Son of Man and Judge of the World announced by John the Baptist. He accepted the title "Messiah" in the circle of his disciples, but he wanted to live his earthly life in humility as the Suffering Servant of God by sacrificing himself for "the many" (cf. Isa 43:3–4; 53:11–12). Finally, Jesus openly confessed his messianic mission before his Jewish judges and expressed his expectation that he would be exalted

to the right hand of God according to Ps 110:1 and installed in the end-time office of the Son of Man to execute the final judgment "coming with the clouds of heaven" (Dan 7:13). *As the messianic Son of Man, Jesus combined in himself the being of the true human before God, of the Suffering Servant, and of the Son of God who truly accepts people.* He represented humanity to God in his obedience as the Son and his obedience to suffering, and he represented God to humanity as messianic evangelist to the poor, as completer of the Torah of Sinai, and as self-sacrificing Servant. Jesus was in one and the same person the true "human" or "(son of) man" who lives in the fear of God (Ps 8:5–6 [ET vv. 4–5]) and the messianic "Immanuel" (Isa 7:14).

One final point may be added: Before Easter Jesus' messianic consciousness of deity was shrouded by a *threefold veil of secrecy*: First, Jesus remained a controversial figure throughout his public ministry (cf. Mark 3:21–22; 6:1–6; Luke 7:33–34/Matt 11:18–19; Luke 13:31–33; 13:34/Matt 23:37; Mark 14:61–62 par.). Secondly, Jesus spoke about his special mission mainly in riddles, parables, and internal teachings among his disciples, which were met with reservations and lack of understanding even there (cf. Mark 8:32–33 par.; 9:9–10 par.; 9:32 par.; Luke 22:31–34). Finally, the new setting that Jesus gave to the titles Messiah and Son of Man from the perspective of Isa 43:3–4 and 53:11–12 was so unusual, and the fact of his execution on the cross against the background of Deut 21:22–23 so shocking, that an understanding of Jesus' true historical being could only be established from the perspective of the Easter events, in the circle of those who remembered Jesus' teaching and believed him to be the Lord and Messiah (Acts 2:36), raised by God and exalted to his right hand according to Ps 110:1 (Acts 2:33).

Part 5

Jesus: Major Events

Introduction

SCOT McKNIGHT

Recent historiography, especially of a postmodern flavor, has pointed to the difficult but unavoidable conviction that "what we make" of someone's life, a biography, is just as much "interpretation" as it is "description" at an objective level. If the postmodernist historian contends that this "linguistic turn" goes all the way down, even to the point that historical description of Jesus is nothing but interpretation, more moderate voices contend that the early Christians did "remember" Jesus and that this memory correlates not only with what the early Christians believed about Jesus but also with what Jesus said and did (McKnight 2005). But, as one of the editors of this volume reminds us (Dunn 2003; 2005), there never was a time when there was not Jesus of faith. In other words, the "memory" of Jesus was itself a "linguistic turn" as well.

Even if the Jesus now embedded deeply in the Gospels is the "remembered Jesus," that memory was solid when it came to major events in the life of Jesus. Shelving for the moment a discussion of which events are to be enlisted as major, one can affirm that Jesus' reputation as a miracle worker, his provocative action of practicing table fellowship with the wrong sorts, his action in the temple, his death, and his resurrection are events that must be dealt with thoroughly if one is to understand who Jesus was and what his mission of the kingdom meant. For this section, we have focused on the miracles and on the events of the last week.

Miracles have played an enormous role in Christian apologetics, but that role shifted in the days of Spinoza, Thomas Hobbes, John Locke, and the Deists from a confirmative to a defensive stance. The orthodox have dug in their heels, while the skeptical turn of mind has had more than its fair share of volleys, and all of this has been neatly described by Colin Brown (1984) and recently summed up by J. P. Meier (1994) and set in ancient context by Howard Clark Kee (1983). There seems to a general consensus today that Jesus did things that were otherwise inexplicable.

While the apologists and skeptics argued, a very fine analysis has been taking place in which the miracles of Jesus have been studied from every angle to discover the various "forms" that were "used" by early Christians to tell stories about Jesus. The first major form-critical analysis was that of Rudolf Bultmann, in his *History of the Synoptic Tradition*, but even Bultmann's analytical method would be impressed with the analyses of Gerd Theissen. Theissen isolates 33 "motifs," 6 "themes," and then examines the permutations of motifs and themes. Only then does he subject the miracle stories to a study about historical intention. In historical Jesus studies, form analysis usually precedes historical description.

The last week of Jesus begins with what some call the "temple tantrum" of Jesus. E. P. Sanders, whose work on Judaism and Paul established an entirely new day for our historical understanding of the relationship between Jesus, Paul, and Judaism (1977), argued convincingly that historical Jesus scholarship will never come to anything approaching a consensus on the sayings of Jesus, so the place to begin is with incontestable events and facts in the life of Jesus that shed light on his mission and intention. Arguing that, where there is "smoke" there must have been some "fire," Sanders contends that one must connect the events from the death of Jesus back to the temple incident, though he also argues that using the term "cleansing" for interpreting this event is a "linguistic turn" without historical warrant. Sanders's view has been hotly contested, but what Jesus did Sanders has also done: he has himself turned over tables and raised the rafters (1985).

If Sanders connects the events of Jesus from the temple incident to his death, then others have asked, *pace* Sanders, if any of Jesus' sayings and teachings also shed light on how he understood his death. It must be said that if Jesus was the scripture prophet everyone thinks he is, and if he undoubtedly came to the conviction that he would die prematurely, it is altogether reasonable to think that Jesus must have "interpreted" his death by appealing to Scripture (McKnight 2005). A significant segment of scholarship contends that the way to understand Jesus and his death is to examine the various "titles" Jesus used to understand both himself and his mission, in particular, titles that are connected to death and vindication. German scholarship of a conservative stripe has pursued the question relentlessly through the themes of Messiah, Son of Man, and Servant, and none represents this field better than Peter Stuhlmacher and his study of how Jesus understood his death.

The resurrection of Jesus, in part because it is both so profoundly central to early Christian preaching (see 1 Corinthians 15) and in part because it is so contrary to the empirical, has become once again a significant discussion (Wright 2004; Allison 2005). An older study (a study by C. E. B. Cranfield and representing a more traditional argument) and a newer study (by G. Luedemann and representing what can only be called a modernist and skeptical study) offers to readers two views of whether or not Jesus was in fact raised from the dead. Both drive the reader to come to a conclusion whether or not the early Christians were proclaiming the truth or telling a lie, and it really cannot be reduced to anything else.

Bibliography

Allison, D.
>   2005   *Resurrecting Jesus: The Earliest Christian Tradition and Its Interpreters.*
>   London: T. & T. Clark.

Brown, C.
>   1984   *Miracles and the Critical Mind.* Grand Rapids: Eerdmans.

Bultmann, R.
>   1963   *History of the Synoptic Tradition,* trans. J. Marsh. Revised ed. New York:
>   Harper & Row.

Dunn, J. D. G.
>   2003   *Jesus Remembered.* Christianity in the Making 1. Grand Rapids: Eerd-
>   mans.
>   2005   *A New Perspective on Jesus: What the Quest for the Historical Jesus Missed.*
>   Acadia Studies in Bible and Theology. Grand Rapids: Baker.

Kee, H. C.
>   1983   *Miracle in the Early Christian World: A Study in Sociohistorical Method.*
>   New Haven, Connecticut: Yale.

McKnight, S.
>   2005   *Jesus and His Death: Historiography, the Historical Jesus, and Atonement
>   Theory.* Waco, Texas: Baylor University Press.

Meier, J. P.
>   1994   *Mentor, Message, and Miracles?* Volume 2 of *A Marginal Jew: Rethink-
>   ing the Historical Jesus.* Anchor Bible Reference Library. New York:
>   Doubleday.

Sanders, E. P.
>   1977   *Paul and Palestinian Judaism: A Comparison of Patterns of Religion.*
>   Philadelphia: Fortress.
>   1983   *Jesus and Judaism.* Philadelphia: Fortress.

Wright, N. T.
>   2003   *The Resurrection of the Son of God.* Christian Origins and the Question
>   of God 3. Minneapolis: Fortress.

GERD THEISSEN

The Historical Intention of Primitive Christian Miracle Stories

[[276]] The primitive Christian miracle stories regard themselves as testimonies to a unique event in the past. They have a "historical" intention.[1] They are aware of the uniqueness of the miracles they recount. The narrators know that where all doctors not only have failed (this is a familiar trope), but have even done harm, Jesus heals. The uniqueness of the miracles is claimed when the crowd [[277]] shouts in acclamation, "We have never seen anything like this" (Mark 2:12; cf. Matt 9:33). The Fourth Gospel insists, "From eternity it has been unheard of that anyone should open the eyes of a blind man" (9:32). It makes Jesus speak of his miracles as feats "which no-one else does" (15:24; cf. 3:2). The intensification of the miracles in the course of their transmission could also be connected with this sense of uniqueness, as could the development of analogies and comparisons with non-Christian miracle stories. In John 5:1ff. the contrast implied with ancient healing shrines is unmistakable.[2] John 2:1ff. is probably trying to outdo other wine miracles.[3] Luke 7:11ff. could be modelled on similar ancient miracle stories (*vita Apoll.* 4.45; Apuleius, *flor.* 19). The stories of liberation from prison in Acts (12:3ff.; 16:22ff.) may be setting out to rival similar liberation miracles in Dionysus traditions.[4] In order to do full justice to this sense of being something unique as regards miracles, primitive Christianity had to tell new miracle stories, elaborate old ones and outdo any rivals. The stories which may perhaps be

Reprinted, with permission, from Gerd Theissen, *The Miracle Stories of the Early Christian Tradition* (trans. F. McDonagh; ed. J. Riches; Edinburgh: T. & T. Clark, 1983) 276–86 and portions of (bibliography) 303–15.

1. As J. Roloff, *Kerygma*, 111ff., has rightly emphasised, though one may disagree with the detail of his argument.

2. K. H. Rengstorf, *Die Anfänge der Auseinandersetzung zwischen Christusglaube und Asklepiosfrömmigkeit*, 1953. I was unable to obtain A. Duprez, "Jésus et les Deux Guérisseurs. A Propos de Jean V," 1970.

3. For critical comments on this, H. Noetzel, *Christus und Dionysos*, 1960.

4. O. Weinreich, "Türöffnung," 309–41.

regarded as attempts to outdo rivals only appear in the later tradition, but all these developments show a sense of the uniqueness of Jesus' miracles.[5] Only retrospective study can relativise this uniqueness by setting them within a larger historical context, and this relativistic approach is in the sharpest possible conflict with the historical intention of the miracle stories. They set out to be evidence of an absolutely valid revelation. Although historical study can in no sense either legitimate or establish this claim, it must nonetheless take note of it as a datum present in the texts. It can do more: it can allow it relative legitimacy. The primitive Christian miracle stories stand out from their historical context as something new, unique and individual. This newness can in no sense substantiate their claim, but it makes it intelligible. This new element must be examined first in Jesus and then in primitive Christianity.

Jesus' Miracles

There is no doubt that Jesus worked miracles, healed the sick and cast out demons, but the miracle stories reproduce these historical events in an intensified form. However, this enhancement of the historical and factual begins with Jesus himself. For Jesus too the [[278]] miracles were not normal events, but elements in a mythical drama: in them the miraculous transformation of the whole world into the βασιλεία θεοῦ [['kingdom of God']] was being carried out. As an apocalyptic charismatic miracle-worker, Jesus is unique in religious history.[6] He combines two conceptual worlds which had never been combined in this way before, the apocalyptic expectation of universal salvation in the future and the episodic realisation of salvation in the present through miracles. This thesis has both an historical aspect relating to the development of religious traditions and a substantive one.

The historical aspect presupposes that before Jesus there was no comparable combination of apocalyptic and the charism of miracle-working. Of course there are miracles in apocalyptic texts and contexts, but they are different in character.

(1) The book of Daniel contains a combination of two different traditions.[7] The legends of the miraculous rescues in the first part are not apocalyptic, and the visions in the second part contain no miracles which take place in the present. This combination of miraculous rescues and apocalyptic visions must naturally be taken seriously as a combination, but in contrast to primitive Christianity we find no charismatic miracle workers active on earth. The miracles are always performed by God.

5. For a different view, W. Schmithals, *Wunder und Glaube*, 13: "They claim neither originality nor uniqueness."

6. The eschatological view of miracles is generally and rightly held to be a peculiarity of Jesus' preaching. See R. M. Grant, *Miracles and Natural Law*, 172; R. and M. Hengel, "Heilungen," 352; R. Pesch, *Taten*, 151ff.; H. Baltensweiler, "Wunder und Glaube im NT," *ThZ* 23 (1967) 241–56; R. H. Fuller, *Miracles*, 44ff. Cf. also W. Grundmann, *Kraft*, 65–68; A. Oepke, *TWNT* 3.213; G. Delling, "Das Verständnis des Wunders im Neuen Testament," *Studien zum NT und zum hellenistischen Judentum*, 1970, 146–59; A. Richardson, *Miracle Stories*, 54.

7. O. Plöger, *Theokratie und Eschatologie*, 1959, 18ff.

(2) In Qumran exorcisms were performed. Abraham and Daniel were regarded as exorcists (*Genesis Apocryphon* XX 16–32; *Prayer of Nabonidus*). This, however, is an art of exorcism and healing based on ancient traditions (cf. Jos. *J. W.* 2.134–36; *Jub.* 10:12f.). There is no intrinsic connection between the future end of the world and the miracles in the present.

(3) Finally we must look again at the messianic prophets active at the same time as Jesus.[8] With them too there were no miracles in the present as initial realisations of the future transition. In addition their view of the future change was different from Jesus." The messianic prophets expected an Israel freed from foreign rule; Jesus and the genuine apocalyptics looked for a cosmic reversal. [[279]] On the other hand, these two tendencies in Judaism, the particularist and the universalist, are much less distinct than is frequently assumed.

Even before Jesus, then, there were various combinations of apocalyptic ideas with miracles, but they were miracles performed by God, traditions of exorcism or miracles announced but not brought about. The elements were there. Jesus combined them in a new way. Nowhere else do we find miracles performed by an earthly charismatic which purport to be the end of the old world and the beginning of a new one.

At the same time, however, the combination of the charism of miracles with apocalyptic creates a substantive problem. Apocalyptic pessimism, as shown in the assumption that the whole universe is in the grip of evil, is in conflict with the hope of a salvation brought about here and there by individual miracles. It is not that the present history is empty of promise in apocalyptic, but that the promise is tied to a fulfilment of the divine will which confers an entitlement to future salvation.[9] Only because apocalyptic and miracles in Jesus' work modify each other can they form a genuine combination: Jesus gives future expectation a root in the present and his miracles become signs of a universal change.[10] This understanding of Jesus' miracles appears only in the sayings-tradition.

The statements of present eschatology are clearest in dualistic contexts. Satan has fallen from heaven (Luke 10:18); his kingdom is disintegrating (Mark 3:24–26), his house being plundered (3:27). The casting out of demons is the first sign of the arrival of the rule of God (Matt 12:28). The end of the negative has already come; the web of evil around this passing world has already been torn. That is why there are no apocalyptic speculations about this web of evil, its duration and its stages. And yet the full establishment of the positive is still to come.

Similarly, the starting point for an eschatological interpretation of the miracles is the exorcisms—that is, miracles with a pronounced dualistic, conflictual character. All four dualistic and present-centred statements appear in

---

8. R. M. Grant, *Miracles and Natural Law*, 166f., here gives insufficient emphasis to the difference from the miracles of Jesus.

9. W. Harnisch, *Verhängnis und Verheissung der Geschichte*, 1969.

10. R. Otto, *Kingdom of God*, 53f., 117f., has drawn attention to this connection.

the context of exorcism. Because Jesus casts out demons he can proclaim that the end has entered into the present. There is a close connection between present eschatology and the eschatological interpretation of the miracles. Apocalyptic and miracles have modified each other. [[280]] Because the negative web of evil has already been broken it is possible for salvation to come in individual instances. Because individual instances of salvation occur, the presence of the end can be proclaimed here and now.[11] Even the Qumran texts provide no parallel for this combination of present and future eschatology.

In a fine study,[12] H. W. Kuhn has shown that present and future eschatology were combined in Qumran, the present deriving from a spiritualised liturgical tradition, the future from an apocalyptic and dualistic tradition. Entry into the community's cultic saving area meant salvation in the present, the expectation of the eschatological battle between God and Belial future salvation. The following differences from Jesus' eschatology should be stressed:

(1) In Qumran the two "eschatologies" coexist without connection. Where God battles with Belial there is no present eschatology. Conversely, "the community songs, whose interweaving of future and present we have examined, never use the dualism of God and devil."[13] In Matt 12:28, however, present eschatology and the dualism of God and Satan's kingdom are coherently combined in a single saying.

(2) In the case of Jesus the dualistic sayings themselves are evidence of present eschatology: the power of Satan is already broken. The references to the Temple, on the other hand, belong to future eschatology. In Qumran it is the exact opposite.

(3) For Jesus the end which has aready come is given a cosmic interpretation: demonic and satanic powers give way. In Qumran present eschatology rests on an individual act, entry into the community.

The combination of eschatology and miracle in Jesus' activity is distinctive. This combination is no less characteristic than that of eschatology and wisdom. Jesus sees his own miracles as events leading to something unprecedented. They anticipate a new world. They seek to be "already here and now a microcosm of a new heaven and a new earth" (Ernst Bloch).[14] The new world has not come, and yet its expectation is intelligible. The primitive Christian charism of miracle-working in fact began a far-reaching restructuring of the ancient world. The cosmic world was not turned upside down, but the world as interpreted by symbolic actions was.

---

11. On Jesus' eschatology, cf. W. G. Kümmel, *Promise and Fulfilment*, 1957; E. Grässer, *Das Problem der Parusieverzögerung in den synoptischen Evangelien und in der Apostelgeschichte*, 1957, 3–75; J. Becker, *Das Heil Gottes*, 1964, 197–217; H. W. Kuhn, *Enderwartung und gegenwärtiges Heil*, 1966, 189–204.

12. *Enderwartung*, esp. 176–88.

13. Ibid., 202.

14. E. Bloch, *Prinzip Hoffnung*, 1959, 1544.

The Primitive Christian Miracle Stories

[[281]] If we move from the sayings tradition, which talks about the miracles, to the miracle stories themselves, it is impossible not to be struck by the complete disappearance of the eschatological interpretation of the miracles. The distinctive feature of Jesus' miracles has disappeared; the eschatological framework is missing. In only one place is the casting out of demons associated with the final judgment: Jesus is said to torment the demons "before the time," that is, before their final destruction at the judgment (Matt 8:29). Only at this secondary point in the developed miracle stories are the miracles presented as signs of the eschaton, nowhere else—a fact which is often overlooked.[15] The development which can be seen here from Jesus to primitive Christianity consists of two contrary tendencies. On the one hand there is a tendency to smooth out characteristic features, a "popular adaptation," which can be observed in other traditions. On the other hand there is a tendency to intensify, to make the miraculous even more striking, which goes well beyond the historical and factual. The process is marked both by a disappearance of distinctive features and at the same time by the appearance of a new character. Both tendencies will be briefly described.

The "popular adaptation" is easier to appreciate when comparable processes are considered. Take for example the traditions about Paul in Acts and about John the Baptist in Mark 6:17ff. In both cases all the unusual and provocative features of these eschatological preachers have been smoothed out. There is no more than a vague echo of what gave their presence distinctiveness and power. What would we learn from Acts about Paul's teaching on justification, its crucial importance and its polemical character? It appears only in Acts 13:38, watered down into an addition to justification by the Law, robbed of its provocative force, the Law-Christ dichotomy. What would we know about Paul's eschatology? In Acts it is "moved from the centre of Pauline belief to the end and turned into a treatise on the last things."[16] John the Baptist appears [[282]] in Mark 6:17–29, made unrecognisable by a popular adaptation. There is no reference to his preaching of repentance, no reference to the threatening, imminent judgment. We see the courageous critic of an Oriental despot, attacking blatant sins, but not the complacency of the religious. That there is little left of historical truth either is shown by a comparison with Jos. *Ant.* 18.116–19, where the Baptist's execution is politically

15. G. Delling, "Botschaft und Wunder im Wirken Jesu," in *Der historische Jesus und der kerygmatische Christus*, 1964, 389–402, admits that the miracle stories show "scant interest" in the eschatological significance of the miracles (p. 401).

16. P. Vielhauer, "Zum Paulinismus der Apostelgeschichte," *Aufsätze*, 18ff., quoted from p. 23. Cf. H. von Campenhausen, *Entstehung*, 57, who suggests that the author of Luke was a travelling companion of Paul's. He admits: "However, the Pauline ideas in their Lucan version are all more muted; they have lost not only their abstruseness but also their original profundity, and seem paler, more ordinary, as though they had been smoothed out for easier assimilation and something had been lost" (p. 57). It is this process that is here called "popular adjustment."

motivated. Is there not a similar popular adaptation in operation when the es-chatological interpretation of Jesus' activity is completely written out of the miracle stories? To attempt to reconstruct a vivid picture of the historical Jesus from the miracle stories would be as nonsensical as to attempt to recon-struct the Pauline teaching on justification from Acts 13:38f. or the Baptist's preaching of repentance from Mark 6:17ff.

This is not an argument for radical historical scepticism. Of course Acts 13:28f. contains an echo of the doctrine of justification. Undoubtedly the Baptist's preaching of repentance lies behind Mark 6:17ff. Even Paul's mir-acles in Acts cannot be explained as simply travel motifs, transferred stories or inventions.[17] After all, we know from the Pauline letters, if only from pass-ing remarks, that Paul had charismatic powers: action at a distance (1 Cor 5:1ff.),[18] visions (2 Cor 12:1ff.), miracles (2 Cor 12:12; Rom 15:18f.), speaking with tongues (1 Cor 14:18), rescue from distress at sea (2 Cor 11:25), survival of a stoning (2 Cor 11:25), miraculous escape (2 Cor 11:32f.). The relevant accounts in Acts undoubtedly have a historical background. But the popular image of the historical kernel is misleading. It suggests that the kernel was transmitted. The truth is that the historical shell was transmitted, all that Paul boasts about in his folly. Applied to the Jesus tradition, this means that, re-duced though the eschatological framework may be, the historical back-ground to the miracle stories cannot be denied. Primitive Christian miracle stories are symbolic actions provoked by the historical Jesus in which the his-torical figure has been intensified out of all proportion. We can still put for-ward hypotheses about where we have echoes of historical truth:

(1) Just as Jesus' exorcisms were closely connected with his eschatological [[283]] view of miracles, so it was the exorcisms which were the stimulus to primitive Christianity to attach christological titles to Jesus: "Holy One of God" (Mark 1:24) and "Son of the Most High" (5:7). The banishment of un-clean demons and idols gave messianic hopes their greatest purchase.[19]

(2) In the rule miracles, the conflicts about the sabbath, there is undoubt-edly an echo of Jesus' freedom with regard to the sacred institutions of his environment.

(3) The idea of faith gained such prominence in the miracle stories be-cause "faith" was a central concept in primitive Christianity. It is not impos-sible that this is directly or indirectly connected with Jesus.

---

17. Cf. R. Otto, *Kingdom of God*, 346ff., who, however, starts from the problematic as-sumption that Luke was an eye-witness. On Paul as a charismatic cf. also H. Windisch, *Paulus und Christus*, passim.

18. K. Thraede, *Grundzüge griechisch-römischer Brieftopik*, 1970, 93–106, esp. 98, sees no more than a traditional trope here, but any trope can be filled with new life in a specific context.

19. R. H. Fuller, *Interpreting the Miracles*, 75–76, interprets this feature of exorcisms as a transition from an implicit to an explicit Christology.

The development from Jesus' understanding of miracles to the interpretation of miracles in the primitive Christian miracle stories cannot be treated just as a process of displacement, smoothing out, toning down and softening of original features. There is rather a simultaneous process of stylisation, enhancement and heightening. In any case it would be one-sided to take isolated motifs and examine their originality and unmistakability. What gives the primitive Christian miracle stories their character is the whole form-critical field of motifs, characters and themes. In the framework of the genre-specific structure of the miracle stories Jesus is seen in a new light. He appears as the miraculously enhanced figure of the historical Jesus. His miracles become increasingly more paradoxical, more miraculous. Their contradiction of normal experience becomes more and more prominent. This enhancement certainly has popular features, but it cannot be treated simply as an assimilation to popular expectations and ideas. Traditional miracle motifs are, on the contrary, developed into an exceptionally striking miracle structure which far exceeds any other contemporary phenomenon. From the miracle-working prophets of the Old Testament to the Coptic legends of the saints, from the inscriptions of Epidaurus to the miracles of the later Neo-Platonists, from the divine men of early Greece to the miracles at Christian shrines, little comparable material has survived. Comparison is possible only at a few points.

The language in which the motifs and structure of the miracles of Epidaurus are presented is terse and brittle. The stories lack internal drama; their religious expressiveness is slight. We have to bear in mind their purpose: they are intended to give suppliants comfort and confidence, to increase expectations and cushion disappointments [[284]]. In this respect they are skilful compositions.[20] Everywhere one sees the hand of an experienced shrine bureaucracy, cleverly managing hope and hopelessness. The mood in the primitive Christian miracle stories is quite different. Where the priests of Epidaurus seem to insist, "Miracles are an everyday event here," in the Christian stories the miracle is presented as something completely improbable: "We never saw anything like this" (Mark 2:12). Miracles are not the object of expectation and hope supported by permanent institutions, but paradoxical events which fly in the face of all experience. In contrast to the miracle stories of Epidaurus, which radiate confidence, in which the accents of fear and despair are silent, we find an often defiant will to live which has to surmount obstacles. In the case of the ancient healing cults, it was left to the Cynic Diogenes to point to other sides of the picture. When someone was admiring the mass of votive tablets in Samothrace, he said, "There would be even more if those who were not saved had put up tablets" (Diog. Laert. 6.59). The inscriptions from Epidaurus are about 300 years older than the primitive Christian miracle stories. It is also interesting to compare the primitive Christian stories with later miracle stories, which we owe to the writers of the second Sophist movement, Aelius Aristides, Lucian and Philostratus. In Lucian the miracles are part of satirical

---

20. On the purpose of the inscriptions cf. R. Herzog, *Epidauros*, 59ff.; M. Dibelius, [[*From Tradition to Gospel*,]] 166ff.

dialogues, partly the object of ridicule, partly a device for intellectual entertainment.[21] Lucian's stories derive their vitality from the narrator's ironical distance from his stories. They are parodies. Miracle stories appear in a quite different form in the "Sacred Discourses" of Aelius Aristides,[22] the great orator of the second Sophist movement, which contain a re-working of an "invalid's diary" composed by Aristides. It is all written in perfectly classical style, but pervaded by a rather cloying sentimentality. The closest parallel to the gospels is Philostratus' *vita Apollonii*, a biography with novelistic features and propagandist intentions.[23] Even here, however, there are large differences. Philostratus' work has a taste for the exotic derived from travellers' tales and an embarrassment about miracles both of which are foreign to the gospels. Philostratus goes to considerable lengths to present Apollonius, not as a [[285]] possessor of magical powers, but as a sage who can do the most amazing things by virtue of his miraculous knowledge. His description of the raising of the dead bride is typical: He ends it with the words, "And whether he had found a spark of life in her which had remained hidden from those who had treated her . . . or whether he rekindled and brought back life which had been extinguished . . ." *(vita* 4.45). He refers previously to the "apparent death" of the young woman, so discreetly hinting at his own view. In his writings miracles are, wherever possible, eliminated by apologetic. The attitude of all the writers of the second Sophistic movement towards miracles is similarly cut through by reflection, irony, sentimentality or apologetic. In them members of educated classes are reproducing popular traditions in different ways. They lack naivety. The repeated assertion that miracles are only ever described outside the New Testament for their own sake should therefore be abandoned. The truth is more nearly the reverse. The attractiveness of primitive Christian miracle stories is due in no small part to their wholehearted appreciation of miracles and to their radical enhancement of them.

This enhancement may have popular features, but its main source is the tension between boundary stressing and boundary crossing which becomes visible in the form-critical field of motifs, characters and themes. It is as if traditional miracle motifs have moved into a new field of force which has brought the potentialities immanent in the genre to their highest development. Here the light falls more sharply than elsewhere on the transcending of human expectations and ordinary logic. In contrast to Epidaurus, we hear the voices of despair and resignation. In contrast to Philostratus, there is not a trace of educated, cautious apologetic. Even the most impossible things appear as quite simply possible. The miracle stories will sooner deny the truth of all human experience than the claim of human distress to be overcome. In contrast to Aelius Aristides, no personal relationship to the saving God is cultivated. "Faith" may be central, but it does not mean a personal relationship

21. On the form of Lucian's dialogues cf. W. Schmid and O. Stählin, *Geschichte der griechischen Literatur*, 1924, 710ff.

22. On these discourses in their literary and historical context, cf. ibid., 698ff.

23. On this characterisation of the genre cf. D. Esser, *Form geschichtliche Studien*, 98ff. He defines the *vita Apollonii* as "a novelistic biography of a 'divine man' written for purposes of religious politics" (p. 98).

with Jesus, but that unconditional desire which receives the promise πάντα δυνατά [['all things can be done']] (Mark 9:23). The miracle itself is the revelation,
the manifestation, of the sacred in fascinating otherness and total uncondi-
tionality. In the face of such a power interference from irony, emotion and
apologetic is silenced. Most typical of all is the absolute denial of experience,
and in this the primitive Christian miracle stories are an extension of Jesus'
own understanding of miracles. Jesus too saw his miracles in the context of a
universal turning point which burst the bounds of experience. This eschatological orientation has faded in the miracle stories, but the [[286]] contradiction of experience, in the form of the miraculous and paradoxical, has been
pushed to an extreme.

This internal heightening of charismatic belief in miracles is combined
with a rejection of all other forms of belief in the miraculous current in the ancient world. The two are closely connected. Charismatic belief in miracles is
probably heightened to such a degree because it now has to absorb all the expectations which otherwise led to magic and soothsaying and were institution-
alised in oracles and healing sanctuaries. Primitive Christianity was not just a
part of the general movement of the age, which led to increased irrationality;
within this movement it offered an alternative which, as the ancient world
drew to a close, took the form of a choice between Neo-Platonic *theourgia*
[['work of God']] and the Christian charisma of miracles. However much we
must place primitive Christianity within a general religious development, it
nonetheless towers above it. The paradoxical feats of charismatic miracle-
workers are here given an aura of religious significance without parallel elsewhere. If we may use for purposes of illustration a periodisation usual in other
contexts, we could say that the primitive Christian miracle stories form the
"classical" pinnacle of the genre, between the archaic brittleness of the Epidaurus inscriptions and the baroque embellishments of the later Empire. No
historical assessment can make good their absolute claim, but it can make it
intelligible: the new way of life which established itself in symbolic actions distinguished itself from all existing ways of life by its claim to absoluteness.

The analysis of contemporary religious influences on primitive Christian
miracle stories and the interpretation of their historical intention leads to a
hermeneutical conflict. Functional analysis cannot resolve this conflict, but it
can make it intelligible. Primitive Christian miracle stories are part of a wider
process, and this relativises their claim. However, they were able to give this
process a new impetus only because they enhanced the historical figure of
Jesus in symbolic actions out of all proportion. Only a figure enhanced in
symbolic transformation could radiate the totally motivating force which was
able to bring about the profound change in ancient consciousness which we
associate with the name of Christianity.

Bibliography

Baltensweiler, H. "Wunder und Glaube im Neuen Testament." *Theologische Zeit-
    schrift* 23 (1967) 241–56.

Becker, J. *Das Heil Gottes: Heils- und Sündenbegriffe in den Qumrantexten und im Neuen Testament.* Studien zur Umwelt des Neuen Testaments 3. Göttingen: [[Vandenhoeck & Ruprecht,]] 1964.

Bloch, E. *Prinzip Hoffnung.* [[Frankfurt am Main: Suhrkamp,]] 1959.

Campenhausen, H. von. *Die Entstehung der christlichen Bibel.* Beiträge zur historischen Theologie 39. Tübingen: [[Mohr,]] 1968 [[trans. J. A. Baker. *The Formation of the Christian Bible.* Philadelphia: Fortress, 1972]].

Delling, G. "Botschaft und Wunder im Wirken Jesu." Pp. 389–402 in *Der historische Jesus und der kerygmatische Christus.* Edited by H. Ristow and K. Matthiae. 3rd ed. Berlin: [[Evangelische,]] 1964.

——. "Das Verständnis des Wunders im Neuen Testament." Pp. 146–59 in *Studien zum Neuen Testament und zum hellenistischen Judentum.* Göttingen: [[Vandenhoeck & Ruprecht,]] 1970.

Dibelius, M. *From Tradition to Gospel.* [[Translated by B. L. Woolf.]] London: [[Nicholson & Watson,]] 1934 [trans. of *Die Formgeschichte des Evangeliums.* 2nd ed. Tübingen, 1933; 4th ed., 1961].

Duprez, A. *Jésus et les Dieux Guérisseurs: A Propos de Jean V.* Cahiers de la Revue Biblique 12. [[Paris: Gabalda,]] 1970.

Esser, D. *Formgeschichtliche Studien zur hellenistischen und zur frühchristlichen Literatur unter besonderer Berücksichtigung der vita Apollonii des Philostrat und der Evangelien.* Ph.D. diss. Bonn, 1969.

Fuller, R. H. *Interpreting the Miracles.* [[London: SCM,]] 1963.

Grässer, E. *Das Problem der Parusieverzögerung in den synoptischen Evangelien und in der Apostelgeschichte.* Beihefte zur Zeitschrift für die neutestamentliche Wissenschaft 22. Berlin: [[Alfred Töpelmann,]] 1957.

Grant, R. M. *Miracles and Natural Law in Graeco-Roman and Early Christian Thought.* Amsterdam, 1952.

Grundmann, W. *Der Begriff der Kraft in der neutestamentlichen Gedankenwelt.* Beiträge zur Wissenschaft vom Alten und Neuen Testament 4, 8. Stuttgart: [[Kohlhammer,]] 1932.

Harnisch, W. *Verhängnis und Verheißung der Geschichte.* Forschungen zur Religion und Literatur des Alten und Neuen Testaments 97. Göttingen: [[Vandenhoeck & Ruprecht,]] 1969.

Hengel, R., and M. Hengel. "Die Heilungen Jesu und medizinisches Denken." Pp. 331–61 in *Medicus Viator: Festschrift R. Siebeck.* Tübingen, 1959.

Herzog, R. *Die Wunderheilungen von Epidauros: Ein Beitrag zur Geschichte der medizin und der Religion.* Philologus Supplements 22/3. Leipzig, 1931.

Kümmel, W. G. *Promise and Fulfilment.* [[Studies in Biblical Theology 23.]] London: [[SCM,]] 1957 [trans. of *Verheissung und Erfüllung.* Abhandlungen zur Theologie des Alten und Neuen Testaments 6. 2nd ed. Zurich, 1953].

Kuhn, H. W. *Enderwartung und gegenwärtiges Heil.* Studien zur Umwelt des Neuen Testaments 4. Göttingen: [[Vandenhoeck & Ruprecht,]] 1966.

Noetzel, H. *Christus und Dionysos.* Arbeiten zur Theologie 1. Stuttgart, 1960.

Oepke, A. "ἰάομαι." *Theologische Wörterbuch zum Neuen Testament* 3.194–215 (*Theological Dictionary of the New Testament* 3.194–215).

Otto, R. *The Kingdom of God and the Son of Man.* Revised ed. [[Translated by F. V. Filson and B. L. Woolf. London: Lutterworth,]] 1943 [trans. of *Reich Gottes und Menschensohn.* Munich, 1934].

Pesch, R. *Jesu ureigene Taten?* Quaestiones Disputatae 52. Freiburg: [[Herder,]] 1970.

Plöger, O. *Theokratie und Eschatologie.* Wissenschaftliche Monographien zum Alten und Neuen Testament 2. Neukirchen-Vluyn: [[Neukirchener Verlag,]] 1959.

Rengstorf, K. H. *Die Anfänge der Auseinandersetzung zwischen Christusglaube und Asklepiosfrömmigkeit.* Münster: [[Aschendorff,]] 1953.

Richardson, A. *The Miracle Stories of the Gospels.* London: [[SCM,]] 1941 [3rd ed., 1948].

Roloff, J. *Das Kerygma und der irdische Jesus.* Göttingen: [[Vandenhoeck & Ruprecht,]] 1970.

Schmid, W., and O. Stählin. *Geschichte der griechischen Literatur.* Handbuch der Altertumswissenschaft 7/2/2. Munich: [[Beck,]] 1924.

Schmithals, W. *Wunder und Glaube.* Biblische Studien 59. Neukirchen-Vluyn: [[Neukirchener Verlag,]] 1970.

Thraede, K. *Grundzüge griechisch-römischer Brieftopik.* Zetemata 48. Munich: [[Beck,]] 1970.

Vielhauer, P. "Zum Paulinismus der Apostelgeschichte." *Aufsätze zum Neuen Testament.* Theologische Bücherei 31. Munich: [[Chr. Kaiser,]] 1965.

Weinreich, O. "Türöffnung im Wunder-, Prodigien- und Zauberglauben der Antike, des Judentums und Christentums. Pp. 200–264 in *Genethliakon Wilhelm Schmid zum 70. Geburtstag.* Tübinger Beiträge zur Altertumswissenschaft 5. Stuttgart: [[Kohlhammer,]] 1929.

Windisch, H. *Paulus und Christus.* Untersuchungen zum Neuen Testament 24. Leipzig: [[Hindrichs,]] 1934.

E. P. SANDERS

Jesus and the Temple

[[61]] Having named Jesus' activity in the temple as the surest starting point for our investigation, I must hasten to say that the question of Jesus and the temple brings with it the amount of uncertainty which is usual in the study of the Gospels. There is neither firm agreement about the unity and integrity of the basic passages concerning the "cleansing of the temple" (Mark 11:15–19 and pars.),[1] nor is there absolute certainty of the authenticity of either or both of the sayings about the destruction of the temple (Mark 13:2 and pars.;[2]

Reprinted, with permission, from E. P. Sanders, *Jesus and Judaism* (Philadelphia: Fortress / London: SCM, 1985) 61–76 and portions of (bibliography) 363–69.

1. Bultmann (*History*, 36): Mark 11:15, 18f. come from the editor; v. 17 is an added saying which has replaced another, which may be preserved in John 2:16. One may conjecture that 11:27–33 followed 11:16 immediately, though probably not as part of the same unit. Roloff (*Der irdische Jesus*, 93): the oldest form of the narrative was Mark 11:15f., 18a, 28–33. Vincent Taylor (*The Gospel according to St. Mark*, 1959, 461): the original unit is 11:15b–17. Mark added vv. 15a, 18f. Boismard (*Synopse des quatre Évangiles en Français* 2: *Commentaire*, 1972, 334–36): Mark 11:27–33 originally followed the "cleansing" scene. Verses 17f., 19 are later insertions. The casting out of the vendors (11:15) was originally followed by a saying better preserved in John 2:16b. Note also Goguel's view, n. 4 below. It should be noted that Mark 11:16, absent from both Matthew and Luke, plays little role in these analyses. It is my own view that this sort of general prohibition (see I. Abrahams, *Studies in Pharisaism and the Gospels*, vol. 1, 1917, reissued 1967, 84f.) does not accord well with overthrowing tables and the like and is probably a later addition, even though it usually passes unquestioned. It may also be doubted that the admonition is appropriate to the temple at Jerusalem, in view of the placement of the gates. In any case, it plays no role in our analysis.

2. For a list of scholars regarding Mark 13:2 as inauthentic (because a weakened form of 14:58, which was embarrassing), see G. R. Beasley-Murray, *A Commentary on Mark Thirteen*, 1957, 23. The passage is often accepted as authentic, however, it being noted that in fact the temple was destroyed by fire (see Taylor, *St. Mark*, 501). Lloyd Gaston (*No Stone on Another*, 1970, 12f., 65, 244, 424f.) has correctly noted that only the redactional framework of Mark 13:2 and parallels mentions the temple, and he proposes that the prophecy of destruction is found in its original form in Luke 19:44, where it refers to the destruction of Jerusalem. He gives (p. 65 n. 1) a bibliography of scholars who combine Mark 13:2 with 14:58 and 15:29

Matt 26:61//Mark 14:58[3]). Despite all this, it is overwhelmingly probable that Jesus did something in the temple and said something about its destruction.[4] The accusation that Jesus threatened the temple is reflected in three other passages: the crucifixion scene (Matt 27:39f.//Mark 15:29f.); Stephen's speech (Acts 6:13f.); and, with post-Easter interpretation, in John 2:18–22. The conflict over the temple seems deeply implanted in the tradition, and that there was such a conflict would seem to be indisputable.[5]

The "Cleansing" of the Temple (Mark 11:15–19 and parallels)

The older understanding of the event, and the one which still predominates, is that it was just what the title of the pericope in modern synopses says: the *cleansing* of the temple. This implies a prior profanation or contamination, and the profanation has been readily found in the conducting of trade in or

---

and consider that Jesus did predict or threaten the destruction of the temple—the view taken here. Gaston's view is discussed further in n. 5 and in the next chapter [[of Sanders, *Jesus and Judaism*]].

3. For both views, that Mark 14:58 is authentic and that it is inauthentic, see Taylor, *St. Mark*, 566. Taylor regards the passage as authentic.

4. M. Goguel, *Jesus and the Origins of Christianity*, vol. 1: *The Life of Jesus*, 412–15, argued that the act and the saying do not form a unity (cf. n. 1), but he proposed that the saying against the profanation of the temple was authentic and that the act of overthrowing the tables was unhistorical and had been created on the basis of the saying. Scholarship has not, however, followed Goguel's proposal. The action against the buyers and sellers and the frequent accusation that Jesus threatened to destroy the temple are mutually supportive.

5. See the survey of opinions by W. D. Davies, *The Gospel and the Land: Early Christianity and Jewish Territorial Doctrine*, 1974, 349–52 nn. 45 and 46. We should note in addition the intriguing proposals of Lloyd Gaston in *No Stone on Another*. He considers that the origin of the threat to destroy the temple is actually to be found in Stephen's position and does not come from Jesus. Jewish opponents of Christianity picked up Stephen's threat and employed it against the Christian movement. Mark 14:58 and 15:29 (and parallels) are then considered to be a defense against Jewish accusations. He believes that the accusation that Jesus threatened to destroy the temple is no more historical than the accusation that Jesus committed blasphemy by claiming to be Son of God (Mark 14:61–64 and parallels); that is, both accusations are later Jewish accusations against the church (pp. 65–69). The two halves of Mark 14:58 and 15:29 (the threat to destroy and the promise to rebuild) are to be taken separately. The threat to destroy goes back only to Stephen (p. 161), while the promise to rebuild the "temple" goes back to Jesus but refers to the founding of the eschatological community as the "temple of God" (pp. 226f., 241, 243). It was only the opponents of Christianity who combined the two traditions, and they appear together in the Gospels because it was necessary to answer the charge (pp. 145f., 162). Gaston considers it conceivable that "a saying against the temple was important in Jesus' condemnation" (p. 68), but is more impressed by the absence of the charge in Luke and John (p. 68 n. 4). Jesus' own attitude towards the temple as a place of cult was one of indifference (pp. 102, 240f.). I shall argue that the threat of destruction appears in too many strata and coheres too well with the "cleansing" of the temple to be denied to Jesus, and I follow the majority of scholars in taking the multiple attestation to indicate authenticity. It should be noted that Gaston finds no background in contemporary Jewish thought for the expectation of the destruction and renewal of the temple, and this buttresses his view that the threat is inauthentic. . . .

around[6] the temple precincts. To many this is self-evidently a debasing of true religion, and Jesus was intending to purify the temple so that it should better fulfil its purpose. Thus, for example, Edersheim was of the view that "the whole of this traffic—moneychanging, selling of doves, and market for sheep and oxen—was in itself, and from its attendant circumstances, a terrible desecration."[7] [[62]] It is noteworthy that Abrahams, in disagreeing with Edersheim, nevertheless accepted his major premises: what is external is bad, and Jesus was right to attack it. Edersheim accepted the charge of corruption ("den of thieves," Mark 11:17) as being necessarily a part of any trading.[8] Abrahams countered with the observation that while some individual abuses might have occurred, a general charge would be unjustified.[9] Yet he himself also wrote that he approved of Jesus' attack on "externalism." "When Jesus overturned the money-changers and ejected the sellers of doves from the Temple he did a service to Judaism."[10] This is a strange position for one to adopt who argued that buying and selling were necessary for the continuation of the temple sacrifices.[11] It shows the pervasiveness of the view that Jesus opposed externals in the name of true religious interiority.[12]

This same view, though now expressed differently, is seen in more recent exegetical remarks. After rejecting (correctly, in my view) what he identifies as the two principal recent interpretations of the "cleansing"—that it expresses the opposition of the early church to the temple cultus[13] and that it represents "the present power of the raised [Christ] in the confession of the post-Easter

6. There is some debate about what took place within the temple precincts and what was relegated to the area outside. According to J. Klausner (*Jesus of Nazareth*, 314), the Pharisees would have permitted no selling or money-changing in the temple, although the Sadducees, then in charge, may have permitted the use of the outer court. See also Abrahams, *Studies*, 86f.: commercial money-changers would not have been allowed in the temple precincts, but those who turned the profits over to the temple would have been permitted inside for one week, from 25 Adar to 1 Nisan. The buying and selling of sacrificial victims ordinarily took place outside. We cannot settle the question of precise location, but we may assume that trade was allowed only in the court of the Gentiles—if anywhere in the temple confines. To the degree to which the view that there was never any exchange of money in the temple precincts rests on *m. Ber.* 9:5 (and parallels), it may now be dismissed. Jeremias has better explained that mishnah as applying to visitors to the temple area (tourists and the like), who are prohibited from carrying money, not to those who came to offer sacrifice. See J. Jeremias, "Zwei Miszellen: 1. Antik-Jüdische Münzdeutungen. 2. Zur Geschichtlichkeit der Tempelreinigung," *NTS* 23, 1977, 179f.

7. Edersheim, *The Life and Times of Jesus the Messiah*, vol. 1, 1936, 370.

8. Ibid.: "Most improper transactions were carried on, to the taking undue advantage of the poor people."

9. Abrahams, *Studies*, 1.87.

10. Ibid., 88.

11. Ibid., 84.

12. Cf. Klausner, *Jesus of Nazareth*, 314: the money-changing was necessary (he compares the sale of candles by Christians), "though such behaviour arouses indignation in the truly devout."

13. Roloff, *Der irdische Jesus*, 89, citing H. Braun, *Spätjüdisch-häretischer und frühchristlicher Radikalismus*, vol. 2, 1957, 12.

community"[14]—Roloff gives his own interpretation: the action was "a prophetic sign which intended to bring about the repentance and return of Israel in the last days."[15] "He charged Judaism with its own recognition of the holiness of the temple as the place of the presence of God and demonstrated that its practice stood in contradiction to that holiness."[16] Jesus' action constituted a "requirement of the absolute maintenance of the holiness of the existing temple."[17] There was, it seems from this remark, an interior holiness which was being besmirched or obscured by the actual conduct of the temple's affairs.

Other recent scholars, without explicitly expressing the view that religion must be devoid of crass materialism, also understand Jesus' action as being a "cleansing" of defiling trade. Thus Jeremias proposed that the "cleansing" was directed against the priestly class because "They misuse their calling . . . by carrying on business to make profit."[18] Similarly Aulén remarked that "To transform the court of the temple to a market place—and for their own profit—was a violation of the law concerning the holiness of the temple. . . ."[19] We may also cite Trocmé's view: the action was "in defence of the honour of God,"[20] which the trade apparently called into question. Harvey speaks of "the abuse of Jewish institutions"[21] which Jesus attacked and characterizes the action as a prophetic one which represents "the divine judgment on a particular use which was being made [[63]] of the temple."[22] That "use" was trading, and Harvey writes that Jesus had good grounds for thinking that trade should not have been taking place in the temple precincts.[23]

Such comments as these are doubtless intended to distinguish the temple ordained by God—which Jesus did not attack—from the Jewish "abuse" of the divine institution—which Jesus did attack. The way in which the distinction is made, however, implies that it is just the trade itself—the changing of money, the purchase of sacrifices, and probably also the charge for their inspection—which is the focus of the action. The assumption seems to be that Jesus made,

14. Roloff, 89, citing A. Suhl, *Die Funktion der alttestamentlichen Zitate und Anspielungen im Markusevangelium*, 1965, 143.

15. Roloff, 95.

16. Ibid., 96.

17. Roloff, 97. One may note here Bousset's view (*Jesus*, 105f.): Jesus attached no value to any outward forms. In exerting himself "for the holiness and purity of the Temple service" he still did not give it any true value. The action just shows his dislike of "pseudo-holiness and hypocrisy." Roloff agrees on what Jesus did: *purify* the service; but he assigns real value to it in Jesus' eyes.

18. Jeremias, *Proclamation of Jesus*, 145. It should be noted that Jeremias accepts Mark 11:17 as authentic, and thus his critical view corresponds to the motive which he attributes to Jesus.

19. Aulén, *Jesus*, 77.

20. E. Trocmé, *Jesus as Seen by His Contemporaries*, ET 1973, 118. Again, compare Davies' analysis of divergent views, *The Gospel and the Land*, 349 n. 45, item 2.

21. Harvey, *Constraints*, 15.

22. Ibid., 131.

23. Ibid., 129.

and wanted his contemporaries to accept, a distinction between this sort of "practice" and the "real purpose" of the temple. This seems to owe more to the nineteenth-century view that what is external is bad than to a first-century Jewish view.[24] Those who write about Jesus' desire to return the temple to its "original," "true" purpose, the "pure" worship of God,[25] seem to forget that the principal function of any temple is to serve as a place for sacrifice, and that sacrifices *require* the supply of suitable animals. This had always been true of the temple in Jerusalem. In the time of Jesus, the temple had long been the only place in Israel at which sacrifices could be offered, and this means that suitable animals and birds must have been in supply at the temple site. There was not an "original" time when worship at the temple had been "pure" from the business which the requirement of unblemished sacrifices creates. Further no one remembered a time when pilgrims, carrying various coinages, had not come. In the view of Jesus and his contemporaries, the requirement to sacrifice must always have involved the supply of sacrificial animals, their inspection, and the changing of money. Thus one may wonder what scholars have in mind who talk about Jesus' desire to stop this "particular use" of the temple. Just what would be left of the service if the supposedly corrupting externalism of sacrifices, and the trade necessary to them, were purged? Here as often we see a failure to think concretely and a preference for vague religious abstractions.

In order to solidify the present point, and to gain perspective on the possible range of meanings of Jesus' action in the temple, we should lay out more thoroughly the common view of the temple, the sacrifices, the changing of money, and the sale of birds. The common view was that the temple was where sacrifices to God were offered, and that these sacrifices were not only appropriate but necessary. Josephus, in commenting on the strategic importance of fortified places in the city, gives clear expression to this view: [[64]]

> Whoever was master of these [fortified places] had the whole nation in his power, for sacrifices could not be made without (controlling) these places, and it was impossible for any of the Jews to forgo offering these, for they would rather give up their lives than the worship which they are accustomed to offer God. (*Ant.* 15.248)

The importance of sacrifice emerges in another way in Josephus, in his account of the beginning of the revolt. One Eleazar persuaded the priests who were then serving "to accept no gift or sacrifice from a foreigner." Josephus continues:

> This action laid the foundation of the war with the Romans; for the sacrifices offered on behalf of that nation and the emperor were in

---

24. Note the argument by Robert Banks (*Jesus and the Law in the Synoptic Tradition*, 1975, 208) that an inner/outer distinction is anachronistic (discussing Matt 5:17).

25. Most explicitly, Bornkamm speaks of the action as "more than an act of reform to restore the temple service to its original purity" (*Jesus of Nazareth*, 158f.), which means that it was also that.

> consequence rejected. The chief priests and the notables earnestly besought them not to abandon the customary offering for their rulers, but the priests remained obdurate. (*J.W.* 2.409f.)

Everyone agreed that sacrifices were integral to the function of the temple. They were essential to the religion of Judaism, and withholding sacrifices for the Romans was the final sign that a true revolt, rather than just another round of rock-throwing, was at hand. The notion that the temple should serve some function other than sacrifice would seem to be extremely remote from the thinking of a first-century Jew.

But could the sacrifices continue without the changing of money and the selling of birds? It is hard to see how.[26] The money changers were probably those who changed the money in the possession of pilgrims into the coinage acceptable by the temple in payment of the half-shekel tax levied on all Jews.[27] The word "levied" itself requires interpretation, for payment of the tax was voluntary, being enforced only by moral suasion.[28] Yet we know that Jews from all parts of the Diaspora paid it out of loyalty to the Jerusalem temple.[29] The desire of the authorities to receive the money in a standard coinage which did not have on it the image of an emperor or king is reasonable, and no one ever seems to have protested this. The money changers naturally charged a fee for changing money,[30] but they can hardly have been expected to secure enough Tyrian coinage to meet the demands of worshippers and to supply their services for free. The buyers and sellers were similarly required for the maintenance of the temple service, and they provided a convenient service for pilgrims. If a Galilean, for example, wished or was required to present a dove as a sacrifice, it was more convenient to sell the dove in Galilee and buy one in Jerusalem which was certified as unblemished than to carry the dove from Galilee to the temple. A charge was made in Jerusalem for the service, [[65]] but this was doubtless to be preferred to the alternative: bringing one's own dove from Galilee and running the risk of having it found blemished after the trip. The charge for inspection would be made in any case. The

26. I believe the best treatment of the particular point at hand to he that of Abrahams, *Studies*, 1.82–89. For a general account of the priesthood and the temple service, see Emil Schürer, ed. Vermes, *The History of the Jewish People in the Age of Jesus Christ*, 2.237–308.

27. On the "Tyrian" coinage accepted by the temple, see Abrahams, p. 83, where there are references to further literature. See also *Bekorot* 8.7 on the requirement of "Tyrian" coins. Here and elsewhere I take the Rabbinic discussions of the temple, the trade, the temple tax, and sacrifices to be somewhat idealized but basically to reflect common thought and practice before 70. Most of the Rabbinic statements about these matters are not peculiarly Pharisaic, and many are confirmed by Josephus and the New Testament. See the discussion of the views of Jacob Neusner and J. N. Epstein in [[Sanders,]] *Paul and Palestinian Judaism*, 63f.

28. See Matt 17:24–27; *Šeqalim* 1:3 (on taking pledges from those who have not paid).

29. That the temple tax was paid follows from the fact that the Romans, after the fall of the temple, assigned the payment to the capital. According to Josephus (*J.W.* 7.218), this resulted in a levy on all Jews, no matter where resident. See further Thackeray's notes in the Loeb edition of Josephus. For Rabbinic theory about how the tax was collected, see *Šeqalim* 1:3 and 2:1.

30. See *Šeqalim* 1:6.

most important point to recognize here is that the requirement to present an *unblemished* dove as a sacrifice for certain impurities or transgressions, was a requirement *given by God to Israel through Moses.*[31] The business arrangements around the temple were *necessary* if the commandments were to be obeyed. An attack on what is necessary is not an attack on "present practice."

If these were the circumstances, was there anything at all about the temple which could give rise to attacks on "present practice" as distinct from the temple service itself? As it happens, we know of attacks which rest on a distinction between "practice" and "ideal" and which have in view the purity of the temple. Will these help us fit Jesus into the mould of a religious reformer, bent on cleansing the temple? It seems not. The attacks otherwise known rest on charges about which the Gospels are silent: the suitability of the priests for their office. Such charges appear already in the biblical period. Thus in Malachi 3 the "messenger of the covenant" will "purify the sons of Levi" until they present "right offerings." This may have been taken in an eschatological sense subsequently, but the thrust of the chapter itself is that the Levites were impure (3:3) and that all Israel was robbing God by withholding part of the tithes (3:6–10). They should mend their ways or face destruction.

Such accusations continue in the later period. In the days of the Hasmoneans, there were objections to their combining the offices of priest and king[32] and against their "usurping" the high priesthood.[33] The author[s] of the *Psalms of Solomon* also objected to the contemporary priests because they served the temple in a state of immorality and impurity. They are accused of committing adultery, robbing the sanctuary, and offering sacrifice when impure because of having come into contact with menstrual blood (8:9–14). God duly punished them (the Hasmonean priests) by sending the Romans (8:15–19). The Dead Sea Sectarians accused the "Wicked Priest" of committing abominable deeds and defiling the temple (1QpHab 12:8f.). He also "robbed the Poor of their possessions" (ibid., 12:10; cf. 9:5), but this apparently refers to his actions as king, as is clear in 8:8–11 (cf. 11:4–7). Similar accusations are seen in the Covenant of Damascus:

> Also they convey uncleanness to the sanctuary, inasmuch as they do not keep separate according to the Law, but lie with her that sees "the blood of her flux." [[66]] And they marry each man the daughter of his brother and the daughter of his sister. . . . (CD 5:6–8; cf. 4:18)

The charge of impurity in part reflects such halakic disputes as the duration of a woman's impurity following her menstrual period,[34] and there were

---

31. Hirsch ("Sacrifice," *JE* 10:617) summarized the uses of the pigeon and turtledove in sacrifices thus: they "served for burnt offerings and sin-offerings in cases of lustrations. They were allowed as private holocausts, and were accepted as sin-offerings from the poorer people and as purification-offerings. . . ." So Josephus, *Ant.* 3.230. Thus numerous unblemished birds were required.

32. *Pss. Sol.* 17:6–8. See Adolf Büchler, *Types of Jewish-Palestinian Piety from 70 B.C.E. to 70 C.E.*, 1922, 170–74.

33. *T. Mos.* 6:1; Büchler, ibid.

34. CD 5:7; *Pss. Sol.* 8:13; cf. *Niddah* 4:2. See [[Sanders,]] *Paul and Palestinian Judaism*, 404.

other halakic disputes. Thus the Dead Sea Sect would have followed a different calendar from that used in Jerusalem, with the result that all the sacrifices were, from their point of view, on the wrong day (see again 1QpHab 11:7).[35] We should also suppose that the Pharisees quarrelled with the Sadducean practice because of halakic disagreements.[36]

Criticism of anyone who handles money or goods is easy and obvious—so much so that the priests of the second temple are still assumed to have been dishonest.[37] Many New Testament scholars quite readily suppose that such concerns lay behind Jesus' demonstration.

If Jesus were a religious reformer, however, bent on correcting "abuse" and "present practice," we should hear charges of immorality, dishonesty and corruption directed *against the priests.*[38] But such charges are absent from the Gospels (except for Mark 11:17), and that is not the thrust of the action in the temple. On the contrary, the attack was against the trade which is necessary for sacrifices no matter who are the priests and without mention of the *halakot* which they follow. Thus far, it appears that Jesus' demonstration was against what all would have seen as necessary to the sacrificial system, rather than against present practice.

If the saying in Mark 11:17 and pars. were Jesus' own comment on why he "cleansed" the temple, however, we would have to accept that it was indeed trade and sacrifice which bothered him, possibly because dishonesty was involved.[39] In that verse the conflated quotation from Isa 56:7 and Jer 7:11 says that the temple should be a house of prayer (Mark has "for all the Gentiles"), while "you" have made it a den of robbers. The saying, however, is quite correctly rejected by most scholars as an addition.[40] Roloff regards

35. For the criticism of the cult on the grounds of different *halakah*, see Yigael Yadin, *The Scroll of the War of the Sons of Light against the Sons of Darkness*, 1962, 198f.

36. *Yoma* 19b; [[Sanders,]] *Paul and Palestinian Judaism*, 151.

37. Nahman Avigad, commenting on a discovery of what he believes to have been a workshop which supplied incense and the like to the temple, describes the owner as having "usurped" the privilege for his own gain. Such information does not come from archaeology, but from applying a generalization to a particular person. The priests in general, he writes "abused their position . . . through nepotism and oppression" (*Discovering Jerusalem*, 1983, 130f.).

38. Gaston (*No Stone on Another*, 85) gives a bibliography of those who see Jesus as a religious reformer and appropriately comments: "In contrast to the manner in which the Essenes would have cleansed the temple, beginning with the High Priest and continuing with a reform of the whole cult, Jesus cannot be seen here as a religious reformer, cleansing the temple of abuses."

39. We noted above (n. 18) that Jeremias, for example, accepts Mark 11:17 as giving Jesus' motive. Cf. also Albert Nolan, *Jesus before Christianity*, 1980, 102: the issue was only the "abuse of money and trade." Nolan continues by stating that there is evidence for fraud and theft, citing Jeremias, *Jerusalem in the Time of Jesus*, 33f. Those pages, however, contain no such evidence, nor do I know of any.

40. See above, n. 1; further the *Ergänzungsheft* to Bultmann's *Geschichte*, ed. G. Theissen and Philipp Vielhauer, [4]1971, p. 29. The authenticity of Mark 11:17 is doubted also by Georg Klinzing, *Die Umdeutung des Kultus in der Qumrangemeinde und im Neuen Testament*, 1971, 209. Note also the view of Maria Trautmann, *Zeichenhafte Handlungen Jesu*, 1980. She never doubts

v. 17 as an addition because of the introductory "and he taught them and said."[41] A. E. Harvey has recently proposed that the quotations in Mark 11:17 cannot represent a saying of Jesus. "House of prayer for all the Gentiles" "could hardly be extracted from the Hebrew version which Jesus would have used." He adds that "robbers' cave" is inappropriate, since "robber" always means raider, never swindler.[42] That these and other scholars who reject v. 17 nevertheless think that Jesus opposed present practice, not the temple itself, shows how deeply embedded is the view that Jesus opposed corrupting externalism. They [[67]] must take it that the mere fact of buying and selling, without any charge of thievery, was seen by Jesus as in contradiction to the purity of the temple.

If one overlooked the "thievery" part of Mark 11:17 and focused on the "house of prayer" part, one could argue that Jesus was against sacrifice itself. This view has occasionally been championed,[43] and it could be supported by citing the quotation of Hos 6:6 in Matt 9:13 and 12:7, "I want mercy and not sacrifice." As Davies points out in correctly dismissing this view, "Matt 5:23–24 and Acts 2:46 become inexplicable on such a view of Jesus."[44] We have here the same problem which we shall meet in discussing Jesus' view of the law. If he actually explicitly opposed one of the main institutions of Judaism, he kept it secret from his disciples.

There is one last possibility for seeing Jesus as bent on purification and reform: he wanted the trade moved entirely outside the temple precincts. If any trade was conducted inside the temple precincts, it was conducted in the court of the Gentiles.[45] We shall immediately consider the question of whether or not it was precisely the Gentiles for whom Jesus was concerned, and we now limit our attention to the fact that the court of the Gentiles was within the temple precincts. Did Jesus differ from his contemporaries simply by wishing to extend the holy area to the outermost court? To my knowledge, no one has proposed this precise interpretation, although one might do so.[46] Such a view could have been suggested by the last sentence of Zech 14:20f.:

> And on that day there shall be inscribed on the bells of the horses, "Holy to the Lord." And the pots in the house of the Lord shall be as the bowls

---

that "cleansing" is the right term, though she argues persuasively against the authenticity of Mark 11:17 (pp. 87–90).

41. Roloff, *Der irdische Jesus*, 93.

42. Harvey, *Constraints*, 132 and notes.

43. For references, see W. D. Davies, *The Gospel and the Land*, 349 n. 45 item 1. See especially the sensitive treatment by Moule, *Birth*, 21–25.

44. Davies, loc. cit.

45. For the sake of argument, we presently accept the view that the trade, or part of it, was conducted in the court of the Gentiles. See n. 6 above and Davies' defence of this location, *The Gospel and the Land*, 350f.

46. Compare, however, the argument of J. D. M. Derrett, "The Zeal of Thy House and the Cleansing of the Temple," *Downside Review* 95, 1977, 79–94. He proposes that the casting out of merchants is something to which the prophets looked forward, citing Zech 14:21 and other passages which do not appear to be directly relevant.

before the altar; and every pot in Jerusalem and Judah shall be sacred to the Lord of hosts, so that all who sacrifice may come and take of them and boil the flesh of the sacrifice in them. And there shall no longer be a trader in the house of the Lord of hosts on that day.

In a context in which all the cooking utensils in Jerusalem are to be ritually pure, so that they can be used in preparing sacrificed meat, there will be no traders in the house; the entire area will be purified.

It is very unlikely that we have here the motive behind Jesus' action. One passage, Mark 7:1–5 and par., depicts Jesus' followers as not accepting an extension to lay people of the biblical purity laws which govern the priests. I doubt the authenticity of this dispute, but in any case there is certainly no evidence for attributing to Jesus a concern to extend the purity code in the way hoped by Zechariah.

This leads us to see once more that the notion behind the discussion of "purity" in New Testament scholarship is a modern one. New Testament [[68]] scholars who write about Jesus' concern for the purity of the temple seem to have in mind a familiar Protestant idea: "pure" worship consists in the Word, and all external rites should be purged. In first-century Judaism, however, a concern to extend purity would almost certainly have involved extending the rites, such as washing, connected with it. I think that we should drop the discussion of Jesus' action as one concerned with purifying the worship of God.[47]

I shall shortly propose an alternative explanation, and one which seems to fit better into the probable outlook of Palestinian Jews of Jesus' day.[48] We should first of all note that other views have been advanced. Principally to be noted are Brandon's view that Jesus' action was part of a carefully planned attempt to take the leadership of the country by arms[49] and Davies' view that what was at stake was the status of Gentiles.[50] On the latter view the key is

47. One could conceivably think that Jesus wanted to purify the temple, but simultaneously to redefine purity in such a way as to eliminate the standard distinction between sacred and profane. The redefinition would involve purging externals (sacrifice) in favour of internals (prayer). One may think, for example, of Käsemann's view that this is what Jesus did in Mark 7:15: it is not food which makes impure, but what comes out of the heart (see [[Sanders, Jesus and Judaism,]] Introduction, 34). I have not noted that anyone explicitly argues this case with regard to the temple, but the widespread discussion of Jesus' action in the temple as cleansing or purifying the service may rest on such a view. I would regard such a proposal, were it to be made, as being too improbable to discuss. Cf. the comment on the inner/outer distinction in the next note.

48. I am not arguing that no Jew of Jesus' day could have made the inner/outer distinction which is often attributed to him. On the contrary, Philo's writings contain this sort of distinction, and it may also be seen in Rom 2:28f. It is more than slightly difficult, however, to find this kind of distinction in literature of Palestinian provenance. Most to the point, I know of no clear example in the synoptic Gospels.

49. S. G. F. Brandon, Jesus and the Zealots, 1967. See Davies, The Gospel and the Land, 349f. n. 45, item 4.

50. Davies, The Gospel and the Land, 350f. n. 46. So also Dodd, Founder, 147; Pesch, "Der Anspruch Jesu," 56. According to the latter, the key passage is the quotation of Isa 56:7 in Mark 11:17, but we have already seen that the verse is most probably a later addition.

given by the fact that trade was conducted in the court of the Gentiles.[51]
Since that was the area that was cleansed, Jesus must have been "concerned
with the right of, and the hopes of Judaism for, the Gentiles as with the
Temple itself."[52] Both of these views rest on reconstructions of Jesus' activity
which are informed by numerous points of evidence, and it would be out of
place to discuss them fully in this chapter. Brandon's view, in fact, will get no
full airing at all, since I consider that it has been sufficiently refuted;[53] it cannot in any case be said to have influenced many.

Jesus' attitude towards the Gentiles, on the other hand, will be discussed
in more detail in chap. 7 [[not reprinted here]]. Meanwhile, it will have to suffice to say that Jesus does not seem to have made a definite gesture in favour
of including Gentiles in the kingdom, although he may well have envisaged
their inclusion at the eschaton. The evidence to be discussed below will show
Jesus not to have been *directly* concerned with the Gentiles. In light of this,
the place of the trade, and consequently of Jesus' action, should be seen as
coincidental and not determinative for the meaning of the event.[54] Any public action must have been performed in a place in which activities related to
the temple were carried out and to which Jesus had access. In order to derive
the meaning of the event directly from the place where it was carried out
(presumably the court of the Gentiles), or from the particular activity which
was attacked (the trade necessary as a preliminary to sacrifice), we would
have to think that Jesus selected the place and the activity from among several available. This, however, seems not to have been the case. Jesus might
have gained access to the Priests' Court, and thus to a place more directly
connected with the preparation of sacrifices, had he pretended to have a sin-
or guilt-offering to present; but apart from [[69]] the employment of such a
ruse there would seem to be nothing other than the trade in the court of the
Gentiles which he could have attacked.

The proposal that Jesus' action was in favour of the Gentiles, however, has
the merit of understanding it as symbolic, a point to which we shall return.

There is one other frequently met scholarly assertion about the significance of Jesus' action at the temple which should be noted. It is generally
thought that Jesus' action would have been primarily resented by the temple
hierarchy, those who had a vested interest in the profit derived from the sale
of bird-offerings and the exchange of money. Thus, for example, Trautmann
argues that Jesus objected to the *Sadducean* priesthood for combining politics
and economics with the temple and also opposed *their* theology of atonement
by means of sacrifice and the cult[55]—as if other Jews did not believe in atonement through sacrifice. We have seen that a distinction has often been made
between Jesus' attack on the law, which is believed to have been directed

51. Trade in the court of the Gentiles: see above, nn. 6 and 45.
52. Davies, *The Gospel and the Land*, 351.
53. See especially Hengel, *Was Jesus a Revolutionist?*, ET 1971.
54. Gaston (*No Stone on Another*, 87) has strongly objected to drawing far-reaching conclusions from the possibility that the "cleansing" took place in the court of the Gentiles.
55. Trautmann, *Zeichenhafte Handlungen*, 120–22.

against the Pharisees and scribes, and his attack on the temple trade, directed against the priests and the Sadducees.[56] This distinction, which is often made sharply, is quite misleading. The law was generally revered, while the temple was the focus of religious hope and devotion throughout Judaism. I earlier pointed out that there is no indication that Jesus' action was directed only against some particular practice. Now we must note that it would not have been offensive to only one group. More than just the priests thought that the sacrifices were ordained by God and atoned for sins. We shall return to this point later in this chapter . . . when assessing Jesus' opponents and the points of opposition.

Thus far we have seen reason to doubt many of the prevalent views about the event in the temple area: that the action was that of a religious reformer, bent on "purifying" current practice; that the locale, the court of the Gentiles, indicates that the action primarily had to do with opening the worship of the temple to non-Jews; that the action was, and was perceived to be, primarily against the temple officers and the Saducean party.

There is another frequently met interpretation, however, which I regard as entirely correct. Jesus' action is to be regarded as a symbolic demonstration.[57] The question, of course, is what the action symbolized. We have already considered and rejected the principal proposal, that it symbolized the inclusion of Gentiles.

Let us first consider how the action must have looked to others. Jesus did not actually bring all buying and selling to a halt. As Hengel has pointed [[70]] out, any real effort to stop the trade necessary to the temple service would have required an army, and there is no evidence of a substantial martial conflict.[58] It is reasonable to think that Jesus (and conceivably some of his followers, although none are mentioned) overturned some tables as a demonstrative action. It would appear that the action was not substantial enough even to interfere with the daily routine; for if it had been he would surely have been arrested on the spot. Thus those who saw it, and those who heard about it, would have known that it was a gesture intended to make a point rather than to have a concrete result; that is, they would have seen the action as symbolic.

The discussion of whether or not Jesus succeeded in interrupting the actual functioning of the temple points us in the right direction for seeing what

56. Examples are given throughout the section on the "State of the Question" in [[Sanders, *Jesus and Judaism*,]] Introduction. Recently see Jeremias, *Proclamation*, 145; Meyer, *Aims*, 238; H. W. Bartsch, *Jesus. Prophet und Messias aus Galiläa*, 1970, 48; Boismard, *Synopse*, 2.408: it was the sacerdotal caste which became exasperated at seeing Jesus pose as a religious reformer with regard to cultic practice.

57. Thus, for example, Roloff, *Der irdische Jesus*, 95; Brandon, *Jesus and the Zealots*, 338; cf. Meyer, *Aims*, 170: "Jesus' act was symbol-charged"; Gaston, *No Stone on Another*, 86: the action was symbolic.

58. Hengel, *Was Jesus a Revolutionist?*, 16f. Cf. Dodd, *Founder*, 144f. "The force which effected it was simply the personal authority which made itself felt when Jesus confronted the crowd."

the action symbolized but did not accomplish: it symbolized destruction. That is one of the most obvious meanings of the action of overturning itself. Some have seen this, but the force and obviousness of the point are obscured as long as we continue to think that Jesus was demonstrating against the Sadducees for profiting and in favour of purifying the temple of externalism.[59] Had Jesus wished to make a gesture symbolizing purity, he doubtless could have done so. The pouring out of water comes immediately to mind. The turning over of even one table points towards destruction.

Professor Moule has proposed to me that overturning one or more tables is not an entirely self-evident symbol of destruction. He quite correctly points to the broken pot of Jer 19:10. Would breaking something not have been a better symbol? Perhaps so. I must leave to others the assessment of "overturning" as a self-evident symbol of destruction, though it appears to me to be quite an obvious one. My view, however, depends in part on further considerations.

Let us continue by pursuing the question of how the action would have been understood by others. The import to those who saw or heard of it was almost surely, at least in part, that Jesus was attacking the temple service which was commanded by God. Not just priests would have been offended, but all those who believed that the temple was the place at which Israel and individual Israelites had been commanded to offer sacrifice, to make atonement for their sins. Further, it is hard to imagine how Jesus himself could have seen it if not in these terms. We should suppose that Jesus *knew what he was doing*: like others, he regarded the sacrifices as commanded by God, he knew that they required a certain amount of trade, and he knew that making a gesture towards disrupting the trade represented an attack on the divinely ordained sacrifices. Thus I take it that the action [[71]] at the very least symbolized an attack, and note that "attack" is not far from "destruction."

But what does this mean? On what conceivable grounds could Jesus have undertaken to attack—and symbolize the destruction of—what was ordained by God? The obvious answer is that destruction, in turn, looks towards restoration.[60] This will be better seen when we consider the sayings about the destruction of the temple, which complement and help us understand the action.[61]

59. See the next note.

60. In favour of this interpretation of the action, see for example R. J. McKelvey, *The New Temple. The Church in the New Testament*, 1969, 66 ("it points to the coming of the kingdom of God"); pp. 71f. ("The new age would have its temple . . ."); James D. G. Dunn, *Unity and Diversity in the New Testament*, 1977, 324 (Jesus' disciples understood the action as pointing towards "eschatological renewal centred on Mount Zion and on an eschatologically renewed or rebuilt temple"); Trautmann, *Zeichenhafte Handlungen*, 124, 126f., 129, 386. On p. 130 she argues that the action was not "prophetic," since there was no appeal to the Lord, which I take to be a distinction without much of a difference. Trautmann's position is interesting, since she holds that Jesus intended to purify the temple of present corrupting practice, but yet manages to see that the action points towards a new temple. The real force of the event stands out even more sharply when it is not confused with another, competing interpretation.

61. Note the setting of Jer 19:10 in a lengthy spoken prediction of destruction.

The Sayings about the Destruction of the Temple

The first form in which the reader of the Gospels meets a saying about the destruction of the temple is in the form of a simple *prediction*, with no implication of a threat:

> As he was leaving the temple, one of his disciples exclaimed, "Look, Master, what huge stones! What fine buildings!" Jesus said to him, "You see these great buildings. Not one stone will be left upon another; all will be thrown down." (Mark 13:1f.)

To this prediction all three synoptists append the "little apocalypse." It is likely that the saying was originally independent of this entire context (both the introduction, which, as Bultmann observed, seems designed to elicit the saying,[62] and the attached apocalypse), but it would seem likely that Jesus said something of the sort and applied it to the temple. For one thing, other traditions contain the charge that he *threatened* the temple. One of these is the trial scene:

> And some stood up and bore false witness against him, saying, "We heard him say, 'I will destroy this temple that is made with hands, and in three days I will build another, not made with hands.'" (Mark 14:57f.)
> At last two [false witnesses] came forward and said, "This fellow said, 'I am able to destroy the temple of God, and to build it in three days.'" (Matt 26:60f.)

The reports of what was said at the trial scene are notoriously difficult to verify. In fact, it may even be wondered whether or not the entire "trial" before the high priest and others is largely fictional.[63] Even if the entire scene were composed after Easter, however, it would still seem likely that this specific accusation is based on an accurate memory of the principal point on which Jesus offended many of his contemporaries. One can imagine a subsequent Christian penning *de novo* [['afresh']] the scene in which Jesus [[72]] is charged with blasphemy for claiming to be the Son of God (Mark 14:61–64), but it is hard to imagine a purely fictional origin for the accusation that he threatened to destroy the temple. For one thing, it leads nowhere. According to the evangelists, the testimony of the witnesses as to what Jesus said did not agree, and the charge was apparently dropped. For another, the implication of physical insurrection which the charge seems to contain would scarcely have been something that a Christian author would spontaneously have thought of. Luke drops the charge from the trial scene, and Matthew and Mark characterize it as false. Mark's contrast "made with hands," "not made with hands" may also be an attempt to water down this implication.[64]

---

62. Bultmann, *History*, 36.
63. See chap. 11 below [[in Sanders, *Jesus and Judaism*]].
64. The principal alternative for understanding Mark's meaning has been well argued by Donald Juel, *Messiah and Temple: The Trial of Jesus in the Gospel of Mark*, 1977. His chief conclusion is that the author of Mark had in mind the Christian community as the temple not

Most striking, however, is the reappearance of the charge in other traditions. In the crucifixion scene both Matthew (27:40) and Mark (15:29) (but again not Luke) depict the crowd as calling Jesus "the one who would destroy the temple and rebuild it in three days." According to Acts 6:14 the charge against Stephen was that he said—even after Jesus' death and resurrection—that "this Jesus of Nazareth will destroy this place" (the temple). If we could be absolutely sure of the historicity of this charge against Stephen, it would be clear that Jesus had spoken so firmly that Christians continued to expect the imminent destruction of the temple. It is noteworthy that the author of Acts says that the charge against Stephen was brought by false witnesses (Acts 6:13). This is further evidence of early Christian reluctance to admit the accusation, and it helps confirm that Jesus actually said something which was taken as a threat.

Finally, we should quote John 2:18–22:

> The Jews then said to him, "What sign have you to show us for doing this?" Jesus answered them, "Destroy this temple, and in three days I will raise it up." The Jews then said, "It has taken forty-six years to build this temple, and will you raise it up in three days?" But he spoke of the temple of his body. When therefore he was raised from the dead, his disciples remembered that he had said this; and they believed the scripture and the word which Jesus had spoken.

In John's account, this exchange immediately follows the "cleansing" of the temple. This passage is especially striking. We see here the characteristic Johannine device of having Jesus say something which his interlocutors understand on one level, which gives the evangelist the opportunity of explaining the true meaning, which resides on another level. For our purposes, however, the statement of John 2:19 shows how deeply embedded in the tradition was the threat of destroying and the promise of [[73]] rebuilding the temple. It was so firmly fixed that it was not dropped, but rather interpreted. John, it is to be noted, does drop the threat, "I will destroy," in favour of the second person statement which implies a condition, "[If] you destroy." The change is necessary for the evangelist's explanation that the temple is Jesus' body. Jesus could not have said that he would destroy his own body.[65] It is reasonable to see the change in subject as John's and to suppose that John had the tradition contained in Mark 14:58, Matt 26:61, Mark 15:29, Matt 27:40, and Acts 6:14: Jesus threatened the destruction of the temple (and perhaps predicted its rebuilding after three days).

We seem here to be in touch with a very firm historical tradition, but there is still uncertainty about precisely what it is. Did Jesus *predict* the destruction of the temple (Mark 13:1f. and pars.) or *threaten* it (Mark 14:58 and

---

made with hands (see, for example, pp. 168f.). See also Dodd, *Founder*, 89f.; Klinzing, *Umdeutung*, 202f. (with bibliography). Klinzing (p. 204) also argues that the phrases "made with hands" and "not made with hands," absent from Matthew, are secondary additions.

65. Cf. Gaston, *No Stone on Another*, 71.

elsewhere)?[66] Did he mention destruction and rebuilding, or only the former? The christological use of the prediction that it would be rebuilt after three days is evident, but even so Jesus may have predicted just that, for the application to the resurrection is not always explicit (e.g., Mark 15:29 and par.). If Jesus either threatened or predicted the destruction of the temple and its rebuilding after three days, that is, if the saying in any of its forms is even approximately authentic, his meaning would be luminously clear: he predicted the imminent appearance of the judgment and the new age.

The saying and the deed would then correspond. Both point towards the destruction of the present order and the appearance of the new. We should probably think that his expectation was that a new temple would be given by God from heaven, an expectation which is not otherwise unknown during the period, even if it may not have been universal.[67] In this case the characterization of the temple as "made without hands" could be original, rather than a spiritualizing interpretation. But if (following Mark 13:1f.; Acts 6:14) there was no prediction of a rebuilding, the meaning would be only slightly less concrete. Jesus either threatened or predicted that *God* would put an end to the present temple: that is, that the end was at hand. If he said "I will destroy," he saw himself as God's agent.

We have thus far not attempted to determine the original form of the saying, nor is it likely that this can be done with certainty. Some possibilities, however, can be excluded. We should first observe that the existence of the threat form ("I will destroy," Mark 14:58; implied by Mark 15:29 and Acts 6:14, and probably by John 2:19) makes it virtually incredible that the entire saying could be a *vaticinium ex eventu*, a "prophecy" after the event. [[74]] After the temple was in fact destroyed by the Romans in the year 70, the Christians would not have composed a threat by Jesus that he would destroy it, nor would they have turned an existing prophecy that the temple would be destroyed into such a threat. If we had only the prediction, we could believe it to be a *vaticinium* [['prophecy']], though perhaps not a very likely one,[68] but we cannot explain the origin of the double form in this way. One would then have to suppose that the prediction was composed after it was fulfilled in 70, that an evangelist or someone in the pre-Gospel tradition creatively turned the prediction into a threat and made it the object of a charge before the high

66. Thus Bultmann: a saying about the temple goes back to Jesus, but we must remain uncertain about the form (*History*, 120f.; *Ergänzungsheft*, 46f., with bibliography). In the *Ergänzungsheft* he corrected his earlier view that the saying has a mythological basis and correctly placed it in the framework of Jewish apocalyptic (in the sense of eschatology). Dieter Lührmann's discussion of the sayings is quite instructive. He points out that Mark regarded the threat of Mark 14:58 as inauthentic, but accepted the prediction of 13:2. One can be certain that there was *a* saying and suspect that the version in 14:58 is closer to the original. See Lührmann, "Markus 14.55–64. Christologie und Zerstörung des Tempels im Markusevangelium," *NTS* 27, 1981, 457–74, here 466–69.

67. See the next chapter [[in Sanders, *Jesus and Judaism*]].

68. Gaston (*No Stone on Another*, 45) cites a true *vaticinium ex eventu* on the destruction of Jerusalem from Lactantius, *Divine Institutions* 4.21. It is much more explicit and detailed than anything in the Gospels.

priest which failed for lack of agreement in the testimony, that one of Luke's sources for the early chapters of Acts independently arrived at the same charge (for Luke can scarcely have composed it, having twice dropped it in the Gospel), and that the fourth evangelist found the threat form of the saying to be so well known that it had to be taken account of. All of this, especially the change from a prediction based on facts to a threat which became the object of a charge, strains the imagination too much. It is better to believe that Jesus said something which lies behind the traditions. But did *he* predict a military disaster? It is not inconceivable that as a sagacious man he saw where zealotism would lead the nation one generation later, but there is no reason to think that this sort of commonplace observation (if you fellows keep up your trouble-making, it is bound to lead to disaster) lies behind the double tradition of prediction and threat as we have it. Even if we push the prediction back to Jesus, it is still unlikely that the threat form derived from a simple prediction of disaster. It seems far better to suppose that Jesus either threatened the destruction of the temple, with himself playing a role, or predicted its destruction in such terms that the prediction could be construed as a threat, than that he made a general prediction that foreign arms would some day take Jerusalem and destroy the temple. It is hard to know how such a prediction could have led to the traditions in the Gospels and Acts.

If Jesus did not predict the conquest of the temple by foreign arms, and if he himself was not planning armed insurrection, then it follows that he must have either predicted or threatened the destruction of the temple *by God*. In this case there would still be the question, though it probably cannot be resolved, of his own role in the destruction. Mark 13:1f. and pars. give him no role, while the other passages, including John 2:18f. by inference, do. Even if he said "I will destroy," however, he could only have meant that he would act as God's agent and do so in the context of the arrival of the eschaton.

Finally, we can note that whatever Jesus said became public in some [[75]] way or other. Mark has the prediction of destruction made to one disciple (13:1), while Matthew has "his disciples" (24:1). Luke gives the saying a wider setting (21:5). Here as elsewhere we must suppose that the settings are secondary. The public nature of the statement is implied by its being used in charges against Jesus and Stephen.

Thus we conclude that Jesus publicly predicted or threatened the destruction of the temple, that the statement was shaped by his expectation of the arrival of the eschaton, that he probably also expected a new temple to be given by God from heaven, and that he made a demonstration which prophetically symbolized the coming event.

Roloff took the "cleansing" of the temple and the prediction of its destruction to be "obviously contradictory" to each other in a way suitable to the words and deeds of a prophet. Jesus *both* saw the temple as the place of God's presence which should be purified for present use and predicted its destruction.[69] Others have interpreted the action as "cleansing" and have then

---

69. *Der irdische Jesus*, 97; cf. Meyer, *Aims*, 170.

allowed this meaning to submerge the force of the saying about destruction. Thus Bornkamm wrote that the temple "cleansing" is "more than an act of reform to restore the temple service to its original (sic!) purity." Jesus was also "cleansing the sanctuary for the approaching kingdom of God."[70] Here the threat to destroy is dropped and thus the radical connection with eschatology.

On the hypothesis presented here the action and the saying form a unity. Jesus predicted (or threatened) the destruction of the temple and carried out an action symbolic of its destruction by demonstrating against the performance of the sacrifices. He did not wish to purify the temple, either of dishonest trading or of trading in contrast to "pure" worship. Nor was he opposed to the temple sacrifices which God commanded to Israel. He intended, rather, to indicate that the end was at hand and that the temple would be destroyed, so that the new and perfect temple might arise.[71]

Our hypothesis receives partial confirmation from the embarrassment of Matthew and Mark about the threat to destroy and the embarrassment of all three synoptists about the action in the temple. Matthew and Mark explain that the threat to destroy was testified to only by false witnesses (Matt 26:59f.; Mark 14:56f.); and all three synoptists, by use of the quotation about a "den of robbers," make it appear that Jesus was quite reasonably protesting against dishonesty (Mark 11:17 and pars.). They attempt to make the action relatively innocuous, and they deny the force of the saying—while reporting both. Despite their efforts, we should take both the action and the saying at full value. We see immediately behind [[76]] the surface of the Gospels that Jesus threatened (or predicted) the destruction of the temple and that he acted to demonstrate it.

Our interpretation has the additional advantage of making sense of the acceptance of temple worship by the early apostles (Acts 2:46; 3:1; 21:26). They did not think that Jesus had considered it impure, but only that the days of the present temple were numbered.

The only question which remains outstanding at this point is whether or not Jesus' contemporaries would have clearly understood the prophetic symbolism. I have previously urged that pious Jews, not just the supposedly profiteering priestly class, would have been offended at the action in the temple. This follows both from intrinsic probability and from the sequel—Jesus was put to death, apparently with the approval of many in Jerusalem. But would the crowd have understood without ambiguity that Jesus intended to symbolize the impending eschatological act of God? We recall here the question of whether or not the meaning of the symbolic action was self-evident. To this question no certain answer can be given.[72] The chapter which immediately

70. Bornkamm, *Jesus of Nazareth*, 158f.

71. The view that Jesus expected a new, end-time temple is by no means unique, although, as I have indicated, it is often mixed—I think uncomfortably—with the interpretation of the action as cleansing (e.g., Trautmann and others, cited in n. 60; Roloff and Meyer, cited in n. 67). For the view that Jesus expected a new temple, see recently Klinzing, *Umdeutung*, 205 (citing further literature); Meyer, *Aims*, 168–70; 181–85; 197f.

72. Harvey (*Constraints*, 133f.) proposes that the action was not immediately understood, but that it would have been at least seen as a claim to authority.

follows argues that there was current in some circles the expectation of the destruction and rebuilding of the temple. Thus it is at least reasonable that the intent of Jesus' action was clear to his contemporaries. Even if he was understood, however, the action and saying were still highly offensive. Jesus still attacked the functioning temple, where the sins of Israel were atoned, and the crowd could simply have disbelieved his eschatological prediction or resented his personal self-assertion. To attempt a real answer to the question posed in this paragraph, however, would be to press hypothetical reconstruction too far. In the subsequent chapters supporting evidence for the interpretation of Jesus' word and deed will be presented. I doubt that we can ever securely know how well Jesus was understood by how many of his contemporaries.

Bibliography

1. Texts and Reference Works Cited or Quoted

The Apocrypha and Pseudepigrapha of the Old Testament in English. 2 vols. Edited by R. H. Charles. Oxford: [[Clarendon,]] 1913 (repr. 1963).
The Old Testament Pseudepigrapha I: Apocalyptic Literature and Testaments. Edited by James H. Charlesworth. New York: [[Doubleday,]] 1983.

The Dead Sea Scrolls in English. Geza Vermes. Harmondsworth: [[Penguin,]] 1962.
The Scroll of the War of the Sons of Light against the Sons of Darkness. Edited by Yigael Yadin. [[London: Oxford University Press,]] 1962.
Die Texte aus Qumran: Hebräisch und Deutsch. 2nd ed. Edited by Eduard Lohse. [[Munich: Kösel,]] 1971.

Shishah Sidre Mishnah (The Six Orders of the Mishnah). Edited by Chanoch Albeck. 6 vols. Jerusalem and Tel Aviv, 1958–59.
The Mishnah. Translated by Herbert Danby. Oxford: [[Clarendon]], 1933.

Josephus. Translated and ed. by H. St. J. Thackeray (vols. 1–5), Ralph Marcus (vols. 5–8), and Louis Feldman (vols. 9–10). Loeb Classical Library. [[Cambridge: Harvard University Press,]] 1926–65.
Philo. Translated and ed. by F. H. Colson (vols. 1–10) and G. H. Whitaker (vols. 1–5). Loeb Classical Library. [[Cambridge: Harvard University Press,]] 1929–43.

2. General

Abrahams, I. *Studies in Pharisaism and the Gospels: First and Second Series.* Cambridge, 1917, 1924. Reprinted New York: [[Ktav,]] 1967.
Aulén, G. *Jesus in Contemporary Historical Research.* [[Translated by Ingalill H. Hjelm. Philadelphia: Fortress,]] 1976.
Avigad, Nahman. *Discovering Jerusalem.* [[New York,]] 1983.
Banks, Robert. *Jesus and the Law in the Synoptic Tradition.* Society for New Testament Studies Monograph Series 28. Cambridge: [[Cambridge University Press,]] 1975.
Bartsch, H. W. *Jesus: Prophet und Messias aus Galiläa.* Frankfurt a.M.: [[Stimme,]] 1970.

Beasley-Murray, G. R. *A Commentary on Mark Thirteen.* London: [[Macmillan,]] 1957.

Boismard, M.-É. *Commentaire.* Vol. 2 of *Synopse des quatre Évangiles en Français.* Paris: [[Cerf,]] 1972.

Bornkamm, G. *Jesus of Nazareth.* [[Translated by Irene McLuskey and Fraser McLuskey.]] New York: [[Harper,]] 1960.

Bousset, W. *Jesu Predigt in ihrem Gegensatz zum Judentum.* Göttingen, 1892.

———. *Jesus.* 2nd ed. [[Translated by J. P. Trevelyan.]] Edited by W. D. Morrison. [[London: Williams & Norgate,]] 1906.

Brandon, S. G. F. *Jesus and the Zealots.* [[Manchester: Manchester University Press,]] 1967.

Braun, H. *Spätjüdisch-häretischer und frühchristlicher Radikalismus.* 2 vols. Tübingen: [[Mohr,]] 1957.

Büchler, Adolf. *Types of Jewish-Palestinian Piety from 70 B.C.E. to 70 C.E.: The Ancient Pious Men.* London, 1922. Reprinted New York: [[Ktav,]] 1968.

Bultmann, R. *Die Geschichte der synoptischen Tradition.* 7th ed. Göttingen: [[Vandenhoeck & Ruprecht,]] 1967. *Ergänzungsheft.* 4th ed. Edited by Gerd Theissen and Philipp Vielhauer. Göttingen: [[Vandenhoeck & Ruprecht,]] 1971.

———. *The History of the Synoptic Tradtion.* Translated by John Marsh. New York: [[Harper & Row,]] 1963.

Davies, W. D. *The Gospel and the Land: Early Christianity and Jewish Territorial Doctrine.* Berkeley: [[University of California Press,]] 1974.

Derrett, J. D. M. "The Zeal of Thy House and the Cleansing of the Temple." *Downside Review* 95 (1977) 79–94.

Dodd, C. H. *The Founder of Christianity.* New York: [[Macmillan, 1970]].

Dunn, James D. G. *Unity and Diversity in the New Testament: [[An Inquiry into the Character of Earliest Christianity.* Philadelphia: Westminster,]] 1977.

Edersheim, Alfred. *The Life and Times of Jesus the Messiah.* 2 vols. Grand Rapids: [[Christian Classics Ethereal Library,]] 1936.

Gason, Lloyd. *No Stone on Another: Studies in the Significance of the Fall of Jerusalem in the Synoptic Gospels.* Novum Testamentum Supplements 23. Leiden: [[Brill,]] 1970.

Goguel, Maurice. *The Life of Jesus.* Vol. 1 of *Jesus and the Origins of Christianity.* [[Translated by O. Wyon. New York: Macmillan, 1933.]]

Harvey, A. E. *Jesus and the Constraints of History.* London: [[Duckworth,]] 1982.

Hengel, Martin. *Was Jesus a Revolutionist?* [[Translated by W. Klassen. Philadelphia: Fortress,]] 1971.

Hirsch, Emil G. "Sacrifice." Pp. 615–28 in vol. 10 of *Jewish Encyclopedia.*

Jeremias, J. "Zwei Miszellen: 1. Antik-Jüdische Münzdeutungen. 2. Zur Geschichtlichkeit der Tempelreinigung." *New Testament Studies* 23 (1977) 177–80.

———. *Jerusalem in the Time of Jesus.* [[Translated by F. H. Cave and C. H. Cave. Philadelphia: Fortress,]] 1969.

———. *The Proclamation of Jesus.* Vol. 1 of *New Testament Theology.* [[Translated by John Bowden. New York: Scribner / London: SCM,]] 1971.

Juel, Donald. *Messiah and Temple: The Trial of Jesus in the Gospel of Mark.* Society of Biblical Literature Dissertation Series 31. Missoula, Montana: [[Scholars Press,]] 1977.

Klausner, J. *Jesus of Nazareth*. [[Translated by Herbert Danby. New York: Macmillan,]] 1925.

Klinzing, Georg. *Die Umdeutung des Kultus in der Qumrangemeinde und im Neuen Testament*. Studien zur Umwelt des Neuen Testaments 7. [[Göttingen: Vandenhoeck & Ruprecht,]] 1971.

Lührmann, Dieter. "Markus 14.55–64: Christologie und Zerstörung des Tempels im Markusevangelium." *New Testament Studies* 27 (1981) 457–74.

McKelvey, R. J. *The New Temple: The Church in the New Testament*. [[London: Oxford University Press,]] 1969.

Meyer, B. F. *The Aims of Jesus*. London: [[SCM,]] 1979.

Moule, C. F. D. *The Birth of the New Testament*. 3rd ed. [[San Francisco: Harper & Row, 1982]].

Nolan, Albert. *Jesus before Christianity: The Gospel of Liberation*. Cape Town: [[Philip,]] 1976 / London, 1977.

Pesch, R. "Der Anspruch Jesu." *Orientierung* 35 (1971) 53–56, 67–70, 77–81.

Roloff, J. *Das Kerygma und der irdische Jesus*. Göttingen: [[Vandenhoeck & Ruprecht, 1970]].

Sanders, E. P. *Paul and Palestinian Judaism*. [[Philadelphia: Fortress,]] 1977.

Schürer, Emil. *The History of the Jewish People in the Age of Jesus Christ*. 3 vols. [[Edited by Geza Vermes, Fergus Millar, and Matthew Black. Edinburgh: T. & T. Clark, 1973–87]].

Suhl, A. *Die Funktion der alttestamentlichen Zitate und Anspielungen im Markusevangelium*. Gütersloh: [[Mohn,]] 1965.

Taylor, Vincent. *The Gospel according to St. Mark*. London: [[Macmillan, 1952]].

Trautmann, Maria. *Zeichenhafte Handlungen Jesu: Ein Beitrag zur Frage nach dem geschichtlichen Jesus*. Forschung zur Bibel 37. Würzburg: [[Echter,]] 1980.

Trocmé, E. *Jesus and His Contemporaries*. [[Translated by R. A. Wilson. London: SCM,]] 1973 = *Jesus as Seen by His Contemporaries*. Philadelphia: [[Westminster,]] 1973.

C. E. B. CRANFIELD

The Resurrection of Jesus Christ

[[167]] About the importance accorded to the resurrection of Jesus Christ in the New Testament there can hardly be any doubt. It is referred to explicitly and with emphasis in seventeen of the twenty-seven books. These seventeen include all four Gospels, the Acts of the Apostles, Romans and 1 and 2 Corinthians,[1] while the ten which do not explicitly mention it include the seven shortest and slightest books.[2] And those New Testament books, which contain no explicit reference to the Resurrection, may anyway be said to imply it. It may truly be said that they "breathe the Resurrection."[3] Without the existence of belief in Jesus as risen from the dead, their existence is hardly explicable.

Many passages indicate very clearly the centrality of the Resurrection. One of the most striking is Rom 10:9 ("Because if thou shalt confess with thy mouth Jesus *as* Lord, and shalt believe in thy heart that God raised him from the dead, thou shalt be saved"); for it makes it abundantly clear that, for Paul, belief that God has raised Jesus from the dead is the decisive and characteristic belief of Christians. Similarly clear is his statement in 1 Cor 15:14 that "if Christ hath not been raised, then is our preaching vain, your faith also is vain." We may set beside these Pauline examples the words of 1 Pet 1:3 ("Blessed *be* the God and Father of our Lord Jesus Christ, who according to his great mercy begat us again unto a living hope by the resurrection of Jesus Christ from the dead") and the characterization by the author of Acts of the apostles' preaching as "their witness of the resurrection of the Lord Jesus."[4] If then the

---

Reprinted with the permission of T. & T. Clark from *Expository Times* 101 (1989–90) 167–72.

1. The rest of the seventeen are Galatians, Ephesians, Philippians, Colossians, 1 Thessalonians, 2 Timothy, Hebrews, 1 Peter and Revelation. On the fact that the only direct reference to the resurrection of Christ in Hebrews is in 13:20 see C. E. B. Cranfield, *The Bible and Christian Life* (Edinburgh [1985]) 146.

2. Namely, 2 Thessalonians, Titus, Philemon, 2 Peter, 2 and 3 John and Jude.

3. The Epistle of James might seem to be an exception; but on it see Cranfield, op. cit., 151ff.

4. Acts 4:33; cf. 1:22; 2:32; 3:15; 5:32; 10:41; 13:31.

Resurrection is so central to the faith of the New Testament, it clearly matters tremendously whether the affirmation that Jesus was raised from the dead is true or not. If our study of the New Testament is serious, we are bound sooner or later to ask, "Was Jesus of Nazareth really raised from the dead?" Can we, or can we not, respond to the Easter greeting, "Christ is risen," with our own "He is risen indeed," with intellectual and moral integrity?

I shall attempt here, first, to consider the main objections urged against the truth of the affirmation that Jesus was raised from the dead; secondly, to set out the main arguments which may be brought in support of it; and, thirdly, to indicate the conclusion to which I, personally, come.

I

1. The New Testament contains no narrative of the actual raising of Jesus (according to the New Testament that was an event which no mortal eye saw), but it does contain several accounts of incidents associated with it, namely, the discovery of the empty tomb and the resurrection appearances. The first of the objections which have to be considered is that there are a number of apparent discrepancies between these accounts.

(i) Luke 23:56 seems to indicate that it was before the sabbath began that the women prepared their spices and ointments, whereas according to Mark 16:1 [[168]] they waited till the sabbath was over before buying their spices.

(ii) As to the time when the women came to the tomb on the first day of the week, Mark surprisingly qualifies his "very early" by "when the sun was risen," which seems to contradict it (the Western variant which gives the sense "as the sun was rising" looks like an attempt to remove the difficulty). The "at early dawn" of Luke 24:1 and "while it was yet dark" of John 20:1 agree with Mark's "very early," but not with his "when the sun was risen." Matthew's "late on the sabbath day, as it began to dawn toward the first day of the week" (28:1) would seem to indicate Saturday evening after sundown, when (according to Jewish reckoning) the first day of the week was beginning.

(iii) According to Mark 16:1 (compare Luke 24:1) the women's purpose was to anoint the body; but Matt 28:1 gives as their intention simply "to see the sepulchre."

(iv) As to the number and names of the women who came to the tomb there is a puzzling variation. According to Mark there were three, Mary Magdalene, Mary the mother of James, and Salome; according to Matt 28:1 there were two, Mary Magdalene and "the other Mary." Luke 24:10 names three women, two of whom are the same as in Mark, while Joanna replaces Salome (there is also a reference to "the other women with them"). According to John 20:1, 11 and 18, Mary Magdalene was apparently alone.[5]

(v) According to Mark 16:5 and Matt 28:5, one angel appears to the women: in Luke 24:4 (compare v. 23) and John 20:12 two angels are seen.

---

5. Though the first person plural in John 20:2 ("we know not") is possibly a trace of the involvement of more than one woman.

(vi) The effect of the angel's (or angels') words on the women is variously represented. Mark 16:8 tells us that the women "went out, and fled from the tomb; for trembling and astonishment had come upon them: and they said nothing to any one; for they were afraid." Matthew also mentions their fear, but couples with it "great joy," and adds that they "ran to bring his disciples word" (28:8). Luke says that they "returned from the tomb, and told all these things to the eleven, and to all the rest" (24:9). In John the angels do not give the command, but Jesus himself gives it and Mary obeys.

(vii) In contrast with all four Gospels, Paul says nothing of any visit of women (or of a woman) to the tomb.

(viii) While all four Gospels testify to the tomb's being empty, Paul does not mention the tomb at all.

(ix) 1 Cor 15:5 seems to imply that the first person to see the risen Lord was Peter. Luke 24:34 agrees with this. But Matt 28:9 (compare 28:1), John 20:14–17 and the Markan appendix (Mark 16:9) agree that Jesus appeared first either to Mary Magdalene alone or to her and "the other Mary." Mark 16:1–8 says nothing about an appearance of Jesus himself to the women.

(x) Mark 14:28 and 16:7 point to a resurrection appearance in Galilee, though Mark's own text stops at 16:8 without any appearance's having been related. Matthew does record such an appearance (28:16ff.), preceded by one to the women In Jerusalem (28:9f.). John 20 relates appearances in Jerusalem, John 21 appearances in Galilee. Luke stands apart somewhat awkwardly, in that he not only records appearances only in Jerusalem and its neighbourhood, but also by his omission of any parallel to Mark 14:28, his pointed alteration of Mark 16:7 (Luke 24:6f.) and his inclusion of the command to tarry in Jerusalem in 24:49 (compare Acts 1:4) seems to be deliberately ruling out the possibility of a Galilean appearance.

Some further discrepancies can be discerned; but these which have been listed would seem to be the most significant. Of these the first six are not, I think, particularly serious. Differences between the accounts of eye-witnesses of quite ordinary events are a common enough phenomenon. And, if the Resurrection really did happen, the incidents associated with it were certainly not just ordinary events. That there should be signs of disturbance and strain in the human testimony would not be surprising. With regard to (vii), we need not infer that Paul did not know of the part played by the women. His omission of them in 1 Cor 15:4ff. is adequately explained on the assumption that he specially wanted to cite witnesses who would be as generally acceptable as possible. In Jewish legal practice women were not accepted as credible witnesses except in certain limited areas of life, and in Gentile society too their position in regard to the law was inferior to that of men.[6] With regard to (viii), Paul's omission of any reference to the tomb goes naturally with his not mentioning the women as witnesses. To conclude from it that Paul and

6. That Paul's not mentioning the women here was due to a personal antipathy to women is disproved by, among other things, the notable prominence of female names in Romans 16.

the earliest tradition must have known nothing of the empty tomb is quite unjustifiable. The emptiness of the tomb is almost certainly implied by the mention of burial between "died" and "hath been raised" in 1 Cor 15:4. With regard to (ix), the disagreement as to who was the first to see the risen Lord, the part played by concern that the testimony should be generally acceptable is to be recognized. With regard to (x), it is to be noted that Luke, who appears to be intent on excluding the tradition of appearances in Galilee, is also the one who, by specifying forty days as the period between the resurrection and the ascension, underlines the fact that there was ample time to allow for appearances both in Jerusalem and its neighbourhood and also in Galilee.

2. The presence of an angel or angels in the Gospel Easter narratives is probably for a good many people [[169]] an additional reason for doubting the truth of the Resurrection. On this it may simply be said that, while angels as generally depicted in Christian art are indeed incredible, the possibility that the angels of the Bible may be a quite different matter should not be ignored. It would be wise at least to consider Karl Barth's discussion of the angels in *Church Dogmatics* 3/3, 369–519,[7] before we decide either to dismiss the Easter angel as a legendary accretion or to appeal to his presence in the story as a reason for rejecting the truth of the resurrection itself.

3. But the most important objection of all is, without doubt, simply the apparent sheer, stark, utter impossibility of the thing. For Jews of New Testament times, who believed in the final, eschatological resurrection, the idea that that final resurrection had, in the case of one man, been accomplished already was unthinkable. For the vast multitudes of modern men and women, to whom it seems perfectly obvious that death is the end, the manifest, incontrovertible, irreversible termination of a human life, the claim that Jesus was raised from the dead is nonsense, its folly apparent as soon as it is uttered. And this conviction that death is the end does seem to give modern man a certain sense of security. At least, when things are going well for him, he can enjoy his brittle triumphs, strut a while in pride and forget about his limits. But the message of the Resurrection threatens even this illusory sense of security. It opens up a vast vista of the unknown, mocking man's self-importance. To entertain the thought of it is to suffer all one's ordinary preconceptions to be called in question. No wonder it is so earnestly resisted. Whether this third and strongest objection is outweighed by what will be set out below remains to be seen.

II

The main things which may be said in support of the truth of the Resurrection must now be indicated.

1. The transformation of the disciples may be mentioned first. There is no reason to question the historicity of their frightened and dejected condition at the time of the death of Jesus, as portrayed in the Gospels (e.g., Mark

7. For a brief account of this, reference may be made to W. A. Whitehouse, *The Authority of Grace* (Edinburgh [1981]) 47–52.

14:50, 66–72; John 20:19). It is not something which the early church would have been inclined to invent. Besides, it is something we could safely have taken for granted, even without the testimony of the Gospels, as the natural, the inevitable, consequence of what they had experienced. But it is evident that within a few weeks of the Crucifixion these same disciples had become bold and energetic witnesses of a risen Christ. Leaving aside the testimony of the early chapters of Acts, we have firm enough evidence of this transformation in what Paul says of his own persecution of the church (1 Cor 15:9; Gal 1:13). Already within—at the very most—five or six years of the Crucifixion so many had been won by the disciples' witness, that the young Pharisee was moved to mount a strenuous and energetic campaign against the followers of Jesus. This astounding transformation of the disciples presupposes a sufficient cause, something which was enough to convince them that Jesus was alive.

2. The second piece of evidence is the conversion and subsequent life and work of the apostle Paul. His most extended testimony to the fact of the Resurrection is in 1 Corinthians 15. Here, writing in A.D. 53 or 54 (more than a decade before the earliest of the Gospels), he reminds the Corinthian Christians of the tradition which he had passed on to them when he was in Corinth (probably in A.D. 50–51). As he indicates that the tradition he passed on he had himself received, the implication would seem to be that what is said in the latter part of v. 3 and in vv. 4–7 is the church's basic tradition which he had received in the earliest days of his Christian life. In v. 8 he adds his personal testimony: "And last of all, as unto one born out of due time,[8] he appeared also to me." In connection with Paul's conversion a number of points must be made. (i) It cannot be maintained at all plausibly that this zealous persecutor of the disciples was in any way predisposed to accept the truth of the Resurrection. Having committed himself so publicly to the attempt to root out the new movement as something mischievous, he had a personal interest in not believing. For him to accept that Jesus had been raised from the dead was a volte-face involving a high degree of personal humiliation. (ii) As one who had been working in conjunction with the Jewish authorities, he is

8. The sense of "as unto one born out of due time" is uncertain. Is Paul alluding to the difference between his seeing the risen Lord after the Ascension and the pre-Ascension Resurrection appearances? But the natural significance of *ektrōma* [['untimely, premature']] has to do not with unduly late, but with unduly early, birth, denoting that which is not yet properly formed and ready to be born. C. K. Barrett, *A Commentary on the First Epistle to the Corinthians* (London [1968]) 344, suggests that it could be said that "in comparison with other apostles who had accompanied Jesus during his ministry he had been born without the due period of gestation." Could it perhaps be that Paul's thought is rather of the fact that he was still a furious persecutor of the disciples when he was apprehended by Christ—so in a real sense extremely unprepared, something not properly formed, an ugly thing? The way Paul continues in v. 9 (note the "For") might seem to support this suggestion: "For I am the least of the apostles, that am not worthy to be called an apostle, because I persecuted the church of God." This seems preferable both to the suggestion that Paul is taking up a reproach levelled against him by his opponents and also to the suggestion that Paul means "that he has seen by anticipation the glory of Christ as that will be manifest in the *Parousia*" (S. Neill and T. Wright, *The Interpretation of the New Testament 1861–1986* [Oxford (1988)] 308 n. 1).

likely to have been well acquainted with their views on the ministry of Jesus and subsequent events. He must surely have known what answer or answers they were giving to the claim that he was risen. (iii) His unquestionable intellectual power (about which no one who has been at all seriously engaged in the study of the Epistle to the Romans is likely to have any doubts) must be taken into account. (iv) He was clearly a deeply religious man, fully aware how serious a thing it would be to bear false witness about God by proclaiming that God raised Jesus from the dead, if in fact he did not raise him (compare 1 Cor 15:15). The testimony of this man, with his background, his qualities, his character, with his mind which has left us so much authentic evidence of its workings (in—at the very least—1 and 2 Corinthians, Galatians and Romans), I personally find extraordinarily convincing.

3. A third thing to mention is the striking prominence of women in the Gospel Easter [[170]] narratives. Reference has already been made, in connection with Paul's omitting female witnesses in 1 Cor 15:4ff., to the fact that women were not acceptable witnesses in Jewish legal practice. It made sense to cite only those whose testimony stood a real chance of being taken seriously. The fact that these traditions, in which women featured so prominently, were nevertheless preserved would seem to indicate the presence of a high regard for historical truthfulness. That such traditions could be inventions of the community seems inconceivable, since they flouted accepted ideas about credible witness, were liable to attract ridicule[9] and, furthermore, ran counter to the natural tendency to magnify the apostles (since they represent the women as receiving the news of the resurrection before them). This third thing, then, which is inexplicable except as genuine historical reminiscence, would seem to be a further pointer to the truth of the Resurrection.

4. The undisputed fact that, in spite of all that the sabbath meant to Jews and although Jesus himself had loyally observed it all his life (even if not always in such a way as to satisfy his critics), Jewish as well as Gentile Christians soon came to regard the first day of the week as the special day for Christian worship[10] is highly significant. The replacement of sabbath by Lord's day presupposes a sufficient cause—nothing less than, at the very least, an extraordinarily strong conviction of an event's having taken place on the first day of the week which could be seen as transcending in importance even God's "rest" after completing his work of creation.

5. Another thing to be said in support of the truth of the Resurrection is that, before the event, neither the women nor the disciples had the slightest expectation of their Master's being raised from the dead before the general

9. We catch a glimpse in the New Testament itself of the sort of ridicule which could have been expected, in the reference to "old wives' fables"; in 1 Tim 4:7 and in what is said about the fecklessness of "silly women" and the ease with which they can be led astray in 2 Tim 3:6f. For material illustrative of ancient Jewish, Greek and Roman attitudes to women reference may be made to the article on γυνή [['woman']] in G. Kittel and G. Friedrich (eds.), *TWNT* (Stuttgart [1933–79]) Vol. 1 (Eng. tr. by G. W. Bromiley, *TDNT*, 1964ff.).

10. Cf. Acts 20:7; 1 Cor 16:2; Rev 1:10 (perhaps); *Didache* 14:1.

eschatological resurrection. The early church, convinced that Jesus had been raised, certainly searched the Old Testament for passages which could be taken to foretell the Resurrection; but there is no reason to believe that the Old Testament had suggested to the disciples, before the first Easter Day, any hope of this sort. That the various predictions of the Passion (in particular, Mark 8:31; 9:31; 10:32–34), if in their present form made by Jesus himself (something which is, of course, strongly denied by many), were not understood by the disciples at the time, seems clear enough.

6. There is also the highly significant fact that neither the Jewish nor the Roman authorities ever produced evidence to disprove the claim that Jesus had been raised. The Jewish authorities, in particular, had every reason to want to do so, and they must surely have been in a position to interrogate and search thoroughly. Rumours of what the disciples were saying can scarcely have failed to get to the ears of authority within a few days of the Crucifixion, even if the audacious public proclamation of the Resurrection did not start till Pentecost. The chances of finding the body, if the claim that Jesus was risen was not true, must surely at that early date have been quite good. The Sanhedrin must have known that the most effective way to be rid of what they regarded as a dangerous movement would be to produce the body, and knowing this they must surely have instituted an energetic search. The fact that, with the will and the powers and resources they surely had, they never produced the body must count as a significant consideration in favour of the truth of the Resurrection.

7. Last of all must be mentioned the continuance of the Christian church through nineteen and a half centuries, in spite of bitter and often prolonged persecution, in spite of all its own terrible unworthiness and incredible follies, in spite of its divisions, and in spite of all the changes which the passing years and centuries have brought. The fact that the church still produces today (as it has produced in all the past centuries of its existence) human beings, who, trusting in Jesus Christ crucified, risen and exalted, show in their lives, for all their frailty, a recognizable beginning of being freed from self for God and neighbour, is a not unimpressive pointer to the truth of the Resurrection.

III

It will, I think, be helpful at this point to attempt some clarification of the two basic alternatives between which we have to choose: (a) Jesus was raised from the dead; and (b) Jesus was not raised from the dead. With regard to (a), it must be said that we are concerned with the affirmation *of the New Testament and of the church's creeds* that Jesus *was raised*. We must therefore put aside two views of the Resurrection which are sometimes proposed: first, that according to which it is possible to believe in the Resurrection without believing that the crucified body was raised; and, secondly, that which insists that the risen body is simply the crucified body resuscitated, possessed of exactly the same properties as it had before death. Both these views must, I believe, be rejected as inconsistent with the witness of the New Testament. In support of the former, appeal is made to Paul's failure to mention the empty tomb; but the sequence "died . . . was buried . . . hath been raised" in 1 Cor 15:3f. surely implies it, as does Paul's use of the language of "raising" here and elsewhere. It would seem that there [[171]] never was in the early church a belief in the Resurrection which did not involve belief that the tomb was empty. A supposed belief in the Resurrection without belief that the tomb was empty must surely be classified as acceptance of basic alternative (b), not as acceptance of basic alternative (a). As to the latter view, it is contradicted by the way the New Testament represents the risen Jesus as appearing and vanishing, becoming less or more recognizable (e.g., Luke 24:16, 31; John 20:14–16), and passing through closed doors (John 20:19, 26: cf. vv. 6 and 7, in which it seems to be suggested that the body had been mysteriously withdrawn from the cloths, leaving them collapsed where they were). The New Testament attests the risen body's being the same body as was crucified (Luke 24:39–40; John 20:27), but the same body wonderfully changed, transformed into a glorious body, no longer subject to the limitations of Jesus's historical life.[11]

With regard to basic alternative (b), clarification is achieved when we recognize that to accept it means coming to one of three conclusions: either, the church's belief that Jesus was raised from the dead is based on a fraud; or, it is based on a mistake; or, it is based on some combination of fraud and mistake.

It would seem, then, that there are, in all, four alternatives from which we have to choose: (i) The Christian affirmation of the Resurrection has its origin in a fraud; (ii) It has its origin in a mistake; (iii) It has its origin in some sort of combination of fraud and mistake; (iv) It is true.

With regard to (i), Matt 27:62–66 and 28:11–15 are evidence that the explanation of the Resurrection as a fraud perpetrated by the disciples, who had stolen the body of Jesus and then announced that he had been raised from the dead, was current among the Jews at the time of the composition of Matthew. We may accept that, were a fraud really at the bottom of the matter, the disciples (and the women) would be the only—even remotely—likely perpetrators of it. No one else is at all likely to have had an interest in the propagation of such a falsehood. The Jewish and Roman authorities had, in fact, a very strong interest in Jesus's being securely dead. But the objections to this first alternative are formidable indeed. What motive could the disciples have had for embarking upon such a fraud? Is it really likely that they would have succeeded not only in disposing of the body (in the circumstances, perhaps itself not a very easy task) but also in convincing a large number of people that they had seen the risen Jesus (1 Cor 15:5–8)? Do not the discrepancies and unevennesses between the various accounts of the visits to the tomb and of the Resurrection appearances weigh against the credibility of such a theory

11. It is scarcely fair to press Luke 24:42f. and Acts 10:41 as proof that the author of Luke and Acts must have entertained a different view. Why should we assume that he could not have thought that the risen Jesus could partake of earthly food and drink, not because his risen body needed them, but for the sake of his disciples?

(one would have expected the perpetrators of a concerted deception to have taken more care to make their stories agree)? Would such a fraud account for that transformation of the disciples to which reference has already been made? And, last and most telling of all, is it possible to reconcile responsibility for the conception and carrying out of such a fraud with what we know of the character and conduct of the earliest Christians?[12]

Alternative (ii) can take more than one form. There is the explanation of the Resurrection appearances as hallucinatory experiences. But there is no evidence to suggest that the disciples or the women were in such a state of mind as would have made them liable to this sort of hallucination. They were not expecting any resurrection before the final one at the end of history (the reflection attributed to the chief priests and Pharisees in Matt 27:63 hardly accords with the disciples' understanding of Jesus' teaching during his ministry); and their Jewish background would hardly have made them susceptible to such hallucinations. Moreover, the experiencing of hallucinations by so many different individuals and groups as are listed in 1 Cor 15:5–8 or are represented in the Gospels as seeing the risen Jesus, and in such varied situations, is hard to envisage. There is also the suggestion that the women went to the wrong tomb by mistake. But it is extremely difficult to imagine how the mistake would not have been quickly corrected. Is it really plausible to maintain that the transformation of the disciples was simply the result of a misunderstanding or of an illusion born of hallucination? Does such an explanation of belief in the Resurrection do justice to the fact that the earliest church included at any rate one or two people of the intellectual calibre of the apostle Paul?

With regard to (iii), it is possible to imagine various combinations of mistake and deception: for example, a mistake about the identity of the tomb combined with the invention of appearances, or a stealing and secretly disposing of the body combined with hallucinatory appearances; but none seems at all plausible. In fact, alternative (iii) seems even less convincing than (i) or (ii). Would not such a mixture of mistake and deceit have had even less chance of being sustained for long than either the one thing or the other?

It seems to me that alternative (iv), hard to accept though it undoubtedly is, is the least incredible of the four—by a long way.

The position seems, then, to be that, while the discovery of the dead bones of Jesus would indeed, as C. K. Barrett has rightly maintained,[13] conclusively disprove the church's doctrine of the Resurrection and utterly destroy Christian faith, no amount of scientific, historical-critical or other [[172]] scholarly activity can prove conclusively that the Resurrection is true. A positive proof of its truth is just not to be had by such means. Certainty with regard to it can come to us only by the work of the Holy Spirit making us free to

12. The suggestion, which has been made, that Jesus was not really dead, but mistaken for dead, and revived in the tomb, does indeed offer a motive for the disciples' deception (to protect Jesus); but otherwise it is exposed to all the objections to alternative (i), and to others besides.

13. Op. cit., 349.

believe. But it seems to me that the evidence available to us—and I have tried now a good many times to weigh it as carefully and honestly and objectively as I can—is such that, though I cannot prove that God raised Jesus from the dead by historical-critical methods, I can believe it without in any way violating my intellectual or moral integrity. For myself, I must declare that I do indeed confidently believe it.

PETER STUHLMACHER

Jesus' Readiness to Suffer and His Understanding of His Death

Literature: J. Ådna, "The Servant of Isaiah 53 as Triumphant and Interceding Messiah: The Reception of Isaiah 52:13–53:12 in the Isaiah Targum with Special Reference to the Concept of the Messiah," in *The Suffering Servant*, ed. B. Janowski and P. Stuhlmacher (2004) 189–224; **D. P. Bailey**, "Concepts of *Stellvertretung* in the Interpretation of Isaiah 53," in *Jesus and the Suffering Servant*, ed. W. H. Bellinger and W. R. Farmer (1998) 223–50; **G. Barth**, *Der Tod Jesu Christi im Verständnis des Neuen Testaments* (1992); **W. H. Bellinger** and **W. R. Farmer**, eds., *Jesus and the Suffering Servant: Isaiah 53 and Christian Origins* (1998); **O. Betz**, "Jesus and Isaiah 53," in *Jesus and the Suffering Servant*, ed. W. H. Bellinger and W. R. Farmer (1998) 70–87; **G. Bornkamm**, *Jesus of Nazareth* (ET 1960) 153–68; **R. Bultmann**, "The Primitive Christian Kerygma and the Historical Jesus" (1959), in *The Historical Jesus and the Kerygmatic Christ*, ed. C. E. Braaten and R. A. Harrisville (1964) 15–42; **J. D. G. Dunn**, *Jesus Remembered* (2003) 765–824; **K. F. Euler**, *Die Verkündigung vom Leidenden Gottesknecht aus Jes 53 in der Griechischen Bibel* (1934); **R. T. France**, "Servant of Yahweh," in *Dictionary of Jesus and the Gospels*, ed. J. B. Green and S. McKnight (1992) 744–47; **G. Friedrich**, *Die Verkündigung des Todes Jesu im Neuen Testament* (1982); **H. Gese**, "Die Sühne," in idem, *Zur biblischen Theologie* (1977; 1989³) 85–106 = ET, "The Atonement," in idem, *Essays on Biblical Theology* (1981) 93–116; **J. B. Green**, *The Death of Jesus: Tradition and Interpretation in the Passion Narrative* (1988); "The Death of Jesus, God's Servant," in *Reimaging the Death of the Lucan Jesus*, ed. D. D. Sylva (1990) 1–28, 170–73; **W. Grimm**, *Die Verkündigung Jesu und Deuterojesaja* (1981²) 231ff.; **V. Hampel**, *Menschensohn und historischer Jesus* (1990) 246–342; **W. Haubeck**, *Loskauf durch Christus* (1985) 226ff.; **M. Hengel**, *The Atonement* (1981); **M. Hengel** with **D. P. Bailey**, "The Effective History of Isaiah 53 in the Pre-Christian Period," in *The Suffering Servant*, ed. B. Janowski and P. Stuhlmacher (2004) 75–146; **H. J. Hermisson**, "The Fourth Servant Song in the Context of Second Isaiah," in *The Suffering Servant*, ed. B. Janowski and P. Stuhlmacher (2004) 16–47; **M. D. Hooker**, *Not Ashamed of the Gospel: New Testament Interpretations of the Death of Christ* (1994); "Did the Use of Isaiah 53 to Interpret His Mission Begin with Jesus?" in *Jesus and the Suffering Servant*, ed. W. H. Bellinger and W. R. Farmer (1998) 70–87; **B. Janowski**, *Sühne als Heilsgeschehen* (1982; 2000²);

Reprinted, with permission, from Peter Stuhlmacher, *Biblical Theology of the New Testament* (trans. D. P. Bailey; Grand Rapids, Michigan: Eerdmans, forthcoming) chap. 10; because this printing precedes the official publication by Eerdmans, minor differences may exist, and the page numbers of that printing are not cited. Translated from *Biblische Theologie des Neuen Testaments*, vol. 1 (3rd ed.; Göttingen: Vandenhoeck & Ruprecht, 2005) 124–47.

"Auslösung des verwirkten Lebens," in idem, *Gottes Gegenwart in Israel* (1993) 5–39; *Stellvertretung* (1997); "He Bore Our Sins: Isaiah 53 and the Drama of Taking Another's Place," in *The Suffering Servant*, ed. B. Janowski and P. Stuhlmacher (2004) 48–74; **B. Janowski** and **P. Stuhlmacher**, eds., *The Suffering Servant: Isaiah 53 in Jewish and Christian Sources* (ET 2004); **J. Jeremias**, *Heiligengräber in Jesu Umwelt* (1958); *The Eucharistic Words of Jesus* (ET 1966); "Der Opfertod Jesu Christi," in idem, *Jesus und seine Botschaft* (1976) 78–92; **K. T. Kleinknecht**, "Johannes 13, die Synoptiker und die 'Methode' der johanninischen Evangelienüberlieferung," *ZTK* 82 (1985) 361–88; **T. Knöppler**, *Sühne im Neuen Testament* (2001); **K. Koch**, ed., *Um das Prinzip der Vergeltung in Religion und Recht des Alten Testaments* (1972); "Is There a Doctrine of Retribution in the Old Testament?" (1955), in *Theodicy in the Old Testament*, ed. J. L. Crenshaw (1983) 57–87; **B. Kollmann**, *Ursprung und Gestalten der frühchristlichen Mahlfeier* (1990); **E. Lohse**, *Märtyrer und Gottesknecht* (1963[2]); **W. Manson**, *Jesus the Messiah: The Synoptic Tradition of the Revelation of God in Christ* (London, 1943, repr. 1956, 200 pp./Philadelphia, 1946, 267 pp.) chap. 7, pp. 121–46 (London) = 169–201 (Philadelphia); **S. McKnight**, "Jesus and His Death: Some Recent Scholarship," *CurBS* 9 (2001) 185–228; *Jesus and His Death: Historiography, the Historical Jesus, and Atonement Theory* (2005); **H. Merklein**, "Erwägungen zur Überlieferungsgeschichte der neutestamentlichen Abendmahlstraditionen," in idem, *Studien zu Jesus und Paulus* (1987) 157–80; "Der Tod Jesu als stellvertretender Sühnetod," ibid., 181–91; **D. J. Moo**, *The Old Testament in the Gospel Passion Narratives* (1983); **J. W. Olley**, "'The Many': How Is Isaiah 53:12a to Be Understood?" *Bib* 68 (1987) 330–56; **H. Patsch**, *Abendmahl und historischer Jesus* (1972); **R. Pesch**, *Das Abendmahl und Jesu Todesverständnis* (1978); **G. Röhser**, *Stellvertretung im Neuen Testament* (2002); **L. Ruppert**, *Jesus als der leidende Gerechte?* (1972); **H. Schürmann**, *Jesus—Gestalt und Geheimnis: Gesammelte Beiträge*, ed. K. Scholtissek (1994); **O. H. Steck**, *Israel und das gewaltsame Geschick der Propheten* (1967); **P. Stuhlmacher**, "Jesus von Nazareth und die neutestamentliche Christologie im Lichte der Heiligen Schrift," in *Mitte der Schrift?* ed. M. Klopfenstein, U. Luz, S. Talmon, E. Tov (1987) 81–95; "Zur Predigt an Karfreitag," in *Anfänge der Christologie: Festschrift für Ferdinand Hahn zum 65. Geburtstag*, ed. C. Breytenbach and H. Paulsen (1991) 447–72; *Was geschah auf Golgotha?* (1998); "Isaiah 53 in the Gospels and Acts," in *The Suffering Servant*, ed. B. Janowski and P. Stuhlmacher (2004) 147–62, esp. 147–53, 160–62; **G. Theissen** and **A. Merz**, *The Historical Jesus* (ET 1998) 405–39; **H. W. Wolff**, *Jesaja 53 im Urchristentum* (1984[4]); **N. T. Wright**, *Jesus and the Victory of God* (1996).

If we want to understand Jesus' passion, we must first recognize that his death on the cross was the historically inevitable consequence of his provocative ministry as the messianic Son of Man. While the historical event and causes of the passion will be dealt with in the next chapter [[not reprinted here]], in this chapter we follow up our presentation of Jesus' understanding of his identity (see chap. 9 [[in this volume, pp. 325–344]]) by asking what we can know about his understanding of his death.

1. Like many other problems of Jesus research, the question of Jesus' understanding of his suffering and death is answered in extremely different ways today. In his 1959 study "The Primitive Christian Kerygma and the Historical Jesus," R. Bultmann claimed that "we cannot know how Jesus understood his end, his death" (p. 23). Bultmann considered all the Gospel passion predictions to be *vaticinia ex eventu* ("prophecies after the event"), and he regarded E. Fuchs's claim that Jesus had the Baptist's demise in mind during his final

journey to Jerusalem to be merely an "improbable psychological construc-
tion" (ibid.). Bultmann was also not convinced by G. Bornkamm's thesis that
Jesus went to Jerusalem purposely to seek a final verdict in the Holy City.
Even if this was the case, Bultmann continues,

> [Jesus] scarcely reckoned on execution at the hands of the Romans, but
> only on the immanent appearing of the kingdom of God. But these are
> only assumptions. What is certain is merely that he was crucified by the
> Romans, and thus suffered the death of a political criminal. This death
> can scarcely be understood as an inherent and necessary consequence of
> his activity; rather, it took place because his activity was miscontstrued as
> a political activity. In that case it would have been, historically speaking, a
> meaningless fate. We cannot tell whether or how Jesus found meaning in
> it. We may not veil from ourselves the possibility that he suffered a col-
> lapse. (ibid., 24)

Nevertheless, several of Bultmann's prominent students did not follow him
in this principled historical skepticism. E. Fuchs and especially G. Bornkamm
assumed that Jesus faced the possibility of his martyrdom already on his way
to Jerusalem. But because they joined Bultmann in considering the passion
predictions, the ransom saying in Mark 10:45 par., and the eucharistic texts
to be products of the early church, Jesus' own understanding of his death remained historically inaccessible to them.

On the other hand scholars including W. Manson, H. W. Wolff, J. Jeremias, and L. Goppelt have used precise analyses of the passion predictions,
Mark 10:45 par., and the Lord's Supper tradition to defend the thesis that
Jesus not only counted on his suffering, but also understood his death as a
sacrificial one for the sins of "the many." In view of these texts, H. W. Wolff in
his dissertation *Jesaja 53 im Urchristentum* (1984[4]) concludes: "Jesus in describing himself with the words of the prophecy of Isaiah 53 speaks of something completely self-evident" (p. 69). J. Jeremias's judgment is very similar:

> Everywhere we find the explanation of this suffering to be the vicarious
> act (*Stellvertretung*) for the many (Mark 10.45; 14.24). The only answer to
> the question how it could be possible that Jesus attributed such unlimited
> atoning power to his death must be that he died as the servant of God,
> whose suffering and death is described in Isa. 53. It is innocent (v. 9), vol-
> untary (v. 10) suffering, patiently borne (v. 7), willed by God (vv. 6, 10)
> and therefore vicariously atoning [i.e., atoning for others] (vv. 4f.). Be-
> cause it is life with God and from God that is here given over to death,
> this death has an unlimited power to atone. (*New Testament Theology*,
> trans. J. Bowden, 299 [modified])

Recent investigations by O. Betz, M. Hengel, and R. Pesch have confirmed
this view.

2. In order to arrive at one's own opinion, one must first turn to the following Jesus sayings: the saying about the death of the prophets in Luke 13:31–

33, the passion prediction in Mark 9:31 (Luke 9:44b), and the ransom saying in Mark 10:45 (par. Matt 20:28). The contribution of the Lord's Supper tradition in Mark 14:22–26 par. must also be investigated.

2.1 Luke 13:31–33 belongs to Luke's special material:

> At that very hour some Pharisees came and said to him, "Get away from here, for Herod wants to kill you." He said to them, "Go and tell that fox for me, 'Listen, I am casting out demons and performing cures today and tomorrow, and on the third day I finish my work. Yet today, tomorrow, and the next day I must be on my way, because it is impossible for a prophet to be killed outside of Jerusalem.'"

From its wording the scene's originality can hardly be doubted. It shows that, like John the Baptist, Jesus had to fear persecution from his local ruler Herod Antipas, but that he paid no attention to the warnings about this from well-meaning Pharisees. *Jesus reckoned with the possibility of his death in Jerusalem, understanding it by analogy to the martyrdom of the prophets (cf. also Luke 13:34/Matt 23:37).*

Jesus' language about martyrdom becomes comprehensible when one looks at the Jewish *Lives of the Prophets* from the first century B.C. or A.D. (*OTP* 2:385–99) and at the Deuteronomistic sayings about the fate of the prophets who warned Israel against falling away (cf. Neh 9:26; 2 Chr 24:17–22; 36:14–16). According to early Jewish legends the great prophets of Israel, above all Isaiah, Jeremiah, and Ezekiel, became victims of their own proclamation. In Jesus' day they were venerated in Jerusalem as martyrs whose souls had already taken up into heaven (cf. Rev 6:9) and whose (undecayed) bodies were awaiting the resurrection of the dead and future glorification (Dan 12:3). People made pilgrimages to the tombs of these martyred prophets and prayed to them (cf. *Liv. Pro.* 71:9 with Matt 23:29–30). They saw them as helpers in time of need, whose heavenly intercession could bring God's mercy to Israel (*Liv. Pro.* 12:13; 42:14). Jesus knew these ideas and practices and foresaw his own death in Jerusalem. Yet he also knew that with his own arrival, something "more than Jonah" was on the scene (Matt 12:41).

2.2 We have already briefly analyzed the passion prediction about the Son of Man being "betrayed" or "delivered up" in Mark 9:31 par. and the ransom saying in 10:45 par. (cf. pp. 339–40 in this volume). These are authentic sayings of Jesus, based on Isa 43:3–4 and 53:11–12. The soteriological dimension of both sayings is determined by the early Jewish tradition about a "ransom" and by the Suffering Servant of Isaiah 53. As the Son of Man, Jesus saw himself called to follow the way of the Servant who suffers vicariously for "the many," whose life is delivered up by God as an end-time ransom for Israel.

2.2.1 B. Janowski has shown that the term "ransom" (כֹּפֶר) in Isa 43:3–4 is an example of judicial language. In Exod 21:29–30 the ransom is a substitute payment of damages to an injured party, offered instead of payment by the offender's own life. It is the *"redemption of a forfeited individual life, . . . a substitution of existence, a life-equivalent"* (Janowski, *Gottes Gegenwart*, 14). In the Septuagint כֹּפֶר is translated partly by τὸ λύτρον "ransom," partly by τὸ (ἀντ)άλλαγμα, something "given in exchange" and therefore a ransom, equivalent, or substitute. In Isa 43:3 the idea of a ransom is carried over into the realm of God's final judgment of Israel and the nations, but is used in a special sense: the ransom is paid by God for Israel, even though God himself is the injured party because of Israel's sins (cf. 43:24). The payment is his act of redemption out of pure love for his chosen people (43:4, 25). The formulations "for you" and "for your life" in 43:4 show that the act of paying the כֹּפֶר actually involves a "substitution of existence" (*Existenzstellvertretung*). According to Isa 43:3, "Yahweh gives Cyrus (as recipient of the כֹּפֶר) Egypt, Ethiopia, and Seba, the whole of the then-known northeast Africa, for the release of Jacob-Israel from the exile, thus preserving the life of Israel (cf. also Isa 45:14–17)" (Janowski, ibid., 29). Isa 43:3–4 is applied to the final judgment in early Judaism, with the understanding that the wicked will be given as a ransom for Israel in the judgment of annihilation (cf. 1Q*Liturgical Prayers* [1Q34 + 1Q34bis] frag. 3, col. I, lines 5–6, *DSSSE*, 144–45; *Sifre* §333 on Deut 32:43, in J. Neusner, trans., *Sifre to Deuteronomy*, 2:382 §333.V.2). According to rabbinic texts the wicked Gentiles are delivered over to Gehinnom, the fiery hell, for Israel's sake (cf., e.g., *Mekilta* on Exod 21:30, in J. Z. Lauterbach, *Mekilta de-Rabbi Ishmael*, 3:87–88).

If one views Mark 9:31 (Luke 9:44) and Mark 10:45 from this early Jewish perspective, it becomes clear that *Jesus was prepared to perform a "substitution of existence" for Israel, or more precisely for the ungodly who were supposed to be handed over for Israel's salvation in the final judgment*. Perhaps Jesus already had the ungodly Gentiles in mind here. In any case Mark 9:31 (Luke 9:44) and Mark 10:45 par. provide a precise pattern for God's incredibly loving act of surrendering his own son to death for the ungodly, proclaimed by Paul in Rom 5:6 (cf. 8:32).

Jesus' readiness to die must be seen in terms of the *final judgment*. This is clear from Mark 8:36–37 par.: "For what does it profit a man [or woman], to gain the whole world and forfeit his life? For what can a man give in return [lit., as an exchange, ἀντάλλαγμα] for his life?" (RSV). Verse 37 alludes to Ps 49:8–9 ("the ransom of life is costly"), and in early Judaism from *1 En.* 98:10 onward, this psalm passage, partly combined with Isa 43:3–4 (cf. *Mekilta* on Exod 21:30), is applied to the situation of the final judgment: No one can pay a ransom for his or her forfeited life in the final judgment; all the wicked are destined for demise. Only God can and will protect Israel from eternal separation from him by means of the ransom he himself has chosen (cf. Isa 43:3–4). Jesus affirms this principle of judgment. Acting on God's behalf, he was prepared to die, making his life the divinely appointed ransom for the salvation of "the many."

2.2.2 In the background of Mark 9:31 par. and 10:45 par. stands not only Isa 43:3–4 but also the *Song of the Suffering Servant* of Isaiah 53 (i.e., Isa 52:13–53:12). Mark 9:31 alludes to the Lord's delivering up the Servant in Isa 53:6, while Mark 10:45 alludes to Isa 53:11–12.

The Hebrew text of Isa 53:10 speaks of the Servant's אָשָׁם, typically translated as "an offering for sin" (NRSV). The Septuagint similarly understands this as περὶ ἁμαρτίας, a "sin offering" (cf. Rom 8:3, NRSV margin), although it requires the sin offering from a group of people rather than from the Servant (ἐὰν δῶτε [plur.] περὶ ἁμαρτίας, etc.). However, according to R. Knierim, "אָשָׁם," *TLOT* 1:191–95, an אָשָׁם does not involve a ransom or a sin offering per se, but rather the discharging of the *debt* that arises from being guilty before God. When humans behave sinfully, for example by attacking justice or oppressing the righteous, they infringe upon God's rights and privileges on the earth, and a liability arises that needs to be discharged as one would discharge a debt of guilt (Ps 68:22 [ET 21]; Prov 14:9; Jer 51:5). In the cultic arena this discharge is accomplished by sacrificing a guilt offering (cf. Lev 5:14–16; 7:7, 37), whereas outside the cult some type of material restitution is required, such as items of gold (1 Sam 6:3–17). Isa 53:10 is to be understood outside the cultic realm from the perspective of the final judgment. In vv. 11–12 it is interpreted in terms of a theology of justification: "the many" have become guilty before God because of their iniquities, but the obligation arising from their guilt is taken over by the Servant and discharged by his vicarious surrender of his life, so that the guilty escape destruction in the judgment. The Servant or *Ebed* (עֶבֶד) is God's own tool, effecting liberation from guilt and a new life before God for the many; God sends "his" Servant (Isa 52:13; 53:11) and directs him in his course of sacrifice. As in Isa 43:3–5, 22–25 the absolute gulf between God's holiness and human injustice is not simply jumped over; instead out of his free grace God takes care of those destined for death and provides justice for them by surrendering his Servant. Isaiah 53 shows that the ideas of sacrifice, vicarious suffering, and justification were connected in the Old Testament long before the formation of the New Testament message about Christ.

Modern scholarship often identifies the *Suffering Servant* of Isaiah 53 with the prophet Second Isaiah, but sometimes this designation is applied collectively to the "ideal Israel." The context of the book of Isaiah favors the collective interpretation, which applies the passage to Israel, more precisely to that part of Israel deported to Babylon, which gave up its existence vicariously for the whole people of Israel and the world of the nations (cf. Isa 49:3). Isaiah 53 seems to have left its stamp upon the presentation of the priestly figure from the house of Aaron who suffers, but not vicariously, according to the *Aramaic Apocryphon of Levi* 4Q541 (cf. 1QS 9:11). Wis 2:12–20 and 5:1–7 applies Isaiah 53 to a paradigmatic individual suffering righteous person. (For analysis of Wisdom and 4Q541, see M. Hengel with D. P. Bailey, "The Effective History of Isaiah 53 in the Pre-Christian Period," 106–18, 129–32.) According to Acts 8:34 the Greek text of Isaiah 53 could be applied either to the (suffering) prophet Isaiah or to the Messiah (Jesus). In the later Aramaic Targum to Isaiah 53, we once again meet a messianic understanding of the Servant Song, which however reinterprets the suffering to apply to others than the Messiah, e.g., the Gentiles or the wicked in Israel (J. Ådna).

Jesus' application of Isaiah 53 to his own suffering as the messianic Son of Man (which was continued by the early Christian witnesses) *stands at the crossways of the interpretations already being considered in early Judaism.* According to Mark 9:31 (Luke 9:44); Mark 10:45 par. and the difficult but probably authentic logion about the "two swords" and Jesus being "counted among the lawless" (cf. Isa 53:12) in Luke 22:35–38, Jesus saw his path of suffering marked out in Isaiah 53. By vicariously taking the liability of the guilt of the many upon himself and blotting it out by the surrender of his own life, he created for them the righteousness that they need for their life before God. However, Jesus' vicarious discharge of the liability of the guilt of the many is neither a sacrifice to appease God's wrath nor an act of satisfaction for the insult done to God's majesty by the sins of the many (as later in the theology of Anselm). It is rather a substitution of existence made possible by God himself through his Servant Jesus out of God's love and mercy toward Israel. *The Suffering Servant of Isaiah 53 is the mediator and tool of the saving will of God.* Through the surrender of his life he leads the many back into the relationship with God that was broken by their guilt: "The righteous one, my servant, shall make many righteous by bearing their iniquities" (Isa 53:11). This is the "making righteous" or justification that Jesus wanted to put into effect for "the many." *One can therefore see in Mark 9:31 (Luke 9:44); Luke 22:37 and Mark 10:45 that the early Christian and Pauline doctrine of justification has taken up the interpretation of Jesus' sacrifice begun by Jesus himself with the help of Isaiah 53, and has further reflected upon it from a post-Easter perspective.*

3. Mark 10:45 (par. Matt 20:28) stands materially very close to the *words of institution that Jesus spoke to his twelve disciples at the Last (Passover) Supper: Mark 14:22, 24 par.* The analysis of these words is complicated, but helps us to recognize broad salvation-historical and eschatological horizons for the understanding of the death of Jesus.

3.1 That the *Lord's Supper tradition* is not simply a formation of the early church but a tradition that is to be *traced back to Jesus* is the conclusion to be drawn not only from our general method of viewing the synoptic tradition, but also from 1 Cor 11:23. Here Paul expressly says that the Lord's Supper tradition which he handed on was one which he received ἀπὸ τοῦ κυρίου, "from the Lord." The wording of this verse shows clearly that the κύριος is not simply the exalted Christ but simultaneously the earthly Jesus. Paul assumes that the Lord's Supper tradition which he received as teaching and passed on to the Corinthians in 1 Cor 11:23–25 (or 26) goes back to the earthly Lord who was raised by God.

3.2 The *analysis* of the New Testament texts concerning the Lord's Supper must be approached very carefully. The four records of the "words of institution" in the Synoptics and Paul (Matt 26:26–29; Mark 14:22–25; Luke 22:14–20; 1 Cor 11:23–26) are very tersely formulated, and every word is chosen with care. In spite of great similarities, the four reports are nevertheless so variously formulated and stand in such different contexts that one must be prepared for both agreements and differences in the Lord's Supper tradition. If one adds to this the Bread of Life discourse in John 6:52–58 and the Last Supper scene in John 13:1–30, one stands before a highly *complex tradition.*

3.2.1 The most important *differences* in the reports of the Lord's Supper are the following:

(1) The Synoptics relate Jesus' last supper in the context of a continuous passion narrative, whereas Paul presupposes the passion story, alluding only briefly to the events "on the night when he was betrayed (by Judas)" or "delivered up (by God)" (1 Cor 11:23; the passive παρεδίδετο, "he was betrayed/delivered up" bears this double sense; cf. in Rom 4:25 the divine passive παρεδόθη, "he was delivered up," sc. ὑπὸ τοῦ θεοῦ, "by God"), and provides the text as an agenda for the celebration of the Lord's Supper in Corinth.

(2) The three synoptic texts are of different length. Mark and Matthew report about Jesus' passion and the institution of the Lord's Supper in a similarly concise and condensed form. In Luke by contrast we find an extensive report that is firmly embedded in the special passion tradition of Luke's Gospel. The text-critical apparatus at Luke 22:14–20 shows that the text was continually reworked by scribes. Not until the discovery of the famous third century papyrus 𝔓[75] could we even be sure that vv. 19b–20 (including "do this in remembrance of me" and the second cup saying) belonged to the tradition from the beginning. Today we can assume that the so-called long version of Luke's text is original and that it was shortened only subsequently by the elimination of the apparent doublets in vv. 19b–20.

(3) The words of institution that Jesus speaks to his disciples at the Last Supper have different wordings. The formulations of Mark and Matthew are very similar to each other, as are those of Luke and Paul, but these two pairs of texts are so different that it remains undecided until today whether the oldest form of the words of institution is preserved by Mark (and Matthew), or by Paul (and Luke).

(4) Jesus' declaration that he will henceforth refrain from drinking wine until he can drink it "new in the kingdom" is placed at the end of the Last Supper according to Mark and Matthew: "Truly I tell you, I will never again drink of the fruit of the vine until that day when I drink it new in the kingdom of God" (Mark 14:25; cf. Matt 26:29). But the corresponding declaration that he will not drink wine or eat the Passover until the kingdom of God comes is placed at the start of Luke's account (cf. Luke 22:16, 18). Moreover, whereas one gets the impression from Mark and Matthew that Jesus ate his Passover meal together with his disciples, interpreted the bread and wine during the meal, distributed both to the disciples, and turned his attention to the heavenly table fellowship only at the conclusion, in Luke Jesus was looking forward to the end-time meal of fulfillment in the βασιλεία right from the beginning of the meal. He no longer ate together with the disciples—cf. "I will not eat it [the Passover] until it is fulfilled in the kingdom of God" (NRSV, Luke 22:16, worded absolutely over against the adverb in the NIV: "I will not eat it *again*," i.e., after this Passover)—but rather distributed only to them the bread and wine over which he had previously spoken the words of institution.

(5) To compound the difficulties, the Gospel of John narrates Jesus' last supper very differently from the Synoptics. While they report that Jesus kept the Passover with his disciples and celebrated the Lord's Supper in this

context, Jesus was already resting in the grave on Passover evening according to the Johannine passion chronology. The final supper presented in John 13 takes place on the eve before the Passover, and centers on the foot washing; nothing hints at the institution of the Lord's Supper. Instead of this the bread discourse of John 6:22–59 alludes so clearly to eating Jesus' flesh and drinking his blood (cf. John 6:[51b] 52–58) that one suspects that the Johannine interpretation of the Lord's Supper is to be found here; but in part one also assumes that the questionable verses were added to the bread discourse only later.

3.2.3 The New Testament texts about the Lord's Supper therefore raise quite a few historical questions, not every one of which is finally solvable. Not a few researchers therefore believe that the tradition is so opaque that one must refrain from reconstructing the original situation of the supper and the words of institution spoken by Jesus himself. But while it should be admitted that every attempt at reconstruction remains saddled with considerable uncertainty, in view of the generally reliable continuum of transmission of the synoptic tradition, wholesale skepticism over against the texts is once again out of place.

3.3 A historically plausible result can be obtained when one takes into account not only the differences but also the *commonalities* of the tradition and considers the following factors:

3.3.1 All the New Testament texts of the Lord's Supper stem, from a literary standpoint, from the testimony of the post-Easter witnesses. It is possible to reason backwards from these texts to the history of the Lord's Supper only to the extent that the texts lie close to the post-Easter witnesses. Because the synoptic reports and the Pauline Lord's Supper tradition explicitly want to explain what Jesus said and did on the evening before his death, they themselves suggest a historical quest for the Last Supper.

3.3.2 In the reconstruction of the Lord's Supper not only a single strand of the tradition, let alone a single text, is to be followed; rather all the available data that the Lord's Supper texts offer are to be brought together.

3.3.3 As a rule one comes closer to the teaching of the earthly Jesus through the continuum of the synoptic tradition than through the Johannine tradition, whose main accent lies on the Spirit-inspired post-Easter understanding of Jesus (cf. John 14:26). Because the synoptic passion reports assume that Jesus' last supper was a *Passover* supper, this presentation is to be laid at the foundation initially, then departed from only when historically necessary.

3.3.4 According to the Gospel of John, Jesus dies as the true Passover lamb at the time when the Passover lambs were slaughtered in the temple (cf. John 1:29, 36; 18:28; 19:36). Because of its interest in this christological presentation, the Gospel cannot offer a report of the institution of the Lord's Supper;

instead we find the Johannine interpretation of the Lord's Supper in John 6:52–58 (see above). Because John 13 dramatically speaking follows the Lukan report in Luke 22 (K. T. Kleinknecht) and John 13:10, 26 points to a Passover meal tradition that also underlies John's presentation, there is *no reason* to prefer the presentation of John 13 over that of the Synoptics. [[While the "Passover amnesty" for Barabbas is sometimes thought to favor John's passion chronology, this problem is dealt with in P. Stuhlmacher, *Biblical Theology of the New Testament*, chap. 11 §4.3.3.]]

3.3.5 In the quest for the original wording of the words of institution, the shortest and most difficult version deserves the preference in as far as this most readily explains the origin of the other versions. *The briefest and most difficult form of the words of institution lies in Mark 14:22–24.*

4. If one wishes to understand Jesus' last supper with his closest disciples in the light of these considerations, one must first recall that for Jesus and his Jewish contemporaries, the celebration of a meal in God's presence was the essence of the βασιλεία τοῦ θεοῦ or "kingdom of God." The end-time feast of the nations upon Zion (cf. Isa 25:6–8) is something Jesus repeatedly held before his disciples (cf. Luke 13:29/Matt 8:11f.; Luke 14:15–24/Matt 22:1–14). Anticipation of this feast marked the Last Supper in Jerusalem as well (cf. Mark 14:25 par.). *Jesus' last supper is different from his table fellowship with tax gatherers and sinners in that it was a Passover meal and included only the Twelve who were gathered around Jesus.* According to Luke 22:28–30/Matt 19:28 the Twelve represent the end-time people of the twelve tribes.

The Passover meal is for the Jews until today much more than a festal family gathering around a meal; it is rather the *re-enactment of the deliverance of Israel from Egypt in the form of a shared ritual meal.* At the time of Jesus the slaughter of the Passover lambs was only possible and allowed in the temple in Jerusalem (cf. Deut 16:5–6). Outside Jerusalem Passover evening had to be celebrated without a Passover lamb. (After the destruction of the temple in the year A.D. 70, this type of celebration necessarily became the general manner of celebration for all Jews; only the Samaritans on Mount Gerizim have retained the slaughter of the Passover lambs.) For this reason every year thousands of Jews made the pilgrimage to Jerusalem for Passover in order to celebrate it there in its fullest form. The festival pilgrims had a custom of forming meal parties big enough to consume one Passover lamb in the evening (Exod 12:43–46). The meal had to be held in Jerusalem, and the concluding Passover night also had to be spent there (cf. Deut 16:7). Jesus adopted this custom. He instructed his disciples to prepare everything for the meal (perhaps in the house of John Mark and his mother? Cf. Mark 14:12–16 par. with Acts 1:13; 12:12). Then in the evening he himself came to Jerusalem in order to celebrate the meal in the circle of his closest confidants. Luke 22:15 emphasizes that this last shared Passover celebration before his suffering lay especially on his heart.

According to the Old Testament Passover regulations in Exod 12:1–14; 13:3–10; Deut 16:1–8 as well as the Jewish Passover *haggadah* (the "telling" of the Passover story, but also the order of the Passover liturgy), one practices in this festival an act of *remembrance*: One recalls Israel's departure from Egypt and the ratifying of the covenant at Sinai according to Exodus 24 (and also the gift of the Torah, guidance into the promised land, and the building of the Jerusalem temple for atonement for sins). People sang together Psalms 113–18, the Passover *hallel*, and mutually encouraged each other in the hope of final salvation. *Mishnah Pesaḥim* 10:5 says: "In every generation a man must so regard himself as if he came forth himself out of Egypt, for it is written, *And thou shalt tell thy son in that day saying, It is because of that which the Lord did for me when I came forth out of Egypt* (Exod 13:8)." During the Passover celebration the past and the present become one: present celebrants participate in the exodus from Egypt and experience that past event of salvation as their own history.

Regarding Jesus' behavior at his last Passover meal, the synoptic Lord's Supper texts and the Pauline tradition are concerned only with the actions and statements of Jesus that went beyond the usual custom for the festival and that were important for the post-Easter celebration of the Lord's Supper.

According to the reconstruction of J. Jeremias (*The Eucharistic Words of Jesus* [1966] 85–86), the Passover meal at the time of Jesus took the following course:

Preliminary Course
    Word of dedication (blessing of the feast day [קִדּוּשׁ = *kiddûš*] and of the cup) spoken by the *paterfamilias* [['head of family (father)']] over the first cup (the *kiddûš* cup).
    Preliminary dish, consisting among other things of green herbs, bitter herbs and a sauce made of fruit purée.
    The meal proper (see the third item) is served but not yet eaten; the second cup is mixed and put in its place but not yet drunk.

Passover Liturgy
    Passover *haggada* by the *paterfamilias* (in Aramaic).
    First part of the Passover *hallēl* = Psalms 113–14 (in Hebrew).
    Drinking of the second cup (*haggadah* cup).

Main Meal
    Grace spoken by the *paterfamilias* over the unleavened bread.
    Meal, consisting of passover lamb, unleavened bread, bitter herbs (Ex. 12.8), with fruit purée and wine.
    Grace (*birkat hammaṣon*) over the third cup (cup of blessing).

Conclusion
    Second part of the passover *hallēl* = Psalms 115–18 (in Hebrew).
    Praise over the fourth cup (*hallēl* cup).

Mark 14:17, 22 simply presupposes this knowledge of the course of a Passover celebration, and even Luke's more extensive account only hints at it in 22:14–

20. Therefore, during the process of handing down the New Testament reports, the Jewish Passover was eventually forgotten, and early church celebrations of the Lord's Supper became separated from the date and custom of the Passover. Consequently the original embedding of Jesus' last supper in the context of a Passover meal also became controversial. The controversy continues to draw strength from John's different witness to the Lord's Supper and therefore remains until today.

If one follows the united witness of the first three Gospels and fits Jesus' words and actions into the ritual course of the Passover meal, then two results emerge: *Jesus enacted with the Twelve the festival of Israel's deliverance from bondage in Egypt. Yet in so doing he celebrated much more than just the redemption of Israel from Egyptian slavery.*

As any reader who is familiar with the Jewish custom can see from Mark 14:17–25 par., but especially from Luke 22:14–20, Jesus concentrated his special actions at the beginning and end of the main course of the Passover meal. The first two parts of the celebration, the preliminary course and the Passover liturgy, were apparently celebrated by Jesus in the customary fashion; the unleavened bread and the bitter herbs will have been interpreted at this time. But for the main course, the Passover *haggadah* no longer gave any fixed rules. The only customary feature was for the father of the house to say grace at the beginning over the (unleavened) bread, then to break it and distribute it to the table guests. Jesus took advantage of this custom in order to add his bread saying after the usual blessing. The whole Passover meal was connected to this saying. At the end of this time it was customary for the master of the table to take the third cup "after supper" (μετὰ τὸ δειπνῆσαι; cf. Luke 22:20; 1 Cor 11:25) and to say over it the grace or blessing for the meal. This third cup was therefore called "the cup of blessing," τὸ ποτήριον τῆς εὐλογίας (1 Cor 10:16), and the blessing was called the בִּרְכַּת הַמָּזוֹן (grace after a meal with bread). Then all participants in the meal normally emptied their glasses individually. But this custom gave Jesus the opportunity of first speaking the cup saying and then, against the usual custom, allowing the twelve to drink from a single cup of blessing.

According to early Jewish expectation, at the end-time feast of the nations on Mount Zion, all Israel will be given to drink from a single great "cup of salvation" (Ps 116:13), over which David will say the blessing to God's glory (cf. Str-B 4/2:1163–65). Jesus had the twelve drink from the common cup in the anticipation of their drinking from it together in the βασιλεία [['kingdom']]. This fits well with the anticipation of the messianic banquet of thanksgiving on Zion in Mark 14:25/Luke 22:15–16.

Jesus celebrated his last meal with the twelve at the borderline between his upcoming death and the new life in the messianic fulfillment of the kingdom of God (Luke 22:16, 18). In so doing he openly declared that his vicarious death makes his table companions participants in the new covenant, which replaces and completes the Sinai covenant (cf. Exod 24:1–8 with Jer 31:31–34 and Mark 14:24/Matt 26:28 with Luke 22:20/1 Cor 11:25). As a result they may participate in the eschatological feast in the βασιλεία of Zion, which according to Isa 24:23; 25:6–8 corresponds to the meal that Moses, Aaron, and the seventy elders of Israel were allowed to eat before God on Mount Sinai (cf. Exod 24:9–11).

5. In the interpretation of the *words of institution* it is best to follow the wording of the texts as exactly as possible, neither deconstructing them prematurely through literary criticism, nor giving them meanings that they are known to have only in the interpretation of the early church.

5.1 First of all it is striking that Jesus never compares himself directly with the slaughtered Passover lamb, either in the bread saying or in the cup saying. We do indeed find such a comparison in 1 Cor 5:7; 1 Pet 1:19; John 1:29, 36; 19:36 and (according to many interpreters) Rev 5:6, 12 and 13:8. But this comparison seems to stem only from the post-Easter perspective on Jesus' completed passion and resurrection. Therefore the original interpretation of the words of institution is, if possible, to be sought without reference to the Passover lamb.

5.2 As far as the bread saying is concerned Jesus spoke the usual blessing over the bread at the beginning of the main meal. But then he immediately added that his disciples were not merely eating the unleavened bread that the Passover liturgy calls the "bread of affliction" (Deut 16:3). Rather, by eating the bread that Jesus broke and distributed to them, they were gaining a share in Jesus himself, who was about to go to his death for them.

In its simplest form, transmitted in Mark, Jesus' word of institution says: λάβετε, τοῦτό ἐστιν τὸ σῶμά μου, "Take; this is my body" (Mark 14:22). Matthew adds to this "taking" (λάβετε) the idea of "eating" (φάγετε): "Take, eat . . ." (Matt 26:26), while in the tradition of Luke and Paul, the bread saying is clarified by a further addition, involving ὑπέρ: τοῦτό ἐστιν τὸ σῶμά μου τὸ ὑπὲρ ὑμῶν (διδόμενον) = "This is my body *for* you" (1 Cor 11:24) or "*given for* you" (Luke 22:19). To the Greek word σῶμα corresponds most nearly the Hebrew גּוּף or the Aramaic גּוּפָא, "body, person." The equation of σῶμα with σάρξ, "flesh" (Hebrew בָּשָׂר or Aramaic בִּשְׂרָא), is indeed possible from the perspective of John 6:52–58, but somewhat artificial: the bread with which Jesus identifies himself and which he distributes is not simply his "flesh," but himself in person.

Because in Hebrew and Aramaic as a rule no copulative verb is required, the bread saying and the cup saying were originally nominal clauses in which the Greek verb "is," ἐστίν, was lacking. The original meaning of the sayings should therefore not be sought from this ἐστίν (even though this has traditionally caused debate in historical discussions about the nature of the elements of communion, i.e., transubstantiation, in which the consecrated element actually becomes or "is" the body or the blood). For Jesus the supper involved a total life-giving procedure: by hearing Jesus' blessing of the bread and his additional words to them, then taking and eating the bread he broke and distributed to them, the disciples gain a share in him who is about to go to death for them vicariously. The "bread" that Jesus distributes to his table guests is he himself, who gives them new life before God through his sacrificial death and prepares them a place at the heavenly table. Jesus' blessing of the bread, the breaking of the bread, the word of institution, the distribution to the disciples, and the eating combine to form a messianic symbolic act in which fellowship (κοινωνία) is established before God between Jesus and his table companions, for whom he offers up his life (cf. 1 Cor 10:16–17).

The whole Passover meal time was connected to this initial bread saying. The time could have been spent in "table talk" about the question of what Jesus meant by his word of institution, and what sorts of hopes and obligations might follow for the disciples from Jesus' readiness for sacrifice. Luke 22:21–38 seeks to give an impression of such parting conversations, including Peter's rash offer to accompany Jesus to his death and Jesus' advice that his disciples buy swords in the face of coming persecution.

5.3 Matters with the cup saying at the end of the main Passover meal are very similar to those associated with the bread saying at the beginning. The Jewish table custom provided only for a short word of prayer or blessing to be spoken at the end over the "cup of blessing." But Jesus raised the cup, spoke this blessing, then added: τοῦτό ἐστιν τὸ αἷμά μου τῆς διαθήκης τὸ ἐκχυννόμενον ὑπὲρ πολλῶν, "This is my blood of the covenant, which is poured out for many" (Mark 14:24). He then had the Twelve drink from this one cup. As with the bread saying, the Markan version of the cup saying is the most primitive and its content the most difficult. It explains the parallel versions more easily than the assumption that the wording of Mark 14:24 (Matt 26:28) developed only subsequently from Luke 22:20 or 1 Cor 11:25. What Mark's saying means becomes clear only when one exactly follows the biblical language and expectation surrounding it.

Exegetically it is to be observed that the Greek phrase τοῦτό (γάρ) ἐστιν, "this is," in Mark 14:24 (Matt 26:28) refers by metonymy to the cup and its contents, and that the helping verb ἐστίν once again was added only at the stage of translation into Greek. (The same holds for 1 Cor 11:25 if one seeks to translate the Pauline text back into Aramaic.) Again it is important to pay attention not only to the identification of the cup's contents with Jesus' blood, but also to the whole context of action surrounding the cup saying: Jesus' blessing over the cup, the common drinking of all disciples from this one cup, and the word of institution once again form a messianic symbolic action.

What this symbolic action means is shown by the individual formulations. As we have seen, the *common cup* that Jesus passed around the table already has great symbolic value: In anticipation of the messianic feast on Zion, Jesus gives each of his twelve disciples a drink from the one "cup of salvation" that will be extended to Israel (cf. Ps 116:13). But this cup gives a share in Jesus' "blood of the covenant" that is "poured out for many." Again Jesus gives himself to his disciples with the greatest thing he has to give—his life, contained in his shed blood, offered up for "the many." By their common drinking from the one cup, Jesus' disciples gain a share in his atoning death's saving power. This opens the way to their participation in the end-time feast of the thanksgiving sacrifice on Mount Zion (Isa 25:6–8).

In the context of a Passover meal the language of the *blood of the covenant* recalls the ritual of Exod 24:8: After the reading the book of the covenant

Moses sprinkled the "blood of the covenant" upon the assembled people in order to seal the covenant (= obligation) which God established (and made obligatory) for Israel at Sinai. Although the connection of this blood with atonement (cf. כפר) is not made in the Hebrew text of Exodus 24, the ancient Aramaic Targums already speak about the atoning power of the blood of the covenant. *Targum Onqelos* on Exod 24:8 says: "Moses took the blood and sprinkled it upon the altar in order to make atonement for the people, and he said: See, this is the blood of the covenant which the Lord has made with you on the basis of all these words." The presentation of *Targum Yerushalmi* I is literally almost the same.

From this historical standpoint there need be no controversy about the *atonement-theological meaning of Jesus' "blood of the covenant."* That such controversy nevertheless continues to flares up today depends above all on the sense of theological foreignness that the biblical atonement tradition has aroused since the enlightenment in Europe. But exegetically and dogmatically this ought not keep us from facing up to the idea of atonement that is constitutive for the biblical understanding of the death of Jesus.

In order to understand the biblical *atonement tradition* one must have a clear historical idea of two contexts: the Old Testament and early Jewish view of the life-order determining all creaturely being, and the atonement texts themselves.

The payment of a "ransom" for the forfeited life of an individual or the entire people is required because otherwise the life-order destroyed by human misdeeds cannot be restored. Behind this practice lies a concept encountered particularly in the wisdom texts of the Old and New Testaments of a *fixed connection between a human action and its results*, to which K. Koch has drawn attention by speaking of "a deed's fate-determining sphere" (*schicksalwirkende Tatsphäre*). In the essay collection he edited in 1972, *The Principle of Retribution in the Religion and Justice of the Old Testament* (*Um das Prinzip der Vergeltung in Religion und Recht des Alten Testaments*), Koch describes the fundamental principle of the wisdom literature's understanding of order as follows: "[T]he deed forms an invisible sphere around the doer through which the corresponding fate will be effected; the deity watches over this interpersonal order and continually reinforces it where it threatens to weaken" (ibid., xi; cf. further K. Koch, "Is There a Doctrine of Retribution in the Old Testament?"). This so-called "action-consequences connection" (*Tun-Ergehen-Zusammenhang*) determines biblically speaking not only the social world of experience but also the transcendental realm: Only the vicarious surrender of life by the innocent Servant made possible by God, understood partly as a discharge of guilt (Isa 53:10), partly as a ransom, is able to deprive the misdeeds of the many of their force, thus creating for the many a new right of existence before God. Because the Old Testament word for a "ransom," כֹּפֶר, is derived from the root כפר, "to make atonement," certain commonalities exist between the ideas of ransom and atonement.

Atonement is spoken of in the Old Testament and early Judaism in non-cultic and cultic contexts. As far as cultic atonement is concerned there can be no talk whatsoever of the idea summarized by the Latin phrase *do ut des*, "I give in order that you might give," i.e., the human attempt to appease the wrath of God with the help of a ritual sacrifice, as assumed in research up to and including L. Köhler, *Theologie des Alten Testaments* (1953³) 188. (Unfortunately, Köhler's emphasis on the cultic aim of the "appeasement" or *Beschwichtigung* of God is completely lost on the English translator, A. S. Todd. He understands a *Beschwichtigungsgeruch* or "appeasing fragrance" as nothing more than a "sweet savour," and *was zur Beschwichtigung Gottes dient*, "what serves for the appeasement of God," as simply, "what God likes"! Cf. Köhler, *Old Testament Theology* [ET 1957] 196–97.) Atonement rather involves appropriating something God himself has instituted: Yahweh allows and enables Israel to meet with him despite all their iniquity, without requiring that the nation or the individual perish before him in their earthly guilt and fallibility. The nonnegotiable founding principle of the cultic-priestly type of thinking is that God in his holiness cannot and will not coexist with sin and its effects. Impurity, sin, and unrighteousness must rather perish before God (cf. Isa 6:5; Exod 33:20). The helpful and wonderful thing about the atoning cult is that it makes possible a meeting between the holy God and the unholy people: God has allowed and made a way for things that are evil and unholy to be deprived of their force and destroyed through priestly mediation, so that new fellowship is established between God and Israel. This happens through the transfer of both the personal subject and the personal guilt of an individual or group onto a pure, ritually unblemished sacrificial animal. Instead of the person or persons, the animal is killed and its blood dedicated to the holy altar. This symbolic sacrificial consecration is both a "surrender of life to the holy" (*Lebenshingabe an das Heilige*) and a "coming to God that consists of passing through the death sentence" (*ein Zu-Gott-Kommen durch das Todesgericht hindurch*), as H. Gese has nicely formulated it in his essay "Die Sühne" (pp. 98, 104; cf. ET: "The Atonement," 107, 114).

By means of the *tamîd* offering (עֹלָה תָמִיד), the "regular" or "perpetual" burnt offering that had to be offered every day at morning and evening (cf. Num 28:3–8; Exod 29:38–42; *Jub.* 6:14; 50:11), Israel could daily be redeemed from its guilt. The atoning cult reaches its high point on the *Day of Atonement* ceremony which is to be performed once a year, and whose ritual is described in a rudimentary form in Leviticus 16 (and in the Mishnah tractate *Yoma*). The place of "atonement" (German: *Versühnung* [cf. *Sühne*]) and therefore also of "reconciliation" (*Versöhnung*) between God and humanity is this time not the altar alone, but includes also the temple's most holy place, the Holy of Holies. Within this sacred chamber, withdrawn in the dark from all human eyes, is the so-called ark of the covenant. Upon this chest containing the covenant is a "top piece" (ἐπίθεμα) consisting of a flat golden plate or surface fitted with cherubim at either end (for ἐπίθεμα, cf. Exod 25:17; Philo, *Vit. Mos.* 2.95, 97; *Fug.* 100; Josephus, *Ant.* 3.135, 137). While this object is physically a "top piece" upon the ark, theologically it is a one-of-a-kind artifact that has always been given a special name—Hebrew: כַּפֹּרֶת; Greek: ἱλαστήριον; Latin: *propitiatorium*; German: *Gnadenstuhl*; English: "mercy seat" (the term "cover" in REB, NJPS, and NRSV margin at Exod 25:17–22 is philologically inappropriate to the Hebrew כַּפֹּרֶת and too pedestrian to capture the object's significance). According to Exod 25:22 the mercy seat is the place where Yahweh will meet his people and from which he will deliver his commands to them. On the Day of Atonement the high priest, as the representative of Israel, enters the Holy of Holies, fills it with incense, and sprinkles the blood of the sin-offering goat delivered to death in place of the people seven times before the mercy seat and once upon the mercy seat. With this rite of sacrificial consecration the priest establishes new fellowship between God and Israel. Returning from the Holy of Holies he gives the blessing of Aaron to the people waiting before the temple as a sign of their having been atoned for (cf. Sir 50:20–21).

How little this cultic procedure has to do with a human attempt to appease the angry God is shown by the wording of Lev 10:17 and 17:11. According to Lev 10:17 the sin offering is "given" by God, while Lev 17:11 says in the form of a divine address:

> For the life of the flesh is in the blood; and I have given it to you for making atonement for your lives on the altar; for, as life, it is the blood that makes atonement.

The blood is the carrier of the life that belongs to God, and the atonement ritual (of Lev 16:14) is accomplished by the medium of blood that God has both ordained for atonement (Lev 17:11) and withheld from all human use (Lev 17:10). The whole atonement procedure is therefore a symbolic act of grace: *God himself opens the way of the cultic ritual; he establishes sacrifice and provides blood as the means of atonement. By this means the people that is otherwise under the judgment of death is atoned for and reestablished in its existence before God. Atonement, forgiveness of sins, and new creation belong most closely together in the atonement ritual (cf. Heb 9:22).*

If the idea of atonement is transported into the extra-cultic realm nothing changes in its basic conception. The intercessions of Moses (Exod 32:30), Aaron (Num 17:11–12), or the Levites (Num 8:19) likewise did not appease God's wrath but rather pleaded for God's forgiveness and gracious dealings on behalf of those concerned. Atonement remains to God's own act of grace. Therefore we may compare the confession of the worshiper in 1QS XI 13–15 (cf. 1QH IV 35–37) (trans. G. Vermes, *The Complete Dead Sea Scrolls* [1997] 116):

> He will draw me near by His grace,
>   and by His mercy will He bring my justification.
> He will judge me in the righteousness of His truth
>   and in the greatness of His goodness
>   He will pardon all my sins.
> Through His righteousness He will cleanse me
>   of the uncleanness of man
>   and of the sins of the children of men,
> that I may confess to God His righteousness,
>   and His majesty to the Most High.

The cup saying of Mark 14:24 is clearly at home in the extra-cultic realm and is to be related to the events of the end. Jesus' "blood of the covenant" is therefore credited with the power to make atonement in the end times: Jesus' life is contained in the blood of the covenant, and he gives it up vicariously in order to open a new life before God to the "many." In the Old Testament the expression *to shed blood* (שָׁפַךְ דָּם) means "to bring a person violently to death" (cf., e.g., Gen 9:6; Num 35:33; Deut 21:7, etc.). Therefore when Jesus speaks in Mark 14:24 par. of his "blood of the covenant poured out for many," he is thinking about the violent death he has to undergo and the vicarious surrender of life to be accomplished in this death "for many"–ὑπὲρ (Matthew: περὶ) πολλῶν. The expression οἱ πολλοί means the uncountable, great throng and alludes (as in the Mark 10:45) to Isa 53:11: "by his suffering my servant will justify *many* by taking their guilt upon himself." Although the πολλοί are to be understood as including first and foremost Israel according to Isa 53:11, from the perspective of Isa 52:14–15 the Gentile nations are also in view.

In the cup saying Jesus appears again as the Lord's Servant, who through his vicarious suffering and death establishes end-time justification for Israel and the nations. If one takes together the passion prediction of Mark 9:31, the ransom saying of Mark 10:45 par., the bread saying, and the cup saying, then it shows that the ideas of an end-time ransom, of discharge of guilt or of the guilt offering, of justification through the vicarious death of the Servant, and of eschatologically effective atonement through Jesus' blood of the covenant all belong most closely together. As in Second Isaiah (cf. Isa 43:1–5; 53:5–6, 10–12), these ideas formed a unit in the proclamation of Jesus that functioned as a pre-existent given for the kerygma of the early church.

Exod 24:9–11 relates that Moses together with Aaron and his sons and seventy of the elders of Israel climbed Mount Sinai after the people were sprinkled with the blood of the covenant. At the top they were able to behold God and have a meal before him without perishing as sinners before his glory: "God did not lay his hand on the chief men of the people of Israel; also they beheld God, and they ate and drank" (Exod 24:11). In his cup saying Jesus apparently had this meal scene in view, and from its perspective he looked forward to the end-time table fellowship before God (cf. Isa 25:6–8). The perspectival combination of the meal on Mount Sinai with the meal of the nations on Mount Zion is already present in Isaiah 24–27: In Isa 24:23 the anticipation of the eschatological meal of the nations in Isa 25:6–8 is typologically connected to God's manifestation of his glory before the elders in Exod 24:9–11. As the messianic Son of Man whom he will yet declare himself to be this very night before the high priest (cf. Mark 14:61–62), Jesus does not wish to lend force only to the Sinai covenant of Exodus 24 with his "blood of the covenant." Rather, beginning with the Twelve whom he has symbolically gathered around him, Jesus wants to make the "many" into his table guests at the end-time fellowship meal upon Mount Zion, corresponding to the meal on Mount Sinai in Exod 24:11. This is the meal of "fulfillment" to which Jesus looks forward in Luke 22:16; Mark 14:25 par. Jesus' blessing over the cup, his word of institution, his passing of the one cup around the circle, and the common drinking from it belong together: *by hearing Jesus' word, taking the cup of blessing offered to them as the cup of salvation (Ps 116:13), and drinking together out of it, the Twelve gain a share in Jesus' blood of the covenant, experiencing the saving power of Jesus' death that freshly and finally unites them with God. A place is reserved for them at the messianic table, at which they may live in peace with God and their meal companions, singing the thanksgiving song of Isa 26:1ff.*

The *(Markan) cup saying* is unusually densely formulated, with each expression full of meaning and content. Although it needs no literary correction or decomposition, it does need to be followed exactly. One cannot very well claim that the bread and the cup saying are schematically parallel in Mark if one wishes to allow each its original wording.

The Markan cup saying (Mark 14:24) is once again the origin of the parallel versions. This can be seen by the further interpretation of the Markan version both in Matthew and in the tradition of Paul and Luke. Matthew provides the saying of Mark 14:24 with an addition about *forgiveness*: τοῦτο γάρ ἐστιν τὸ αἷμά μου τῆς διαθήκης τὸ περὶ πολλῶν ἐκχυννόμενον εἰς ἄφεσιν ἁμαρτιῶν, "for this is my blood of the covenant, which is poured out for many *for the forgiveness of sins*" (Matt 26:28). This expanded interpretation is materially fully justified, because the goal of the event of atonement that God put into effect through Jesus is the establishment of new life through the forgiveness of sins.

The striking similarity between Luke's and Paul's text is explained most readily by the assumption that both go back to the proto-Lukan passion tradition that was at home in Antioch and originated in the tradition of the Jerusalem "Hellenists" around Stephen. Both Luke 22:20 and 1 Cor 11:25 point out that Jesus took the cup only "after supper." In Luke's narrative this means that the cup Jesus took was the third cup, which concludes the main Passover meal—the so-called "cup of blessing," τὸ ποτήριον τῆς εὐλογίας (1 Cor 10:16). But his interpretation does not dwell on this—liturgically by no means unimportant—detail. Instead it addresses the question that remains open at the superficial level of the texts in Mark 14:24/Matt 26:28: For what type of "covenant" has Jesus shed his "blood of the covenant" (Exod 24:8)? The fully correct biblical answer involves the new covenant according to Jer 31:31–34, opened through Jesus' vicarious surrender of his life. Therefore the cup saying in 1 Cor 11:25 reads: τοῦτο τὸ ποτήριον ἡ καινὴ διαθήκη ἐστὶν ἐν τῷ ἐμῷ αἵματι, "This cup is the new covenant (sealed) in my blood," while Luke clarifies it by the addition of a ὑπέρ clause: τοῦτο τὸ ποτήριον ἡ καινὴ διαθήκη ἐν τῷ αἵματί μου τὸ ὑπὲρ ὑμῶν ἐκχυννόμενον, "This cup is the new covenant (sealed) in my blood, *which is poured out for you*" (Luke 22:20). With this formulation the tradition of Paul and Luke leads forward in a sensible way, yet at the same time avoids the suspicion that could easily arise for Jewish ears in Mark's version that Jesus required the Twelve at his last supper to drink his own blood (prohibited in Lev 17:10–11). The content of Luke and Paul's version of the cup saying is more easily understood than that of Mark and Matthew, and less offensive for both Jewish and Gentile Christians. It thereby shows itself to be a further development, perfectly understandable in a missionary context, of the old but potentially offensive cup saying of Jesus preserved by the apostles' memory and contained in Mark.

It is often assumed that the Pauline-Lukan cup saying is original and took on the more difficult and readily misunderstood form in Mark and Matthew only in the course of transmission. But this assumption can hardly be verified: in its original setting the tradition of the "new covenant" that later appears in Paul and Luke was inherently connected neither with the motif of the blood (of the covenant) nor with the messianic feast of Isa 25:6–8. The connection of the new covenant with both of these themes in 1 Cor 11:25 and Luke 22:20 results only from Mark 14:24–25, where Exod 24:8–11; Isa 24:23 and 25:6–8 are coupled with Jesus' end-time act of atonement in the form of the shedding of his "blood of the covenant." Because Paul by his formulation in 1 Cor 10:16–17 also betrays a knowledge of the Markan tradition of institution, from the tradition historical standpoint there is much more in favor of proceeding from Mark to Paul and Luke than vice versa.

Jesus' cup saying (like the bread saying) may have been followed by a series of conversations with his disciples at the last Passover (cf. Luke 22:21–38). When the conversations were over, the disciples together with Jesus sang the second part of the Passover *hallel* (Psalms 115–18) and drank the fourth or *hallel* cup. Then they went out to the Mount of Olives (Mark 14:26). The fact that Jesus did not spend the night as usual in Bethany (cf. Mark 11:11b par.) but in the Garden of Gethsemane finds its explanation in the regulation of Deut 16:5–7 that the Passover night should be spent in the place of God's choosing, which by this time meant the city precincts of Jerusalem. In order to make room for the pilgrim masses that streamed to Jerusalem for the Passover festival, the city area was extended for Passover night to the Mount of Olives on which the garden lies. Judas, who obviously knew Jesus' plan, gained his opportunity to betray Jesus to the temple guard in this way (cf. Mark 14:32ff. par.).

How the early Christian "Lord's Supper" (1 Cor 11:20) developed out of Jesus' last (Passover) supper is a topic for later discussion. The aim here has merely been to reconstruct what Jesus said and did during his last Passover supper with the Twelve in Jerusalem, and what can be inferred from this about his understanding of his suffering and death.

This reconstruction is nevertheless decisively important for the *understanding and formation of Christian celebrations of the Lord's Supper*: ever since the church has existed the celebration has been determined not in the first instance by Jesus' symbolic table fellowship with tax gatherers and sinners or by the symbolic feeding of the people of God (cf. Mark 6:24–44; 8:1–8 par.), but by Jesus' supper activities "on the night when he was delivered up (by God)" (1 Cor 11:23; cf. Rom 4:25). The remembrance (ἀνάμνησις) expressly required of the celebrating church in 1 Cor 11:24–25 and Luke 22:19 corresponds to the requirement in Exod 12:14; 13:3, 8 and Deut 16:3 that the Passover celebration include remembrance of Israel's salvation history, and it constitutes the Christian counterpart to the remembrance required of later

Jewish generations in *Mishnah Pesaḥim* 10:5 (see above, p. 402). In the act of remembering during the Lord's Supper, the Christian church, as the vanguard of the new people of God, continues the remembrance of Israel's salvation history and expands it to include Jesus' passion. The church practices this remembrance under the hope expressed by the prayer μαράνα θά, "Our Lord, come!" (1 Cor 16:22), until the day of the Parousia (1 Cor 11:26). Looking back from the perspective of Easter upon Jesus' mission, passion, and resurrection, the church once again takes part in Jesus' last supper and the events "on the night when he was betrayed (by Judas)" and "delivered up (by God)." In this way the church becomes aware of its salvation-historical place on the way of the people of God from Sinai to the end-time Zion, and is strengthened in its hope of the Parousia.

6. Looking back it can be seen that the question of how Jesus understood his suffering and death need not remain unanswered. The conclusion to be drawn from the tradition of the death of the prophets in Luke 13:31–33, the passion prediction of Mark 9:31 par., the ransom saying of Mark 10:45 par., and the two words of institution of Mark 14:22, 24 par. is clear and unmistakable: *Jesus knowingly and willingly went to his death. He understood this as a vicarious atoning death for the many, both Israel and the nations.* The atoning death of Jesus is not an act of appeasement or satisfaction over against the angry God. Rather, it is the vicarious saving act of the messianic Son of Man in the name and authority of the God who out of love for his chosen people Israel (cf. Isa 43:3–4) wants to bring justification and salvation to the guilty many through the sacrifice of his Servant.

This result is of great theological significance: the soteriological interpretation of the death of Jesus in the early Christian kerygma (cf., e.g., 1 Cor 15:3b–5; Rom 4:25) does not in the first instance originate from the interpretive will of the post-Easter church to explain the event of the cross on Golgatha from Isa 43:3–4; 52:13–53:12 and the Old Testament atonement tradition. Rather, it corresponds to the messianic will of Jesus to complete his mission and sacrifice, about which he told his disciples already before Easter. The saving dimensions of the early Christian missionary gospel are therefore precisely prefigured for the church in Jesus' teaching and destiny. If one wants to summarize this content in a christologically precise way, one can say that *Jesus took suffering and death upon himself out of love for God and humanity. Because he was the messianic "mediator and reconciler"* (to borrow the language of the Reformation), *the apostolic missionary gospel became the "word of reconciliation,"* ὁ λόγος τῆς καταλλαγῆς *(2 Cor 5:19).*

GERD LUEDEMANN

The History and Nature of the Earliest Christian Belief in the Resurrection

[[173]] According to the evidence of all the New Testament Gospels the Roman prefect Pontius Pilate had Jesus crucified on a Friday—probably around 30 C.E. The group of male disciples who had come up from Galilee to Jerusalem with him for the passover abandoned him in flight either before or at the arrest; after initial hesitation even including Simon Peter, one of the Twelve, who had a pre-eminent position among Jesus' disciples. By contrast, women followers of Jesus, who had also travelled with him from Galilee to Jerusalem for the passover, stayed with the Master longer.

The motives for the execution of Jesus by the Roman Pilate are clear. He saw him as a political troublemaker, who had to be put out of action politically. Evidently Jesus was falsely accused of being a political agitator by elements of the Jerusalem priesthood who were hostile to him, in reaction to his eschatological and messianic activity, which perhaps included a claim that he was identical with the coming judge–Son of Man. How far a disciple (Judas) was also involved in this—probably for other motives—need not be discussed further here.

The trial, execution and death of Jesus took place on one and the same day. This was followed by the sabbath, which in that year coincided with the first day of the feast of passover.[1] This presented the Jews with the problem what to do with the body of Jesus, since according to Jewish custom it was against the law to leave a dead body on the cross overnight (Deut 21:23) and moreover on a sabbath, which in addition coincided with the first day of the feast of the passover. At all events, the Jews were given permission by Pilate to

---

Reprinted, with permission, from Gerd Luedemann, *The Resurrection of Jesus: History, Experience, Theology* (Minneapolis: Fortress, 1994) 173–79, 248–50.
1. Cf. John 18:28; 19:13; 13:1. According to the Synoptics the Friday is already the first day of the passover. But the first day of the passover as a date for an execution is extremely improbable.

take the body of Jesus down from the cross. Either the Jews entrusted Joseph of Arimathea with putting Jesus in a tomb, or Jews unknown to us buried the body at a place which can no longer be identified. That settled matters for the relevant Jewish authorities [[174]] and Pilate, in whose view Jesus of Nazareth was only one of many Jewish messianic pretenders.

Women followers of Jesus kept as near as possible to him in his last hours, even if they could not avert his fate. They certainly included Mary from the Galilean fishing village of Magdala (whom Jesus had cured of a serious illness [Luke 8:2]).

No one knows what Jesus felt in his last hours. The words attributed to him during the trial and on the cross are certainly later creations. Nor, for example, can it be said that he really collapsed inwardly, as is often suggested,[2] though the opposite cannot be said either.

So Good Friday ended in silence as in a dark cave, and thus the torch lit by Jesus was evidently snuffed out in an ice-cold way. However, not long after the death of their master on the cross and the return of the disciples to Galilee a new spring unexpectedly dawned. We do not know precisely when this happened. That it was on the third day, i.e., on the Sunday after the sabbath, can be ruled out above all because the breakthrough took place in Galilee and the disciples cannot have got back there in one or two days (and moreover during the sabbath). But not long after the Friday on which Jesus died, Cephas saw Jesus alive in a vision which also had auditory features, and this event led to an incomparable chain reaction. If Cephas had seen and heard Jesus, the content of the vision (and the audition) was passed on to others. The news went round like lightning that God had not abandoned Jesus in death, indeed had exalted Jesus to himself and that Jesus would soon be appearing as Son of Man on the clouds of heaven.[3] That created a new situation, and the Jesus movement embarked on a tremendous new beginning. Now the women and men around Jesus could go back again to Jerusalem and there take up the work which their master had left uncompleted, and call on both the people and the authorities to repent. (Perhaps the present was understood as the very last reprieve that God had given.) The first vision to Peter proved formally "infectious,"[4] and was followed by others. The group of

2. Cf. David Friedrich Strauss, *Der alte und der neue Glaube. Ein Bekenntnis*, [4]1873, 77: "We are not even certain whether in the end he was not wrong about himself and his cause," also Rudolf Bultmann, "Das Verhältnis der urchristlichen Christusbotschaft zum historischen Jesus" (1960), in id., *Exegetica*, 1967, 445–69: 453: "We must not disguise the possibility that he collapsed."

3. Cf. Martin Hengel, "Psalm 110 und die Erhöhung des Auferstandenen zur Rechten Gottes," in Villiers Breytenbach and Henning Paulsen (ed.), *Anfänge der Christologie (FS Ferdinand Hahn)*, 1991, 43–73: 67f.: "Those 'sent by the Messiah Jesus' were to announce . . . the crucified Messiah Jesus of Nazareth as the one who had been raised from the dead and exalted to God."

4. There is polemic against this in Erich Fascher, "Die Auferstehung Jesu und ihr Verhältnis zur urchristlichen Verkündigung," *ZNW* 26, 1927, 1-26: 5: "Anyone who believes that at any rate according to the old tradition (viz., 1 Cor 15:3–8) this was a series of appearances is at liberty to think that Peter had an 'infectious' effect here." Here Fascher refrains from the

twelve which had been called into being by Jesus during his lifetime was carried along by Cephas and also saw Jesus. And probably at the feast of weeks
which followed the passover at which Jesus died, there took place that appearance to more than 500. Women, too, were now among those who saw Jesus.
Indeed when opponents on the Jewish side objected and asked where the
body of Jesus was, it could immediately be reported that the women [[175]]
had found the tomb empty and later that Jesus had even appeared to the
women at the tomb.

We cannot underestimate the explosive dynamic of the beginning. So in
addition the physical brothers of Jesus (cf. 1 Cor 9:5) were caught up in the
whirlpool, and went to Jerusalem; James even received an individual vision—
that James who had not thought much of his brother during Jesus' lifetime
(Mark 3:21; John 7:5).

We should reckon that the events mentioned (apart from the "discovery"
of the empty tomb and the appearance of Jesus there) took hardly more than
six months. Here many things were going on side by side. In addition to the
experience of the risen Christ in the present the following elements of the
development can be clearly grasped historically: (a) in the breaking of the
bread the assembled community immediately relived for itself the fellowship
with the Messiah Jesus who had been so wretchedly executed and had now
been all the more powerfully endorsed; (b) the recollection of Jesus' activity
and his word immediately came alive; (c) "the eschatological-messianic word
of scripture present to their minds, here above all the messianic songs of the
psalter, which people had long known by heart" were now sung "as psalms of
present fulfilment, to the glory of the exalted Messiah–Son of Man."[5]

The movement achieved a new stage when Greek-speaking Jews joined it
in Jerusalem. That may already have happened at the feast of weeks following
the passover at which Jesus died, when people from all countries were in Jerusalem and heard of Jesus. At all events, the message of Jesus spread into
areas outside Jerusalem and attracted the attention of the Pharisee Saul. He
went into action in a way which was at first to prove extremely successful, and
suppressed the new preaching until he too was overcome by Jesus and saw
and heard him. With this event an outer point is reached in the earliest Easter faith, although Jesus kept appearing in the subsequent period. Paul's calling was not recognized by many in Jerusalem, but also as a result of his
missionary success, at a later stage he could achieve a temporary accommodation with some of the people there. Three years after he had seen (and
heard) Jesus he visited Cephas in Jerusalem and learned from him further details of the preaching and activity of Jesus.[6]

---

task of translating traditions into history. But already previously, he had to say that he had
given up on the task of saying what happened at Easter, "the effects of which it is possible
for the historian to note, even if he cannot grasp their cause" (p. 4).

5. Hengel, "Psalm" (n. [[3]]) 69.

6. Paul "presumably knew well enough whose 'cause' he was fighting when he persecuted the Hellenistic Jewish-Christian community, and without doubt he asked Peter about

Doubtless one or other point of this historical outline of the earliest Christian belief in the resurrection needs to be corrected. The reason for this is not only the relatively meagre amount of source material, but also the nature of the event itself.

> During these [[176]] momentous months of the beginning, which are so obscure to us but which shone out so splendidly for the disciples, many movements and discoveries alongside and with each other and sometimes confusingly 'through each other' were possible. The encounters with the Risen Christ formed a complex knot along with the formation of the earliest exaltation christology; but we can no longer neatly untangle the individual strands and put them in chronological order, especially as the world of ideas of the first disciples, shaped by eschatological enthusiasm, did not correspond to the rules of our analytical method.[7]

However, there is no gap here, nor anything of the kind, as is often said,[8] but the beginning of a religious enthusiasm[9] with its own dynamic. The oldest history of early Christianity runs almost logically (see below), and at any rate it would be over-hasty to say, as is often done, that the resurrection of Christ, as earliest Christianity proclaimed it, was something absolutely new.[10] Such a view is over-hasty in its systematizing and is evidently looking for a metaphysical anchor instead of first discovering the individual facts and then looking at them from its level of experience, transposing them into a historical sequence.[11]

At this point the question arises: "What was the nature of the earliest Christian belief in the resurrection?" The central point is that it was said of the

---

Jesus, even if he hardly states any real Jesus tradition in his letters" (Nikolaus Walter, " 'Historischer Jesus' und Osterglaube," *TLZ* 101, 1976, 321–38: 331). "Certainly Paul and Peter did not spend all the time 'talking about the weather' " (C. H. Dodd, *The Apostolic Preaching and Its Development*, 1936, 256 [[on Gal 1:18]]).

7. Hengel, "Psalm" (n. [[3]]) 73.

8. Cf., e.g., C. F. D. Moule and Don Cupitt, "The Resurrection: A Disagreement," *Theology* 75, 1972, 507–19: 509. Moule thinks that in connection with the Easter events he must be concerned with "something beyond history," "something transcendent," and continues: "The NT calls it the resurrection of Jesus." But here he is presupposing a theory of the event which corresponds to a philosophical realism that has been untenable since Kant. Cf. the remarks by Don Cupitt in *Christ and the Hiddenness of God*, 1985, 138–53.

9. Cupitt thinks that the Easter faith precedes the Easter experiences: "The arguments that led to the Easter faith are logically prior to the Easter appearances" (Cupitt, *Christ*, 8). But this thinking is too rationalistic. A vision is a primary experience and bears the religious truth completely in itself.

10. Cf. Friedrich, "Die Auferweckung [[Jesu, eine Tot Gottes oder ein Interpretation der Jünger," *Auf das Wort kommt es an: Gesammelte Aufsätze zum 70. Geburtstag* (ed. J. H. Friedrich; Göttingen: Vandenhoeck & Ruprecht, 1978)]] 335f.

11. What is correct in Friedrich's view above is that "the Jewish future hope nowhere knows an appointment to messianic-eschatological dignity through resurrection" (Hengel, "Psalm," 68). But as Hengel rightly states, the claim to be Messiah—whether explicit or implicit—was made by Jesus himself. "Without a messianic claim of Jesus the rise of christology would be completely inconceivable" (ibid.). Cf. also Martin Hengel, *Studies in the Gospel of Mark*, 1985, 31–60: 45f.

crucified Jesus of Nazareth that God had taken him to himself or exalted him, in other words that God had put himself at the side of Jesus, which was unexpected after Jesus' death on the cross. To that is attached the conclusion that God speaks to human beings in the crucified Jesus. Because Peter had this experience as his guilt feeling was broken through, it is certain, *first*, that the experience of the crucified Jesus is directly connected with the forgiveness of sins. In other words, the experience of the forgiveness of sins is an essential point of the earliest Christian Easter faith. *Secondly*, the earliest Christian Easter faith is the experience of the overcoming of death, i.e., the experience of life which from then on is at work in the community as Spirit. This life was seen as present in a vision; real eternal life was experienced here and now, the future as present. To this degree, *thirdly*, the earliest Christian Easter faith is also an eternity faith and as such an end faith.[12] Time and eternity have become one, but in such a way that the heart looks into eternity (Emanuel Hirsch). So eternal life has become the life of human beings. These three essential characteristics also relate to Paul–as [[Luedemann, *Resurrection of Jesus*,]] 83f. above show–and were [[177]] concisely summed up by Martin Luther in the Small Catechism: "Where there is forgiveness of sins, there too is life and blessedness."[13]

The three core points of the earliest Christian Easter faith were put in different frameworks of theological ideas. First, the resurrection of Jesus was understood as the beginning of the general resurrection of the dead (cf. 1 Cor 15:20: Jesus as the firstfruits of those who sleep), then that God has exalted Jesus to himself (Phil 2:9), or even in a combination of both statements (1 Thess 1:10). But the issue is not these different theological ideas; even without them the content of the first experience has become clear.

A further point needs clarification: as is well known, a wealth of different narratives were in circulation about the encounter with the Risen Christ, . . . How do these relate to the original Easter experience? In the analysis it has proved that all are in some way removed from the real Easter situation and historically speaking no longer contain primary reports. But some express in narrative form the content of the original Easter experience: the forgiveness of sins (John 20:19–23; Luke 5/John 21), the experience of life (John 20:11–18), the experience of eternity (Luke 24:13–31). Others represent Jesus in the flesh and in this respect are even more remote from the Easter situation, though we must immediately add that the Easter experiences in the Spirit, say of the Pharisee Paul, necessarily contain pre-existent material features because of the world view: the heavenly body of Jesus (and of Christians) is a body which is pneumatic and imagined in material form, even if it has been

---

12. For the terms eternity faith and end faith cf. Hirsch, *Osterglaube:* [[*Die Auferstehungsgeschichten und der christlichen Glaube* (ed. H. M. Müller; Tübingen: Mohr, 1940)]] 74–80, 206–12.

13. In *Martin Luther's Basic Theological Writings*, ed. Timothy F. Lull, Minneapolis 1989, 471–96 (cf. Gerhard Ebeling, *Wort und Glaube* 2, 1975, 33f.). "Lutheran" does not automatically mean "un-Pauline," as is thought in some places today.

changed. However, that does not in any way alter the fact that the original experience of a visionary kind happened in the Spirit, in rapture (1 Cor 15:6;
cf. Rev 1:10), and that the Gospel narratives mentioned above have little to
do with the Pauline conceptual material. (According to Paul "the Risen
Christ" did not eat, he was not with his disciples for forty days; Jesus entered
God's presence directly at the moment of his death [cf. Luke 16:22; 23:43]; he
was exalted directly from the cross to God.)[14]

Now one could make the criticism that the main points of the earliest
Christian belief in the resurrection depicted in this way are an expression of
wishes, in other words a projection. This argument of a reductionist hermeneutic which locates the centre of the meaning of faith as it were behind the
backs of those who convey it has beyond question some degree of justification and must be [[178]] looked at seriously. At any rate this argument is more
honest than the claim of a conservative hermeneutic that behind the resurrection faith stands the testimony of divine revelation which tolerates no
questions.[15] That happens even in Hans Grass's book, truthful though it is:
he speaks of an objective resurrection vision and connects this, in contrast to
subjective visions, with revelation[16] (cf. similarly Theodor Keim's thesis of a
"telegram from heaven").[17] In this and other cases scholars know a priori
what needs to be proved or to be shown to be probable, and questions are
not asked at the decisive point.

The objection to reductionist hermeneutics is closely connected with the
concept of symbol which underlies it. Thus for example according to Sigmund Freud symbols are concealments of unconscious, suppressed wishes.[18]
But the question is whether symbols do not contain more, all the more so
since the positivistic philosophy which underlies the reductionist hermeneu-

14. Cf. Johannes Weiss, *Earliest Christianity* (1917), 1959, 27.

15. For the hermeneutical conflict cf. Gerd Theissen, *The Miracle Stories of the Earliest
Christian Tradition*, 1983, 32–40.

16. "Where historical criticism is taken seriously, so seriously that even the most critical
possibilities are taken into account, i.e., in the case of the resurrection that it is impossible to
demonstrate an empty tomb and appearances of the risen Christ in the 'spatially physical
world,' but only visions of the disciples; and where on the other hand the belief cannot be surrendered that Christ lives as the exalted Lord, because without a living and exalted Lord the
church would no longer have the right to exist, an attempt must be made to think of the two
together. The objective vision hypothesis has made this attempt and done so in a theological
way; for in contrast to the subjective vision hypothesis it is a theological and not a historical
hypothesis, because it maintains the trans-subjective origin of the Easter vision and Easter
faith and the transcendent reality of what is seen and believed in these visions" (Grass, *Oster-
geschehen* [[*und Osterberichte* (Göttingen: Vandenhoeck & Ruprecht, 1964)]] 248). The thesis of
an "objective vision" has rightly found no echo in more recent scholarship, but Grass does
more in his excellent book than provide a basis for the objective vision hypothesis.

17. Theodor Keim, *Geschichte Jesu von Nazara III: Das Jerusalemische Todesostern*, 1872,
605; "The sign that Jesus was alive, the telegram from heaven, was necessary after this unprecedented and convincing destruction in the childhood of humanity" (Keim gives an introduction to the vision hypothesis on pp. 578–603 which is still worth reading).

18. Cf. Sigmund Freud, *New Introductory Lectures on Psychoanalysis*, Freud Penguin Library 2, 1962, 46; Paul Ricoeur, *Freud and Philosophy: An Essay on Interpretation*, 1962.

tic takes no note of spiritual, artistic and religious content and such a form is now no longer advocated by any perceptive contemporaries. Thus Paul Tillich understands symbol in a different way, in the framework of Schelling's idealistic philosophy.[19] First of all he distinguishes symbols from signs and metaphors, but also from dream symbols, "which in reality are symptoms" (p. 3). For clarification he calls them "representative symbols," which display five characteristics:

> The first and fundamental characteristic of all representative symbols is their property of pointing beyond themselves. . . . The second characteristic of all representative symbols is that the symbol participates in the reality of that to which it points. . . . This notion leads to the third characteristic of all representative symbols: they cannot be invented arbitrarily (p. 4). The fourth characteristic of representative symbols is their power to disclose dimensions of reality which are usually concealed by the domination of other dimensions. One could also add a fifth characteristic of representative symbols: their power to build up and order, and their power to divide and destroy . . . (p. 5).

Now of course it should be noted that this does not yet say anything about the truth of the resurrection faith of the first Christians, which perhaps is to be understood symbolically. (Tillich regarded the resurrection as a symbol which shows "the New Being in Jesus as the Christ as victorious over the existential estrangement to [[179]] which he has subjected himself."[20]) But the attack of a reductionist hermeneutic can for the moment be warded off by the indication of another possible (and plausible) understanding of symbol. Now at last we get to the heart of the matter.

19. Paul Tillich, *Symbol und Wirklichkeit*, [2]1966. Further references to this work are given in the text.
20. Paul Tillich, *Systematic Theology* 2, 1957, 159.

Part 6

Jesus and Others

In contemporary scholarship of an interdisciplinary nature, perhaps nothing is more discussed than the "other." A good example of this is Daniel Boyarin's recent study of the development of the concept of *heresy* and *orthodoxy*: the need for both (and at the same time, as he points out!) Judaism and Christianity to define themselves over against the "other" led them both to create the ideological notions of *heresy* and *orthodoxy*. Prior to the "discoveries" of them as the "other," the boundary lines between the two were fuzzier (Boyarin 2004). E. P. Sanders argued famously (1977) that Martin Luther needed the Roman Catholics to argue with, and to bolster his case he made the Jews who stood opposed to Jesus and the early Christians into a cipher for the Roman Catholics. Thus, he handed on to Protestant scholarship a view of the faith shaped by the "other." No one, of course, argues these things without careful consideration, but what is being argued today is that "others" are needed for both self-consciousness and self-definition. The insight calls into question whether or not we can be objective enough to describe anything if we are in need of others to define ourselves.

Consequently, when it comes to historical Jesus studies, Jesus is frequently contrasted to and compared with his contemporaries and frequently in terms of negating the "other." Because modern scholarship's sensitivity radars are on full readiness, at times the lines between groups are so blurred that one wonders if it is possible to make distinctions at all. We are fond today of discussing "Judaisms" and of even making the first Christians a form of Judaism. All of this illustrates the need to be especially careful in making comparisons, though the troubles that Jesus experienced and the efforts that were undertaken by some to thwart the missionary efforts of the Apostle Paul lead us to think that distinctions need to be made, even if they must be made with sensitivity and an abundance of nuance.

One of the most neglected "others" at the time of Jesus, and one about whom we do have plenty of solid Christian memory, is John the Baptist. And, if we may be so bold, his "otherness" is minimized in the tradition as well as (at crucial points) emphasized. The statement in the Gospel of John that "He must increase, but I must decrease" (John 3:30), whether ever said by John or not, is certainly true of the Christian faith, for John is barely known. Several recent studies on John are excellent examples of the recovery of John's significance, of historical research and the need to set Jesus in his historical relations to others (Webb 1991; Meier 1994; Taylor 1997), but the catalyst for this scholarship seems to be the fine chapter of Ben F. Meyer, in his fundamentally important and philosophically nuanced study, *The Aims of Jesus*. Perhaps the noteworthy item of Meyer's chapter on John (below, pp. 426–443) is that Jesus' own eschatological hope for the restoration of Israel is established in his relationship to John and even in what he learned from John. While some scholars today are skeptical of the historical value of the traditions about John and his parents, not to mention the traditions about Mary and Joseph, there is a growing trend to see these folk as the nest out of which Jesus flew.

The major "others" for Jesus include the Pharisees, the Essenes at Qumran, various prophets at the time of Jesus, and the emerging model of wisdom and Torah that come to fruition in the Mishnah. A study of each is found in this volume. Jesus' relationship to the Pharisees has been misunderstood, mostly because of the influence of theological categories and the need to sit in judgment, but a good approach to seeing both the nuance and the need for careful discernment can be seen in the seminal essay of James D. G. Dunn on "Pharisees, Sinners, and Jesus" (below, pp. 463–488). Paul Barnett's careful analysis of how Jesus can be seen in the context of the Jewish "sign prophets," known almost entirely through the writings of Josephus, has no rival, and it pays several readings (pp. 444–462). As Jacob Neusner pointed out so carefully in his three-volume study of the Pharisees (1971), Hillel takes the sides of the "victors" in the rabbinic sources, and it was a benefit to scholarship when a number of historians recently gathered to study how Jesus was related to Hillel. One study, that of Philip Alexander (pp. 489–508), has been chosen as a fresh example of what we are learning about how Jesus related to the emerging rabbinic praxis and theory.

It will be observed that we have not included the "Zealots," and this is not because we think the studies of either Brandon (1967) or Buchanan (1984)—not to mention the full-scale examination of the multiauthored volume edited by Bammel and Moule (1984)—are not worthy of inclusion. But space prohibits covering everything, and Horsley's study in part 4 above may be seen as one example of the discussion taking place today. Furthermore, there is considerable debate, even after Martin Hengel's massive work (1989), whether or not the Zealots even existed at the time of Jesus. It will also perhaps be noted that we have nothing on the Sadducees or priests, though we suggest that E. P. Sanders's essay (above, pp. 361–381) may lead the reader into this largely neglected field of "otherness" study.

The storm center in the last three decades, however, has not revolved around Jesus and the Pharisees so much as it has around Jesus and women. The foundational study of Elisabeth Schüssler Fiorenza, which itself provoked an entire branch of historical research, established a theory that Jesus was more egalitarian than the Gospels themselves reveal (1985). There has been a notable lack of feminist full-scale historical Jesus books, but perhaps the most influential scholar in the field today is Amy-Jill Levine, and her essay included here (pp. 509–23) is an exemplary specimen of sensitivity to both history and faith, as well as witty rhetoric that stings as it heals the wounds that have been inflicted by male hegemony.

Bibliography

Bammel, E., and Moule, C. F. D., eds.
   1984   *Jesus and the Politics of His Day*. Cambridge: Cambridge University Press.
Boyarin, D.
   2004   *Border Lines: The Partition of Judaeo-Christianity*. Philadelphia: University of Pennsylvania Press.
Brandon, S. G. F.
   1967   *Jesus and the Zealots: A Study of the Political Factor in Primitive Christianity*. Manchester: Manchester University Press.
Buchanan, G. W.
   1984   *Jesus: The King and His Kingdom*. Macon, Georgia: Mercer University Press.
Hengel, M.
   1989   *The Zealots: Investigations into the Jewish Freedom Movement in the Period from Herod I until 70 A.D.*, trans. D. Smith. Edinburgh: T. & T. Clark. [original pub., 1976]
Meier, J. P.
   1994   *Mentor, Message, and Miracles*. Volume 2 of *A Marginal Jew: Rethinking the Historical Jesus*. Anchor Bible Reference Library. New York: Doubleday.
Meyer, B. F.
   1979   *The Aims of Jesus*. London: SCM.
Neusner, J.
   1999   *The Rabbinic Traditions about the Pharisees before 70*. 3 vols. South Florida Studies in the History of Judaism 202–4. Atlanta: Scholars Press. [original pub., 1971]
Sanders, E. P.
   1977   *Paul and Palestinian Judaism: A Comparison of Patterns of Religions*. Philadelphia: Fortress.
Schüssler Fiorenza, E.
   1985   *In Memory of Her: A Feminist Theological Reconstruction of Christian Origins*. New York: Crossroad.
Taylor, J. E.
   1997   *The Immerser: John the Baptist within Second Temple Judaism*. Grand Rapids: Eerdmans.
Webb, R. E.
   1991   *John the Baptizer and Prophet: A Socio-Historical Study*. Journal for the Study of the New Testament Supplement Series 62. Sheffield: Sheffield Academic Press.

BEN F. MEYER

The Judgment and Salvation of Israel

Understanding the Baptist

[[115]] The beginning of Jesus' public career is inextricably bound up with the public career of John the Baptist. Both careers were prophetic appeals to the nation. Both were short, abruptly ended by execution. But we have to do here with more than "parallel lives," for the two were significantly related.

Initial Sketch

John "appeared" in the wilderness north of the Dead Sea "in the fifteenth year of the reign of Tiberius Caesar" (Luke 3:1); i.e., not earlier than the autumn of A.D. 27 nor later than midsummer of 29.[1] Travellers found themselves startled and stopped by a warning voice, a proclamation of judgment and a summons to repentance which soon brought visitors, then crowds, out to the wilderness to see and hear. Here was no theologian, no enthusiast, but a prophet. And this alone was taken as a persuasive sign of the truth of his message, a sign of the imminence of the end; for by now Israel had lived so long without prophecy that common expectation postponed its appearance to the day of definitive salvation.[2] The very phenomenon of the return of prophecy made John

---

Reprinted, with permission, from Ben F. Meyer, *The Aims of Jesus* (London: SCM, 1979) 115–28, 281–86.

1. The Syrian mode of calendrical calculation, presumably adopted by Luke, designated as the first year of a new ruler's reign the period from his accession to power to the next New Year's day (1 October). In this system Tiberius's first regnal year fell between 19 August and 30 September A.D. 14; his fifteenth year, between 1 October A.D. 27 and 30 September A.D. 28. (But it is at least possible that Luke followed the common Roman computation, according to which the first year of Tiberius's reign ran from August A.D. 14 to August A.D. 15 and the fifteenth from August A.D. 28 to August A.D. 29.)

2. On the quenching of prophecy cf. 1 Macc 4:46; 9:27; 14:41; *Syr. Bar.* 85:3; Josephus, *Ag. Ap.* 1.41; [[Str-B]] 1.127–34; 2.128–34. On the return of prophecy as a sign of messianic salvation, cf. the identification of "prophet" in Deut 18:15–18 with "Messiah" (*Sifre*, ad loc.); see also [[Str-B]] 2.134 t; 615f.

an eschatological symbol freighted with powerful, if ambiguous, meaning. Indeed, his career is unintelligible apart from the interwoven symbols in which it was realized: the pelt clothing that recalled Elijah;[3] the striking asceticism that made Jesus say, "John came neither eating nor drinking" (Matt 11:18a par.) and made the Christian community remember that "his food was locusts and wild honey" (Mark 1:6 par.); the imagery of judgment that filled his preaching (Spirit and fire, wheat and chaff, winnowing fork and threshing floor, axe and root). Two symbols especially defined his career: the encircling wilderness and, at its centre, the water rite of baptism.

[[116]] The wilderness (the word says simply "uninhabited land") that was John's "primary locale was the lower Jordan valley, east of Jerusalem.[4] But "wilderness" was filled with connotation and symbolic meaning. It connoted, first of all, the impure, the demonic, the lethal. In the scriptures, however, wilderness (*midbar*) had become a multivalent symbol. In the wilderness Yahweh tested Israel and Israel rebelled and was punished. Above all, the wilderness signified the return to God by return to where God's transactions with his people began.[5]

It can be no accident that the wilderness chosen by John was within easy distance of Jerusalem.[6] Bent on confronting the whole of Israel with his proclamation, he was no doubt acutely conscious that the way Jerusalem went the nation would go. But John would not himself go to Jerusalem, e.g., to preach in the temple. No; he called Jerusalem out to him, to the wilderness, away from the whole network of current structures and commitments. He called the nation to a new beginning.[7]

The rite which won John the surname "Baptizer" coheres with this interpretation. It was designed to symbolize and seal the conversion of Israel in the face of the approaching judgment—"the wrath about to come" (Matt 3:7 par.). In John's view, evidently, the supremely critical moment had come for Israel, a *kairos* [['time']] charged with imperatives of purification. It is equally evident that in John's view the standing religious resources of Israel, e.g., cultic means of expiation, could not meet these imperatives. God called for the conversion and washing of the whole nation. It would only be by repentance and baptism that a renewed Israel could meet judge and judgment and survive.

3. See M. Hengel, *Nachfolge und Charisma* [[Berlin: Alfred Töpelman, 1968) 39 n. 71; ET, *Charismatic Leader and His Followers* (New York: Crossroad, 1981)]].

4. G. Dalman, *Orte und Wege Jesu*, Gütersloh: Mohn, [4]1924; reprinted, Darmstadt: Wissenschaftliche Buchgesellschaft 1967, 89–107, esp. 97–99. ET, *Sacred Sites and Ways. Studies in the Topography of the Gospels*, tr. P. Levertoff; London: SPCK 1935, 81–100, esp. 89–91.

5. Hos 2:16f. (EVV 2:14f.); 12:10 (EVV 12:9); Mic 7:15; Isa 11:11; 48:20f. The ties between messianism and the desert are a development of the theme; see [[Str-B]] 1.85–88.

6. See A. Schlatter, *Der Evangelist Matthäus. Seine Sprache, sein Ziel, Seine Selbstständigkeit*, Stuttgart: Calwer 1948, 62, on Matt 3:5.

7. See A. Schlatter, *Matthäus*, 54f., on Matt 3:1. "New beginning" is meant to imply not rupture and renewal of covenant but the discontinuity between history and eschaton in accordance with the *Urzeit/Endzeit* [['prehistory/end times']] schema. Both Jesus and the earliest Christian tradition saw John as belonging to the scenario of eschatological fulfilment. Cf. below, pp. [[440–442]]; 220f. [[not reprinted here]].

This radical eschatology, grounded like classical prophecy in the conviction that the judgment to be turned against Israel would he unsparing, is implicit in the whole circle of symbols within which John operated. It is confirmed by a stinging word:

> Do not start saying to yourselves
> "We have Abraham for our father."
> I tell you:
> God can raise up sons to Abraham out of these stones!
>
> (Luke 3:8; Matt 3:9)

God was now summoning the children of Abraham[8] to enter the scenario of the end-time. By repentance and baptism he would reconstitute his people for the messianic visitation.

> I baptize you with water for repentance;[9]
> but one comes after me mightier than me
> whose sandals I am unworthy to carry;[10]
> he will baptize you[11] with the holy Spirit and fire.[12]

8. On the possibility that the Baptist preached to Samaritans as well as to Jews, see W. F. Albright, "Some Observations Favouring the Palestinian Origin of the Gospel of John," *HTR* 17, 1924, 189–95, esp. 194. B. Bagatti, "Ricordi di S. Giovanni Battista in Samaria," *ED* 25, 1972, 294–98, offers a more probable account of the archaeological data (tombs, place names) connecting the Baptist with Samaria. Not the Baptist himself but his disciples account for the ties. They buried their master outside the territory of Antipas and, settling there (Samaria), they named their settlements after the places where they had been with him (a practice attested for other sectarian groups in Palestine).

9. With baptism "for repentance" compare (a) baptism "of repentance for the forgiveness of sins" (Mark 1:4; Luke 3:3) and (b) the confession of sins that accompanied baptism (Mark 1:5; Matt 3:6). The rite signified a twofold object: the break with sin (now) and acquittal at the judgment (soon). "Repentance" thematizes the first; "forgiveness," the second. That John conceived his baptism as already (sacramentally) effecting the forgiveness of sins is unlikely, for, as Schlatter, *Matthäus*, 79, argues: "If he had had a consciousness of himself as the dispenser of forgiveness, he would not have described his relation to the coming one as one of total powerlessness." By the same token the Baptist could hardly have understood himself as "saviour." This is confirmed by the exclusively future role of purification through "the holy Spirit and fire," as well as by the historicity of the Baptist's question to Jesus. See [[Meyer, *Aims of Jesus*,]] 295 n. 96; cf. also John 1:19–34; 5:33–35. Contrast H. Thyen, *Studien zur Sündenvergebung*, FRLANT 96, 1970, 131–45.

10. The theme of the holy Spirit relates to "the mightier one" and may well account for the epithet. That "the mightier one" was John's circumlocution for "God" is practically excluded by the comparative form of the present *māšāl*. Rather, John must have belonged to an esoteric stream of Judaic tradition, comparable, perhaps, to Enoch, Baruch, *II* (4) *Ezra* and the *Sibylline Oracles*, which attributed the coming judgment of the world to an apocalyptic figure to come. Cf. 11QMelch 9–15. On the sense of the image: when a master arrives home, his slave removes and takes away his sandals. But John completely effaces himself. With reference to the mightier one he is not even worthy to perform a slave's service.

11. The repeated verb ("baptize") indicates that the role of the messianic judge stood in positive and essential relationship to the role of John. This is likewise indicated by "you": The Messiah will effect the final purification of the selfsame persons John has baptized.

His winnowing fork is in his hand [[117]]
and he will clear his threshing floor
and gather his wheat into the granary
but the chaff he will burn with unquenchable fire.

(Matt 3:11 par.)

These words supposed a scheme of salvation in two phases: the water baptism of John and the "mightier one's" baptism in "the holy Spirit and fire." The two phases were related as prologue to judgment and judgment itself. The second baptism would sort out, gather up, and purify the righteous. But the unrepentant ("the chaff") would be doomed to hell-fire.

John's career had a public dimension (the call to the nation) and an esoteric dimension (the guidance of disciples). Three traits typify the latter: fasting, prayer, and teaching. On the basis of specific fasting practices John's discipleship was at least externally comparable to the Pharisaic brotherhood (Mark 2:18; Matt 9:14; Luke 5:33). More significant, no doubt, for his followers' self-understanding were the prayers John composed for them (Luke 11:1; cf. 5:33) but of which we have no vestige. Finally, the heart of John's esoteric instruction was surely his prophetic expectations of the messianic judge to come. We have too little of his descriptive indications to match them with any eschatological figure of biblical or Judaic tradition. The clear points are two: (1) John's own mission was wholly relative to that of the coming judge (2) whose messianic epiphany was imminent.

Analysis

How are we to understand the aims of John? It is clear that the world of meaning within which he lived and operated was essentially shaped by expectation of the eschatological judgment (Mark 1:2f. pars.; Matt 3:7 par.; 3:10 par.; 3:11f. par.).[13] But his own role with reference to the judgment is revealed by "the wilderness" where he took his stand and by the baptizing which in contemporary estimation quintessentially defined him. Hence, the question "What were the aims of John?" is reducible to "What was the meaning of his baptizing in the wilderness?" Generically, the answer must be: "to make Israel ready for the judgment." But the challenge is so to sharpen the focus of

12. Here the judgment is conceived with exclusive reference to purification of the saved. That either phrase, "the holy Spirit" or "and fire," is a Christian addition is gratuitous and unlikely. The combination is distinctive and probably original with John, though each element separately finds relevant attestation elsewhere. The eschatological cleansing and life-giving role of the Spirit of Yahweh is a motif found in the Psalms and prophets, especially Ezekiel (36:26f.; 37:14). It is likewise attested with reference to eschatological judgment in Qumran, 1QS 4:21. On judgment as *refining* fire, see Isa 1:25; Zech 13:9; Mal 3:2; *2 Bar.* 48:39; 1 Cor 3:13–15. The judge to come does not simply pronounce the acquittal of the repentant; his judgment is a baptism, i.e., an apocalyptic cleansing.

13. The un-eschatological description of the Baptist in Josephus (*Ant.* 18.116–19) is a conscious accommodation to Hellenistic categories. See P. Vielhauer, "Johannes, der Taufer," *RGG*[3] 3.804–8, col. 804.

both question and answer as to arrive at a differentiated understanding of John's presuppositions and purposes.

It is historically out of the question that John conceived judgment along the individualistic lines characteristic of later Western thought. Rather, he conceived judgment in collective, or better, "ecclesial," terms, i.e., in terms of "God's people, Israel." To miss this is to miss the context—a massive tradition— in which John consciously and publicly situated himself and out of which came his every word and act. In Torah and prophets alike the [[118]] drama of history is the covenantal dialogue of God and people. Judgment is turned against *Israel* and *Israel* is the object of salvation. John's summons to baptism in the wilderness was accordingly directed not simply to all Israelites but to all Israel, i.e., to the nation as an ecclesial entity or to Israel as people of God. The response to his summons therefore could not be merely so many re- sponses of individuals within Israel; it had to be the response of Israel as such. "Prophet" is locked, as always, in engagement with "people." It would be a great mistake, then, to suppose that diversity of response could cancel the ec- clesial character of the encounter. On the contrary, the diversity of response would concretely determine the destiny of Israel as such: its division (cf. the coming separation of wheat and chaff) and restoration (the wheat gathered into the granary). For the issue now was the judgment that would bring his- tory to an end. Can John have supposed that, in the final act of the drama of God and people, some in Israel would be lost and some saved, but that Israel as such, neither lost nor saved, would simply cease to be a factor? Such a con- ception is totally alien to ancient Judaism as to the whole biblical tradition.

If it is Israel that is judged, it is Israel that is saved. But as judgment means the burning of the chaff, saved Israel is, in respect of its past collective selfhood, a remnant.

Prophetic tradition had converted "the remnant of Israel" into a powerful symbol of restoration.[14] In and through the remnant of Israel God reconsti- tuted his holy people. This both illuminates and is illuminated by "wilderness" and "baptism."

In the language and imagery of John prophetic and apocalyptic schemes of thought went easily together and cohered. For all John's apocalyptic horizons (e.g., the definitive judgment and the mysterious figure of "the mightier one" coming to judge), the wilderness thematic derived from prophetic sources. Apocalyptic threat invested John's prophetic themes with new urgency. In the face of judgment Israel was to be reconstituted as in the beginning:

> So I will allure her;
>   I will lead her into the wilderness
>   and speak to her heart. . . .
> She shall respond there as in the days of her youth
>   when she came up from the land of Egypt.
>   (Hos 2:16f.; EVV 2:14f.)

---

14. See [[Meyer, *Aims of Jesus*,]] 227–29.

By making his career "in the wilderness" and so presenting Israel with a charged symbol (the *Urzeit/Endzeit* schema) by which to understand him, John purposefully evoked themes of eschatological restoration. This would seem to be the real thrust of the symbolic act of appearing and preaching "in the wilderness." As in the beginning Israel was made God's covenant people in the wilderness and so made ready for entry into the land of [[119]] promise, so in the end-time Israel, renewed in the wilderness, would be made ready for the messianic judge. Moreover, this interior drama of reform was to be sealed by a rite of symbolic immersion in water:[15] Israel's "baptism of repentance" (Mark 1:4; Luke 3:3) prophetically sponsored by John and designating in advance a people whose positive response to his call destined it for acquittal.

The analysis can be recapitulated in three points: (1) The question "What were the aims of John?" is reducible to "What was the meaning of his baptizing in the wilderness?" (2) It was in view of eschatological judgment that John summoned Israel as such to baptism in the wilderness. But: if John's mission (a) was undertaken precisely with reference to the coming judgment, (b) was directed to Israel as such (though envisaging a diversity of response to it among Israelites) and (c) consisted in proclaiming and realizing the condition on which Israel's survival of judgment hinged, it follows that John's goal was to gather the remnant of Israel destined for salvation.[16] (3) The symbols "wilderness" and "baptism" illuminate and support this conclusion.

Objections and Precisions

Biblical criticism has failed to reach unanimity on the issue of John and the remnant of Israel because of numerous misunderstandings. We will mention five. It has been repeatedly but mistakenly supposed, first, that "remnant" must signify a separate and organized community and, second, that the community

15. See J. Jeremias, *Verkündigung*, 51; ET, *NT Theology* [[vol. 1: *The Proclamation of Jesus* (tr. J. S. Bowden; London: SCM / New York: Scribner's, 1971)]] 44: "To answer the question what led John to administer his baptism, we shall rather have to begin from the Jewish doctrinal statement (which can be traced back to the beginning of the first century A.D.) that on Sinai Israel was prepared for receiving salvation by means of a bath of immersion (cf. 1 Cor 10:1f.). [Cf. J. Jeremias, "Der Ursprung der Johannestaufe," *ZNW* 28, 1929, 312–20, pp. 314f.] According to a stereotyped apocalyptic pattern of thought, the Israelites in the wilderness were regarded as a type of the eschatological community of salvation; thus the tenet of their bath of immersion included the expectation that in the end-time Israel would again be prepared for salvation by a bath of immersion." G. Friedrich, "*prophētēs* (NT)," *TWNT* 6.829–58, p. 839; *TDNT* 6.828–61, p. 838, remarks apropos of 1 Cor 10:1ff. that inasmuch as use of the Moses/Messiah schema is atypical of Paul (it crosses the grain of his theology of righteousness), the connection of primitive Christian baptism with Moses "must go back to an ancient tradition which regarded baptism as a prophetic eschatological act." Cf. John 1:25.

16. Among those whose views converge at this point: J. Jeremias, "Der Gedanke des 'Heiligen Restes' im Spätjudentum und in der Verkündigung Jesu," *ZNW* 42, 1949, 184–94, p. 191, reprinted in *Abba* [[J. Jeremias, *Abba: Studien zur neutestamentlichen Theologie und Zeitgeschichte* (Göttingen: Vandenhoeck & Ruprecht, 1966)]] 121–32, p. 129; A. Oepke, *Das neue Gottesvolk in Schrifttum, bildender Kunst und Weltgestaltung*, Gütersloh: Mohn 1950, 176; P. Nepper Christensen, *Wer hat die Kirche gestiftet?* SBU 12, 1960, 23–35, p. 30.

so constituted must be a closed corporation. Third, it has been thought that remnant theology must suppose previous rupture of covenant. It has been unconsciously assumed, fourth, that John need not have conceived Israel as such to be the object of salvation, and fifth, that before specifying the aims of John as exactly as we have, we must first be able to settle all history-of-religions (*religionsgeschichtlich*) questions relating to him, his eschatology, and his baptismal rite. But none of these suppositions (which we will now take up in order) is well grounded; rather, all of them are misleading or false.

It is striking that the prophets who converted the age-old conception of the remnant into a vehicle of parenetic warning (*Drohpredigt*) and, eventually, into a potent symbol of survival and restoration, did not themselves undertake to gather the remnant of Israel prior to the outbreak of catastrophe. Perhaps they thought that this would be to presume to anticipate God's sovereign judgment. Nevertheless, two developments followed the prophetic use of the remnant theme, each exhibiting a distinctive "realized eschatology."[17] First, the exiles returning to the Holy Land from Babylon saw "the remnant of Israel" realized in themselves in so far as they were indeed survivors of judgment. "Remnant theology" became thereby a vehicle of national hope. Second, the Hellenistic crisis of the second century B.C. [[120]] prompted the public appearance of more or less markedly apocalyptic communities of the pious which characteristically sought to realize in themselves the scriptural attributes of the holy remnant. Here the realized eschatology was of a distinct kind. Like the returning *gola* [['diaspora']], they came to see "true Israel" realized in themselves, but unlike the *gola*, they did not understand themselves as survivors of an already realized judgment of God in history. Rather, they made themselves ready by a right observance of the Torah for the judgment which would bring history to an end. The realized element in their eschatology lay in the very existence of the community as the realization of scriptures now read as law for the last days.

The summons of the Baptist, though tolerating a certain structural comparison with the eschatological self-understanding and purposes of these latter groups, was distinctive in virtue of its simplicity and incisiveness. The Baptist "assembled" the remnant of Israel only in the sense that he sponsored a public and external rite to seal the decision of repentance and reform. Though the Johannite remnant, like contemporary remnant groups such as the Essenes or the Therapeutae,[18] was thereby "assembled" in advance of the judgment, unlike them it did not exist as a separate, organized community. In this respect as in others the key to the distinctiveness of John's movement lay in its genuine openness to all Israel.

This introduces the second point differentiating John from contemporary movements. The one condition of acquittal at the impending judgment was repentance. The last hour had come, the blade of the axe was already sunk in the root of the tree. There was no time, no need, no place for long

---

17. See [[Meyer, *Aims of Jesus*,]] 229–35.
18. See ibid., 233f.

study of the Torah, for priestly robes, for isolation in *élite* groups, for a massively detailed *halaka* [['the body of Jewish oral laws']] to guide the conduct of life. Indeed, there was no point in any of this. God's demand was radical and urgent. He called the whole people to a decisive break with sin. If this was to require less than did the mass of elitist prescriptions cultivated by the Pharisees, the Essenes, and like groups, it was also to require much more. Simple, urgent, incisive, the summons of the Baptist was keyed to evoke a response at a different and deeper level. The result is tangible. Other remnant groups were closed. The Johannite remnant was open.

In the sectarian groups contemporary with John the desire to embody "true Israel" inspired (probably on the basis of Exod 19:5f.) the self-imposition of a priestly standard of ritual purity. This separatist stance generated the Pharisees' condemnation of the unobservant and the Essenes' exclusion (from the final battle with the Gentiles) of the lame, the halt, the blind, and the dumb. John's mission was strikingly independent of such exclusivism. His call was addressed to all as a possibility for all. He proposed no special ritual code, no set of separatist rubrics, no distinguishing creed. He had disciples but organized no community. Whereas the self-understanding of the contemporary groups implied great claims, John [[121]] insisted on the renunciation of claims. His work was consciously preparatory and provisional.

"Remnant," therefore, was not defined by the limitation of John's mission to a given group. It was defined by the diversity of response (i.e., acceptance and rejection) vis-à-vis a summons addressed to all Israel. In so far as John realistically foresaw that his appeal would divide the nation, his goal was to bring into being the "remnant of Israel." In so far as this remnant was the destined object of salvation, his goal was to make Israel ready for its messianic restoration. Though John's controlling vision of things was finally apocalyptic, both these facets of his purpose prolonged the classic tradition of prophecy in Israel.

The third point: Our conclusion on the aims of John does not mean that his summons necessarily presupposed previous rupture and collapse of the covenantal relationship of God and Israel. In the face of judgment all claims to salvation on the basis of racial solidarity with Abraham were unavailing. This is the force of what we have called John's "stinging word" (Luke 3:8; Matt 3:9). "We have Abraham for our father" implied that descent from Abraham was a guarantee of salvation. If the retort "God can raise up sons to Abraham out of these stones" meant that for John sonship to Abraham was a matter of no consequence, then we are no doubt confronted with the motif of covenant-rupture. But more probably the sense of the retort was: "Sonship to Abraham is not physical descent!" On this hypothesis the Baptist did not void "sonship to Abraham" of its positive thrust; rather, he affirmed the positive thrust[19] but, taking a stance in radical continuity with themes of classical

19. See J. Jeremias, [[*Jesu Verheissung für die Völker* (Stuttgart: Kohlhammer, 1956)]] 52 n. 195; ET [[*Jesus' Promise to the Nations* (tr. S. H. Hooke; SBT 24; London: SCM / Naperville, Ill.: Allenson, 1958)]] 60 n. 3.

prophecy, he repudiated the superficial reduction of sonship to mere racial solidarity. Those destined for salvation were indeed sons to Abraham, and the baptism of John related positively to the covenant, bringing it eschatological affirmation and fulfilment.

The fourth point is the total implausibility of the assumption that John might have conceived salvation in other than collective and ecclesial terms. There is, of course, room in biblical and Judaic soteriology for the important question of the individual, but the form of the question is distinctive. It asks whether or not the individual belongs to the people to be saved. In the traditional biblical conception, "the saved" (survivors of judgment whether past or future) are the reconstituted ecclesial entity, Israel (cf., e.g., Isa 1:2; Mic 4:6f.). On this the biblical testimonies are impressively at one.[20]

Lastly the validity of our position on John's aims is not conditioned by the antecedent need to answer all questions relative to his eschatological vision and specifically to his baptismal rite. To suppose the contrary is to forget that the conditions of the truth of any proposition are limited and that the first step whether in the elaboration or testing of a hypothesis is [[122]] the selective determination of these conditions. The task, that is, is to find out what questions must be put and what answers verified to settle some prospective matter of fact. Related questions and answers may well have independent value; but, while potentially testing the hypothesis, they may also receive illumination from it.

Jesus and the Baptist

Among those from whom John's summons to baptism elicited a positive response was Jesus of Nazareth. But the baptism of Jesus,[21] unlike that of the many others who answered John's call, marked the beginning of a public religious career.

Jesus as Baptizer

The synoptic gospels date the start of Jesus' public career from the arrest of John (Mark 1:14; Matt 4:12; less clearly, Luke 3:19), leaving unexplained why Jesus had remained in Judaea until John's arrest (Mark 1:14; Matt 4:12) and

20. The biblical conception has had an impact on but is nevertheless to be distinguished both from Paul's *pas Israēl sōthēsetai* ('all Israel will be saved', Rom 11:26) and from the traditional dictum *kol yiśrā'ēl yēš lāhem ḥēlek bā'ōlām habbā'* ('all Israel has a share in the age to come', *m. Sanh.* 10:1). The first promised that, once the appointed measure of the salvation of the Gentiles had been reached, the whole empirical people Israel would enter into its historic heritage of salvation (i.e., the messianic community or church of Christ). The second asserted that every Jew (with specified exceptions) would eventually find final salvation in the age to come. The biblical conception, on the other hand, does not say who or how many will be saved but rather affirms that in the saved the ecclesial reality "Israel" is realized. Cf. the use of "Israel" in Gal 6:16.

21. Historicity is established by the index of discontinuity. Jesus' baptism crossed the grain of primitive Christianity insofar as it could suggest subordination to the Baptist and need of repentance (hence the didactic dialogue of Matt 3:14f.).

why the arrest should have had particular and decisive significance for him.[22] The lacuna is filled by data given in the Fourth Gospel: Jesus' public career had two phases, of which that opened by John's arrest and Jesus' return to Galilee (and recounted by the synoptists) was the second. Before the arrest he had already gathered followers about himself and with them worked as baptizer in alliance with (though apparently not alongside [John 3:26b]) John.[23]

In the context of our inquiry into the aims of Jesus these data immediately invite two questions. How, concretely, did Jesus' career as baptizer correlate with the career of John? And what in Jesus' career as baptizer correlated with his own later career?

The fact that Jesus could actively associate himself as he did with the Baptist's movement suggests that "the baptism of John" (Mark 11:30 pars.; Luke 7:29; Acts 1:22; 18:25; 19:3f.; cf. 10:37; 13:24) be understood as "the rite which John sponsored and whose sense and purpose he defined" but not as "the rite which John had personally and physically to administer."[24] Like

---

22. The *paradothē* of Matt 4:12 (cf. *paradothēnai* in Mark 1:14; cf. Matt 17:22; 20:18; 26:2, 45) is a "divine passive," i.e., a circumlocution employing for reverential reasons a passive verb form rather than an active form which would require "God" as subject. See A. Schlatter, *Matthäus*, 112. The text equivalently says that Jesus acts (goes to Galilee) not simply in reaction to the initiative of Herod but on a signal from God (cf. Luke 4:14: "by the power of the Spirit").

23. A claim to historicity for some of the data on Jesus' career as baptizer is established by the index of discontinuity: (a) The career of Jesus as baptizer is suggestive of subordination to the Baptist (in John 3:26 Jesus is interpreted as a rival of John); John 4:2, designed to soften the scandal, is a late addition; see J. Jeremias, *Verkündigung*, 53; ET, *NT Theology*, 45; (b) details apparently quite unrelated to post-paschal Christianity are given in John 3:23, 25. R. Schnackenburg, "Das vierte Evangelium und die Johannesjunger," *HJ* 77, 1958, 21–38, p. 23 remarks: "The debate is . . . over the question of 'purification' *(katharismos,* cf. 2:6); it is, then, an intra-Jewish controversy, but one having no follow-up [in the Fourth Gospel]." See also C. H. Dodd, *Historical Tradition in the Fourth Gospel*, Cambridge: Cambridge University Press 1965, 280f. For a trenchant critique of Bultmann's literary and historical judgment of the Johannine text, see E. Linnemann, "Jesus und der Täufer," *Festschrift für Ernst Fuchs*, ed. G. Ebeling, E. Jüngel and G. Schunack; Tübingen: Mohr 1973, 219–36, pp. 221–23. (c) It does not seem possible, however, to resolve the question of the historicity of one significant datum in the Johannine account; namely, that Jesus already had followers before the arrest of John. On the one hand, a synoptic omission of all data on the ministry of Jesus as baptizer is to be inferred. But might not the Johannine representation of the first disciples (particularly the representation that they were former followers of the Baptist) simply derive from the emphatic Johannine theme of the Baptist's testimony to Jesus? A marked stylization of traditions in the narrative sequence following the Prologue (John 1:19ff.) is evident. If, however, a circle of disciples actually did surround Jesus during his career as baptizer, this will have accorded well with the general principle laid down by Anton Fridrichsen [["Jesus, St. John and St. Paul," *The Root of the Vine: Essays in Biblical Theology* (ed. A. Fridrichsen et al.; London: Black / New York: Philosophical Library, 1953)]] 55) that "the man of God" in the ancient Orient "is never isolated. He is always the centre of a circle taught by his words and example . . ." It is, moreover, likely that like Jesus himself the disciples of Jesus underwent "the baptism of John" (cf. Acts 1:21f.) and the hypothesis of the historicity of the Johannine data on the first disciples accords well with this.

24. The contrary is, to be sure, supposed by John 4:2, a late addition (see the reference in the previous note). But Aramaic *ṭᵉbal* to which *baptizesthai* corresponds, means, not 'to be

John, Jesus preached repentance and baptism in the face of imminent judgment and stood as witness to the conversion of the repentant and its ritual sealing in water. We know of nothing distinctively his own in Jesus' participation in the call to baptism; only that it was effective. Some of John's disciples complained to their master that "here he is, baptizing, and all are going to him" (John 3:26c.).

That Jesus not only responded positively to the Baptist's call to the nation but actively shared in it as an ally already stamps his horizons as [[123]] eschatological and "preparationist." Moreover, intimate association with the Baptist's movement argues participation in his aim: the reconstitution of Israel in view of the eschaton. It was an aim that involved Jesus in the dangerous business of calling the powerful and the righteous to repentance, From the start, then, a seed of conflict was sown between him and the religious *élite* of Israel as between the same *élite* and John (Matt 11:18f par.; Mark 11:29–34 pars.). These would seem the most significant of the correlations between Jesus' ministry as baptizer and his post-Johannite ministry. To them we should add a final remark on the repentance attested as a demand both of John and Jesus.

Repentance was not an arbitrary requirement, not a ticket to be turned in for admission to salvation. Rather, it intrinsically conditioned salvation by generating a new recognition of one's sins and sinfulness (Matt 3:7b–8 par.;[25] Mark 1:5; Matt 3:6; Matt 3:11d par.[26]) and a new recognition of one's neighbour (see especially Luke 3:11–14). Radical repentance—the renunciation of claims and the opening of the heart to others—remains among the most compelling facets of the Baptist's religious stance. Jesus refined and extended it. To the representatives of Torah piety, repentance was supremely difficult for professional sinners such as publicans.[27] John's ministry showed the opposite (Luke 3:12–14; 7:29; Matt 21:32). Repentance in the Baptist's sense, with its

---

baptized', but 'to undergo immersion, to immerse oneself'. (*Baptizein* renders the causative form of the same verb.) Nor can one argue from the Greek termination *-tēs* (pl., *-tai*) in *baptistēs* that John 'performed' a rite on others, for the *ṭôbᵉlê šᵉḥārîn* (*t. Yad.* 2.20), who immersed themselves, were called in Greek *hēmerobaptistai*. J. Jeremias, *Verkündigung*, 58; ET, *NT Theology*, 51, refers to Luke 3:7 D *it*, "where it is said that those who were baptized immersed themselves *enōpion autou* 'in the presence' of the Baptist. Accordingly, John the Baptist had the function of a witness, as in proselyte baptism."

25. This word of the Baptist was designed to provoke a realistic facing of the issue of judgment. The symbolic rite of baptism would be empty if there were lacking the repentance and will to reform which it was meant to signify and seal. Real flight from "the wrath about to come" consisted in repentance and the break with sin, by which one escaped liability to condemnation at the impending judgment.

26. If the one mightier than John would effect the final purification from sinfulness "by the holy Spirit and fire," it is clear that John conceived the reform God required now as a radical orientation to the good which did not, however, suppose perfect purity from sinfulness.

27. "The repentance of tax collectors and publicans is hard . . ." *t. B. Meṣiʿa* 8.26 (Zuckermandel 1875, repr. Jerusalem 1963, 390); supported by *y. B. Meṣiʿa* 11a; a *baraita* in *b. B. Qam* 94b adds herdsmen to the list. Repentance was hard for them because they could not know all whom they had cheated and to whom they accordingly owed restitution.

renunciation of all claims on God, proved supremely difficult to the professionally holy (Mark 11:29–33 pars.; Matt 11:18f. par.; 21:32).

Is there still more which the opening phase of Jesus' career can tell us of his "aims"?

As the Baptist's career evidences a prophetic self-understanding (see John 1:23; Mark 1:2 pars.; cf. Luke 3:15), so do the beginnings of the career of Jesus. Both his embarking on a ministry within the cadre of the Baptist's call to Israel and, even more, his withdrawal to Galilee on the signal of the Baptist's arrest[28] only to inaugurate a new proclamation and ministry of his own, point to an eschatological and prophetic self-understanding. Texts such as the baptism (Mark 1:9–11 par.; Luke 3:2a f.) and temptation (Mark 1:12f.; Matt 4:1–11 par.) narratives are designed to meet the questions which naturally arise from the fact of such activities: "Who is this Jesus and what is he about?" Both the baptism and the temptation narratives depict him as Spirit-filled Servant of God and obedient Messiah, leaving open the specific contours of his vocation and destiny.

But these texts, it would seem, could give us data *immediately* relevant to our question on the aims of Jesus only if, biographical in intention, they ultimately derived from his personal testimony. This condition is not a priori impossible; but since the main thrust of the texts is situated on another plane, it is not easy to vindicate a genuinely biographical [[124]] dimension.[29] We will therefore deal with the texts later, in terms of the community's interpretation of Jesus.[30]

Words of Jesus on the Baptist[31]

The work of the Baptist in the Christian view (Mark 1:3 pars.) as, no doubt, in his own self-understanding (John 1:23),[32] was to cry out in the wilderness to

28. *Anachōrein* in Matt 4:12 implies that the journey to Galilee is temporary, a withdrawal (cf. Matt 2:22) until the moment for return to Judaea and Jerusalem; see A. Schlatter, *Matthäus*, 113. Like the Baptist, Jesus is evidently conceived here as understanding the encounter with Israel to be peculiarly mediated by and concentrated in encounter with the capital city. (Unlike the Baptist, he would provoke the encounter on the spot, by symbol-charged public acts.)

29. The question has been clarified by considerations relevant to definition of the *Gattung* of the synoptic texts on Jesus' baptism. See F. Lentzen-Deis, *Die Taufe Jesu nach den Synoptikern. Literarkritische und gattungsgeschichtliche Untersuchungen*, Frankfurt: Knecht 1970. On the significance of these considerations for the history of Jesus, see esp. pp. 286–89.

30. See [[Meyer, *Aims of Jesus*,]] 240f.

31. We omit discussion of the complicated problem of the Baptist's testimony to Jesus, for, unlike the question of Jesus' stance toward the Baptist, the topic has little immediate relevance to the definition of Jesus' aims. See [[ibid.,]] however, on the question which the Baptist posed to Jesus (p. 295 n. 96).

32. That John himself invoked the Isaian text (Isa 40:3) to define his mission is a probable inference. First, the traditions on the Baptist provided by the Fourth Gospel have a special claim to independence (see C. H. Dodd, *Historical Tradition*, 248–301). This has rightly inclined numerous critics to account for Johannine variations from synoptic tradition on the Baptist by positing a historical component in both the evangelist's intention and in his

Israel to prepare the Lord's "way" (Isa 40:3; Mal 3:1). More, "John brought[33] you the way of righteousness" (Matt 21:32), i.e., the way of repentance and baptism in view of the eschaton. A logion originally isolated in the gospel tradition,[34] this succinctly stated Jesus' understanding of the Baptist's career as the divinely commissioned role of revealing God's will for his people in the last days.

For our purposes this theme is among the most significant in Jesus' teaching, for his testimony to the Baptist cannot but throw a powerful if indirect light on his own self-understanding and intentions. This testimony was not wholly public. One element of it was esoteric, i.e., reserved, as apocalyptic secret, for his disciples. We will begin with public testimony and, first of all, that addressed to critics as self-defence and counter-attack.

> To what shall I compare this generation?
> It is like children sitting in the market place
> and calling to their playmates
>> "We piped to you and you did not dance,
>> we wailed and you mourned not."
> For John came[35] neither eating nor drinking
> and they say, "He is mad."
> Then along comes one[36] who eats and drinks
> and they say, "Behold, a glutton and drunkard,
> a friend of tax-collectors and sinners."
>   (Matt 11:16–19b; cf. par. Luke 7:31–34)[37]

---

performance (see, for example, J. Schmitt, "Les écrits du Nouveau Testament et les textes de Qumrân," *RevSR*, 1955, 381–401, esp. 394–97). Second, the text of John 1:23 in particular is independent of synoptic tradition (Dodd, op. cit., 31–46; 252). Finally, the likelihood of the notion that the tie between the Baptist and the Isaian text was a stroke of finely calibrated Christian inventiveness designed to give John a fully eschatological but less than messianic role collapses in the face of the Essene use of the text of Isaiah (1QS 8:12–14; 9:19f.).

33. 'To come with' = 'To bring' ($b\bar{o}'b^e$). See the Lukan parallel (7:30). See also A. H. McNeile, *The Gospel According to St Matthew*, London: Macmillan 1915, 308.

34. See J. Jeremias, *Gleichnisse*, 78f.; ET, *Parables*, 80f.

35. 'To come': to appear, be there, be here. Bultmann's view (*Synoptische Tradition*, 167; ET, *Synoptic Tradition*, 155f. [[reprinted in this volume, pp. 96–97]]) to the effect that *ēlthon* of itself implies viewing the life of the one named as subject of the verb *as a totality in the past* was influential but mistaken. On the senses ('to intend', 'to will', 'to have as one's task', etc.) of *ēlthon* as rendering $b\bar{o}'$ l^e or $'\bar{a}t\bar{a}'$ le with the infinitive, see J. Jeremias, "Die älteste Schicht der Menschensohn-Logien," *ZNW* 58, 1967, 159–72, pp. 166f.

36. 'Then along comes'; this translates an underlying Aramaic perfect ($'\bar{a}t\bar{a}'$). See C. Colpe, "ó uíos tou anthropou," *TWNT* 8.434; *TDNT* 8.432. 'One': ó uíos tou anthropou renders *bar* $'\check{e}n\bar{a}\check{s}\bar{a}'$, which doubtless carried here an original indefinite sense. Cf. J. Jeremias, "Die älteste Schicht . . . ," 165; earlier, T. W. Manson, *The Teaching of Jesus*, Cambridge: Cambridge University Press 1931, ²1935, 216–18.

37. The historicity of the text is established by a variety of indices: discontinuity (John and Jesus are placed on a par; the charge, especially "glutton and drunkard" [cf. Deut 21:18–21 on execution of the rebellious son] was hardly devised by the post-Easter Christian tradition); resistive form (parable; the originality of the context is peculiarly attested by the

The image is one of pouting children who, unwilling to join in with their playmates, sit on the sidelines grumbling that the others do not follow their whims. So "this generation" piped and John did not dance; it wailed and Jesus did not mourn. Both violated the sanctity of custom: to feast and to fast in accord with specified tradition. But John's whole life-style was a break with this world of customary practices, and so was that of Jesus (Mark 2:19 pars.).[38] John and Jesus alike were signs of the eschatological break in the times. Though the signs were different—it is interesting that Jesus should indicate how fully conscious he was of the sharp difference between John's life-style and his own—they were signs pointing to one and the same thing: the coming of the consummation of history. The two were allied in common repudiation by a generation of sour critics satisfied to be installed in the assurances of holy routine.

[[125]] Jesus' royal entry into Jerusalem for the pasch at which he would die, his cleansing of the temple, and the question about his authority to do these things, originally formed a single literary unit.[39] Its third and last element consisted in speech and counter-speech: his critics' demand for credentials ("By what authority are you doing these things, or who gave you this authority to do them?") and Jesus' response, posing a dilemma which reduced them to silence:

> I will ask you a question. Answer me and I will tell you by what authority I do these things. Was the baptism of John from heaven or from men? (Mark 11:29f. pars.).

The answer finally given was "We do not know" (Mark 11:33 pars.).

Jesus' question may have been designed simply to stymie his critics. If so, it is still significant as incidentally implying that, for his part, Jesus considered John's baptism to be "from heaven." But there may be more here, namely, a veiled answer to the question posed by his critics. They asked by what authority he did these things ("these things": the royal entry into city and temple

---

refractoriness of the image, i.e., by the *difficulty* of exactly correlating the image of the children with its application to "this generation"); Aramaic substratum (indefinite sense of underlying *bar 'ĕnāšā'*; on retro-translation of the children's singsong into Aramaic and into *kinâ* rhythm, see J. Jeremias, *Verkündigung*, 36; ET, *NT Theology*, 26; *ekopsasthe* in Matt 11:17 and *eklausate* of Luke 7:32 are translation variants of *'arqēdtun*); multiple and multiform attestation of some aspects of the text (see Mark 2:16; Luke 7:27f.).

38. O. Linton, "The Parable of the Children's Game," *NTS* 22, 1976 159–79, pp. 174–77. Scriptural background on "asocial" behaviour as a prophetic sign to the nation: Jer 16:1–4, 5–7; Ezek 24:15–24. Cf. M. Hengel, *Nachfolge* . . . ,13.

39. For illuminating parallels to the sequence "royal entry–temple cleansing," see J. Jeremias, *Jesus als Weltvollender* [[Gütersloh: Bertelsmann, 1930]] 35–54. This was originally followed by the question about Jesus' authority (cf. John 2:18). Literary analysis (J. Jeremias, *Abendmahlsworte*, 83–87; ET, *Eucharistic Words*, [[New York: Scribner, 1966]] 89–93) indicates the likelihood that in early oral tradition the cleansing of the temple immediately followed the account of the royal entry into the city. (That the goal of the pilgrimage procession should have been nothing other than the temple is an inference from age-old practice. It is also explicit in the texts: Mark 11:11; Matt 21:10; Luke 19:45.)

and the cleansing of the temple). Jesus' counter-question also turned on the
authority theme, viz., that which authorized John's baptism. The element of
"veiled answer" lies in the implication: If John's baptism was "from heaven,"
so is my doing "these things." The middle term in this logic remains to be
specified. Why should the divine authority of Jesus to do "these things" follow logically from recognition of the divine authority of John's baptism? The
answer must be: Because the symbolic acts of both men converged perfectly
on one and the same goal: the eschatological restoration of Israel.

Another tantalizing testimony is that which Jesus addressed to a general
audience with the intent of defining for them, albeit cryptically, the sense of
the Baptist's mission:

> What did you go out to the wilderness to see?
> A reed being shaken by the wind?
> Then, what did you go out to see?
> A man clothed in soft raiment?
> Behold, men wearing soft raiment are in the houses of kings.
> Why, then, did you go out? To see a prophet?
> Yes, I tell you, and more than a prophet!
> This is he of whom it is written:
>> "Behold, I send my messenger before your face
>> who shall prepare your way before you."
>> (Matt 11:7–10; cf. par. Luke 7:24–27).

The main thrust here is the interpretation of the Baptist's career as a fulfilment event. God's messenger before the outbreak of judgment, John begins
the fulfilment of eschatological prophecy. But the tantalizing element in this
testimony is the mysterious identification of John as Elijah. "If [[126]] you are
willing to accept it," says Jesus, "he is Elijah who is to come" (Matt 11:14); but
that this disclosure was itself filled with hidden meaning is indicated by the
formula which immediately followed: "He who has ears to hear, let him hear"
(Matt 11:15).

Eschatological speculation formed the background of this designation of
the Baptist. The prophet called Malachi, seizing on the Deutero-Isaian motif
of "preparation for the Day" implicit in the text "In the wilderness clear the
way of Yahweh!" (Isa 40:3), specified this preparation as the task of Elijah returned to earth:

> Behold, I will send you Elijah the prophet
> before the coming of the great and terrible day of Yahweh;
> and he shall turn the hearts of fathers to their sons
> and the hearts of sons to their fathers
> lest I come and smite the land with a curse.
>> (Mal 3:23f.; EVV 4:5f.)

The preparation consisted in purifying the priesthood (Mal 3:1–3) and in
putting an end to familial wrangling and strife in the face of judgment (Mal

3:24). Ben Sira (48:10) adds that Elijah stood in readiness for the chosen time when he would not only "appease the wrath before it breaks out" but also "re-establish the tribes of Jacob" (so fulfilling the mission of the Servant of the Lord, Isa 49:6). Here, returning Elijah is the key figure of the end-time. In the Pseudepigrapha, on the other hand, the importance of Elijah has receded, and by the time of Jesus his eschatological role was variously conceived. But Elijah was thought of mainly, perhaps, as the "forerunner" of the Messiah.[40] In the gospels the hidden sense of the identification of John as Elijah is its messianic reference: If the Baptist was Elijah, how imminent must the epiph-any of the Messiah be!

Another and deeper meaning of the identification is disengaged and highlighted in an esoteric teaching (Mark 9:11–13 par. Matt 17:10–13) which typically remained charged with enigma.

> "Why [asked the inner circle of Jesus' disciples[41]] do the scribes say: 'First, Elijah must come'?" and he said to them, "Elijah does indeed come first to restore all things. And how is it written of the Son of Man that he should suffer much and be despised? But I tell you Elijah has come, and they did to him whatever they pleased, as it is written of him."
>
> (Mark 9:11–13)

The text seems to have taken shape as a variation on a basic theme in the po-lemic between orthodox Jews and Jewish Christians. The basic theme: Jesus could not have been the Messiah, for Elijah has not come. Answer: Elijah *has* come—in the person of John. The variation on this theme: Jesus could not have been the Messiah, for Elijah's mission excludes a suffering Messiah. The answer to this objection rests on two presuppositions; namely, that no proph-ecy is to be fulfilled in a way which would exclude fulfilment of another proph-ecy, and that we have to do here with two sets [[127]] of prophecies: Elijah is to come before the Messiah to reconcile (Malachi 3) and restore (Sir 48:10) Is-rael; and the Messiah is to suffer much and be "despised."[42] On these presup-positions, the answer to the objection consists in interpreting the Baptist's historic destiny as the fulfilment of Elijah's mission. This not only denies that Elijah's mission rules out a suffering Messiah; it also presents John's (= Elijah's) martyrdom as a prophetically attested paradigm for the Messiah.

In the Markan text the disciples do not so much pose their own question as cite a scribal view of messianic eschatology according to which Elijah's

40. See J. Jeremias, *"El(e)ias," TWNT* 2.930–43, esp. 933, 938–40; *TDNT* 2.928–41, esp. 931, 936–38. Both Matthew and Mark unambiguously define the Elijah-role as one of prepa-ration for the Messiah: cf. *sou* in Matt 11:10 (par.)! Cf. Mark 1:2.

41. Represented as privileged witness to mysterious revelation in Mark 5:37–43 (the raising of the daughter of Jairus); 9:2ff. (the Transfiguration and the present scene); 14:33–42 (Gethsemane); and, with Andrew, 13:3ff. (eschatological discourse).

42. 'Despised': *exoudenēthē*, probably reflecting *nibzeh* of Isa 53:3a,d. Aquila, Symma-chus, and Theodotion (but not LXX) draw on the same Greek word to render *nibzeh*, in Isa 53:3a,d. See J. Jeremias, *"Pais(Theou)"* in the New Testament," W. Zimmerli, J. Jeremias, *The Servant of God*, SBT 20, [[London: SCM / Naperville, Ill.: Allenson,]] ²1965, 90.

mission of restoration would preclude any intelligible context for a suffering Messiah. Jesus' answer first brings out the point of the objection: "Elijah does indeed come first to restore all things; [but, if so] how is it written of the Son of man that he should suffer much and be despised?" He then gives the solution: John fulfilled the Elijah role and it included his death!

Elijah, then, is (so to speak) demythologized. His return is not a literal re-incarnation but a role in the eschatological scenario, and his mission of restoration is concretely accomplished by John's preaching and baptizing—not a restoration necessarily precluding a suffering Messiah. The last aspect of Jesus' answer—the affirmation that John's death was itself comprehended in the Elijah role—underlines this, alluding to the tradition that Elijah was destined for martyrdom.[43] Indeed, it would hardly be possible to align Jesus more closely and rigorously with John than does this early Christian reflection, or to imagine a level of alignment more profound.

There can be no reasonable doubt about the decisive significance of the Baptist in the scheme of the eschaton as Jesus understood it. "The baptism of John" (Mark 11:30 pars.) was heaven-sent; "the days of John" (Matt 11:12) epitomized the inauguration of eschatological fulfilment. But "the days of John" were no more than an inauguration. The *consummation* would transform the world. This may well be the sense of Jesus' eschatological riddle:

> No one greater has arisen among men than John
> and the least in the reign of God is greater than he.
>
> (cf. Matt 11:11; Luke 7:28)

Conclusion

To recover the meaning of the Baptist's mission is to win an insight into the perspectives of Jesus, for Jesus' response to the Baptist was unequivocally positive. Epitomized as "a voice crying in the wilderness" to prepare for God's final visitation, the Baptist was first of all the bearer of an urgent warning. But this warning, and the confession, conversion, and washing to which it summoned its hearers, evoked a scheme of [[128]] eschatological hope. Accents of warning and images of judgment (the felling of the tree, the winnowing of the chaff) yielded ultimately to promise-motifs and images of hope: the apocalyptic purification in holy Spirit and fire, the gathering of the wheat into the barn. The mission of the Baptist belonged to a scenario of fulfilment. His role was to assemble by baptism the remnant of Israel destined for cleansing and acquittal and so, climactically, for restoration.

The first observable act of Jesus' own career was to enter unreservedly into this scheme of prophetic meaning, sharing not only in the response to the Baptist's call but in the call itself. The legacy of Jesus' words on the Baptist supports this inference. He clearly affirmed the divine authenticity of the Baptist's mission. More: In particulars of the Baptist's career he read divine

---

43. See J. Jeremias, "*El(e)ias*," *TWNT* 2.942; *TDNT* 2.940.

signs bearing on himself. He significantly aligned himself in the closest possible way with the trajectory of the Baptist's mission. The fact that Jesus was explicitly conscious of how sharply he differed from the Baptist in style of career gives particularly incisive definition to his alliance with the Baptist's purposes. There remains more to be said both about the distinctiveness of Jesus vis-à-vis John and about his words on John's mission. But without going further than we have already gone we are ready to offer the first formulation of a hypothesis on Jesus' own aims, i.e., on how he conceived his life's role. Like the Baptist, he understood his own role in terms of the age-old scriptural promise of the restoration of Israel; and, like the Baptist, he understood this restoration not as a divine act exclusively reserved for post-historical realization (located, that is, on the far side of a still future judgment) but as called for now and already begun! Its beginning was effected by "the baptism of John." As an ally of John, Jesus had already plunged into the prophetic and eschatological task he took to be his destiny.

P. W. BARNETT

The Jewish Sign Prophets

The Jewish Sign Prophets

[[679]] As we read those parts of Josephus'[1] works which coincide with the Apostolic Age (in round figures A.D. 30–70) we encounter a number of references to certain prophetic[2] figures. In the absence of existing descriptive titles we will refer to them as the Jewish Sign Prophets.

Reprinted, with the permission of Cambridge University Press, from *NTS* 27 (1980) 679–97.

1. Quotations, translations and citations from Josephus are taken from the Loeb Classical Library.

2. Apart from the references in Josephus there is scanty evidence for the activities of the Jewish Sign Prophets.

    a. A Theudas is mentioned in Acts 5:36 though it is a matter of debate whether he is one and the same as the Theudas who arose under Cuspius Fadus.

    b. The Egyptian prophet is referred to in:
        (i) Acts 21:38
        (ii) Eusebius, *H.E.* 2.21 (where Josephus, *Ant.* is closely followed)
        (iii) *b. Sanh.* 67a (?).

    c. It is possible that Matt 24:11–12, 24–26 refers to the prophets who arose under Felix and Festus.

The various "source blocks," taken as a whole, are silent about the activities of the Jewish Sign Prophets:

    a. Philo makes frequent reference to προφήτης [['prophet']] (and cognates) but these relate to the Biblical period and never to contemporary figures. (But cf. *De Spec. Leg.* 4.51 where ψευδοπροφήτης [['pseudoprophet']] refers to divination.)

    b. The classical Graeco-Roman writers make no reference to the Jewish Sign Prophets.

    c. Patristic authors, except as in b (ii) above, are silent.

    d. The Mishnah, to our knowledge, contains no reference.

    e. The rabbinic sources, except as in b (iii) (?) above, so far as we can see, are silent.

In c. A.D. 36 an unnamed Samaritan encouraged large numbers of his countrymen to accompany him to Mt. Gerizim promising to reveal the location of the temple vessels which Moses had hidden there (*Ant.* 18.85–87). In popular Samaritan belief the recovery of these vessels was expected to mark the beginnings of the Eschatological Age.[3] A decade or so later during the procuratorship of Cuspius Fadus (A.D. 44–48) Theudas *(Ant.* 20.97–99) persuaded the "majority of the masses to take up their possessions and follow him to the Jordan." He claimed to be a prophet and that, at his word, Jordan would divide, thus affording safe passage for his followers.

While Antonius Felix was procurator (A.D. 52–60) some unnamed persons "called upon the mob to follow them to the desert" (*Ant.* 20.167–68, *J.W.* 2.259). Many accompanied them since it was promised that "unmistakable marvels" (*Ant.*), "signs of freedom" (*J.W.*) would be displayed.

Also within Felix's period of rule there arose another prophet, an Egyptian (*Ant.* 20.168–72, *J.W.* 2.261–63; cf. Acts 21:38). He led his followers from the desert to the Mount of Olives where, he claimed, the walls of Jerusalem would collapse at his command. He proposed to overwhelm the Roman garrison and establish himself as ruler.

Shortly afterwards, while Porcius Festus was procurator (A.D. 60–62), an unnamed man persuaded people to "follow him to the wilderness" where, he promised, they would receive "salvation and rest from troubles" (*Ant.* 20.188).

At the end of the Roman siege while the temple was ablaze (August, A.D. 70), six thousand refugees fled to the remaining portico in the outer court. A prophet had informed them that they would receive the "tokens of their deliverance" and "help from God" (*J.W.* 6.285–86).

The Verdict of Scholarship

No single study focusing on the Jewish Sign Prophets has been undertaken, though it is true that they are often referred to in short sections[4] [[680]] of

---

3. The Samaritan is on the periphery of our study since it is convenient to limit our attention to Palestinian Jews. The weaver Jonathan of Cyrene (*J.W.* 7.438) who in A.D. 73 promised 'signs and apparitions' (σημεῖα καὶ φάσματα) in the 'wilderness' (ἔρημος) is not included in these studies, being outside Palestine.

4. In general terms these prophets have been discussed in two classes of literature.

a. In standard histories of the New Testament period, for example:

> Ch. Guignebert, *The Jewish World in the Time of Jesus* (E.T., S. H. Hooke) (London, 1939) 132–33.
>
> F. F. Bruce, New *Testament History* (London, 1969) 319–31, passim.
>
> E. Schürer, *The History* of the *Jewish People in the Age of Jesus Christ* (rev. and ed. by G. Vermes and F. Millar) (Edinburgh, 1973) 455–70, passim.
>
> S. Safrai and M. Stern (eds.), *The Jewish People in the First Century* (Assen, 1974) 360–72, passim.
>
> E. M. Smallwood, *The Jews under Roman Rule* (Leiden, 1976) 256–92, passim.

larger works. Wide variety of opinion exists among scholars about the self-awareness and intentions of the Sign Prophets.

S. Zeitlin[5] regarded these prophets as "sincere and pious people" who were "opposed to acts of terror" and who "preached love." According to Zeitlin they "believed that God would re-establish Israel under his anointed *Mashiah* [['Messiah']]" and that these prophets "introduced the idea of a supernatural *Mashiah.*"

S. Mowinckel,[6] however, asserts that Theudas, the Egyptian and the unnamed prophet in the time of Festus were hailed by their contemporaries as Messiahs. Mowinckel classified them, without distinction, along with Judas the Galilean, Menahem and bar Cochba as Messianic.

J. Jeremias[7] specifically affirms that these prophets were Mosaic Messiahs.

> All these messiahs follow the example of Moses by calling for an exodus into the wilderness and promising signs and wonders and also deliverance. The series is an impressive testimony to the strength with which the idea that the Messiah would be a second Moses was anchored in popular expectation.

Certainly there is considerable support[8] for the view which associates these prophets with the Exodus-Conquest. Nevertheless there is no scholarly consensus about the role or the intentions of the Sign Prophets.

---

b. In articles or monographs devoted to various themes, for example:

J. Jeremias, "Μωυσῆς," *TDNT* 4.848–73.
F. Young, "Jesus the Prophet," *JBL* 68 (1949) 285–99.
S. Mowinckel, *He That Cometh* (E.T., G. W. Anderson) (Oxford, 1956) 284–85.
W. R. Farmer, *Maccabees, Zealots and Josephus* (New York, 1956) 116–17.
H. M. Teeple, *The Mosaic Eschatological Prophet* (Philadelphia, 1957) 63–66.
R. W. Funk, "The Wilderness," *JBL* 78 (1959) 205–14.
R. Meyer, "προφήτης," *TDNT* 6.812–28.
M. Hengel, *Die Zeloten* (Leiden, 1961) 235–51.
U. Mauser, *Christ in the Wilderness* (London, 1963) 56–58.
C. H. Dodd, *Historical Tradition in the Fourth Gospel* (Cambridge, 1963) 213–21.
J. L. Martyn, *History and Theology in the Fourth Gospel* (New York, 1968) 85 n. 13.
W. A. Meeks, *The Prophet-King* (Leiden, 1967) 163–64.
S. G. F. Brandon, *Jesus and the Zealots* (Manchester, 1967) 65–145, passim.
F. Hahn, *The Titles of Jesus in Christology* (E.T., H. Knight and G. Ogg) (London, 1969) 358–59.
W. Nicol, *The Sēmeia in the Fourth Gospel* (Leiden, 1972) 82–83.
S. Zeitlin, "The Origin of the Idea of the Messiah," *Studies in the Early History of Judaism* (New York, 1973) 2.403–5.
G. Vermes, *Jesus the Jew* (London, 1973) 98–99.
T. Crone, *Early Christian Prophecy: A Study of Its Origin and Significance* (Baltimore, 1973) 131–39.

5. Op. cit., 403–4.
6. Op. cit., 284–85. For a *contra* view see F. Hahn, op. cit., 358.
7. Op. cit., 862. See also S. G. F. Brandon, op. cit., 100.
8. See F. Hahn, op. cit., 359. W. A. Meeks, op. cit., 163. J. L. Martyn, op. cit., 85 n. 134.

Context and Comment

Theudas: During the Procuratorship of Cuspius Fadus (A.D. 44–48)

Context. The death of Herod Agrippa I (A.D. 44) represented a watershed in First Century Judaean History. Never again was a Jewish King to reign, even as the Emperor's client, over the people of Judaea. Agrippa I had striven to make himself acceptable to the people,[9] and he appears to have achieved a considerable measure of popularity. The memory of Gaius' reign must have been fresh in Jewish minds throughout the whole eastern Mediterranean. Gaius had been callously indifferent[10] to the plight of Alexandrian Jews during the pogrom of A.D. 38 and had actually ordered[11] that a statue of himself be placed within the Temple in Jerusalem. One major reason the desecration was not executed is that Agrippa[12] interceded with his old friend Gaius. After the death of the anti-Semite Gaius, Agrippa petitioned[13] Claudius to issue an edict to the Alexandrians and Syrians granting the Jews equal citizenship rights. The general edict to the "rest of the world"[14] concerning the Jews was in all probability also issued at the behest of Agrippa.

Clearly the Jews had lost in Agrippa I not only a pious and popular king, but also a Herodian Dynast of great influence with successive Julio-Claudians [[681]] in Rome. On the death of Agrippa I Claudius allowed himself to be advised against appointing the (sixteen year old) younger Agrippa, then in Rome, in succession to the large kingdom of his father. Accordingly the decision was taken to re-annex Judaea and with it Galilee, now for the first time under Roman rule. Claudius therefore despatched Cuspius Fadus[15] in A.D. 44 as Procurator of "Judaea and of the whole kingdom."

Thus the events of A.D. 44 represented a double disappointment to the people of Judaea. They were deprived of a Jewish king and they were subjected

9. *Ant.* 19.328–330, Acts 12:3.

10. Philo, *Legatio ad Gaium*, 349–67.

11. The sources of this incident (Philo, *Legatio ad Gaium*, 184–333; Josephus, *Ant.* 18.261–301, *J.W.* 2.185–201) are in conflict as to the sequence. Various authors have attempted to resolve the matter. See E. M. Smallwood, "The Chronology of Gaius' Attempt to Desecrate the Temple," *Latomus* 16 (1957) 3–17. V. Tcherikover and A. Fuks, *Corpus Papyrorum Judaicarum* (Cambridge, Mass., 1957) 69 affirm that: "had this order been carried out, the entire Jewish population of the Empire would have revolted."

12. Philo, op. cit., 276–333, Josephus, *Ant.* 18.289–301.

13. *Ant.* 19.279–85. The nature of the *Isēs Politeias (Ant.* 19.281) is much debated in view of the *Letter of Claudius to the Alexandrians*, ed. H. I. Bell (London Papyrus, 1913), lines 75ff. where the status of Jews appears to be inferior to that of the Alexandrians. For a discussion of this complex question see:

E. M. Smallwood, op. cit., 6–14.

L. H. Feldman, Josephus, *Jewish Antiquities* (Cambridge, Mass., 1963), books 18–20 (LCL) p. 346 n. (b) 344 n. (d) and pp. 583–85 (Appendix Q "Select literature on the Citizenship of the Alexandrian Jews and on Claudius' 'edict'").

14. *Ant.* 19.286–91.

15. *Ant.* 19.363.

again to direct Roman rule (mediated by the High Priest-in-Council). It meant a severe blow to Jewish nationalism, for the appointment of Cuspius Fadus also inevitably entailed all the outward evidences of Roman subjection—the visible presence of the cohorts, the use of Roman coinage and the levy of the tribute. Just as disturbances occurred at the "changeover" situation after the death of Herod (4 B.C.) and the exile of Archelaus (A.D. 6) so too the return of Roman Rule in A.D. 44 witnessed a significant incident—the rise of Theudas, the prophet.

The situation in Judaea to which Cuspius Fadus came called for sympathetic diplomacy such as that displayed by Vitellius[16] after the removal of Pontius Pilate. Cuspius Fadus, however, appears to have arrived bent on keeping order in Judaea by means of discipline and coercion,[17] so that Josephus wrote ominously, "these . . . are the events which befell the Jews during the time that Cuspius Fadus was procurator."[18]

Comment (Ant. 20.97–99). Josephus' description of Theudas and other Sign Prophets as "charlatans" (γόητες [['sorcerer, juggler']]—*Ant.* 20.97; 20.167, *J.W.* 2.261, *Ant.* 20.188) must be read against the background of the historian's own description of the Exodus and the γοητεία and μαγεία [['magic']] of the Egyptian Court magicians.[19] Likewise the self-designation of Theudas and the Egyptian[20] as "prophet" and the reference to the unnamed prophet[21] of A.D. 70 as 'false prophet' (ψευδοπροφήτης) must be understood in relationship with Josephus' presentation of Moses[22] (? and Joshua)[23] as the true prophet(s) of the Exodus. Certainly, Theudas' claim that "at his command the (Jordan) river would be parted and would provide them an easy passage" is clearly in reference to Moses' division of the Red Sea and/or Joshua's division of Jordan.

Unnamed Goëtes and The Egyptian: During the Procuratorship of Antonius Felix (A.D. 52–60)

Context. The appointment of a new procurator in A.D. 52[24] was necessitated by the dismissal of Ventidius Cumanus who was found guilty of favouring the Samaritans in a serious dispute between them and the Galileans. In these [[682]] tense and emotion-laden circumstances Claudius appointed one of his favourite freedmen, Antonius Felix, brother of Pallas (Claudius' *a rationibus* [['financial secretary']]). Josephus indicates that an ex–High Priest, Jonathan (incumbent in A.D. 37), who was in Rome for the Cumanus affair, sought the

16. *Ant.* 18.88–90, 121, 123 cf. Tacitus, *Annals* 6.32.
17. *Ant.* 20.2–4, 13.
18. *Ant.* 20.99.
19. *Ant.* 2.286 cf. 2.302, 332, 336.
20. *J.W.* 2.261.
21. *J.W.* 6.285–87.
22. *Ant.* 2.327 cf. *Ag. Ap.* 2.145, 161.
23. *Ant.* 4.165.
24. For discussion whether the year of appointment was A.D. 52 or 53 and whether Roman Palestine was divided or not see E. Schürer, op. cit., 460 n. 17 and 459 n. 15, respectively.

appointment of Felix.[25] Thus Felix was able to perpetrate his excesses shielded by Pallas[26] in Rome and supported by Jonathan[27] in Jerusalem. It is significant that Jonathan was the first aristocrat to fall to the newly formed terrorist organization, the *sicarii*.[28]

In public affairs it is evident that Felix was both brutal[29] and corrupt.[30] Under him the High Priest Ananias was allowed to plunder the tithes of the poor priests,[31] a practice which subsequently drove many priests into the arms of the more radical elements. Bearing in mind Felix's servile origins Tacitus[32] wrote of Felix that he practised "every kind of cruelty and lust" and that he wielded royal power with the instincts of a slave.

Felix's private affairs must also have shocked the sensibilities of the Jewish population. Each of Felix's three wives belonged to Royal families. The third was Drusilla, daughter of Agrippa I and sister of Agrippa II. To marry Felix it was necessary for Drusilla to divorce her first husband. Drusilla's marriage to the hated pagan procurator, in defiance of the Law, must have scandalized the Jewish people.

Although Felix was successful in ridding Judaea of the bands of robber chieftains like Eleazar, son of Deinaeus,[33] his excesses provoked the rise of the political terrorist organization, the *sicarii*. The *sicarii* were active in striking down anyone who collaborated with the Romans which inevitably meant certain of the Jewish aristocracy.[34]

Josephus claims that the political fanatics were followed by religious fanatics "with cleaner hands but wickeder intentions."[35] We know neither the number nor the names of these Sign Prophets, except that one is referred to as "the Egyptian,"[36] for whom the apostle Paul was mistaken.[37]

The extremes of political and prophetic activism in the days of Felix are a reflection of the bitterness of the Jewish people towards him. Schürer wrote:

> Felix's term of office manifestly constitutes the turning point in the drama which started in A.D. 44 and reached its bloody climax in A.D. 70. Whereas the period of the first two procurators was comparatively peaceful, and

25. *Ant.* 20.162.

26. Tacitus, *Ann.* 12.54 comments that Felix "believed that he could commit all kinds of enormity with impunity."

27. For the influence wielded by Jonathan see E. M. Smallwood, "High Priests and Politics in Roman Palestine," *JTS* 13 (1962) 23–25.

28. F. F. Bruce, *New Testament History* (London, 1969) 327 rightly rejects the version that Felix had Jonathan removed (*Ant.* 20.162–64) in favour of the view that the plan originated from the *sicarii* (*J.W.* 2.256).

29. *J.W.* 2.270.

30. Acts 24:26.

31. *Ant.* 20.206.

32. *Hist.* 5.9.

33. *J.W.* 2.252 cf. 2.235.

34. *J.W.* 2.255–57.

35. *J.W.* 2.258.

36. *J.W.* 2.261, *Ant.* 20.169.

37. Acts 21:38.

under Cumanus more serious uprisings occurred only sporadically, set off by individual malcontents, under Felix, rebellion became permanent.[38]

Comment

The Unnamed Goētes (J.W. 2.258–59; Ant. 2.167–68).   In leading the multitude to 'the desert' (τὴν ἐρημίαν) these unnamed *goētes* also select a significant locale from the Exodus–Conquest. It was their belief that God would display in the desert 'signs of freedom' (σημεῖα ελευθερίας), [[683]] a phrase which Josephus employs in his Exodus narrative (τῶν . . . τὴν ἐλευθερίαν αὐτοῖς σημείων [['all those . . . tokens of their liberation']][39] of the plagues which foreshadowed the coming "liberation" of God's people.

Yet again the Sign Prophets are identified with the Egyptian Court magicians who in the Exodus account of Josephus are contrasted with God's true prophet Moses.[40] Thus these Sign Prophets seek to display τέρατα καὶ σημεῖα[41] [['marvels and signs']] which will 'accord with God's plan' (κατὰ τὴν τοῦ θεοῦ πρόνοιαν γινόμενα), a phrase which Josephus specifically applied to the signs wrought by Moses in contrast to those attempted by the court magicians[42] which are attributed to 'magic' (μαγεία) and 'witchcraft' (γοητεία).

What, specifically, the Sign Prophets proposed to do is not known. Were they expecting manna and/or quails to drop from the heavens? Would a "Moses" figure strike a rock for the water to gush forth? Perhaps the Jordan would turn to blood? No certain answer is possible; but σημεῖα in the manner of Moses or Joshua are quite likely. It should not pass unnoticed that these Sign Prophets were preceded by a Prophet who sought to divide Jordan in the manner of Joshua (i.e., Theudas) and that they were followed immediately by a Prophet (i.e., the Egyptian) who sought to make the city walls collapse, also in the manner of Joshua.

The Egyptian (J.W. 2.261, Ant. 20.169, Acts 21:38).   As with Theudas and the unnamed prophets previously studied there is the deliberate almost stylized manner in which the Egyptian set himself up as a prophetic figure. He claimed to be a (? the) prophet; he ordered his hearers to accompany him to 'the desert' (τῆς ἐρημίας) whence they would make their way back to Jerusalem by a "circuitous route."[43]

Like his predecessors who sought to perform "signs" the Egyptian Sign Prophet claimed that 'at his command' (ὡς κελεύσαντος αὐτοῦ) the walls of Jerusalem would collapse.

The similarities with Joshua are unmistakable; but why should the walls of Jerusalem, as opposed to Jericho, collapse?

A clue is perhaps provided in 4QTest, where Joshua's original curse on the one who rebuilds Jericho (Josh 6:26) is applied not to Jericho but Jerusa-

38. Op. cit., 460.
39. *Ant.* 2.327.
40. *Ant.* 2.286 cf. 2.327.
41. *Ant.* 20.168.
42. *Ant.* 2.286.
43. Does περιάγειν mean 'circuitous route' around Jerusalem, as with Joshua's forces?

lem. In this Qumran extract the destruction of Jerusalem is an act of judgement on an apostate people. Was the Egyptian seeking to enact a "sign" of judgement against what he regarded as a pagan-dominated and apostate city in the manner of Joshua's overthrow of Jericho?

Unlike the other Sign Prophets the Egyptian prophet portrayed himself as the fulfilment of the "sign." Thus, after overpowering the Roman garrison, he would 'set himself up as tyrant of the people' (τοῦ δήμου τυραννεῖν). Thus the Egyptian is both a "prophet" and also a "king" and as such unique among the Sign Prophets. [[684]]

Unnamed Goēs: During the Procuratorship of Porcius Festus[44] *(A.D. 60–62)*

Context. Although Festus was "a man of honest intentions"[45] affairs in Judaea continued to deteriorate. Festus' death after so short a period in office suggests that he may have experienced ill-health for some or all of his two year appointment.

It is probable that the inadequacies of the Emperor Nero were now gravely affecting the conduct of the provinces. For although he began his principate well enough, by A.D. 60 the procurators were virtually responsible to no-one except themselves.[46] B. H. Warmington comments that

> In the last analysis . . . Nero's personal responsibility seems to have ended with the choice of governors for the provinces in which there were military forces, and the approval of measures to back them up if trouble occurred.[47]

Although Nero was not notably antipathetic towards the Jews he struck a severe blow against them by annulling their *isopoliteia* [['equal civic rights']][48] in Caesarea. In A.D. 59 members of both the Graeco-Syrian and the Jewish communities appealed to the emperor to resolve a long-standing dispute.[49]

Whilst the matter was as yet unheard Festus had replaced Felix and a Jewish delegation had arrived in Rome to accuse Felix before Nero. The Emperor's advisers so influenced him that he delivered a double blow to the Jews. Thus Pallas secured the acquittal of Felix and Beryllus persuaded Nero to revoke the Jews' *isopoliteia* in Caesarea. The news of the Emperor's decisions must have profoundly embittered and discouraged the Jews regarding the Roman attitudes towards them.

Since A.D. 50 an unworkable system of administration had been allowed to occur in Judaea. From that time the appointment of the High Priest was

44. The date for the arrival of Festus is a matter of debate. See E. Schürer, op. cit., 465 n. 42.

45. E. Schürer, op. cit., 467.

46. B. H. Warmington, *Nero: Reality and Legend* (London, 1969) 59–62, points out that although there are records of numerous prosecutions of governors between A.D. 54 and 61, there is no record of prosecutions thereafter.

47. Op. cit., 72.

48. *Ant.* 20.183–84 cf. *J.W.* 2.270.

49. *J.W.* 2.270.

the prerogative, not of the procurator, but of Agrippa II, king of Chalcis. Thus, from that date the Sanhedrin was responsible to two masters instead of one—procurator and client king. After A.D. 59 when Ananias, son of Nebedaios was dismissed there was a rapid turn-over of High Priests, probably to secure competing financial inducement from would-be incumbents. Inevitably, political instability must have accompanied this rapid turn-over of high priests.

In particular, the removal of Ananias and the appointment of Ishmael, son of Phabi in A.D. 59 led to

> mutual enmity and clan warfare between the high priests, on the one hand, and the priests and leaders of the populace in Jerusalem on the other. Each of the factions formed and collected for itself a band of the most reckless revolutionaries and acted as their leader . . . it was as if there was no one in charge of the city.[50]

Stability in Judaean–Roman relationships depended on the effectiveness [[685]] of emperor, procurator and high priest. In previous times one or two of these key figures had been defective but Judaea continued on account of the strength of the remaining figure. Between A.D. 60–62 Porcius Festus alone kept any measure of stability. With his passing the days would soon come when the Romans were forced to invade Judaea only to witness a process of destruction from within Judaea by the recklessly warring factions.

Comment (Ant. 20.188). Once again 'the wilderness' (τῆς ἐρημίας) is the special locale to which this *goēs* led his followers. Although there is no reference to 'signs' (σημεῖα) there can be no doubt that these were promised. Specifically the prophet 'promised' (ἐπαγγελλομένου) 'salvation' (σωτηρίαν) and 'rest from troubles' (παῦλαν κακῶν).

Both these concepts are employed by Josephus in his account of God's great act of redemption in the Exodus. We read[51] that "Aaron with his company . . . chanted hymns to God as the author and dispenser of their salvation (σωτηρίας) and their liberty (ἐλευθερίας)." Thus σωτηρία and ἐλευθερία are virtually synonymous;[52] both are promised,[53] apparently interchangeably, by the Sign Prophets.

'Trouble' (κακόν) was the opposite of 'salvation' (σωτηρία). Thus God would 'deliver' (σώσειν) his people and bring disaster (κακοῖς) on the Egyptians.[54] It is concluded that παῦλαν κακῶν [['rest from troubles']] is to be equated with σωτηρία and ἐλευθερία. Josephus does not reveal what the Sign Prophet meant to convey by the promise of 'salvation' (= 'rest from troubles'). It is difficult to escape the conclusion that the people were promised a re-run of the Exodus–Conquest event.

50. *Ant.* 20.179–81.
51. *Ant.* 3.64.
52. Cf. *Ant.* 2.327, 345; 4.42.
53. *J.W.* 2.259; *Ant.* 20.188; *J.W.* 6.286.
54. *Ant.* 2.276 cf. *Ant.* 3.219.

Unnamed pseudoprophētēs: *While the Temple Was Alight (10th Ab* A.D. *70)*

Context.   During the Passover in A.D. 70 John of Gischala and his supporters, by means of a subterfuge, ousted Eleazar, son of Simon, and the Zealots from the temple.[55] Although individual zealots are subsequently referred to[56] the Zealot *faction* disappeared leaving two factions—those led by John of Gischala and Simon bar Gioras.[57]

However, by the 8th Ab (July–August) Titus gained access to the Temple area by firing the gates of the Temple.[58] Although Titus persuaded his generals to spare the Temple on 9th Ab a soldier disobediently threw a torch into one of the chambers.[59] The soldiers ignored the commands to extinguish the blaze and actually set fire to the inner Temple as well. With the Temple burning fiercely other edifices were also fired, including porticoes and treasury chambers. Many women and children were sheltering in [[686]] the one remaining portico of the outer court. These, numbering six thousand, lost their lives when the soldiers put this area to the torch.

Comment (J.W. 6.284–86).   In the days leading up to and during the war a number of 'portents' (τέρατα) were reported[60]—a sword-shaped comet which hung over the city, weird lights in the temple, and such like. The 'inexperienced'[61] (ἀπείροι = ἰδιῶται, 'uninitiated'),[62] among whom apparently were "numerous (Sign) Prophets,"[63] interpreted these portents as pointing to 'salvation'[64] (σωτηρία). Josephus, supported by the "sacred scribes" declared that the portents were in fact omens of doom.[65]

There was also an oracle, apparently based on Num 24:17, which affirmed "at that time one from their country would become ruler of the world."[66] Josephus, the true prophet,[67] pointed to Vespasian[68] as the fulfilment of the oracle whereas the "wise men" (i.e., "the sacred scribes") argued that the ruler must be a Jew.

It is probable that the so-called "false prophet(s)" in fact regarded the appearance of the world-ruler in the oracle as the fulfilment of the 'salvation'[69] (σωτηρία) which they promised. They may have regarded the portents as

55. *J.W.* 5.99–105.
56. *J.W.* 5.358; 6.92, 148.
57. *J.W.* 5.105; Tacitus, *Hist.* 5.12.
58. *J.W.* 6.220–35.
59. *J.W.* 6.254–66. On the question of Roman intention to burn the temple, see J. Neusner, *From Politics to Piety* (Ingleside Cliffs, 1973) 149–50.
60. *J.W.* 6.285,Tacitus, *Hist.* 5.13.
61. *J.W.* 6.291.
62. *J.W.* 6.295.
63. *J.W.* 6.286.
64. Cf. *J.W.* 6.310.
65. *J.W.* 6.291.
66. *J.W.* 6.313.
67. *J.W.* 3.350–54, 3.401; Suetonius, *Vesp.* 5.6.
68. *J.W.* 6.313.
69. *J.W.* 6.285 cf. 6.310.

"messianic woes" which would, they believed, surely foreshadow the appearance of the world-ruler.

Once again Exodus–Conquest imagery is employed by the Sign-Prophet. He promised the 'signs of salvation' (τὰ σημεῖα τῆς σωτηρίας), a phrase clearly interchangeable with the 'Signs of freedom' (σημεῖα ἐλευθερίας) employed by the Sign Prophets[70] in the days of Felix (but equally unclear as to its precise meaning).

The Intentions of the Jewish Sign Prophets

Certain possibilities can be excluded.

a. They were neither Zealots nor *Sicarii*.

It is now widely held[71] that the Zealots emerged as a party only after the war with Rome had begun. Clearly the Sign Prophets could not have been partizans of the Zealots. In any case, Josephus[72] specifically differentiates them from those whose methods were marked by violence and bloodshed, in particular the *sicarii*.

b. They were not "Christs."

The almost complete lack of reference to χριστός[73] in Josephus is interpreted as due to his unwillingness to associate any Jewish pretender with his patron Vespasian. Nevertheless there are a number of persons who are called or referred to as 'kings'[74] (βασιλεῖς) and it is probable that they were, in fact, "messianic" figures. Thus Josephus possessed a word which he could have applied to the Sign Prophets. Josephus' failure to refer to [[687]] them as βασιλεῖς is surely evidence that the Sign Prophets did not claim to be "Messiahs."

The Egyptian Prophet, however, is an interesting exception. He alone is a self-styled prophet-king.

c. They were not Pious Charismatics.

Should such Pious Ones as Onias the Righteous (First Century B.C.) and Hanina ben Dosa[75] (late First Century A.D.?) be regarded as possessing the same intentions as the Sign Prophets? Miracles are credited to both men. Thus it rained when Onias prayed (*Ant.* 14.22–24—but cf. *m. Ta'an.* 3:8 where he is referred to as "Honi the Circle Drawer" and described in a somewhat

---

70. *J.W.* 2.259.

71. See, e.g., M. Smith, "Zealots and Sicari. Their Origins and Relation," *HTR* 64 (1971) 1–19.

72. *J.W.* 2.258.

73. See *Ant.* 18.63; 20.200 both referring to Jesus; though the former reference is questioned by many.

74. Unnamed βασιλεῖς [['kings']] 4 B.C.ᵀ(*Ant.* 17.285), Judas Son of Ezekias (*Ant.* 17.271), Simon (*Ant.* 17.273), Athronges (*Ant.* 17.278), Menahem (*J.W.* 2.434), Simon bar Gioras (*J.W.* 4.510).

75. On whom see G. Vermes, "'Hanina ben Dosa,' I," *JJS* 23 (1972) 28–50, "'Haninsa ben Dosa,' II," *JJS* 24 (1973) 51–64.

derogatory manner). Whilst Onias resembles the Prophet Elijah in that God answered his prayer, the likeness ends at that point. Onias does not bring a prophetic message as from God to recall the people to the covenant, nor does he perform any eschatological sign. Hanina ben Dosa is credited with healings and miracles, yet they are related to everyday problems and domestic needs (sickness, snake bite, missing livestock, building and furniture repairs, oil shortage for Sabbath lamp, etc.); they are hagiographic in style, not unlike the miracles of the boy Jesus in the Apocryphal Gospels. The miracles of Hanina are in the nature of "miraculous" answered prayer. Hanina, in fact, attempted no "sign" of an eschatological nature and actually denied that he was a prophet (*b. Yeb.* 121b).

It is difficult to see any similarity of intention between the Pious Charismatics and the Sign Prophets.

What then were the intentions of the Sign Prophets? What were they hoping to accomplish?

It is evident that the Sign Prophets anticipated some great act of eschatological redemption. Thus the *goētes* in the days of Felix promised to show the multitudes 'Signs of *Freedom*' (ἐλευθερία). Similarly the *goēs* in the days of Festus promised '*Salvation*' (σωτηρία). The *pseudoprophētēs* of A.D. 70 spoke of 'Signs of *Salvation*' (σωτηρία). The Sign Prophets' expectation, therefore, was 'freedom' (ἐλευθερία) = 'salvation' (σωτηρία).

As to the questions of the nature or form of their "freedom" = "salvation," it has to be admitted that sheer lack of evidence precludes certainty. It is suggested that the World Ruler of the troublesome oracle may have been envisaged as the instrument of the "salvation" about which the prophet(s) of A.D. 70 spoke. It is likely, too, that the Egyptian Prophet saw the fulfilment of his activities in his own person as he assumed the rule of Jerusalem. The precise expectations of the other Sign Prophets remain hidden from view. However, it is likely that they looked for "liberation" from their current political bondage and a re-acquisition of the land.

What then was the point of the σημεῖα attempted by these prophets? The suggestions are discounted that the Sign Prophets were "charlatans," [[688]] hoaxers or political activists in disguise. There can be little doubt that the Sign Prophets were both convinced and convincing in their prophetic claim. Frequently they paid for their convictions with their own lives.

God's gift of a σημωῖον was the pledge of "something" greater which He would bring to pass. With reference to the plagues which preceded the Exodus, Josephus[76] wrote of 'those miracles wrought by God in token of their liberation' (τῶν ἐκ θεοῦ πρὸς τὴν ἐλευθερίαν αὐτοῖς σημείων). Likewise Isaiah promised King Hezekiah that God would heal him of a serious illness whereupon a σημεῖον was given to the king to signify that the healing miracle would soon take place.[77]

76. *Ant.* 2.327.
77. *Ant.* 10.28, cf. 2 Kgs 20:8.

However, it seems unlikely that the Sign Prophets intended their σημεῖα merely as pledges of a vague fulfilment in the remote future. The Exodus "signs" were close in time to their fulfilment. Once the "sign" is effected then the fulfilment will inexorably follow, and soon afterwards. It is suggested that these Prophets believed that if only a "sign" of the Exodus–Conquest could be performed, then the wheels of God would be set in motion for a re-run of His Great Saving Act. Thus the Sign Prophets appear to have regarded their "Signs" as "levers" by which to activate, even force, the hand of God to speedily bring his "Salvation." The Romans, certainly, viewed the gathering of otherwise harmless prophets in "the wilderness," etc., as a very serious matter and reacted with speed and ferocity.

It will perhaps be objected that the notion of "forcing" the salvation of God is an impossibility given the determinism of Post-Restoration Judaism as reflected in the Pseudepigraphical literature.[78] The *Assumption of Moses*, however, conveys the idea that the Kingdom of God is capable of being "forced" or "hastened."[79] If the godly Taxo and his seven sons will cleave to the law and then expose themselves to martyrdom then—

> Our blood shall be avenged before the Lord
> And then His kingdom shall appear throughout His creation.[80]

Whilst there is no reference here to "signs" as instruments in "forcing" or "hastening" God's Kingdom, it is clear that the Kingdom is capable of being "forced" into existence, in this case by the martyrdom of godly men. Such a clear doctrine of "forcing" the Kingdom of God, so close to the time of the Jewish Sign Prophets, makes it distinctly possible that they too held such a belief.

It is suggested that the Sign Prophets were possessed of a related twofold intention. In seeking to perform "signs" they sought both to herald God's "salvation" and also to "force" it into existence.

Thus Theudas and those who came after him cannot be classified as Zealots or *Sicarii*. Nor are they able to be regarded as "Messiahs"—except perhaps the Egyptian. Nor do they easily fit into the mould of the Pious charismatics. They are, it is argued, rightly referred to as *Sign* Prophets [[689]] whose style of operation is modelled upon the great figures of Israel's Exodus–Conquest, Moses and Joshua.[81]

---

78. E.g., *1 En.* 9:11, *4 Ezra* 4:36–37.

79. Thus J. Licht, "Taxo, or The Apocalyptic Doctrine of Vengeance," *JJS* 12 (1962) 97.

80. *As. Mos.* 9:7. Cf. Luke 19:11.

81. Why should Josephus depict these prophets, who by his descriptions he clearly abhors (γόητες [['sorcerers']], ψευδοπροφῆτου [['pseudoprophets']], etc.), in terms of the typology of Exodus–Conquest which he so evidently reveres? In favour of Josephus' credibility in this matter, it is noted that there were current expectations of a New Mosaic Age and also the coming of the Prophet like Moses (see P. W. Barnett, "The Jewish Eschatological Prophets A.D. 40–70 in their Theological and Political Setting," Unpublished Dissertation, University

The Origins of the Jewish Sign Prophets

A Pattern

It will be obvious by now that a common pattern exists in this sequence of Prophetic figures in Judaea A.D. 40–70. Each clearly was a *prophet*. A "*Sign*" was attempted by each man. A significant *locale* was involved on each occasion and a *crowd* of people was present.

It is striking that Jesus, too, belongs to this sequence. In one notable incident He too was hailed as a *prophet* who performed an Exodus–Conquest "*Sign*" (the loaves) in a significant *locale* (the wilderness) and in the presence of a *crowd* (John 6:1–15).

If enquiry is made into the possibility of a similar pattern in persons earlier than Jesus in Jewish history, the interesting result is that none can be found![82] Investigation into attempted miracle-signs and crowds attending prophetic figures leads to the conclusion that Jesus was, in the context of immediate Jewish history, the first in the sequence. (John the Baptist did no sign.)

It is possible to tabulate the sequence and its pattern as follows:

Prefect/ Procurator	Prophet	Sign	Location	Crowd
Pilate	John the Baptist	John did no sign (John 10:41)	Jordan	"Jerusalem, all Judaea and the region around Jordan"
Pilate	Jesus	e.g., Feeding 5,000 men	Wilderness	"5,000 men"
Pilate	Samaritan	Reveal hidden temple vessels	Mt. Gerizim	"a great crowd"
Fadus	Theudas	Divide Jordan	Jordan	"a great crowd"
Felix	Unnamed prophets	Signs of Freedom	Wilderness	"a great crowd"
Felix	Egyptian	Walls of Jerusalem collapse	Wilderness to the Mt. of Olives	"4,000 men"
Festus	Unnamed prophet	? of salvation	Wilderness	not specified
A.D. 70	Unnamed prophet(s)	Signs of salvation	Temple	"6,000 people"

[[690]] Why is this sequence of *prophets* who fulfil the *Sign, place, crowd* pattern and which began with Jesus, not noticed by historians? The answer

of London (1977) 47–74. In Josephus' narratives, the consistent failure of these prophets to execute their promised "Signs" is, by implication, proof positive of their γοητεία [['sorcery']].

82. This, broadly, is the position of W. Nicol, *The Semeia in the Fourth Gospel* (Leiden, 1972). In summing up the debate on miracles precedent to or contemporary with Jesus, Nicol states that: "Jesus with his miraculous powers would have been a unique appearance in the Palestine of His time" (p. 56 n. 2).

may be that the sources, Josephus and the Gospels–Acts, are so dissimilar in their interests and emphases that scholars have not sought any historical continuity between them. Josephus is primarily a political propagandist who in any case makes but brief reference to these Prophets. The New Testament is primarily theological, focusing our interest on Jesus. The sequence of prophets for whom a common pattern is true in both the New Testament and Josephus is easily missed.

Such a reconstructed sequence inevitably raises the question of the relationship between the Sign Prophets and Jesus, who in the "feeding of the multitude" is so similar to them. Is the relationship merely coincidental or is it, in some way, causal?

Coincidence or Causality?

It is possible that the theological setting, in which a New Mosaic Age and "the Prophet" were expected, was such that Jesus and the Sign-Prophets were "thrown up" independently of each other. Perhaps the combination of theological expectation and the worsening political circumstances were sufficient in themselves, to precipitate the rise of prophetic figures like Jesus and Theudas without the former exercising any influence over the latter.

On the other hand the common elements in the pattern are so puzzling as to warrant an investigation of the hypothesis that the activities of Jesus were in some way a causal factor in the rise of the Sign Prophets.

A Threefold Test. Was there, in the period after Jesus and before Theudas, a propagation of ideas about Jesus which could be said to represent an influence on the thought and behaviour of Theudas? Our method is to ascertain whether the first Christians proclaimed Jesus in terms which genuinely correspond with the thought-world of Theudas and those who came after him. The elements listed for investigation are *Signs, Exodus–Conquest imagery* and *The Prophet like Moses.*

Signs (σημεία) in Acts 1–12. It is noted that all but three references to σημεῖον in Acts occur within the critical period (? 33–44) represented by Acts 1–12.

σημεῖον			4:16, 22, 8:6
σημεῖον		δύναμις	8:13
σημεῖον	τέρας		2:43, 4:30, 5:12, 6:8, 7:36
σημεῖον	τέρας	δύναμις	2:22

[[691]] Whenever "sign"-activity is referred to, whether in speeches about the signs of Jesus (2:22, 7:36)[83] or in descriptions about the signs of the Apostles or the seven, it is, according to W. Nicol "always in the context of missionary work."[84]

---

83. Referring to Moses but really in reference to Jesus.
84. Op. cit., 77.

If it could be established that the Signs Source(s) in the Fourth Gospel was written earlier rather than later and from a Jewish milieu, it would tend to corroborate the picture in Acts 1–12 where σημεῖα occupy such an important place in the life of the Christians in Palestine in the period prior to A.D. 44. John 20:30–31 certainly suggests that "signs" played an important part in the gospel witness of the author and his circle.

Did Theudas know about the σημεῖα of Jesus and His first followers? The evidence from Acts 1–12 possibly corroborated by Heb 2:3–4 and John 20:31 suggests that by A.D. 44–48, during which period Theudas led his followers to Jordan, the news of the σημεῖα of Jesus and His followers must have been well known throughout Judaea–Galilee.

Exodus–Conquest Imagery. The speech of Stephen (Acts 7) to the Sanhedrin has been widely recognized as reflecting a clear typological relationship between Moses and Jesus. The Israelites rejected Moses (vv. 25, 35, 39) just as their descendants now reject Jesus (v. 51). Like Jesus, Moses came as λυτρωτής [['redeemer']] (v. 35) bringing σωτηρία [['salvation']] (v. 25). Moses worked τέρατα καὶ σημεῖα [['marvels and signs']] (v. 36) as did Jesus (2:22).

Quite clearly, Stephen and the community which he represented believed and affirmed that Jesus was a Mosaic figure.

It is possible that the ἀρχηγός [['Leader']] Christology of Acts 3:5, 5:31 (cf. Heb 2:10 and 12:2) reflects an early correspondence seen to exist between Jesus and Joshua.[85] Conceivably a Joshuanic Christology would fall out of fashion once Theudas and the Egyptian applied Joshua imagery to themselves. Did the very name Jesus = Joshua suggest a Joshuanic style of vocation to Theudas and the Egyptian? Certainly the name "Jesus" (without the addition of "Christ") figures extensively[86] in Acts 1–12, both in kerygmatic references and also in audience response.

ὁ προφήτης *in Acts 1–12.* Jesus is depicted twice in Acts 1–12 as "The Prophet" like Moses. The two references (Acts 3:22–23 and Acts 7:37), are so similar to each other and yet so clearly different to LXX Deut 8:1–5, 18 as to suggest that there was a firm tradition among the first Christians which held that Jesus was "The Prophet."[87]

We have now seen that these three elements which unquestionably belong to the Sign Prophets were part of the complex of ideas propagated by the [[692]] first Christians during the critical period (? A.D. 33–44) and over a wide ranging area within Palestine.

It is impossible to establish beyond doubt that Theudas was influenced by such concepts. Nevertheless there is the distinct possibility that a causal relationship existed between (the news about) Jesus and Theudas along with those who followed him.

---

85. Thus W. L. Knox, *Some Hellenistic Elements in Primitive Christianity* (London, 1944) 26 n. 1. See also *Sib. Or.* 5.256–59.

86. Acts 2:22, 32; 3:13; 4:13, 18, 30; 5:30, 40; 6:14; 8:16, 35; 9:17, 20, 27; 10:38; 11:20.

87. On which see M. Wilcox, *The Semitisms of Acts* (Oxford, 1965) 54–55.

For all his exaggerations, A. Schweitzer[88] revealed considerable insight when he wrote:

> The Baptist and Jesus are not . . . borne upon the current of a general eschatological movement. The period offers no events calculated to give an impulse to eschatological enthusiasms. They themselves *set the times in motion* by acting, by creating eschatological facts.

The Activities of Jesus Were Widely Known.   Peter on two occasions is recorded as informing his hearers that they already "knew" about Jesus. To the crowds in Jerusalem at Pentecost Peter is recorded as saying: Ἰησοῦν τὸν Ναζωραῖον, ἄνδρα ἀποδεδειγμένον ἀπὸ τοῦ θεοῦ . . . καθὼς αὐτοὶ οἴδατε [['Jesus of Nazareth, a man attested to you by God . . . as you yourselves know']] (Acts 2:22). Then, to the household of Cornelius in Caesarea he said: οἴδατε τὸ γενόμενον ῥῆμα καθ᾽ ὅλης τῆς Ἰουδαίας ἀρξάμενος ἀπὸ τῆς Γαλιλαίας . . . Ἰησοῦν τὸν ἀπὸ Ναζαρέθ [['that message spread throughout Judea, beginning in Galilee . . . Jesus of Nazareth']] (Acts 10:37–38).

Information about Jesus and his followers had come to the ears of the Roman Procurator, Felix, of whom Luke writes: ἀκριβέστερον εἰδὼς τὰ περὶ τῆς Ὁδοῦ [['rather well informed about the Way']] (Acts 24:22). Herod Agrippa II was also aware of Christians and presumably of Jesus, as Paul reminded him: ἐπίσταται γὰρ περὶ τούτων ὁ βασιλεύς, πρὸς ὅν καὶ παρρησιαζόμενος λαλῶ. λανθάνειν γὰρ αὐτὸν τούτων οὐ πείθομαι οὐθέν, οὐ γάρ ἐστιν ἐν γωνίᾳ πεπραγμένον τοῦτο [['Indeed the king knows about these things, and to him I spreak freely; for I am certain that none of these things has escaped his notice, for this was not done in a corner']] (Acts 26:26).

E. Trocmé[89] states that there were only two episodes which could have made Jesus into a public figure—the "entry" into Jerusalem (which Trocmé minimises, wrongly we believe, on account of its place in the traditions) and the "expulsion" of the merchants from the Temple. This twofold action (the "entry" and the "expulsion") may well have provided an influential model to Menahem (son or grandson of Judas the Galilean)[90] who entered Jerusalem with a bodyguard 'like a veritable king' (οἷα δὴ βασιλεύς)[91] whereupon he "became the leader of the revolution, and directed the siege of the palace."[92] J. H. Yoder[93] refers to Jesus' triumphant procession as a "recurrent symbolic pattern of Zealot political activity." But who in the first century does this before Jesus? If there is a "pattern," did not Jesus create it?

Trocmé is overly restrictive in the events which may have constituted Jesus as a "public figure." The "feeding" of the multitude and its aftermath must surely have had the same effect, even though the significance for us

---

88. *The Quest of the Historical Jesus* (E.T., W. Montgomery) (London, 1911) 368. My italics.
89. *Jesus and His Contemporaries* (London, 1971) 110–20.
90. *J.W.* 2.433.
91. *J.W.* 2.434, 444, 426–27.
92. *J.W.* 2.427.
93. *The Politics of Jesus* (Grand Rapids, 1973) 48 n. 31.

[[693]] only begins to emerge when we carefully compare Mark 6:30–46 with John 6:1–15. Mark writes of "many" who from "every town" in Galilee "ran together" to meet Jesus in the "wilderness." John tells us the outcome: 5,000 "men" attempt to "force" Jesus to become "king." H. W. Montefiore[94] is correct in regarding this event as a "messianic uprising."

As such it must have been widely known. There can be little doubt that Jesus became widely known within Galilee and Judaea as a "public figure" in respect of the "feeding" in the "wilderness" and also of the "entry" to Jerusalem and the accompanying "expulsion" of the merchants from the Temple. It is equally probable that as a "public figure" Jesus was accorded popular support by those who saw in Jesus a political liberator.

Indeed it is possible that a curious reference in the "Slavonic" Josephus may express, from their own point of view, the hopes and aspirations of those who saw in Jesus a kingly political liberator. The "wonderworker" having gone to the Mount of Olives along with the multitude and one hundred and fifty of his "ministers," "they made known to him their will that he should enter into the city and cut down the Roman troops and Pilate and rule over us. . . ."[95] Do we have here, embodied within the perplexing material of the "Slavonic" Josephus, a surviving first person fragment (". . . he should . . . rule over *us*") in which is expressed devotion to Jesus from a group whose interest in Jesus was primarily political and whom the Fourth Evangelist systematically depicts as possessed of "inadequate belief"?[96] Does the "wonderworker" extract in the first person suggest the possibility of a *continuing* interest in Jesus as a prophet and (political) king? Is it possible that the Egyptian prophet knew of such a tradition and indeed modelled himself upon it? Such a suggestion would help explain the otherwise baffling similarities[97] between the "wonderworker" of "Slavonic" Josephus and the Egyptian prophet. If the Egyptian Prophet was modelling himself upon tradition about Jesus as "Wonderworker" it would perhaps explain the later identification[98] ben Stada (The Egyptian) = ben Pandira (Jesus).

94. "Revolt in the Desert?" *NTS* 8 (1965) 135–41.

95. Addition 12; quoted in H. St. J. Thackeray, *The Jewish War* (Cambridge, Mass., 1968) 648–49.

96. E.g., John 2:23; 4:48 (cf. v. 45); 6:26 (cf. vv. 14–15); 7:31; 8:30 (but cf. vv. 37, 40); 12:37 and 42–43 (cf. 11:45, 48; 12:9–11, 17–19) and discussion thereon in W. Nicol, op. cit., 99–102.

97. (a) Both were followed by (or sought the following of) a *multitude.*
   (b) Both positioned themselves on the *Mount of Olives overlooking Jerusalem which was in Roman hands.*
   (c) Both worked (or sought to work) a *sign(s) by a word* (command).
   (d) Both sought (or were desired to secure) *the destruction of the Romans.*
   (e) Both sought to be (or were urged to become) *"king."*

It should not pass unnoticed that in the "feeding" incident recorded in the Fourth Gospel Jesus is hailed as "the prophet" whereupon an attempt is made to force him to become "king" (John 6:14–15).

98. Certain editions of the Talmud contain a passage inserted within *b. Sanh.* 67a in which ben Stada (probably The Egyptian—[ὁ] ἀναστατώσας [Acts 21:38]) and ben Pandira (i.e.,

Conclusion

The Jewish Sign Prophets heralded, and by their attempted "signs" sought to activate God's eschatological salvation. Their activities over three decades in such a significant period merit closer attention than has hitherto been devoted to them. It is hoped that what is now written will stimulate further discussion. In particular, enquiry into possible relationship between Jesus and the Sign Prophets may illuminate both Jesus and the prophets. Not least, more research may well throw light upon such shadowy figures as the βιασταί [['the violent']] (Matt 11:12–13) and the ψευδοπροφῆται [['false prophets']] (Matt 7:15 and 24:13) and indeed upon the whole religious ethos of the period of Judaean history encompassed by the ministry of John Baptist through to the Fall of Jerusalem.

Jesus as in certain Talmudic references—see J. Klausner, *Jesus of Nazareth*, E.T. [London, 1925] 46) are *identified*: "thus they did to Ben Stada . . . they hung him on the eve of Passover. Ben Stada was Ben Pandira."

JAMES D. G. DUNN

Pharisees, Sinners, and Jesus

[[61]] One of the most striking features of the study of Christianity's beginnings in the past ten years or so has been the reassessment of Jesus' relationship with his native faith, particularly with the Pharisees, and the increasing
impact of the reassessment. It is, of course, part of a much larger reappraisal
of the relationship between Christianity and Judaism, a central element of
which has been a growing realization that Christian attitudes towards Judaism have been deeply tainted and indeed warped by centuries of misunderstanding and prejudice. Already before the Second World War individual
voices had been raised in protest on the non-Jewish side.[1] But the horror of
the Holocaust forced a much wider circle of Christians to re-examine the nature and roots of anti-Semitism and to face up to the stark issue of whether,
and if so to what extent, anti-Semitism is endemic to Christianity and rooted
in its own sacred Scriptures.[2] Since the Pharisees are the most immediate
predecessors of rabbinic Judaism, which became Judaism's enduring form
(and so the object of anti-Semitism through the centuries), it was inevitable
that Christian perception of the Pharisees, not least in the Gospels, would
have to come under particularly close scrutiny. And since Jesus is the founder
of Christianity, which came to display such regrettable antagonism towards

Reprinted, with permission, from James D. G. Dunn, *Jesus, Paul, and the Law: Studies in Mark
and Galatians* (Louisville: Westminster/John Knox, 1990) 61–88.

1. Particularly G. F. Moore, "Christian Writers on Judaism," *HTR* 14 (1921) 197–254;
R. T. Herford, *The Pharisees* (London: George Allen & Unwin, 1924; Boston: Beacon, 1962);
and J. Parkes, *The Conflict of the Church and the Synagogue* (1934; New York: Atheneum, 1969).

2. See especially the debate occasioned by R. Ruether's *Faith and Fratricide: The Theo-
logical Roots of Anti-Semitism* (New York: Seabury, 1974); A. T. Davies, ed., *AntiSemitism and the
Foundations of Christianity* (New York: Paulist, 1979); and J. G. Gager, *The Origins of Anti-
Semitism* (New York: Oxford University Press, 1983); *Anti-Judaism in Early Christianity*, Vol. 1
Paul and the Gospels, ed. P. Richardson, Vol. 2 *Separation and Polemic*, ed. S. G. Wilson, Studies
in Christianity and Judaism (Waterloo, Ontario: Wilfrid Laurier University, 1986). Note also
C. Klein, *Anti-Judaism in Christian Theology* (Philadelphia: Fortress, 1978); and from the Jew-
ish side S. Sandmel, *Anti-Semitism in the New Testament* (Philadelphia: Fortress, 1978).

its founder's ancestral faith, it was equally inevitable that Jesus' relationship to the Pharisees should be a crucial issue within the larger debate.

As the reassessment of Jesus' relationship with the Pharisees has gathered strength a number of important claims have been staked out:

1. The Pharisees, the contemporaries of Jesus, have been misrepresented in at least some degree in the Gospels, particularly in Matthew and John, which reflect the growing antagonism between Christianity and rabbinic Judaism after 70 C.E. This judgement would now command a widespread consensus within New Testament as well as Jewish scholarship.[3]
2. The Pharisees were not responsible for and had no part in the death of Jesus—a view long championed by Jewish scholars (H. Maccoby: the "Jewish view of Jesus").[4]
3. Pharisees would not have been hostile to Jesus. Indeed, on the Jewish side the claim is quite often made that Jesus, far [[62]] from being an opponent of the Pharisees, was himself a Pharisee.[5]

The high-water mark, so far, in this tide of re-evaluation is the work of E. P. Sanders. In his *Jesus and Judaism*[6] he re-expresses all the claims so far outlined in his own terms and develops especially the last. In Sanders' judgement there was no substantive point of disagreement between Jesus and the Pharisees. In particular, the Pharisees would not have regarded the ordinary people (*'am ha-aretz*) as "sinners" beyond the pale of the law and would not have criticized Jesus for associating with them. The Pharisees did not have the power to exclude others from the social and religious life of Judaism. And the depiction of the Pharisees as super-bigots attacking Jesus for offering forgiveness to the common people is ridiculous and offensive.[7]

All this can be summed up under the head of Jewish-Christian rapprochement: on the one hand, the Jewish attempt to reclaim Jesus; on the other, the Christian attempt to demonstrate the Jewishness of Jesus.[8] The proponents

---

3. See, e.g., W. D. Davies, *The Setting of the Sermon on the Mount* (New York and Cambridge: Cambridge Univ. Press, 1964) 256–315, esp. 290–92; J. Koenig, *Jews and Christians in Dialogue* (Philadelphia: Westminster, 1979) chaps. 4 and 6; and F. Mussner, *Tractate on the Jews* (London: SPCK, 1984) 164–76.

4. The most recent proponents are H. Maccoby (*The Mythmaker: Paul and the Invention of Christianity* [London: Weidenfeld & Nicolson, 1986] 45–49 [the phrase is used on pp. 208–10]) and E. Rivkin (*What Crucified Jesus?* [Nashville: Abingdon, 1984]). For earlier literature, see esp. D. R. Catchpole, *The Trial of Jesus* (Leiden: E. J. Brill, 1971).

5. Most recently by H. Falk (*Jesus the Pharisee* [New York: Paulist, 1985]) and Maccoby (*Mythmaker*, 29–44). So also J. T. Pawlikowski (*Christ in the Light of the Christian-Jewish Dialogue* [New York: Paulist, 1982]). The claim is usually firmly denied on the Christian side; see, e.g., S. Westerholm, *Jesus and Scribal Authority*, Coniectanea biblica, New Testament (Lund: C. W. K. Gleerup, 1978) 128.

6. E. P. Sanders, *Jesus and Judaism* (Philadelphia: Fortress, 1985).

7. See ibid., especially chap. 7, "The Sinners," which is a reworking of "Jesus and the Sinners," *JSNT* 19 (1983) 5–36.

8. For other literature, see D. A. Hagner, *The Jewish Reclamation of Jesus* (Grand Rapids: Zondervan, 1984) 23–39; and Mussner, *Tractate*, 109–14.

on both sides are usually well aware of the corollary: that the "blame" for any anti-Jewish element within the Christian Scriptures is to be shifted well beyond Jesus to a later stage—to Paul (as in Maccoby), or beyond 70 C.E. (as in Sanders).[9] The problem and consequences of thus separating Jesus from subsequent Christianity, however, have not been fully worked out. Nor has it been sufficiently appreciated that to replace the wedge between Jesus and Judaism with a wedge between Jesus and Gentile Christianity has an unnerving echo of the equivalent attempts at the turn of the last century to isolate Jesus as a purveyor of a purer and less offensive gospel from the "Hellenization" begun by Paul and his successors.[10] Before the echoes of the last Jesus-v.-Paul debate have died away there seems to be a growing need for a re-match.

Obviously there are too many issues caught up in the whole affair to be dealt with in a single essay. Here we can look at only one: the question of Jesus' relationship with the Pharisees as posed most recently and most challengingly by Sanders. In particular, is it the case that opposition between Jesus and the Pharisees as portrayed in the Gospels is all a retrojection of later controversies, without historical foundation within the ministry of Jesus? And is it the case that the "sinners" Jesus was criticized for befriending were the "truly wicked"?[11] These are only two of the many issues raised by Sanders' important work, but they provide a sizeable enough agenda for the moment.

Pharisees . . .

Despite repeated studies of the Pharisees there are still an astonishing [[63]] number of disputed claims and unresolved questions on the subject. Here we confine ourselves to the single issue of the Pharisees' character and influence in the period prior to 70 C.E., with the years of Jesus' ministry particularly in mind. Only if we can gain a reasonably clear picture here will we be in any position to answer our question as to whether the opposition between Jesus and the Pharisees as portrayed in the Gospels reflects the historical realities of Jesus' ministry. We have in fact *four* potential sources from which to glean the relevant information: the rabbinic traditions themselves, Josephus, Paul, and the Gospels.

---

9. Though some Jewish scholars are willing to shift "blame" for the hostility to Jesus from one group within first-century Judaism to another: from Pharisees to high priests (Rivkin, *What Crucified Jesus?*) or to Pharisees over against charismatics (G. Vermes, *Jesus the Jew* [London: William Collins, 1973] 80–82), or from Pharisees in general to the house of Shammai in particular (A. Finkel, *The Pharisees and the Teacher of Nazareth* [Leiden: E. J. Brill, 1964] 134–43; Falk, *Jesus*). Cf. J. Bowker, *Jesus and the Pharisees* (New York and Cambridge: Cambridge Univ. Press, 1973): Pharisees/*perushim* as a more extreme wing of the Hakamim (sages). For older discussion, see, e.g., J. Jocz, *The Jewish People and Jesus Christ* (London: SPCK, 1954) 17–42.

10. See, e.g., A. Harnack, *What Is Christianity?* (London: William & Norgate, 1901); and W. Wrede, *Paul* (London: Green, 1907) 177–80.

11. Sanders, *Jesus*, 210.

The Pharisees from the Perspective of the Rabbinic Traditions

Here we are bound to start with the work of Jacob Neusner. Whatever issues
he has left unresolved, and however one may dispute particular findings, it
cannot be denied that he has made a decisive beginning in the too long delayed task of providing a tradition-historical analysis of the amazingly rich
and diverse traditions of the rabbis.[12] In particular, we must refer to his careful study of the traditions regarding the Pharisees before 70 C.E.[13] These traditions naturally have a first call on our attention, if only for the important
fact that they provide *a picture of the Pharisees as the later rabbis chose to remember them.*

Neusner's findings are very striking. The traditions about the Pharisees
before 70 C.E. specifically attributed to individuals or houses (the houses of
Hillel and Shammai) consist of approximately 371 separate items. "Approximately 67% of all legal pericopae deal with dietary laws: ritual purity for
meals and agricultural rules governing the fitness of food for Pharisaic consumption."[14] In his numerous subsequent writings, Neusner has continued to
maintain the same point: this much-repeated concern with rules on agricultural tithes and ritual purity all focuses on table-fellowship; the attempt to
maintain in everyday life the purity laws designed for the temple was most at
risk at the meal table.[15] The pre-70 strata of the Mishnaic law bear witness to
a group where food taboos were the chief mode of social differentiation by
which they maintained their continued existence as a group:

> The Mishnah before the wars begins its life among a group of people
> who are joined by a common conviction about the eating of food under
> ordinary circumstances in accord with cultic rules to begin with appli-
> cable . . . to the Temple alone. This group, moreover, had other rules
> which affected who might join and who might not . . . [which] formed a
> protective boundary, keeping in those who were in, keeping out those
> who were not.[16]

Sanders, however, finds Neusner's analysis of the rabbinic texts "unper-
suasive" and "made especially dubious by the evidence from [[64]] Josephus."
In more detail, Sanders' objection is that Neusner's conclusions are drawn
only from the tradition explicitly assigned to individuals or to houses. "The

---

12. For questions of methodology, see, e.g., J. Neusner, "The Use of the Later Rabbinic
Evidence for the Study of First-Century Pharisaism," in *Approaches to Ancient Judaism: Theory
and Practice*, Brown Judaic Studies 1 (Missoula, Mont.: Scholars Press, 1978) 215–28. But
P. S. Alexander's protest ("Rabbinic Judaism and the New Testament," *ZNW* 74 [1983] 237–
46) is evidently still necessary.

13. J. Neusner, *The Rabbinic Traditions about the Pharisees before 70*, 3 vols. (Leiden: E. J.
Brill, 1971).

14. Ibid., 3:303–4.

15. J. Neusner, *From Politics to Piety: The Emergence of Pharisaic Judaism* (Englewood
Cliffs, N. J.: Prentice-Hall, 1973) 81–96.

16. J. Neusner, *Judaism: The Evidence of the Mishnah* (Chicago: Univ. of Chicago Press,
1981) 69–70.

summary does not reflect the numerous anonymous laws which probably represent *common* belief and practice, including large bodies of law on civil matters, worship, feasts and the temple cult." And Josephus shows the Pharisees to be simply lay experts in the law and says nothing about their having peculiar food and purity laws.[17]

There is some force in both points. But Neusner is by no means so vulnerable to the criticism as might at first appear. In his original treatment of the tradition attributed to the houses he had allowed the possibility that they were "relatively small and constituted only one part of the Pharisaic group in Jerusalem, a still smaller segment of Pharisaism as a whole."[18] And in *Judaism* he is scrupulously careful not to identify this early stage of the Mishnaic tradition with a particular named group. In the face of Josephus' silence regarding any concern on the part of the Pharisees for the purity of the meal table, he had made the important observation that on this point the Pharisaic group were different from the Qumran covenanters (not to mention the Christians latterly). For they "evidently did not conduct table-fellowship meals *as rituals*. The table-fellowship laws pertained not merely to group life, but to daily life quite apart from a sectarian setting and ritual occasion."[19] Consequently, they would be less distinctive for a readership looking at Judaism from outside, for whom the Jewish food laws would be striking enough,[20] so that the refinements of subgroups within Judaism would be lost on them (cf. Mark 7:3: ". . . the Pharisees and *all* the Jews . . ."). Besides this, Josephus with his strong Roman contacts would be well aware of Roman suspicion that special dietary laws were an indication of strange cults[21] and would not be anxious to highlight this aspect of Pharisaism in writings that take such pains to conceal the less acceptable (in Roman eyes) features of Pharisaism (see below).[22]

As for Sanders' former criticism, no doubt many of the unattributed traditions do go back to the pre-70 period. But even so, that should not be allowed to detract so much from Neusner's findings. It may simply mean that there was a strand of Pharisaism which, among other things, emphasized dietary rules at the daily meal table. But in fact the evidence calls for a stronger conclusion. For despite Sanders, it must be significant that such a high percentage of the attributed traditions focus upon one main aspect of practical piety. It strongly suggests that these rulings were sensitive matters or matters of dispute among the predecessors of the rabbis, so that relevant rulings were

17. Sanders, *Jesus*, 188 n. 59.

18. Neusner, *Rabbinic Traditions* 3:279. See also idem, "The Fellowship (חבורה) in the Second Jewish Commonwealth," *HTR* 53 (1960) 125, 128.

19. Neusner, *From Politics to Piety*, 87–88.

20. See, e.g., Philo *Leg.* 361; Plutarch *Quaest. Conviv.* 4.5; Tacitus *Hist.* 5.4.2.

21. Seneca *Ep. Mor.* 108.22: "Abstinence from certain kinds of animal food was set down as a proof of interest in the strange cult." Cicero *Pro Flacco* 28.67: "barbarous superstition." Tacitus *Ann.* 2.85.4: ". . . Jewish rites . . . that superstition."

22. Josephus, on the other hand, can give an extensive account of the Essenes (*J.W.* 2.119–261) since he had distinguished them from the Pharisees and since they were no longer a factor within Judaism in the post-70 period.

remembered by the post-70 dominant party by their attribution to leading figures of the past or as part of the houses' disputes. The clear implication is that
the purity of table-fellowship [[65]] was thus remembered as a matter of great
importance within pre-70 Pharisaic circles or by a group or faction of Pharisees.[23] And whatever their numerical size in that period, they were strong
enough not only to survive the catastrophe of 70 c.e. but also to stamp their
authority on the tradition preserved by the rabbis.

In short, the evidence of the rabbinic traditions points clearly to the conclusion that *the purity of the meal table was an important concern among many of the
Pharisees of Jesus' time*, or at least within a significant faction of the Pharisees.

The Pharisees in Josephus

Here the main question is twofold: how to account for the differences in the
pictures of the Pharisees which emerge from Josephus and from the rabbinic
traditions; and what weight to give to the different emphases present in the
various accounts of the Pharisees provided by Josephus himself.

The answer to the first is probably fairly straightforward, as we have already suggested. Josephus writes of the Pharisees, as on other matters, with
an eye to his wider readership in sophisticated Greek-speaking society. This is
particularly clear in what is his most consistent emphasis when be makes a
point of describing the Pharisees: they are a "philosophy" (*J.W.* 2.119, 166;
Ant. 18.11); their beliefs are described in philosophical terms (*J.W.* 2.163;
Ant. 13.172); they resemble quite closely (παραλήσιος) the Stoic school or sect
(*Life* 12). Clearly evident here is a deliberate and sustained strategy of com-
mending the Pharisees as a philosophical school. Josephus was hardly likely
to put that strategy in jeopardy by also presenting the Pharisees in the contrasting and much less appealing terms of a foreign superstition.[24]

When we consider the internal tensions between Josephus' various references to the Pharisees, particularly as between the *Jewish War* and *Antiquities*,
the issue that comes to the fore is whether and, if so, to what extent the Pharisees were a significant influence on the religious and political life of the nation. The issue is posed by M. Smith:

> In the *War* [Josephus] says nothing of the Pharisees having any influence
> with the people. . . . In the *Antiquities*, however, written twenty years
> later, the picture is quite different. Here whenever Josephus discusses the

---

23. Note also that the very name "Pharisees" (the 'separated') points to their having a
characteristic practice that set them apart from their fellow Jews. See esp. E. Schürer, *The
History of the Jewish People in the Age of Jesus Christ*, rev. and ed. G. Vermes et al., vol. 2 (Edinburgh: T. & T. Clark, 1979) 396–98: "A separation from uncleanness is always a simultaneous
separation from unclean persons." "The Pharisees must have obtained their name from a
separation in which the main body of the people did not participate, in other words, from
having set themselves apart, by virtue of their stricter understanding of the concept of purity
. . . from that uncleanness which, in their opinion, adhered to a great part of the people itself." See also nn. 29, 53 below.

24. See again n. 21 above.

Jewish sects, the Pharisees take first place, and every time he mentions them he emphasizes their popularity. . . .[25]

From this Neusner concludes, "We must discount all of [Josephus's] references to the influence and power of the Pharisees [in the Herodian period]."[26] They *had* been deeply involved in politics during the Hasmonean period, but at the time of Jesus they were a [[66]] relatively small sect concerned primarily with matters of ritual purity.

This position must, however, be regarded as something of an over-statement. For one thing, the contrast between *War* and *Antiquities* is not so marked as Smith argues. *Whenever* Josephus mentions the three sects of the Jews, he always names the Pharisees "first," with Sadducees "second" and Essenes "third," in *War* as much as in *Antiquities*, as also in his *Life* (*J.W.* 2.119, 162, 164; *Ant.* 13.171; 18.11; *Life* 10). On this point Josephus is again consistent: the Pharisees were the leading or most important of the different factions within first-century Judaism.

As to the difference in emphasis between *War* and *Antiquities* on the matter of the Pharisees' popularity and influence, an obvious explanation lies near to hand here too. In the immediate aftermath of the Jewish revolt (assuming the consensus view that *War* was published in the 70s), it would hardly be wise for Josephus to highlight the political influence of the Pharisees in the period leading up to the revolt. In fact he does note that "distinguished Pharisees' were consulted as the crisis deepened (*J.W.* 2.411). And in his later writings it is not only the Pharisees' popularity with the people on religious matters of which he speaks (as in *Ant.* 18.15, 17) but also of Pharisaic involvement in the revolt against Rome (*Ant.* 18.4; *Life* 21, 191, 197; note also *Ant.* 18.23). It would be unwise, therefore, wholly to discount the *Antiquities'* picture of Pharisaic influence and popularity: it is as likely that such an emphasis has been suppressed in *War* as that it has been exaggerated in *Antiquities*; apologetic considerations would play an important role in both cases. The truth probably lies somewhere in between.[27]

In short, the strong impression given by Josephus is that the Pharisees were the most important of the three or four main factions in Jewish social and religious life, outside the temple, of this period, and that the Pharisees were divided among themselves on the question of active involvement in the growing political crisis, with some leading Pharisees having influence in the highest Jewish councils and others active in the developing resistance. Even if the depiction of Pharisaic influence in *Antiquities* is exaggerated, therefore, the Pharisees cannot be discounted as a merely quietistic, purity sect without significant influence beyond their own circles. On the contrary, if we can speak of

25. M. Smith, "Palestinian Judaism in the First Century," in *Israel: Its Role in Civilization*, ed. M. Davies (New York: Jewish Theological Seminary of America, 1956) 75–76.

26. Neusner, *From Politics to Piety*, 65.

27. Cf. Schürer, *History*, 395: "However indifferent to politics Pharisaism was to begin with, the revolutionary trend which gained increasing ground among the Jews in the first century C.E. is to be attributed, indirectly at least, to its influence."

them as a coherent sect (as not only Josephus consistently does but also Acts 15:5; 26:5), we have to recognize *the likelihood that their influence reached well beyond their own ranks.*[28]

In addition, we should note the point made by A. I. Baumgarten: that when Josephus speaks of the Pharisees he regularly describes them as the party of ἀκρίβεια (*J.W.* 1.110; 2.162; *Ant.* 17.41; [[67]] *Life* 191; cf. *Ant.* 20.201, and note again the striking correlation in Acts 22:3; 26:5). The word denotes "exactness or precision," and when used in connection with "law" is most naturally taken in a sense like "strictness or severity" (*Greek-English Lexicon*, ed. H. Liddell and R. Scott). So when we read, for example, in *J.W.* 2.162, that the Pharisees interpreted the laws or customs μετ᾽ ἀκρίβείας [['with exactness']], the implication is clear that *they were well known as those who interpreted the law with scrupulous exactness and strictness in detail.*[29] This strongly suggests that the Pharisees also saw themselves in an important sense as *guardians of the law and of the ancestral customs* (*Ant.* 13.297, 408; 17.41; *Life* 198). Moreover, if Josephus, the self-confessed Pharisee, is any guide, they naturally wished to commend such "strictness" to others (*Ant.* 1.14; 4.309; 5.132; 8.21; 18.345; *Ag. Ap.* 2.149, 187, 227–28). The implications of this for their relationship to a movement like that of Jesus are potentially important, but the picture is too incomplete to say more at this stage.

Paul the Pharisee

It is very surprising that in such discussions the potential evidence of Paul is rarely taken into account.[30] For Paul is the only first-century Pharisee apart from Josephus from whom we have any firsthand evidence. And Paul is the only Pharisee who speaks to us with his own voice from the period under scrutiny. Of course, Paul's testimony has to be discounted to some extent at least, since he can be regarded as a "hostile witness." But the testimony should certainly not be ignored or disparaged out of hand.[31]

---

28. According to Neusner (*Judaism in the Beginning of Christianity* [London: SPCK, 1984] 53), the Pharisees "claimed the right to rule all the Jews by virtue of their possessing the 'Oral Torah' of Moses"; so also Schürer, *History*, 389–91; and Rivkin, *What Crucified Jesus?* 41, 44–47. Sanders (*Jesus*, 188) thinks that Josephus has exaggerated the success of the Pharisees but accepts that "there is every reason to think that the Pharisees tried to have their views of the law carry the day."

29. A. I. Baumgarten, "The Name of the Pharisees," *JBL* 102 (1983) 413–17. Baumgarten goes on to argue that the name "Pharisees" probably also involved a play on the sense *parosim* 'specifiers', during our period (pp. 422–28).

30. Regrettably Maccoby chooses to ignore or to discount Paul's own testimony in Rom 11:1; Gal 1:13–14; Phil 3:4–6; and to argue the fanciful thesis that Paul was a Greek/Gentile on the basis of a reference in Epiphanius (*Pan.* 30.16.6–9), whose tendentiousness is not hard to detect. Since Paul's role as persecutor would require political sanction, it must certainly have enjoyed high priestly backing, and co-operation between high priest and Pharisee on such a matter is entirely plausible (cf. *Ant.* 2.411, 4.159–60; *Life* 21, 191–94).

31. So, e.g., Neusner (*Judaism in the Beginning*, 45–61; and "Three Pictures of the Pharisees: A Reprise," in *Formative Judaism: Religious, Historical, and Literary Studies*, 5th ser., Brown Judaic Studies 91 [Chico, Calif.: Scholars Press, 1985] 51–77) still confines his discussion of

The passages which obviously call for consideration are the two where he speaks of his own pre-Christian past: Gal 1:13–14; Phil 3:5–6. In addition, however, there are one or two passages where he speaks of his fellow Jews and where the most obvious interpretation is that he is thinking of the Judaism he knew best: especially Rom 10:2–3, but also Rom 2:17ff. In Gal 1:13–14 he briefly describes his "way of life when he was in Judaism" in three clauses: he persecuted the church of God καθ' ὑπερβολήν; he progressed in Judaism beyond many of those of his own age among his people; he was much more of a zealot (ζηλωτής) for the traditions handed down from the fathers. In Phil 3:5–6 the most relevant part again has three elements: in terms of the law, a Pharisee; in terms of zeal (ζῆλος), a persecutor of the church; in terms of righteousness which is in the law, blameless (ἄμεμπτος). In Rom 10:2–3, Paul bears personal testimony (no doubt on the basis of his own experience) to Israel's zeal for God (ζῆλον θεοῦ) and concern "to establish their own righteousness."

There are two features which recur in each description and which are worthy of special note. One characteristic of Judaism [[68]] which Paul recalls and most naturally thinks of as typical of Judaism is "zeal"—zeal for God, zeal for the traditions of the fathers. In Jewish circles the classic examples of such zeal were well known: Simeon and Levi (Genesis 34; Jdt 9:4; *Jub.* 30:5–20), Phinehas (Num 25:10–13; Sir 45:23–24; 1 Macc 2:54; 4 Macc 18:12), Elijah (Sir 48:2; 1 Macc 2:58), and the Maccabees (1 Macc 2:19–27, 50, 58; 2 Macc 4:2; Josephus *Ant.* 12.271). It is notable that in each case this zeal led to taking the sword to maintain Israel's distinctiveness as God's covenant people. It is certainly just such zeal which motivated the Zealots, and it was also such zeal which Paul had in mind in Phil 3:6 ("in terms of zeal a persecutor") when he recalled his own past.[32] But Gal 1:14 indicates that "zeal for God," "zeal for the law," could be a relative thing ("much more a zealot") and could therefore presumably express itself in dedication to observing and maintaining the law as the mark of Israel's distinctiveness without necessarily resorting to the sword (cf. 1QS 4:4; 9:23; 1QH 14:14; *T. Ash.* 4:5). The implication is that Paul was comparing himself with his fellow students or younger Pharisees as all "zealous," but he much the more so because he resorted to the sword.

The other feature of these Pauline passages is the strong conviction of a secure status sustained not least by such zeal—of a progress beyond others (Gal 1:14), of a righteousness sustained without reproach (Phil 3:6), of a confidence of possessing light and knowledge to higher advantage than others by virtue of having the law (Rom 2:17–20, 23). All this is most naturally understood as tied into and as a corollary to the "strictness" which, according to

---

the Pharisees to our other three sources. E. Rivkin (*A Hidden Revolution* [Nashville: Abingdon, 1978]) recognizes the importance of Paul's testimony but devotes only a little over two pages to it.

32. See further J. D. G. Dunn, "Righteousness from the Law" and "Righteousness from Faith": Paul's Interpretation of Scripture in Romans 10:1–10," in *Tradition and Interpretation in the New Testament* (E. E. Ellis Festschrift), ed. G. F. Hawthorne (Grand Rapids: Wm. B. Eerdmans, 1987) 216–28. See also my *Romans*, Word Biblical Commentary 38 (Waco: Word, Inc., 1988) 586–87. In the Mishnah note particularly *Sanh.* 9:6.

Josephus, characterized the Pharisees. The point seems to be confirmed beyond reasonable dispute by the corroborative evidence of two other witnesses:
Acts 22:3 confirms that "zeal for God" and "strictness" in observing the ancestral law are closely synonymous concepts in the description of a Pharisee; and
in *Ant.* 17.41, Josephus provides the nearest parallel to what Paul implies in
the passages cited—that the Pharisees were a group of Jews who prided themselves on the strict observance (ἐξακριβώσει) of their ancestral law(s).

The picture which emerges from Paul, therefore, is what one might fairly
call a Pharisee's view of Judaism. Or to be more precise, in such passages Paul
recalls his self-understanding as a Pharisee and uses language and sentiments
which must have been characteristic of the Pharisee as "sect" (and which, of
course, Paul now regards as mistaken). This should *not* be taken as evidence
for the old interpretation of Pharisaism as boastful of self-achievement and
consumed with meritorious point-scoring. In speaking of his life as a Pharisee
as "blameless" (Phil 3:6), Paul most likely meant that he had lived to the full in
the terms laid down for members of [[69]] the covenant people (κατὰ δικαιοσύνην τὴν ἐν νόμῳ), including the law's provision for atonement and forgiveness.[33] And in talking of Israel's "seeking to establish its own righteousness"
(Rom 10:3), the thought is of *Israel's* righteousness—not available to those outside the covenant people—not of a righteousness achieved by Paul (τὴν ἰδίαν
δικαιοσύνην).[34] Nor does it follow that Paul speaks in these passages for all
Pharisees, or for Pharisees alone. But he probably does speak as a Pharisee
and express views typical of Pharisees of his own day. From such evidence,
therefore, we may fairly conclude that *in the middle decades of the first century,
Pharisees were characterized by zeal for the law and concern to practise that pattern of
life which maintained the righteousness of the covenant and Israel's status as the
people of God.*

The Pharisees in the Synoptic Gospels

On this issue, Sanders is at his most confrontational: "It is incorrect to make
purity the issue between Jesus and his critics." "Jesus' eating with the sinners
probably did not involve him in a dispute with a superscrupulous group
(whether called *haberim* or Pharisees)." "It is very probable that the issues of
food and Sabbath are so prominent in the Gospels because of the importance
which they assumed in the church." "There was no substantial conflict between
Jesus and the Pharisees with regard to Sabbath, food, and purity laws."[35] A repeated claim is that the stories of such conflict are "obviously unrealistic."

---

33. For the importance of atonement and forgiveness within Judaism, see esp. E. P.
Sanders, *Paul and Palestinian Judaism: A Comparison of Patterns of Religion* (Philadelphia: Fortress, 1977), index: "atonement" and "forgiveness."

34. See ἴδιος, in *Greek-English Lexicon of the New Testament*, ed. W. Bauer, W. F. Arndt,
and F. W. Gingrich. Cf. E. P. Sanders, *Paul, the Law, and the Jewish People* (Philadelphia: Fortress, 1983) 38: "Their own" righteousness, then, is not characterized as being self-righteous-
ness, but rather as being the righteousness which is limited to followers of the law" (further
literature in n. 107). See also Dunn, *Romans*, pp. 587–88.

35. Sanders, *Jesus*, 199, 209, 264.

The extraordinarily unrealistic settings of many of the conflict stories should be realized: Pharisees did not organize themselves into groups to spend their Sabbaths in Galilean cornfields in the hope of catching someone transgressing (Mark 2:23–24), nor is it credible that scribes and Pharisees made a special trip to Galilee from Jerusalem to inspect Jesus' disciples' hands (Mark 7:1f.). Surely stories such as these should not be read as describing actual debates between Jesus and others.[36]

There are a number of issues here to which we must come in due course (particularly the identity of the "sinners" and the likelihood of Pharisees seeking to influence religious practice in Galilee). For the moment, however, we will confine ourselves to the issue of whether the Synoptic testimony, and if so how much of it, can be admitted as evidence for Pharisaic attitudes in the period before 70 C.E., and particularly in regard to Jesus.

There is no question that many of the references to "Pharisees" in the Synoptic accounts are redactional: we need think only of such passages as Matt 3:7; 5:20; 9:34; 12:24; 21:45; Luke 5:17, 21; 7:30; 19:39; not to mention the strong sequence of references found only in one of the evangelists (particularly Matthew 23 passim; Luke 14:1, 3; 15:2; 16:14; 18:10–11). Few would dispute that at least a [[70]] considerable portion of this testimony has to be read in the light of the increasing conflict between Christianity and rabbinic Judaism in the 80s of the first century, and that traditions have been shaped and particularized to make them more serviceable for congregations (usually Jewish Christian congregations) who felt themselves under threat from the successors of the Pharisees. But that still leaves a core of references strongly attested in the triple tradition, that is, including Mark—particularly Mark 2:16, 18, 24 pars.; 7:1 pars. And it is a good deal more difficult to treat these as the product of disputes of the post-70 period.

1. It is of course arguable that Mark was written after 70 C.E.,[37] though most scholars find the late 60s more compelling.[38] But even if a post-70 date for Mark should be accepted, that may still be inadequate for the case. In the aftermath of the destruction of Jerusalem the rabbinic school at Jabneh did not immediately leap into prominence. The probability is that they took time to find their feet and that their influence took many years to spread.[39] The hypothesis that rabbinic pressure on the Christian congregations of the post-70 period left its imprint on the Jesus-tradition used by Mark probably requires a date for Mark into the early 80s before it becomes realistic. Such a date is not impossible, but the later Mark has to be dated the weaker the hypothesis becomes.

36. Ibid., 178, 265.
37. So Sanders would maintain; for others, see W. G. Kümmel, *Introduction to the New Testament* (London: SCM, 1975) 98 n. 65.
38. Kümmel, *Introduction*, 98; and see now esp. M. Hengel, *Studies in the Gospel of Mark* (Philadelphia: Fortress, 1985) 1–30, nn.
39. See esp. G. Alon, *The Jews in Their Land in the Talmudic Age*, vol. 1 (Jerusalem: Magnes, 1980).

2. Few would want to argue that the material in Mark 2:15–28 and 7:1–5 was created *de novo* at the final stage of the Gospel. Apart from anything else, there are too many indications of editorial work on a pre-formed tradition: in particular, Mark 2:20 as a qualification added in the light not least of the Christian congregations' continuation (or resumption) of the practice of fasting some time after Jesus' death; and Mark 7:3–4 as added to explain Pharisaic practice to a Gentile readership, making it necessary for 7:5a to recapitulate the introduction (7:1–2). There is clear evidence in these chapters of Mark's having taken over an *earlier* tradition in which Christian congregations in the period before 70 C.E. felt it necessary to defend themselves from criticism particularly on matters of table-fellowship, ritual purity, and sabbath observance, and in which the criticism is explicitly attributed to Pharisees.[40]

3. Looked at from a slightly different angle, the same evidence also indicates that at the pre-Markan level of the tradition it is *internal Jewish* disputes which are in view: a dispute over *how* the sabbath should be observed, not yet *whether* it should be observed (Mark 2:27–28; contrast Rom 14:5), and a dispute where the indisputably Jewish use of κοινός in the sense of "impure, defiled" has also to be explained to Gentiles (7:2). The indication again is of *Jewish* Christian congregations, who from within Judaism or as [[71]] part of Judaism felt the need to explain and defend themselves to other Jews.

4. This evidence accords well with other indicators of intra-Jewish concerns in the period prior to 70 C.E. (apart from those already reviewed above). On the one hand there is the evidence of both *Jub.* 2:29–30, 50:6–13 and CD 10:14–11:18 that concern to protect the sabbath by means of particular *halakoth* [[the body of Jewish oral law]] was already well developed before the time of Jesus.[41] On the other there is the strong testimony of Gal 2:11–14 that pressure was exerted on the Antioch congregation from within the Jerusalem leadership anxious to maintain the traditional dietary laws. Mark's portrayal of Pharisees concerned about issues of sabbath observance and ritual purity fits much more closely into the period of Jesus' ministry than Sanders allows,[42] as does Mark's depiction of Pharisees' high regard for ancestral traditions (Mark 7:3, 5; cf. Gal 1:14; Josephus *Ant.* 13.297, 408; 17.41; *Life* 198).

40. See the much fuller tradition-history analysis in J. D. G. Dunn's "Mark 2:1–3:6: A Bridge between Jesus and Paul on the Question of the Law," *NTS* 30 (1984) 395–414; reprinted [[in Dunn, *Jesus, Paul, and the Law,*]] chap. 1. See also idem, "Jesus and Ritual Purity: A Study of the Tradition History of Mark 7:15," in *A cause de l'Evangile*, Festschrift J. Dupont, Lectio Divina 123 (Paris: Editions du Cerf, 1985) 251–76; reprinted [[in Dunn]] chap. 2. Among other literature, see, e.g., H. Merkel, "Jesus und die Pharisäer," *NTS* 14 (1967–68) 194–208, esp. 202–6; H. F. Weiss, φαρισαῖος, in *TDNT* 9:41; Westerholm, *Jesus*, 71–75, 96–103; and Mussner, *Tractate*, 176–79.

41. In his various studies (see nn. 13, 15, 16, 28 above), Neusner notes that in the pre-70 rabbinic traditions, concern for observances of sabbaths and festivals follows rulings on ritual purity and agricultural matters in frequency.

42. C. Thoma (*A Christian Theology of Judaism* [New York: Paulist, 1980] 113) summarizes the position fairly: "Not only the final, redacted parts of the New Testament but even the earlier ones indicate opposition as well as affinity between Jesus and Pharisees."

To sum up, when the four strands of testimony regarding the Pharisees examined above are put together, a remarkably coherent picture emerges of Pharisees as a sufficiently clearly defined group to be described as a 'sect', αἵρεσις, whose most characteristic concern was to observe the law and ancestral traditions with scrupulous care, with a deep desire to maintain Israel's identity as the people of the law, as expressed not least in developing *halakoth* regarding the sabbath and particularly ritual purity. To attempt to undermine this picture by setting Neusner's findings aside, by failing to follow through the logic of Josephus' description of the Pharisees as ἀκρίβεις, by ignoring the testimony of Paul, or by banishing all the evidence of the Synoptics to as late a date as possible must be counted a policy of desperation. It is not necessary to argue that the picture applies equally to all Pharisees ("the Pharisees"). Nor does the precise relation of the *haberim* in particular to the Pharisees in general (or of Pharisees/*perushim* to sages, or of scribes to Pharisees) need to be resolved.[43] But *that there were at the time of Jesus a number of Pharisees, and probably a significant body of Pharisees, who felt passionately concerned to preserve, maintain, and defend Israel's status as the people of the covenant and the righteousness of the law, as understood in the already developed* halakoth, *must be regarded as virtually certain.*

. . . Sinners . . .

The thrust of Sanders' attack on older positions, however, is that the Pharisees would not have been critical of those who did not observe the law in the way and to the degree they accepted as their own obligation. In particular, they would not have condemned the ordinary people as "sinners" because they failed to observe all the [[72]] *halakoth* they took upon themselves. The "sinners" with whom Jesus consorted were genuinely "wicked" and "traitors."[44] And contraction of impurity did not constitute one a "sinner" or exclude from the covenant; it simply prevented participation in the temple cult for the period of impurity, and lack of concern about impurity outside the temple

---

43. Sanders questions whether *haberim* and Pharisees were identical but accepts that "before 70 there was probably an appreciable overlap between Pharisees and *haberim*" (*Jesus*, 187). Bowker (*Jesus*, 35) expresses the point neatly: "There is no indication that all Pharisees were members of a fellowship, although all members were Pharisees and accepted their views on Jewish law." See also A. Oppenheimer, *The 'Am Ha-aretz* (Leiden: E. J. Brill, 1977) 118–19; and Westerholm, *Jesus*, 13–15. It is worth noting that the more one discounts Josephus' picture of the Pharisees as widely influential (as Sanders does; see n. 28 above), the more closely they will tend to approximate to the *haberim*—whereas the less significant the *haberim* were within the important Pharisee sect, the more difficult it is to account for the strong influence they had on subsequent rabbinic ideals. In fact *haberim* and "Pharisee" are usually regarded as to all intents and purposes synonymous terms (see esp. Schürer, *History*, 398–99). On Pharisees and sages, scribes and Pharisees see Bowker, *Jesus*, esp. 13–15, 21–23. Rivkin (*Hidden Revolution*) sees "scribes" and "Pharisees" as synonymous terms; contrast J. Jeremias, *Jerusalem in the Time of Jesus* (Philadelphia: Fortress, 1969) 254–56.

44. Sanders, *Jesus*, esp. 177–80; see n. 68 below.

simply made one a non-*haber*.[45] Here again Sanders is justified in reacting against overstatements by too many New Testament scholars about Pharisaic hostility to the ordinary people.[46] But here too the question has to be asked whether Sanders in turn has *over*-reacted and tried to push the pendulum too far in the opposite direction.

The Role of Social Conflict in Group Self-Definition

We may consider, first of all, the insights of sociology and social anthropology into the nature of groups and their self-definition. Once we realize that the social identity of a group depends to a large extent on the distinctiveness of its practices and beliefs, it also becomes evident that the corollary of "identity" is "boundary," that self-definition involves self-differentiation.[47] In all this, ritual as a visible expression of social relationships usually plays a particularly important role.[48] Moreover, wherever there are other groups whose distinctives differ, each group is liable to be particularly protective of its identity and react strongly to any perceived threat to its boundaries.[49] Indeed, group conflict can play an important role in binding a group more closely together[50] and will often cause it to put still greater emphasis on the distinctiveness of its rituals. And particularly where groups are close to one another in origin or character or distinctives, the conflict is liable to be all the more intense.[51] It is the brother who threatens identity most ("sibling rivalry"); it is the party most like your own which threatens to draw away your support and undermine your reason for existence as a distinct entity.

Such generalized observations provide a remarkably close fit with the data we have already gleaned: the Pharisees as a distinct "sect" whose distinctives included particularly their zeal for scrupulous interpretation and observance of the law and, for at least a large proportion of their number, concern to maintain temple purity at the meal table (the "separated ones").[52] It is in-

---

45. Ibid., esp. 180–87.

46. Sanders' criticism is directed particularly against J. Jeremias, *New Testament Theology*, vol. 1, *The Proclamation of Jesus* (London: SCM, 1971) 108–13; see Sanders, *Jesus*, esp. 385 n. 14. But see also n. 68 below.

47. See esp. H. Mol, *Identity and the Sacred* (Oxford: Basil Blackwell, 1976) 57–58: "It is precisely the boundary . . . which provides the sense of identity."

48. Mol, *Identity*, 233; and M. Douglas, *Purity and Danger* (London: Routledge & Kegan Paul, 1966) 62–65, 128.

49. Douglas, *Purity*, 124. Cf. P. L. Berger and T. Luckman, *The Social Construction of Reality* (Baltimore: Penguin Books, 1967) 126: "The appearance of an alternative symbolic universe poses a threat because its very existence demonstrates empirically that one's own universe is less than inevitable."

50. See esp. L. A. Coser, *The Foundations of Social Conflict* (London: Routledge & Kegan Paul, 1956).

51. Coser, *Foundations*, 67–72.

52. See above, n. 23. As J. Neusner ("The Pharisees in the Light of the Historical Sources of Judaism," in *Formative Judaism*, Brown Judaic Studies 37 [Chico, Calif.: Scholars, 1982] 71–83) notes, since Pharisees lived among their fellow Jews (contrast the Qumran covenanters), "this made the actual purity-rules and food-restrictions all the more important, for

herently likely that such zeal would cause friction with other groups, not least with the other main "sects" of the time—Sadducees and Essenes. And so the evidence indicates, as we shall see. But it would also be unsurprising if at least some Pharisees refused to settle quietly behind their boundaries or opt merely for self-defence but sought to maintain their identity by taking the offensive. This was all the more true when there was any sense of conviction that what the Pharisee or *haber* practised was what God [[73]] required of Israel as a whole.[53] Certainly wherever the zeal of a Phinehas or a Mattathias was lauded and the concern of such heroes to preserve Israel's integrity as the people of God was taken as an ideal, a highly likely corollary would be a sharp criticism of any who seemed to threaten Israel's birthright or to deny Israel's obligation under the covenant—if not outright persecution of the offenders. None of this goes beyond the evidence already examined. On the contrary, the portrayal of the Pharisees in Mark 2 and 7 is shown to have considerable plausibility, and Paul's persecuting zeal to be not necessarily exceptional. The alternative of a quietistic group wholly absorbed in their own affairs and completely uncritical of others becomes increasingly unrealistic.[54]

Finally we should note that Sanders' argument is in danger of rebounding on him. For the effect of arguing that Jesus was very close to the Pharisees, not least on matters of the law, is to *increase* the likelihood of tension between Jesus and the Pharisees, not to lessen it. A Jesus who sat wholly loose to the law would pose little threat: he was self-condemned. But a successful Jesus who was observant of the law and yet not a Pharisee or *haber* was bound to be regarded as some sort of competitor and to cause some friction and conflict.[55] And a Jesus who was as loyal to the covenant but who had different ideas of what covenant loyalty involved would almost certainly pose a threat to Pharisaic self-understanding and identity. In particular, where issues such as sabbath or purity *halakoth* were put in question by Jesus' conduct, critical and defensive questions were bound to arise for those who prized such *halakoth*.

In short, given the data we have regarding the Pharisees in the period prior to 70 C.E., it would be very surprising had they *not* been critical of Jesus and his disciples.

---

only they set the Pharisee apart from the people among whom he constantly lived." Jeremias (*Jerusalem* 259–62), however, makes the surprising assumption that the regulations regarding the Qumran community can be used to build up a picture of "Pharisaic communities." But see Oppenheimer, *ʿAm Ha-aretz*, 147–51.

53. Bowker, *Jesus*, 21: "In *theory* the extent of the Hakamic movement was coterminous with the Jewish people. . . . The movement was not intended to be a party within Israel. It was intended to be Israel itself." There is all the difference, however, between such a self-perception or ideal and the social reality of such a movement. Bowker also notes that "Pharisees/*perushim*" probably first appeared as a description of the Hakamic movement used by *others* (p. 15). See also n. 63 below.

54. Neusner shows keen awareness of the sociological dimensions of his discussion; see, e.g., *Judaism*, 69–75.

55. For the possibility of quite serious conflict among the Pharisees themselves, see above, n. 9. That Pharisees would also differ in their attitudes to Jesus (cf. esp. Luke 13:31) is also inherently probable.

Who Were the Sinners?

But what about the "sinners"? Was the "offence" of Jesus at this point that he consorted with the wicked and promised them the kingdom even though they remained unrepentant of their wickedness?[56] Certainly Sanders is on good ground when he questions the too simplistic equation of "sinners" and "people of the land." In the Old Testament the word (ἁμαρτωλός) occurs most frequently in the Psalms, almost always translating רָשָׁע, and the rendering 'wicked' is wholly appropriate. Similarly with the word's most common use in the apocryphal writings (Sirach). But Sanders ignores the fact that the word is also used in a *factional* context to denote those outside the boundary of the group who use it, where wickedness, by definition, is conduct outside the boundary, conduct unacceptable to those inside.[57]

The most obvious example of this is where "sinner" is used more [[74]] or less as a synonym for "Gentile" (Ps 9:17; Tob 13:8[6]; *Jub.* 23:23–24; *Pss. Sol.* 1:1; 2:1–2; Luke 6:33 = Matt 5:47; Mark 14:41 pars.; Gal 2:15). In such passages the unifying concept is not that Gentiles are by definition murderers and robbers. Rather it is that their conduct lay outside the boundary of the law. They were literally lawless: they did not have the law because they did not belong to the covenant people, the people of the law. And so, not knowing the Torah, naturally they did not keep it.

More to the present point, however, is the fact that boundaries could also be drawn *within* the people of Israel, with "sinners" used to describe those of whom a particular faction disapproved. So in the case of 1 Maccabees, where the "sinners and lawless men" (1:34; 2:44, 48) certainly at least include those whom the Maccabeans regarded as apostate Jews, as Israelites who had abandoned the law.[58] Of course, what is in view here is no mere breach of sabbath or purity *halakoth* but full-scale apostasy, conduct no longer contained within the bounds of the covenant. Nevertheless, the fact remains that this is a factional viewpoint: "sinners" is language used by one group of Israelites to describe another.

What is at issue here is the definition of what conduct proper to the covenant actually involves and who determines it. In the case of 1 Maccabees the issue was fairly clear cut, at least for the Maccabeans: the Syrian sympathizers among the Jews had departed too far from the Torah. But in the subsequent period the issue became more blurred as different heirs of the first wave of Maccabean resistance sought to define in their own terms what walking in the ways of the Torah meant. For example, *Jubilees* shows that the calendar became an important bone of contention. The implication is clear:

56. Sanders, *Jesus*, 206.

57. In one place, Sanders does define "sinners" quite properly as "those beyond the pale and outside the common religion by virtue of their implicit or explicit rejection of the commandments of the God of Israel" (ibid., 210). But the question is, What counted as implicit rejection of the commandments? And in whose eyes?

58. J. A. Goldstein, *I Maccabees*, Anchor Bible 41 (New York: Doubleday & Co., 1976) 123–24.

that observance of a festival or ordinance whose date had been wrongly com-
puted was regarded (by those for whom *Jubilees* speaks) as *non*observance, as
failure to maintain the covenant, as walking in the errors of the Gentiles (particularly *Jub.* 6:32–35; also 23:16, 26).[59] *Jubilees* does not use the pejorative
"sinner" in the context, but the connotation is the same: those Jews who disagreed on the calendar showed disregard for the law of festivals and so put
themselves outside the covenant, made themselves like Gentile sinners.

A similar attitude is evident in the earliest parts of the *Enoch* corpus and
provides further evidence of a bitter calendrical dispute which divided Judaism probably in the second century B.C.E. "The righteous," "who walk in the
ways of righteousness," clearly marked themselves off from those who "sin
like the sinners" in wrongly reckoning the months and the feasts and the
years (82:4–7).[60] Less specific is the accusation of *1 Enoch* 1–5, where again a
clear line of distinction is drawn between the "righteous/chosen" and the
"sinners/impious" (1:1, 7–9; 5:6–7). But here too an internal Jewish [[75]] factional dispute is clearly in view: the sinners are addressed directly and
roundly rebuked—"You have not persevered, nor observed the law of the
Lord"—5:4). "Sinners" here are Jews who practised their Judaism differently
from the "righteous."[61]

A more virulent usage of the same kind occurs regularly, as we might have
expected, in the Dead Sea Scrolls. Again and again the political and religious
opponents of the sectarians are attacked as the wicked, the men of the lot of
Belial, who have departed from the paths of righteousness, transgressed the
covenant, and suchlike (e.g., CD 1:13–21; 1QS 2:4–5; 1QH 2:8–19; 1QpHab
2:1–4; 5:3–8). And again and again it is clear that the touchstone which divides "righteous" from "sinner" was not what the typical non-Essene would regard as blatant wickedness but the Torah as interpreted within the community
(e.g., CD 4:8; 1QS 5:7–11; 1QH 7:12)—that is, a sectarian interpretation which
would doubtless have been disputed at many points by the nonsectarians, who
were categorized in turn as "those who seek smooth things" and "deceivers"
(1QH 2:14–16; 4:6–8; 4QpNah 2:7–10). If we follow the usual view of these
opponents, such denunciations were directed particularly against the Pharisees:[62] in this case it is the Pharisees themselves who are the "sinners"! The
point, however, is that once again we have clear evidence that in the period
leading up to the time of Jesus, and in a community in existence during Jesus'

59. We need not presuppose that a clear rupture had already taken place within Israel
at this time such as the establishment of the Qumran community involved (see, e.g., Sanders,
Paul, 367–74; and J. C. VanderKam, *Textual and Historical Studies in the Book of Jubilees* [Mis-
soula, Mont.: Scholars, 1977] 281–83), but a factional attitude is clearly evident.

60. Sanders, *Paul*, 360; and G. W. E. Nickelsburg, *Jewish Literature between the Bible and
the Mishnah* (Philadelphia: Fortress, 1981) 48.

61. Cf. L. Hartman, *Asking for a Meaning: A Study of I Enoch 1–5*, Coniectanea biblica,
New Testament (Lund: C. W. K. Gleerup, 1979) 132.

62. See, e.g., M. Black, *The Scrolls and Christian Origins* (London: Thomas Nelson &
Sons, 1961) 23–24; G. Vermes, *The Dead Sea Scrolls* (London: William Collins & Co., 1977)
152; and Nickelsburg, *Jewish Literature*, 131.

ministry and beyond, "sinner" was used as a sectarian word to denounce those outside the bounds of the sect itself.[63]

A further example is the *Psalms of Solomon*, written less than a century before Jesus' ministry. They too clearly have been composed by those who regarded themselves as the "righteous," the "devout" (e.g., 3:3–7; 4:1, 8; 9:3; 10:6; 13:6–12; 15:6–7). But the "righteous" are not the covenant people as a whole; the usage is again clearly factional and amounts to a claim that only this faction properly "live in the righteousness of [the Lord's] commandments" (14:2). Similarly with the obverse in the repeated attacks on "sinners." Once again "sinners" are not synonymous with Gentiles or the blatantly wicked. On the contrary, "sinners" often refers to the Jewish opponents of the "devout," probably the Hasmonean Sadducees who had usurped the monarchy and defiled the sanctuary (1:8; 2:3; 7:2; 8:12–13; 17:5–8, 23).[64] According to 4:1–8 they sit in the Sanhedrin, they live in hypocrisy, they try to impress the people, they deceitfully quote the law. They do not maintain proper standards of ritual purity (8:12).[65] In the reckoning of the devout, such sinners have no part in Israel's inheritance: the promise was not made to them (17:5, 23). Here, then, is another case where "sinners" was used by Jews for other Jews who did not live by the standards of righteousness which the devout held before themselves.

[[76]] A similar internal Jewish polemic is evident in the document which of all the "intertestamental" literature is usually dated (in its present form) closest to the time of Jesus: the *Testament* (or *Assumption*) *of Moses*. In *T. Mos.* 7 (set in the final author's own time) there is a forthright attack on "godless men, who represent themselves as being righteous," "with hand and mind" they "touch unclean things" even though they themselves say, "Do not touch me, lest you pollute me" (7:3, 9–10). In view of our earlier findings we may well have to recognize here another attack on the Pharisees themselves, where

---

63. See further M. Newton, *The Concept of Purity at Qumran and in the Letters of Paul*, SNTSMS 53 (Cambridge: Cambridge Univ. Press, 1985), esp. 15–19. We need not attempt any further clarification on the very difficult question of whether the Qumran covenanters regarded themselves as the people of the covenant *in toto*, and so Pharisees, etc., as those outside the covenant ("sinners"); or as representative of the eschatological people of the covenant whose boundaries at least in principle stretched beyond the membership of the sect (see Sanders, *Paul*, 240–57). Either way the point remains the same: they regarded others as sinners who saw themselves as full, law-abiding members of the covenant people and who were so regarded by the bulk of their fellow Jews.

64. R. B. Wright, "Psalms of Solomon," in *The Old Testament Pseudepigrapha*, ed. J. Charlesworth, vol. 2 (New York: Doubleday & Co., 1985) 642. Sanders warns against a simple lumping-together of Sadducees with Hasmoneans (*Paul*, 403–4). A straightforward equation of the psalmist(s) with the Pharisees should also be avoided, although of the Jewish sects known to us "it is the Pharisees whom they most closely approximate" (Nickelsburg, *Jewish Literature*, 212).

65. The accusations of a passage like 8:11–13 should not be read as an impartial and objective testimony. This is factional propaganda and polemic, with a fair degree of exaggeration, reflecting the priority which the "righteous" placed on the correct observance of rituals laid down in the Torah.

different interpretations of ritual purity requirements were at the heart of the dispute.[66]

It should not escape notice that we have just reviewed a sequence of documents which include those having the strongest claim to represent attitudes of Jewish groups in Palestine contemporaneous with Jesus. And a common feature of them all is a factional conflict within the Judaism of their time. In view of this evidence we may well have to conclude that no period of ancient Judaism was so riven with factional dispute as the time of Jesus. Nor should we regard those labelled "sinners" simply as "apostates"[67]—those who in the eyes of all Jews had abandoned the covenant. That they *had* done so is certainly the view of the various authors; but that is simply to underline the factional character of these documents. From the perspective of those with a narrower definition of what covenant righteousness required it was natural to accuse those who disagreed with that definition of having abandoned the covenant. Such has been the attitude of rigorists and traditionalists throughout the ages. But those (i.e., sinners) who viewed things from *outside* the circle of the "righteous" would doubtless have a different understanding of the matter.

Against this background it has to be said that the Gospel usage of "sinners" makes perfect sense. It is wholly plausible to see "sinners" functioning in the Gospels as a *factional term*, describing those whose conduct was regarded as unacceptable to a sectarian mentality—that is, not just the blatantly wicked but those who did not accept the sect's interpretation of the law or live in sufficient accord with that interpretation. This fits too well with what we have learned of the Pharisees to be easily ignored. It is precisely those who were "scrupulous" in their adherence to the law and the ancestral customs who would be most liable to criticize others whose observance was, in their eyes, significantly less scrupulous (= *un*scrupulous). It is precisely those who were earnest in their practice of ritual purity who would be most likely to count others as sinners who did not share that zeal or who blatantly disregarded matters of purity. The fact that "tax collectors" are linked with "sinners" in the Synoptic testimony (Mark 2:15–16 pars.; Matt 11:19//Luke 7:34) should not be counted as evidence that "sinners" [[77]] meant blatant lawbreakers: tax collectors were despised more for national and political than religious reasons; only the Zealots would have regarded the job of tax collecting for the Romans as antithetical per se to a life lived in accordance with the law. More relevant is Mark 2:16 pars.: "sinners" as the antithesis of the "righteous." This is precisely the language of sectarianism reviewed above: the sin of the "sinners" is that they stand outside the boundaries of righteousness as defined by the "righteous." We need not assume that the Pharisees were as rigid on this matter as the Essenes: they did not necessarily regard all non-

---

66. Where opponents are identified, the usual assumption is that Pharisees are in view. See, e.g., D. Flusser, *Jesus* (New York: Herder & Herder, 1969) 47; and Jeremias, *Jerusalem,* 250.

67. As Sanders (*Paul*) tends to do—though, of course, he is treating the texts on their own terms.

Pharisees as sinners—perhaps only those who made light of Pharisaic concerns.[68] Nevertheless, the conclusion presses upon us: *The more that members of the Jewish community departed from the standards which the Pharisees as a rule saw to be necessary to maintain covenant righteousness, the more likely these Pharisees would be to dub them "sinners."*

Pharisees in Galilee?

One other issue cannot be ignored: whether the Gospel's portrayal of Jesus coming under attack from Pharisees *in Galilee* is credible. Sanders questions it, following the conclusion of Smith: "There is strong evidence that there were practically no Pharisees in Galilee during Jesus' lifetime."[69] But Smith's reading of the evidence is at least open to question, and may have to be discounted as tendentious.[70]

1. It is certainly the case that the only Pharisees Josephus speaks of in Galilee had been sent from Jerusalem (*J.W.* 2.569; *Life* 189–98). But in these accounts Josephus was not attempting to describe social or religious life in Galilee; he was writing a military history, and the Pharisees in question are mentioned because they served as emissaries from Jerusalem. For the same reason he speaks of synagogues only in the context of narrating factional disputes (*Life* 276–80, 293–303) and mentions the sabbath only when it inhibited military action (*Life* 159, 275–79; *J.W.* 2.634). A more accurate description of Josephus' testimony on this matter, therefore, would be that the only Pharisees Josephus had *cause* to mention in these passages were from Jerusalem. Since the matter of whether there were or were not Pharisees in Galilee is irrelevant to his purpose, his silence on the score means nothing.

2. Smith plays down the significance of the fact that the great Pharisee Yohanan ben Zakkai lived in Galilee—in a village called 'Arav—for eighteen years (probably between 20 and 40 C.E.), during which time only two cases of *halakah* were brought to him.[71] But as Neusner has noted, the explanation for this may simply be that Yohanan was not yet well known and that the Galileans preferred to seek *halakic* rulings elsewhere.[72] We may note in addition that [[78]] Hanina ben Dosa, who is once described as Yohanan's pupil (*b. Ber.*

---

68. The antagonism between Pharisees (or *haberim*) and the people of the land should not be exaggerated; see Oppenheimer, *'Am Ha-aretz*, 156–69; and Sanders, *Jesus*, esp. 177–80. We should note also the references in Luke 7:36; 11:37; 14:1, which speak of Pharisaic hospitality. But Jeremias has not overstated the position as much as Sanders claims (see n. 46 above).

69. M. Smith, *Jesus the Magician* (New York: Harper & Row, 1978) 157; cited by Sanders, *Jesus*, 292, 390 n. 90. Josephus (*Ant.* 18.15) does imply that the Pharisees' influence was greatest in the cities, though in the same context he refers to their influence on the people, the multitude (18.15, 17).

70. I owe several observations in what follows to a working paper prepared by my research student Paul Trebilco.

71. Smith, *Jesus*, 157.

72. J. Neusner, *A Life of Rabban Yohanan ben Zakkai*, 2nd ed. (Leiden: E. J. Brill, 1970) 47.

34b), also came from ʿArav.[73] Yohanan's period of residence in Galilee may not therefore be read as evidence for Pharisaic disengagement from Galilee. On the contrary, it may be evidence of a deliberate Pharisaic strategy to station some of the most promising younger Pharisees in different parts of the country to ensure that *halakic* rulings were readily available.[74] Indeed, if part of Pharisaic motivation in practising temple purity outside the temple was to demonstrate and maintain covenant righteousness throughout Israel, a natural corollary would be for some at least to follow the Pharisaic *halakoth* in different population centres throughout the promised land.

3. Smith has overlooked a further piece of evidence of potential importance. In *Ant.* 20.38–48, Josephus narrates the conversion of Izates, king of Adiabene, who initially had been told that circumcision would not be necessary. But then another Jew arrived, one Eleazar, who came from Galilee and who had a reputation for being very strict (πάνυ ἀκριβής) concerning the ancestral laws (20.43). When he learned of the situation he sternly warned Izates against committing the impiety of offending against the law and thereby against God (20.44). Since ἀκριβής is Josephus' characteristic description of the Pharisees (see above, "The Pharisees in Josephus"), the most obvious conclusion is that Eleazar was a Pharisee. And even if he was not so designated he clearly shared the typical Pharisaic concern to maintain the law and the traditions with scrupulous care. Either way, Eleazar confirms that at the time of Jesus Galilee was by no means devoid of those who observed the law with Pharisaic strictness. Moreover, the episode provides some confirmation that such a one would also and naturally be concerned that others who yoked themselves to Israel should be properly observant of the law. The issue here, of course, is that of circumcision, but in the perspective of the devout, proper observance of food laws and sabbath were equally obligatory for the member of the covenant people.[75] And the readiness to find fault with others who failed to maintain that observance would likely be equally vocal.

4. Finally, we may simply repeat the point already made: that the evidence of the Gospels themselves cannot *all* be dismissed or postponed to a post-70 context. Passages like Mark 2 and 7 in particular must be allowed as testimony at least for the presence of *some* Pharisees on *some* occasions in Galilee in the period before 70 C.E. No more than that is needed.[76] It is not even necessary to argue for many Pharisees having residence in Galilee. As Mark

---

73. Ibid., 47, 51.

74. Ibid., 48; and Sean Freyne, *Galilee from Alexander the Great to Hadrian, 323 B.C.E. to 135 B.C.E.: A Study of Second Temple Judaism* (Wilmington, Del.: Michael Glazier, n.d.) 317, 321–23, 341 n. 78. I. Abrahams (*Studies in Pharisaism and the Gospels*, ser. 1 [1917; New York: Ktav, 1967]) refers to Büchler's conjecture that Shammai was a Galilean. See further Freyne, *Galilee*, 341 n. 74.

75. Circumcision: esp. Gen 17:9–14. Food laws: esp. Leviticus 11; Deuteronomy 14; 1 Macc 1:62–63; cf. Acts 10:14; 11:3. Sabbath: esp. Exod 31:12–17; Isa 56:6–8.

76. Smith's talk of "the synoptics' picture of a Galilee swarming with Pharisees" (*Jesus*, 157) is an unnecessary exaggeration.

7:1 indicates, Pharisees may have been sent or have come down from Jerusalem to view the new phenomenon which Jesus represented.[77] In short, the relative lack of reference to Pharisees in Galilee [[79]] constitutes very little of a case for rejecting the Gospels' own testimony on the point. There is evidence that some Pharisees, or equally strict devotees to the law and the customs, did live in or come from Galilee. And the likelihood that such a popular movement as the one represented by Jesus would attract attention from the larger grouping of Pharisees in Jerusalem must be considered rather high, and certainly much higher than either Smith or Sanders allows.

We may conclude, therefore, that Pharisees were liable to be critical of conduct and teaching which called into some question the priorities they regarded as covenant imperatives. Those who sat light to this righteousness they would regard as unrighteous, or "sinners." If Jesus was seen to encourage such attitudes they would be likely to criticize him too. All the more so if on other points Jesus and the Pharisees shared similar concerns: the closer Jesus was to the Pharisees, the more he would actually constitute a threat to their identity and boundaries, and the more hostile they would be to him. There is no good reason to doubt that Jesus came under such criticism already during his period of success and popularity in Galilee. The Gospel pictures offered in Mark 2 and 7 are at this point wholly plausible and should not be lightly discarded. There is no need to exaggerate Pharisaic influence on religious attitudes and practices of the day,[78] or Pharisaic hostility to non-Pharisees or to "people of the land" in particular. But neither is it helpful to resort to caricature, as though the Gospels' portrayal depended on the assumption that the Pharisees were "supersnoopers" who spent their time looking for infringements of sabbath or purity *halakoth*. All that the data require is that there were Pharisees in Galilee at some points during Jesus' ministry who were critical of his conduct, in respect of sabbath, ritual purity, and table-fellowship with those whom the Pharisees regarded as "sinners." That portrayal fits too well with all the available data to be set aside.

. . . And Jesus

Despite the objection raised most recently by Sanders, the earliest portrayal of Jesus in relation to Pharisees and sinners is remarkably consistent with what we know of his Pharisaic contemporaries. The degree to which the evidence is mutually supportive has not been given sufficient weight.

1. The Pharisees were scrupulous in their interpretation of the law and maintenance of the customs handed down (so Josephus; and Paul and the Gospels agree).

---

77. Apart from Josephus' accounts of Pharisees being sent to Galilee (*J.W.* 2.569; *Life* 189–98), there is a rabbinic tradition that one of Johanan's pupils was sent to investigate a *hasid* living at Beth Rama (probably Galilee) who is said to have been strangely ignorant of purity regulations (Freyne, *Galilee*, 316). See also Vermes, *Jesus*, 56–57.

78. See again n. 28 above.

2. One very important aspect of that strictness in relation to law and tradition was a concern to maintain temple purity at the daily meal table (so rabbinic tradition, which is strongly supported by [[80]] the Gospels and consistent with a view which Paul had abandoned [contrast Gal 1:13–14; Rom 14:14]).

3. Such zeal for the law as expressed not least in ritual was probably one of the chief identity markers of the "sect" of the Pharisees, which marked them off from other Jews at least in the degree of their devotion. Where any threat to that identity and boundary was perceived, Pharisees were liable to react against that threat; the more zealous they were, the more violent the reaction (as Paul himself confirms; and again the Gospels cohere).

4. As a sect with clear ideas of what character of life and conduct was required to maintain the covenant righteousness of the people of God, Pharisees were highly likely to regard as "sinners" those who disagreed with them and who lived in open disregard of this righteousness—as had the groups behind the early *Enoch* writings, the *Psalms of Solomon*, and the Dead Sea Scrolls (so again the Gospels).

5. Other scattered evidence refutes the notion that the Pharisees would have avoided Galilee, and suggests rather that at least some Pharisees would have been concerned enough about a movement in Galilee like that around Jesus to inquire more closely into it and to criticize it for failure on sensitive points where they saw their interpretation of Israel's heritage being disregarded or threatened (as, once again, the Gospels narrate).

In short, it is very likely, after all, that the portrayal of Pharisees, sinners, and Jesus in passages like Mark 2 and 7 accords very closely with the historical realities of Jesus' ministry and may not be discounted as a retrojecton of later controversies into the period of Jesus' ministry.

Indeed, far from being left with an uncomfortable wedge between Jesus and Gentile Christianity, the overall perspective we have gained from our study enables us to recognize an important line of continuity between Jesus and his successors. For behind the particular objections and charges levelled against Jesus was the central fact that Jesus was ignoring and abolishing boundaries which more sectarian attitudes had erected *within* Israel. This is in no way an anti-Semitic conclusion, nor should it be regarded as a blanket criticism of all Pharisees. It simply attempts to reckon seriously with what was an *internal* Jewish dispute, a confrontation between Jewish factions. Nor does it necessarily implicate the Pharisees in Jesus' crucifixion: that is a further question requiring further discussion. Nor does it solve all problems regarding the transition from Jesus to Paul: that too requires more careful delineation. But at least it does help us see how a Christianity which broke through the boundaries of Israel's own distinctiveness sprang from a Jesus who posed such a challenge to the boundary between Pharisee and sinner. In other words, the recognition of [[81]] the Jewishness of Jesus need not separate Jesus from the Christianity he founded, just as the recognition of the Christian significance of Jesus need not separate him from the faith of his own people.

Additional Note

For another critique of Sanders' *Jesus and Judaism*, in some degree complementary with [[the present essay]], see B. D. Chilton, "Jesus and the Repentance of E. P. Sanders," *Tyndale Bulletin* 39 (1988) 1–18.

A. I. Baumgarten, "The Pharisaic *Paradosis*," *HTR* 80 (1987) 63–77, argues that "the terms *paradosis* [['tradition']] of the elders and of the fathers were deliberate attempts by the Pharisees to give their tradition a pedigree it might have seemed to lack. As such, they hoped to defend their tradition at a vulnerable point, and raise it from merely that of a school to the patrimony of the nation" (p. 77).

R. A. Wild, "The Encounter between Pharisaic and Christian Judaism: Some Early Gospel Evidence," *NovT* 27 (1985) 105–24, takes up Neusner's view of Pharisaism at the time of Jesus as a "sectarian movement rather than the dominant form of Judaism." From this he deduces the unlikelihood of Pharisees being so concerned about the observance of Jesus' disciples as the Jesus-tradition depicts (referring particularly to Mark 7:1–23 and 2:15–17), unless "Jesus and his disciples actually did follow the Pharisaic way of life" (p. 118; similarly p. 122). Wild thus shows no awareness of the factionalism or concern to define and defend boundaries evidenced in the talk of "sinners," as demonstrated above, but he rightly detects something of the "in-house" nature of such passages—"in-house" as reflecting debates both between fellow Jews (Christian and non-Christian) and between fellow Christians.

C. Tuckett, "Q, the Law and Judaism," *Law and Religion. Essays on the Place of the Law in Israel and Early Christianity*, ed. B. Lindars, Cambridge: James Clarke (1988) 90–101, is sympathetic with Wild's suggestion, that

> Originally Jesus' disciples had close links with the pharisaic movement, so that other Pharisees apparently expected the disciples to conform to their own mores. Such a picture emerges from both the Markan and Q material examined. However it is only in Q that Jesus himself emerges as one who affirms these links positively. . . . It would thus appear that the community which preserved the Q material also preserved positive links with the pharisaic movement in a way that most other primitive Christian groups about which we have any evidence did not. . . . Certainly Q reflects a strongly conservative Jewish-Christian group within primitive Christianity.

He concludes that

> at some stage at least, the Q community may have had a close relationship with the small sectarian movement in pre-70 Judaism which we call Pharisaism. No doubt this relationship was a dialectical one in that non-Christian Pharisees were evidently hostile to the Christian group. But the very existence of such hostility may well be evidence that the Christian group was claiming to be a genuine part of the pharisaic movement. (p. 100)

Similarly K. Berger, "Jesus als Pharisäer und frühe Christen als Pharisäer," *NovT* 30 (1988) 231–62, maintains that the Jesus-tradition evidences a degree of mutual concern between Pharisees and Jesus, both in matters on which they agreed (Mark 12:19–34) and in matters which they thought worthy of discussion (p. 237). Particularly important was the issue of purity, with its social implications for group identity and boundaries (p. 238). Where Jesus differed from Pharisees was in his understanding of the positive power of purity/holiness ("offensive Reinheit/Heiligkeit"), a power to overcome impurity, through table-fellowship, physical contact, etc. In effect Jesus lived a new kind of Pharisaism, "an eschatological-pneumatic Pharisaism," where purity and the question of boundaries were still the central problem, but where Jesus' power actually achieved the objectives of the Pharisees (pp. 246–47). So too Jesus did not contest the Pharisees' standing with God. The problem lay not with their lacking righteousness but with their unwillingness to rejoice over the acceptance of sinners (p. 249). "According to the Synoptics, the Pharisees failed not through their achievements-righteousness, but in that they did not go along with Jesus' openness to the sinners and impure" (p. 250). Although I am not entirely happy with Berger's broad use of "Pharisaism" ("Jesus is a Pharisee with authority"—p. 247), my main dispute with him would be over his assumption of a "diaspora-Pharisaism" particularly marked by law-observance (p. 232)—again not giving enough weight to the factionalism of Palestinian Judaism.

L. W. Countryman, *Dirt, Greed and Sex*, London: SCM (1989) sums up the significance of purity ritual well and in a way which reinforces the argument of the final paragraph of [[the present essay]], though without any engagement with Sanders:

> For the Hellenistic Jew of the Diaspora, purity continued to function almost entirely as a way of distinguishing Jew from Gentile. . . . In Palestine, by contrast, the purity code was, to a large extent, simply the way of life of the dominant population group. It served . . . as a daily reminder of Israelite identity. Of more importance, however, was that particular interpretations of the purity code, especially those of the Essenes and Pharisees, became ways of distinguishing one Jew from another, both in terms of their understanding of the code and in terms of their devotion to the keeping of it. In both cases, the code was still serving its intrinsic function of establishing and keeping boundaries; the boundaries thus guarded, however—ethnic in one case, sectarian in the other—were significantly different. (pp. 64–65)

Similarly A. J. Saldarini, "The Social Class of the Pharisees in Mark," *The Social World of Formative Christianity and Judaism*, ed. J. Neusner et al., Philadelphia: Fortress (1988) 69–77. He takes up J. Neyrey, "The Idea of Purity in Mark's Gospel, *Semeia* 35 (1986) 91–128, who shows that the purity rules in Mark function as boundary-setting mechanisms for the community. Saldarini concludes:

Thus the Pharisees were the defenders of a certain kind of community, and Jesus challenged the Pharisees' vision of community by attacking their purity regulations concerning washing and food as well as Sabbath practice. The effect of Jesus' teaching was to widen the community boundaries and loosen the norms for membership in his community. (p. 72)

Compare and contrast H. Maccoby, *Judaism in the First Century*, London: Sheldon (1989), who, as usual, drives his own line of argument through the evidence with single-mindedness. The Pharisees were "a three-tiered movement consisting of Sages, rank-and-file Pharisees, and 'people of the land.' . . . The Pharisees never regarded themselves as a sect, but as the religious leaders of the whole people. . . . [They were] the religious leaders of the overwhelming majority of the nation" (pp. 12–13). "Jesus was probably a member of that movement [the Pharisees]" and "his hostile critics were probably not the Pharisees but the Sadducees," with "Pharisees" later substituted for "Sadducees" in the tradition (pp. 42–51). "Jesus' policy towards tax gatherers . . . was perfectly in accord with Pharisee thinking" (pp. 100–102). Despite his knowledge of rabbinic Judaism, Maccoby's grasp of the realities of pre-70 Judaism is exceedingly tenuous.

P. S. ALEXANDER

Jesus and the Golden Rule

[[363]] Any comparison of Hillel and Jesus must address, sooner or later, the problem of the Golden Rule. Both Hillel and Jesus are credited with having quoted the Rule and both are said to have used it in rather similar situations as a summary of the law. This apparent agreement between these two influential Palestinian Jewish teachers from the turn of the eras is striking and merits close investigation. Obvious questions arise. Are the traditions which attribute the Rule to Hillel and to Jesus reliable? What does the Rule mean and who was its author? What is involved in the claim that the Rule is the sum of the law? Does the Rule throw any light on first-century Judaism or on the relationship between Judaism and Christianity? We shall try to answer some of these questions in the present essay. But first we must define the Rule itself.

The Golden Rule is not a fixed form of words, but a proposition which can be expressed in a variety of ways. The origins of the term are surprisingly obscure. Though it was probably first attached to the saying in Matt 7:12, "All things whatsoever ye would that men should do to you, do so even to them" (KJV), it was rapidly extended to cover all other forms of this moral maxim. It is commonly quoted, both in everyday speech and in literature, not in its classic Matthean wording, but in shorter, crisper versions, such as, "Do as you would be done by."[1]

Reprinted, with permission, from P. S. Alexander, "Jesus and the Golden Rule," in *Hillel and Jesus: Comparative Studies of Two Major Religious Leaders* (ed. J. H. Charlesworth and L. L. Johns; Minneapolis: Fortress, 1997) 363–88.

1. The epithet "golden" expresses the value, excellence, or utility of the Rule (cf. Golden Mean, Golden Section, Golden Number, Golden Age). The designation "Golden Rule" was first applied to Matt 7:12, for it is there, not in the parallel in Luke 6:31, that the excellence of the maxim is implied ("for this is the law and the prophets"). This use of the term is apparently modern. The earliest example cited is Gibbon, *Decline and Fall of the Roman Empire*, chap. 54, footnote: "Calvin violated the golden rule of doing as he would be done by." The usage is, however, anticipated by Isaac Watts in 1741 ("that golden principle of morality which our blessed Lord has given us") and by R. Godfrey in 1674 ("that Golden Law

[[364]] The fact that the Golden Rule embraces a range of verbally different utterances, which are thought of as expressing the same basic idea, means that it is defined primarily in terms of concepts. Thus, in tracing its history, we are tracing the history of an idea. We should be in no doubt at the outset of our inquiry that this will complicate matters, since the history of an idea is much more difficult to unravel than the transmission of a stable and distinctive form of words.

The Golden Rule, the Historical Hillel, and the Historical Jesus

What evidence do we have for linking the Hillel and the Jesus of history with the Golden Rule? In the case of Hillel, it is much weaker than has sometimes been supposed. There is only one text in the whole of classic rabbinic literature which attributes the saying to him, namely, *b. Šabbat* 31a. This simple fact should give us pause for thought. The Babylonian Talmud was redacted at least five hundred years after the time of Hillel. We should be extremely wary of basing deductions regarding the historical Hillel on so late a source.

This caution is amply reinforced by an analysis of the literary context in which the attribution is found. To clarify the range and depth of the problems concerning the historicity of the attribution, we must set out the relevant text in full. The language of the passage is, for the most part, simple, elegant Hebrew. But certain words and phrases (indicated in the translation by underlining) are in Aramaic.

(A) Our Rabbis taught (*tānû rabbānan*): A man should always be gentle like Hillel, and not impatient like Shammai. [[365]]

(B) It once happened (*ma'aśeh be*) that two men made a wager with each other, saying, "He who goes and makes Hillel angry shall receive four hundred zuz." One of them said, "I will make him angry."

That day was the Sabbath eve and Hillel was washing his head. The man went, passed by the door of Hillel's house, and called out, "Is Hillel here? Is Hillel here?" Hillel robed, went out to him and said, "My son, what do you seek?" "I have a question to ask," said he. "Ask, my son," he said to him. He asked, "Why are the heads of the Babylonians round?" "My son, you have asked a great question," said he. "It is because they do not have skillful midwives."

The man departed, tarried awhile, returned, and said, "Is Hillel here? Is Hillel here?" Hillel robed, went out to meet him, and said, "My son,

---

do as you would be done by"). For R. Recorde in 1542 "the Golden Rule" referred, not to Matt 7:12, but to the mathematical rule of proportions, the rule of three; cf. *Oxford English Dictionary*, 2nd ed., 6.656, s.v. "golden." Attempts to trace the term back to the Renaissance or the Middle Ages (see A. Dihle, "Goldene Regel," *Reallexikon für Antike und Christentum*, 11 [Stuttgart, 1981], col. 930) are purely speculative. The designation of the maxim in Matt 7:12 as "the Golden Rule" probably originated in England. From there it passed over to Germany and France. See L. J. Philippidis, *Die "Goldene Regel" religionsgeschichtlich untersucht, Inaugural-Dissertation zur Erlangung der Doktorwürde der Hohen Philosophischen Fakultät der Universität Leipzig* (Leipzig, 1930) 11–15.

what do you seek?" "I have a question to ask," said he. "Ask, my son," he said to him. He asked, "Why are the eyes of the Palmyrenes bleary?" "My son, you have asked a great question," said he. "It is because they live in sandy places."

The man departed, tarried awhile, returned, and said, "Is Hillel here? Is Hillel here?" Hillel robed, went out to meet him, and said, "My son, what do you seek?" "I have a question to ask," said he. "Ask, my son," he said to him. He asked, "Why are the feet of the Africans wide?" "My son, you have asked a great question," said he. "It is because they live in watery marshes." The man said, "I have many questions to ask, but I am afraid that you may become angry." He robed, sat before him, and said, "Ask all the questions you have to ask." He said, "Are you the Hillel whom they call the Nasi of Israel?" "Yes," he said. "If that is so," said he, "may there not be many more like you in Israel!" "Why, my son?" asked he. "Because I have lost four hundred zuz through you," complained he. "Control your-self!" he answered. "It is better that you should lose four hundred zuz on account of Hillel, and a further four hundred zuz, than that Hillel should lose his temper."

(C) Our Rabbis taught (*tānû rabbānan*): Once (*ma᾽aseh be*) a certain heathen came before Shammai and asked him, "How many Torahs do you have?" "Two," he replied, "the Written Torah and the Oral [[366]] Torah." The heathen said, "I believe you about the Written Torah, but not about the Oral. Make me a proselyte on condition that you teach me only the Written Torah." Shammai scolded him and angrily ordered him to get out.

When he went before Hillel, he made him a proselyte. On the first day Hillel taught him ᾽*alef, bêt, gîmel, dālet*. The following day he reversed the order of the letters. The heathen protested, "But yesterday you did not teach them to me thus." "Must you not rely upon me in this matter?" Hillel replied. "Then rely on me with respect also to the Oral Torah."

(D) On another occasion it happened (*šûv ma᾽aśeh be*) that a certain heathen came before Shammai and said to him, "Make me a proselyte on condition that you teach me the whole Torah while I stand on one foot. Shammai drove him out with the builder's cubit which was in his hand. When he went before Hillel, he made him a proselyte. He said to him, "What is hateful to you, do not do to your neighbor. That is the whole Torah. The rest is commentary. Go and learn!"

(E) On another occasion it happened (*šûv ma᾽aśeh be*) that a certain heathen was passing behind a school and heard the voice of a teacher recit-ing, "And these are the garments which they shall make: a breastplate and an ephod" (Ex 28:4). Said he, "For whom are these?" "For the high priest," said they. The heathen said to himself, "I will go and become a proselyte, so that I may be appointed a high priest." So he went before Shammai and said to him, "Make me a proselyte on condition that you appoint me high priest." Shammai drove him out with the builder's cubit which was in his hand.

When he went before Hillel, he made him a proselyte. Hillel said to him, "No one is appointed king who does not know the arts of government. Go and study the arts of government!" So he went and read. When he came to the words, "The stranger that comes nigh shall be put to death" (Num 1:51), he asked Hillel, "To whom does this verse apply?" "Even to David, king of Israel," was the answer. Thereupon the proselyte reasoned *a fortiori*, "If the words, 'The stranger that comes nigh shall be put to death,' are applied in Scripture to [[367]] Israel, who are called sons of the Omnipresent, and whom in his love he designated, 'Israel, my firstborn son' (Ex 4:22), how much more do they apply to a mere proselyte, who comes with his staff and his bag!" So he went before Shammai and said to him, "Could I ever have been eligible to be high priest? Is it not written in the Torah, 'The stranger that comes nigh shall be put to death'?" He went before Hillel and said to him, "O gentle Hillel, may blessings rest on your head for bringing me under the wings of the Shekhinah!"

(F) Some time later, when the three proselytes met in one place, they said, "Shammai's impatience nearly drove us out of the world, but Hillel's gentleness brought us under the wings of the Shekhinah!"

This unusually long pericope is clearly demarcated by the inclusio of the superscription (section A) and the subscription (section F). The purpose of the unit is to illustrate, by a series of exempla (*maʿaśîm*), the proposition that "a man should always be gentle like Hillel and not impatient like Shammai." The exempla fall into two groups, the first of which is represented by section B, and the second by sections C, D, and E—a fact signalled by the repetition of *tānû rabbanān* at the beginning of section C. Section B concerns Hillel alone, whereas sections C, D, and E are structurally similar, they contrast Hillel and Shammai, and they are linked by the theme of conversion. All the individual anecdotes may once have existed independently, but they have been marshalled here into an effective and coherent unity.

There can be little doubt that this pericope was not composed by the redactor of the Babli, but was taken over by him more or less intact from tradition. Evidence for this may be found not only in the formula *tānû rabbānan*, which shows that he claimed the material was Tannaitic in origin, but also in the strange fact that the pericope bears absolutely no relationship to the Mishnaic lemma to which it is now attached. It cannot have been generated or influenced by the lemma, but must have come as a block from elsewhere.

Two similar blocks of material are, in fact, found in ARN A 15 and B 29. They are completely at home there. Large narrative structures, such as we have here, are comparatively rare in rabbinic literature, but are characteristic of ARN. Moreover, the pericope is attached in ARN to an appropriate lemma from *m. ʾAbot*: "Be not easily [[368]] angered." It is not inconceivable that this lemma generated the pericope. The versions of the pericope in ARN A and B differ considerably from each other and from the version in *b. Šab*. The Babli version is much closer to that in ARN A and is most plausibly explained as a reworking of it.[2]

---

2. Sections A and B of the pericope are paralleled in the late sources Kallah Rabbati 10:3 and Sefer Ha-Maʿaśiyyôt 84 (ed. M. Gaster, *The Exempla of the Rabbis* [New York, 1968] 55f.). Section E is paralleled in SefMaʿas 31 (Gaster, p. 23). The intrusion of Aramaic into

Interestingly, section D of the Babli version (the story of Hillel and the Golden Rule) is absent from the ARN versions, though it would have been totally appropriate to the ARN context. The conclusion seems unavoidable: section D is a post-ARN intrusion into the pericope. We can only speculate about its origins, but it is surely rather curious that a similar story is told in ARN B 26 about Aqiba. It seems likely that the Babylonian redactor of the tradition, whether deliberately or through faulty memory, transferred the Aqiba story to Hillel.

Tradition-historical analysis of the pericope suggests the late and unhistorical character of the anecdote about Hillel and the Golden Rule. The style of the pericope points in the same direction. The unit reflects the unmistakable elements of hagiography and is most plausibly dated to a time when Hillel and Shammai belonged to the distant past and had been reduced to stereotypes—the former to a paragon of scholarly virtue, the latter to his foil. The stereotypical nature of section A is particularly strong. There Hillel is depicted as playing the age-old role of the sage who is able to answer conundrums and riddles.

Thus, the case against the historicity of the tradition is very strong. But nothing can be conclusively proved. There will doubtless always be some who will remain unmoved by the kind of argument just advanced and who will invoke the rabbis' extraordinary powers of [[369]] memory to argue that this Talmudic unit contains early, reliable tradition, and may even preserve the Aramaic *ipsissima verba* [['very words']] of Hillel. What of it if a similar story is told of another early authority? Could not both Hillel and Aqiba have cited the Golden Rule?

In the last analysis, such views cannot be decisively refuted, historical scholarship is not a matter of proof, or even of argument, but of judgment. Having weighed all the evidence, I can only conclude that there are no good historical grounds for stating that Hillel himself ever cited the Golden Rule; he cites it only in later rabbinic fiction.

The evidence that Jesus quoted the Golden Rule is much stronger. The Rule is found both in the Sermon on the Mount (Matt 7:12) and in the Sermon on the Plain (Luke 6:31). It is not possible here to do justice to the complex source- and redaction-critical problems raised by the comparison of these two texts. It must suffice to present Fitzmyer's plausible conclusion:

---

the predominantly Hebrew text is puzzling. The fact that the Golden Rule itself is quoted in Aramaic is easily explained: Aramaic seems to have been the language in which the maxim was current in rabbinic circles. The form of the maxim is close to that found in the Book of Tobit (4:15). Though it is still an open question whether Tobit was composed originally in Aramaic or in Hebrew, Jerome knew only the Aramaic. This suggests that by the Amoraic period, the Aramaic text had prevailed in Palestine. Some older writers assume that Hillel was consciously quoting Tobit, but it is more likely that the maxim had entered general parlance. More puzzling is the fact that some of the narrative framework is in Aramaic. This phenomenon occurs in all three recensions of the pericope.

Despite the many differences in the two sermons, there is a basic similarity in them which makes one argue for a nucleus sermon that was inherited by "Q" and that the two evangelists have reworked each in his
own way. The similarities are such that they suggest that the tradition preserved something of an extended sermon delivered by Jesus towards the
beginning of his ministry.[3]

The Golden Rule belongs to the "nucleus sermon."

Though the substance of the Rule in both Gospels is patently the same, the
exact wording differs. The differences may be displayed graphically as follows:

Matthew: πάντα οὖν ὅσα ἐὰν θέλητε ἵνα τοιῶσιν ὑμῖν οἱ ἄνθρωποι,

Luke: καθὼς θέλετε ἵνα ποιῶσιν ὑμῖν οἱ ἄνθρωποι,

Matthew: οὕτως καὶ ὑμεῖς ποιεῖτε αὐτοῖς

Luke: ποιεῖτε αὐτοῖς ὁμοίως

Matthew: [['In everything, then, whatever you would have people
                    do to you, thus also you do to them']]

Luke: [['just as you would have people
                    do to you,   do to them']]

Of the variants here, the Matthean πάντα οὖν [['in everything, then']] is probably secondary. The Matthean οὕτως and the Lukan ὁμοίως may both be secondary, [[370]] since both words are characteristic of their authors. The
resumptive adverb is not strictly necessary, though it improves the style in
Greek. In comparison to the Matthean ὅσα ἐὰν [['whatever']], the Lukan καθὼς
[['just as']] is, on the face of it, more likely to be original. Thus behind the two
versions may stand the formulation, καθὼς θέλετε ἵνα ποιῶσιν ὑμῖν οἱ ἄνθρωποι,
ποιεῖτε αὐτοῖς [['just as you would have people do to you']], which each Gospel
writer has styled in his own distinctive way.[4] There is no problem retroverting
this statement into Aramaic, the vernacular of Jesus, and the language in
which the Golden Rule apparently circulated among Palestinian Jews.[5]

There is an indirect line of argument which lends some support to the
view that the tradition of Jesus' use of the Golden Rule is sound. It would be a
truism to say that the concept of love plays an important part in early Christian teaching. This stress on love is found in diverse early Christian texts. It is

---

3. J. A. Fitzmyer, *The Gospel According to Luke* (AB; New York, 1981) 1.627.

4. On the redactional problems, see W. D. Davies and D. C. Allison, *The Gospel According to St. Matthew* (ICC; Edinburgh, 1988) 1.688; I. H. Marshall, *The Gospel of Luke* (Exeter,
1978) 261.

5. G. Dalman, *Jesus-Jeshua: Studies in the Gospels*, trans. P. P. Levertoff (London, 1929)
226, offers the following retroversion: *kol ma de-ʾattun baʿayin de-yaʿbedun lekhon bene nasha
hakheden ʾuph ʾattun hawon ʿabedin lehon*. In the light of our discussion of the redaction of the
saying, we may refine this to *kema de-ʾattun baʿayin de-yaʿbedun lekhon bene nasha hawon ʿabedin
lehon*. See further, T. W. Manson, *The Sayings of Jesus* (London, 1949) 18–19.

so ubiquitous that it is reasonable to suppose that it reflects something in the teaching of Jesus himself. More specifically, evidence suggests that Jesus laid great store in the Love Command of Lev 19:18 and that the early Christian writers remembered this fact and pondered upon it. In Gal 5:14 Paul asserts that the whole law is fulfilled by keeping the Love Command. In Gal 6:2 he picks up this idea again in the following terms: "Bear one another's burdens, and so fulfil the law of Christ." Could the "law of Christ" here refer in an historical sense to the law which Christ himself established as the most fundamental of all the laws, namely, the Love Command? Paul returns to this theme in Rom 13:9, where he claims that all the other commandments are summed up in the sentence, "You shall love your neighbor as yourself." James, writing from a different standpoint, also stresses the importance of the Love Commandment. It is "the royal law": "If you really fulfill the royal law, according to the Scripture, 'You shall love your neighbor as yourself,' you do well" (Jas 2:8). The Gospels of Matthew (22:34–40) and Mark (12:28–34) take up the same refrain.

[[371]] This agreement is impressive and points to a very early element of Christian tradition, probably deriving from Jesus himself. But as we shall see below, the Golden Rule tended to be regarded in early Judaism as simply a variant of the Love Command. Indeed, it is noteworthy that Paul in Rom 13:10 glosses the Love Command with what sounds like an echo of the negative form of the Golden Rule: "love does no wrong to a neighbor." Consequently, the Golden Rule fits snugly into Jesus' teaching and is consonant with his emphasis on the centrality of the Love Command.

We are left, then, with an asymmetry in our evidence. That Jesus cited the Golden Rule is well-attested and highly probable. That Hillel quoted it cannot absolutely be ruled out, since we are in no position to assert such a negative. But there is no reliable evidence that he did. The conclusion is unavoidable: there is no logic in comparing and contrasting how the historical Hillel and the historical Jesus used the Golden Rule. The Rule may enlighten us as to the teachings of Jesus, but it cannot enlighten us as to the teachings of Hillel.

Origins and Originality of the Golden Rule

We turn now to the question of the originality of the Golden Rule. For the sake of argument, we will lay aside the foregoing reservations and assume that Hillel and Jesus did indeed quote the Golden Rule. Would the formulations of either teacher have been original to them? Does the Rule mark a breakthrough in religion or ethics? Would the Rule be of any use in defining what was distinctive in the teaching of either Hillel or Jesus?

The answer to all these questions must be an emphatic negative. The Golden Rule is found long before the time of Hillel and Jesus. It was so widespread in the ancient world that if either Hillel or Jesus did use it, they would have been citing an ethical commonplace which, however true it may be, cannot in their day be seen as enunciating an original or distinctive moral principle. Indeed, in both the Christian (Matt 7:12) and the Jewish sources (*b. Šabb.* 31a), any claim to originality is explicitly denied. The Rule is offered as a summation of age-old teaching—a point too often ignored by Christian commentators.

In its classic formulation, the Golden Rule is not found in the Hebrew Bible nor in the literature of the ancient Near East. The common [[372]] view, argued at length by Dihle,[6] is that it was formulated in the Greek world and from there passed over into Jewish writings in the Hellenistic period. If we set aside Diogenes Laertius' attribution of the Rule to Thales (LEP 1.36), the reliability of which must be in serious doubt, then the earliest allusion to it in the Mediterranean world is in the *Histories* of Herodotus. Herodotus (3.142) depicts Maenandrius as telling the Samians: "It is known that I have sole charge of Polycrates' sceptre and dominion; and it is in my power to be your ruler. But, so far as in me lies, I will not do myself that which I account blameworthy in my neighbor."

Another echo of the Rule may be detected in Herodotus' report of Xerxes' reply to the Spartan emissaries (7.136). The obliqueness of these two early references is noteworthy. It suggests that already in the time of Herodotus the Rule was a commonplace. Further references to it occur later in the writings of Isocrates, and from then on it is fairly widespread in both Greek and Latin literature.[7]

The earliest Jewish attestation of the Rule is probably in the collection of wisdom sayings which constitute the teaching of Tobit (frequently dated around 200 B.C.E.): "Take heed to yourself, my child, in all your works, and be discreet in all your behavior. And what you [yourself] hate, do to no one." Another early reference (c. 150 B.C.E.) is Aristeas 207:

> The king received the answer with great delight and looking at the next guest said, "What is the teaching of wisdom?" He replied, "As you wish no evil to befall you, but to partake of every blessing, so you should act on the same principle toward your subjects, including wrongdoers, and you should mildly admonish the noble and the good. For God draws all men to himself in his mercy."

The application here of the Golden Rule specifically to the relationship between a ruler and his subjects may reflect its frequent use in political [[373]] contexts in earlier Greek writers.[8]

---

6. A. Dihle, *Die 'Goldene Regel': Eine Einführung in die Geschichte der antiken und frühchristlichen Vulgärethik* (Göttingen, 1962). See further the valuable review by D. A. Russell in *Gnomon* 35 (1963) 213–15.

7. For a list of references, see Dihle, *Goldene Regel*, 85–102; cf. his summary article in *Reallexikon für Antike und Christentum*, vol. 11, cols. 933–36. Further, Philippidis, *Goldene Regel religionsgeschichtlich untersucht*, 42–55.

8. Herodotus 3.142; Isocrates, *Nicocles* 49 and 61; *To Nicocles* 24; *Panegyricus* 81; cf. Cassius Dio 52.34.

Although chronology appears to favor the view that the Golden Rule passed over from the Greek world into Judaism, it would be wrong to be too dogmatic on this point. This cultural transfer—if transfer it be—should be evaluated with great care. The Greek culture from which the Jews may have borrowed the Golden Rule was not an autonomous entity, cut off from the general culture of the Levant and the ancient Near East.

The absence of the Rule in the surviving literature of the ancient Near East may be accidental. A version of the Rule is found in the Armenian Wisdom of Ahiqar.[9] Its presence there may, of course, be due to Christian influence. On the other hand, the Armenian version at this point may preserve early Ahiqar material not attested in the other recensions. It is hard to tell. Moreover, it should be borne in mind that the date of Tobit is by no means certain. If, as has been argued, Tobit was composed in the Persian period, then the Greek origin of the Golden Rule loses its force.[10]

The earliest attestation of the Rule may be in the Analects of Confucius (551–479 B.C.E.): "Tsze-Kung asked, saying, 'Is there one word which may serve as a rule of practice for all one's life?' The Master said, 'Is not reciprocity such a word? What you do not want done to yourself, do not do to others" (Analects 15:23).[11] If the attribution to Confucius is historically accurate, this reference effectively destroys any simple diffusionist model for the spread of the Golden Rule, for how on this model could we explain the occurrence of the Rule in Greece (Herodotus) and China (Confucius) at roughly the same time. The Rule is found in many cultures—a fact noted already by Voltaire: "La raison universelle qui contrebalance les passions . . . imprimie cette loi dans tous les coeurs: ne fait pas ce que tu ne voudrais [[374]] pas qu'on te fit" [['The universal reason that counterbalances passions . . . imprints this law in all hearts: do not do to others what you do not want done to you']].[12] To suggest that there is something quintessentially Hellenic about the Rule—in that it seems to imply that the human, or self, is the measure of things (cf. Protagoras in Plato, *Theaetetus* 160D)—would be grossly to overinterpret it.

Furthermore, even if the Rule was borrowed from the Greeks, it was easily domesticated within Judaism. The ease of this domestication is a direct reflection of the fact that the ideas contained in the Rule were not alien to Judaism. Though none of its precise formulations are found, the substance of the Rule was attested. As we have already hinted, the so-called Love Command of Lev 19:18 ("You shall love your neighbor as yourself") appears to

---

9. "Son, that which seems evil unto thee, do not do to thy companion; and what is not thine own give not to others" (F. C. Conybeare, J. R. Harris and A. S. Lewis, *The Story of Ahiqar* [London, 1898] 34). The absence of obvious verbal echoes here of the Gospels is noteworthy.

10. See C. A. Moore, "Tobit," *ABD* (New York, 1992) 6.591, for a recent survey of the problem of the date of Tobit.

11. Trans. J. Legge, *The Chinese Classics* (Hong Kong, 1960) 1.301.

12. Voltaire, "Essai sur les moeurs et l'esprit des nations" (1765), in *Oeuvres Complètes* (Paris, 1784) 4.289.

have played a central role in this process of domestication. The Golden Rule seems to have been treated as a comment on—or restatement of—this commandment. A few examples will illustrate this phenomenon.

(1) Luke 6:31 quotes the Golden Rule, but the commentary on the Rule in Luke 6:32–38 seems to be formulated with reference to the Love Command. We noted above that early Christian literature sometimes defines the *summum ius* [['highest law']] in terms of the Love Command (Rom 13:9) and sometimes in terms of the Golden Rule (Matt 7:12). It is unlikely that these were two mutually exclusive or contradictory points of view. Rather the Golden Rule and the Love Command would have been seen simply as alternative statements of the same principle.

(2) *Did.* 1:2: "The way of life is this: first of all, you shall love the God who made you, and secondly your neighbor as yourself. And all things whatsoever you would not befall yourself, neither do to another." In the juxtaposition here of the Love Command and the Golden Rule, the latter is intended to throw light on the former.

(3) *Tg. Jon.* to Lev 19:18: "You shall not take revenge, nor shall you bear a grudge against the children of your people, but you shall love your neighbor [*ḥābēr*]. What you hate for yourself, you shall not do to him." Note how here the Golden Rule functions specifically to clarify the sense of כָּמוֹךָ [['as you']] in the original Hebrew.

(4) A possible fourth example of the equation of the Golden Rule with the Love Command may be implicit in *b. Šabb.* 31a. It is paradoxical that the Gentile who asks Hillel to summarize the whole Torah while he [[375]] stands on one foot is answered with a maxim—the Golden Rule—which is not actually found in the Torah. Perhaps the point is that Hillel, in trying to draw the Gentile under the wings of the Shekhinah, cunningly chooses to summarize the Torah in terms of a principle the Gentile would readily recognize.

Is there behind this passage a doctrine akin to that enunciated by Paul in Rom 2:14–15: "When the Gentiles who have not the law do by nature the things contained in the law, they are a law unto themselves, even though they do not have the law. They show that the work of the law is written in their hearts"? Is Hillel appealing to an innate, God-given moral sense in the Gentile?[13] This may be pressing the text too hard. One thing is certain: the text makes no sense if the Golden Rule is not a reasonably satisfactory statement of the essence of the Torah. Such a use of the Golden Rule as a summary of the Torah is best explained by supposing that it is being taken as a restatement of the Love Command. Elsewhere in rabbinic literature the Love Command is cited as the *summum ius* (*Gen. Rab.* 24:27; SifQed 4:12 [ed. Weiss

---

13. Cf. J. Jeremias: "Hillel benutzt offensichtlich die stoische Lehre vom ἄγραφος νόμος (vgl. Röm. 2,14), wenn er die G.R. für das gottliche Urgesetz erklart"("Goldene Regel," *Die Religion in Geschichte und Gegenwart*, vol. 2 [Tübingen, 1958], col. 1688). Cf. also Jeremias, "Paulus als Hillelit," *Neotestamentica et Semitica: Studies in Honour of Matthew Black*, E. E. Ellis and M. Wilcox, eds. (Edinburgh, 1969) 89f. On the "unwritten law" in Judaism, see I. Heinemann, "Die Lehre vom ungeschriebenen Gesetz im jüdischen Schrifttum," *HUCA* 4 (1927) 149–71.

89b]; *y. Ned.* 9.3 [41 c. 36–38]). This is not contradictory to Hillel's view in *b. Šabb.* 31a, since the rabbis, like the early Christians, may have seen the Golden Rule and the Love Command as different formulations of the same fundamental principle.

Treating the Golden Rule as a reformulation of the Love Command helps to resolve some of the linguistic ambiguities of the Love Command and favors a universalizing interpretation of it. The Love Command is surprisingly ambiguous. Does כָּמוֹךָ modify וְאָהַבְתָּ ('and you shall love your neighbor in the same manner as you love yourself'), or does it qualify רֵעֲךָ ('and you shall love your neighbor who is like yourself')? And what is meant by רֵעֲךָ? Does it mean, "your fellow Jew"? Or, "your friend but not your enemy"? Or, "your fellowman or woman, whoever they may be"? All these interpretations are found in [[376]] early Jewish tradition. But the Golden Rule seems to sit easiest with the view that כָּמוֹךָ expresses the manner of the love and that the love command should be given a universal reference.

Although the Golden Rule may have been used to formulate the universalizing interpretation, it would be going too far to suggest that it generated the universalizing interpretation. The early Jewish sages were perfectly capable of following their own strong moral sense and of reaching such a universal interpretation without the help of the Golden Rule.

The indications are, then, that the Love Command played a major part in domesticating the Golden Rule in Judaism. But it is by no means the only maxim in early Jewish literature to express the principle of reciprocity which lies at the heart of the Rule. Even if we confine ourselves to the rabbinic corpus, we can find there numerous sayings which can be seen simply as applications of the Rule to concrete situations. The following will illustrate this point:

1. "Let the honor of your friend [*ḥābēr*] be as dear to you as your own honor" (*m. 'Abot* 2:10).
2. "Even as a man looks out for his own home, so should he look out for the home of his fellow. And even as no man wishes that his own wife and children be held in ill repute, so should no man wish that his fellow's wife and his fellow's children be held in ill repute" (ARN A 16).
3. "Let your neighbor's property be as dear to you as your own" (*m. 'Abot* 2:12).
4. "If you do not want a man to take what is yours, do not take what is his" (ARN B 30).
5. "If you do not wish to be slandered, do not slander another" (ARN B 29).
6. "If you do not want a man to hurt you or what is yours, then you too should not hurt him" (ARN B 26). [[377]]
7. "Do a kindness that one may be done to you. Attend a funeral that people should attend your funeral; mourn for others so that others should mourn for you; bury so that others should concern themselves with your burial; act benevolently so that benevolence should be done to you" (*Eccl. Rab.* 7.2.5; cf. *t. Meg.* 4(3):16; *t. Ketub.* 7.6; *y. Ketub.* 7.5 [31b.54]).

There can be no denying that the sentiments expressed by the Golden Rule were thoroughly at home in early Judaism. Even if the Rule was borrowed from outside, it found a ready acceptance in Jewish circles.

A final, thorny question needs to be addressed regarding the originality of the Golden Rule. Hillel quotes the Rule in its negative form ("Do not do to others what you would not want them to do to you"), Jesus in the positive ("Do to others as you would want them to do to you"). Is there a significant difference between these two formulations?

Christian writers have commonly asserted that there is. They have argued that the positive form is much superior to the negative in that it contains a positive injunction to love one's neighbor, whereas the negative does not. Some have gone so far as to assert that Jesus was actually the first to use the positive form. On this view a gap opens up between Hillel and Jesus. Hillel may well have been citing an ethical commonplace, but Jesus was not. One nineteenth-century Christian writer puts the case thus:

> The merest beginner in logic must perceive that there is a vast difference between the negative injunction, or the prohibition to do to others what is hateful to ourselves, and the positive direction to do unto others as we would have them do unto us. The one does not rise above the standpoint of the Law, being as yet far removed from that love which would lavish on others the good we ourselves desire, while the Christian saying embodies the nearest approach to absolute love of which human nature is capable, making that the test of our conduct to others which we ourselves desire to possess.[14]

[[378]] There are a number of reasons why this position is untenable. In the first place, it is not true that Jesus was the first, or the only one, to formulate the Rule in its positive form. Aristeas 207 combines both the negative and the positive forms: "As you wish that no evil should befall you, but to partake of every blessing, so you should act on the same principle toward your subjects, including wrongdoers." According to Diogenes Laertius (5.21), Aristotle, when asked how we should act toward our friends, replied, "As we would they should act toward us." Even if this logion is not genuinely Aristotle's, it is unlikely that Diogenes, or his source, was influenced by Christian texts. Christian influence can equally be ruled out in *2 En.* 61:2, where we have, in effect, a positive version of the Golden Rule: "That which a person makes request for from the Lord for his own soul, in the same manner let him behave toward every living soul." However, it is intriguing that the majority of the instances of the Golden Rule in both Jewish and pagan authors in antiquity are in the negative form.

Second, even if the concept of generosity of action toward others is not expressed explicitly in the negative form of the Golden Rule, that concept itself is not alien to Judaism. The performing of acts of loving-kindness (*gemîlût ḥasādîm*) is as much a part of Jewish as of Christian ethics. To imply otherwise is absurd. The positive injunction to love one's fellows is found not only in

---

14. A. Edersheim, *The Life and Times of Jesus the Messiah* (London, 1906) 1.535–36.

the Hebrew Bible, in the Love Command and its parallels (e.g., Lev 19:34), but in rabbinic literature as well: "Hillel says: 'Be of the disciples of Aaron, loving peace and pursuing peace, loving mankind and drawing them to the Torah" (*m. 'Abot* 1:12; cf. ARN A and B, ad loc.). "If Israel would but look closely at what their father Jacob said to them (cf. Gen 49:28), no nation or kingdom could dominate them. What did he say to them? Accept upon yourselves the kingdom of heaven, vie with each other in the fear of heaven, and act toward each other with loving-kindness."[15]

Third, if the difference between the two formulations is so obvious and so important, it is surprising that more was not made of it in antiquity. As we noted earlier, Paul in Rom 13:10 seems to echo the negative form. The negative form is found in the *Gospel of Thomas* (Logion 6) and is common in the church fathers, despite the fact that the [[379]] two occurrences of the Rule in the New Testament are positive.[16] This indifference toward nuancing the forms continued down through the Middle Ages to the philosophers of the seventeenth and eighteenth centuries, such as Hobbes, Locke, and Kant. The philosophers show little interest in the Rule and seem unaware of any profound differences between its positive and negative versions.[17]

Only in the nineteenth and twentieth centuries do Christian writers begin to insist on the superiority and originality of the positive form. The context of the assertion was polemical. It was part of a concerted attempt to maintain—in the face of the new historical-critical approach to the Bible—the traditional claim that Christianity was distinct from and had transcended its Jewish origins. Some Jewish writers replied in kind. Aḥad Ha-Am, for example, urged the superiority of the negative form, arguing that the positive formulation stands in direct contradiction to the moral basis of Judaism, since it deprives man of an objective moral value.[18]

---

15. SifDeut §323 (Finkelstein ed., 372).

16. See Dihle, "Goldene Regel," *Reallexikon für Antike und Christentum*, vol. 11, cols. 938–39.

17. Locke, *Essay on Human Understanding*, Book 1, chap. 3, §4 (ed. Nidditch, 1975, p. 68) quotes the Rule in its positive form: ". . . that most unshaken Rule of Morality, and foundation of all social Virtue, That one should do as he would be done unto. . . ." Hobbes, *Leviathan*, Part 1, chap. 15 (ed. Oakeshott, 1955, p. 103) quotes it in the negative: ". . . to leave all men inexcusable, they [the laws of nature] have been contracted into one easy sum, intelligible even to the meanest capacity; and that is, Do not that to another, which thou wouldest not have done to thyself." Kant, *Grundlagen zur Metaphysik der Sitten*, chap. 2 (Gesammelte Schriften, Berlin, 1903, 4.421) restates the Rule in a more rigorous form: "Handle so also ob die Maxime deiner Handlung durch deinen Willen zum algemeinen Naturgesetze werden sollte" [['Conduct yourself as if the maxim of your conduct would become through your will the general law of nature']]. For a useful survey of the use of the Rule in medieval and modern times, see Heinz-Horst Schrey, "Goldene Regel III. Historisch und ethisch," *Theologische Realenzyclopädie* (Berlin, 1984) 13.575–78.

18. Aḥad Ha-Am's powerful critique deserves to be quoted at some length: "Christian commentators point proudly to the positive principle of the Gospels: 'Whatsoever ye would that men should do to you, do ye even so to them' . . . and thereby disparage Judaism, which has only the negative principle of Hillel: 'What is hateful to thyself do not unto thy neighbour.'

[[380]] Finally, the Rule is too imprecise a principle to bear much philosophical weight. It should not be overnuanced. Despite its sophisticated linguistic form, it is unsophisticated in content. As Dihle rightly saw, it is not a philosophical principle, but a piece of Vulgärethik.[19] Philosophers have never been much interested in it. What little philosophic interest has existed in the twentieth century has been provoked by the theological debate. Bultmann put his finger on the philosophical weakness of the Rule when he said that it "embodies the morality of a naive egoism."[20]

To make one's own ego—its needs and desires—the standard of one's actions toward others is clearly fraught with danger. The philosopher L. J. Russell stated the problem boldly when he argued that

> the rule as its stands gives no hint of the kind of person it is desirable you should be, if you are to be trusted to carry it out. It authorizes the [[381]] quarrelsome person, who loves to be provoked, to go about provoking others, and the person who hates friendliness and sympathy to be cold and unsympathetic in his dealings with others; it authorizes the man who

---

Mr. Montefiore debates the matter, and cannot make up his mind whether the positive principle really embraces more in its intention than the negative, or whether Hillel and Jesus meant the same thing. But of this at least he is certain, that if Hillel's saying were suddenly discovered somewhere in a positive form, the Jews would be 'rather pleased' and the Christians would be 'rather sorry.' . . . But if we look deeper, we shall find that the difference between the two doctrines on this point is not one of more or less, but that there is a fundamental difference between their views as to the basis of morality. It was not by accident that Hillel put his principle in the negative form; the truth is that the moral basis of Judaism will not bear the positive principle. If the positive saying were to be found somewhere attributed to Hillel, we should not be able to rejoice; we should have to impugn the genuineness of the 'discovery' which puts in Hillel's mouth a saying opposed to the spirit of Judaism. The root of the distinction lies here also, as I have said, in the love of Judaism for abstract principles. The moral law of the Gospels beholds man in his individual shape, with his natural attitude towards himself and others and asks him to reverse this attitude, to substitute the 'other' for the 'self' in his individual life, to abandon plain egoism for inverted egoism. Altruism and egoism alike deny the individual as such all objective moral value, and make him a means to the subjective end; but egoism makes the 'other' a means to the advantage of the 'self,' while altruism does just the reverse. Now Judaism removed this subjective attitude from the moral law, and based it on an abstract, objective foundation, on absolute justice, which regards the individual as such as having moral value, and makes no distinction between the 'self' and the 'other.' Just as I have no right to ruin another man's life for my own sake, so I have no right to ruin my own life for the sake of others. Both of us are men, and both our lives have the same value before the throne of justice." See: "Judaism and the Gospels (1910)," *Ten Essays on Judaism by Achad Ha-Am*, trans. L. Simon (New York, 1973) 235–36. The original Hebrew can be found in the essay, "ʿAl šetê ha-seʿippîm" ("Halting between Two Opinions") in *Kol Kitbê Aḥad Ha-ʿAm* (Tel Aviv, 1947) 374. For Claude Montefiore's views on the Golden Rule, see his *Synoptic Gospels* (London, 1917) 2.119–20, and his *Rabbinic Literature and Gospel Teaching* (London, 1930) 150f. Cf. also I. Abrahams, *Studies in Pharisaism and the Gospels*, First Series (Cambridge, 1917) 18–29.

19. Dihle, *Goldene Regel*, 30–40.
20. R. Bultmann, *The History of the Synoptic Tradition*, trans. J. Marsh (Oxford, 1963) 103.

loves to find himself in a network of intrigue and sharp dealing, to deal with others habitually in this way.[21]

Norms of behavior should transcend the self and have some sort of universality. This problem was noticed early on by Christian commentators. The Old Latin translates Matt 7:12 "Whatsoever good things . . ." (*omnia ergo quaecumque vultis ut faciant vobis homines bona, ita et vos facite illis* [['Whatever good things you want men to do to you, do also to them']]). The addition is significant and attempts to introduce an objective moral standard. In his commentary on the Sermon on the Mount, Augustine argues that a distinction should be drawn between "desiring" and "wishing." He claims that a man, however much he may desire it, cannot will or wish for himself anything which is not good.[22]

Two popular nineteenth-century Christian commentaries illustrate two other ploys for getting round the problem. One urges that

> the precise sense of the maxim is best referred to common sense. It is not, of course, what—in our wayward, capricious, grasping moods—we should wish that men would do to us, that we are to hold ourselves bound to do to them; but only what—in the exercise of an impartial judgment, and putting ourselves in their place—we consider it reasonable that they should do to us, that we are to do to them.[23]

Another proposes that the self envisaged in the Rule is not any or every self, but the purified, redeemed self:

> [[382]] There is, of necessity, an implied limitation. We cannot comply with all men's desires, nor ought we to wish that they should comply with ours, for those desires may be foolish and frivolous, or may involve the indulgence of lust or passion. The rule is only safe when our own will has been first purified, so that we wish only from others that which is really good. Reciprocity in folly is obviously altogether alien from the mind of Christ.[24]

21. L. J. Russell, "Ideals and Practice (I)," *Philosophy* 17 (1942) 110.

22. Augustine, *De Sermone Domini in Monte secundum Matthaeum* 2.74 (Patrologia Latina 34, col. 1303): "Intelligendum est ergo plenam esse sententiam et omnino perfectam, etiam si hoc verbum [bona] non addatur. Id enim quod dictum est, *quaecumque vultis*, non usitate ac passim, sed proprie dictum accipi oportet. Voluntas namque non est nisi in bonis: nam in malis flagitiosisque factis cupiditas proprie dicitur, non voluntas. Non quia semper proprie loquuntur Scripturae, sed ubi oportet ita omnino proprium verbum tenent, ut non aliud sinant intelligi" [['It is to be understood, therefore, that the clause is complete and altogether perfect, even if this word be not added. For the expression used, "whatsoever ye would," ought to be understood as used, not in a customary and random sense, but in a strict sense. For there is no will except for good deeds: for in the case of bad and wicked deeds, desire is, strictly speaking, not will. Not that the Scriptures always speak in a strict sense; but where it is necessary, they take such care to ensure a precise meaning that nothing else could be understood']].

23. D. Brown, *A Commentary, Critical, Experimental and Practical, on the Old and New Testaments*, ed. R. Jamieson, A. R. Fausset and D. Brown (Grand Rapids, Mich., 1976) 3.47f.

24. E. H. Plumptre, *A New Testament Commentary for English Readers*, ed. C. J. Ellicott (3rd ed., London [c. 1881]) 1.41.

All this special pleading serves only to highlight the deficiencies of the Rule and the dangers of pressing it too hard. Theologians and philosophers can nuance the Rule to their hearts content, but the fact remains that it is a popular saying and should not be asked to bear the weight of a theological or philosophical system. If Jesus' positive formulation of the Golden Rule marked a profound moral breakthrough, then it is very odd that no one— whether theologian or philosopher—seems to have spotted the fact till the nineteenth century.

The Golden Rule as the *Summum Ius*

Our analysis leads inevitably to the conclusion that the Golden Rule is of no use whatsoever in comparing the historical Hillel and the historical Jesus. The evidence that Hillel quoted the Rule is shaky in the extreme. Even if he did, he would only have uttered a maxim which would have sprung readily to the lips of any street-corner moralist in antiquity. There are better grounds for believing that Jesus quoted the Rule, but his positive formulation of it is not so innovative as has often been claimed.

The fact remains that Jewish and Christian tradition claim that Hillel and Jesus quoted the Golden Rule and that both teachers proposed that the Rule could be seen in some sense as a summation of the law. This striking agreement calls for explanation. It suggests that there is a valid and illuminating comparison to be made, not between the historical figures, but between the images of those figures which have been projected by the religious communities which they have influenced. We can legitimately compare and contrast the traditions about Hillel with [[383]] the traditions about Jesus. A comprehensive comparison cannot be undertaken here. We will content ourselves with trying to clarify what might be meant in both traditions by asserting that the Golden Rule is the *summum ius* [['highest law']].

In *b. Šabb.* 31a the Gentile asks Hillel to teach him the whole Torah while he stands on one foot. Clearly he wants Hillel to sum up the Law, to put it in a nutshell. Hillel obliges by quoting the Golden Rule and by claiming that it is "the whole Torah." The implication appears to be that the Rule is the fundamental principle which underlies the whole Torah: the rest of the Torah is but "commentary" (*pērûš*) on the principle, which draws out its meaning and applies it to concrete situations. The analogy of text and commentary to explain the relationship between the Golden Rule and the Torah is suggestive but vague.

In ARN B 26, however, the language is more precise. There the Golden Rule is described as "the great principle (כלל גדול) of the whole Torah." *Kelāl* is a technical term in rabbinic literature for a general principle underlying a series of concrete rulings. *M. Ketub.* 3:9 provides a simple example:

> If a man said, "I have seduced the daughter of such-a-one," he must pay [compensation for] indignity and blemish on his own admission, but he does not pay the [prescribed] fine.

If a man said, "I have stolen," he must repay the value on his own admission, but he does not make double or fourfold or fivefold restitution.
[If he said], "My ox has killed such-a-one," or "the ox of such-a-one," he must make restitution on his own admission.
[If he said], "My ox has killed the bondsman of such-a-one," he does not make restitution on his own admission.
This is the general principle (*zeh ha-kelāl*): whosoever must pay more than the cost of damage does not pay on his own admission.

Here the *kelāl* clearly has the function of stating succinctly the principle embodied in the bill of particulars.

[[384]] The *kelāl* in *m. Ketub.* 3:9 is of limited scope and will cover only a limited bill of particulars. However, once one has started looking for *kelālîm*, the question of ever more comprehensive principles naturally arises. Faced with a number of limited *kelālîm*, one could ask if there is a more general *kelāl* which would embrace them all. These second-order *kelālîm*, of wider application, appear to be called "great principles" (*kelālîm gedōlîm*) in rabbinic literature.[25]

There is no logical stopping place on this road till one has asked the ultimate question of whether there is a single "great *kelāl*" underlying the whole Torah. This is clearly the issue in ARN B 26. It is also the issue in *Gen. Rab.* 24:7 (cf. SifQed 4:12 [ed. Weiss 89b]), where Ben Azzai states that the creation of man in God's image (Gen 5:1) is the "great principle" of the Torah, whereas Aqiba claims that the Love Command (often identified, as we have seen, with the Golden Rule) has that status. The context and the parallels with *b. Šab.* 31a and ARN B 26 indicate that the dispute is not about *a* great principle, but about the greatest principle of all.

This search for the ultimate principle of the Torah is vividly illustrated by *b. Mak.* 23b–24a:

> R. Simlai, when preaching, said: Six hundred and thirteen precepts (*miṣvôt*) were communicated to Moses, three hundred and sixty-five negative (corresponding to the days of the solar year), and two hundred and forty-eight positive (corresponding to the number of a man's limbs). . . .
> David came and based them upon eleven [precepts], as it is written: "Lord, who shall sojourn in your tent, who shall dwell in your holy mountain? (1) He who walks uprightly, and (2) does righteousness, and (3) speaks the truth in his heart. (4) He who has no malice on his tongue, (5) nor wrongs his fellow, (6) nor tells tales against his neighbor; (7) in whose eyes a reprobate is despised, (8) but who honors [[385]] those who fear the Lord. (9) He who swears to his own hurt, and does not change; (10) he who does not put out his money to usury, (11) nor takes a bribe against the innocent. He who does these things shall never be moved" (Ps 15:1–5). . . .

25. See, for example, *m. Šabb.* 7:1, "A great principle have they laid down concerning the Sabbath [*kelāl gādôl 'āmerû*]." The *kelāl* which follows appears to embrace virtually all the complex Sabbath legislation. Likewise, when in *b. B. Qam.* 46a the principle that "the burden of the proof lies with the plaintiff" (cf. *m. B. Qam.* 3:11) is described as a "great principle of jurisprudence" (*kelāl gādôl ba-dîn*), the *kelāl* in question is clearly of a high order of generality.

Then Isaiah came and based them upon six, as it is written: "(1) He who walks in righteousness, and (2) speaks the truth; (3) he who scorns to enrich himself by extortion, (4) and who keeps his hands clean from bribes; (5) who stops his ears against talk of murder, and (6) shuts his eyes against looking at evil" (Isa 33:15).

Then Micah came and based them upon three, as it is written: "The Lord has told you, O man, what is good, and what it is that the Lord requires of you: only (1) to act justly, (2) to love mercy, and (3) to walk humbly with your God" (Mic 6:8). . . .

Again Isaiah came and based them upon two, as it is written: "Thus says the Lord: (1) Keep judgment, and (2) do righteousness" (Isa 56:1).

Then came Amos and based them upon one: "Thus says the Lord, Seek me and you shall live" (Amos 5:4).

To this R. Naḥman b. Isaac objected: [Might not the sense be,] seek me by observing the whole Torah and [thus] live? Rather, Habakkuk came and based them all upon one [precept], as it is written: "The righteous man shall live by his faith" (Hab 2:4).

Interest in the underlying principles of the Torah is not confined to rabbinic texts. It surfaces also in Philo. Philo distinguishes between the Decalogue and the "special laws" (i.e., the concrete *miṣvôt*, including the ritual laws and the laws of *kašrût*). He argues that the latter may be subsumed under the former: "We must not forget that the Ten Words are summaries of the special laws which are recorded in the sacred Books and run through the whole of the legislation" (*De Decalogo* 154; cf. *De Specialibus Legibus* 1.1).

We find similar concerns in early Christian texts. In Mark 12:28ff. a scribe asks Jesus, "Which is the first commandment of all?" [[386]] Jesus replies, "Hear, O Israel: the Lord our God, the Lord is one; and you shall love the Lord your God with all your heart, and with all your soul, and with all your mind, and with all your strength" (Deut 6:4–5). He then goes on to add that the second commandment is, "You shall love your neighbor as yourself" (Lev 19:18). *First* here is probably to be taken in a hierarchical sense: which law contains the first and fundamental principle of the Torah underlying all the other laws? The parallel in Matt 22:34ff. speaks of the whole law and the prophets "depending" on the commandments to love God and to love one's neighbor. The sense appears to be that the former are derived from, or give expression to, the latter.

Gal 5:14 uses slightly different language: "The whole law is fulfilled in one word, 'You shall love your neighbor as yourself.'" Rom 13:8–10 introduces the notion of a single law as the "summation" of the rest of the laws:

He who loves his neighbor has fulfilled the law. The commandments, 'You shall not commit adultery, You shall not kill, You shall not steal, You shall not covet,' and any other commandment, are summed up in this sentence, 'You shall love your neighbor as yourself.' Love does no wrong to a neighbor; therefore love is the fulfilling of the law.

In Matt 7:12 (though not in Luke 6:31) the Golden Rule is given as the essence of the Torah: "for this is the law and the prophets." A similar idea may lie behind the Western text of Acts 15:29, where the negative form of the Golden Rule is inserted. The purpose of the interpolation may be quite simple. The context is concerned with the question of what commandments of the Torah should Gentile converts be required to observe. The interpolator wished to suggest that if they kept the Golden Rule, they would, in effect, be observing the whole Law. He could have quoted as effectively the Love Command, but perhaps, as in the story of Hillel in *b. Šabb.* 31a, the Golden Rule was deliberately chosen as the "Gentile" version of this command.

Many of the *kelālê ha-Tôrāh* [['principles of the Torah']] are propositions drawn from the Bible. They may, indeed, themselves be biblical *miṣvôt* [['precepts']]. In this case, some laws of the Torah would be more universal and fundamental than others and may lie behind the more concrete and specific pieces of legislation. But it also appears permissible to formulate independent [[387]] principles not explicitly stated in the Bible through extrapolation from the concrete laws. No obvious distinction is drawn between these two types of *kelālîm:* the "nonbiblical" *kelāl* is treated as being as valid as the "biblical" *kelāl.*

The search for the *kelālê ha-Tôrāh* is linked to the long-running debate within Judaism concerning the "reasons for the commandments" (*ṭaʿamê ha-miṣvôt*). It is natural to ask why a given piece of legislation has been enacted. What is its purpose? One answer to this question is that the specific law gives concrete expression to a moral or rational principle. If one pursues the *kelālê ha-Tôrāh* to a sufficiently high level of abstraction, then almost inevitably one will identify them with moral propositions, since only moral propositions have a sufficiently universal and abstract character to embrace a wide variety of different, concrete laws. On this view, the reason for a given commandment is simply to apply the moral principle in the everyday world. Thus a view of the Torah emerges in which it is seen to comprise both eternal, universal truths, and the working out of those truths in the form of specific legislation.

The potential for radicalism in this position is obvious. It opens the way for the argument that what is important is not the concrete law but the eternal truth. The concrete law is valid only insofar as it successfully expresses—under the conditions of space and time—the underlying universal principle. If it fails to do this, then it should be abolished or modified. Thus the *kelālîm* can be used as a platform for a radical critique of the legislation. Some early Christian writers seem drawn to this position,[26] but, not surprisingly, it held few attractions for the Rabbis.

The words used by Hillel in *b. Šabb.* 31a, in which the *kelāl* is compared to the text and the remaining legislation to the commentary, *could* be given a radical twist. Nevertheless, halakhists [['Jewish legal experts']] would reject

---

26. For example, the argument in Mark 2:23–27 appeals to a *kelāl* ("the Sabbath was made for the benefit of humanity") and plays it off against a concrete (Pharisaic) ruling that plucking ears of corn on Sabbath constituted forbidden work (cf. *b. Šabb.* 73a–b).

drawing radical conclusions from such a haggadah [['explanatory matter in rabbinic literature']]. A more normative halakhic view would be that the concrete halakhot are primary, the *kelālîm* secondary. That is, the halakhot are the "text," the *kelālîm* the [[388]] "commentary." The direction of the critique must always be from the halakhot to the *kelālîm*, not vice versa.[27]

There is also a significant tendency among halakhists to resist the idea that every *miṣvāh* must have a moral or rational basis. Some *miṣvôt*, such as the laws of the Red Heifer, have no such basis, but must nevertheless be obeyed.[28] The authority of the *miṣvāh* lies not in its morality or rationality, but in its fundamental character as a *ius divinum* [['divine law']].

Conclusion

Comparing the historical Hillel and the historical Jesus is a questionable exercise. Comparing the traditions regarding these two great teachers is not. As we have seen, such comparison can be illuminating and can draw out the nuances of both traditions. At the end of our analysis, the overriding feeling is one of astonishment at the convergence of the two traditions. Christians have commonly regarded Jesus' teaching on love as the heart of the gospel. Yet similar ideas are found in rabbinic literature. Here, arguably, is a significant community of belief, which imparts substance to the notion of a Judeo-Christian tradition.

27. *B. Qidd.* 34a: *'en lemēdîn min ha-kelālôt va-'afîlû bemāqôm še-ne'emar bô ḥûṣ* ('no inference may be drawn from general rulings, even where an exception is actually specified'). Cf. also *y. Ter.* 1.2 (40 c. 36): *lêt kelālîn de-Rabbî kelālîn* ('the general statements made by Rabbi are not general statements'). Cf. Paulus, *Digest* 50.17.1: Regula est, quae rem quae est breviter enarrat. Non ex regula ius sumatur, sed ex iure quod est regula fiat. Per regulam igitur brevis rerum narratio traditur, et, ut ait Sabinus, quasi causae coniectio est, quae simul cum in aliquo vitiata est, perdit officium suum [['A rule is something that briefly describes how a thing is. The law is not to be derived from a rule, but a rule must come from the law as it already is. By means of (establishing) a rule, thus, a brief description of something is made; as Sabinus says, it is, as it were, the element of a case that loses its force as soon as it becomes defective in any way']].

28. This is the point of the story about Yoḥanan ben Zakkai and the Red Heifer in *Pesiqta de Rab Kahana* 4:7.

AMY-JILL LEVINE

The Word Becomes Flesh: Jesus, Gender, and Sexuality

[[62]] In the initial planning both for Florida Southern's 1998 Biblical Symposium and for the published proceedings of that gathering, I was asked to address the question, What do we get when investigating the historical Jesus in
a historically informed way? I knew I would be sharing the podium and these
pages with Professors James H. Charlesworth, John Dominic Crossan, and
E. P. Sanders; I also knew that composing an essay that would substantively,
comprehensively, and equitably summarize my colleagues' methods and emphases would likely be impossible. The path to the answer of What do we
get? was already riddled with stumbling blocks.

My problem encompassed more than the technical difficulties of epito-
mizing complex approaches and subtle conclusions. [[63]] I can reconstruct
my colleague's views from their publications, my notes on their talks, reviews
by others, and in the cases of Crossan and Charlesworth, from long-standing
personal friendships, but the pictures I develop may not be, at least to my
colleagues' self-perceptions, accurate. I risk emphasizing the wrong issues,
misquoting statements or taking them out of context, and otherwise distort-
ing their positions. I may even find myself unconsciously adapting their material to fit my own ideological perspectives or what I perceive to be the
interests of my audience. Even if I cite directly from their books and articles,

Reprinted, with permission, from Amy-Jill Levine, "The Word Becomes Flesh: Jesus, Gender,
and Sexuality," in *Jesus Two Thousand Years Later* (ed. J. H. Charlesworth and W. P. Weaver;
Faith and Scholarship Colloquies; Harrisburg, Pa.: Trinity, 2000) 62–83.

Author's note: My gratitude to Nashville's Hillsboro Presbyterian Church and to the
priests of the Roman Catholic Diocese of Middle Tennessee for their thoughtful questions
and trenchant suggestions on earlier versions of this essay in its oral form. For elaboration
on the themes in this paper, with particular attention to the divorce sayings and anti-Jewish
interpretations, see Amy-Jill Levine, "Jesus, Gender, and Sexuality: A Jewish Critique," in
[[*Women and Judaism* (Studies in Jewish Civilization 14; ed. L. J. Greenspoon, R. A. Simkins,
and J. A. Cahan; Omaha: Creighton University Press, 2003)]].

problems continue. First, scholars sometimes modify their views as they refine their methods, respond to critics, and find new evidence. Consequently,
any summary risks obsolescence. Second, even the most careful editors make
mistakes. For example, the program distributed to the participants at Florida
Southern's Biblical Symposium contained errors about my publications (my
next book is forthcoming from Harvard, not Cambridge) and my editorial
work (for the *Journal of Biblical Studies*, not the *Journal of Biblical Literature*);
whether error or not, my children say that the publicity photograph in the
program does not even look like me.

If it is difficult to locate with full confidence the historical Crossan, Sanders, Charlesworth, or even Levine, then *Qal v'homer*,[1] how much more so is
it difficult to locate the historical Jesus? How much trustworthiness should we
grant the Gospels, written after the crucifixion, not by eyewitnesses, and in
Greek rather than Aramaic?

I think we should grant them a great deal. While the specifics of the symposium program were incorrect, overall the impression given of me—of a
writer and teacher who is interested in gender roles on the one hand and the
relationship between Church and Synagogue on the other and who usually
smiles—was correct. Similarly, while the words and deeds the Gospels attribute to Jesus have been modified, edited, and expanded by the Evangelists to
fit the needs of the developing Church, I think much of their general depiction of Jesus' words and deeds has good claims to credibility.

Finally, since my editors have no desire for a monograph, I [[64]] cannot
give a comprehensive picture of the Jesus who emerges from the application
of various methods, let alone offer critiques or develop pastoral implications.
For manageability, and given my particular interests, I shall focus on two interrelated categories often absent from studies of the historical Jesus: gender
and sexuality. Our understanding of these issues in turn may contribute to
our views of matters pressing in today's political climate: attitudes towards
marriage and divorce, procreation, and male/female relationships.

The timeliness of these issues and their absence from much of what has
come to be known as the "third quest of the historical Jesus" are not the only
reasons I have for my focus. At Vanderbilt's Divinity School, I serve as the di-
rector of the Carpenter Program in Religion, Gender, and Sexuality, whose
mandate is to encourage education and communication on these controversial topics.[2] In this capacity, I get a number of phone calls and letters. Here
are three examples (paraphrased slightly):

1. "When all those Jews were thanking God for not making them women,
   slaves, or gentiles, Jesus was talking with women, healing them, encouraging them. The Church has sunk back into Paul's Rabbinic Judaism
   rather than followed Jesus' break with patriarchy."

---

1. A Rabbinic expression equivalent to the *a fortiori* argument "how much more."
2. Http://divinity.lib.vanderbilt.edu/Carpenter/index.htm.

2. "I got pregnant when I was in junior high and had to get married. My husband never loved me. He beat me, and when he got tired of that, he moved out. We haven't been together for over two years. I've become a Christian, and in church I met a man I love. My pastor says I can't get divorced, and if I remarry, I'll be committing adultery. What would Jesus say?"

3. "The Bible is my guide for how to live, and my girlfriend and I often study it together. Everything was fine until we started making wedding plans, and we checked to see what Jesus says about marriage. I'm not sure I like what I've found. Jesus wasn't married, he praised 'eunuchs for the kingdom of Heaven' (Matthew 19), and he told husbands to leave their wives and follow him. Now I'm [[65]] thinking of calling off the wedding, or at least telling my fiancée that we shouldn't have sex. She thinks I'm nuts. What do you think?"

Engagement

Responses to such questions should address not only the content of Jesus' teaching but also the rationale. Pronouncement is often insufficient apart from explanation; as the mother of two children, I am well aware that the reply "Because I said so" is unhelpful for developing moral responsibility or religious commitment. This extension is necessary even for those who claim, "If the Bible says it, I believe it." The most literal of readers needs to judge whether a statement is imperative, ideal, metaphor, even sarcasm; whether it applies to both men and women, to only one group or an individual, to all people for all times.

The question *why* greatly occupies those engaged in historical Jesus research: whether we see Jesus as expecting an apocalyptic end to the world or a new form of social organization brought about through human endeavor, as a peasant addressing social evils or a prophet seeking spiritual renewal, necessarily impacts our interpretation of his sexual ethic and his view of gender roles. However, compared with the numerous works on Jesus' parables, healings, view of *Halachah* (literally: "the way"; generally: following Torah), and the circumstances of his crucifixion, there remains little written by academic "questers" on his view of sex and gender.

Few biblical scholars before the 1970s talked about sexuality or gender at all, let alone Jesus' sexuality. Even the article titled "Sex and Sexuality" in the recent *Anchor Bible Dictionary* only considers the Hebrew Scriptures (demonstrating thereby to the literalist that there is no sex in the New Testament).[3] On sexual ethics, Paul was and remains the more frequently evoked; this is appropriate since he has more to say on the topic. Still others did not find the issues relevant. Noting that Jesus had a message for all people, they saw little reason to concentrate on his message to or relationships with women.

3. Tikva Frymer-Kensky, "Sex and Sexuality," *Anchor Bible Dictionary* (New York: Doubleday, 1992) 5:1144–46.

[[66]] Another contingent may have been discouraged by the Evangelists' lack of sustained detail on women's roles. The Gospel accounts of women and discussions of sexuality are, to use J. Cheryl Exum's term, "fragmented."[4] Whereas, the stories of Jesus, and to a great extent of the disciples and even the Pharisees, develop from scene to scene, women lack a progressive story line; like guest stars on a television show, they appear, make a noteworthy contribution, and then vanish. Topics concerning sexuality, such as marriage, family structures, divorce, celibacy, and procreation, occur sporadically, but they are diffused throughout the texts.

Finally, until very recently, scholars either did not find the topics of gender and sexuality of interest or, if they did, feared such study would be labeled faddish, inflammatory, or—heaven forbid—"feminist." These were not the sorts of subjects that would enhance a tenure file. Consideration of what scholars find interesting and valuable should not be passed over too quickly. Our questions, methods, and conclusions are products, implicitly or explicitly, consciously or unconsciously, of our academic contacts and cultural contexts.

Recent studies of peasant cultures and the effects of urbanization on agrarian economic and social structures inform Crossan's works. Innovative approaches to Rabbinic texts and increasing familiarity with the diversity of Second Temple Judaism underlie Sanders's studies. Placing Jesus in his Jewish context, particularly through investigation of the Pseudepigrapha and the Qumran scrolls, determines much of Charlesworth's corpus. Biblical scholars today bring literary-critical approaches to the parables, cross-cultural anthropology to Galilean village life, studies of millenarian movements and cult formation to the community Jesus called forth, etc. Moreover, many of those who study Jesus, including my three colleagues, recognize that what biblical scholars say both informs and is informed by what clergy communicate to their congregations: for example, contemporary implications of the Jesus quest have enormously high stakes for those worried about anti-Semitism and sexism.

Correspondingly, from the '70s "women's lib" to the '90s "backlash," feminists and nonfeminists—self-proclaimed and [[67]] otherwise—have brought the categories of gender and sexuality to biblical studies. As increasing numbers of women find a home in pulpits and lecterns, and as various groups celebrate or condemn this presence, it is not surprising that questions of gender and sexuality are finally being asked of Jesus and the Gospels.[5]

Whether Jesus himself would have seen these questions as of interest is another matter. Difficult as it is to locate his views of *Halachah* or the temple, it is more difficult to determine his attitude toward women as *women* and harder still to conceptualize the history of the women he encountered: his

4. J. Cheryl Exum, *Fragmented Women: Feminist (Sub)versions of Biblical Narratives* (Sheffield: JSOT Press, 1993).
5. The opening of such questions as academically viable topics is due in great measure to Elisabeth Schüssler Fiorenza, *In Memory of Her: A Feminist Theological Reconstruction of Christian Origins* (New York: Crossroad, 1984); *Jesus: Miriam's Child, Sophia's Prophet: Critical Issues in Feminist Christology* (New York: Continuum, 1994).

followers, those he healed, those who regarded him as possessed, or those who dismissed him. Nevertheless, lack of sustained detail, clear sources, a fully viable method, and other components of the historiographical task has never been a preventative when it comes to talking about Jesus.

In popular literature, studies of Jesus, gender, and sexuality tend to be based less on rigorous historical method and less on knowledge of the primary Jewish, Christian, and pagan sources than on stereotype (e.g., Jesus was married because Jesus was a rabbi and all rabbis were married) or apologetic (Jesus didn't really mean what he said about divorce, remarriage, etc.). Worse, both stereotype and apologetics frequently lead to or are characterized by anti-Judaism.

Christian feminists seeking a supportive Jesus had little evidence of his attempt to overthrow gender bifurcation; they had no women among the Twelve; they had no call of a woman comparable to that of Peter or Matthew; they had no pronouncement such as "in me there is neither male nor female" (cf. Gal 3:28). While women may have been at the Last Supper, their presence is unrecorded (the silence of the sources may indicate either presence suppressed or absence unremarked). But these feminists did have one of the "master's tools," which they used to great effect: they focused on women the lenses ground by those supersessionist interpreters who saw Jesus overturning a Judaism categorized as obsessively concerned with legal minutiae while lacking morality, love, and compassion.[6] So, they concluded, Jesus came to correct Jewish views on women. The [[68]] worse these scholars painted Jesus' Jewish context, the more feminist he looked.[7]

Correction of this view on both feminist and nonfeminist fronts has come, in great thanks to the work of E. P. Sanders. His *Paul and Palestinian Judaism* was a watershed treatment of the problems with stereotyping Second Temple Judaism as monolithic and atavistic.[8] But even in the better studies, Sanders's lessons are forgotten or ignored when the subject turns, if it turns at all, to women. For example, although N. T. Wright's magisterial *The New Testament and the Victory of God* does present brief treatments of Mary and

6. Remnants of this view appear in much of the work of Marcus Borg, which has served to awaken in many Christians new interest in and respect for the Jesus tradition. Ben Witherington III, with whom I frequently disagree, here cogently recognizes that Borg's Jesus, "in his advocacy of compassion, was opposed to purity systems of all sorts." Witherington then demonstrates why Borg's view is untenable. See Witherington, *The Jesus Quest: The Third Search for the Historical Jesus*, 2nd ed. (Downers Grove, Ill.: InterVarsity, 1997) 104.

7. Judith Plaskow, "Blaming the Jews for the Birth of Patriarchy," *Lilith* 7 (1980) 11–12, 14–17; "Anti-Judaism in Feminist Christian Interpretation," in *Searching the Scriptures*, vol. 1, *A Feminist Introduction*, ed. E. Schüssler Fiorenza (New York: Crossroad, 1993) 117–29; Susannah Heschel, "Anti-Judaism in Christian Feminist Theology," *Tikkun* 5.3 (1990) 25–28, 95–97; Amy-Jill Levine, "Yeast of Eden: Jesus, Second Temple Judaism, and Women," *Biblical Interpretation* 2 (1994) 8–33; "Lilies of the Field and Wandering Jews: Biblical Scholarship, Women's Roles, and Social Location," in *Transformative Encounters: Jesus and Women Re-viewed*, ed. I. R. Kitzberger (Leiden: Brill, 1999) 329–52.

8. E. P. Sanders, *Paul and Palestinian Judaism: A Comparison of Patterns of Religion* (Philadelphia: Fortress, 1977).

Martha and of Jesus' pronouncements on divorce, it does not integrate gender or sexuality into its larger picture of Jesus. What Wright does say is typical of modern mainstream comments on Jesus and women. Appealing to
cross-cultural anthropology and the broadly termed "social sciences" to propose a model of "a first-century Palestinian village," he interprets Luke 10:38–
42 to reveal not simply that Mary is "spiritual" and Martha "practical" but to
sound "a much more subversive note. . . . Mary has refused to be confined to
the women's quarters."[9] This citation seems an endorsement of my first caller:
Jesus combats misogynistic Judaism.

It is true that Mary is not confined to the complex of rooms called *gynaikonitis* (women's quarters), which were not just for women but also for
slaves and various domestic activities.[10] True, Jesus has praise for Mary, who
sits at his feet. Martha, needing help—probably in food preparation—and
seeking Mary's aid, he rebukes. But I still find Wright's reading wrong. For example, why assume that the house had women's quarters? Where are archaeological reports of Judean villages and analyses of social class? Only the very
wealthy had the luxury of such separate quarters; further, were Martha this
well-off, surely she would have had a wealth of household help. On the other
hand, why assume that upper-class women, in *gynaikonitis*, were confined
within their own homes? Where is classical history and cross-cultural analysis
of gender-bifurcated societies? Given the active manner in which she is portrayed, who would have confined Martha? Indeed, who would have [[69]]
dared? The only other family member Luke mentions is her sister, Mary.
Even in John's narrative, which identifies her brother as Lazarus, there is still
no indication either that someone is constraining Martha or that her actions,
including those at Lazarus's tomb, are anomalous. Finally, the house belongs
to Martha (Luke 10:38); classical and Rabbinic sources as well as several early
Christian texts too indicate women's economic independence.

To claim that Jesus, or Luke, drew Mary and Martha out of a system of
separation and suppression replaces history with theology. It is as unsubtle
and as apologetic as the counterclaim, based on the same story and made by
those disenchanted with Christianity, that Jesus permitted women followers
as long as they remained silent, servile, and sitting at his feet.

When we reconstruct Second Temple social history by looking at Jewish
Law from Jesus to the Mishnah or at Judaism's practice and beliefs, from say
63 B.C.E. (Pompey's entry into Jerusalem) until 70 C.E. (the destruction of the
Second Temple),[11] when we search the Dead Sea Scrolls and the Pseudepigra-

---

9. N. T. Wright, *Jesus and the Victory of God*, Christian Origins and the Question of God
2 (Minneapolis: Fortress, 1996) 52, following Bruce Malina and Jerome Neyrey, in *The Social
World of Luke–Acts: Models for Interpretation*, ed. Jerome Neyrey (Peabody, Mass.: Hendrickson, 1991).

10. Cf. John 11:1–12:8. See the helpful descriptions by Carolyn Osiek and David L.
Balch, *Families in the New Testament World: Households and House Churches*, The Family, Religion and Culture Series (Louisville: Westminster/John Knox, 1997) 6–11.

11. Cf. E. P. Sanders, *Jewish Law from Jesus to the Mishnah: Five Studies* (London: SCM;
Philadelphia: Trinity International, 1990); *Judaism: Practice and Belief 63 B.C.E.–70 C.E.* (London: SCM; Philadelphia: Trinity International, 1992).

pha to locate Jesus within Judaism,[12] and when we broaden our historical focus to include the Mediterranean world and peasant life,[13] we find a Galilee and Judea that was patriarchal and androcentric (what wasn't?). The issue, however, is one of degree. While social roles and religious responsibilities differed for men and women, Second Temple Judaism in its various forms did not epitomize misogynism. The Rabbinic materials should not be selectively chosen, retrojected back to pre-70 Jewish practice, and read therein as descriptive rather than prescriptive (any more than Tertullian's misogynism should be attributed to Jesus). To learn anything about Jesus' attitude toward women, let alone gender roles and human sexuality, we cannot begin by stacking the deck against Second Temple Judaism.

The Gospels in fact appear to counter this view of Jewish repression. They find quite unremarkable women's public presence (Mark 5:24–34; 12:42; Luke 7:11–15; 8:1–3; 11:27; etc.); they present no indication of a society obsessed with laws of family purity.[14] These impressions are confirmed by sources as varied as Josephus and Philo, the Apocrypha, the Pseudepigrapha, [[70]] papyrus collections, a substantial bulk of Rabbinic writings, etc.[15]

Conversely, the Gospels offer no evidence that Jesus questioned what has come to be called the "sexual division of labor." The parables and sayings reflect traditional gender roles: the woman who seeks the lost coin in her house is paired with the shepherd in the field; the woman who puts yeast into dough matches the man who plants the mustard seed. The women grind meal; the men recline on the dining couch (Luke 17:35) or, in Matthew's version, work in the field. Even the birds of the air and the lilies of the field may be gendered images. In turn, no women in the Gospels explicitly seek to escape the demands of the so-called "oppressive patriarchal family."

Much of what Jesus said and did, as best as I can reconstruct his message and mission, had revolutionary potential: mandates like forgiving all debts, giving without expectation of return, thinking less about social convention and personal honor, resisting oppression without resorting to violence, basing identity on deed rather than family name or economic assets. But I cannot agree with my first caller who would accept Crossan's claim that the "Sophia-Christ" drew forth a "radically egalitarian [kingdom that] rendered sexual and social, political and religious distinctions completely irrelevant and anachronistic."[16] Jesus did not combat androcentrism and did not seek

12. Cf. James H. Charlesworth, ed., *Jesus' Jewishness: Exploring the Place of Jesus within Early Judaism* (Philadelphia: American Interfaith Institute; New York: Crossroad, 1991); *Jesus within Judaism: New Light from Exciting Archaeological Discoveries*, Anchor Bible Reference Library (Garden City, N.Y.: Doubleday, 1988).

13. John Dominic Crossan, *The Historical Jesus: The Life of a Mediterranean Jewish Peasant* (San Francisco: HarperSanFrancisco, 1991).

14. Amy-Jill Levine, "Discharging Responsibility: Matthean Jesus, Biblical Law, and Hemorrhaging Woman," in *Treasures New and Old: Contributions to Matthean Studies*, ed. D. R. Bauer and M. A. Powell, SBL Symposium Series (Atlanta: Scholars, 1996) 379–97.

15. See Levine, "Yeast of Eden," 8–33.

16. Crossan, *Historical Jesus*, 298. Wright, following an unpublished paper by Jerome Neyrey, condemns Crossan for "celebrating sexual ambiguity or homosexuality" in relation

to break down gender roles. He likely advocated celibacy, as we shall see, but it is not necessarily the case that sexual asceticism would be congenial to all women (or all men). My first caller was very well motivated, but his attempt to reform the Church by negatively categorizing early Judaism as misogynistic and positively categorizing Jesus as proactive on women's rights is both bad history and bad theology.

Marriage and Divorce

What I have so far unveiled applies directly to my second interlocutor, the young woman who wanted to remarry. I wish I had easy answers for her. [[71]] Jesus forbade both divorce and remarriage. His pronouncements are multiply attested in the canonical tradition (Mark 10:2–12; 1 Cor 7:10–11; Matt 5:31f.; 19:3–9; Luke 16:16–18; cf. 17:1–2 [Q]). Similar comments appear in the prophet Malachi (2:13–16) and the Dead Sea Scrolls, so the legislation is not anomalous in its cultural context.[17] There is no evidence of Jesus or his followers being charged with encouraging divorce (as there is, for example, with associating with prostitutes or sinners).[18] Finally, the topic of divorce was of general interest at his time, such that it is likely someone would have asked his opinion.

Less certain are rationale and result: why forbid divorce, and what effect does this interdiction have on women? The answer most often given to the first question is that the proscription responds to a particular social problem: namely, Jewish men were divorcing their wives at whim and leaving them destitute. Such a construct makes Jesus congenial to those groups who want to institute covenantal marriage, restrict divorce, and otherwise legislate "family values" given what they perceive to be an increasingly decadent society. This approach, once again, relies on a derogatory stereotype in order to explain Jesus' radical demand.[19]

---

to the historical Jesus (*Jesus and the Victory*, 54); this is not Crossan's point. His *Historical Jesus* discusses Secret Mark but divorces the historical Jesus from the erotic overcoat worn by the naked young man in the garden (330ff.).

17. Some commentators claim that Mark's note that women cannot divorce their husbands must be an addition to Jesus' original words (now found in Matthew and Luke or, for some, Q) because Jewish women in the Second Temple period did not have this right. But this claim has been demonstrated false for Diaspora settings, and quite likely within the wider Mediterranean culture that also engulfed Judea, some women there too sought divorce (perhaps from Roman courts).

18. Jesus' association with prostitutes remains debated among historians. Matt 21:31 associates John the Baptist with "tax collectors and prostitutes," but the phrase may be an expression of inclusivity for male and female sinners. It is not clear that the woman "of the city" who anoints Jesus (Luke 7:36–50) is a prostitute.

19. See Marcus Borg, *Meeting Jesus Again for the First Time: The Historical Jesus and the Heart of Contemporary Faith* (San Francisco: HarperSanFrancisco, 1994) 57. Cf. Crossan, *Historical Jesus*, 301–2, incorrectly, on Jewish women's inability to obtain a divorce and, following John Kloppenborg, on the attack on "androcentric honour whose debilitating effects

Ironically, this convention categorizes Second Temple Judaism, not as a retrograde Puritanism in which women are confined to their quarters, but as a sexual hedonism in which women are cast out into the street. Like that other stereotype, however, it is not well supported by the sources. First, we have no evidence that divorce was rampant in the period. The primary support for this view is the statement attributed to Rabbi Akiva (d. 135 C.E.) that a husband can divorce for any reason, such as his finding a woman prettier than his wife.[20] This is Rabbinic rhetoric demonstrating what is possible given certain legal presuppositions. It is no more descriptive of Second Temple Jewish life than Jesus' exhortations to pluck out the offending eye and chop off the offending hand are indicative of a first-century group of blind and maimed messianists.[21]

Second, Jewish women received marriage contracts (*Ketubot*), which both made divorce prohibitive and assured them [[72]] some financial security when it did occur.[22] Referring to the early second-century marriage and divorce documents from Murabbaʿat and Nahal Hever, John Collins remarks: "Both types of contract . . . are concerned for the economic well-being of the wife. This concern remains central to the well-documented development of Jewish marriage contracts in later tradition."[23] It is as historically problematic and theologically vapid to praise a command against divorce by positing a Jewish society out of moral control as it would be to suggest that Jesus' interdiction is designed to maintain relationships that begin in or disintegrate into abuse, violence, and hate.

Third, arguments against divorce and remarriage are consistent with Jesus' interest in reconfiguring the formation and role of kinship groups: "Who are my mother and my brothers? . . . Whoever does the will of God" (Mark 3:33–35, NRSV). Such social planning puts Jesus at odds with most, but not all, Jews of his time.[24] The Qumran scrolls posit such a community, as do Philo's Therapeutae/Therapeutrides and several Greek philosophical schools. Like a number of these other groups as well, Jesus endorses separation from the biological kinship group. Luke 18:29–30 reads, "Truly I tell you, there is no one who has left house or wife or brothers or parents or children, for the

---

went far beyond the situation of divorce." On Jewish women obtaining divorce (e.g., Salome, the sister of Herod the Great: Herodias, daughter of Agrippa I, and perhaps Shelamzion of Nahal Hever fame), see John J. Collins, "Marriage, Divorce, and Family in Second Temple Judaism," in *Families in Ancient Israel*, ed. L. G. Perdue and others, The Family, Religion, and Culture Series (Louisville: Westminster/John Knox, 1997) 120.

20. Detailed discussion in Collins, "Marriage, Divorce," 117–20. The pronouncements appear in the context of a debate between the Houses of Hillel and Shammai (see *m. Giṭ.* 9–10).

21. Divorce may have increased under the pressures of the Bar Cochba Revolt of the early second century C.E. On divorce documents, see Collins, "Marriage, Divorce," 111.

22. Ibid., 107–12, 115–19.

23. Ibid., 112.

24. This notice is similar to his citation of Mic 7:5–6 on disruption between parents and children (cf. Matt 10:34–39; Luke 12:51–53; 14:25–27; and cf. *Gospel of Thomas* 55, 101).

sake of the kingdom of God, who will not get back very much more in this age, and in the age to come eternal life."[25]

If Jesus was convinced—as were Paul, the authors of several Dead Sea Scrolls, and apparently John the Baptist—that a new way of living was breaking in, then his endorsing of fictive kinship groups and countercultural views of the family should not be unexpected. This is what millenarian groups do, from Africa to Melanesia to the Shakers and the group known as Heaven's Gate. A reformist sexual ethic with strongly ascetic (or strongly libertinistic) content is often the hallmark of apocalyptic communities, as is a move toward recreating the golden age.[26] This explanation also accounts for Jesus' appeal to Adam and Eve in grounding his proscription: millenarian communities frequently associate the age to come (*Endzeit*) with the past's golden age (*Urzeit*). Jesus apparently expected, even as he attempted to create a new Eden, a setting where humanity lived [[73]] at peace with nature, where ownership of property and family connections were not the ground of being. As Mark puts it:

> Because of your hardness of heart he [Moses] wrote this commandment [concerning the opportunity of divorce] for you. But from the beginning of creation, "God made them male and female." "For this reason a man shall leave his father and mother and be joined to his wife, and the two shall become one flesh." So they are no longer two, but one flesh. Therefore what God has joined together, let no one separate. (Mark 10:5–9)

Not all the studies of Jesus subscribe to this eschatological-apocalyptic explanation. However, the other constructs are less convincing. If Jesus were a Cynic, uninterested in apocalyptic eschatology but very interested in social critique, he may have issued a prohibition against remarriage. For Cynics, marriage would be seen as demanding attention to producing heirs, toward sexual intercourse, toward the constraints that come with family life. Marriage is then the opposite of the freedom that men should have and that the Cynics sought. According to the Stoic Epictetus, the unmarried Cynic makes it his duty to comment on the morality of the marriages of others.[27] Why a Cynic would legislate the maintenance of the marital arrangement, which is clearly a cultural construct, is a more difficult question. Then again, Cynics took their name from the Greek term for "dog"; Diogenes received the epithet because of his "public defecation and immodest, public sexual

25. Most commentators assume Luke added "wife," although separation of spouses in the context of millenarian piety is hardly unusual. On the replacement of traditional families with fictive kin by millenarian groups and sectarian movements generally, see Dale C. Allison Jr., *Jesus of Nazareth: Millenarian Prophet* (Minneapolis: Fortress, 1998); and sources cited there. This volume, just published, is the first sustained study of Jesus and asceticism.

26. Wright connects the injunction with Jesus' vision of the "new heart" and the inauguration of the "new covenant" (*Jesus and the Victory*, 285–87). Wright also suggests that the teaching was cryptic, given the political liability of arguing against divorce with Antipas's rule (*Jesus and the Victory*, 397–98; cf. Mark 6:18, 21–29).

27. Osiek and Balch, *Families*, 124.

behavior."[28] To press the Cynic analogy given Jesus' sexual asceticism would therefore be barking up the wrong tree.

Perhaps Jesus was a Mediterranean peasant dedicated to social justice apart from apocalyptic or millenarian considerations. In this case, he may have resisted divorce, recognizing as destructive the separation of families caused by increasing urbanization and the attendant loss of peasant land. However, this model does not help account for the commands to leave families and follow him.

Antidivorce legislation may also have been a matter of practicality. The pronouncements are less focused on spousal separation than on one of the partners remarrying: "Whoever divorces his wife and marries another commits adultery against [[74]] her, and if she divorces her husband and marries another, she commits adultery" (Mark 10:11–12). Where husbands and wives are following Jesus, the last thing he and his movement need are charges of, or temptations to, adultery, nor does he, apparently, want loyalty to a spouse or the sexual availability that comes with marriage to interfere with his mission.[29] Of the various options regarding Jesus' divorce pronouncements, the apocalyptic-eschatological prophet of Jewish restoration theology provides the most convincing explanation. While the other modes can accommodate the prohibition, they do not as sufficiently account for its relationship to other pronouncements, cross-cultural parallels, and the almost immediate revision of its radicality (e.g., Paul's "if she does separate" in 1 Cor 7:11 and Matthew's *porneia* clause).[30]

Where then is our second interlocutor? I'd like to think that if she asked Jesus directly, he would tell her to follow her heart; he would tell her that in cases of abuse, divorce is not only appropriate but necessary (cf. 1 Cor 7:15). I would like to think that he would attend her second wedding—and even provide the wine. But a Jesus who provides comforting answers is, while more palatable, often less historical.

I think he would say she should call no man "lord" and remain celibate, and this because of his apocalyptic, eschatological perspective. For my conservative caller, alas, such historical contextualization was irrelevant. More helpful to her was discussion of Matthew's *porneia* clause (of which the husband was clearly guilty), appeal to John's "woman taken in adultery" (since it was the "sin of fornication" that prompted the first marriage), and the questions, "Do you think God brought together you and your first husband; did God bring together you and the man you met in church?" I also gave her the phone numbers of several local ministers. I do not know what she decided.

---

28. Witherington, *Jesus Quest*, 59.

29. Materials cited in support of marriage, such as John 2, are not decisive. The historicity of the singularly attested account is debatable, and attendance at a wedding is no more an endorsement of the marriage than eating at the home of a tax collector or sinner is an endorsement of tax collecting or sin.

30. The clause may have addressed (gentile) marriages rendered illegal by Levitical consanguinity legislation. It may also reflect Augustan law making adultery a crime, such that the man who did not divorce and prosecute his adulterous wife could be accused of pimping.

Consummation

Then there is my third caller, the fiancé who hears a message of celibacy. Again, the tradition is not as supportive of [[75]] contemporary concerns as I would wish. That is, I think he heard correctly.

The tradition presumes Jesus is unmarried. His designation as "bridegroom" reinforces rather than compromises his virginity; it is the husband—a role Jesus does not fulfill—not the groom who consummates the relationship. And, like Jesus, the majority of his followers appear outside marital structures. The disciples speak of leaving their families to follow Jesus (e.g., Matt 19:27–29), and no spouses are listed for Martha and Mary, Mary Magdalene, or the other women from Galilee. Even the Syro-Phoenician woman (implicitly) and the Samaritan woman (explicitly) are outside marital structures. No account depicts Jesus speaking directly with a woman expressly embedded in a marriage save for Jairus's wife, present at the healing of her daughter (Mark 5:40).

The tradition also cautions against sexual desire. Matt 5:27–28 not only forbids adultery but asserts that "everyone who looks at a woman with lust has already committed adultery with her in his heart." It may caution also against self-gratification related to that desire. Mark 9:43 exhorts, "If your hand causes you to stumble, cut it off; it is better for you to enter life maimed than to have two hands and to go to hell," and Matthew juxtaposes this saying to the pronouncement on lusting (Matt 5:29). There are some Rabbinic hints of at least one tradition that advocated cutting off the hand for masturbation (cf. in a different context Deut 25:11–12),[31] and in Semitic languages, "hand" can function as a euphemism for "penis."[32]

Among the more controversial sayings attributed to Jesus are ones in Matt 19:10–12: "There are eunuchs who have been so from birth, and there are eunuchs who have been made eunuchs by others, and there are eunuchs who have made themselves eunuchs for the sake of the kingdom of heaven. Let anyone accept this who can" (v. 12). This statement has been seen as a prohibition against remarriage by widowers (although why a widower would be called a "eunuch" or how the status of widower relates to birth remains unclear) and as a call to self-castration (which is both contrary to *Halachah* and unattested in the earliest traditions). It is, however, consistent with [[76]] Mark 12:18–27, which describes the ideal (resurrected) state as a celibate one where "[men] neither marry nor are [women] given in marriage" because they will be "like angels in heaven."[33] It is also consistent with Jesus' concern

31. For texts and discussion, see W. D. Davies and Dale C. Allison Jr., *A Critical and Exegetical Commentary on the Gospel according to Saint Matthew*, New International Critical Commentary Series 1 (Edinburgh: T. & T. Clark, 1988) 524.

32. See Hans Dieter Betz's denial that the idiom lies behind the verse in question; *The Sermon on the Mount*, Hermeneia Series (Minneapolis: Fortress, 1995) 238 n. 335.

33. See Josephus *J.W.* 3.374, on the "chaste bodies" of the world-to-come. Witherington sees the comparison as indicating not "asexuality or lack of married condition" but "immortality" (*Jesus Quest*, 169). His appeal to Philo is inconsequential, his emphasis is not supported by other textual materials, and his view erases the specifics of the comparison itself.

that followers become like little children (Mark 10:15; Matt 19:14; Luke 18:17): usually seen as representing innocence or helplessness, children are also marked by virginity and lack of sexual shame. As Crossan puts it, "a kingdom of children is a kingdom of the celibate."[34] The consistency is only slightly indirect: eunuchs could marry, and they did have sexual relationships, but they did not produce children. In a world where the dominant ethos was to have children—to preserve the family name, to inherit family property—Jesus' statement echoes his concern for humility and self-abnegation. The "eunuch for the kingdom" then was one who did not seek children, and this means the one who abstained from sexual intercourse.[35]

Matthew did not expect all church members to follow the pronouncement in 19:12, as the line "Let anyone accept this who can" indicates. I do not think, however, the line is authentic: the rest of the Jesus tradition does not appear to make radical demands conditional: do it if you can, but if you can't, don't worry.

Similarly, the Gospels do not privilege childbearing. According to Luke 11:27–28 (NRSV), "A woman in the crowd raised her voice and said to him [Jesus], 'Blessed is the womb that bore you and the breasts that nursed you!' But he said, 'Blessed rather are those who hear the word of God and obey it!'" This statement, also cited in *Gospel of Thomas* 79 (where Luke 23:29 is added), recollects Jesus' ideal of the new family.[36] The major point of the saying is, probably, that honor and blessing should not be based on family lines; for women as well, one's ethic rather than one's fertility is to be valued. But the saying is also consistent with a negative view of procreation. In an apocalyptic context, Jesus correspondingly blesses the wombs that never gave birth and the breasts that never nursed (Luke 23:29). Unlike his prophetic predecessors, the one miracle Jesus does *not* do is cure infertility.

Jesus' sexual asceticism may be seen as part of a tradent [[77]] in early Christianity and Judaism: much of 1 Corinthians,[37] Revelation's 144,000 male virgins (14:4), and Philip's virgin daughters (Acts 21:9) all indicate a preference for celibacy.[38] Although the Dead Sea Scrolls themselves do not

---

Also unconvincing are those arguments that see Jesus as looking forward to the end of "patriarchal" marriage in which women are objectified as tokens of exchange; this may be the result of the statement, but less clear is its function as motivation.

34. Crossan, *Historical Jesus*, 267, in discussion of *Thomas*; the comments here extend Crossan's point back to the historical Jesus.

35. There is no indication that birth control is intended.

36. Crossan, *Historical Jesus*, 299–300.

37. Paul's notice that other apostles take a "sister-wife" (*adelphēn gynaika*, 1 Cor 9:5), although not often cited as an example of celibacy, is likely to be precisely this.

38. Matters would also be clearer if we knew which, if any, of the noncanonical gospels contain comments from Jesus' lips. For example, in the *Gospel of Thomas*, Jesus suggests that Mary Magdalene must become "male" (give up her female identity, probably through radical asceticism, and thereby become an androgyne, like *ha-adam*, "the earthling" in Eden, prior to the separation into male and female bodies) to enter the kingdom. Even for those who see *Thomas* as reflecting historical material, this verse is usually seen as part of a later redactor's

prohibit intercourse, Josephus, Philo, and Pliny agree that the Essenes were celibate.[39] Sexual asceticism is likewise consistent with Jesus' interest in a new Eden. While Rabbinic sources read Genesis as indicating that Adam and Eve had sexual relations in the Garden, earlier Jewish texts do not (*2 Bar.* 56:6; *Jubilees* 3; perhaps 4Q265).[40]

As with the question of divorce, Jesus' preference for celibacy is, finally, less the issue. The major question is its rationale. Intimately familiar with the Hebrew Scriptures, Jesus may have considered himself a new Moses or (less likely) a true priest seeking a true Temple. In either case, he might endorse celibacy. Before Matt Sinai, the people of Israel were told to refrain from intercourse (in gendered terms, "Do not touch a woman"; cf. Exod 19:15), and priests needed to keep themselves apart from sexual intercourse before performing specific Temple duties. However, his various comments on human sexuality (celibacy, divorce, separation of families, childbirth, etc.) do not all match these models.

As a resident of the Hellenized Mediterranean world, Jesus may have subscribed to the prevailing medical views that semen production is at best a necessary evil and that intercourse occasions for both men and women weakness and loss of spiritual vigor.[41] Yet the "professional" medical opinion may not have been shared by popular culture, and there is no evidence Jesus even knew of such ideas.

Likely among Jesus' followers were fellow Galileans whose familial structures had been disrupted by the increasing pressures of urbanization and colonialism. In this context, abstinence is practical: given disintegration of family ties and land ownership, children are an economic burden. Then again, disruption of peasant life or even familial separation under economic pressure does not necessarily create an ascetic impulse. The contrary effect is equally plausible if not more likely. Apart from millenarian implications, the problems of colonialism do [[78]] not typically translate into calls for asceticism. We therefore return to our thesis that Jesus be seen as an apocalyptic, eschatological prophet. In this worldview, asceticism would be expected.

Jesus commended celibacy. What then should the third caller do? He might, for example, follow the Church and the canon and not just statements in the Gospels taken out of context. Although celibacy remained a major impulse in Church development, those who compiled the canon decided to include the Pastoral Epistles but not the Apocryphal Acts: childbirth, and therefore sexual intercourse, became not only encouraged but necessary for salvation (1 Timothy 2). Also to the caller's relief, I noted that celibacy is,

---

interests (e.g., it is consistent with other concerns about celibacy and asceticism in *Thomas*; then again, this is hardly a definitive reason for elimination).

39. Sources and discussion in Collins, "Marriage, Divorce," 128–35.

40. See discussion and notes in ibid., 128–29; C. Anderson, "Celibacy or Consummation in the Garden? Reflections on Early Jewish and Christian Interpretations of the Garden of Eden," *Harvard Theological Review* 82 (1989) 121–48.

41. See Osiek and Balch, *Families*, 104–7. The ancient medical view has, ironically, been preserved primarily by athletes.

even in Matthew 19's saying on eunuchs, a spiritual gift. Finally, I advised him to see both a pastoral-care specialist and a caterer.

Likely I will soon get a call citing Gen 1:28 and asking about birth control.

Reception

Jesus gathered a small but loyal following of fellow Jews who sought to incarnate the *basileia*, the kingdom of heaven, on earth. They preached a joyous attitude toward life, community support and solidarity and a view of others based on actions, not on pronouncements, birth, or wealth. With this message and this lifestyle, women took their place among Jesus' followers. His association with women, in and of itself, is unremarkable.

But the times were dangerous for popular prophets and their followers, as the preemptive strike Herod Antipas took against John the Baptist testifies. In such times and for such people, marriage is a luxury, and children are a liability. But Jesus' sexual ethic stems from more than political challenge: he anticipated major change through divine intervention into history. Marriage would soon pass away as we all become angels in heaven.

For those Christians who want the Word to become flesh in the twentieth century, it seems to me that the turn toward [[79]] the celebration of marriage and childbirth for those lacking the spiritual gift of celibacy, a more open view of divorce especially in cases of domestic abuse, and the increasing role of women in the Church would not be inconsistent with the scriptural model beginning with Genesis. Would the historical Jesus agree? I would like to think so, given his willingness to make unpopular pronouncements, his concerns for justice, and his prophetic critique of exploitation and of self-righteous religious leadership. Then again, this may be my wish, not his view.

For those who seek to enact the more radical statements, such as those on divorce, into law, historical inquiry provides some context at least for those willing to consider it. If we do not live in the same culture, and with the same worldview, as Jesus and his earliest followers, then we must, necessarily, adapt. This has always been the role of the Church. And for those who are not interested in history, in interpretation, in human needs, for those who insist on their own literalistic interpretation of *select* passages in the canon, then before they spout a historical anti-Jewish apologetic, condemn those seeking exit from abusive relationships, and forbid committed partners from sanctifying their relationships, my advice remains, "Sell all you have and give to the poor; leave your parents, children, and spouse; pluck out your eye and cut off your hand; be perfect, and then come back and make your case."

Part 7

Conclusion

Conclusion

SCOT MCKNIGHT

Jesus asked Peter en route: "Who do you say I am?" For historical Jesus scholars, Jesus' question cannot be entertained until an altogether different question is asked: "Who do you think I thought I was?" Or, put differently, "Who *was* he?" must be asked before one can ask, "Who *is* he?"

This sort of question was called the "last tabu" by the inimitable J. A. T. Robinson, in an essay included in this volume (below, pp. 553–566). This sort of "tabu," an investigation into the "self-consciousness" of Jesus, is both at the heart and the periphery of historical Jesus scholarship. It is at the heart because nearly every major study of Jesus is saying as much about who Jesus thought he was as it is about what we can know about what Jesus did and said. But, at the same time, it remains at the periphery because, methodologically, scholars today are nervous about what we can really know about the *intention* of the Evangelists, let alone the intention of the one about whom they wrote. Robinson says that the previous generation had inquired into this hot topic and "had its fingers burnt" (1984: 155). In addition, Robinson noted that his generation was not permitted—and the permission slip is still hard to obtain— to use the Fourth Gospel for learning things about Jesus. As he said it, "One must not be caught using *those* texts even with a long spoon!" (1984: 157). Robinson, who was a lightning rod within the Anglican Church, was one of those who thought one's conclusions about the historical Jesus had direct bearing on one's theology. And so he argues: "the *self-knowledge* of Jesus is the indispensable heart of the mystery: to regard it as a matter of indifference [and he's going toe-to-toe here with Kähler and Bultmann] or as a 'no go' area is to leave a blank at the centre of Christian theology" (below, p. 558). And, as his readers know, Robinson thought John's Gospel was worthy of consideration for understanding that self-knowledge.

The reasons generations have been warned about using John as a source for historical mining are manifold, not the least of which is that John operates with a powerful and high Christological hermeneutic. Such a Christology implies questions about truth and significance, and these are not (we have been warned time and again) questions historians can answer. It is the implication of "who *is* Jesus?" that shapes the essays of this concluding section to this anthology.

Historical Jesus scholars other than Robinson have indeed asked such questions, they have answered them, and what is more, the questions and their answers are inevitable, for the non-asking and the non-answering are forms of asking and answering. Questions and answers of this sort, of course, do not lead inexorably to the Nicene Creed or the variations of its themes over the next four centuries. But they do lead to profound starting points that can help the "disinterested" as well as the interested. There is a living scholarly tradition that the Christology of the Church owes its origins to the "past" of Jesus, and that past "really matters" for understanding that Christology.

Bultmann thought history mattered. To be sure, he is known for the opposite:

> I do indeed think that we can now know almost nothing concerning the life and personality of Jesus, since the early Christian sources show no interest in either, are moreover fragmentary and often legendary; and other sources about Jesus do not exist. (Bulmann 1958: 8)

But, any reading of this passage in *Jesus and the Word* in situ, or of the entire book, leads the reader to know two things: first, Bultmann is not denying knowledge about Jesus' teachings but about the inner development of his life; and second, Bultmann indeed thought he knew a fair share of what Jesus did teach. And this is where Bultmann can be deconstructed: if he claimed that theology was not determined by historical study, his own "theology" of Jesus was itself deeply rooted in what he thought was historically defensible about Jesus' teachings.

The issue is what to make of one's historical conclusions and how to carry it off. Nothing is more central to this task than the eschatological imminency so many think is central to the vision of Jesus (e.g., McKnight 1999). It proved a test-case for Bultmann in his landmark *Jesus Christ and Mythology*, two chapters of which are included in what follows. Bultmann's observations say it all: "the conception 'Kingdom of God' is mythological," and the "course of history has refuted mythology" (1958: 14; below, p. 533). His solution, which dominated German and continental theology for decades, was this: "We must ask whether the eschatological preaching and the mythological sayings as a whole contain a still deeper meaning which is concealed under the cover of mythology" (1958: 18; below, p. 534). Bultmann developed an entire program that he called "de-mythologizing." Bultmann believed that beyond the process, a process that in its newer form is called "deconstruction," there is hope for a theology that will speak the Word to a new generation.

If Bultmann thought Christological reflection needed to transcend the past of Jesus and the historically verifiable, G. N. Stanton, who here represents a moderate stance, argued in the late 60s and early 70s (and is still doing so today; see 2002; 2004) that the Christology of the Gospel traditions, which show some continuity with later Christian theological developments, owes its origins to the earliest Christian concerns with the "past" of Jesus. Stanton was then waging battle with *Redaktionsgeschichte* (the editorial concerns of the Evangelists) in full bloom. He applied the brakes gently and suggested that in fact the Gospels have a concern with the past of Jesus. And this means that the significance of Jesus is not just a late imposition, but from the very beginning the earliest Christians were pressing the button of Christology.

No one has placed his finger on this theological button more deftly than Robert Morgan in his inquiry into the significance of the historical Jesus for doing a "theology" of the New Testament. Morgan puts his finger on the proper dilemma: ". . . the central problem of a modern New Testament theology, which may be summarized as the necessity and the impossibility of including the 'historical Jesus'" (see p. 570 below). Because I do not want to usurp his study, I will flesh out this dilemma with only two more quotations:

> But since Jesus *was* a historical figure, and Christians find salvation in this life and this death, they *are* interested in the actual history. (below, p. 570)

> The objection to this procedure, and what some would call its theological *impossibility* [here alluding to Bultmann], is that it substitutes a religiously indeterminate historical presentation of Jesus for the Gospels and most Christians' theological evaluation of him. (below, p. 570)

If I may be so bold as to call attention here to my co-editor and mentor's newest thesis, I would point out that Dunn's own work addresses precisely this problem (Dunn 2003; 2005). If we are to do theology and if we are to do historical Jesus studies, we must recognize up front that the Gospels themselves are crystallized memories of what early Christians thought and believed about Jesus but that we cannot expect to find in those Gospels anything other than a faith-based memory, behind which we cannot go to find some "neutral" or "uninterpreted" Jesus.

A variant on this view, which owes some of its origins to Martin Kähler but which has since been seriously chastened and nuanced, is what we are learning from postmodernist challenges to historiography. Namely, every "conceptualizing" scheme of doing history (which is what history can only be—a historian's capturing of the past into a narrative) leads to the same result: the Gospels themselves are "histories" in the sense that they conceptualize the past of Jesus into a coherent narrative, and this narrative is itself an interpretation of Jesus, a faith-based one (McKnight 2005). There is, in other words, a door through which anyone must enter who wants to study Jesus historically or theologically.

Bibliography

Bultmann, R.
    1958   *Jesus and the Word*, trans. L. P. Smith and E. H. Lantero. New York: Scribner's.
Dunn, J. D. G.
    2003   *Jesus Remembered*. Christianity in the Making 1. Grand Rapids: Eerdmans.

2005   *A New Perspective on Jesus*. Acadia Studies in Bible and Theology. Grand Rapids: Baker.

McKnight, S.

1999   *A New Vision for Israel: The Teachings of Jesus in National Context*. Grand Rapids: Eerdmans.

2005   *Jesus and His Death: Historiography, the Historical Jesus, and Atonement Theory*. Waco, Texas: Baylor University Press.

Stanton, G. N.

2002   *The Gospels and Jesus*. Oxford: Oxford University Press.

2004   *Jesus and Gospel*. Cambridge: Cambridge University Press.

RUDOLF BULTMANN

The Message of Jesus and the Problem of Mythology

1

[[11]] The heart of the preaching of Jesus Christ is the Kingdom of God. During the nineteenth century exegesis and theology understood the Kingdom of God as a spiritual community consisting of men joined together by obedience to the will of God which ruled in their wills. By such obedience they sought to enlarge the sphere of His rule in the world. They were building, it was said, the Kingdom of God as a realm which is spiritual but within the world, active and effective in this world, unfolding in the history of this world.

The year 1892 saw the publication of *The Preaching of Jesus about the Kingdom of God* by Johannes Weiss. [[12]] This epoch-making book refuted the interpretation which was hitherto generally accepted. Weiss showed that the Kingdom of God is not immanent in the world and does not grow as part of the world's history, but is rather eschatological; i.e., the Kingdom of God transcends the historical order. It will come into being not through the moral endeavour of man, but solely through the supernatural action of God. God will suddenly put an end to the world and to history, and He will bring in a new world, the world of eternal blessedness.

This conception of the Kingdom of God was not an invention of Jesus. It was a conception familiar in certain circles of Jews who were waiting for the end of this world. This picture of the eschatological drama was drawn in Jewish apocalyptic literature, of which the book of Daniel is the earliest still extant. The preaching of Jesus is distinguished from the typical apocalyptic

Reprinted with permission from Rudolf Bultmann, *Jesus Christ and Mythology* (New York: Scribner's, 1958) 11–34.

pictures of the eschatological drama and of the blessedness of the coming new age in so far as Jesus refrained from drawing detailed pictures. He confined himself to the statement that the Kingdom of God will come and that men must be prepared to face the coming judgment. Otherwise he shared the eschatological expectations of his contemporaries. That is why he taught his disciples to pray,

> Hallowed be thy name,
> Thy Kingdom come,
> Thy will be done on earth as it is in heaven.

Jesus expected that this would take place soon, in the immediate future, and he said that the dawning of that [[13]] age could already be perceived in the signs and wonders which he performed, especially in his casting out of demons. Jesus envisaged the inauguration of the Kingdom of God as a tremendous cosmic drama. The Son of Man will come with the clouds of heaven, the dead will be raised and the day of judgment will arrive; for the righteous the time of bliss will begin, whereas the damned will be delivered to the torments of hell.

When I began to study theology, theologians as well as laymen were excited and frightened by the theories of Johannes Weiss. I remember that Julius Kaftan, my teacher in dogmatics in Berlin, said: "If Johannes Weiss is right and the conception of the Kingdom of God is an eschatological one, then it is impossible to make use of this conception in dogmatics." But in the following years the theologians, J. Kaftan among them, became convinced that Weiss was correct. Perhaps I may here refer to Albert Schweitzer who carried the theory of Weiss to extremes. He maintains that not only the preaching and the self-consciousness of Jesus but also his day-to-day conduct of life were dominated by an eschatological expectation which amounted to an all-pervading eschatological dogma.

Today nobody doubts that Jesus' conception of the Kingdom of God is an eschatological one—at least in European theology and, as far as I can see, also among American New Testament scholars. Indeed, it has become more and more clear that the eschatological expectation and hope is the core of the New Testament preaching throughout.

The earliest Christian community understood the [[14]] Kingdom of God in the same sense as Jesus. It, too, expected the Kingdom of God to come in the immediate future. So Paul, too, thought that he would still be alive when the end of this world was to come and the dead were to be raised. This general conviction is confirmed by the voices of impatience, of anxiety and of doubt which are already audible in the synoptic gospels and which echo a little later and louder, for example, in the Second Epistle of Peter. Christianity has always retained the hope that the Kingdom of God will come in the immediate future, although it has waited in vain. We may cite Mark 9:1, which is not a genuine saying of Jesus but was ascribed to him by the earliest community: "Truly, I say to you, there are some standing here who will not taste death before they see the kingdom of God come with power." Is not the meaning of this verse clear? Though many of the contemporaries of Jesus are already dead, the hope must nevertheless be retained that the Kingdom of God will still come in this generation.

2

This hope of Jesus and of the early Christian community was not fulfilled. The same world still exists and history continues. The course of history has refuted mythology. For the conception "Kingdom of God" is mythological, as is the conception of the eschatological drama. Just as mythological are the presuppositions of the expectation of the Kingdom of God, namely, the theory that the world, although created by God, is ruled [[15]] by the devil, Satan, and that his army, the demons, is the cause of all evil, sin and disease. The whole conception of the world which is presupposed in the preaching of Jesus as in the New Testament generally is mythological; i.e., the conception of the world as being structured in three stories, heaven, earth and hell; the conception of the intervention of supernatural powers in the course of events; and the conception of miracles, especially the conception of the intervention of supernatural powers in the inner life of the soul, the conception that men can be tempted and corrupted by the devil and possessed by evil spirits. This conception of the world we call mythological because it is different from the conception of the world which has been formed and developed by science since its inception in ancient Greece and which has been accepted by all modern men. In this modern conception of the world the cause-and-effect nexus is fundamental. Although modern physical theories take account of chance in the chain of cause and effect in subatomic phenomena, our daily living, purposes and actions are not affected. In any case, modern science does not believe that the course of nature can be interrupted or, so to speak, perforated, by supernatural powers.

The same is true of the modern study of history, which does not take into account any intervention of God or of the devil or of demons in the course of history. Instead, the course of history is considered to be an unbroken whole, complete in itself, though differing from the course of nature because there are in history [[16]] spiritual powers which influence the will of persons. Granted that not all historical events are determined by physical necessity and that persons are responsible for their actions, nevertheless nothing happens without rational motivation. Otherwise, responsibility would be dissolved. Of course, there are still many superstitions among modern men, but they are exceptions or even anomalies. Modern men take it for granted that the course of nature and of history, like their own inner life and their practical life, is nowhere interrupted by the intervention of supernatural powers.

Then the question inevitably arises: is it possible that Jesus' preaching of the Kingdom of God still has any importance for modern men and the preaching of the New Testament as a whole is still important for modern men? The preaching of the New Testament proclaims Jesus Christ, not only his preaching of the Kingdom of God but first of all his person, which was mythologized from the very beginnings of earliest Christianity. New Testament scholars are at variance as to whether Jesus himself claimed to be the Messiah, the King of the time of blessedness, whether he believed himself to be the Son of Man who would come on the clouds of heaven. If so, Jesus understood himself in the light of mythology. We need not, at this point, decide one way or the other. At any rate, the early Christian community thus regarded him as a mythological figure. It expected him to return as the Son of Man on the clouds of heaven to bring salvation and damnation as judge of the world. His person is viewed in the light of mythology when he is [[17]] said to have been begotten of the Holy Spirit and born of a virgin, and this becomes clearer still in Hellenistic Christian communities where he is understood to be the Son of God in a metaphysical sense, a great, pre-existent heavenly being who became man for the sake of our redemption and took on himself suffering, even the suffering of the cross. It is evident that such conceptions are mythological, for they were widespread in the mythologies of Jews and Gentiles and then were transferred to the historical person of Jesus. Particularly the conception of the pre-existent Son of God who descended in human guise into the world to redeem mankind is part of the Gnostic doctrine of redemption, and nobody hesitates to call this doctrine mythological. This raises in an acute form the question: *what is the importance of the preaching of Jesus and of the preaching of the New Testament as a whole for modern man?*

For modern man the mythological conception of the world, the conceptions of eschatology, of redeemer and of redemption, are over and done with. Is it possible to expect that we shall make a sacrifice of understanding, *sacrificium intellectus*, in order to accept what we cannot sincerely consider true—merely because such conceptions are suggested by the Bible? Or ought we to pass over those sayings of the New Testament which contain such mythological conceptions and to select other sayings which are not such stumbling-blocks to modern man? In fact, the preaching of Jesus is not confined to eschatological sayings. He proclaimed also the will of God, which is God's demand, the demand for [[18]] the good. Jesus demands truthfulness and purity, readiness to sacrifice and to love. He demands that the whole man be obedient to God, and he protests against the delusion that one's duty to God can be fulfilled by obeying certain external commandments. If the ethical demands of Jesus are stumbling-blocks to modern man, then it is to his selfish will, not to his understanding, that they are stumbling-blocks.

What follows from all this? Shall we retain the ethical preaching of Jesus and abandon his eschatological preaching? Shall we reduce his preaching of the Kingdom of God to the so-called social gospel? Or is there a third possibility? We must ask whether the eschatological preaching and the mythological sayings as a whole contain a still deeper meaning which is concealed under the cover of mythology. If that is so, let us abandon the mythological conceptions precisely because we want to retain their deeper meaning. This method of interpretation of the New Testament which tries to recover the deeper meaning behind the mythological conceptions I call *de-mythologizing*—an unsatisfactory word, to be sure. Its aim is not to eliminate the mythological statements but to interpret them. It is a method of hermeneutics. The meaning of this method will be best understood when we make clear the meaning of mythology in general.

3

It is often said that mythology is a primitive science, the intention of which is to explain phenomena and incidents [[19]] which are strange, curious, surprising, or frightening, by attributing them to supernatural causes, to gods or to demons. So it is in part, for example, when it attributes phenomena like eclipses of the sun or of the moon to such causes; but there is more than this in mythology. Myths speak about gods and demons as powers on which man knows himself to be dependent, powers whose favor he needs, powers whose wrath he fears. Myths express the knowledge that man is not master of the world and of his life, that the world within which he lives is full of riddles and mysteries and that human life also is full of riddles and mysteries.

Mythology expresses a certain understanding of human existence. It believes that the world and human life have their ground and their limits in a power which is beyond all that we can calculate or control. Mythology speaks about this power inadequately and insufficiently because it speaks about it as if it were a worldly power. It speaks of gods who represent the power beyond the visible, comprehensible world. It speaks of gods as if they were men and of their actions as human actions, although it conceives of the gods as endowed with superhuman power and of their actions as incalculable, as capable of breaking the normal, ordinary order of events. It may be said that myths give to the transcendent reality an immanent, this-worldly objectivity. Myths give worldly objectivity to that which is unworldly. (In German one would say, "Der Mythos objektiviert das Jenseitige zum Diesseitigen" [['Myth objectifies the future into the now']].)

[[20]] All this holds true also of the mythological conceptions found in the Bible. According to mythological thinking, God has his domicile in heaven. What is the meaning of this statement? The meaning is quite clear. In a crude manner it expresses the idea that God is beyond the world, that He is transcendent. The thinking which is not yet capable of forming the abstract idea of transcendence expresses its intention in the category of space; the transcendent God is imagined as being at an immense spatial distance, far above the world: for above this world is the world of the stars, of the light which enlightens and makes glad the life of men. When mythological thinking forms the conception of hell, it expresses the idea of the transcendence of evil as the tremendous power which again and again afflicts mankind. The location of hell and of men whom hell has seized is below the earth in darkness, because darkness is tremendous and terrible to men.

These mythological conceptions of heaven and hell are no longer acceptable for modern men since for scientific thinking to speak of "above" and "below" in the universe has lost all meaning, but the idea of the transcendence of God and of evil is still significant.

Another example is the conception of Satan and the evil spirits into whose power men are delivered. This conception rests upon the experience, quite apart from the inexplicable evils arising outside ourselves to which we are exposed, that our own actions are often so puzzling; men are often carried away by their passions and are no longer master of themselves, with the [[21]] result that inconceivable wickedness breaks forth from them. Again, the conception of Satan as ruler over the world expresses a deep insight, namely, the insight that evil is not only to be found here and there in the world, but that all particular evils make up one single power which in the last analysis grows from the very actions of men, which form an atmosphere, a spiritual tradition, which overwhelms every man. The consequences and effects of our sins become a power dominating us, and we cannot free ourselves from them. Particularly in our day and generation, although we no longer think mythologically, we often speak of demonic powers which rule history, corrupting political and social life. Such language is metaphorical, a figure of speech, but in it is expressed the knowledge, the insight, that the evil for which every man is responsible individually has nevertheless become a power which mysteriously enslaves every member of the human race.

Now the question arises: is it possible to de-mythologize the message of Jesus and the preaching of the early Christian community? Since this preaching was shaped by the eschatological belief, the first question is this: *What is the meaning of eschatology in general?*

4

[[22]] In the language of traditional theology eschatology is the doctrine of the last things, and "last" means last in the course of time, that is, the end of the world which is imminent as the future is to our present. But in the actual preaching of the prophets and of Jesus this "last" has a further meaning. As in the conception of heaven the transcendence of God is imagined by means of the category of space, so in the conception of the end of the world, the idea of the transcendence of God is imagined by means of the category of time. However, it is not simply the idea of transcendence as such, but of the importance of the transcendence of God, of God who is [[23]] never present as a familiar phenomenon but who is always the coming God, who is veiled by the unknown future. Eschatological preaching views the present time in the light of the future and it says to men that this present world, the world of nature and history, the world in which we live our lives and make our plans is not the only world; that this world is temporal and transitory, yes, ultimately empty and unreal in the face of eternity.

This understanding is not peculiar to mythical eschatology. It is the knowledge to which Shakespeare gives grand expression:

> The cloud-capp'd towers, the gorgeous palaces,
> The solemn temples, the great globe itself,

> Yea, all which it inherit, shall dissolve,
> And like this insubstantial pageant faded,
> Leave not a rack behind. We are such stuff
> As dreams are made on; and our little life
> Is rounded with a sleep. . . .
>
> *Tempest* IV, 1

It is the same understanding which was current among the Greeks who did not share the eschatology which was common to the prophets and to Jesus. Permit me to quote from a hymn of Pindar:

> Creatures of a day, what is anyone? what is he not?
> Man is but a dream of a shadow.
>
> *Pythian Odes* 8, 95–96

and from Sophocles: [[24]]

> Alas! we living mortals, what are we
> But phantoms all or unsubstantial shades?
>
> *Ajax* 125–26

The perception of the boundary of human life warns men against 'presumption' (ὕβρις) and calls to 'thoughtfulness' and 'awe' (σωφροσύην and αἰδώς).' Nothing too much' (μηδὲν ἄγαν), 'of strength do not boast' (ἐπὶ ῥώμη μὴ καυχῶ) are sayings of Greek wisdom. Greek tragedy shows the truth of such proverbs in its representations of human destiny. From the soldiers slain in the Battle of Plataeae we should learn, as Aeschylus says, that

> Mortal man needs must not vaunt him overmuch . . .
> Zeus, of a truth, is a chastiser of overweening pride
> And corrects with heavy hand.
>
> *Persians* 820–28

And again in the *Ajax* of Sophocles Athene says of the mad Ajax,

> Warned by these sights, Odysseus, see that thou
> Utter no boastful word against the gods,
> Nor swell with pride if haply might of arm
> Exalt thee o'er thy fellows, or vast wealth.
> A day can prostrate and a day upraise
> All that is mortal; but the gods approve
> Sobriety and frowardness abhor.
>
> 127–33

5

If it is true that the general human understanding of the insecurity of the present in the face of the future [[25]] has found expression in eschatological thought, then we must ask, *what is the difference between the Greek and the Biblical understanding?* The Greeks found the immanent power of the beyond, of the gods compared with whom all human affairs are empty, in "destiny." They do not share the mythological conception of eschatology as a cosmic event at the end of time; and it may well be said that Greek thought is more similar to that of modern man than to the Biblical conception, since for modern man mythological eschatology has passed away. It is possible that the Biblical eschatology may rise again. It will not rise in its old mythological form but from the terrifying vision that modern technology, especially atomic science, may bring about the destruction of our earth through the abuse of human science and technology. When we ponder this possibility, we can feel the terror and the anxiety which were evoked by the eschatological preaching of the imminent end of the world. To be sure, that preaching was developed in conceptions which are no longer intelligible today, but they do express the knowledge of the finiteness of the world, and of the end which is imminent to us all because we all are beings of this finite world. This is the insight to which as a rule we turn a blind eye, but which may be brought to light by modern technology. It is precisely the intensity of this insight which explains why Jesus, like the Old Testament prophets, expected the end of the world to occur in the immediate future. The majesty of God and the inescapability of His judgment, and over [[26]] against these the emptiness of the world and of men were felt with such an intensity that it seemed that the world was at an end, and that the hour of crisis was present. Jesus proclaims the will of God and the responsibility of man, pointing towards the eschatological events, but it is not because he is an eschatologist that he proclaims the will of God. On the contrary, he is an eschatologist because he proclaims the will of God.

The difference between the Biblical and the Greek understanding of the human situation regarding the unknown future can now be seen in a clearer light. It consists in the fact that in the thinking of the prophets and of Jesus the nature of God involves more than simply His omnipotence and His judgment touches not only the man who offends Him by presumption and boasting. For the prophets and for Jesus God is the Holy One, who demands right and righteousness, who demands love of neighbour and who therefore is the judge of all human thoughts and actions. The world is empty not only because it is transitory, but because men have turned it into a place in which evil spreads and sin rules. The end of the world, therefore, is the judgment of God; that is, the eschatological preaching not only brings to consciousness the emptiness of the human situation and calls men, as was the case among the Greeks, to moderation, humility and resignation; it calls men first and foremost to responsibility toward God and to repentance. It calls them to perform the will of God. Thus, the characteristic difference between [[27]] the eschatological preaching of Jesus and that of the Jewish apocalypses becomes evident. All the pictures of future happiness in which apocalypticism excels are lacking in the preaching of Jesus.

Though in this connection we do not examine other differences between Biblical and Greek thought, as, for instance, the personality of the one holy God, the personal relationship between God and man, and the Biblical belief that God is the creator of the world, we must consider one more important point. The eschatological preaching proclaims the imminent end of the world, not only as the final judgment, but also as the beginning of the time of salvation and of eternal bliss. The end of the world has not only a negative but also a positive meaning. To use nonmythological terms, the finiteness of the world and of man over against the transcendent power of God contains not only warning, but also consolation. Let us ask whether the ancient Greeks also speak in this way about the emptiness of the world and of this-worldly affairs. I think that we can hear such a voice in Euripides' question,

> Who knows if to live is really to die,
> and if to die is to live?
>
> Frg. 638 (ed. Nauck)

At the end of his speech to his judges, Socrates says,

> But now the time has come to go away. I go to die and you to live; but which of us goes to the better lot, is known to none but God.
>
> *Apol.* 42A

[[28]] In a similar vein the Platonic Socrates says,

> If the soul is immortal, we must care for it, not only in respect to this time, which we call life, but in respect to all time.
>
> *Phaed.* 107c

Above all, we should think of this famous saying,

> practice dying.
> *Phaed.* 67e

This, according to Plato, is the characteristic feature of the life of the philosopher. Death is the separation of the soul from the body. As long as man lives, the soul is bound to the body and to its needs. The philosopher lives his life detaching his soul as much as possible from communion with the body, for the body disturbs the soul and hinders it from attaining the truth. The philosopher looks for cleansing, that is, for release from the body, and so he "gives heed to dying."

If we may call the Platonic hope in life after death an eschatology, then the Christian eschatology agrees with the Platonic eschatology in so far as each expects bliss after death and also in so far as bliss may be called *freedom*. This freedom is for Plato the freedom of the spirit from the body, the freedom of the spirit which can perceive the truth which is the very reality of being; and for Greek thinking, of course, the realm of reality is also the realm of beauty. According to Plato, this transcendent bliss can be described not only in negative and abstract, but also in positive terms. Since the [[29]] transcendent realm is the realm of truth and truth is to be found in discussion, that is, in dialogue, Plato can picture the transcendent realm positively as a sphere of dialogue. Socrates says that it would be best if he could spend his life in the beyond in examining and exploring as he did on this side. "To converse and associate with them and examine them would be immeasurable happiness" (*Apol.* 41C).

In Christian thinking freedom is not the freedom of a spirit who is satisfied with perceiving the truth; it is the freedom of man to be himself. Freedom is freedom from sin, from wickedness, or as St. Paul says, from the flesh, from the old self, because God is Holy. Thus, obtaining bliss means obtaining grace and righteousness by God's judgment. Moreover, it is impossible to depict the ineffable blessedness of those who are justified, save in symbolic pictures such as a splendid banquet, or in such pictures as the Revelation of John paints. According to Paul, "the kingdom of God does not mean food and drink but righteousness, and peace, and joy in the Holy Spirit" (Rom 14:17). And Jesus said, "when they rise from the dead, they neither marry nor are given in marriage, but are like angels in heaven" (Mark 12:25). The physical body is replaced by the spiritual body. To be sure, our imperfect knowledge will then become perfect, and then we shall see face to face, as Paul says (1 Cor 13:9–12). But that is by no means knowledge of truth in the Greek sense, but an untroubled relationship with God, as Jesus promised that the pure in heart shall see God (Matt 5:8).

[[30]] If we can say anything more, it is that the action of God reaches its fulfilment in the glory of God. Thus the Church of God in the present has no other purpose than to praise and glorify God by its conduct (Phil 1:11) and by its thanksgiving (2 Cor 1:20; 4:15; Rom 15:6f.). Therefore, the future Church in the state of perfection cannot be thought of otherwise than as a worshiping community which sings hymns of praise and thanksgiving. We can see examples of this in the Revelation of John.

Surely both conceptions of transcendent bliss are mythological, the Platonic conception of bliss as philosophical dialogue as well as the Christian conception of blessedness as worship. Each conception intends to speak about the transcendent world as a world where man reaches the perfection of his true, real essence. This essence can be realized only imperfectly in this world, but nevertheless it determines life in this world as a life of seeking, and longing and yearning.

The difference between the two conceptions is due to different theories of human nature. Plato conceives the realm of spirit as a realm without time and without history because he conceives human nature as not subject to time and history. The Christian conception of the human being is that man is essentially a temporal being, which means that he is an historical being who has a past which shapes his character and who has a future which always brings forth new encounters. Therefore the future after death and beyond this world is a future of the totally new. This is the *totaliter aliter*. [[31]] Then there will be "a new heaven and a new earth" (Rev 21:1, 2 Pet 3:13). The seer of the future Jerusalem hears a voice, "Behold, I make all things new" (Rev

21:5). Paul and John anticipate this newness. Paul says, "If any one is in Christ, he is a new creation; the old has passed away, behold, the new has come" (2 Cor 5:17), and John says, "I am writing you a new commandment, which is true in him and in you, because the darkness is passing away and the true light is already shining" (1 John 2:8). But that newness is not a visible one, for our new life "is hid with Christ in God" (Col 3:8), "it does not yet appear what we shall be" (1 John 3:2). In a certain manner this unknown future is present in the holiness and love which characterize the believers in the Holy Spirit which inspired them, and in the worship of the Church. It cannot be described except in symbolic pictures: "for in this hope we were saved. Now hope that is seen is not hope. For who hopes for what he sees? But if we hope for what we do not see, we wait for it with patience" (Rom 8:24–25). Therefore, this hope or this faith may be called readiness for the unknown future that God will give. In brief, it means to be open to God's future in the face of death and darkness.

This, then, is the deeper meaning of the mythological preaching of Jesus—to be open to God's future which is really imminent for every one of us; to be prepared for this future which can come as a thief in the night when we do not expect it; to be prepared, because this future will be a judgment on all men who have bound [[32]] themselves to this world and are not free, not open to God's future.

6

The eschatological preaching of Jesus was retained and continued by the early Christian community in its mythological form. But very soon the process of demythologizing began, partially with Paul, and radically with John. The decisive step was taken when Paul declared that the turning point from the old world to the new was not a matter of the future but did take place in the coming of Jesus Christ. "But when the time had fully come, God sent forth his Son" (Gal 4:4). To be sure, Paul still expected the end of the world as a cosmic drama, the *parousia* [['advent']] of Christ on the clouds of heaven, the resurrection from the dead, the final judgment, but with the resurrection of Christ the decisive event has already happened. The Church is the eschatological community of the elect, of the saints who are already justified and are alive because they are in Christ, in Christ who as the second Adam abolished death and brought life and immortality to light though the gospel (Rom 5:12–14; 2 Tim 1:10). "Death is swallowed up in victory" (1 Cor 15:54). Therefore, Paul can say that the expectations and promises of the ancient prophets are fulfilled when the gospel is proclaimed: "Behold, now is the acceptable time [about which Isaiah spoke]; behold, now is the day of salvation" (2 Cor 6:2). The Holy Spirit who was expected as the gift of the time of blessedness has already been given. In this manner the future is anticipated.

[[33]] This de-mythologizing may be observed in a particular instance. In the Jewish apocalyptic expectations, the expectation of the Messianic kingdom played a role. The Messianic kingdom is, so to speak, an *interregnum* between the old world time (οὗτος ὁ αἰών) and the new age (ὁ μέλλων αἰών). Paul explains this apocalyptic, mythological idea of the Messianic *interregnum*, at the end of which Christ will deliver the Kingdom to God the Father, as the present time between the resurrection of Christ and his coming *parousia* (1 Cor 15:24); that means, the present time of preaching the gospel is really the formerly expected time of the Kingdom of the Messiah. Jesus Is now the Messiah, the Lord.

After Paul, John de-mythologized the eschatology in a radical manner. For John the coming and departing of Jesus is the eschatological event. "And this is the judgment, that the light has come into the world, and men loved darkness rather than light, because their deeds were evil" (John 3:19). "Now is the judgment of this world, now shall the ruler of this world be cast out" (12:31). For John the resurrection of Jesus, Pentecost and the *parousia* of Jesus are one and the same event, and those who believe have already eternal life. "He who believes in him is not condemned; he who does not believe is condemned already" (3:18). "He who believes in the Son has eternal life; he who does not obey the Son shall not see life, but the wrath of God rests upon him" (3:36). "Truly, truly, I say to you, the hour is coming, and now is, when the dead will hear the voice of the Son of God, and those who hear will live" (5:25). "I am the resurrection and the life; he [[34]] who believes in me, though he die, yet shall he live; and whoever lives and believes in me shall never die" (11:25f.).

As in Paul, so In John de-mythologizing may be further observed in a particular instance. In Jewish eschatological expectations we find that the figure of the anti-Christ is a thoroughly mythological figure as it is described, for example, in 2 Thessalonians (2:7–12). In John false teachers play the role of this mythological figure. Mythology has been transposed into history. These examples show, it seems to me, that de-mythologizing has its beginning in the New Testament itself, and therefore our task of de-mythologizing today is justified.

G. N. STANTON

The Gospel Traditions and Early Christological Reflection

[[191]] It is not surprising that motifs such as "Jesus as the Man for others," and, indeed, the humanity of Jesus in general, should be so prominent in the recent work of systematic theologians, whether or not one agrees that the most adequate modern christology will start "from below." Much more surprising is the width of the gap between this current interest in the life and character of Jesus of Nazareth and the conclusions of many New Testament scholars. For many New Testament specialists are becoming more and more vociferous in their insistence that there was no close relationship between early christological reflection and the life and character of Jesus; the most primitive christologies did not arise from the church's interest in or memory of the type of person Jesus showed himself to be in his teaching, actions, and relationships with others, but from expectations of an imminent *parousia* [['advent']] which were deeply influenced by apocalyptic.

If the primitive church was not interested in the "past" of Jesus, why, then, did the church produce gospels which, at a cursory glance at least, look so much like lives of Jesus? A wide variety of answers has been given, all of which argue that only at a relatively late stage in the long development from the earliest preaching of the gospel to the church's acceptance of four gospels did the church understand its traditions about Jesus as historical or biographical reminiscence of any sort. Some point to the important step taken by Mark when he first linked gospel traditions together to make a "story" about Jesus; many others insist that Luke is the innovator, for he has carefully placed his biography of Jesus within the framework of his overall understanding of the Christian message; others point to the effect of the so-called delay of the *parousia*, to the needs of the Hellenistic churches or to a reaction [[192]] which set in

---

Reprinted, with permission, from G. N. Stanton, "The Gospel Traditions and Early Christological Reflection," in *Christ: Faith and History* (ed. S. W. Sykes and J. P. Clayton; Cambridge Studies in Christology; Cambridge: Cambridge University Press, 1972) 191–204.

against primitive *Christian Enthusiasmus* which had partly overlooked the earthly Jesus. When the gospel traditions did eventually come to play a more central role in the life and faith of the church, they were understood in the light of firmly established christological convictions; convictions which, it is often argued, deeply influenced or even largely created the church's traditions about Jesus.

The systematic theologian is placed in something of a quandary by expositions of the development of the christology of the early church which proceed along these lines. If the humanity of Jesus is to be central in christological thinking and if the christology of the New Testament is to be taken at all seriously, the earliest stages of christological reflection must be by-passed deliberately and attention paid to later developments. Just conceivably, the systematic theologian may be tempted to throw his hands in the air and conclude that since New Testament scholars cannot provide a consensus of opinion and since the various christologies in the New Testament arose at different stages and clash so strongly with one another, he is forced to work out his christology in isolation from historical uncertainties.

I should want to argue that various lines of evidence, taken cumulatively, indicate that Luke and Mark have done little more than use their literary and theological talents to refine a pattern which is very much earlier: in its proclamation of Jesus, especially in its initial missionary proclamation, the primitive church included reference to the past of Jesus of Nazareth, to his life and character, and often used gospel pericopae for this very purpose. Opponents will immediately retort that this is a naïve view which can be defended, firstly, only by reading the gospels and the traditions they enshrine as biographical documents, thus totally misunderstanding their perspective, and, secondly, only by assuming that the primitive church was interested in the "past" of Jesus, for which there is in fact no *Sitz im Leben*.

I make no apology for advancing an unfashionable point of view by re-examining these two widely cherished convictions. New Testament scholarship has moved so quickly in recent decades that reconsideration of generally accepted conclusions is very much [[193]] the order of the day. New theories may or may not emerge, but an intensive resifting of the evidence will, by indicating which conclusions are well grounded and which not, provide firmer foundations for further research.

I

The often-repeated dictum "the gospels are not biographies" needs careful reappraisal. I certainly do not want to argue that the clock must now be turned back many decades and the gospels read as biographies. The gospels are unique. There is little point in considering which ancient biography is closest in form to the gospels. But a comparison of the gospels with roughly contemporary biographical writing is by no means irrelevant, for it underlines some important characteristics of the gospels which have often been overlooked in recent discussion.

The fundamental difference between the gospels and all biographical writing, whether ancient or modern, has often been used as a quick way of confirming that the gospel traditions were not originally understood as "historical reminiscence" or "biographical" portrait of Jesus.

> The gospel form [writes Norman Perrin] was created to serve the purpose of the early Church, but historical reminiscence was not one of those purposes. So, for example, when we read an account of Jesus giving instruction to his disciples, we are not hearing the voice of the earthly Jesus addressing Galilean disciples in a Palestinian situation but that of the risen Lord addressing Christian missionaries in a Hellenistic world.[1]

Standard New Testament textbooks usually point out that the gospels are not at all comparable with Hellenistic biographies, for they make no attempt to set out a detailed chronological record of the events in the life of Jesus, nor do they depict the main stages in the psychological development of Jesus or a description of his appearance, nor do they set Jesus against the wider historical background of his time; Luke, it is admitted, is a partial exception. [[194]] The gospels and the gospel traditions which circulated in the church before and after Mark wrote are not related to any biographical interest on the part of the early church. They are proclamation, not report. Such conclusions are usually taken, if not as an axiom, then at least as an assured result of the form critical revolution; the word "biographical" has become to a form critic like a red rag to a bull. But this general understanding of the perspective of the gospels is bound up with a quite surprisingly inaccurate assessment of ancient biographical writing.

Greek and Roman biographical writing reached its zenith shortly after the gospels were written, in the work of Tacitus, Plutarch and Suetonius; but all three writers drew, in different ways, on traditional techniques. When some of the literary conventions used in depicting the life of a significant person in the Graeco-Roman world of the first and early second centuries are examined, the profound difference which emerges is not so much between ancient biographical writing and the gospels, as between all forms of ancient biographical writing and its modern counterpart.

The gospels do show comparatively little interest in chronological order when compared with modern biographical writing, but the loose structure of the gospels is by no means unique. It was once customary for classical scholars to divide ancient biographical writing into two streams: chronological order was a feature of the Peripatetic biographers by whom Plutarch was deeply influenced; the Alexandrian biographers, and later Suetonius, dealt with a life *per species*, grouping together material on topics such as conduct, business, family, attitude towards society, friends. However, since the discovery of fragments of Satyrus' *Life of Euripides*, the only firsthand Peripatetic biography extant, this division is seen to have been an oversimplification. Although Satyrus was one of the last Peripatetic biographers, writing in the second half

---

1. N. Perrin, *Rediscovering the Teaching of Jesus* (1967) 15f.

of the third century B.C., the extant sections of his work reveal a clear tendency towards an orderly grouping of material, but only one section which can in any way be called chronological. There is now little doubt that the Peripatetics, who so strongly influenced both Greek and Roman [[195]] biographical writing of the first century A.D. and later, ordered their material by topics, not chronologically.

Nor does Plutarch make any attempt to adopt a precise chronology; the chronological expressions he does use are nearly all vague, phrases such as "about this time," "some time after this," being common. Campaigns are presented chronologically, but Plutarch's basic method is *per species*. Later writers, such as Arrian, Philostratus and Diogenes Laertius present a similar picture. Concern for chronological order was not a characteristic of ancient biographical writing; Tacitus and Cornelius Nepos are partial exceptions who prove the rule. As a stylistic technique, presentation of material *per species* is much more common than a precise chronological order or framework.

Since chronological order was not common, it is not surprising to find that to trace development of character was not a *sine qua non* of ancient biographical writing. Early encomiasts, such as Isocrates and Xenophon, were not interested in development of character, for they attempted to delineate their subjects in terms of their own notions of exemplary character traits. Nor did Peripatetic biographers, and those who later inherited their techniques, trace development of character or personality, though the phenomenon of human alteration was not unknown. Instead of tracing character development, ancient biographical writing from Plato onwards generally started and finished with the mature character of the person concerned. The idea that a person can be understood only by tracing the development of his personality is modern and is hardly found in the ancient world.

Nor is the brief character sketch a common convention in ancient biographical writing. Plutarch, for example, sometimes does include a character summary, but he makes no attempt to analyse internal development of personality. Plutarch aimed to "paint personality," but he did not always do this in his own words.

Much more prominent as a method of character portrayal is the recognition that a person's actions and words sum up his character more adequately than the comments of an observer. This is a deeply rooted tradition in ancient biographical writing. In his [[196]] *Agesilaus* Xenophon states that the deeds of a man best disclose the stamp of his nature. Direct analysis of the subject's character was almost certainly rare in Peripatetic biography; the actions and words of a person were allowed to speak for themselves. At the beginning of his life of Alexander Plutarch expounded the principles on which he worked: "In the most illustrious deed there is not always a manifestation of virtues and avarice, nay, a slight thing like a phrase or a jest often makes a greater revelation of character than battles where thousands fall, or the greatest armaments or sieges of cities." This method of indirect characterisation, in which the personality of the author himself remained in the background, was a widely practised technique in ancient biography generally.

The gospels also show little interest in character development, portraying Jesus from the beginning to the end of his ministry in essentially the same way and allowing his actions and words to show the sort of person he was. While it is impossible to find clear traces of ancient biographical conventions in the gospel traditions, the gospels' presentation of the life of Jesus is much less distinctive than has been claimed.

Attention has often been drawn to the fact that, unlike ancient biographical writing, the gospels fail to set Jesus against the wider historical background of his time. But this feature of modern biographical writing was not known among the Greeks, for consciousness of different historical epochs was lacking in antiquity. Biography and history were carefully held apart.

There is a little more justification for drawing attention to the absence of personal descriptions of Jesus from the gospels, but even this was not a universal feature of ancient biographical writing. Xenophon only rarely mentions traits of physical appearance. Both Plutarch and Diogenes Laertius have descriptions in some but not all of their biographies. Tacitus gives only a very brief account of the appearance of Agricola, while Nepos omits such a description of Atticus.

It is not difficult to draw attention to the wide gulf between the gospels and ancient biographical writing; the gospels have nothing comparable to the many personal anecdotes, some of which were [[197]] widely used "stock" situations which Plutarch and Suetonius included simply to satisfy the curiosity of their readers. The travellers' tales cast in biographical form perform a similar function in Philostratus' *Life of Apollonius of Tyana*.

The gospels must be read against the backdrop, not of modern biographical writing, but of their own times. When this is done, the gospels do not emerge as biographies of Jesus, but their presentations of the life of Jesus are seen to be much less distinctive than is usually believed. Recognition of the fact that, unlike Plutarch, Suetonius and other ancient biographers, they do not draw on a long literary tradition, supports this conclusion. For if the modern preoccupation with chronological precision, historical background, personal appearance and character development are all largely missing in ancient biographical writing with its *literary* tradition, their absence is even less surprising in the gospels, which can scarcely be described as literary productions. "Sophisticated" ancient biographical writing very often used the simple technique of portraying character by allowing the actions and words of a person to speak for themselves; hence there is no reason to agree that "unsophisticated" gospel traditions can appear to portray the character of Jesus by reporting his words and actions only if their intention is misunderstood.

However Hellenistic the gospels may be, they are firmly anchored in the Jewish world. But Jewish accounts of the life and character of a person comparable in any way with the gospels are almost non-existent. The Qumran literature, for example, reminds us that it was by no means the usual practice in the ancient world to compile an account of the life of a founder of a community such as Qumran, nor even of many other types of significant figures. In spite of the influence and importance of Qumran's Teacher, the community seems to have survived on a minimum of tradition about him. The nature and extent of material relating to the life and character of the Teacher show clearly that by comparison the gospels are rich in material about Jesus, however the historian may evaluate it. Similarly, the variety and richness of the gospels' materials about *one* person stand out when they are placed alongside the rabbinic literature. We [[198]] know exceedingly little about the life of Yohanan Ben Zakkai, one of the most important and influential rabbinic teachers. Rabbinic traditions refer to almost as many different rabbis as there are pericopae.

That the uniqueness of the gospels lies primarily in the impact of the resurrection on the primitive church is not in doubt. But the uniqueness of the gospels also lies not so much in the ways they differ from Greek and Roman biographical writing, as many have insisted, but in the fact that in Jewish writings, from the Old Testament right through to the rabbinic corpus, there is nothing comparable to the gospels' concentration on the words, actions and relationships of one person.

The dictum "the gospels are not biographies" is still as firmly established as the standard solution to the synoptic problem, but this dictum cannot be used to deny that the gospels and the gospel traditions were intended to portray the life and character of Jesus. If, as one of his main purposes, Mark had wished to set out an account of significant aspects of the life of Jesus and to indicate the sort of person Jesus was, would the end result have been strikingly different from the gospel we now have?

Once this understanding of the perspective of the gospels is acknowledged as plausible, it is by no means difficult to accept that there is a good deal of material in the four gospels which portrays the character of Jesus. Many traits emerge from the gospel accounts of the actions and teaching of Jesus, and of his relationships with others. To this extent the gospel traditions may be described as "biographical." However, this expression has so many modern connotations (especially concerning personality) which are foreign to the ancient world that (if it is not to be misleading) it can be used of the gospel traditions only with careful definition.

But it is certainly true that no tradition about Jesus was retained by the church *solely* out of historical interest or biographical curiosity, for the traditions are kerygmatic and were used in the service of the preaching of the primitive church. There is no reasons either to quarrel with this general conclusion or to rehearse the reasons which lie behind its widespread acceptance since the [[199]] rise of form critical study of the gospels. But the very commonly suggested corollary, that since the gospel traditions are kerygmatic they are neither "historical" nor "biographical" in their perspective, is untenable: the kerygmatic role of the gospel traditions has not smothered interest in the life and character of Jesus. The dual perspective of the gospel traditions is inescapable: they intend to proclaim Jesus, they are also concerned with his life and character. To by-pass or minimise either aspect is to miss the finely-held balance of the traditions themselves: they are neither purely "biographical" nor "historical," nor are they kerygmatic to the exclusion of concern with more than the mere fact of the historical existence of Jesus.

The earliest preaching of the Christian message must surely have taken pains to sketch out briefly the kind of person Jesus was, in the context of its call to commitment to the one raised by God from the dead. Since the gospel traditions "report" the life of Jesus and "portray" his character, they were particularly appropriate for use in the initial missionary preaching of the church. This is not to deny that gospel traditions were used in ethical instruction, in apologetic, in instruction of believers, in worship, and in a variety of other ways in the life of the church.

II

In the preceding paragraphs we have been using the dual perspective of the gospel traditions to establish their *Sitz im Leben* in the primitive church. This procedure looks dangerously like a circular argument: the interest of the primitive church in the past of Jesus is established from the *form* of the traditions, but the very form of the traditions is interpreted in the light of their use in the primitive church. At this point we must also take up briefly the objection that since the primitive church was at first uninterested in the life of Jesus, the gospel traditions cannot have been understood and used in the way we have described. However, there are other lines of evidence which minimize the risk of a circular argument and also suggest that the early church, especially in its missionary preaching, was interested in the past of Jesus and that [[200]] traditions about Jesus were understood and used, as far back as we can trace them, as both proclamation and report about Jesus.

The only explicit accounts of initial missionary preaching in the New Testament period are to be found in Acts.[2] While it is impossible to date the traditions lying behind the speeches in Acts with any precision, these speeches (especially Acts 10:36–43 and Acts 13:16–41) are certainly pre-Lucan and seem to stem from a very early period. Luke indicates that as soon as the gospel was preached to audiences unfamiliar with the story of Jesus, the first evangelists included in their preaching a sketch of the life and character of Jesus. Peter's speeches in Acts make it quite clear that the primitive church did not proclaim the risen Christ and overlook the pre-resurrection events and the character of Jesus of Nazareth.

As Paul refers to the content of his initial missionary preaching only rarely in his epistles, he may well have used gospel traditions in his preaching—but there is, of course, no explicit evidence for this in the epistles. Paul's knowledge and use of gospel traditions must be left as a partially open question. But even if Paul did not refer to the life of Jesus precisely in the *form* of the gospel traditions which have come down to us, there are good grounds for maintaining that Paul was neither ignorant of, nor uninterested in the life

---

2. The arguments which are advanced briefly in the following paragraphs have been explained and defended in much greater detail in my forthcoming book, *The Primitive Preaching and Jesus of Nazareth* [[later published as *Jesus of Nazareth in New Testament Preaching* (SNTSMS 27; London: Cambridge University Press, 1974)]].

and character of Jesus and that his preaching included some reference to the sort of person Jesus was.

The proclamation of Jesus was used in the primitive church to proclaim him. Jesus' message is already, *in nuce,* a message about himself; his actions and words are inseparable. Jesus' message is very much bound up with his conduct and character, his "obscure" background and the unpromising outward circumstances of his ministry. The nature of Jesus' proclamation encouraged the primitive church to sketch out his life and character—including the "scandal" of his background—as part of its proclamation of him.

The very fact that Jesus could not be fitted into any of the categories of the day meant that the primitive church could not [[201]] simply make a theological pronouncement about him, and assume that no further explanation either of what sort of a person he was or of what sort of a life he had lived was necessary. For Jesus broke all Jewish preconceptions about the promised one; Hellenistic categories were no more adequate.

III

If then, the primitive church included a sketch of the character of Jesus in its preaching, it had a stake in transmitting and using traditions which it understood as referring to the past of Jesus; it was also much more aware of the distinction between the "past" and the "present" of Jesus than many scholars have recently argued, and it was therefore less likely to confuse its own understanding and experience of the risen Christ with its account of who Jesus of Nazareth was. And if the earliest christological proclamation and traditions about Jesus were not at first separate entities which were only later linked together, there are still further implications for our understanding of primitive christology.

What were the factors which influenced the earliest christological reflections of the church? The church's experience of the risen Christ, its apocalyptic expectations of an imminent *parousia* [['advent']] and its interpretation of the Old Testament are all seen as influential at particular points. But the christological terminology employed by the primitive church in its confession and proclamation of Jesus Christ was partly developed in the light of its traditions of the teaching, actions and character of Jesus.

Take, for example, the confession "Jesus is Messiah," one of the earliest, if not the earliest, ways in which Jesus was proclaimed. Why was Jesus called Messiah? Whether Jesus avoided the title completely (either because it was politically dangerous or because he did not consider himself to be Messiah), or whether he was simply extremely reticent about using it, there is a gulf between the explicit teaching of Jesus and the preaching of the primitive church. One currently popular answer argues that the Palestinian church used Messiah of Jesus in the specific context of his *parousia,* [[202]] as an equivalent for the apocalyptic title, Son of Man; hence there was no danger of confusing the title with the political type of Messiah.[3] This view places a great

---

3. R. H. Fuller, *The Foundations of New Testament Christology* (1965) 159.

deal of weight on Acts 3:20 which is understood to mean that at the *parousia* Jesus will return as "the Christ appointed for you." But this is not the most natural interpretation; the immediate context confirms that Jesus is already Messiah, not merely at his *parousia*. And in addition there are serious objections to be raised against the view that Son of Man was an apocalyptic title first used by the church in connection with its *parousia* expectations, then of the passion and resurrection of Jesus, and finally applied to the ministry of Jesus. The hypothesis that the primitive church's christological reflection (especially its use of Messiah–Christ, Son of Man, and even its interpretation of Old Testament passages) moved "backwards" from the *parousia* to the life of Jesus is surely an oversimplification of the evidence.

Nor can one answer the question "Why was Jesus called Messiah?" merely in terms of the resurrection. What was there about the resurrection which led the earliest believers to make a link between Jesus and Messiahship? One may legitimately insist that the resurrection confirmed, declared or even revealed the Messiahship of Jesus, but the resurrection alone did not *make* Jesus Messiah.

Peter's speech to Cornelius points us in a rather different direction: "God anointed Jesus of Nazareth with the Holy Spirit and with power (made him Messiah–Christ, *echrisen*). He went about doing good and healing all who were oppressed by the devil, for the active presence of the Holy Spirit of God was with him" (Acts 10:38).[4] The primitive church announced the Messiahship of the one raised by God from the dead because of its conviction, now confirmed by the resurrection, that this Jesus had been anointed by God's Spirit, for his life and ministry were not merely consistent with this claim, but provided evidence that God had begun to act in a new and decisive way in Jesus of Nazareth. The proclamation of Jesus as Messiah was no doubt filled out and [[203]] supported by traditions about the life of Jesus—for example, by traditions which showed that his relationships with others, which were so revolutionary as to prompt constant critical questioning, were grounded in his unique relationship to God, and by traditions which claimed that Jesus' actions were not those of a madman but were done by the finger or Spirit of God. The kind of person Jesus showed himself to be by his actions and relationships with others, and not merely such explicit teaching as he gave about his own person, may very well have influenced the kind of christological confessions the church made about Jesus.

But there remains the possibility that this understanding of Messiahship in terms of the anointing of Jesus with God's Spirit is Luke's theological achievement, for it is certainly an important theme in Luke–Acts. At the opening of Luke's account of Jesus' ministry, Jesus announces in the synagogue at Nazareth: "The Spirit of the Lord is upon me, because he has anointed (*echrisen*) me, he has sent me to announce good news to the poor" (Luke 4:18f.). Isa 61:1f. lies at the heart of both Acts 10:38 and Luke 4:18f. But in both passages

---

4. See W. C. van Unnik, "Jesus the Christ," *New Testament Studies* 8 (1961–62) 101ff., and "'Dominus Vobiscum': The Background of a Liturgical Formula" in A. J. B. Higgins (ed.), *New Testament Essays in Memory of T. W. Manson* (1959) 270ff.

Isa 61:1f. is tightly woven together with other Old Testament passages in a way which is typical of early Christian exegesis of Old Testament texts, but not typical of Luke himself. In addition, both passages contain a number of features which are not characteristic of Luke, but point to pre-Lucan tradition.[5]

And it would be rash to argue that the portrait of Jesus has been created by the church, for many aspects of the gospels' portrait of Jesus are represented so widely in various sources, strata and forms of the gospel traditions that their substantial reliability is established on the basis of the criteria of multiple attestation, coherence and consistency.

Perhaps we shall never know *precisely* the influences at work in [[204]] the earliest christological reflections of the church. To claim that the christological beliefs of the primitive church have not left their mark upon the gospel traditions would be to fly in the face of clear evidence to the contrary. But we may be sure that traditions about the life and character of Jesus played an important part not only in the preaching of the primitive church, but also in its christological reflection: both began with Jesus of Nazareth.

---

5. Luke 7:22 (Q) also weaves together Isa 61:1f. with other Old Testament passages. Isa 61:1f. is alluded to in another Q passage, Luke 6:20f. H. Schürmann has recently suggested that Luke 4:16–30 contains some material, including the citation of Isa 61:1f., which is characteristic of the Q material, but not of Luke or his L material. ("Zur Traditionsgeschichte der Nazareth-Perikope Luke 4,16–30," in *Mélanges Bibliques en homage au R. P. Béda Rigaux*, ed. A. Descamps and A. de Halleux [1970] 187ff.) If this is so (and Schürmann's case is strong), Isa 61:1f. must have deeply influenced the theology of the Q material.

JOHN A. T. ROBINSON

The Last Tabu?
The Self-Consciousness of Jesus

[[155]] Each generation of students inherits from its predecessor certain "no go" areas that have been thoroughly worked over and had warning notices erected. There is little point in going over *that* ground again: it has been exhausted and declared barren. Certain negative results are implicitly communicated to the undergraduate beginning on his search. There are issues, it is suggested, which may be set aside as a waste of time to reopen; and slogans are passed on which it would not be intelligent or respectable to question. Some of those with which my generation was brought up, beginning its theology more or less with the Second World War, were:

> The parables are not allegories;
> The gospels are not biographies;
> It is impossible to write a life of Jesus;
> We can never get behind the Christ of the church's faith;

and above all

> Of the self-consciousness of Jesus we may say nothing.

The previous generation had been through all that and had its fingers burnt. So there was no need to read it up or to work it through for oneself. All of us, I suppose, are worst read in any field in the period immediately prior to our own, which our own is struggling to leave behind. And this came as a special relief to my generation, since so much of it was in German and still untranslated. Indeed, until the spate of Continental theology made available by the post-war SCM Press under Ronald Gregor Smith we were unbelievably insular.

Reprinted, with permission, from John A. T. Robinson, *Twelve More New Testament Studies* (London: SCM, 1984) 155–70.
   Given as the Presidential Address to the Cambridge Theological Society, 12 May 1983.

Jülicher on the parables (which had given the quietus to allegory) is [[156]] un-translated (and as far as I am concerned unread) to this day. Wrede, whom my supervision pupils still serve up to me as "Reade" (this always seems to me the best argument for getting them to read their essays, quite apart from what one is saved in hand-writing and spelling)—Wrede on the Messianic Secret, published in 1901, was translated only in 1971. Bultmann's *History of the Synoptic Tradition* remained in "the decent obscurity of a learned language" for forty-two years and Martin Kähler's most influential book of all, *The So-Called Jesus of History and the Historic Biblical Christ*,[1] for nearly seventy. If we had read Schweitzer's *Quest of the Historical Jesus*, it was only the last chapter. That area could safely be relegated to the background of one's studies and a censor posted at the threshold, secure in the reassurance, to quote the verdict of Kähler's translator, that "the Life of Jesus movement" had proved itself "historically impossible, theologically illegitimate and apologetically irrelevant." So who in his senses would wish to revive that corpse?[2]

Above all was this true of the self-consciousness of Jesus—and instinctively it rose to the mind as *Selbstbewusstsein*, though there was a perfectly good English equivalent, as there was for *Sitz im Leben* (though not for the elusive, and often one suspects deliberately obfuscating, distinction between *Historie* and *Geschichte*). But somehow to give the monster a German name put it in its place and made it easier to tame. "We can, strictly speaking, know nothing of the personality of Jesus," declared Bultmann in his *Jesus and the Word*, by which alone he was known in English until after the war. There was no gold there. And still the area was fenced off by Bornkamm in pioneering "the new quest." The "messianic consciousness" of Jesus, he wrote in his *Jesus of Nazareth*, is "all too psychological" for theological investigation. So the sensible student is advised to this day to give it wide berth if he does not wish to tread on mines still lying around.

Intimately bound up with this issue was the use, or rather the non-use, to be made of the evidence of the Fourth Gospel. This too had been put away into an isolation ward labelled "Christian mysticism" and severely discounted in any reconstruction of the historical Jesus. Even the so-called "bolt from the Johannine blue" in the Q logion of Matt 11:17 and Luke 10:22 was pronounced guilty by association. [[157]] For the pre-critical use made of the Fourth Gospel in the history of christology had given scholars a bad conscience, which has still not been exorcized. Since the Johannine material was so heavily affected, not to say infected, by this "history," it could not be approached dispassionately. One must not be caught using *those* texts even with a long spoon! But cut out the Johannine texts, and even Johannine sounding texts, and could the question of Jesus' inner life ever be asked, let alone answered? For in the classical debates of the Christian church it was taken for granted that texts from this gospel were primary data of the problem to be

---

1. W. Wrede, *The Messianic Secret*, ET London 1971; R. Bultmann, *The History of the Synoptic Tradition*, ET Oxford and New York 1963; *Der sogennante historische Jesus und der geschichtliche, biblische Christus*, Leipzig 1892; ²1896, ET Philadelphia 1964.

2. E. Bratten, Introduction to ET, 36.

solved.[3] No christology which did not do justice to both the sayings "I and the Father are one" (10:30) and "my Father is greater than I" (14:18), or which failed to posit in Jesus both genuine limitations, like tiredness, tears and thirst (4:6; 11:35; 19:28), as well as a memory of pre-existent glory (8:58; 17:5), could satisfy the "facts." It was material from the Gospel of John which more than any other compelled, and tested, the doctrine of the Two Natures in its different presentations, and most of the patristic examples of what it meant for Christ to do some things as God and some things as man were drawn from this Gospel. Still as late as the nineteenth century so liberal a theologian as Schleiermacher used as an argument for the priority of John the authority of its eyewitness to the person of Christ. "It is, according to him," wrote Schweitzer, "only in this Gospel that the consciousness of Jesus is truly reflected." "The contradictions," Schleiermacher maintained, between this and the others "could not be explained if all our Gospels stood equally close to Jesus."[4] But if John stands closer than the others, as he believed, then the problem could be resolved. Even up to the First World War it was possible for Bishop Frank Weston to write his great book *The One Christ* as though the data for the self-consciousness of Jesus were still basically set, largely by the Fourth Gospel, in the way they had been for Cyril of Alexandria. What Weston claimed to do, not without some success, was to produce a more adequate hypothesis to account for the same data: he did not question, let alone set aside, the Johannine material. "The most important evidence," he wrote, "to the divine nature of Christ is that which is based upon the revelation of His self-consciousness, His knowledge of His pre-existence, and His memory of the state of eternal glory."[5]

[[158]] The swing away from this position, which of course had set in in liberal circles long before Weston, has been almost total. Yet nothing has been put in its place. In respect of what Clement of Alexandria called "the bodily facts," John's evidence has again come back into serious contention. But what lay at the centre of Jesus' life has been left a blank, and indeed been regarded as forbidden territory. We can say what the church said about him, but we cannot say—or apparently be allowed to care—what he thought about himself. He could have meant something entirely different, or been a deluded megalomaniac. But what if he did not understand himself as anything like what the church proclaimed him to be? Is it possible to be content with—let alone to believe—a Christ *malgré lui* [['in spite of himself']]? "Do you think you're what they say you are?" asks the chorus in *Jesus Christ Super-Star*, representing, as choruses are supposed to, the ordinary man. And if he did not, then it is difficult to persuade the ordinary man or "the simple believer" that it is a matter of complete indifference.

---

3. I have drawn in what follows on some material reprinted in chap. 10 [[in Robinson, *Twelve More New Testament Studies*,]] 138ff.

4. *The Quest of the Historical Jesus*, 66, quoting Schleiermacher, *Über die Schriften des Lucas*, Berlin 1817.

5. *The One Christ*, [[London: Longmans, Green, 1914]] 38.

Yet the scholars, particularly those grasping the relief afforded by
Kähler's book, which seemed to offer indemnity from what Tillich called "historical risk" and to secure churchmen from being at the mercy of the latest
deliverances of the Herr Professor, have thought it possible to ring off for
faith what Kähler called an "invulnerable area" from "the papacy of scholarship." Bultmann's statement of this position in his *Theology of the New Testament* could stand for many:

> The acknowledgment of Jesus as the one in whom God's word decisively
> encounters man, whatever title be given him—'Messiah (Christ)', 'Son of
> Man', 'Lord'—is a pure act of faith independent of the answer to the his-
> torical question of whether Jesus considered himself to be the Messiah.
> Only the historian can answer this question—as far as it can be answered
> at all—and faith, being personal decision, cannot be dependent on a his-
> torian's labour.[6]

One may agree that only the historian can answer this question, and grant
too that the historian's labour cannot give faith, but still question whether it
may not take it away, by rendering what lay at the heart of the truth about
Jesus so uncertain, so vacuous or so culturally conditioned that men and
women cease in fact to find it worth believing. I am not persuaded that it is
possible to remain indifferent to the findings of the historian on how Jesus
understood [[159]] himself, nor that an ultimate scepticism is either tolerable
or necessary. Yet are we in a position to give any answer? Have we the materials? Is it not inaccessible, even if not invulnerable?

At this point a distinction needs to be made. The materials clearly fail for
reconstructing Jesus' self-consciousness in psychological terms, for analysing
his psyche, its history or its type. The gospels are no more in the business of
supplying answers to psychological questions than they are to sociological or
economic questions—though this does not mean that it is illegitimate *for us* to
ask them. They do not even tell us what he looked like. Nor do they concern
themselves with the dawning or development of his self-awareness. They are
not biography, in the sense of writing about his life as βιός, let alone providing fragments of autobiography from the lips of Jesus. But this does not
mean that they presuppose there *was* no development in his apprehension of
God or himself, or that his was a static perfection. They would surely have
agreed with Cullmann that "the life of Jesus would not be fully human if its
course did not manifest a development."[7] Indeed the writer to the Hebrews is
quite clear that he learned obedience through the things that he suffered,
that he had to become what he was, to be made perfect, to go through the
process of individuation and maturation like every other human being (2:10,
17f.; 4:15; 5:5, 8f.; 6:20; 7:28). Luke certainly recognized its beginning in the
boy Jesus (2:52) in words that deliberately echo the growth of the child Samuel (1 Sam 2:26) and which Barth delighted to observe is described by the

---

6. ET London and New York 1952–55, 1.26.
7. *The Christology of the New Testament*, ET London and Philadelphia ²1963, 97.

word προχόπτειν, meaning "to extend by blows, as a smith stretches metal by hammers."[8] But the gospels are not interested in continuing to trace this process. One only gets glimpses of it, for example, in the story of the Syrophoenician woman, where under pressure Jesus comes through to a position he has apparently no intention of adopting at the outset (Matt 15:21–28; Mark 7:24–30), or in Gethsemane, where he struggles to align his will with that of his Father (Mark 14:32–42 and pars.; Heb. 5:7). But even here of course the accounts are not written with an interest in tracing the psychological processes involved.

In John, for all the concentration on Jesus' inner life and relationship to the Father, there is even less attention to questions of psychic development or to the human factors that obedience involved. Yet they can be read between the lines of a number of [[160]] passages, such as 7:1–10 (his prevarication about going up to Jerusalem for Tabernacles: life is easy for those for whom "any time is right," he must abide his "hour"; cf. 2:4; 12:23; 13:1); or 11:1–16 (where again in the conflict brought to a head by Lazarus' illness the reluctance to face a return to Judaea comes through); or 12:27–31 (the Johannine equivalent of Gethsemane, with its turmoil of soul and inner dialogue). Indeed the marks of emotional strain and psychic disturbance in Jesus are quite as evident in John as they are in Mark—though this is not the time to set them out in detail.[9] It would, I believe, be quite false to conclude that John supposed there *was* no development in his subject, or that the static effect and the semblance of effortless superiority which his gospel has conveyed *when read from the viewpoint of modern psychology* was his intention.

Nevertheless a distinction needs to be made in the case of Jesus as of every other human being between his ego and his self, his *ego-consciousness* and his *self-knowledge*. Unhappily the Greek ἐγώ like the English 'I' has to stand for both. Who, deep down, was the person who said ἐγώ εἰμί [['I am']] or αμην λέγω ὑμῖν [['truly I say to you']]? How are we to understand such words, and with what aim are they recorded? There is an important difference to be drawn at this point between psychological verisimilitude and theological verity. None of the gospels is primarily interested in the former; all are deeply concerned with the latter. And particularly of course is this true of John. If the distinction is not grasped, then the misunderstanding in his case will be the greater. If the Jesus of John and his words are taken at the level of psychological verisimilitude, then the impression is indeed left that never did any true man speak as he spoke, or, as those openly say in this gospel who *do* take him at this level, that he was mad (2:17; 6:42; 7:20; 8:48, 52; 10:20) or bad (7:12; 9:16, 24; 10:21, 33; 18:30). And to many since the Johannine Christ has come through as intolerable or repellent.

Yet at the level of theological verity John is simply deepening the question posed by all the gospels, Who is this man? (Mark 4:41 and pars.; cf. 1:27; 2:7). Where is he *from*, that he speaks and acts with such authority, direct

---

8. *Church Dogmatics*, ET Edinburgh and Grand Rapids, Michigan 1936–69, 1/2.158.
9. Cf. my forthcoming *The Priority of John* [[later published in London: SCM, 1985]].

'from source' (ἐξ-ουσία)? *"Quis et unde?"* [['who and where?']]: so Krister Stendahl has brilliantly elucidated the two questions behind the opening chapters of Matthew's Gospel. And these two questions, τίς χαὶ πόθεν? [['where do you come from']], are those round which the whole of John's Gospel may be said to be written. "Where do you come from?" asks Pilate in desperation and not a little apprehension (19:8f.). At one level [[161]] Jesus' contemporaries claim to know this well enough (7:27f.)—they are perfectly familiar with his parentage and his home (6:42)—and in irony they are represented as saying that if he *were* the Messiah they would *not* know: for "no one is to know where *he* comes from" (7:27). Yet at a deeper level they do not and cannot know (8:14; 9:29f.). *But he knows* (7:29; 8:14; 13:3). This last is a presupposition of the whole gospel, which is written to draw it out for its readers. In this sense the *self-knowledge* of Jesus is the indispensable heart of the mystery: to regard it as a matter of indifference or as a "no go" area is to leave a blank at the centre of Christian theology. Rather, John's concern is to take the reader into the very heart of this relationship, to disclose the inside story, what was really going on and who he really was, ἀληθινῶς [['true']], at the level of πνεῦμα [['spirit']] rather than ψυχή [['psyche']].

In the synoptists the relation of Jesus to God, the distinctive relationship which allows him to speak of "my Father" and to know himself called in a unique manner to the vocation of sonship, is everywhere presupposed. It is declared by the heavenly voice at his baptism, tested in the wilderness temptations, reiterated at the Transfiguration, and summed up at the close of his public teaching in the distinction between the servants and the son in the parable of the Wicked Husbandmen. The relation to source, the freedom and the authority with which Jesus speaks and acts, the intimacy of his union with God as Father: all these are presupposed and taken for granted. Yet, apart from hints from supernatural powers "in the know" (Mark 1:24, 34; 3:11; 5:7 and pars.), there is really only one point at which we are permitted a glimpse into the inside of that reality. That is when a door is opened into the relationship between Jesus and his Father which forms the centre and core of his being:

> At that time Jesus spoke these words: I thank thee, Father, Lord of heaven and earth, for hiding these things from the learned and wise, and revealing them to the simple. Yes, Father, such was thy choice. Everything is entrusted to me by my Father; and no one knows the Son but the Father, and no one knows the Father but the Son and those to whom the Son may choose to reveal him. (Matt 11:25–27)

This mutual "knowledge" is of course that of *connaitre* [['to know a person']], not *savoir* [['to know information']], even in the Lukan version, "no one knows who the Son is but the Father, or who the Father is but the Son" (10:21f.). It is the knowledge of personal intimacy, and has been shown to have its closest parallel not in Hellenistic "gnosis" but in the "knowledge" of [[162]] the Dead Sea Scrolls.[10] Indeed the precedence given to the Father knowing the Son, in

10. Cf. W. D. Davies, *Christian Origins and Judaism*, London and Philadelphia 1962, 119–44; especially 141–44.

contrast to what we should instinctively think of or quote, shows that it is grounded in the Hebraic understanding of God's prevenient knowledge and covenant-love (as the presence of the word εὐδοχία, or choice, in the context clearly indicates): "You only have I known of all the families of the earth" is the presupposition of Yahweh's judgment of Israel (Amos 3:2). Similarly in Isaiah the charge that "Israel does not know" rests on the divine premise, "Sons have I reared and brought up" (1:2f.). And within the new covenant the same order still holds: "I shall know even as also I have been known" (1 Cor 13:12). So in John, the order is "the Father knows me and I know the Father" (10:15); and the good shepherd knows his sheep before they know him (10:14).

That Jesus is thus known or loved (for the two are practical equivalents) by the Father, that he is "the son of his love" (Paul's equivalent in Col 1:13 of υἱὸς ἀγαπητός or ἐκλεκτός [['chosen']]), that he finds his entire life and being in responding to this relationship, is, as Jeremias contended, his secret, his revelation, the clue to his whole mission, which, as he tells Peter, flesh and blood cannot reveal, but only his Father in heaven (Matt 16:17). Without this clue we should miss everything. The synoptic gospels, as we have said, presuppose it, but they do not expose it. And in this, we may judge, they are true to Jesus. It is not, as G. Bornkamm states,[11] because they are "extremely indifferent and evasive" to the consciousness of Jesus. It is because they respect the privacy and intimacy of the relationship with the one he called "my Father." Like Socrates of his δαιμόνιον [['demon']], he evidently did not talk of it freely. Yet that Socrates had this inner conviction of a reality that was always with him is deeply embedded in our sources, in Xenophon (*Mem.* 1.1.2; 4.8.1, 5; *Apol.* 4, 12f.) as well as Plato (*Apol.* 40A; *Theaet.* 151A; *Euthyd.* 272E; *Euthyphr.* 3B), and has to be regarded as one of the most certainly remembered facts about him. Equally, with Jesus, this inner relationship as the umbilical cord of his life must be accepted as irreducibly necessary to the understanding of who and what he was, and, Riesenfeld has insisted,[12] to the authority of his teaching. Though the passage which brings it to the surface may appear in the synoptic gospels to stick out like a sore thumb and "gives the impression of a thunderbolt fallen from the Johannine sky,"[13] recent critical study has shown that there is less [[163]] and less ground for doubting its genuineness as a saying of Jesus. This is especially true if, with Jeremias again, we recognize that on Jesus' own lips the "the" of "the father" and "the son" is the generic "the" constantly to be found in parables, like "the sower" that went out to sow (Mark 4:3) or "the grain of wheat" that falls into the ground (John 12:24). In these cases we should use the indefinite article, so Jeremias renders: "Just as only a father (really) knows his son, so only a son (really) knows his father." It is still indeed a parable of Jesus' unique relationship to God, like "the son" in the story of the Wicked Husbandmen. But, as James Dunn has rightly said, it does not by itself commit us to any particular interpretation of "divinity":

11. *Jesus of Nazareth*, [[London: Hodder and Stoughton, 1960]] 169.

12. *The Gospel Tradition and Its Beginnings*, London 1957, 28f.

13. K. von Hase, *Die Geschichte Jesu*, Leipzig ²1876, 422.

"Schweitzer's claim that Matt. 11.27 'may be spoken from the consciousness of pre-existence' is never more than a possibility, neither finally excluded nor positively indicated by careful exegesis."[14] To the content of what is or is not here being claimed I shall come back. At this point we are simply concerned with whether such insight into the self-knowledge of Jesus is a legitimate or important quest. And on this Dunn is unequivocal:

> Can the historian hope to penetrate into the self-consciousness (or self-understanding) of a historical individual? The answer must be in the affirmative, otherwise history would be nothing more than a dreary catalogue of dates and documentation.[15]

He goes on to illustrate from Louis XIV and Winston Churchill how particular utterances or revealing comments, especially at crucial moments, may "provide as it were a key which unlocks the mystery of the historical personality, a clue into his or her character, a window into his or her soul." He asks whether there are any statements of Jesus which provide similar windows into his inner feelings and consciousness, and he replies: "In my judgment the answer is almost certainly yes." He cites those sayings of Jesus which express "what Bultmann himself called 'the immediacy of eschatological consciousness'" (Matt 11:5f. = Luke 7:22f.; Matt 13:16f. = Luke 10:23f.; Matt 12:41f. = Luke 11:31f.; Luke 12:54–56; and he adds Matt 12:28 = Luke 11:20).[16] But none of these begins to take one inside his relationship to God in the manner of Matt 11:27 = Luke 10:22. Yet remarkably this saying is never cited anywhere in Bultmann's *Theology of the New Testament*; and it is [[164]] significant that he always speaks of Jesus' "messianic self-consciousness," asking whether he saw himself as Messiah or Son of Man or Lord. His relationship to the Father as Son, which Jeremias rightly saw as central, is not even discussed.

But what is so rare as to be almost unique in the synoptists is normative in John. And if, as I am convinced, there is no literary interdependence it is surely very significant that the one synoptic window should be thoroughly Johannine in colouring. It suggests strongly that the Johannine picture of Jesus' self-understanding as "the unique Son of God who has a unique knowledge of the Father, and a unique function as Mediator of that knowledge" is not simply of his creation but a taking up and drawing out of what surfaces so sketchily elsewhere.

This aspect of "St John's Contribution to the Picture of the Historical Jesus" was stressed in an inaugural lecture of that title (the source of my last quotation), given by T. E. Pollard at Knox Theological Hall, Dunedin, in 1964. Since it has appeared only in a privately circulated journal for ministers of the Presbyterian Church in New Zealand,[17] I should like to give it wider circulation by some more extended citation than would otherwise be appropriate.

14. *Christology in the Making*, London and Philadelphia 1980, 29; so Cullmann, *Christology of the New Testament*, 288.
15. Op. cit., 25.
16. Op. cit., 26.
17. *Forum* 16.6, August 1964, 2–9.

He believes that the paucity of synoptic reference to the consciousness of Jesus represents a faithful reflection of his own reticence.

> If he avoids using Messianic categories, it is not because he did not believe himself to be Messiah; but because, as the sequel to Peter's confession of him as the Messiah shows so clearly, there was a vast difference between what Peter and the rest understood by the title and the meaning it had for Jesus himself. Luke testifies to the failure of the disciples to understand the significance of Jesus and his words in the disillusionment and perplexity of the two disciples on the road to Emmaus. The Synoptics give an accurate picture of this failure on the part of the disciples to understand the personality and the words and deeds of Jesus. They are recording the consciousness and personality of Jesus as they dimly apprehended it in the days of his ministry.
>
> On the other hand, John writes in order to bring out the real personality of Jesus and the real nature of his ministry, which had been there all the time, but which, during Jesus' sojourning with them, they had failed to see clearly. . . . It is not that John is reading [[165]] back into the earthly life something that was not there; rather, with the penetrating insight born of reflection and faith, he sees the personality of Jesus as it really was, and as the disciples would have seen it had their eyes not been blinded by preconceptions and misunderstanding. As he writes his Gospel John is saying in effect, 'This is what Jesus was really like; we did not realise it then, but now we know it.'

Pollard goes on to use R. G. Collingwood's distinction between the "outside" and the "inside" of the same event, between "everything belonging to it that can be described in terms of bodies and their movements" and "that in it which can only be described in terms of thought."[18]

> Applying this distinction I would say that the Synoptists are more concerned with the 'outside' of the events they record, even though they record them because they believe that they have a theological or soteriological significance. John, on the other hand, is concerned with the 'inside' of the events; to use Collingwood's words, he 'remembers that the events were actions, and that his main task is to think himself into these actions, to discern the thoughts of the agent'.[19] In other words, the Synoptists see Jesus and his words and actions from the outside through the eyes of the disciples: John 'enters sympathetically into the mind' of Jesus, or 'puts himself into the shoes' of Jesus.

He draws the conclusion that

> On Collingwood's definition of the real task of the historian, it could well be argued that John is a better historian than the Synoptists. John portrays Jesus as the one who at every point is conscious of his Messianic function

18. *The Idea of History*, Oxford and Toronto 1959, 174.
19. Loc. cit.

as Son of God, whose every action, thought and word are governed by this consciousness. There is no need to interpret this portrait as an invention by John or a falsification of what Jesus really was. Rather it is an attempt to portray Jesus as he was, in his earthly life, in and for himself. It is not that this Jesus of St John is any less human than the Jesus of the Synoptics; it is rather that John penetrates with deeper insight into the inner springs of the personality of Jesus. Nor was John's portrait a more highly developed theological interpretation; [[165]] rather because of his deeper insight he makes explicit what is implicit, and, for the most part, veiled in the synoptics.

And he ends by predicting that, as I am trying to work out at every level in my forthcoming Bampton Lectures,

> As the New Quest progresses, the Gospel of John must come into its own again as a primary source. To quote E. M. Sidebottom 'The Fourth Gospel is . . . best understood as a complement to the others not in the sense that it interprets them but that it shows us how to interpret them'.

So with this in mind let us look very summarily[20] at the content of the statements about the "I" of Jesus in the gospels and especially the Fourth.

First it must be stressed again that what we are dealing with in all the gospels (and not only the Fourth) is theological interpretation of his person, not a transcript of his words. This does not mean that we may not catch the *ipsissima vox* [['actual voice']], but it certainly does not commit us to claiming the *ipsissima verba* [['actual words']]. The Johannine "I am" sayings above all demand to be understood as interpretative clues of the evangelist to his essential self-understanding, not as materials from a psychologist's note-book for piecing together a reconstruction of his consciousness.

Secondly, I would want to insist again that what John is doing here as elsewhere, is drawing out and deepening what is already there in the Christian tradition, making explicit what is implicit. For the "I" of this gospel is already in principle that of the synoptics. It is the "I" of the numerous "I have come" sayings that declare the purpose of his mission and which are common to all the gospels; it is the "I" to whom everything is committed by his Father in whose person and deeds God's rule are made present; who in the name of the divine Wisdom speaks the invitation of God and sends his emissaries; the "I" of the Sermon on the Mount who goes behind what was said, not merely (as in the AV), *by* them of old time, but to them (by God); who as the Son of Man on earth is lord of the Sabbath, enjoying the same superiority to its rest (as John draws out) as the Creator himself; who pronounces the forgiveness of sins, thereby putting himself in the place of God; who quells the powers of demons and of nature, and exercises before the time the prerogatives of the last judgment; the "I" who in Luke, as well as in John, will dispense the Father's Spirit and who in Matthew can promise his own abiding presence.

---

20. Again for a fuller analysis I must refer to *The Priority of John*.

[[167]] All of this is in the synoptists; and John is portraying and project-
ing it in categories, already, it is becoming clear, well understood in Jewish
apocalyptic mysticism, of primacy and ultimacy, before and after, above and
below. For what is here is a greater than Solomon or Moses, than Jacob or
Abraham, and so must be recognized as being before them and above them–
and indeed before all and above all. But what is here is a *man*, who has been
given an authority, as the authentic son of man, reaching back to the very beginning of God's purpose and extending to its end. Even the most exalted Johannine affirmations of timeless pre-existence and heavenly ascendency, like
those of the more prophetically-based categories of foreordination and eschatology common to the synoptists, are made not to question his humanity
but to enhance it. In fact when the Baptist reiterates the assertion of Jesus'
priority in [[John]] 1:30 he adds the word ἀνήρ: to say that Jesus is 'before'
him is not to lift him out of the ranks of humanity but to assert his unconditional precedence. To take such statements at the level of "flesh," to imply, as
"the Jews" interpret him, that, at less than fifty, Jesus is claiming to have lived
on this earth before Abraham (8:52, 57), is to be as crass as Nicodemus who
understands rebirth as an old man entering his mother's womb a second time
(3:4). These are not assertions about the ego of the human Jesus, which is no
more pre-existent than that of any other human being. Nor are statements
about the glory that he enjoyed with the Father before the world was to be
taken at the level of psychological reminiscence. As such they would clearly
be destructive of any genuine humanness, whereas for the Johannine Jesus
the revelation of "what I saw in my Father's presence" (8:38) is described unequivocally only two verses later as the work of "a *man* who told you the truth
as I heard it from God" (8:40). Again, to confuse theological verity with psychological verisimilitude is to confound everything. Yet at the level of spirit
and truth (4:23; 3:6), of ζωή [['life']] (6:63) rather than βίος [['life']], the voice
with which Jesus speaks and the authority with which he acts and claims allegiance is that of the Word which transcends time and space.

There are two ways in which Jesus' way of speaking (λαλιά) is misunderstood and his word therefore cannot be "heard" (8:43) that are reflected in
the Fourth Gospel and its subsequent interpretation. The first is to take the
"I" of such utterances at the level of the ego of Western empiricism, and so
make nonsense of his humanity. The other is to go in the opposite direction
and see him as usurping the divine name, as for instance E. Stauffer[21] does
when he interprets the "I am" [[168]] of this Gospel as claiming identification
with the 'I am he' (*ani hu*) of Yahweh in the Old Testament. But this I believe
to be an equal misreading and can be shown to be such by careful attention
to the text.

Of the "I am" sayings in this gospel, those with a predicate ("I am the
bread of life," "the door," "the way," "the good shepherd," etc.) certainly do
not imply that the subject is God. As Barrett rightly says, "ἐγώ εἰμί does not
identify Jesus with God, but it does draw attention to him in the strongest

---

21. *Jesus and His Story*, [[New York: Knopf, 1960]] 142–49.

possible terms. 'I am the one—the one you must look at, and listen to, if you would know God.' "[22] If there is a proto-Gnostic style to this formula (which must remain doubtful, since all the evidence, especially the Mandaean on which Bultmann relied so heavily, is later), it is that of the mystagogue, the initiator into and revealer of the divine secrets, not of God himself.

Of the "absolute" uses of ἐγώ εἰμι, the majority are simply establishing identification: "I am he." This is so of 4:26 (the Messiah you speak of); 6:20 (confirming Jesus' identity on the lake at night, exactly as in Mark 6:50; Matt 14:27); 9:9 (on the lips not of Jesus but of the blind man); and 18:5–8, the "I am your man" at the arrest (cf. Acts 10:21), even though it evokes awe (though *not* the reaction to blasphemy) in the arresting party. There is the same usage in the resurrection scene of Luke 24:39, "It is I myself," where John does *not* have it just where we might expect it, any more than he has an equivalent to the "I am" of Mark 14:62 at the climax of the Jewish trial. Three other occurrences (8:24, 28; 13:19) are I believe correctly rendered by the NEB "I am what I am," namely, the truth of what I really am. They do not carry with them the implication that he is Yahweh (indeed in the latter two especially there is *contrast* with the Father who sent him) but, in Johannine terms, "the Christ, the Son of God." The sole remaining instance is 8:58, "Before Abraham was born, I am." This certainly asserts pre-existence, as in the Baptist's statement of 1:15 and 30, but there, as we saw, the subject is specifically designated "a man." That Jesus is arrogating to himself the divine name is nowhere stated or implied in this gospel. Even "the Jews" do not accuse him of this—only of calling God "his own Father," and thereby implying equality with god (or as H. Odeberg[23] interprets this from rabbinic parallels, rebellious independence, being "as good as God") (5:18). What they take to be the blasphemy of making himself "a god" in 10:33 is again made clear to be a misunderstanding of Jesus calling himself "God's son" (10:36). It is inconceivable, if Stauffer's interpretation [[169]] were the correct one, either in the evangelist's intention or in the mind of Jesus' opponents, that it should not come out in the charges against him at the trial, where again the worst that can be said about him is that he claimed to be "God's son" (19:7) again without the article.

If then the "I" with which Jesus speaks is neither that simply of the individual ego nor of the divine name, what is it? I suggest that it is to be understood as the totality of the self, of which Jung spoke in contrast with the ego. As he saw it,[24] the Christ-figure is an archetypal image of the self, the God-image in us, "consubstantial" alike with the ground of our being and with our own deepest existence. It is the "I" of the mystics, who make the most astonishing claims to be one with God, without of course claiming to *be* God, the

22. *The Gospel According to St. John*, London and Philadelphia 1978, 342; cf. 98.
23. *The Fourth Gospel*, [[Amsterdam: Grüner, 1968]] 203.
24. As he is always careful to insist, *he* is writing at the level of psychology not theology, but these categories can usefully be employed in a theological context to what is true at the level of πνευνα [['spirit']] and not simply σαρχ [['flesh']].

"I" of Meister Eckhart and Angelus Silesius, of the Sufis and the Upanishads, where *atman* and *Brahman* are completely "one," as in John 10:30. Such is Bede Griffiths' interpretation, born of long exposure to this tradition. In his latest book he says of Jesus,

> In the depths of his being, like every human being, he was present to himself, aware of himself, in relation to the eternal ground of his being. In most people this intuitive awareness is inchoate or imperfect, but in the great prophet and mystic, in the seer like Gautama Buddha or the seers of the Upanishads, this intuitive knowledge of the ground of being becomes a pure intuition, a total awareness. Such according to the tradition of St John's Gospel (which in its origin is now considered to be as old as that of the other gospels) was the nature of the knowledge of Jesus. He knew himself in the depth of his spirit as one with the eternal ground of his being.[25]

Westcott indeed believed that the great commentary on St John waited to be written by an Indian—though I doubt if this will happen until Indian theology has risen above its tendency to depreciate the historical or to absorb the "thou" of personal union to the "that" of impersonal identity. But it is Buber the Jew—shall we say "the Israelite without guile" of this gospel?—who perhaps gets nearest to what John is indicating by his ἐγώ εἰμι:

> How powerful, even to being overpowering, and how legitimate, [[170]] even to being self-evident, is the saying of *I* by Jesus! For it is the *I* of unconditional relation in which the man calls his *Thou* Father in such a way that he is simply Son, and nothing else but Son. Whenever be says *I* he can only mean the *I* of the holy primary word that has been raised for him into unconditional being.[26]

There is nothing here that is not utterly and "superly" human, as well as being totally transparent of God. To have seen the one is to have seen the other, without either being dissolved in the other. The "I" that says "I and the Father are one" is as unequivocally human as the "I" that says "I thirst." There can be no residue or trace of a christology that says that Jesus said or did some things as God and some things as man. That is wholly alien to the interpretation of John. He did everything as the integral human being who was totally one with his Father and with all other men so that in him the fullness of deity as well as the fullness of humanity becomes visible. The distinctive thing about that "I" is not that it was *not* human but that it was *wholly* one with the self-expressive activity of God, and thus *uniquely* human. What he was the Logos was and what the Logos was God was, so that in his "I" God is speaking and acting. Bultmann in his commentary on John gets it succinctly by making a careful distinction: "In Jesus' words God speaks the ἐγώ εἰμι. We should, however reject the view that ἐγώ εἰμι means 'I (Jesus) am God.'"[27]

---

25. *The Marriage of East and West*, London and New York 1982, 189.
26. *I and Thou*, ET, R. Gregor Smith, Edinburgh 1937, 66f.
27. *The Gospel of John*, [[Philadelphia: Westminster, 1971]] 327 n. 5.

Thus I believe that we must insist that the human filial self-awareness of Jesus is the linch-pin of John's christology (what, to return to the jargon of our theological youth, constitutes *Anknüpfungspunkt*, or point of contact, between God and man), and that here as elsewhere John is but drawing out and making explicit what is central to the entire gospel tradition. To declare it tabu is to risk missing everything and to be thrown back on the false alternative of a "mere man" christology with no unique divine relationship or one which sees him as a heavenly visitant whose genuine humanity is constantly in question. Both I believe are false not only to John but, more importantly, to Jesus.

ROBERT MORGAN

The Historical Jesus and the Theology of the New Testament

[[187]] When George Caird died suddenly on Easter Eve 1984, he had written only a part of his eagerly awaited *New Testament Theology*. How well the rest can be constructed from lecture notes and other sources remains a matter of hope.[1] Meanwhile, one way in which friends and former colleagues can honour his memory is by continuing a discussion in which his own last word is not yet public: on the scope and character of a New Testament theology, as this is illuminated by the central structural decision whether to include a historical reconstruction of the ministry or teaching of Jesus. Major recent and reprinted New Testament theologies diverge sharply in shape and proportions. Some evoke the traditional "Lord and apostle" shape of the canon with an entire first volume on "the history of the Christ" (Schlatter), or "the proclamation of Jesus" (Jeremias), or "the ministry of Jesus in its theological significance" (Goppelt). At the other end Bultmann and Conzelmann in principle exclude the historical message of Jesus from New Testament theology, though Bultmann includes a brief sketch as a "presupposition" and Conzelmann brings it back (also briefly) as part of "the synoptic kerygma."

New Testament theologies have generally tried to summarize those of their authors' scholarly conclusions which are considered most directly relevent to the life and faith of the contemporary Christian Church. For all their attempts to do justice to the historical distance of the New Testament, these textbooks have also been guided by the religious concern of their authors and readers to speak of God through their interpretation of their Scriptures.

Reprinted, with permission, from Robert Morgan, "The Historical Jesus and the Theology of the New Testament," in *The Glory of Christ in the New Testament: Studies in Christology in Memory of George Bradford Caird* (ed. L. D. Hurst and N T. Wright; Oxford: Clarendon, 1987) 187–206.

1. At the time of Caird's death less than half of the first draft of his *New Testament Theology* had been written. The Oxford University Press and Mrs V. M. Caird have commissioned Professor L. D. Hurst with the task of editing and completing the work posthumously [[since published by Oxford: Clarendon, 1994]].

The phrase New Testament *theology* both reflects that aim and highlights the tension between historical critical scholarship and Christian *theology* which has been characteristic of the mediating discipline. When Wrede proposed renaming it "the history of early Christian religion and theology,"[2] he exposed his generation's tendency to abandon the tension and surrender theology [[188]] to history. The master of historical theology, F. C. Baur, had been able to set it on its "purely historical" foundation because for him the history of religious ideas was the disclosure of divine reality. But once this consistently historical conception was cut loose from Baur's Hegelian metaphysics it drifted into a positivistic historiography which had no intrinsic connection with theology. Wrede was only acknowledging and calling for clarity about what had happened in biblical scholarship.

But most German biblical scholars still thought of themselves as theologians. Working in theological faculties with ecclesiastical responsibilities they were under some pressure to forge connections between their historical scholarship and the responsible leadership in the Church for which their students were preparing. The challenge implicit in Wrede's position was therefore taken up after the First War in renewed efforts to do *theology* through the interpretation of Scripture. Bultmann accepted Wrede's criticisms of the historical flaws in Holtzmann's classic, but himself renewed Baur's attempt to do *theology* through his own rather different way of penetrating the meaning of Christian origins.[3] His synthesis of New Testament scholarship (linguistic, literary, and historical), Dilthey's philosophy of history, Heidegger's language for analysing human existence, and a recognizably Lutheran type of kerygmatic theology, constituted a New Testament *theology* properly so called, with all the systematic and philosophical underpinning that theology requires.

Baur and Bultmann both rooted their New Testament theologies in major philosophical and theological options of their day because like many modern theologians they accepted Kant's account of the impossibility of traditional ways of speaking about God. Not all New Testament scholars have shared Baur's or Bultmann's (or Schlatter's) philosophical and theological competence in addition to their necessary linguistic, literary, and historical skills. Neither have they been persuaded about the propriety of introducing a modern philosophical apparatus into their New Testament theologies. This has always been a factor pressing the discipline towards Wrede's "purely historical" programme. Doing *theology* through one's interpretation of the New Testament involves these wider questions, once the difficulties of simply repeating traditional doctrinal language are recognized. Only very unmodern theologians can do New Testament *theology* today without attention to philosophical theology, because only they can naïvely assume [[189]] that the New

2. *Über Aufgabe und Methode der sogenannten neutestamentlichen Theologie* (Göttingen, 1897), ET in *The Nature of New Testament Theology* (London, 1973) 116.

3. He indicates the close relationship of his own existential interpretation to Baur's in "Zur Geschichte der Paulus-Forschung," *TRu* NS 1 (1929) 26–59, reprinted in K. H. Rengstorf (ed.), *Das Paulusbild in der neueren deutschen Forschung* (Darmstadt, 1964), esp. p. 310.

Testament assertions coincide with their own beliefs. Once the distance between the ancient and the modern world is fully acknowledged, hermeneutics becomes essential for any theological interpretation of Scripture. Naïve theological use of Wrede's purely historical view of the discipline, common in the heyday of the "biblical theology" movement, could in any case only be sustained where Wrede's critical conclusions were resisted. When the historical dyke built by learned conservative scholars against radical criticism began to crack, and historical differences between Jesus and even early Christology were accepted, the theologies this had protected were an endangered species. Their vulnerability was exposed by biblical scholarship itself and could therefore not be ignored so easily as earlier philosophical criticism had been. Hermeneutics has now been taken up by conservative as well as by radical biblical theologians.

On the other hand, Wrede's purely historical view of New Testament theology remains attractive to the positivist and empiricist mind-set of both liberals, who are impatient of the claim of ancient texts to instruct them in anything that ultimately matters, and of conservatives who prefer their revelation tangible—if not in clearly formulated propositions then in hard historical facts. It has also been encouraged by a secularism that wanted university theology restricted to the history of theology and (incongruous alliance) by the deep-rooted English optimism about the apologetic potential of historical research.

There are also more sophisticated reasons for preferring Wrede's conception. Krister Stendahl's restriction of biblical theology to its historical and descriptive dimensions,[4] assigning the normative aspects of scriptural interpretation to subsequent applications, was theologically motivated in part by the concern to preserve Scripture's capacity to surprise the Church by saying something different from what was expected. Whether or not it is an adequate theory for interpreting religious, philosophical, or literary texts, this two-stage model, which distinguishes sharply between what the text once meant and what it means to me now, was a healthy corrective to both the conservative ecclesiastical bias of the "biblical theology" movement and the equally ideological tendencies of existentialist theology, not to mention materialist and psychoanalytic theologies. Finally, partly for lack of any comparable synthesis, even New Testament theologians most sympathetic to Bultmann's aims have lately placed more emphasis upon the historical than upon the hermeneutical dimensions of their discipline. Nevertheless, as these various uses of Wrede's position show, the [[190]] practical theological interest of this mediating discipline has remained a defining characteristic.

It follows from this practical aim that the decision about what to include depends upon what the theological interpreter considers religiously important, as well as on what the texts are thought to be saying. Disagreement over whether to include a section on the historical Jesus stems from a difference

---

4. "Biblical Theology, Contemporary" in the *Interpreter's Dictionary of the Bible* (Nashville, 1962) 1.418–32. Reprinted with some further comments in *Meanings* (Philadelphia, 1984).

of opinion about the theological importance of the "historical Jesus" which runs deep through contemporary Christianity.

It is possible to argue quite simply that an interpretation of the New Testament documents which aims to further their theological witness should be guided by the fact that the "historical Jesus" is a modern construction not envisaged by the evangelists, and that one should not be sidetracked or "introduce into the text any alien problems."[5] Admittedly the four accounts of Jesus' ministry form an important part of the New Testament and must be given due weight in any interpretation of this collection of writings. The ministry of Jesus is also important for most Christians' understanding of their faith, and this is a further reason for giving it prominence in a New Testament theology which seeks some correspondence between the interpreter's own theological interests and the texts given in the tradition. But precisely here lies the central problem of a modern New Testament theology, which may be summarized as the necessity and the impossibility of including the "historical Jesus."

Even though the modern historical quest was unknown to the evangelists and remains unimportant to most believers today, the necessity of theologians attending to anything that historians can say about Jesus is widely recognized. However uncritical they may have been, believers have always known that the ministry of Jesus was a historical fact, and once the question is raised most insist that it does broadly matter what really took place, even if the historical details are now lost. They would admit to some perplexity if it could be shown that Jesus had never existed, or that he was a bad man; or that the post-Resurrection proclamation of the disciples was a fraud, as Reimarus suggested. It is not easy to specify how much historical truth Christians require, nor even precisely why it is important to them. The saying that the Son of man *must* suffer was probably an early Christian inference from what *had* happened. Similarly, there is no a priori reason why salvation had to be achieved through a real human life and death, as opposed to a myth. But since Jesus *was* a historical figure, and Christians find salvation in this life and this death, they *are* interested in the actual history, and can [[191]] reasonably expect a textbook which answers to their theological interest in the New Testament to include such good historical information about Jesus as is currently available. Several recent New Testament theologies have therefore reverted to some form of the older liberal model classically exemplified by Holtzmann who began his presentation with a historical reconstruction of Jesus' teaching.

The objection to this procedure, and what some would call its theological *impossibility*, is that it substitutes a religiously indeterminate historical presentation of Jesus for the Gospels and most Christians' theological evaluation of him. That is not an objection to historical research as such, neither does it excuse theologians from facing the results of this, but it poses a question about the propriety of including them in a textbook which aims to interpret and advance the theological witness of these classical Christian writings.

---

5. H. Conzelmann, *An Outline of the Theology of the New Testament* (London, 1969) xviii.

There would be no problem if the history of Jesus somehow included Christology, or even if the history led smoothly into theology. But 150 years of liberal theologians' attempts to relate their historical reconstructions of Jesus to the Christian Church's faith in him give reasons for doubting whether historical research leads smoothly into an adequate Christ of faith.[6] Historical constructions contain information which a modern Christology must include, and may thus be admitted by Christians to contain part of the truth about Jesus. The problem is that they constitute not partial but complete interpretations of him, and that these tend to compete with Christological interpretations. In the ensuing clash between faith and historical reason the latter inevitably proves victorious, at least in the context of rational theological argument.

In what remains the most interesting attempt to resolve the difficulties and exploit the opportunities posed for Christian thought by modern history and philosophy, D. F. Strauss threw a lifebelt to the sinking religion of his childhood. In the concluding dissertation to his misnamed *Life of Jesus* ("critically examined," that is, destroyed) of 1835 he suggested that his cognitively strong Hegelian "idea" could keep theology afloat after historical criticism had torpedoed patristic Christology. But nobody wanted to rescue the dogmatic hull at the expense of the person which it enshrined. In proposing a substitute for Jesus as the subject of Christological predication, Strauss was abandoning Christian faith. If the metaphysical hull of classical Christian doctrine was indeed beyond repair, it was better to preserve the human figure at the [[192]] heart of it all, if necessary in an idiom all but forgotten in the religious haze that surrounded his death. The "historical Jesus" was thus the next move in theology, Strauss having failed to strangle the quest at birth by replacing the Christian affirmation of God in Jesus with a quite different suggestion of God in humanity as a whole. This novelty was naturally rejected, but it had the merit of recognizing the scale of the Church's Christological affirmation. Strauss could not apply "God" language which spoke of reality as a whole to a single individual; he therefore substituted for Jesus of Nazareth what seemed to him a more appropriate subject for these metaphysical claims. His successors, by contrast, kept Jesus as subject, but reduced the Christological predicates to expressions of believers' faith. That was not quite such a break with traditional Christianity, but a break it certainly was.

In rejecting the modern "historical Jesus" Strauss (with Hegel) may be said to have reminded his successors of the scope of Christology even as he abandoned the subject of Christian faith and clung instead to the "idea" of the God-man. The refusal of subsequent liberalism to hear his warning marks a deep division in contemporary Christianity, and this is the issue in our problem of the structure of a New Testament theology. Those who place a historical reconstruction of Jesus at the head of their presentations are wittingly or

---

6. On their tendency towards a Christological dualism see my "Historical Criticism and Christology: England and Germany," in S. W. Sykes (ed.), *England and Germany: Studies in Theological Diplomacy* (Frankfurt, 1982), esp. p. 104.

unwittingly placing a question mark against all traditional Christian ways of understanding Jesus. Anyone who wishes to maintain some essential continuity with historic Christianity is bound to look for alternative ways of integrating modern historical knowledge of Jesus into New Testament theology, and so avoiding this head-on collision between Christological faith and historical reason.

The tension between a "historical Jesus" and New Testament theology only became acute with the widespread acceptance of a fairly radical Gospel criticism. So long as conservative conclusions are maintained, a historical presentation of Jesus can remain more or less in tune with the synoptic evangelists and Christian consciousness. Schlatter's first volume is appropriately called "The History of the Christ." But once the full extent of the gap between the historical Jesus and the evangelists' witness is perceived, the Christological problems faced by nineteenth-century Protestant liberalism confront modern New Testament theology also. The issue has not been much discussed in relation to the structure of a New Testament theology, but it has always been present and provides the key to Bultmann's celebrated (or notorious) opening sentence, that "the message of Jesus is a presupposition for the theology of the New Testament rather than a part of that theology itself."

The brief argument with which Bultmann supports his structural decision [[193]] sidesteps the important theological question of the significance of Jesus' earthly ministry, and the consequent relevance of the critical historical quest, for Christianity. But when, in the 1950s and 1960s, some of his pupils reopened the question of the historical Jesus, the central issue was again the theological significance of New Testament scholarship's historical investigation of Jesus. Bultmann's polemical stance in both contexts reflected Martin Kähler's protest against the liberals' "so-called historical Jesus."[7] He had himself sharpened Kähler's supporting argument about the speculative character of all these constructions, but for him as for Kähler the decisive objection was theological, not historical: constructions which stripped off the post-Resurrection Christology that the evangelists and their precursors and successors considered necessary for understanding Jesus aright inevitably conflict with what most Christians consider essentially Christian. Once the full difference between the historical reality of Jesus and the early Church's and evangelists' theological interpretations is acknowledged, purely historical reconstructions are inevitably at odds with traditional Christianity.

So much the worse for traditional Christianity, responded the liberals and their Enlightenment predecessors. The Incarnation has become incredible in the modern world and had better be replaced with a historical view of Jesus as a religious teacher pointing mankind to God. In retrospect, that judgement was at best premature—as the title of this memorial volume [[*The*

---

7. Even his more constructive *Jesus* (1926) contrived to avoid Kähler's strictures. Bultmann interprets the teaching of Jesus kerygmatically as a call to decision, and leaves open the question of how adequately these earliest Christian traditions represent Jesus' earthly ministry. Outside the theological context, *Das Urchristentum* (1949) correctly sets Jesus historically in Judaism, but distorts primitive Christianity by underestimating its interest in Jesus.

Glory of Christ in the New Testament]] implies. Some apologetic arguments for the divinity of Christ were destroyed by historical criticism, and some traditional ways of understanding and expressing the doctrine were shown to be inadequate and dated, as Schleiermacher had already insisted. Kähler himself was critical of "Byzantine" Christology and appreciated the clarification of Christian belief in Jesus' humanity brought by historical study. But what the fourth evangelist expressed in the confession of Jesus as "my Lord and my God," what Christians have narrated in mythical terms ("he came down from heaven"), defined doctrinally ("true God, true man"), learned through legends (some of the miracle-stories of the Gospels, and the birth narratives), and from discourses placed on Jesus' lips ("he who has seen me has seen the Father"), what they have confessed in Christological hymns and enacted in rituals—the point of all this remains the heart and centre of Christian belief: that in having to do with Jesus we have to do with God.

This Christological belief is constitutive and definitive for orthodox [[194]] Christianity, and in a sense its only "dogma." To replace it with a historical statement about Jesus, however true in its own terms, is no mere modification but a radical break with historical Christianity. Kähler did less than justice to the historical insights of the liberals, and Bultmann to the importance of these for Christology, but both recognized the startling novelty of the Enlightenment proposal and were surely right to resist it on account of its lack of essential continuity with what had hitherto been called Christianity. Like Ritschl, they recognized the potential of purely historical accounts of Jesus for subverting Christian faith. There was no reason to argue that the historical quest is impossible, nor that its results are theologically irrelevant; nor was Bultmann justified in assuming that any interest in this represented an attempt to prove the kerygma.[8] But they were surely right to insist that Christian faith and theology are concerned with the Christ of faith, whatever further questions then arise about the relationship of this to the historical reality of Jesus and (what is not the same thing) to such approximations as historical research can provide.

If that is true for Christology generally, it is doubly true for New Testament theology, since this is bound faithfully to reflect the documents it aims to interpret theologically. Christians who resist presentations of Jesus which remove all post-Resurrection theological interpretation can find rational support for rejecting such presentations from New Testament theology: namely, in the character and aims of the text being interpreted. The difference between historians' reconstructions]] of Jesus and theologians' interpretations of the New Testament is that the latter reflect the intentions of the texts whose witness they seek to advance.

Bultmann's argument for excluding the message of Jesus in any form from the theology of the New Testament is admittedly unsatisfactory. We have seen the necessity for including the ministry of Jesus and respecting the

---

8. So E. Käsemann, *New Testament Questions of Today* (1964; ET, London, 1969) 35–65, esp. 47.

historical truth about it. The only question is how to present this in a way that avoids the liberals' repudiation of the evangelists' Christologies. Even Bultmann's argument is correct in that context and against those opponents. He points out that Christian faith did not exist until there was a kerygma of Christ crucified and risen. That is not a reason for excluding from hristology the historical ministry of Jesus, but it is a good reason for not substituting this for Christology. Even his misleading espousal of Wellhausen's tendentious (though historically true) dictum that Jesus was not a Christian but a Jew, can be defended as polemic against the Enlightenment proposal. It is necessary (against Bultmann) to relate Christian belief in the living Lord [[195]] Jesus to the earthly reality investigated by historical research. But that is not a reason for removing what traditional Christology expresses and replacing it with a historical construction devoid of (and so in effect opposed to) Christology.[9] In resisting the "historical Jesus" Bultmann and Conzelmann emerge as *fidei defensores* [['defenders of the faith']].

These considerations reflect Käsemann's theological criticism of Jeremias's continuation of the liberals' historical Jesus theology.[10] Those criticisms have even greater force against the form of Jeremias's New Testament theology (1971), however valuable its content may be. They apply also to Kümmel's inclusion of the historical Jesus as a "major witness" to the theology of the New Testament (1972). Kummel agrees with Käsemann that a historical portrait of Jesus is both possible and theologically significant. But, unlike Käsemann, Bornkamm, and Conzelmann, he writes a New Testament theology which includes a section on the historical Jesus. He apparently fails to see that the corrections to Bultmann and Kähler made by the "new quest" do not weaken the theological reason for excluding historical reconstructions of Jesus from Christology and New Testament theology. It is one thing to be interested in the historical reality of Jesus, and to see there the criterion of the kerygma (Ebeling), but quite another matter to substitute a purely historical for a kerygmatic presentation of Jesus in this context.

9. *Editors'* [[L. D. Hurst and N. T. Wright's]] *note*: George Caird's own approach to this perennial problem is worth mentioning. As he asks in the introduction to his *New Testament Theology*—

> But what of Jesus himself? Is he not our primary witness? According to Bultmann "the message of Jesus is a presupposition for the theology of the New Testament rather than a part of that theology itself." If by the theology of the New Testament we mean the ideas held by the various authors, this statement is obviously true, since Jesus lived, thought, taught and died before any of them set pen to paper. But if by the theology of the New Testament we mean the modern academic research into the ideas of the New Testament writers, then his statement puts the cart before the horse. *The message of Jesus is not one of the data of New Testament study; we have only the message of Jesus according to Mark, Luke, Matthew or John.* Research must begin with the documents and their theology and arrive *only at the end of its course* at the teaching of Jesus. [Editors' italics]

Caird's decision to place Jesus' message *last* in the outline grew out of a sensitivity to the problems of relating Christological considerations to the Jesus of history.

10. Op. cit., 24–35.

Goppelt's attempt (1975) to meet Kähler's objection by refusing to separate the history of Jesus from the theological significance it had for those
who followed him during the ministry also fails to solve the structural problem of including a historical picture of the ministry without subverting the
Church's Christological confession. His criticism of the nineteenth-century
quest misses the main point, which is not the trivial one that all reconstructions involve presuppositions, but the substantive one that any view of Jesus
which abstracts from his saving death and Resurrection is theologically inadequate. That is true even of the [[196]] disciples' pre-Easter perceptions (so
Mark, rightly!). Goppelt's new factor, the pre-Easter reponse of the disciples,
is only indirectly relevant to New Testament theology. The discipline is concerned with the Christian truth about Jesus. That includes historical information, but above all elucidates how Jesus is understood in the New Testament
itself. This was no doubt partly dependent upon how he was understood by
his followers during the ministry, but that has no independent importance or
theological (as opposed to historical) interest today. Goppelt's presentation is
more illuminating in practice than it is in theory, because his conservative historical judgements bring an element of post-Resurrection perspective into his
account of the ministry. But including theological interpretation in his "historical" account of the ministry and (unlike Kümmel) including a chapter on
the death and Resurrection of Jesus in this same section yields suspect history
and inadequate theology, as well as depending upon an improbable assessment of what is authentic material. It also reduces the impact of each evangelist's witness, though that must also be accounted to the uncompleted state of
Goppelt's manuscript when he died. Finally, the critical task of assessing each
evangelist's theology by reference to the historical reality of Jesus is impeded
by Goppelt's structure.

The importance of this critical function of historical knowledge of Jesus
in Christology and New Testament theology will be considered below. The
point to note here is that a theological criticism which uses historical research as its instrument[11] presupposes the legitimacy of the theological perspective which it seeks to correct. It is thus very different from the historian's
rationalist criticism which replaces Christological interpretation of Jesus with
its own description in purely human terms.

The reason why historical accounts of Jesus threaten Christology is
summed up by the opening sentence of Conzelmann's encyclopaedia article,
"Jesus Christ": "The historical and substantive presupposition for modern research into the life of Jesus is emancipation from traditional Christological
dogma on the basis of the principle of reason.[12] This declared hostility to traditional Christianity neither invalidates the quest nor excuses theologians
from taking it seriously—if only for apologetic reasons. Since Reimarus produced a historical account of Jesus and Christian origins which (if accepted)

---

11. On this see M. Pye and R. Morgan, *The Cardinal Meaning: Buddhism and Christianity
in Comparative Hermeneutics* (The Hague, 1973) esp. 90–100.

12. *RGG*³ (1959) ET, *Jesus* (Philadelphia, 1973) 5.

would falsify Christian faith, theologians have had no choice but to meet him on his own ground of rational investigation. They have had to write better, more rational accounts which show that what can be known about Jesus by [[197]] historical research is at least compatible, perhaps even congruent, with Christian faith. Bornkamm's *Jesus of Nazareth* shows that this can be achieved even where the Gospels are treated fairly sceptically, and even Bultmann claimed that the proclamation of the historical Jesus implied a Christology. But neither Bultmann nor his pupils saw this as reason for doing Christology "from below." There are strong reasons for *not* including such defensive apologetic constructs in positive Christian theological attempts to say who Jesus is and was. Purely historical constructions of Jesus are theologically at best defective and probably misleading. The historical information which (against Bultmann) must be included in Christology and New Testament theology has to be presented in those contexts in a way that does not undermine the faith that is being expressed.

This argument only sharpens the problem of how to include the historical information that must be included. But even this first step of excluding from a New Testament theology all reconstructions of the "historical Jesus" may cause unease. A historical description of Jesus admittedly falls short of Christian confession because it mentions neither the Incarnation (in the broad Christian sense of a claim that Jesus represents God finally and uniquely) nor the Resurrection (vindication by God). But to call conscientious historical reconstructions of Jesus "non-Christian," as is implied by our contrasting Christian (Christological) interpretations of Jesus with historical ones, must arouse the suspicion of pitching faith against reason, which good theology seeks to avoid. Most Christians would assume that whatever historical truth about Jesus can be unearthed ought to illuminate their faith. So far as it goes such information is valuable; to *contrast* it with Christian belief is counter-intuitional. This reaction can be supported by the testimony of many Christians whose faith has been nourished by historical accounts of Jesus.

This last observation suggests that Christians typically read these books through the lens provided by their own Christology. Since both history and Christology refer to the same Jesus, historical accounts can be read from the perspective of a religious pre-understanding. Information quarried from the Gospels and pieced together into a historical narrative is again taken piecemeal by believers and built into their own symbolically heightened mosaic. Christology is thus enriched or challenged by historical insights without being replaced by a rival perspective.

The legitimacy of Christian apologists assisting this process by writing histories which relate Jesus positively to post-Resurrection faith is not our present concern. Provided these are open to rational assessment [[198]] by other historians there can be no objection in principle, though some theologians will prefer to keep their history free of apologetics.[13] But whatever one

---

13. See L. E. Keck's criticisms of Bornkamm's *Jesus of Nazareth, JR* 49 (1969) 1–17.

thinks about these historical accounts of Jesus, how Christians read them implies a solution to the structural problem of a New Testament theology.

The solution is for a New Testament theology to retain the evangelists' own Christological frameworks, but to build into its interpretations further historical information. This piecemeal insertion of reliable historical information does not aim at a complete historical account of Jesus, for which the data is in any case too fragmentary, but remains subject to the aims of theological interpretation. It is motivated and can be justified as the necessary second part of the theological interpretation of each evangelist. Firstly the interpreter must summarize the content of an evangelist's presentation of Jesus' ministry and teaching, elucidating the Christological framework within which it is set. This summary will contain some good historical information about Jesus, but will not identify it as such by separating it from what is historically less reliable. However, a critical New Testament theology cannot stop at a presentation of each author's thought. If it is *theology*, and not simply the history of early Christian theology, it must go on to assess each author's contribution. This task of critical evaluation provides the theologian with a theological reason to bring in further historical information. For one way that an evangelist's theology can be criticized is by reference to the historical reality of the man the evangelist is seeking to interpret.

This cautious use of historical criticism as an instrument of theological criticism, or critical theological interpretation, introduces further historical information about Jesus into what remains a Christologically oriented picture. It does not substitute a purely historical interpretation of Jesus for what remains a christologically orientated picture. It interprets the evangelists, but interprets them critically, where necessary challenging their interpretations by reference to the modern theologian's own understanding of Jesus, which is dependent upon the larger theological tradition and upon rational historical thought.

This process of theological evaluation and appropriation presupposes the validity of the evangelists' theological interpretations of Jesus in principle, even though it challenges them with the help of public historical information at particular points. Historical reconstructions of Jesus, by contrast, challenge the evangelists' Christological presentations wholesale and substitute a historian's Jesus. The intellectual prestige of historical research has tempted some to assume that this [[199]] "historical Jesus" is the real Jesus. That is a mistake fostered by the ambiguity of the phrase which can mean either the now largely inaccessible historical reality of Jesus, or the historians' approximations which are as close as human reason can come to that on the basis of public evidence and inference. But these approximations are as surely interpretations of Jesus as the presentations of the evangelists are, and they contain a large element of hypothesis and guesswork, as well as some "hard" historical information.

These historians' constructions are in some circles preferred to those of the evangelists on the grounds that they remain within the limits of reason alone. Modern European rationalism judges them cognitively superior. Christians, however, continue to assert the presence of God in Jesus, disputed

though this Christological claim is, and one task of theology, including New
Testament theology, is either to defend these claims of faith from rationalist
attacks or, if that is impossible, to advise the Church to alter or abandon its
claims.

The present proposal is a defence of the Christian claim and a criticism
of the liberals' surrender of Christology. The proposal depends upon distinguishing between the good historical information which is true and must be
included in a New Testament theology, and the highly speculative reconstructions of modern historians, which can make no such high claims to truth or
knowledge. These constructions are legitimate, indeed necessary, in historical research. But they are as fragile as Christological assertions, though for
quite different reasons, and as they confront Christians' understandings of
the influential reality of Jesus they are not necessarily more persuasive.

It once appeared that rational accounts of Jesus must overcome faith's interpretations because the theological interpretations of the evangelists actually
contradicted what could be rationally known about Jesus. But the approach
suggested here builds all this good historical material into modern Christology
and critical interpretations of the evangelists. The conflict is thus no longer between faith and reason but between a reasonable faith and a faithless reason.
The outcome will depend not on historical evidence, now respected by both
sides, but on a total view of reality and one's own place within it.

To repeat: in the early days of modern historical study historians' interpretations of Jesus seemed more true than the evangelists' interpretations because at many particular points the history that these purported to relate was
inaccurate. But these vulnerable points which once discredited the truth of
the Gospels have now been covered. The Gospels are agreed to contain both
historical information and the results of subsequent Christological reflection;
the resulting amalgams [[200]] sometimes contradict human reason's best approximations to the historical reality. Historians and theologians alike therefore now distinguish between the historical information they can quarry from
the Gospels and the secondary, generally Christologically motivated developments. Historians also make the distinction, important to our proposal, between what they can know with some certainty and where they can only guess.

What the historian judges secondary, Christologically motivated, developments of the tradition are of primary importance to the Christian theologian, who shares the faith of the evangelists and aims to communicate this.
New distinctions are necessary, to avoid unwarranted historical claims.
Whereas the Gospels were once read as an accurate account of what happened, much of their material has now been reclassified as the vehicle and
expression of post-Resurrection faith. But Christian theologians continue to
assert what this material is saying: that in Jesus we have to do with God. The
truth of this claim cannot be established by historical research. But finding
God in Jesus was no more rationally defensible when Paul wrote 1 Cor 1:18–
25 than it is today, whatever the additional problems faced by theistic belief
in a secular culture. Interpretations of Jesus which speak of reality as a whole
and make serious moral claims upon their hearers (and speakers) naturally

come harder than historical interpretations which profess metaphysical ag-
nosticism. But New Testament theology has to articulate what Christian faith
is, not replace it with what modern positivists and empiricists might prefer it
to be.

Historical research cannot establish Christology. It might even erode or
conceivably destroy it. If Jesus were discovered to contradict anything that
Christians can believe about God[14] (beyond what has always been implied by
the fact of his humanity), then traditional Christianity would be falsified, and
depending on what the historians discovered there might be a case for basing
a new religion on the historical Jesus. Since this has not happened, and only
some historically conditioned Christological formulations have been discredited by rationalist criticism, it is possible to retain the traditional Christian
framework for understanding Jesus, and to incorporate the new historical information into that.

An orthodox New Testament theology[15] must therefore reject the [[201]]
liberals' break with historic Christianity and retain the New Testament writers' Christological frameworks, introducing modern historical knowledge
piecemeal, in and through critical assessment of each evangelist. This approach enables us to include relatively secure historical knowledge while excluding the more speculative constructions necessary for writing a historical
narrative. These hypotheses which bind the fragments of evidence into a
meaningful whole belong to the historian's art, but cannot claim to be more
than possibly true and therefore have no particular claim to be included in a
Christology or a New Testament theology. This does not mean that they are
unimportant. New Testament theologians need some provisional historical
sketch of Jesus' ministry in their minds as they interpret the Gospels. It helps
them to make sense of the material and to assess each evangelist's use of it.
But it is mental scaffolding, helpful in the construction of a critical theological interpretation of each evangelist, not part of the final product, which includes only those pieces of hard historical information which the scaffolding
enabled the theologian to place.

The Christological accounts of Jesus contained in a critical New Testament
theology differ from the interpretations of historians while including their
good historical information. But these differently motivated constructions
speak of the same Jesus. They therefore confront and challenge one another in
contemporary New Testament scholarship. The New Testament theologian's
first task here is to demolish the historian's claim to possess "the truth" about

14. Even the doctrine of God might be modified as a result of historical study. The
Christian understanding of God is partly shaped by how the story of Jesus is heard, which
varies somewhat from age to age. This small element of plasticity allows developments in
faith's understanding of Jesus to be incorporated without abandoning the fundamental
Christian assertion of the presence of God in Jesus.

15. Alan Richardson's much criticized remark about some New Testament theologies
being orthodox and others heretical has the merit of indicating that a New Testament theology is a theological interpretation, and so is open to such description. But Richardson misplaced the labels when he judged Bultmann heretical.

Jesus, and so to make room for Christological claims which assert a fuller and obligatory truth about Jesus, not simply an optional preference of believers. The aim of this essay in prolegomenon to New Testament theology is to propose a shape for the discipline once purely historical reconstructions of Jesus have been banished from its domain.

The argument thus far has accepted the main point of Kähler and Bultmann against the liberals, but also that of the "new quest" against Bultmann. Kähler's kerygmatic emphasis upon "the preached Christ" (of faith) was taken over by the early Barth and by Bultmann to stress the divine act in Jesus. But they achieved this at the expense of its human content. Barth and Bultmann recovered the grammar of traditional Christology (truly human, truly divine) at the price of "no longer knowing Christ according to the flesh" (misusing 2 Cor 5:16). Barth subsequently corrected this Christological deficiency and indirectly influenced Käsemann, Bornkamm, and Fuchs, who later sought to correct [[202]] their still too Kierkegaardian teacher by renewed attention to the Synoptic Gospels and the historical ministry of Jesus. However, these properly kerygmatic theologians had no desire to revert to the liberals' displacement of Christology. It was actually rather appropriate that their discussion petered out when it had established that the historical investigation of Jesus was both possible and theologically necessary. Bornkamm wrote a fine book and Conzelmann an article, but both ensured that these would not replace Christology. Engaging in historical research and reaching some fragmentary conclusions is part of the work of Christology. Total success in this (were it possible) would presumably remove all mystery from the historical figure and so weaken the pressure towards symbolic heightening (expressed in Christology) experienced by the earliest disciples and their successors.

Of Bultmann's pupils only Conzelmann wrote a New Testament theology, and he did not place his encyclopaedia article on Jesus at its head. But neither did he relegate it to the presuppositions of the discipline. By including it as part of his section on the "synoptic kerygma" he respected Bultmann's injunction that "theological thinking—the theology of the New Testament—begins with the *kerygma* of the earliest church, and not before" (Bultmann, [[*Theology of the New Testament* (2 vols.; trans. K. Grobel; New York: Scribner, 1951–55)]] vol. 1, section 1).

But why should a New Testament theology begin with the kerygma of the earliest Church, rather than with its proper business of interpreting the New Testament writings? In including the necessary preparatory work in their finished products Bultmann and Conzelmann both continued to pay tribute to Wrede's purely historical conception. But Wrede was discussing a different (though overlapping) discipline. He disowns both parts of the phrase, "New Testament" and "theology."

Including the necessary historical scaffolding in the finished product is most clear in Bultmann's inclusion of extra-canonical witnesses, namely the Apostolic Fathers. It is true that the New Testament theologian must be a historian, and cannot understand the New Testament adequately without paying the close attention that Wrede devoted to the Apostolic Fathers. It is also true that Bultmann does not introduce the Apostolic Fathers in their own right, but to build up a picture of the development after Paul. Nevertheless, this has the effect of focusing on the period rather than on the canonical texts. That is reminiscent of Wrede's quip about no New Testament writing being born with the predicate "canonical" attached (op. cit., p. 70). Wrede's remark was relevant to "the history of early Christian religion and theology," but is quite irrelevant to New Testament theology, which (as the name implies) focuses on the collection of writings designated canonical by the Christian community.

[[203]] This same canonical principle, which does not limit the range of material to be studied historically, but does prescribe what documents the theologian has to interpret as guidance for the contemporary Church, rules out independent sections on "the kerygma of the primitive community and the Hellenistic community" (Conzelmann's Part 1) and "the synoptic kerygma" (his Part 2).[16] Again, the historian inside every New Testament theologian attends closely to all this. No historically responsible study of the New Testament today can avoid trying to reconstruct the history of early Christian religion through the history of traditions. But this is no reason for including such preparatory work or scaffolding in one's theology of the New Testament. The task of this theological discipline is to interpret the canonical witnesses theologically, and so inform the life and thought of the Christian Church. The evangelists cannot be adequately understood or assessed apart from their prehistory. But it is Matthew, Mark, Luke, and so on, or rather the New Testament documents bearing their names, which constitute the New Testament. The material of Q, M, L, and so on, has been incorporated into the writings of the evangelists, and our understanding of the evangelists is enriched by identifying (however hypothetically) the traditions they used, and studying their redactional activity. But the theology of Q and the rest is not itself part of the theology of the New Testament. These pre-canonical stages belong to its historical presuppositions.

The beginnings of Christian theology are of interest to the historian, and thus indirectly relevant to New Testament theology. But to make these hypothetically reconstructed early experiments normative for Christian faith and life today would be an extraordinary novelty.

The canonical principle leaves a few loose ends, such as textual variants (notably Mark 16:9–20, John 7:53–8:1) which may be considered canonical but are not part of the canonical evangelists' compositions and therefore at best peripheral to New Testament theology.[17] The same principle of identifying the witness applies where the probabilities are more finely balanced. Thus scholars who believe there are redactional additions in the fourth Gospel, or glosses in Romans, are right to exclude these from their interpretations of John and

16. Some brief account of these will appear in the exposition and criticism of Luke's narrative theology.

17. This proposal thus stops well short of the canonical criticism of B. S. Childs, while sharing its ecclesial orientation.

Paul. New Testament theology is based on the canon, but does not read it un-critically. However, its task of interpreting the canonical documents excludes both their prehistory and their textual post-history, even [[204]] where (Mark 16:9–20) this post-history probably belongs to the process of canon formation. The canon has a harmonizing effect within Christian consciousness, but theological interpretation instructs the community by attending to the individuality of particular witnesses. If a witness is judged theologically defective the critical theological interpreter can express this judgement without the help of earlier ecclesiastical redactors.

A more important "loose end" left stranded by the approach advocated here is the Old Testament. Orientation to the canon must face the objection that there never was a New Testament scripture without the Old. A New Testament theology must therefore become a Christian biblical theology. But contrary to current proposals for this a Christian biblical theology can only be a New Testament theology. Christian interpreters' understanding of the Old Testament should ideally be built into their theological interpretation of the New. The practical difficulties and architectural problems cannot be elaborated here. Mention of the canonical principle in New Testament theology simply arose, in passing, out of the case for excluding the "historical Jesus" from this discipline.

In the structure proposed here all the available historical information about Jesus is found in the same places as in the New Testament itself: buried in the theologies of the four evangelists and exposed by the critical interpreter. Since the evangelists constitute four of the (arguably) seven major witnesses that should dominate any New Testament theology, their accounts of Jesus' ministry and Passion, and particularly his teaching according to the Synoptic Gospels, will receive due prominence in an interpretation that respects their narrative character and content. But critical theological interpretation involves assessment, and it is here that a theological role for historical knowledge has been identified and a method for inserting it without cutting across the Christological grain of the documents being interpreted proposed. The Gospels are interpreted and evaluated in terms of their Christological aims. But since they aim to speak Christologically of the man Jesus their interpretations can be criticized by reference to independent information (gained by historical methods) concerning Jesus. Thus John's alleged docetism can be criticized through reference to his astonishing freedom with the tradition, or Matthew's alleged legalism by denying the authenticity of certain material. Both these evangelists must be criticized for their treatment of the Jews, and this can be done by criticizing their history at certain points.

This piecemeal approach allows modern historical judgements to be introduced individually and with due awareness of their often uncertain [[205]] character, whereas a historical reconstruction necessarily includes more than can be known. But, above all, this approach avoids substituting a non-Christian interpretation of Jesus for a Christian one. The canonical emphasis in our proposal for a New Testament theology might seem to give Scripture priority over the Lord. In fact it is designed (as is Scripture itself) to protect Christology, which is lost if a "historical Jesus" is preferred to the Lord of faith. The method of introducing critical historical judgements at the secondary stage of assessment, after the evangelist's message has first been interpreted in its own terms, allows that when necessary "urgemus Christum contra Scripturam" [['to urge Christ against Scripture']] (Luther). But it does not begin by substituting a human historical interpretation of Jesus for Jesus the Christ. Understanding a document precedes criticism in principle, though in practice they interpenetrate; most theological interpreters have a provisional historical idea of Jesus in their minds from the start. More importantly, like their readers they approach these texts with a theological view of Jesus which may be challenged or reinforced by further study. The most religiously valuable historical accounts of Jesus are very sparing in their appeal to historical causality. They can be absorbed piecemeal and integrated into their readers' Christological frameworks because they are written somewhat piecemeal. They are perhaps not intended to be so "purely historical" as they appear. Goppelt repudiates the phrase, and Jeremias refers to "the mystery of the mission of Jesus" (p. 76). Even if Jeremias intended to refer to its historical obscurity he has been read with a fuller religious seriousness. There is a place for such apologetic books, as well as for historical works like those of Caird's Oxford colleague Dr Geza Vermes, and his successor in Dean Ireland's chair, Professor E. P. Sanders, which abjure all apologetic interests.

But there is no room for either (pace Jeremias) as part of a New Testament theology.[18] Our argument has been that this discipline should [[206]] follow the logic of the New Testament authors and their ancient and modern Christian readers. The reason is that, contrary to Wrede's conception, New Testament theology, like other forms of theology, is a matter of faith seeking understanding of its object, using whatever rational instruments are available to help it. Historical criticism is one such *Hilfswissenschaft* [['aid to knowledge']]. Generations of Oxford undergraduates have learned how to use

18. *Editors'* [[Hurst and Wright's]] *note*: George Caird was sympathetic to this twofold warning. While he was less attracted than some to the lure of historical scepticism (he believed firmly that the task of the modern scholar who tries to reconstruct the original message of Jesus is not hopeless), he maintained that a New Testament theology should be sensitive to the problems of recreating past events on the basis of testimony. It should seek rather to set up a *dialogue* ("apostolic conference") between the New Testament writers which allows each, in his turn, to give his own understanding and interpretation of the event. This "conference" model likewise allowed little room for apologetic concerns. As he says in the introduction—

> It is one thing to ask what the New Testament teaches, and quite another to ask whether that teaching is credible to ourselves or to others. The nineteenth century writers of lives of Jesus assumed that if they could strip from the gospel story the accretions of ecclesiastical dogma they would find a Jesus in whom it would be possible for a rational person to believe. More recently Bultmann, believing that even the earliest gospel was couched in thought forms and language which make is unacceptable to "the modern mind," has demanded the demythologizing of the New Testament. But to make the New Testament intelligible is not the same thing as making it credible.

these instruments but have also learned of the New Testament theologian's witness to the glory and the humility of Christ as this was expressed in the work and in the life of George Bradford Caird.

INDEX OF AUTHORS

Index of Scripture

Old Testament

New Testament

Hebrews (cont.)
10:37 97
12:2 76, 459
12:3 76
13:7 340
13:17 340
13:20 382
13:24 340

James
2:8 495
5:12 129

1 Peter
1:3 80, 382
1:19 404
2:6 168
5:5 340

2 Peter
1:15 170
3:2 170
3:13 540

1 John
1:1 67, 77, 170
1:2 169
2:1 77

1 John (cont.)
2:1-2 343
2:7 170
2:8 541
2:24 170
3:2 541
3:11 170
4:14 169
5:4 76

2 John
5-6 170

Jude
14 97, 337

Revelation
1:7 97
1:10 387, 418
1:13 337
2:5 97
2:25 97
3:3 170
3:20 100, 103
3:21 100
5:6 404
5:12 404
5:14 113

Revelation (cont.)
6:9 395
7:10 114
7:11 114
7:12 113-114
7:20 114
9:4 32
9:5 32
11:15 110
12:8 102
13:8 404
13:9 210
13:16 32
14:1 32
14:4 521
14:14 337
14:14-16 342
14:15 22, 342
14:16 22
16:15 103-104
19:4 113
20:4 32
21:1 540
21:5 541
21:14 171
22:17 97
22:20 97, 113-114

DEUTEROCANONICAL LITERATURE

Apocrypha

1 Esdras
8:70 213
8:88 213

2 Esdras
6:54 318

Judith
9:4 471
16:25 114

1 Maccabees
1:34 478
2:44 478
2:48 478
2:50 471
2:54 471
2:58 471
4:46 426
9:27 426
14:41 426
1:62-63 483

1 Maccabees (cont.)
2:19-27 471
2:19-58 471
2:29-42 230

2 Maccabees
4:2 471

Sirach
7:9 228
23:1 202, 203

Pseudepigrapha

INDEX OF OTHER ANCIENT SOURCES

Dead Sea Scrolls

Ancient Jewish Writers

Apostolic Fathers

Greek and Latin Writers

Midrash

Genesis Rabbah
56 (36c)   102
24:7   505
79:6   317
Kallah Rabbati
10:3   492
Mekilta Exodus
12:1   111
17:14   118
Mekilta de Rabbi Ishmael
on Exodus
21:30   396

ʾAbot de Rabbi Nathan
A   501
A 15   492
A 16   499
B   501
B 26   493, 499, 504–
505
B 29   492, 499
B 30   499
Ecclesiastes Rabbah
7.2.5   499
Genesis Rabbah
24:27   498

Pesiqta de Rab Kahana
4:7   508
Sefer Ha-Maʿaśiyyôt
31   492
84   492
Sifra Qedošim
4:12   498, 505
Sifre Deuteronomy
18:15-18   426
32:43   205, 396
§323   501

Miscellaneous

Akhnaton's Hymn to the Sun
18   100
Analects of Confucius
15:23   497
Apocryphon of James
6:11   211
8:1   211, 220

Freer Logion   103
Oxyrhynchus Papyri
I, 3   103
I, 4   104
654.5   219
Peshitta on Exodus
24:8   244

Thomas Aquinas
Commentary on the Epistle to the Galatians
4:7   249

Talmud

Babylonian
Baba Qamma
46a   505
94b   436
Berakot
34b   482
40a   205
55b–56a   205
Makkot
23b–24a   505
Pesaḥim
112a   319
Qiddušin
34a   508

Šabbat
31a   226, 490, 496,
498–499, 504,
505, 507
118a   319
Sanhedrin
48a   335
67a   444, 461
70b   205
97a   95
Taʿanit
23b   204
Yebamot
121b   455
Yoma
19b   368

Jerusalem
Baba Meṣiʿa
11a   436
Ketubbot
7.5   499
Nedarim
9.3   499
Niddah
49b 42f.   205
Taʿanit
1.1   122
Terumot
31a   508

Targums